HINDU MANNERS, CUSTOMS AND CEREMONIES

HINDU MANNERS, CUSTOMS AND CEREMONIES

BY THE

ABBE J. A. DUBOIS

TRANSLATED FROM THE AUTHOR'S LATER FRENCH MS. AND EDITED WITH NOTES, CORRECTIONS, AND BIOGRAPHY

BY

HENRY K. BEAUCHAMP

WITH A PREFATORY NOTE BY THE RIGHT HON. F. MAX. MULLER
AND A PORTAIT

GYAN

Published by

Gyan Publishing House
5, Ansari Road
Daryaganj, New Delhi-110002
Phone: 011-47034999, 9811692060
E-mail: books@gyanbooks.com

Distribution Network
gyanbooks.com
India, USA, Canada, UK, Australia, France

ISBN : 978-81-212-2676-9 (HB)
First Published, 1897

2nd Impression 2021

Printed at: Gyan Press, Delhi.

Hindu Manners, Customs and Ceremonies
Author: ABBE J. A. Dubois

HINDU MANNERS, CUSTOMS AND CEREMONIES

BY THE

ABBÉ J. A. DUBOIS

TRANSLATED FROM THE AUTHOR'S LATER FRENCH MS. AND EDITED WITH NOTES, CORRECTIONS, AND BIOGRAPHY

BY

HENRY K. BEAUCHAMP

WITH A PREFATORY NOTE BY THE RIGHT HON. F. MAX MÜLLER AND A PORTRAIT

Oxford

AT THE CLARENDON PRESS

1897

J. A. Dubois Missionary
Seringapatam 1st December 1820

From a Painting in the Library of the Madras Literary Society.

PREFATORY NOTE

It is difficult to believe that the Abbé Dubois, the author of *Mœurs, Institutions et Cérémonies des Peuples de l'Inde*, died only in 1848. By his position as a scholar and as a student of Indian subjects, he really belongs to a period previous to the revival of Sanskrit studies in India, as inaugurated by Wilkins, Sir William Jones, and Colebrooke. I had no idea, when in 1846 I was attending in Paris the lectures of Eugène Burnouf at the *Collége de France*, that the old Abbé was still living and in full activity as *Directeur des Missions Étrangères*, and I doubt whether even Burnouf himself was aware of his existence in Paris. The Abbé belongs really to the eighteenth century, but as there is much to be learnt even from such men as Roberto de' Nobili, who went to India in 1606, from H. Roth, who was much consulted by Kircher in his *China Illustrata* (1667), and others, so again the eighteenth century was by no means devoid of eminent students of Sanskrit, of Indian religion, and Indian subjects in general. It is true that in our days their observations and researches possess chiefly a historical interest, but they are by no means to be neglected. They make us see how the acquaintance of

European scholars with India began, and under what circumstances the first steps were taken by these pioneers, chiefly missionaries, towards acquiring a knowledge of the ancient language of India, Sanskrit, and through it, towards gaining an acquaintance with one of the most interesting peoples and one of the richest and most original literatures of the world. The reports sent from India by the Père Cœurdoux (1767), and published by Barthélemy in the *Memoirs of the French Academy*, the letters of the Père Calmette (1733), and of the Père Pons (1740), are full of curious information, anticipating on many points the later discoveries of Sir William Jones and other members of the Asiatic Society of Bengal, founded in 1784. It should be remembered also that the first Sanskrit grammar was published at Rome in 1790 by Paolino de S. Bartolommeo, four years before the death of Sir William Jones (1746–1794).

The Abbé Dubois, though born about 1770 and therefore considerably the junior of Sir William Jones, belonged by his place in the history of Sanskrit scholarship to the period that came to an end with the beginnings of the Asiatic Society of Bengal, which had been founded by Sir William Jones in 1784. Nor must it be forgotten that while the real revival of Sanskrit studies took place in Bengal, the Abbé Dubois spent the whole of his life in the Dekhan and in the Madras Presidency. He was therefore, as may be seen by his translation of the *Pancha-tantra*, under the title of *Le Pantchatantra ou les cinq ruses*, Fables du Brahme Vichnou-Sarma; Aventures de Paramarta et autres contes, le tout traduit pour la première fois, Paris, 1826, a Tamil far more than a Sanskrit scholar, and well acquainted with Tamil literature, which hitherto has been far too much neglected by students of Indian literature, philosophy, and religion.

Though little is known of the Abbé Dubois' life beyond the fact that he lived retired from the world, and retired even from his fellow-labourers and a stranger, it would seem, to the researches which were carried on all around him by the devoted and enthusiastic scholars of Sanskrit literature in France, England, and Germany, his principal book, *Description of the Character, Manners, and Customs of the People of India, and of their Institutions, religious and civil*, published both in French and in English, has always continued to be read and to be quoted with respect, as containing the views of an eye-witness, of a man singularly free from prejudice and of a scholar with sufficient knowledge, if not of Sanskrit, yet of Tamil, both literary and spoken, to be able to enter into the views of the natives, to understand their manners and customs, and to make allowance for many of their superstitious opinions and practices, as mere corruptions of an originally far more rational and intelligent form of religion and philosophy. Few men who were real scholars have hitherto undertaken to tell us what they saw of India and its inhabitants during a lifelong residence in the country, and in spite of the great opportunities that India offers to intelligent and observant travellers, we know far less of the actual life of India than of that of Greece and Rome. There are few men now left who, like the Abbé Dubois, have actually been present at the burning of widows, or who can give us, as he does, the direct reports of eye-witnesses who saw a king burnt with two of his queens joining hands on the burning pile over the corpse of their husband. In the south these Suttees were far less frequent than in Bengal, where in the year 1817 no less than 706 cases of Suttee had been officially reported, and where this practice had at last to be put down by the law during the Governor-Generalship of Lord William Bentinck (1825–1835), thanks chiefly to the active exertions and the moral influence of Ram Mohun Roy.

As a trustworthy authority on the state of India from 1792 to 1823 the Abbé Dubois' work will always retain its value, and in its final and complete form now offered to the public it will be welcome not only to Sanskrit scholars, but to all who take an intelligent interest in that wonderful country. As the Abbé went to India as a missionary, and was a man remarkably free from theological prejudices, missionaries in particular will read his volume with interest and real advantage.

F. M. M.

EDITOR'S PREFACE

In the Library of the Madras Literary Society and Auxiliary of the Royal Asiatic Society may be seen, in a conspicuous position above one of the doorways, a striking portrait in oil-colours. This portrait at a distance one takes to be that of some Hindu, clothed in white, wearing a white turban, and holding in one hand the bamboo staff that tradition assigns to a Hindu pilgrim. A closer inspection, however, shows that in reality it is the portrait of a European, albeit the face is so tanned, and so furrowed with the lines of age and thought, that the first impression that one receives of it is not easily dispelled. It is a face that literally speaks to you from the canvas. The broad forehead, the well-shaped but somewhat prominent nose, the firm but kindly mouth, and above all the marvellously intelligent eyes, all bespeak a man of no common mould. Whoever the artist was (and I have not been able to discover his name or the circumstances which led to his executing the work), there can be no doubt that he has succeeded in depicting a countenance that is full of character; while as a background to his picture he has painted a low range of bare, rugged hills that seem to be in thorough keeping with his subject, and to suggest, as a kind of inspiration, the hard, self-denying, but solid life-work of him whose features he has handed down.

This portrait is that of the Abbé J. A. Dubois, a Christian Missionary who laboured for some thirty-one years in India, striving to fulfil the task which his sense of religious duty imposed upon him. Merely in this respect one can claim for him no special merit, for the annals of Christian Missions in India are full of the names of those who spent themselves and were spent in the service of their Master. His special claim to recognition will be found elsewhere, namely, in the wonderful record which he compiled of the manners, customs, institutions, and ceremonies of the people among whom he lived and moved and had his being for so great a portion of his life. He seems to have recognized from the very first day of his arrival in India that Christian Mission work meant something more than the mere preaching and expounding of the Gospel; that it included among its chief essentials to success a long and thorough study of the innermost life and character of the people amidst whom it was to be carried on. In his day, it must be remarked, there were no royal roads to such knowledge. There were no text-books to prepare the way by their critical analyses of the sacred Hindu writings. Such knowledge had to be gained at first hand, and by the more laborious (though, it must be confessed, more sure) method of personal inquiry *in situ*. 'I had no sooner arrived amongst the natives of India,' the Abbé himself tells us, 'than I recognized the absolute necessity of gaining their confidence. Accordingly I made it my constant rule to live as they did. I adopted their style of clothing, and I studied their customs and methods of life in order to be exactly like them. I even went so far as to avoid any display of repugnance to the majority of their peculiar prejudices. By such circumspect conduct I was able to ensure a free and hearty welcome from people of all castes and conditions, and was often favoured of their own accord with the most curious and interesting particulars about themselves.'

Unfortunately such details concerning the Abbé's personal history as we possess are extremely meagre. His modesty is so extreme that he rarely appears in his own person throughout his work, and those particulars that I have been able to obtain have been culled from various other sources—chiefly from the Madras Government Secretariat, from the British Museum, and from the Missions Étrangères. The absolute retirement of the Abbé from European society for a long series of years after his arrival in India, though it qualified him, as was said when his work first appeared, 'for penetrating into the dark and unexplored recesses of the Hindu character,' also veiled him in an equal degree from the curiosity of his readers. Major Mark Wilks, the accomplished historian of Mysore, who in those days was British Resident in that province, in introducing the Abbé's work to the notice of the Government of Fort St. George, remarked: 'Of the history and character of the author, I only know that he escaped from one of the fusillades of the French Revolution and has since lived amongst the Hindus as one of themselves: and of the respect which his irreproachable conduct inspires it may be sufficient to state that when travelling, on his approach to a village, the house of a Brahmin is uniformly cleared for his reception, without interference, and generally without communication to the officers of Government, as a spontaneous mark of deference and respect.' Subsequently, however, Major Wilks became much more intimate with the Abbé, and the latter speaks of him years afterwards in terms of great affection as his patron and friend. With regard to the circumstance mentioned above as having induced him to leave France and come to India, the Abbé remarked afterwards: 'It is quite true that I fled from the horrors of the Revolution, and had I remained I should in all probability have fallen a victim, as did so many of my friends who held the same religious and political opinions as myself; but the truth is I embarked for India some two years before the fusillades referred to took place.'

Be this as it may, I have ascertained that the Abbé was

ordained in the diocese of Viviers in 1792, at the age of twenty-seven, and left France in the same year. He entered on his Mission work under the guidance of the Missions Étrangères. On reaching India he was attached to the Pondicherry Mission; and for the first few years he seems to have laboured in what are now the Southern Districts of the Madras Presidency. He must have quickly made for himself a name, for on the fall of Seringapatam he was specially invited, on the recommendation, it is said, of Colonel Wellesley, afterwards Duke of Wellington, to visit the capital of Mysore in order to reconvert and reorganize the Christian community which had been forcibly perverted to Mahomedanism by Tippu Sultan. *En passant*, I may mention that, through the influence of the Abbé in Mysore, not a single priest of the Missions Étrangères was persecuted by Tippu. For these apostates, we learn, he pleaded eloquently before Mgr. Champenois, the Bishop, and with such good effect that he once more gathered the lost sheep, of whom there were 1,800 in Seringapatam alone, into the Christian fold, and established on a permanent basis the Roman Catholic Church in the province of Mysore. Of the practical farsightedness which guided him in his work, we may judge by two incidents that have been incidentally recorded of him. He met the problem of the poverty of the people committed to his care by founding agricultural colonies on the lines that have during these past few years been advocated by the Salvation Army and others, his principal colony being at Sathalli, near Hassan; and he used his influence to such good effect in preventing epidemics of small-pox by promoting vaccination (then, be it remembered, a comparatively novel idea) that he was afterwards granted a special pension by the East India Company. But the records of his labours in the Mission field, distinguished as they may have been in many respects, are unhappily wrapt in obscurity, though his own general conclusions with regard to them, after thirty-one years of incessant toil and struggle, will be commented upon directly.

For the moment let us return to the great descriptive work which he compiled during his hours of leisure. That the Abbé was from the first a close observer of the people among whom he lived and a keen student of their religious and social institutions is perfectly apparent. But the idea of putting the results of his investigations into writing originated, as he tells us, 'in consequence of notices in the public papers calling for authentic documents regarding these people for the use of the historiographers of the Honourable Company engaged in writing the history of India.' The idea once formed, he set to work with characteristic thoroughness, though with too much modesty he remarks: 'I aim not at the rank of an author, which is suited neither to my talents nor to the secluded state in which my profession confines me amongst the natives of the country.' He remarks further, however: 'During my long sojourn in India I never let slip any opportunity of collecting materials and particulars of all sorts. My information has been drawn partly from the books which are held in highest estimation amongst the people of India and partly from such scattered records as fell by chance into my hands and contained facts upon which I could thoroughly rely. But in regard to the majority of the materials which I now offer to the public I am chiefly dependent on my own researches, having lived in close and familiar intercourse with persons of every caste and condition of life. Probably many Europeans settled in India would have been more capable than myself of performing the same task; but I may be permitted to doubt whether there has been any person more favourably situated for gleaning information or more zealous in his pursuit of knowledge.'

At the same time he disclaims for his work any general applicability to the whole of India. His observations extend, broadly speaking, to the India that lies south of the Vindyan Range; and even within those limits he is careful to remark that local differences are so many and so marked that 'there is no class or sect or community of Hindus that has not, in addition to the general rules of Hindu society, some domestic usages peculiar to itself.' So that, as he says, it is impossible to generalize with complete accuracy on any subject connected with them.

But though the Abbé with characteristic modesty leaves to 'the many learned Europeans residing in the country' the task of compiling from authentic documents 'a more methodical and comprehensive history of the Hindus,' his own work possesses special merits of its own and is far superior to any that could be compiled from books of reference and literary investigations, for, as Major Wilks said of it, 'it was meditated and composed in the midst of the people whom it describes, and in writing it the author followed the only path that has ever yet led to a true delineation of national character, namely, the path of original research and personal observation.'

The French MS. of the work which the Abbé compiled under the circumstances and according to the design above described has a somewhat remarkable history. In its original form it was placed in the hands of Major Wilks in the year 1806, when the Abbé had been some fourteen years in the country. Major Wilks appears to have kept it by him and studied it for more than a year, and then to have forwarded it to the Government of Fort St. George with a letter of warm recommendation, in which he remarked: 'So far as my previous information and subsequent inquiry have enabled me to judge, it contains the most correct, comprehensive, and minute account extant in any European language of the customs and manners of the Hindus.' This judgement was heartily endorsed by Sir James Mackintosh, to whom Major Wilks would appear to have sent it for his opinion, and also by Mr. W. Erskine, of Bombay, a man of distinguished talents and an acknowledged authority in everything connected with the mythology, literature, customs, and institutions of the people of India. Fortified in his own opinion of its high merits by the concurrence of these two eminent men, Major Wilks had no difficulty in persuading Lord William Bentinck, who was then at Madras, to purchase the MS. on behalf of the East India Company, the sum eventually agreed upon being 2,000 star pagodas (i. e. in the present currency some 8,000 rupees). In accordance with the Abbé's request this sum was invested in Government paper and the interest paid to him regularly afterwards—a modest sum, no doubt, judged by latter-day standards of literary remuneration; but, then, the Abbé's wants were modest. According to Major Wilks all that he hoped for was 'a recompense sufficient to shield his future life from those miseries of extreme want which he had once already encountered.'

In summing up his own opinion of the Abbé's work Lord William Bentinck remarked with characteristic candour and good sense:—

> 'The result of my own observation during my residence in India is that the Europeans generally know little or nothing of the customs and manners of the Hindus. We are all acquainted with some prominent marks and facts, which all who run may read; but their manner of thinking, their domestic habits and ceremonies, in which circumstances a knowledge of the people consists, is, I fear, in great part wanting to us. We understand very imperfectly their language. They perhaps know more of ours; but their knowledge is by no means sufficiently extensive to give a description of subjects not easily represented by the insulated words in daily use. We do not, we cannot, associate with the natives. We cannot see them in their houses and with their families. We are necessarily very much confined to our houses by the heat; all our wants and business which would create a greater intercourse with the natives is done for us, and we are in fact strangers in the land. I have personally found the want of a work to which reference could be made for a just description of the native opinions and manners. I am of opinion that, in a political point of view, the information which the work of the Abbé Dubois has to impart might be of the greatest benefit in aiding the servants of the Government in conducting themselves more in unison with the customs and prejudices of the natives.'

The purchase of the MS. was reported by the Madras Government to the Board of Directors in 1807 as 'an arrangement . . . of great public importance'; and the MS. itself was transmitted to London at the same time for translation and publication. It was not until 1816, however, that the English translation was actually published, with the sanction of the East India Company and under the personal supervision of Major Wilks. Meanwhile a copy of the MS. in the records of Fort St. George had in 1815 attracted the attention of Mr. A. D. Campbell, Superintendent of the Local Board of Examiners, who, in apparent ignorance of the fact that the original copy had been sent to England for publication, proposed to publish an annotated edition of it in Madras. Accordingly he commenced the task; but almost immediately he reported to the Local Government as follows:—

'I soon found enough to satisfy me that it would be unfair to proceed further in this pursuit without first affording the author an opportunity of revising his work, being convinced that the increased experience of the Abbé Dubois and his further acquaintance with the customs and habits of the Hindus would enable him to correct many parts of the MS., and to add new information on the very curious and interesting subjects on which it treats. I have now the honour of submitting to the Board the reply of the Abbé Dubois to a reference which I made to him on this subject, and it will thence be perceived that, notwithstanding the very favourable manner in which the accuracy of the facts stated in the MS. has been mentioned by Colonel Wilks, the author admits that the work requires "considerable alterations" and "many additions," and that "there are chapters which ought to be entirely made again."'

It is from this point that the history of the MS. becomes most interesting. It appears from a careful examination which I have made of the records in the Madras Government Secretariat (which records include several letters in the Abbé's own handwriting) that the MS. was sent back to the Abbé for his additions, excisions, and corrections, and that these were very considerable. Indeed the MS. was completely altered, recast and enlarged, until it bore hardly more resemblance to the original work than a rough outline sketch does to a finished picture.

And yet this rough sketch, so to speak, has up to this

day been all that English readers have had presented to them of the Abbé's work. I do not for one moment desire to detract from the artistic and literary value of that sketch, admirable as it is, and as it has been acknowledged to be by the authorities quoted above. But what I do mean to say is that that sketch is only an extremely poor representation of what the Abbé's great work really was.

The true history was this. When the MS. was returned to him in 1815, the Abbé put into it all the additions and corrections suggested by many years of additional study and investigation; and when he sent it back to the Government of Madras, it was, practically speaking, a different work altogether. On receipt of the revised MS. the Government of Madras decided that the only course open to them was to send it to the Court of Directors in England, as the original MS. had been. Unfortunately, however, before the revised MS. could reach England the original draft had been translated and published; and it is this edition which has been sold ever since, and upon which the Abbé's reputation has rested.

It is true that a so-called 'revised' edition was published some thirty odd years ago, but it was merely a reprint (and unfortunately a very considerably curtailed reprint) of the original English edition. The only sign that I have been able to discover of the revised MS. in the Fort having been consulted, is the inclusion of a dedicatory page that had been added by the Abbé when he sent his finally corrected copy to the Madras Government before leaving India. As far as I can ascertain the chief effect of this new edition was a demand for a *verbatim* reprint of the original edition which had been so arbitrarily cut down; and this was almost immediately supplied by the publishers.

The Abbé, the Local Government, and Mr. Campbell, it may be remarked, were all in hopes that a second revised edition would be published containing the corrections and additions that had subsequently been made;

but for some reason or another this has never hitherto been done.

The view which the Abbé took of the edition, as it appeared, is expressed in a letter in English (of which he had a good knowledge) addressed to the Madras Government, dated Seringapatam, February 20, 1818, with which letter he submitted still further revisions. The Abbé remarked therein :—

'Since I wrote my last additions and corrections, a gentleman in the place having favoured me for my perusal with a copy of the English translation of the work, I was sorry to observe that, owing perhaps to some oversight on the part of the copyists of my original MS., or other accidents, many interesting, authentic, and quite unexceptionable paragraphs, and in some instances whole pages, had been passed over, which circumstance occasions chasms in the narrative and otherwise renders the descriptions very imperfect, and in a few instances contradictory.. These differences are pointed out and corrected in the accompanying sheets; and the other inaccuracies to be found in the original MS. and the translation were fully corrected and the work considerably enlarged in the additions sent before to Government. I therefore request that the accompanying accounts may be sent without delay to the Hon'ble the Court of Directors to be added to the former ones, in order that if the work goes through a second edition it may be made as interesting and curious as it lies in my power to do.'

Nor were these the last corrections made in the text of his work by the good Abbé, for three years later, and a short time before he left India for good and all, he sent a fair copy of his 'finally corrected' work to the Madras Government, which, like the two former MSS., was sent to England and is now in the India Office Library. One copy of this, I may mention, was taken by the Abbé to France and was published in the original French. The number issued was however small, and copies of it are now almost unprocurable. And another copy of the MS. was left in the records of Fort St. George. This last-named copy I have carefully compared with the English translation which has hitherto been available to the public, and the comparison has shown me how vastly superior in every way (I might say in every page) is the Abbé's later and unpublished work as contrasted with his first draft, composed sixteen years earlier, which despite its imperfections has enjoyed so much popularity amongst English students of Hinduism.

It is certainly very strange that all the facts which I have detailed above have never before attracted attention, and that although copies of the Abbé's finally completed work are to be found in the records of the India Office and of the Government of Madras, it has never before been discovered that the published English edition is not in reality a complete or true representation of the Abbé's long labours in the field of original research. For all that, however, this edition has been largely drawn upon by English writers, chief amongst whom we may mention Mill, the historian of India, while Oriental students like Professor Wilson have acknowledged the assistance it afforded them, and in the British Museum there is a copy of it containing a manuscript note by Coleridge which shows that the poet had gone to it for inspiration.

Now, if this faulty English edition has been so widely consulted and so frequently extolled, an English edition of the Abbé's revised work ought to be infinitely more valuable. This was the thought which presented itself to me when I discovered, almost accidentally, while looking through the French MS. in the Madras Government's records, that the good Abbé had never had justice done to him. Accordingly, with the permission and with the aid of the Madras Government, I have made a verbatim translation of the work in its complete form which I here present to the public, together with such notes and observations as seem necessary to put the text into line with later developments and research.

As to the intrinsic value of the Abbé's work, I have no hesitation in saying that it is as valuable to-day as ever it was, even more valuable in some respects. It is true that a mass of learned literature on the religious and civil life of the Hindus has accumulated since the Abbé's days, and is still accumulating; and the impression may be felt in many minds that a book written so long ago can be of little practical use at present; but the fact is that the Abbé's work, composed as it was in the midst of the people themselves, is of a unique character, for it combines, as no other work on the Hindus combines, a recital of the broad facts of Hindu religion and Hindu sociology with many masterly descriptions, at once comprehensive and minute, of the *vie intime* of the people among whom he lived for so many years. With any other people than the Hindus such a work would soon grow out of date; but with them the same ancestral traditions and customs are followed nowadays that were followed hundreds of years ago, at least by the vast majority of the population. I do not deny that some of the Abbé's statements require to be modified in the light of changes that have taken place amongst the educated classes since the introduction of Western learning, but such necessary modifications, which, as remarked above, I have introduced in the form of notes, are surprisingly few. Enumerated separately by themselves, no doubt these changes might furnish material for a substantial volume, for no person would now be so foolish as to repeat the assertion so long maintained unchallenged that the Hindu nation is completely apathetic, unchanging, and non-progressive in the modern sense. But in editing the Abbé's work I have confined myself to modifying such statements as seemed to require modification, and have avoided as far as possible any digressions that were not suggested by the text itself.

Petty local differences in civil and religious affairs are a marked feature of Hinduism, just as almost innumerable subdivisions and sub-sections and sub-sub-sections are a marked feature of the caste system. Hence it is that much which is perfectly true of one locality is false of another; and accordingly it is impossible to describe the many details of Hindu life and character without mental reservations as to possible exceptions. Nevertheless, there are certain broad, fundamental principles underlying these many differences and inequalities; and it is upon these that the Abbé rears the fabric of his extraordinary work. Moreover, the Abbé appears to me to avoid the many pitfalls of this uneven field of investigation with peculiar skill. It would be wrong to say that all his observations are generally applicable or perfectly just, but, taken as a whole, they are remarkably true and unprejudiced.

I am here tempted to quote at some length the observations concerning the Abbé and his researches made by a prominent Hindu, the Honourable Dewan Bahadur Srinavasa Raghava Iyengar, C.I.E., at a meeting of the Madras Presidency College Literary Society in May, 1896. This gentleman is well fitted to express an opinion on a subject of the kind, for not only has he been for some years past Inspector-General of Registration in Madras, a department of the public service which in its dealings is in closer touch than any other with the material and social conditions of the people themselves, but he is himself the author of a most authoritative work on the moral and material progress of Southern India under British rule. At the meeting referred to he observed:—

> 'The Abbé was a most remarkable character, and a study of his life cannot fail to be of profit to us all. It has been said, and said truly, that one half of the nation does not know how the other half lives. The difficulties which a foreigner has of understanding the inner life and modes of thought of a people to which he does not belong may indeed be said to be immense. The Abbé surmounted these difficulties by devoting thirty years of his life to his subject. To effect his purpose he adopted the garb, the manners, and, as he says, even the prejudices of the people among whom his lot was cast; won their respect and confidence; and was held by them in quite as much reverence as one of their *yogis* or *gurus*. The quotations from his work show his shrewd common sense, clear-sightedness, and perfect candour. Any account given by such a man of the manners and customs of the people amongst whom he lived must in any case be instructive, and I for one look forward with great interest to the forthcoming revised edition of the Abbé's work.'

In many respects the Abbé displays a truly wonderful insight into things. For instance, in his finally corrected work there is a passage (evidently a late interpolation) in which he sums up in a few brief sentences his opinion of British dominion in India, and which is all the more remarkable as coming from a Frenchman. In that passage he remarks:—

'The European Power which is now established in India is, properly speaking, supported neither by physical force nor by moral influence. It is a piece of huge, complicated machinery, moved by springs which have been arbitrarily adapted to it. Under the supremacy of the Brahmins the people of India hated their government, while they cherished and respected their rulers; under the supremacy of Europeans they hate and despise their rulers from the bottom of their hearts, while they cherish and respect their government. And here I would remark that the rule of all the Hindu princes, and often that of the Mahomedans, was, properly speaking, Brahminical rule, since all posts of confidence were held by Brahmins.

'If it be possible to ameliorate the condition of the people of India I am convinced that this desirable result will be attained under the new *régime*, whatever may be said by detractors who are ready to find fault with everything. Whatever truth indeed there may be in the prejudiced charges, engendered by ignorance and interested motives, which are brought against the new order of things, and which are perhaps inseparable from every great administration, I for one cannot believe that a nation so eminently distinguished for its beneficent and humane principles of government at home, and above all for its impartial justice to all classes alike—I for one cannot believe that this nation will ever be blind enough to compromise its own noble character by refusing participation in these benefits to a subject people which is content to live peaceably under its sway.

'At the same time I venture to predict that it will attempt in vain to effect any very considerable changes in the social condition of the people of India, whose character, principles, customs, and ineradicable conservatism will always present insurmountable obstacles. To make a people happy, it is essential that they themselves should desire to be made happy and should co-operate with those who are working for their happiness. Now, the people of India, it appears to me, neither possess this desire nor are anxious to co-operate to this end. Every reform which is obviously devised for their well-being they obstinately push aside if it is likely in the least degree to disturb their manner of living, their most absurd prejudice, or their most puerile custom.

'Nevertheless the justice and prudence which the present rulers display in endeavouring to make these people less unhappy than they have been hitherto; the anxiety they manifest in increasing their material comfort; above all, the inviolable respect which they constantly show for the customs and religious beliefs of the country; and, lastly, the protection they afford to the weak as well as to the strong, to the Brahmin as to the Pariah, to the Christian, to the Mahomedan, and to the Pagan: all these have contributed more to the consolidation of their power than even their victories and conquests....

'It has been asserted that any great power based neither on a display of force nor on the affection and esteem of subject races is bound sooner or later to topple under its own weight. I am far from sharing this opinion altogether. The present Government is in a position in which it has little or nothing to fear from extraneous disturbance. True it is that like all empires it is subject to possible chances of internal dissension, military revolt, and general insurrection. But I firmly believe that nothing of this sort will happen to it so long as it maintains amongst its troops the perfect discipline and the sense of comfort which at present exist, and so long as it does all in its power to make its yoke scarcely perceptible by permitting its subjects every freedom in the exercise of their social and religious practices.

'It is the poverty of the country which in my opinion gives most cause for apprehension—a poverty which is accompanied by the most extraordinary supineness on the part of the people themselves. The question is, will a Government which is rightly determined to be neither unjust nor oppressive be able always to find within the borders of this immense empire means sufficient to enable it to meet the heavy expenses of its administration? But, after all, God alone can foretell the destiny of Governments!'

Time has but proved incontestably the truth of these far-seeing criticisms. Even the Mutiny is therein anticipated and its chief cause accurately foretold, while nobody will deny the justice, even at the present day, of the Abbé's observations on the attitude of the natives of India towards the British Government and on the difficulties with which that Government has to contend in administering its vast Eastern empire, according to Western notions of civilization and progress, with the resources that it yields for that purpose.

There is one other matter which I feel bound to refer to before concluding this brief notice of the Abbé's sojourn and work in India, and that is the impression he derived after three decades of Mission labour as to the possibility of converting India to Christianity. I have no wish to renew the bitter controversy which ensued on the publication of his *Letters on the State of Christianity in India* soon after his return to France; but no notice of the Abbé's career would be complete without some reference to it. The purport of those *Letters*, as I understand them, was to assert that, under existing circumstances, there is no human possibility of converting the Hindus as a nation to any sect of Christianity; or in the Abbé's own words, 'Let the Christian religion be presented to these people under every possible light, . . . the time of conversion has passed away, and under existing circumstances there remains no human possibility of bringing it back.' It would require a reproduction of the whole text of these *Letters* to explain fully the grounds upon which the Abbé based a decision so humiliating to himself and to his fellow-Christian workers, but the chief cause undoubtedly was the invincible barrier of what we may call nowadays intellectual Hinduism, but which the Abbé called Brahminical prejudice. He refers regretfully to the collapse of the Church, with its hundreds of thousands of converts, many of them of high caste, established by the Jesuits Beschi and de Nobili in Madura; but at the same time he makes no concealment of the real causes of their failure. 'The Hindus soon found that those missionaries whom their colour, their talents, and other qualities had induced them to regard as such extraordinary beings, as men coming from another world, were in fact nothing else but disguised Feringhis (Europeans), and that their country, their religion, and original education were the same as those of the evil, the contemptible Feringhis who had of late invaded their country. This event proved the last blow to the interests of the Christian religion. No more conversions were made. Apostasy became almost general in several quarters, and Christianity became more and more an object of contempt and aversion in proportion as European manners became better known to the Hindus.'

It is necessary to remark that the Abbé's *Letters* were

vehemently answered by the Protestant missionaries, Hough and Townley; but we need not enter into the details of the controversy. In another place the Abbé remarked: 'Should the intercourse between individuals of both nations, by becoming more intimate and more friendly, produce a change in the religion and usages of the country, it will not be to turn Christians that they will forsake their own religion, but rather (what in my opinion is a thousand times worse than idolatry) to become mere atheists; and if they renounce their present customs it will not be to embrace those of Europeans, but rather to become what are now called Pariahs.'

In a word, the Abbé completely despaired of the higher castes ever becoming Christians, though he was ready to acknowledge that there was a harvest-field among the low castes and outcastes. Of his own attempts to convert the Hindus he remarks: 'For my part I cannot boast of my successes in this sacred career during the period that I have laboured to promote the interests of the Christian religion. The restraints and privations under which I have lived, by conforming myself to the usages of the country; embracing, in many respects, the prejudices of the natives; living like them, and becoming all but a Hindu myself; in short, by being made all things to all men, that I might by all means save some—all these have proved of no avail to me to make proselytes. During the long period I have lived in India in the capacity of a missionary, I have made, with the assistance of a native missionary, in all between two and three hundred converts of both sexes. Of this number two-thirds were Pariahs or beggars; and the rest were composed of Sudras, vagrants, and outcastes of several tribes, who, being without resource, turned Christians in order to form connexions, chiefly for the purpose of marriage, or with some other interested views.'

These various quotations from the Abbé's *Letters* are likely to inspire indignation among Christian missionaries, but his general conclusions certainly find a remarkable echo in the following extract on Christianity in Mr. Baines's General Report on the Census of 1891:—

'Its greatest development is found where the Brahmanic caste system is in force in its fullest vigour, in the south and west of the Peninsula, and amongst the Hill tribes of Bengal. In such localities it is naturally attractive to a class of the population whose position is hereditarily and permanently degraded by their own religion, as Islam has proved in Eastern Bengal, and amongst the lowest class of the inhabitants of the Panjab. We have seen that in the early days of Portuguese missionary enterprise, it was found necessary to continue the breach that Brahmanic custom had placed between certain grades of society and those above them; but in later times, and in foreign missions of the Reformed Church, the tendency has been to absorb all caste distinctions into the general commission of the Christianity of that form. The new faith has thus affected the lower classes more directly than the upper, who have more to lose socially, and less to gain.' . . .

It may be mentioned that in the agricultural settlement of reconverted Christians at Sathalli in Mysore, previously alluded to, the inhabitants retained their Hindu caste distinctions; and the following observations in Mr. V. N. Narasimmiyengar's Mysore Census Report (1891) are noteworthy:—

'Roman Catholicism is able to prevail among the Hindus more rapidly and easily, by reason of its policy of tolerating among its converts the customs of caste and social observances, which constitute so material a part of the Indian social fabric. In the course of the investigations engendered by the census, several Roman Christian communities have been met with, which continue undisturbed in the rites and usages which had guided them in their pre-conversion existence. They still pay worship to the *Kalasam* at marriages and festivals, call in the Brahmin astrologer and *purohita*, use the Hindu religious marks, and conform to various other amenities, which have the advantage of minimizing friction in their daily intercourse with their Hindu fellow-caste brethren.'

And yet the Christian native is nowadays but in the ratio of seven in a thousand of the whole population. The remark accordingly made by the Roman Catholic Bishop of Agra to Jacquemont is as applicable now as it was when it was uttered in 1828: 'La caldalja é molto grande, ma la carne é molto poca.'

The last years of the Abbé's life were spent at the head-quarters of the Missions Étrangères at Paris. He left India, never to return, on January 15, 1823, his passage having been paid by the East India Company and a special pension settled upon him for life in recognition of the many services which he had rendered to India. On his return to Paris he was at once made Director of the Missions Étrangères, and from 1836 to 1839 he filled the post of Superior. During his leisure he found time to translate into French the whole of the *Pancha-tantra*, the famous book of Hindu fables, and also a work which he entitled *The Exploits of the Guru Paramarta.* He lived for no less than a quarter of a century after returning to Europe, and died in 1848 at the patriarchal age of eighty-three.

In conclusion I desire to acknowledge the kind assistance and advice which I have received from many Hindu friends and others while editing the Abbé's work: especially do I desire to acknowledge the help rendered to me by Mr. C. V. Munisawmy Iyer, a Brahmin gentleman, who associated himself with me in the revision of the proofs.

H. K. B.

MADRAS,
September, 1897.

CONTENTS

PART II.

The Four States of Brahminical Life.

CHAPTER I.

CHAPTER II.

CHAPTER III.

CHAPTER IV.

CHAPTER V.

CHAPTER VI.

CHAPTER VII.

PART III.

Religion.

CHAPTER I.

CHAPTER II.

CHAPTER III.

CHAPTER IV.

CHAPTER V.

CHAPTER VI.

CHAPTER VII.

CHAPTER VIII.

CHAPTER IX.

APPENDIX I.

APPENDIX II.

APPENDIX III.

APPENDIX IV.

APPENDIX V.

APPENDIX VI.

HINDU MANNERS
CUSTOMS, AND CEREMONIES

AUTHOR'S PREFACE

THOUGH Europeans have possessed settlements in India for more than three centuries, it is only within recent times that authentic details have been obtained with respect to the people who dwell in this vast country and whose ancient civilization, methods of government, manners, creeds, and customs are nevertheless so well worthy of notice. It is impossible to doubt for a moment that science and art flourished amongst these nations at an epoch when our most civilized countries of the West were still plunged in the dark abyss of ignorance. The various forms of their institutions, both political and social; their knowledge of mathematics, especially of astronomy; their systems of metaphysics and ethics: all of these had long ago made the people of India famous far beyond their own borders; while the renown of Hindu philosophers had reached even Europe. The many ill-informed and often contradictory narratives about India which have been published in modern times have deservedly fallen into discredit. Yet, it must be admitted, some good work has been done by certain Literary Societies that have of recent years been established in India, the members of which, possessing access to original sources of information, have begun to survey with a more critical eye these records of divine and human knowledge, whose depositaries have hitherto guarded them with zealous care behind a veil of mystery. Without doubt the members of these Societies, distinguished as they mostly are by their erudition, will continue to devote special study to the languages of the country and to make abundant use of the sources of information open to them. Yet, it must be confessed, the information which we possess about the people of India is very meagre compared with that which it is most important for us to acquire. The ancient history of their country is, for one thing, enshrouded in chimera and fable, and, unfortunately, such incoherence and such obscurity prevail in their written records, which are our only means of really getting at the truth, that it is not too much to presume that we shall never succeed in throwing proper light on all this mass of absurdities. The most popular and best known of these written records are the *Râmâyana*, the *Bhâgavata*, and the *Mahâbhârata*[1]; but the information which their authors give about the dates, events, and duration of the different dynasties; about the heroes of India and their prowess in war; about the various revolutions which occurred in the country and the circumstances which led to them; about the beginnings of Hindu polity; about the discoveries and progress in science and art; in a word, about all the most interesting features of history,—all information of this kind is, as it were, buried amid a mass of fable and superstition.

My readers will see in the following pages to what extremes the people of India carry their belief in and love for the marvellous. Their first historians were in reality poets, who seem to have decided that they could not do better than compose their poems in the spirit of the people for whom they were writing. That is to say, they were guided solely by the desire to please their readers, and accordingly clothed Truth in such a grotesque garb as to render it a mere travesty from an historical point of view. The Indian Muse of History thus became a kind of magician whose wand performed wonders. The successors of these first poet-historians were actuated by the same motives, and even thought that it added to their own glory to improve on their predecessors and to surpass them in the absurdity of their fictions.

While waiting for inquirers, more skilful than myself, to find a way through this labyrinth, which to me is absolutely inextricable, I offer to the public a large number of authentic records which I have carefully collected, and which, for the most part, contain particulars that are either unknown or only partially known, in the hope that they will be found not altogether devoid of interest. I believe, at any rate, that they will be acknow-

[1] These are the three great Hindu Epic poems. Vide Part II, Chapter XXII, and Part III, Chapter V.

ledged to contain some useful materials for future savants who may undertake a complete and methodical treatise on the people of India, a task which is far beyond my powers and which moreover I could not possibly have laid upon myself, seeing that I was without literary aids of any kind during my long and absolute seclusion amongst the natives of the country.

In this new edition the contents of my first MS. have been carefully revised and corrected. They have, moreover, been considerably augmented by many curious details which did not appear in the original document. At the same time, I have made no substantial changes in the order and classification of the contents. Five or six additional chapters, and a number of corrections and improvements in the body of the work, constitute all the difference between this and the earlier draft. Since the English translation of the latter appeared, great political changes have taken place amongst the people whose manners and institutions I have sketched; but, as these changes were not taken into account in my original plan, I have not considered myself bound, when referring to them, to go beyond the limits which I prescribed for myself in the first instance. In all that I say about the administration of the Peninsula my readers will at once perceive that I have in mind the Governments preceding that which has now made itself master of the destinies of the Indian people, and which has freed them from the iron yoke of a long series of arbitrary rulers, under whose oppression they groaned during so many centuries.

This colossal dominion, which a European Government has succeeded in establishing in India without any very great difficulty and without any very violent shocks, has filled the people of India with admiration, and has fully convinced the Powers of Asia of the great superiority of Europeans in every way, and more especially in the art of subjugating and governing nations.

We too may well wonder at a conquest which appears indeed almost miraculous. It is difficult for us to imagine how a mere handful of men managed to coerce into submissive obedience a hundred millions of people, scattered over a country which extends for twenty-four degrees of latitude north and south and for nearly the same number of degrees east and west.

And it is still more difficult to understand how these few men are able to maintain within the bounds of duty and subordination a population whose creeds, habits, customs, and manner of life are so absolutely different from their own.

Yet one will have little or no difficulty in accounting for such a phenomenon if one examines on the one hand the spirit, character, and institutions of the people governed, and on the other the system adopted by those governing them. The people of India have always been accustomed to bow their heads beneath the yoke of a cruel and oppressive despotism, and moreover, strange to say, have always displayed mere indifference towards those who have forced them to it. Little cared they whether the princes under whom they groaned were of their own country or from foreign lands[1]. The frequent vicissitudes that befell those in power were hardly noticed by their subjects. Never did the fall of one of these despots cause the least regret; never did the elevation of another cause the least joy. Hard experience had taught the Hindus to disregard not only the hope of better times but the fear of worse. The fable of the ass urged by its master to escape from approaching robbers is most appropriate to these people. They have always considered themselves lucky enough if their religious and domestic institutions were left untouched by those who by good fortune or force of arms had got hold of the reins of government.

The European Power which is now established in India is, properly speaking, supported neither by physical force nor by moral influence. It is a piece of huge, complicated machinery, moved by springs which have been arbitrarily adapted to it. Under the supremacy of the Brahmins the people of India hated their government, while they cherished and respected their rulers; under the supremacy of Europeans they hate and despise their rulers from the bottom of their hearts, while they cherish and respect their government. And here I would remark that the rule of all the Hindu princes, and often that of the Mahomedans, was, properly speaking, Brahminical rule, since all posts of confidence were held by Brahmins.

If it be possible to ameliorate the condition of the people of

[1] This is illustrated in the familiar proverb, 'What matters it whether Rama reigns or the Rakshasa (Ravana) reigns?'—Ed.

India I am convinced that this desirable result will be attained under the new *régime*, whatever may be said by detractors who are ready to find fault with everything. Whatever truth indeed there may be in the prejudiced charges, engendered by ignorance and interested motives, which are brought against the new order of things, and which are perhaps inseparable from every great administration, I for one cannot believe that a nation so eminently distinguished for its beneficent and humane principles of government at home, and above all for its impartial justice to all classes alike — I for one cannot believe that this nation will ever be blind enough to compromise its own noble character by refusing participation in these benefits to a subject people which is content to live peaceably under its sway.

At the same time I venture to predict that it will attempt in vain to effect any very considerable changes in the social condition of the people of India, whose character, principles, customs, and ineradicable conservatism will always present insurmountable obstacles. To make a people happy, it is essential that they themselves should desire to be made happy and should co-operate with those who are working for their happiness. Now, the people of India, it appears to me, neither possess this desire nor are anxious to co-operate to this end. Every reform which is obviously devised for their well-being they obstinately push aside if it is likely in the least degree to disturb their manner of living, their most absurd prejudice, or their most puerile custom.

Nevertheless the justice and prudence which the present rulers display in endeavouring to make these people less unhappy than they have been hitherto; the anxiety they manifest in increasing their material comfort; above all, the inviolable respect which they constantly show for the customs and religious beliefs of the country; and, lastly, the protection they afford to the weak as well as to the strong, to the Brahmin as to the Pariah, to the Christian, to the Mahomedan, and to the Pagan: all these have contributed more to the consolidation of their power than even their victories and conquests.

There is another circumstance no less remarkable which may account for the stability and power of this Government, and that is the sagacity with which it has chosen persons to fill places of responsibility under it. For uprightness of character, education, and ability it would be hard to find a body of public servants better capable of filling with zeal and distinction the offices, more or less important, that are entrusted to them.

During the thirty years spent by me in the various provinces of India I have had the honour of knowing a very large number of these public servants, and it gives me much pleasure to testify here to the many excellent qualities which I have almost invariably found them to possess. Cast away, as it were, on the shores of this foreign land at a time when my own country was a prey to all the horrors of a disastrous revolution, I never failed to receive from them the warmest hospitality. Even when a desperate war might well have given rise to bitter prejudice against everything French, I never failed to find amongst the rulers of India many friends and benefactors. Would that the fear of offending their modesty did not forbid my mentioning here in testimony of my regard the names of many of them equally distinguished for their high merit and for their commanding position. But even at the risk of appearing indiscreet I cannot pass over one of them in silence. I cannot, in the fullness of my gratitude, abstain from mentioning publicly how much I owe to the Honourable Mr. Arthur Henry Cole, the British Resident in Mysore. This worthy official, whose public and domestic virtues, inexhaustible charity, and polished manners are recognized throughout the whole of the Peninsula, has found a fitting recognition of his fine character in the love and respect of the natives subject to his jurisdiction, who with one voice have hailed him as the *father of their country*. All that he has done for the natives of Mysore will be long remembered by them. As regards myself, nothing can equal the many acts of kindness which he has heaped upon me during my stay of twenty years in the province subject to his authority. If these words ever reach him I trust that he will recognize in them the genuine feelings of respect and gratitude which I shall ever cherish towards him.

One might accuse me of blind prejudice if I went so far as to affirm that everybody vested with authority in this land was without exception worthy of high praise. The fact is, we do not live in an age of miracles. It is probable, it is even certain, that not all of those entrusted with the supervision of this huge political machinery are influenced by the purest motives. And yet the system of watchful control is such that any man who allows himself to be tempted from the path of duty by greed and avarice cannot hope to hide his corrupt doings from the eye of superior authority for any length of time. Every subject of the dominant power, however humble he may be, is allowed the right of free petition; and this is sufficient guarantee that any well-founded grievances will be set right, any well-proven abuses put a stop to.

It has been asserted that any great power based neither on a display of force nor on the affection and esteem of subject races is bound sooner or later to topple under its own weight. I am far from sharing this opinion altogether. The present Government occupies a position in which it has little or nothing to fear from extraneous disturbance. True it is that like all empires it is subject to possible chances of internal dissension, military revolt, and general insurrection. But I firmly believe that nothing of this sort will happen to it so long as it maintains amongst its troops the perfect discipline and the sense of comfort which at present exist, and so long as it does all in its power to make its yoke scarcely perceptible by permitting its subjects every freedom in the exercise of their social and religious practices [1].

It is the poverty of the country which in my opinion gives most cause for apprehension—a poverty which is accompanied by the most extraordinary supineness on the part of the people themselves. The question is, will a Government which is rightly determined to be neither unjust nor oppressive be able always to find within the borders of this immense empire means sufficient to enable it to meet the heavy expenses of its administration [2]? But, after all, God alone can foretell the destiny of Governments!

But I must return to the contents of my work. During my long sojourn in India I never let slip any opportunity of collecting materials and particulars of all sorts. My information

[1] Students of Indian History will bear witness to the wisdom of the Abbé's remarks, which subsequent history has so strikingly tended to confirm.—ED.

[2] Within these few lines the Abbé, with extraordinary insight, has embodied the great problem of British administration in India.—ED.

has been drawn partly from the books which are held in highest estimation amongst the people of India and partly from such scattered records as fell by chance into my hands and contained facts upon which I could thoroughly rely. But in regard to the majority of the materials which I now offer to the public I am chiefly dependent on my own researches, having lived in close and familiar intercourse with persons of every caste and condition of life. Probably many Europeans settled in India would have been more capable than myself of performing the same task; but I may be permitted to doubt whether there has been any person more favourably situated for gleaning information or more zealous in his pursuit of knowledge. I had no sooner arrived amongst the natives of India than I recognized the absolute necessity of gaining their confidence. Accordingly I made it my constant rule to live as they did. I adopted their style of clothing, and I studied their customs and methods of life in order to be exactly like them. I even went so far as to avoid any display of repugnance to the majority of their peculiar prejudices. By such circumspect conduct I was able to ensure a free and hearty welcome from people of all castes and conditions, and was often favoured of their own accord with the most curious and interesting particulars about themselves.

In publishing these records of my researches I have no wish to aspire to literary fame. I have noted down just what I saw, just what I heard, just what I read. I have aimed only at simplicity and accuracy. If I have here and there ventured to give a few opinions and conjectures of my own, I beg that my readers will not suppose that I have done so out of vanity and with the object of posing as a profound scholar, which I am not. However severely critics may attack my work, they cannot be more keenly aware of its imperfections than myself. I know well that my researches might have been presented in a form more agreeable, more animated, and more methodical. There are many matters mentioned by me which called for more profound discussion, clearer criticism, and wider treatment. A more correct and more brilliant style would have concealed the dryness of certain details. But I beg indulgent readers to consider the circumstances which have prevented me from satisfying such conditions. Separated as I was for more than thirty years from all intercourse with my fellow-countrymen, communicating only rarely and occasionally with Europeans, passing my whole life in villages in the midst of rude cultivators of the soil, deprived of all the advantages which great cities offer to those writers who are clever enough to profit by the labours of their predecessors, prevented from invoking the aid and counsel of intelligent men, having no books to refer to except my Bible and a few writings without merit and without interest which chance rather than choice put into my hands, compelled indeed to rely upon the imperfect recollection of what I had read and learned in my youth: with all these disadvantages it was only to be expected that my work would be defective. Nevertheless I am persuaded that the notes which I have taken so much trouble to collect will afford some useful material to others more favourably situated than myself; and I have therefore no hesitation in offering them to the public.

There is one motive which above all others has influenced my determination. It struck me that a faithful picture of the wickedness and incongruities of polytheism and idolatry would by its very ugliness help greatly to set off the beauties and perfections of Christianity. It was thus that the Lacedaemonians placed drunken slaves in the sight of their children in order to inspire the latter with a horror of intemperance.

There is every reason to believe that the true God was well known to the people of India at the time when they first banded themselves together as a nation. For who can doubt that our blessed religion was originally that of the whole world? Who can doubt that it would have exercised universal sway from the days of Adam to the end of time if its original form as established by God Himself and its primitive traditions had been carefully respected? Unfortunately human passion gained the upper hand. Whole nations were corrupted, and men made for themselves a religion more suited to the depravity of their own hearts. Nevertheless, what has now become of the innumerable deities of Greece and Rome? They have vanished like an empty, transitory dream. Let us pray that the Almighty may be pleased to allow the torch of Truth to illumine the countries watered by the Ganges! Doubtless the time is still far distant when the stubborn Hindu will open his eyes to the light and tear himself away from his dark superstitions; but let us not despair, a day will come when the standard of the Cross will be flying over the temples of India as it flies now over her strong places [1].

Certain statements to be found in my work will seem almost incredible to my readers. All that I can say is that I have set down nothing without assuring myself most carefully of its truthfulness. For the rest, my readers will feel much less doubt as to the accuracy of these statements when they have learned to recognize how eminently original the people of India are in their manners and customs. So original are they, indeed, that one may search in vain for types, or anything approaching to types, of them amongst other nations of the world, ancient or modern.

With regard to caste usages I must warn my readers that my researches were confined to the provinces south of the Kistna River, where I passed most of the time that I was in India. I cannot say whether these usages are the same to the north of that river and in Hindustan proper; but if any differences there be it is probable that they exist only in form. There is no place in India which does not possess certain customs and practices of its own, and it would be impossible to give descriptions of them all. Fundamentally, however, caste constitutions are the same everywhere. Furthermore, however many the shades of difference between the various castes, however diversified the customs that control them, only slight differences exist between the various forms of religious belief. Indeed, the religion of the Hindus may be said to form a common centre for the numerous elements which constitute Hinduism in its widest sense. Moreover there is a certain general uniformity of rule and practice in everyday social matters, which compels one to look upon the different masses of the population as belonging in reality to one big family. Nevertheless, whatever I may say in the following pages must not be given a too general meaning, for it is hardly necessary to point out that in such a huge

[1] Yet even now the number of Christians in India is, comparatively speaking, small. They form about ·75 per cent. of the whole population, and nearly 75 per cent. of the total are found in Madras, Travancore, Hyderabad, Mysore, and Cochin. And concerning the native Christians of these parts a distinguished and much-travelled member of the Civil Service recently remarked, 'Their Christianity, as I have seen it, too often breathes but little of the spirit of the Sermon on the Mount.'—Ed.

country there are many peculiarities of language and custom which are purely local in character. For instance, a careful observer would see less resemblance between a Tamil and a Canarese, between a Telugu and a Mahratta, than between a Frenchman and an Englishman, an Italian and a German.

Even when they migrate or travel from one province to another, natives of India never throw off what I may call the characteristics of their natal soil. In the midst of their new surroundings they invariably preserve their own language and customs.

On the Malabar coast one may count five different tribes, established from time immemorial, within a hundred leagues of territory north and south. They are the *Nairs* or *Naimars*, the *Kurgas* or *Kudagas*, the *Tulus*, the *Konkanis*, and the *Kanaras*. Although amalgamated in some degree, each of these tribes still preserves to the present day the language and mode of life peculiar to the place from which it originally sprang. The same thing may be remarked throughout the Peninsula, but especially in the Tamil country and in Mysore, where many families of Telugus are to be found whose ancestors were obliged for various reasons to quit their native soil and migrate thither. The remembrance of their original birthplace is engraved on the hearts of these Telugus, and they always carefully avoid following the peculiar usages of their adoptive country. Yet they are invariably treated with the most perfect tolerance. Indeed, every native of India is quite free to take up his abode wherever it may seem good to him. Nobody will quarrel with him for living his own life, speaking what language he pleases, or following whatever customs he is used to. All that is asked of him is that he should conform generally to the accustomed rules of decorum recognized in the neighbourhood.

The Brahmin caste has seemed to me to merit particular attention. It is the caste whose rules and practices are most scrupulously observed. All persons who have visited India or who have any notion of the character of the Brahmins, of the high esteem in which they hold themselves, and of the distant *hauteur* with which they treat the common people, will be able to appreciate the difficulties which anybody must encounter who would become intimate, or even acquainted, with these proud personages. The hate and contempt which they cherish against all strangers, and especially against Europeans; the jealous inquietude with which they hide from the profane the mysteries of their religious cult; the records of their learning; the privacy of their homes: all these form barriers between themselves and their observers which it is almost impossible to pass[1].

Nevertheless, by much diplomacy and perseverance I have succeeded in surmounting most of the obstacles which have turned back so many others before me. I therefore trust that the minute particulars which I have given in this work will be accepted as a record of all that it is useful to know about the religious ceremonies and ritual of the Hindus.

I have divided this work into three parts. The first presents a general purview of society in India, and contains details concerning all classes of its inhabitants. In the second part I have discussed the Brahmins more particularly, both in themselves and in relation to other castes. The third part contains particulars of the religious tenets and deities of India.

Among the papers which are published separately, as Appendices, there is one on the Jains which I hope will be read not without interest. These schismatics are to be found in great numbers in the western provinces of the Peninsula, and especially in Malabar, where they represent the majority of the population. They form a perfectly distinct class, and differ widely from the Brahmins in many essential points of doctrine and practice.

[1] Since the Abbé wrote, vast stores of Brahminical lore have been brought to light by enterprising savants in Europe, especially by Professor Max Müller.—Ed.

PART I

GENERAL VIEW OF SOCIETY IN INDIA, AND GENERAL REMARKS ON THE CASTE SYSTEM

CHAPTER I

Division and Subdivision of Castes.—Castes peculiar to Certain Provinces.—Particular Usages of some Castes.—Division of Castes founded on Parentage.—Subordination of Castes.—Outward Signs of certain Castes.—Division of Caste-groups into Right-hand and Left-hand.

THE word *caste* is derived from the Portuguese, and is used in Europe to designate the different tribes or classes into which the people of India are divided[1]. The most ordinary classification, and at the same time the most ancient, divides them into four main castes. The first and most distinguished of all is that of *Brahmana*, or *Brahmins*; the second in rank is that of *Kshatriyas*, or *Rajahs*; the third the *Vaisyas*, or *Landholders* and *Merchants*; and the fourth the *Sudras*, or *Cultivators* and *Menials*.

The functions proper to each of these four main castes are: for Brahmins, priesthood and its various duties; for Kshatriyas, military service in all its branches; for Vaisyas, agriculture, trade, and cattle-breeding; and for Sudras, general servitude.

[1] The Sanskrit word is *Varna* = colour, thus showing that upon the difference of colour between the Aryan Brahmins and the aboriginal inhabitants the distinction of caste was originally founded.—POPE.

But I will describe more fully hereafter the several social distinctions which are attached to each of them.

Each of the four main castes is subdivided into many others, the number of which it is difficult to determine because the subdivisions vary according to locality, and a sub-caste existing in one province is not necessarily found in another.

Amongst the Brahmins of the south of the Peninsula, for example, there are to be found three or four principal divisions, and each of these again is subdivided into at least twenty others. The lines of demarcation between them are so well defined as to prevent any kind of union between one sub-caste and another, especially in the case of marriage.

The Kshatriyas and Vaisyas are also split up into many divisions and subdivisions. In Southern India neither Kshatriyas nor Vaisyas are very numerous; but there are considerable numbers of the former in Northern India. Howbeit, the Brahmins assert that the true Kshatriya caste no longer exists, and that those who pass for such are in reality a debased race.

The Sudra caste is divided into most sub-castes. Nobody in any of the provinces where I have lived has ever been able to inform me as to the exact number and names of them. It is a common saying, however, that there are 18 chief sub-castes, which are again split up into 108 lesser divisions.

The Sudras are the most numerous of the four main castes. They form, in fact, the mass of the population, and added to the Pariahs, or Outcastes, they represent at least nine-tenths of the inhabitants. When we consider that the Sudras possess almost a monopoly of the various forms of artisan employment and manual labour, and that in India no person can exercise two professions at a time, it is not surprising that the numerous individuals who form this main caste are distributed over so many distinct branches.

However, there are several classes of Sudras that exist only in certain provinces. Of all the provinces that I lived in, the Dravidian, or Tamil, country is the one where the ramifications of caste appeared to me most numerous. There are not nearly so many ramifications of caste in Mysore or the Deccan. Nowhere in these latter provinces have I come across castes corresponding to those which are known in the Tamil country under the names of *Moodelly, Agambady, Nattaman, Totiyar, Udaiyan, Valeyen, Upiliyen, Pallen,* and several others [1].

It should be remarked, however, that those Sudra castes which are occupied exclusively in employments indispensable to all civilized societies are to be found everywhere under names varying with the languages of different localities. Of such I may cite, amongst others, the gardeners, the shepherds, the weavers, the *Panchalas* (the five castes of artisans, comprising the carpenters, goldsmiths, blacksmiths, founders, and in general all workers in metals), the manufacturers and venders of oil, the fishermen, the potters, the washermen, the barbers, and some others. All these form part of the great main caste of Sudras; but the different castes of cultivators hold the first rank and disdainfully regard as their inferiors all those belonging to the professions just mentioned, refusing to eat with those who practise them.

In some districts there are castes which are not to be met with elsewhere, and which may be distinguished by peculiarities of their own. I am not aware, for example, that the very remarkable caste of *Nairs,* whose women enjoy the privilege of possessing several husbands, is to be found anywhere but in Travancore [2]. Amongst these same people, again, is another distinct caste called *Namburi,* which observes one abominable and revolting custom. The girls of this caste are usually married before the age of puberty; but if a girl who has arrived at an age when the signs of puberty are apparent happens to die before having had intercourse with a man, caste custom rigorously demands that the inanimate corpse of the deceased shall be subjected to a monstrous connexion. For this purpose the girl's parents are obliged to procure by a present of money some wretched fellow willing to consummate such a disgusting

[1] *Moodelly,* 'chief man' or highly respectable trader. *Agambady,* he who performs menial offices in temples or palaces. *Nattaman,* a caste of cultivators. *Totiyar,* a caste of labourers. *Udaiyan,* a potter. *Valeyen,* a fisherman. *Upiliyen,* salt manufacturer. *Pallen,* agriculturist.—ED.

[2] It would be more correct to say West Coast. Moreover, although Nair women are commonly described as polyandrous, they are not really so, for though they enjoy the privilege of changing their husbands, they do not entertain more than one husband *at a time.*—ED.

form of marriage: for were the marriage not consummated the family would consider itself dishonoured [1].

The caste of *Kullars*, or robbers, who exercise their calling as an hereditary right, is found only in the Marava country, which borders on the coast, or fishing, districts. The rulers of the country are of the same caste. They regard a robber's occupation as discreditable neither to themselves nor to their fellow castemen, for the simple reason that they consider robbery a duty and a right sanctioned by descent. They are not ashamed of their caste or occupation, and if one were to ask of a *Kullar* to what people he belonged he would coolly answer, 'I am a robber!' This caste is looked upon in the district of Madura, where it is widely diffused, as one of the most distinguished among the Sudras.

There exists in the same part of the country another caste, known as the *Totiyars*, in which brothers, uncles, nephews, and other near relations are all entitled to possess their wives in common.

In Eastern Mysore there is a caste called *Morsa-Okkala-Makkalu*, in which, when the mother of a family gives her eldest daughter in marriage, she is obliged to submit to the amputation of two joints of the middle finger and of the ring finger of the right hand. And if the bride's mother be dead the bridegroom's mother, or in default of her the mother of the nearest relative, must submit to this cruel mutilation [2].

Many other castes exist in various districts which are distinguished by practices no less foolish than those above mentioned.

Generally speaking, there are few castes which are not

[1] Whatever may have been the case in the days of the Abbé, these customs no longer exist. In regard to this, Mr. W. Logan, in his *Manual of Malabar*, writes thus: 'To make tardy retribution—if it deserves such a name—to women who die unmarried, the corpse, it is said, cannot be burnt till a *tali* string (the Hindu equivalent of the wedding-ring of Europe) is tied round the neck of the corpse, while lying on the funeral pile, by a competent relative. Nambutiris are exceedingly reticent in regard to their funeral ceremonies and observances, and the Abbé Dubois' account of what was related to him regarding other observances at this strange funeral-pile marriage requires confirmation.' —ED.

[2] This custom is no longer observed; instead of the two fingers being amputated, they are now merely bound together and thus rendered unfit for use.—ED.

distinguished by some special custom quite apart from the peculiar religious usages and ceremonies which the community may prescribe to guarantee or sanction civil contracts. In the cut and colour of their clothes and in the style of wearing them, in the peculiar shape of their jewels and in the manner in which they are displayed on various parts of the person, the various castes have many rules, each possessing its own significance. Some observe rites of their own in their funeral and marriage ceremonies: others possess ornaments which they alone may use, or flags of certain colours, for various ceremonies, which no other caste may carry. Yet, absurd as some of these practices may appear, they arouse neither contempt nor dislike in members of other castes which do not admit them. The most perfect toleration is the rule in such matters. As long as a caste conforms on the whole to the recognized rules of decorum it is permitted to follow its own bent in its domestic affairs without interruption, and no other castes ever think of blaming or even criticizing it, although its practices may be in direct opposition to their own.

There are, nevertheless, some customs which, although scrupulously observed in the countries where they exist, are so strongly opposed to the rules of decency and decorum generally laid down that they are spoken of with disapprobation and sometimes with horror by the rest of the community. The following may be mentioned among practices of this nature.

In the interior of Mysore, women are obliged to accompany the male inmates of the house whenever the latter retire for the calls of nature, and to cleanse them with water afterwards. This practice, which is naturally viewed with disgust in other parts of the country, is here regarded as a sign of good breeding and is most carefully observed [1].

The use of intoxicating liquors, which is condemned by respectable people throughout almost the whole of India, is nevertheless permitted amongst the people who dwell in the jungles and hill tracts of the West Coast. There the leading castes of Sudras, not excepting even the women and children, openly drink arrack, the brandy of the country, and toddy, the fermented juice of the palm. Each inhabitant in those parts

[1] If this custom ever existed, the spread of education has effectually put a stop to it.—ED.

has his toddy-dealer, who regularly brings him a daily supply and takes in return an equivalent in grain at harvest time.

The Brahmin inhabitants of these parts are forbidden a like indulgence under the penalty of exclusion from caste. But they supply the defect by opium, the use of which, although universally interdicted elsewhere, is nevertheless considered much less objectionable than the use of intoxicating liquors.

The people of these damp and unhealthy districts have no doubt learnt by experience that a moderate use of spirits or opium is necessary for the preservation of health, and that it protects them, partially at any rate, against the ill effects of the malarious miasma amidst which they are obliged to live. Nothing indeed but absolute necessity could have induced them to contravene in this way one of the most venerable precepts of Hindu civilization.

The various classes of Sudras who dwell in the hills of the Carnatic observe amongst their domestic regulations a practice as peculiar as it is disgusting. Both men and women pass their lives in a state of uncleanness and never wash their clothes. When once they have put on cloths fresh from the looms of the weavers they do not leave them off until the material actually drops from rottenness. One can imagine the filthy condition of these cloths after they have been worn day and night for several months soaked with perspiration and soiled with dirt, especially in the case of the women, who continually use them for wiping their hands, and who never change their garments until wear and tear have rendered them absolutely useless.

Yet this revolting habit is most religiously observed, and, if anybody were so rash as to wash but once in water the cloths with which he or she is covered, exclusion from caste would be the inevitable consequence. This custom, however, may be due to the scarcity of water, for in this part of the country there are only a few stagnant ponds, which would very soon be contaminated if all the inhabitants of a village were allowed to wash their garments in them.

Many religious customs are followed only by certain sects, and are of purely local character. For instance, it is only in the districts of Western Mysore that I have observed Monday in each week kept nearly in the same way as Sunday is among Christians. On that day the villagers abstain from ordinary labour, and particularly from such as, like ploughing, requires the use of oxen and kine. Monday is consecrated to Basava (the Bull), and is set apart for the special worship of that deity. Hence it is a day of rest for their cattle rather than for themselves.

This practice, however, is not in vogue except in the districts where the *Lingayats*, or followers of Siva[1], predominate. This sect pays more particular homage to the Bull than the rest of the Hindus; and, in the districts where it predominates, not only keeps up the strict observance of the day thus consecrated to the divinity, but forces other castes to follow its example.

Independently of the divisions and subdivisions common to all castes, one may further observe in each caste close family alliances cemented by intermarriage. Hindus of good family avoid as far as possible intermarriage with families outside their own circle. They always aim at marrying their children into the families which are already allied to them, and the nearer the relationship the more easily are marriages contracted. A widower is remarried to his deceased wife's sister, an uncle marries his niece, and a first cousin his first cousin. Persons so related possess an exclusive privilege of intermarrying, upon the ground of such relationship; and, if they choose, they can prevent any other union and enforce their own preferential right, however old, unsuited, infirm, and poor they may be[2].

In this connexion, however, several strange and ridiculous distinctions are made. An uncle may marry the daughter of his sister, but in no case may he marry the daughter of his brother. A brother's children may marry a sister's children, but the

[1] Mr. L. Rice, in his *Mysore and Coorg*, remarks: 'Lingayats: The distinctive mark of this caste is the wearing on the person of a *Jangama lingam*, or portable linga. It is a small black stone about the size of an acorn, and is enshrined in a silver box of peculiar shape, which is worn suspended from the neck or tied round the arm. The followers of Basava (the founder of the sect, whose name literally means *Bull*, was in fact regarded as the incarnation of Nandi, the bull of Siva) are properly called Lingavantas, but Lingayats has become a well-known designation, though not used by themselves, the name Sivabhakta or Sivachar being one they generally assume.'—ED.

[2] This custom is gradually giving way now amongst the higher castes. —ED.

children of two brothers or of two sisters may not intermarry. Among descendants from the same stock the male line always has the right of contracting marriage with the female line; but the children of the same line may never intermarry.

The reason given for this custom is that children of the male line, as also those of the female line, continue from generation to generation to call themselves brothers and sisters for as long a time as it is publicly recognized that they spring from the same stock. A man would be marrying his sister, it would be said, if the children of either the male or the female line intermarried amongst themselves; whereas the children of the male line do not call the children of the female line brothers and sisters, and vice versa, but call each other by special names expressive of the relationship. Thus a man can, and even must, marry the daughter of his sister, but never the daughter of his brother. A male first cousin marries a female first cousin, the daughter of his maternal aunt; but in no case may he marry the daughter of his paternal uncle.

This rule is universally and invariably observed by all castes, from the Brahmin to the Pariah. It is obligatory on the male line to unite itself with the female line. Agreeably to this a custom has arisen which so far as I know is peculiar to the Brahmins. They are all supposed to know the *gotram* or stock from which they spring: that is to say, they know who was the ancient *Muni* or devotee from whom they descend, and they always take care, in order to avoid intermarriage with a female descendant of this remote priestly ancestor, to marry into a *gotram* other than their own.

Hindus who cannot contract a suitable marriage amongst their own relations are nevertheless bound to marry in their own caste, and even in that subdivision of it to which they belong. In no case are they permitted to contract marriages with strangers. Furthermore, persons belonging to a caste in one part of the country cannot contract marriages with persons of the same caste in another part, even though they may be precisely the same castes under different names. Thus the Tamil *Yedeyers* and the Canarese *Uppareru* would never consent to take wives from the Telugu *Gollavaru* and the Tamil *Pillay*, although the first two are, except for their names, identical with the second two.

The most distinguished of the four main castes into which the Hindus were originally separated by their first legislators is, as we have before remarked, that of the Brahmins. After them come the Kshatriyas, or Rajahs. Superiority of rank is at present warmly contested between the Vaisyas, or merchants, and the Sudras, or cultivators. The former appear to have almost entirely lost their superiority except in the Hindu books, where they are invariably placed before the Sudras. In ordinary life the latter hold themselves to be superior to the Vaisyas, and consider themselves privileged to mark their superiority in many respects by treating them with contumely.

With regard to the Vaisya caste an almost incredible but nevertheless well-attested peculiarity is everywhere observable. There is not a pretty woman to be found in the caste. I have never had much to do with the women of the Vaisya caste; I cannot therefore without injustice venture to add my testimony to that of others on this subject; but I confess that the few Vaisya women I have seen from time to time were not such as to afford me an ocular refutation of the popular prejudice. However, Vaisya women are generally wealthy, and they manage to make up for their lack of beauty by their elegant attire.

Even the Brahmins do not hold the highest social rank undisputed. The *Panchalas*, or five classes of artisans already mentioned, refuse, in some districts, to acknowledge Brahmin predominance, although these five classes themselves are considered to be of very low rank amongst the Sudras and are everywhere held in contempt. Brahmin predominance is also still more warmly contested by the Jains, of whom I have treated in one of the Appendices to this work.

As to the particular subdivisions of each caste it is difficult to decide the order of hierarchy observed amongst them. Sub-castes which are despised in one district are often greatly esteemed in another, according as they conduct themselves with greater propriety or follow more important callings. Thus the caste to which the ruler of a country belongs, however low it may be considered elsewhere, ranks amongst the highest in the ruler's own dominions, and every member of it derives some reflection of dignity from its chief.

After all, public opinion is the surest guide of caste superiority amongst the Sudras, and a very slight acquaintance with the customs of a province and with the private life of its inhabitants will suffice for fixing the position which each caste has acquired by common consent.

In general it will be found that those castes are most honoured who are particular in keeping themselves pure by constant bathing and by abstaining from animal food, who are exact in the observance of marriage regulations, who keep their women shut up and punish them severely when they err, and who resolutely maintain the customs and privileges of their order.

Of all the Hindus the Brahmins strive most to keep up appearances of outward and inward purity by frequent ablutions and severe abstinence not only from meat and everything that has contained the principle of life, but also from several natural products of the earth which prejudice and superstition teach them to be impure and defiling. It is chiefly to the scrupulous observance of such customs that the Brahmins owe the predominance of their illustrious order, and the reverence and respect with which they are everywhere treated.

Amongst the different classes of Sudras, those who permit widow remarriage are considered the most abject, and, except the Pariahs, I know very few castes in which such marriages are allowed to take place openly and with the sanction of the caste[1].

The division into castes is the paramount distinction amongst the Hindus; but there is still another division, that of sects. The two best known are those of Siva and Vishnu, which are again divided into a large number of others.

There are several castes, too, which may be distinguished by certain marks painted on the forehead or other parts of the body.

The first three of the four main castes, that is to say the Brahmins, Kshatriyas, and Vaisyas, are distinguished by a thin cord hung across from the left shoulder to the right hip. But this cord is also worn by the Jains and even by the *Panchalas*, or five castes of artisans, so one is apt to be deceived by it.

[1] Remarriage in the case of virgin widows is one of the foremost planks in the platform of Social Reform, but it is opposed violently by the orthodox.—ED.

From what has been said it will appear that the name of a caste forms after all its best indication. It was thus that the tribes of Israel were distinguished. The names of several of the Hindu castes have a known meaning; but for the most part they date from such ancient times that it is impossible to find out their significance.

There is yet another division more general than any I have referred to yet, namely, that into Right-hand and Left-hand factions. This appears to be but a modern invention, since it is not mentioned in any of the ancient books of the country; and I have been assured that it is unknown in Northern India. Be that as it may, I do not believe that any idea of this baneful institution, as it exists at the present day, ever entered the heads of those wise lawgivers who considered they had found in caste distinctions the best guarantee for the observance of the laws which they prescribed for the people.

This division into Right-hand and Left-hand factions, whoever invented it, has turned out to be the most direful disturber of the public peace. It has proved a perpetual source of riots, and the cause of endless animosity amongst the natives.

Most castes belong either to the Left-hand or Right-hand faction. The former comprises the Vaisyas or trading classes, the *Panchalas* or artisan classes, and some of the low Sudra castes. It also contains the lowest caste, namely, the *Chucklers* or leather-workers, who are looked upon as its chief support.

To the Right-hand faction belong most of the higher castes of Sudras. The Pariahs are its chief support, as a proof of which they glory in the title *Valangai-Mougattar*, or friends of the Right-hand. In the disputes and conflicts which so often take place between the two factions it is always the Pariahs who make the most disturbance and do the most damage.

The Brahmins, Rajahs, and several classes of Sudras are content to remain neutral, and take no part in these quarrels. They are often chosen as arbiters in the differences which the two factions have to settle between themselves.

The opposition between the two factions arises from certain exclusive privileges to which both lay claim. But as these alleged privileges are nowhere clearly defined and recognized, they result in confusion and uncertainty, and are with difficulty capable of settlement. In these circumstances one cannot hope to conciliate both parties; all that one can do is to endeavour to compromise matters as far as possible.

When one faction trespasses on the so-called rights of the other, tumults arise which spread gradually over large tracts of territory, afford opportunity for excesses of all kinds, and generally end in bloody conflicts. The Hindu, ordinarily so timid and gentle in all other circumstances of life, seems to change his nature completely on occasions like these. There is no danger that he will not brave in maintaining what he calls his rights, and rather than sacrifice a tittle of them he will expose himself without fear to the risk of losing his life.

I have several times witnessed instances of these popular insurrections excited by the mutual pretensions of the two factions and pushed to such an extreme of fury that the presence of a military force has been insufficient to quell them, to allay the clamour, or to control the excesses in which the contending factions consider themselves entitled to indulge.

Occasionally, when the magistrates fail to effect a reconciliation by peaceful means, it is necessary to resort to force in order to suppress the disturbances. I have sometimes seen these rioters stand up against several discharges of artillery without exhibiting any sign of submission. And when at last the armed force has succeeded in restoring order it is only for a time. At the very first opportunity the rioters are at work again, regardless of the punishment they have received, and quite ready to renew the conflict as obstinately as before. Such are the excesses to which the mild and peaceful Hindu abandons himself when his courage is aroused by religious and political fanaticism.

The rights and privileges for which the Hindus are ready to fight such sanguinary battles appear highly ridiculous, especially to a European. Perhaps the sole cause of the contest is the right to wear slippers or to ride through the streets in a palanquin or on horseback during marriage festivals. Sometimes it is the privilege of being escorted on certain occasions by armed retainers, sometimes that of having a trumpet sounded in front of a procession, or of being accompanied by native musicians at public ceremonies. Perhaps it is simply the particular kind of musical instrument suitable to such occasions that is in dispute; or perhaps it may be the right of carrying flags of certain colours or certain devices during these ceremonies. Such at any rate are a few of the privileges for which Hindus are ready to cut each others' throats.

It not unfrequently happens that one faction makes an attack on the rights, real or pretended, of the other. Thereupon the trouble begins, and soon becomes general if it is not appeased at the very outset by prudent and vigorous measures on the part of the magistracy.

I could instance very many examples bearing on this fatal distinction between Right-hand and Left-hand; but what I have already said is enough to show the spirit which animates the Hindus in this matter. I once witnessed a dispute of this nature between the Pariahs and *Chucklers*, or leather-workers. There seemed reason to fear such disastrous consequences throughout the whole district in question, that many of the more peaceful inhabitants began to desert their villages and to carry away their goods and chattels to a place of safety, just as is done when the country is threatened by the near approach of a Mahratta army. However, matters did not reach this extremity. The principal inhabitants of the district opportunely offered to arbitrate in the matter, and they succeeded by diplomacy and conciliation in smoothing away the difficulties and in appeasing the two factions, who were only awaiting the signal to attack each other.

One would not easily guess the cause of this formidable commotion. It simply arose from the fact that a *Chuckler* had dared to appear at a public ceremony with red flowers stuck in his turban, a privilege which the Pariahs alleged to belong exclusively to the Right-hand faction[1]!

[1] These faction fights have gradually disappeared under the civilizing influences of education and good government; and if they ever occur at all, are confined to the lowest castes and never spread beyond the limits of a village. The distinctions between the two factions, however, still exist. —ED.

CHAPTER II

Advantages resulting from Caste Divisions.—Similar Divisions amongst many Ancient Nations.

MANY persons study so imperfectly the spirit and character of the different nations that inhabit the earth, and the influence of climate on their manners, customs, predilections, and usages, that they are astonished to find how widely such nations differ from each other. Trammelled by the prejudices of their own surroundings, such persons think nothing well regulated that is not included in the polity and government of their own country. They would like to see all nations of the earth placed on precisely the same footing as themselves. Everything which differs from their own customs they consider either uncivilized or ridiculous. Now, although man's nature is pretty much the same all the world over, it is subject to so many differentiations caused by soil, climate, food, religion, education, and other circumstances peculiar to different countries, that the system of civilization adopted by one people would plunge another into a state of barbarism and cause its complete downfall.

I have heard some persons, sensible enough in other respects, but imbued with all the prejudices that they have brought with them from Europe, pronounce what appears to me an altogether erroneous judgement in the matter of caste divisions amongst the Hindus. In their opinion, caste is not only useless to the body politic, it is also ridiculous, and even calculated to bring trouble and disorder on the people. For my part, having lived many years on friendly terms with the Hindus, I have been able to study their national life and character closely, and I have arrived at a quite opposite decision on this subject of caste. I believe caste division to be in many respects the *chef-d'œuvre*, the happiest effort, of Hindu legislation. I am persuaded that it is simply and solely due to the distribution of the people into castes that India did not lapse into a state of barbarism, and that she preserved and perfected the arts and sciences of civilization whilst most other nations of the earth remained in a state of barbarism. I do not consider caste to be free from many great drawbacks; but I believe that the resulting advantages, in the case of a nation constituted like the Hindus, more than outweigh the resulting evils.

To establish the justice of this contention we have only to glance at the condition of the various races of men who live in the same latitude as the Hindus, and to consider the past and present status of those among them whose natural disposition and character have not been influenced for good by the purifying doctrines of Revealed Religion. We can judge what the Hindus would have been like, had they not been held within the pale of social duty by caste regulations, if we glance at neighbouring nations west of the Peninsula and east of it beyond the Ganges as far as China. In China itself a temperate climate and a form of government peculiarly adapted to a people unlike any other in the world have produced the same effect as the distinction of caste among the Hindus.

After much careful thought I can discover no other reason except caste which accounts for the Hindus not having fallen into the same state of barbarism as their neighbours and as almost all nations inhabiting the torrid zone. Caste assigns to each individual his own profession or calling; and the handing down of this system from father to son, from generation to generation, makes it impossible for any person or his descendants to change the condition of life which the law assigns to him for any other. Such an institution was probably the only means that the most clear-sighted prudence could devise for maintaining a state of civilization amongst a people endowed with the peculiar characteristics of the Hindus.

We can picture what would become of the Hindus if they were not kept within the bounds of duty by the rules and penalties of caste, by looking at the position of the Pariahs, or outcastes of India, who, checked by no moral restraint, abandon themselves to their natural propensities. Anybody who has studied the conduct and character of the people of this class—which, by the way, is the largest of any in India [1]—will agree with me that

[1] This is true only of Southern India, where the Pariahs number 5,000,000. They form one-seventh of the total population of the Madras Presidency.

a State consisting entirely of such inhabitants could not long endure, and could not fail to lapse before long into a condition of barbarism. For my own part, being perfectly familiar with this class, and acquainted with its natural predilections and sentiments, I am persuaded that a nation of Pariahs left to themselves would speedily become worse than the hordes of cannibals who wander in the vast wastes of Africa, and would soon take to devouring each other.

I am no less convinced that if the Hindus were not kept within the limits of duty and obedience by the system of caste, and by the penal regulations attached to each phase of it, they would soon become just what the Pariahs are, and probably something still worse. The whole country would necessarily fall into a state of hopeless anarchy, and, before the present generation disappeared, this nation, so polished under present conditions, would have to be reckoned amongst the most uncivilized of the world. The legislators of India, whoever they may have been, were far too wise and too well acquainted with the natural character of the people for whom they prescribed laws to leave it to the discretion or fancy of each individual to cultivate what knowledge he pleased, or to exercise, as seemed best to him, any of the various professions, arts, or industries which are necessary for the preservation and well-being of a State.

They set out from that cardinal principle common to all ancient legislators, that no person should be useless to the commonwealth. At the same time they recognized that they were dealing with a people who were indolent and careless by nature, and whose propensity to be apathetic was so aggravated by the climate in which they lived, that unless every individual had a profession or employment rigidly imposed upon him, the social fabric could not hold together and must quickly fall into the most deplorable state of anarchy. These ancient lawgivers, therefore, being well aware of the danger caused by religious and political innovations, and being anxious to establish durable and inviolable rules for the different castes comprising the Hindu nation, saw no surer way of attaining

Of late years the degraded condition of these outcastes has attracted much attention, and a great deal is now being done to elevate them morally and materially.—ED.

their object than by combining in an unmistakable manner those two great foundations of orderly government, religion and politics. Accordingly there is not one of their ancient usages, not one of their observances, which has not some religious principle or object attached to it. Everything, indeed, is governed by superstition and has religion for its motive. The style of greeting, the mode of dressing, the cut of clothes, the shape of ornaments and their manner of adjustment, the various details of the toilette, the architecture of houses, the corners where the hearth is placed and where the cooking pots must stand, the manner of going to bed and of sleeping, the forms of civility and politeness that must be observed: all these are severely regulated.

During the many years that I studied Hindu customs I cannot say that I ever observed a single one, however unimportant and simple, and, I may add, however filthy and disgusting, which did not rest on some religious principle or other. Nothing is left to chance; everything is laid down by rule, and the foundation of all their customs is purely and simply religion. It is for this reason that the Hindus hold all their customs and usages to be inviolable, for, being essentially religious, they consider them as sacred as religion itself.

And, be it noted, this plan of dividing the people into castes is not confined to the lawgivers of India. The wisest and most famous of all lawgivers, Moses, availed himself of the same institution, as being the one which offered him the best means of governing the intractable and rebellious people of whom he had been appointed the patriarch.

The division of the people into castes existed also amongst the Egyptians. With them, as with the Hindus, the law assigned an occupation to each individual, which was handed down from father to son. It was forbidden to any man to have two professions, or to change his own. Each caste had a special quarter assigned to it, and people of a different caste were prohibited from settling there. Nevertheless there was this difference between the Egyptians and the Hindus: with the former all castes and all professions were held in esteem; all employments, even of the meanest kind, were alike regarded as honourable; and, although the priestly and military castes possessed peculiar privileges, nobody would have considered it anything but criminal to despise the classes whose work, whatever it happened to be, contributed to the general good[1]. With the Hindus, on the other hand, there are professions and callings to which prejudice attaches such degradation that those who follow them are universally despised by those castes which in the public estimation exercise higher functions.

It must here be remarked, however, that the four great professions without which a civilized nation could not exist, namely, the army, agriculture, commerce, and weaving, are held everywhere in the highest esteem. All castes, from the Brahmin to the Pariah, are permitted to follow the first three, and the fourth can be followed by all the principal classes of Sudras[2].

These same caste distinctions observable amongst Hindus exist likewise, with some differences, amongst the Arabs and Tartars. Probably, indeed, they were common to the majority of ancient nations. Cecrops, it will be remembered, separated the people of Athens into four tribes or classes, while their great lawgiver, Solon, upheld this distinction and strengthened it in several ways. Numa Pompilius, again, could devise no better way of putting an end to the racial hatred between Sabines and Romans than by separating the body of the people into different castes and classes. The result of his policy was just what he had desired. Both Sabines and Romans, once amalgamated in this manner, forgot their national differences and thought only of those of their class or caste.

Those who instituted the caste system could not but perceive that with nations in an embryonic stage the more class distinctions there are the more order and symmetry there must be, and the more easy it is to exercise control and preserve order. This, indeed, is the result which caste classification amongst the Hindus has achieved. The shame which would reflect on a whole caste if the faults of one of its individual members went unpunished guarantees that the caste will execute justice, defend its own honour, and keep all its members within the bounds of duty. For, be it noted, every caste has its own laws and

[1] See what the illustrious Bossuet says on this point in his *Discours sur l'Histoire Universelle*, Part III.—DUBOIS.

[2] This statement is not quite correct, for in Southern India, at any rate, some classes of Pariahs are most expert weavers, and are honoured as such throughout the country.—ED.

regulations, or rather, we may say, its own customs, in accordance with which the severest justice is meted out, just as it was by the patriarchs of old.

Thus in several castes adultery is punishable by death[1]. Girls or widows who succumb to temptation are made to suffer the same penalty as those who have seduced them. The largest temple of the town of Conjeeveram, in the Carnatic, an immense building, was constructed, so it is said, by a rich Brahmin who had been convicted of having had illicit intercourse with a low-caste Pariah woman. He was, however, sentenced to this severe penalty, not so much on account of the immorality of his action, seeing that in the opinion of the Brahmins it was not immoral at all, but on account of the low-caste person who had been the partner of his incontinence. There are various kinds of delinquencies in connexion with which a caste may take proceedings, not only against the principal offenders, but against those who have taken any part whatever in them. Thus it is caste authority which, by means of its wise rules and prerogatives, preserves good order, suppresses vice, and saves Hindus from sinking into a state of barbarism.

It may also be said that caste regulations counteract to a great extent the evil effects which would otherwise be produced on the national character by a religion that encourages the most unlicensed depravity of morals, as well in the decorations of its temples as in its dogmas and ritual.

In India, where the princes and the aristocracy live in extreme indolence, attaching little importance to making their dependants happy and taking small pains to inculcate in them a sense of right and wrong, there are no other means of attaining these desirable ends and preserving good order than by authoritative rulings of the caste system. The worst of it is, these powers are not sufficiently wide, or rather they are too often relaxed. Many castes exercise them with severity in cases that are for the most part frivolous, but display an easy and culpable indulgence towards real and serious delinquencies. On the other hand, caste authority is often a check against abuses which the despotic rulers of the country are too apt to indulge in. Sometimes one may see, as the result of a caste order, the tradesmen and merchants of a whole district closing their shops, the labourers

[1] This of course is no longer allowed by law.—ED.

abandoning their fields, or the artisans leaving their workshops, all because of some petty insult or of some petty extortion suffered by some member of their caste; and the aggrieved people will remain obstinately in this state of opposition until the injury has been atoned for and those responsible for it punished.

Another advantage resulting from the caste system is the hereditary continuation of families and that purity of descent which is a peculiarity of the Hindus, and which consists in never mixing the blood of one family or caste with that of another. Marriages are confined to parties belonging to the same family, or at any rate the same caste. In India, at any rate, there can be no room for the reproach, so often deserved in European countries, that families have deteriorated by alliances with persons of low or unknown extraction. A Hindu of high caste can, without citing his title or producing his genealogical tree, trace his descent back for more than two thousand years without fear of contradiction. He can also, without any other passport than that of his high caste, and in spite of his poverty, present himself anywhere; and he would be more courted for a marriage alliance than any richer man of less pure descent. Nevertheless, it is not to be denied that there are some districts where the people are not quite so particular about their marriages, though such laxity is blamed and held up to shame as an outrage on propriety, while those guilty of it take very good care to conceal it as much as possible from the public.

Further, one would be justified in asserting that it is to caste distinctions that India owes the preservation of her arts and industries. For the same reason she would have reached a high standard of perfection in them had not the avarice of her rulers prevented it. It was chiefly to attain this object that the Egyptians were divided into castes, and that their laws assigned the particular place which each individual should occupy in the commonwealth. Their lawgivers no doubt considered that by this means all arts and industries would continue to improve from generation to generation, for men must needs do well that which they have always been in the habit of seeing done and which they have been constantly practising from their youth.

This perfection in arts and manufactures would undoubtedly have been attained by so industrious a people as the Hindus, if, as I have before remarked, the cupidity of their rulers had not acted as a check. As a matter of fact, no sooner has an artisan gained the reputation of excelling in his craft than he is at once carried off by order of the sovereign, taken to the palace, and there confined for the rest of his life, forced to toil without remission and with little or no reward. Under these circumstances, which are common to all parts of India under the government of native princes, it is hardly surprising that every art and industry is extinguished and all healthy competition deadened. This is the chief and almost the only reason why progress in the arts has been so slow among the Hindus, and why in this respect they are now far behind other nations who did not become civilized for many centuries after themselves.

Their workmen certainly lack neither industry nor skill. In the European settlements, where they are paid according to their merit, many native artisans are to be met with whose work would do credit to the best artisans of the West. Moreover they feel no necessity to use the many European tools, whose nomenclature alone requires special study. One or two axes, as many saws and planes, all of them so rudely fashioned that a European workman would be able to do nothing with them—these are almost the only instruments that are to be seen in the hands of Hindu carpenters. The working materials of a journeyman goldsmith usually comprise a tiny anvil, a crucible, two or three small hammers, and as many files. With such simple tools the patient Hindu, thanks to his industry, can produce specimens of work which are often not to be distinguished from those imported at great expense from foreign countries. To what a standard of excellence would these men have attained if they had been from the earliest times subjected to good masters!

In order to form a just idea of what the Hindus would have done with their arts and manufactures if their natural industry had been properly encouraged, we have only to visit the workshop of one of their weavers or of one of their printers on cloth and carefully examine the instruments with which they produce those superb muslins, those superfine cloths, those beautiful coloured piece-goods, which are everywhere admired, and which in Europe occupy a high place among the principal articles of adornment. In manufacturing these magnificent stuffs the artisan uses his feet almost as much as his hands. Furthermore, the weaving loom, and the whole apparatus for spinning the thread before it is woven, as well as the rest of the tools which he uses for the work, are so simple and so few that altogether they would hardly comprise a load for one man. Indeed it is by no means a rare sight to see one of these weavers changing his abode, and carrying on his back all that is necessary for setting to work the moment he arrives at his new home.

Their printed calicoes, which are not less admired than their muslins, are manufactured in an equally simple manner. Three or four bamboos to stretch the cloth, as many brushes for applying the colours, with a few pieces of potsherd to contain them, and a hollow stone for pounding them: these are pretty well all their stock in trade.

I will venture to express one other remark on the political advantages resulting from caste distinctions. In India parental authority is but little respected: and parents, overcome doubtless by that apathetic indifference which characterizes Hindus generally, are at little pains, as I shall show later on, to inspire those feelings of filial reverence which constitute family happiness by enchaining the affections of the children to the authors of their existence. Outward affection appears to exist between brothers and sisters, but in reality it is neither very strong nor very sincere. It quickly vanishes after the death of their parents, and subsequently, we may say, they only come together to fight and to quarrel. Thus, as the ties of blood relationship formed so insecure a bond between different members of a community, and guaranteed no such mutual assistance and support as were needed, it became necessary to bring families together in large caste communities, the individual members of which had a common interest in protecting, supporting, and defending each other. It was thus that the links of the Hindu social chain were so strongly and ingeniously forged that nothing was able to break them.

This was the object which the ancient lawgivers of India attained by establishing the caste system, and they thereby acquired a title to honour unexampled in the history of the world. Their work has stood the test of thousands of years, and has survived the lapse of time and the many revolutions to which this portion of the globe has been subjected. The Hindus have often passed beneath the yoke of foreign invaders, whose religions, laws, and customs have been very different from their own; yet all efforts to impose foreign institutions on the people of India have been futile, and foreign occupation has never dealt more than a feeble blow against Indian custom. Above all, and before all, it was the caste system which protected them. Its authority was extensive enough to include sentences of death, as I have before remarked. The story is told, and the truth of it is incontestable, that a man of the Rajput caste was a few years ago compelled by the people of his own caste and by the principal inhabitants of his place of abode to execute, with his own hand, a sentence of death passed on his daughter. This unhappy girl had been discovered in the arms of a youth, who would have suffered the same penalty had he not evaded it by sudden flight.

Nevertheless, although the penalty of death may be inflicted by some castes under certain circumstances, this form of punishment is seldom resorted to nowadays. Whenever it is thought to be indispensable, it is the father or the brother who is expected to execute it, in secrecy. Generally speaking, however, recourse is had by preference to the imposition of a fine and to various ignominious corporal punishments. As regards these latter, we may note as examples the punishments inflicted on women who have forfeited their honour, such as shaving their heads, compelling them to ride through the public streets mounted on asses and with their faces turned towards the tail, forcing them to stand a long time with a basket of mud on their heads before the assembled caste people, throwing into their faces the ordure of cattle, breaking the cotton thread of those possessing the right to wear it, and excommunicating the guilty from their caste [1].

[1] The infliction of such punishments might nowadays be followed by prosecution in the Civil and Criminal Courts.—ED.

CHAPTER III

Expulsion from Caste.—Cases in which such Degradation is inflicted.—By whom inflicted.—Restoration to Caste.—Methods of effecting it.

Of all kinds of punishment the hardest and most unbearable for a Hindu is that which cuts him off and expels him from his caste. Those whose duty it is to inflict it are the *gurus*, of whom I shall have more to say in a subsequent chapter, and, in default of them, the caste headmen. These latter are usually to be found in every district, and it is to them that all doubtful or difficult questions affecting the caste system are referred. They call in, in order to help them to decide such questions, a few elders who are versed in the intricacies of the matters in dispute.

This expulsion from caste, which follows either an infringement of caste usages or some public offence calculated if left unpunished to bring dishonour on the whole community, is a kind of social excommunication, which deprives the unhappy person who suffers it of all intercourse with his fellow-creatures. It renders him, as it were, dead to the world, and leaves him nothing in common with the rest of society. In losing his caste he loses not only his relations and friends, but often his wife and his children, who would rather leave him to his fate than share his disgrace with him. Nobody dare cat with him or even give him a drop of water. If he has marriageable daughters nobody asks them in marriage, and in like manner his sons are refused wives. He has to take it for granted that wherever he goes he will be avoided, pointed at with scorn, and regarded as an outcaste.

If after losing caste a Hindu could obtain admission into an inferior caste, his punishment would in some degree be tolerable; but even this humiliating compensation is denied to him. A simple Sudra with any notions of honour and propriety would never associate or even speak with a Brahmin degraded in this manner. It is necessary, therefore, for an outcaste to seek asylum in the lowest caste of Pariahs if he fail to obtain restoration to his own; or else he is obliged to associate with persons of doubtful caste. There are always people of this kind, especially in the quarters inhabited by Europeans; and unhappy is the man who puts trust in them! A caste Hindu is often a thief and a bad character, but a Hindu without caste is almost always a rogue.

Expulsion from caste is generally put in force without much formality. Sometimes it is due merely to personal hatred or caprice. Thus, when persons refuse, without any apparent justification, to attend the funeral or marriage ceremonies of their relations or friends, or when they happen not to invite the latter on similar occasions, the individuals thus slighted never fail to take proceedings in order to obtain satisfaction for the insult offered to them, and the arbitrators called in to decide the case usually pass a decree of excommunication. When a case is thus settled by arbitration, however, a sentence of excommunication does not bring upon the guilty person the same disgrace and the same penalties which are the lot of those whose offence offers no room for compromise.

Otherwise it matters little whether the offence be deliberate, whether it be serious or trivial, in determining that a person shall pay this degrading penalty. A Pariah who concealed his origin, mixed with other Hindus, entered their houses and ate with them without being recognized, would render those who had thus been brought into contact with him liable to ignominious expulsion from their caste. At the same time a Pariah guilty of such a daring act would inevitably be murdered on the spot, if his entertainers recognized him.

A Sudra, too, who indulged in illicit intercourse with a Pariah woman would be rigorously expelled from caste if his offence became known.

A number of Brahmins assembled together for some family ceremony once admitted to their feast, without being aware of it, a Sudra who had gained admittance on the false assertion that he belonged to their caste. On the circumstance being discovered, these Brahmins were one and all outcasted, and were unable to obtain reinstatement until they had gone through all kinds of formalities and been subjected to considerable expense.

I once witnessed amongst the *Gollavarus*, or shepherds, an instance of even greater severity. A marriage had been arranged, and, in the presence of the family concerned, certain ceremonies which were equivalent to betrothal amongst ourselves had taken place. Before the actual celebration of the marriage, which was fixed for a considerable time afterwards, the bridegroom died. The parents of the girl, who was very young and pretty, thereupon married her to another man. This was in direct violation of the custom of the caste, which condemns to perpetual widowhood girls thus betrothed, even when, as in this case, the future bridegroom dies before marriage has been consummated. The consequence was that all the persons who had taken part in the second ceremony were expelled from caste, and nobody would contract marriage or have any intercourse whatever with them. A long time afterwards I met several of them, well advanced in age, who had been for this reason alone unable to obtain husbands or wives, as the case might be.

Let me relate another instance. Eleven Brahmins travelling in company were obliged to cross a district devastated by war. They arrived hungry and tired in a village, which, contrary to their expectations, they found deserted. They had with them a small quantity of rice, but they could find no other pots to boil it in than some which had been left in the house of the village washerman. To touch these would constitute in the case of Brahmins an almost ineffaceable defilement. Nevertheless, suffering from hunger as they were, they swore mutual secrecy, and after washing and scouring the pots a hundred times they prepared their food in them. The rice was served and the repast consumed by all but one, who refused to partake of it, and who had no sooner returned home than he proceeded to denounce the ten others to the chief Brahmins of the village. The news of such a scandal spread quickly, and gave rise to a great commotion amongst all classes of the inhabitants. An assembly was held. The delinquents were summoned and forced to appear. Warned beforehand, however, of the proceedings that were to be instituted against them, they took counsel together and agreed to answer unanimously, when called upon to explain, that it was the accuser himself who had committed the heinous sin and who had imputed it to them falsely and maliciously. The testimony of ten persons was calculated to carry more weight than that of one. The accused were consequently acquitted, while the accuser alone was ignominiously expelled from caste by the headmen, who, though they were perfectly sure of his innocence, were indignant at his treacherous disclosure.

From what has been said, it will no longer be surprising to learn that Hindus are as much, nay, even more, attached to their caste than the gentry of Europe are to their rank. Prone to using the most disgustingly abusive language in their quarrels, they nevertheless easily forgive and forget such insulting epithets; but if one should say of another that he is *a man without caste*, the insult would never be forgiven or forgotten.

This strict and universal observance of caste and caste usages forms practically their whole social law. A very great number of people are to be found amongst them, to whom death would appear far more desirable than life, if, for example, the latter were sustained by eating cow's flesh or any food prepared by Pariahs and outcastes.

It is this same caste feeling which gives rise to the contempt and aversion which they display towards all foreign nations, and especially towards Europeans, who, being as a rule but slightly acquainted with the customs and prejudices of the country, are constantly violating them. Owing to such conduct the Hindus look upon them as barbarians totally ignorant of all principles of honour and good breeding.

In several cases, at least, restoration to caste is an impossibility. But when the sentence of excommunication has been passed merely by relations, the culprit conciliates the principal members of his family and prostrates himself in a humble posture, and with signs of repentance, before his assembled castemen. He then listens without complaint to the rebukes which are showered upon him, receives the blows to which he is oftentimes condemned, and pays the fine which it is thought fit to impose upon him. Finally, after having solemnly promised to wipe out by good conduct the taint resulting from his degrading punishment, he sheds tears of repentance, performs the *sashtanga* before the assembly, and then serves a feast to the persons present. When all this is finished he is looked upon as reinstated. The *sashtanga*, by the way, is a sign or salute expressing humility, which is not only recognized amongst the Hindus and other Asiatic nations, but was in use amongst more ancient peoples. Instances of it are quoted in Scripture, where this extraordinary mark of respect is known as *adoration*, even when it is paid to simple mortals. (*Vide* Genesis xviii. 2; xix. 1; xxxiii. 3; xlii. 6; xliii. 26; l. 18, &c., &c.) In the same way the Egyptians, Chaldeans, and other nations mentioned in Holy Writ were acquainted with this method of reverent salutation and observed it under the same circumstances as the Hindus. As I shall often have occasion in this work to mention the *sashtanga* I will give here a definition of it. The person who performs it lies prostrate, his face on the ground and his arms extended beyond his head. It is called *sashtanga* from *the prostration of the six members*, because, when it is performed, the feet, the knees, the stomach, the chest, the forehead, and the arms must touch the earth. It is thus that prostrations are made before persons of high degree, such as princes and priests. Children sometimes prostrate themselves thus before their fathers. It is by no means rare to see Sudras of different classes performing *sashtanga* before Brahmins; and it often happens that princes, before engaging an enemy, thus prostrate themselves before their armies drawn up in battle array[1].

When expulsion from caste is the result of some heinous offence, the guilty person who is readmitted into caste has to submit to one or other of the following ordeals: his tongue is slightly burnt with a piece of heated gold; he is branded indelibly on different parts of his body with red-hot iron; he is made to walk barefooted over red-hot embers; or he is compelled to crawl several times under the belly of a cow. Finally, to complete his purification, he is made to drink the *pancha-gavia*. These words, of which a more detailed explanation will be given later on, signify literally *the five things*

[1] Here and elsewhere the Abbé makes the mistake of interpreting *sashtanga* to mean '*the six angas*,' or 'parts of the body.' *Sashtanga* (Sa-ashtanga) really means *with the eight parts of the body*, which are the two hands, the two feet, two knees, forehead, and breast.—ED.

or substances derived from the body of a cow; namely, milk, curds, ghee (clarified butter), dung and urine, which are mixed together. The last-named, urine, is looked upon as the most efficacious for purifying any kind of uncleanness. I have often seen superstitious Hindus following the cows to pasture, waiting for the moment when they could collect the precious liquid in vessels of brass, and carrying it away while still warm to their houses. I have also seen them waiting to catch it in the hollow of their hands, drinking some of it and rubbing their faces and heads with the rest. Rubbing it in this way is supposed to wash away all external uncleanness, and drinking it to cleanse all internal impurity. When this disgusting ceremony of the *pancha-gavia* is over, the person who has been reinstated is expected to give a great feast to the Brahmins who have collected from all parts to witness it. Presents of more or less value are also expected by them, and not until these are forthcoming does the guilty person obtain all his rights and privileges again.

There are certain offences so heinous in the sight of Hindus, however, as to leave no hope of reinstatement to those who commit them. Such, for example, would be the crime of a Brahmin who had openly cohabited with a Pariah woman. Were the woman of any other caste, I believe that it would be possible for a guilty person, by getting rid of her and by repudiating any children he had had by her, to obtain pardon, after performing many purifying ceremonies and expending much money. But hopeless would be the case of the man who under any circumstances had eaten of cow's flesh. There would be no hope of pardon for him, even supposing he had committed such an awful sacrilege under compulsion.

It would be possible to cite several instances of strange and inflexible severity in the punishment of caste offences. When the last Mussulman Prince reigned in Mysore and sought to proselytize the whole Peninsula, he began by having several Brahmins forcibly circumcised, compelling them afterwards to eat cow's flesh as an unequivocal token of their renunciation of caste. Subsequently the people were freed from the yoke of this tyrant, and many of those who had been compelled to embrace the Mahomedan religion made every possible effort, and offered very large sums, to be readmitted to Hinduism. Assemblies were held in different parts of the country to thoroughly consider their cases. It was everywhere decided that it was quite possible to purify the uncleanness of circumcision and of intercourse with Mussulmans. But the crime of eating cow's flesh, even under compulsion, was unanimously declared to be irredeemable and not to be effaced either by presents, or by fire, or by the *pancha-gavia.*

A similar decision was given in the case of Sudras who found themselves in the same position, and who, after trying all possible means, were not more successful. One and all, therefore, were obliged to remain Mahomedans.

A Hindu, of whatever caste, who has once had the misfortune to be excommunicated, can never altogether get rid of the stain of his disgrace. If he ever gets into trouble his excommunication is always thrown in his teeth.

CHAPTER IV

Antiquity and Origin of Caste.

APPARENTLY there is no existing institution older than the caste system of the Hindus. Greek and Latin authors who have written about India concur in thinking that it has been in force from time immemorial; and certainly the unswerving observance of its rules seems to me an almost incontestable proof of its antiquity[1]. Under a solemn and unceasing obliga-

[1] Dr. Muir, in *Old Sanskrit Texts*, vol. i. p. 159, reviewing the texts which he had cited on this subject, says:—'First, we have the set of accounts in which the four castes are said to have sprung from progenitors who were separately created; but in regard to the manner of their creation we find the greatest diversity of statement. The most common story is that the castes issued from the mouth, arms, thighs, and feet of Purusha, or Brāhma. The oldest extant passage in which this idea occurs, and from which all the later myths of a similar tenor have no doubt been borrowed, is to be found in the Purusha Sūkta; but it is doubtful whether, in the form in which it is there represented, this representation is anything more than an allegory. In some of the texts from the Bhāgavata Purāna traces of the same allegorical character may be perceived; but in Manu and the Purānas the mystical import of the Vedic text disappears, and the figurative narration is hardened into a literal statement of fact. In the chapters of the Vishnu, Vāyu, and Mārkandeya Purānas, where castes are described as coeval with creation, and as having been naturally distinguished by different *gunas*, or qualities, involving varieties of moral character, we are nevertheless allowed to infer that those qualities exerted no influence on the classes in which they were inherent, as the condition of the whole race during the Krita age is described as one of uniform perfection and happiness; while the actual separation into castes did not take place, according to the Vāyu Purāna, until men had become deteriorated in the Treta age.

'Second, in various passages from the Brāhmanas epic poems, and Purānas, the creation of mankind is described without the least allusion to any separate production of the progenitors of the four castes. And whilst in the chapters where they relate the distinct formations of the castes, the Purānas assign different natural dispositions to each class, they elsewhere represent all mankind as being at the creation uniformly distinguished by the quality of pas-tion as the Hindus are to respect its usages, new and strange customs are things unheard of in their country. Any person who attempted to introduce such innovations would excite universal resentment and opposition, and would be branded as a dangerous person. The task, however, would be such a difficult one that I can hardly believe that any proposal of the kind would ever enter an intelligent person's head. Everything is always done in exactly the same way; even the minutest details are invested with a solemn importance of their own, because a Hindu is convinced that it is only by paying rigorous attention to small details that more momentous concerns are safeguarded. Indeed, there is not another nation on earth which can pride itself on having so long preserved intact its social customs and regulations.

The Hindu legislators of old had the good sense to give stability to these customs and regulations by associating with them many outward ceremonies, which, by fixing them in the

sion. In one text men are said to be the offspring of Vivasat; in another his son Mami is said to be their progenitor, whilst in a third they are said to be descended from a female of the same name. The passage which declares Manu to have been the father of the human race explicitly affirms that men of all the four castes were descended from him. In another remarkable text the Mahābhārata categorically asserts that originally there was no distinction of classes, the existing distribution having arisen out of differences of character and occupation In these circumstances, we may fairly conclude that the separate origination of the four castes was far from being an article of belief universally received by Indian antiquity.'

The following is the categorical assertion in the Mahābhārata (Santi parvan) above referred to. It occurs in the course of a discussion on caste between Bhrigu and Bharadwaja. Bhrigu, replying to a question put by Bharadwaja, says: 'The colour (*varna*) of the Brahmins was white; that of the Kshatriyas red; that of the Vaisyas yellow, and that of the Sudras black.' Bharadwaja here rejoins, 'If the caste (*varna*) of the four classes is distinguished by their colour (*varna*), then a confusion of all the castes is observable....' Bhrigu replies, 'There is no difference of castes: this world, having been at first created by Brāhma entirely Brahmanic, became (afterwards) separated into castes in consequence of works. Those Brahmins (lit. twice-born men) who were fond of sensual pleasure, fiery, irascible, prone to violence, who had forsaken their duty and were red limbed, fell into the condition of Kshatriyas. Those Brahmins who derived their livelihood from kine, who were yellow, who subsisted by agriculture, and who neglected to practise their duties, entered into the state of Vaisyas. Those Brahmins who were addicted to mischief and falsehood, who were covetous, who lived by all kinds of work, who were black and had fallen from purity, sank into the condition of Sudras.'—ED.

minds of the people, ensured their more faithful observance. These ceremonies are invariably observed, and have never been allowed to degenerate into mere forms that can be neglected without grave consequences. Failure to perform a single one of them, however unimportant it might appear, would never go unpunished.

One cannot fail to remark how very similar some of these ceremonies are to those which were performed long ago amongst other nations. Thus the Hindu precepts about cleanness and uncleanness, as also the means employed for preserving the one and effacing the other, are similar in many respects to those of the ancient Hebrews. The rule about marrying in one's caste, and even in one's family, was specifically imposed upon the Jews in the laws which Moses gave them from God[1]. This rule, too, was in force a long time before that, for it appears to have been general amongst the Chaldeans. We find also in Holy Writ that Abraham espoused his niece, and that the holy patriarch sent into a far country for a maiden of his own family as a wife for his son Isaac. Again, Isaac and his wife Rebecca found it difficult to pardon their son Esau for marrying amongst strangers, that is, amongst the Canaanites; and they sent their son Jacob away into a distant land to seek a wife from amongst their own people.

In the same way to-day, Hindus residing in a foreign country will journey hundreds of leagues to their native land in search of wives for their sons.

Again, as to the caste system, Moses, as is well known, established it amongst the Hebrews in accordance with the commands of God. This holy lawgiver had, during his long sojourn in Egypt, observed the system as established in that country, and had doubtless recognized the good that resulted from it. Apparently, in executing the divine order with respect to it he simply adapted and perfected the system which was in force in Egypt.

The Indian caste system is of still older origin. The Hindu sacred writings record that the author of it was the God Brāhma, to whom they attribute the creation of the world, and who is said to have established this system when he peopled the earth. The Brahmins were the product of his brain; the

[1] Numbers xxxvi. 5–12.

Kshatriyas or Rajahs issued from his shoulders; the Vaisyas from his belly; and the Sudras from his feet.

It is easy to understand the allegorical signification of this legend, in which one can distinctly trace the relative degrees of subordination of the different castes. The Brahmins, destined to fulfil the high functions of spiritual priesthood and to show the way of salvation to their fellow-men, issue from the head of the Creator; the Kshatriyas, endowed with physical force and destined to undergo the fatigues of war, have their origin in the shoulders and arms of Brāhma; the Vaisyas, whose duty it is to provide the food, the clothing, and other bodily necessities of man, are born in the belly of the god: and the Sudras, whose lot is servitude and rude labour in the fields, issue from his feet.

Besides this traditional origin of the different castes, known to all Hindus, there is another to be found in their books, which traces the institution back to the time of the Flood. For, it should be noted, this terrible world-renovating disaster is as well known to the Hindus as it was to Moses. On this important subject, however, I shall have more to say subsequently; suffice it to remark that a celebrated personage, reverenced by the Hindus, and known to them as *Mahanuvu*, escaped the calamity in an ark, in which were also the seven famous Penitents of India. After the Flood, according to Hindu writers, this saviour of the human race divided mankind into different castes, as they exist at the present day[1].

The many subdivisions into which these four great original castes were broken up date undoubtedly from later times. They were due to the absolute necessity of assigning to each person in a special manner his particular place in the social organization. There are some Hindu authors who assert that the individuals composing the first ramifications of the large Sudra caste were the bastard offspring of the other higher castes, and owed their origin to illicit intercourse with the widows of the four great caste divisions. It is said that these bastard children, born of a Brahmin father and a Kshatriya mother, or of a Vaisya father and a Sudra mother, &c., were not recog-

[1] The appellation *Mahanuvu* is well worthy of remark. It is a compound of two words—*Maha* great, and *Nuvu*, which undoubtedly is the same as *Noah*.—DUBOIS.

nized by any of the four primary castes, and so they were placed in other caste categories and were assigned special employments, more or less humble, according to their extraction.

A few of these many subdivisions are said to be of quite recent origin. For instance, the five artisan classes are said to have originally formed only one class, as also the barbers and washermen, the *Gollavarus* and *Kurubas*, and a large number of others who in recent times have split up into new sub-castes.

CHAPTER V

The Lowei Classes of Sudras.—Pariahs.—*Chucklers*, or Cobblers, and others equally low.—Contempt in which they are held.—Pariahs strictly speaking Slaves.—Washermen, Barbers, and some others.—Disrepute into which Mechanical Skill has fallen.—Nomads and Vagabonds.—Gypsies.—Quacks.—Jugglers.—Wild Tribes, &c.

We have already remarked that amongst the immense number of classes of which the Sudra caste is composed, it is impossible to give precedence to any one class in particular; the natives themselves not being agreed on that point, and the social scale varying in different parts of the country. There are certain classes, however, who, owing to the depth of degradation into which they have fallen, are looked upon as almost another race of beings, altogether outside the pale of society; and they are perfectly ready to acknowledge their own comparative inferiority. The best known and most numerous of these castes is the *Parayer*, as it is called in Tamil, the word from which the European name Pariah is derived[1]. The particulars which I am about to give of this class will form most striking contrasts with those I shall relate subsequently about the Brahmins, and will serve to demonstrate a point to which I shall often refer, namely, how incapable the Hindus are of showing any moderation in their caste customs and observances.

Their contempt and aversion for these social outcastes are as extreme, on the one hand, as are the respect and veneration which they pay, on the other, to those whom their superstitions have invested with god-like attributes. Throughout the whole of India the Pariahs are looked upon as slaves by other castes, and are treated with great harshness. Hardly anywhere are they allowed to cultivate the soil for their own benefit, but

[1] *Parayen* means one that beats the drum (*parai*).—Ed.

are obliged to hire themselves out to the other castes, who in return for a minimum wage exact the hardest tasks from them.

Furthermore, their masters may beat them at pleasure; the poor wretches having no right either to complain or to obtain redress for that or any other ill-treatment their masters may impose on them. In fact, these Pariahs are the born slaves of India; and had I to choose between the two sad fates of being a slave in one of our colonies or a Pariah here, I should unhesitatingly prefer the former.

This class is the most numerous of all, and in conjunction with that of the *Chucklers*, or cobblers, represents at least a quarter of the population. It is painful to think that its members, though so degraded, are yet the most useful of all. On them the whole agricultural work of the country devolves [1], and they have also other tasks to perform which are still harder and more indispensable.

However, notwithstanding the miserable condition of these wretched Pariahs, they are never heard to murmur, or to complain of their low estate. Still less do they ever dream of trying to improve their lot, by combining together, and forcing the other classes to treat them with that common respect which one man owes to another. The idea that he was born to be in subjection to the other castes is so ingrained in his mind that it never occurs to the Pariah to think that his fate is anything but irrevocable. Nothing will ever persuade him that men are all made of the same clay, or that he has the right to insist on better treatment than that which is meted out to him [2].

They live in hopeless poverty, and the greater number lack sufficient means to procure even the coarsest clothing. They go about almost naked, or at best clothed in the most hideous rags.

They live from hand to mouth the whole year round, and rarely know one day how they will procure food for the next.

[1] This is the case only in certain districts of Southern India, such as Chingleput and Tanjore. An appreciable percentage of the Pariahs has now migrated to the towns, where they serve as domestic servants in European and Eurasian households.—Ed.

[2] The Christian missionaries in India have done and are doing much to elevate the condition and character of this class. In Madras city there are now Pariah associations, and also a journal specially representing Pariah interests.—Ed.

When they happen to have any money, they invariably spend it at once, and make a point of doing no work as long as they have anything left to live on.

In a few districts they are allowed to cultivate the soil on their own account, but in such cases they are almost always the poorest of their class. Pariahs who hire themselves out as labourers earn, at any rate, enough to live on; and their food, though often of the coarsest description, is sufficient to satisfy the cravings of hunger. But those who are their own masters, and cultivate land for themselves, are so indolent and careless that their harvests, even in the most favourable seasons, are only sufficient to feed them for half the year.

The contempt and aversion with which the other castes—and particularly the Brahmins—regard these unfortunate people are carried to such an excess that in many places their presence, or even their footprints, are considered sufficient to defile the whole neighbourhood. They are forbidden to cross a street in which Brahmins are living. Should they be so ill-advised as to do so, the latter would have the right, not to strike them themselves, because they could not do so without defilement, or even touch them with the end of a long stick, but to order them to be severely beaten by other people. A Pariah who had the audacity to enter a Brahmin's house might possibly be murdered on the spot. A revolting crime of this sort has been actually perpetrated in States under the rule of native princes without a voice being raised in expostulation[1].

Any one who has been touched, whether inadvertently or purposely, by a Pariah is defiled by that single act, and may hold no communication with any person whatsoever until he has been purified by bathing, or by other ceremonies more or less important according to the status and customs of his caste. It would be contamination to eat with any members of this class; to touch food prepared by them, or even to drink water which they have drawn; to use an earthen vessel which they have held in their hands; to set foot inside one of their

[1] Even to this day a Pariah is not allowed to pass a Brahmin street in a village, though nobody can prevent, or prevents, his approaching or passing by a Brahmin's house in towns. The Pariahs, on their part, will under no circumstances allow a Brahmin to pass through their *parcherries* (collections of Pariah huts), as they firmly believe that it will lead to their ruin. —ED.

houses, or to allow them to enter houses other than their own. Each of these acts would contaminate the person affected by it, and before being readmitted to his own caste such a person would have to go through many exacting and expensive formalities. Should it be proved that any one had had any connexion with a Pariah woman he would be treated with even greater severity. Nevertheless, the disgust which these Pariahs inspire is not so intense in some parts of the country as in others. The feeling is most strongly developed in the southern and western districts of the Peninsula ; in the north it is less apparent. In the northern part of Mysore the other classes of Sudras allow Pariahs to approach them, and even permit them to enter that part of the house which is used for cattle. Indeed, in some places custom is so far relaxed that a Pariah may venture to put his head and one foot, but one foot only, inside the room occupied by the master of the house. It is said that still further north the difference between this and other Sudra castes gradually diminishes, until at last it disappears altogether.

The origin of this degraded class can be traced to a very early period, as it is mentioned in the most ancient Puranas. The Pariahs were most probably composed, in the first instance, of all the disreputable individuals of different classes of society, who, on account of various offences, had forfeited their right to associate with respectable men. They formed a class apart, and having nothing to fear and less to lose, they gave themselves up, without restraint, to their natural tendencies towards vice and excess, in which they continue to live at the present day.

In very early days, however, the separation between Pariahs and the other castes does not appear to have been so marked as at present. Though relegated to the lowest grade in the social scale, they were not then placed absolutely outside and beyond it, the line of demarcation between them and the Sudras being almost imperceptible. Indeed, they are even to this day considered to be the direct descendants of the better class of agricultural labourers. The Tamil *Vellalers* and the *Okkala-makkalu-kanarey* do not disdain to call them their children. But one thing is quite certain, that if these classes share a common origin with the Pariahs and acknowledge the same, their actions by no means corroborate their words, and their treatment of the Pariahs leaves much to be desired.

Europeans are obliged to have Pariahs for their servants, because no native of any other caste would condescend to do such menial work as is exacted by their masters. For instance, it would be very difficult to find amongst the Sudras any one who would demean himself by blacking or greasing boots and shoes, emptying and cleansing chamber utensils, brushing and arranging hair, &c.; and certainly no one could be found who for any consideration whatever would consent to cook food for them, as this would necessitate touching beef, which is constantly to be seen on the tables of Europeans, who thereby show an open disregard of the feelings and prejudices of the people amongst whom they live. Foreigners are therefore obliged to have recourse to Pariahs to perform this important domestic service. If the kind of food which they do not scruple to eat lowers Europeans in the eyes of the superstitious native, much more are they lowered by the social status of the people by whom they are served. For it is a fact recognized by all Hindus that none but a Pariah would dare to eat food prepared by Pariahs.

It is undeniable that this want of consideration on the part of Europeans—or rather the necessity to which they are reduced of employing Pariahs as servants—renders them most obnoxious to other classes of natives, and greatly diminishes the general respect for the white man. It being impossible to procure servants of a better caste, foreigners have of necessity to put up with members of this inferior class, who are dishonest, incapable of any attachment to their masters, and unworthy of confidence. Sudras who become servants of Europeans are almost invariably vicious and unprincipled, as devoid of all feeling of honour as they are wanting in resource; in fact, they are the scum of their class and of society at large. No respectable or self-respecting Sudra would ever consent to enter a service where he would be in danger of being mistaken for a Pariah, or would have to consort with Pariahs. Amongst other reasons which contribute largely to the dislike that natives of a better class entertain for domestic service under Europeans, is the feeling that their masters keep them at such a great distance, and are generally haughty and even cruel in their demeanour towards them. But above all things they dread being kicked by a European, not because this particular form of ill-treatment is physically more painful than any other, but because they have a horror of being defiled by contact with anything so unclean as a leather boot or shoe. Pariahs, accustomed from their childhood to slavery, put up patiently with affronts of this kind which other natives, who have more pride and self-respect, are unable to endure.

Under other circumstances, it should be remarked, domestic service in India is by no means regarded as degrading. The servant has his meals with his master, the maid with her mistress, and both go through life on an almost equal footing. The conduct of Europeans being in this respect so totally different, natives who have any sense of decency or self-respect feel the greatest repugnance to taking service with them. One cannot wonder therefore that only the very dregs of the population will undertake the work.

But to return to the Pariahs. One is bound to confess that the evil reputation which is borne by this class is in many respects well deserved, by reason of the low conduct and habits of its members. A great many of these unfortunate people bind themselves for life, with their wives and children, to the ryots, or agricultural classes, who set them to the hardest labour and treat them with the greatest harshness. The village scavengers, who are obliged to clean out the public latrines, to sweep the streets, and to remove all rubbish, invariably belong to this class. These men, known in the south by the name of *totis*, are, however, generally somewhat more humanely treated than the other Pariahs, because, in addition to the dirty work above mentioned, they are employed in letting the water into the tanks and channels for irrigating the rice fields; and on this account they are treated with some consideration by the rest of the villagers. Amongst the Pariahs who are not agricultural slaves there are some who groom and feed the horses of private individuals, or those used in the army; some are in charge of elephants; others tend cattle; others are messengers and carriers; while others, again, do ordinary manual work. Within recent times Pariahs have been allowed to enlist in the European and Native armies, and some of them have risen to high rank, for in point of courage and bravery they are in no way inferior to any other caste. Yet their bringing up put them at a great disadvantage in acquiring other qualifications necessary for the making of a good soldier, for they are induced with difficulty to conform to military discipline, and are absolutely deficient in all sense of honour[1].

Pariahs, being thus convinced that they have nothing to lose or gain in public estimation, abandon themselves without shame or restraint to vice of all kinds, and the greatest lawlessness prevails amongst them, for which they do not feel the least shame. One might almost say that, in the matter of vice, they outstrip all others in brutality, as the Brahmins do in malice. Their habits of uncleanliness are disgusting. Their huts, a mass of filth and alive with insects and vermin, are, if possible, even more loathsome than their persons. Their harsh and forbidding features clearly reveal their character, but even these are an insufficient indication of the coarseness of their minds and manners. They are much addicted to drunkenness, a vice peculiarly abhorrent to other Hindus. They intoxicate themselves usually with the juice of the palm-tree, called toddy, which they drink after it has fermented, as it is then more spirituous. In spite of its horrible stench they imbibe it as if the nauseous liquid were nectar. Drunken quarrels are of frequent occurrence amongst them, and their wives are often sufferers, the unhappy creatures being nearly beaten to death, even when in a state of pregnancy. It is to this brutality and violence of their husbands that I attribute the frequent miscarriages to which Pariah wives are subject, and which are much more common amongst them than amongst women of any other caste.

What chiefly disgusts other natives is the revolting nature of the food which the Pariahs eat. Attracted by the smell, they will collect in crowds round any carrion, and contend for the spoil with dogs, jackals, crows, and other carnivorous animals. They then divide the semi-putrid flesh, and carry it away to their huts, where they devour it, often without rice or anything else to disguise the flavour. That the animal should have died of disease is of no consequence to them, and they sometimes secretly poison cows or buffaloes that they may subsequently feast on the foul, putrefying remains. The carcases of animals that die in a village belong by right to the *toti* or scavenger, who

[1] The Abbé is too sweeping in many of his statements about Pariahs. For instance, in these days at any rate, the Pariah Sepoys in the Madras army are extremely well disciplined, especially the corps of Sappers.—ED.

sells the flesh at a very low price to the other Pariahs in the neighbourhood. When it is impossible to consume in one day the stock of meat thus obtained, they dry the remainder in the sun, and keep it in their huts until they run short of other food. There are few Pariah houses where one does not see festoons of these horrible fragments hanging up; and though the Pariahs themselves do not seem to be affected by the smell, travellers passing near their villages quickly perceive it and can tell at once the caste of the people living there. This horrible food is, no doubt, the cause of the greater part of the contagious diseases which decimate them, and from which their neighbours are free.

Is it to be wondered at, after what has just been stated, that other castes should hold this in abhorrence? Can they be blamed for refusing to hold any communication with such savages, or for obliging them to keep themselves aloof and to live in separate hamlets? It is true that with regard to these Pariahs the other Hindus are apt to carry their views to excess; but as we have already pointed out, and shall often have to point out again, the natural instinct of the natives of India seems to run to extremes in all cases.

The condition of the Pariahs, which is not really slavery as it is known amongst us, resembles to a certain extent that of the serfs of France and other countries of Northern Europe in olden times. This state of bondage is at its worst along the coast of Malabar, as are several other customs peculiar to the country[1]. The reason is that Malabar, owing to its position, has generally escaped the invasions and revolutions which have so often devastated the rest of India, and has thus managed to preserve unaltered many ancient institutions, which in other parts have fallen into disuse.

Of these the two most remarkable are proprietary rights and slavery. These two systems are apparently inseparable one from the other: and, indeed, one may well say, *no land without lord*. All the Pariahs born in the country are serfs for life, from father to son, and are part and parcel of the land on which they are born. The land-owner can sell them along with the soil, and can dispose of them when and how he pleases. This proprietary right and this system of serfdom have existed

[1] Things in this respect have, of course, changed a great deal for the better since the Abbé wrote.—ED.

from the remotest times, and exist still amongst the Nairs, the Coorgs, and the Tulus, the three aboriginal tribes of the Malabar coast. This is, I believe, the only province in India where proprietary right has been preserved intact until the present day. Everywhere else the soil belongs to the ruler, and the cultivator is merely his tenant. The lands which he tills are given to him or taken away from him according to the will of the Government for the time being. On the Malabar coast, however, the lands belong to those who have inherited them from their forefathers, and these in their turn possess the right of handing them down to their descendants. Here the lands may be alienated, sold, given away, or disposed of according to the will of the owners. In a word, the *jus utendi et abutendi*, which is the basis of proprietary right, belongs entirely to them. Every landed proprietor in that country possesses a community of Pariahs to cultivate his fields, who are actually his slaves and form an integral part of his property. All children born of these Pariahs are serfs by birth, just as their parents were; and their master has the right, if he choose, to sell or dispose of parents and children in any way that he pleases. If one of these Pariahs escapes and takes service under another master, his real master can recover him anywhere as his own property. If a proprietor happens to possess more slaves than he requires for cultivating his land, he sells some to other landlords who are less fortunate than himself. It is by no means uncommon to see a debtor, who is unable to pay his debts in hard cash, satisfy his creditors by handing over to them a number of his Pariah slaves. The price of these is not exorbitant. A male still young enough to work will fetch three rupees and a hundred *seers* of rice, which is about the value of a bullock.

But the landed proprietors do not usually sell their slaves except in cases of great emergency; and even then they can only sell them within the borders of their own country. In no case have they a right to export them for sale to foreigners.

Each land-owner in the province of Malabar lives in a house that is isolated in the middle of his estate. Here he dwells, surrounded by his community of Pariah serfs, who are always remarkably submissive to him. Some land-owners possess over a hundred of them. They treat them usually in the most humane manner. They give them only such work as their age or strength permits; feed them on the same rice that they themselves eat; give them in marriage when they come of age; and every year provide them with clothing, four or five yards of cloth for the women and a coarse woollen blanket for the men.

In Malabar it is only the Pariahs who are thus condemned to perpetual slavery; but then there are no free men amongst them. All are born slaves from generation to generation. They have not even a right to buy their own freedom; and if they wish to secure their independence they can only do so by escaping secretly from the country. All the same, I have not heard that they often resort to this extremity. They are accustomed from father to son to this state of servitude; they are kindly treated by their masters; they eat the same food as they do; they are never forced to do tasks beyond their strength; and thus they have no notion of what freedom or independence means, and are happily resigned to their lot. They look upon their master as their father, and consider themselves to belong to his family. As a matter of fact, their physical condition, which is the only thing that appeals to their senses, is much better than that of their brethren who are free. At any rate, the Pariah slave of Malabar is certain of a living, the supreme requirement of nature, whereas the free Pariah of other provinces lives for half his time in actual want of the meanest subsistence, and is often exposed to death from starvation[1].

It is indeed a piteous sight, the abject and half-starved condition in which this wretched caste, the most numerous of all, drags out its existence. It is true that amongst Pariahs it is an invariable rule, almost a point of honour, to spend everything they earn and to take no thought for the morrow. The majority of them, men and women, are never clothed in anything but old rags. But in order to obtain a true idea of their abject

[1] The slaves spoken of here are not Pariahs but Cherumars, who claim to be somewhat superior in rank to the Pariahs. From 1792 the East India Company steadily endeavoured to emancipate the Cherumars. In 1843 an Emancipation Act was passed, but it was explained to the Cherumars that it was their interest, as well as their duty, to remain with their masters if treated kindly. 'Sections 370, 371, &c. of the Indian Penal Code,' writes Mr. Logan in his *Malabar Manual*, 'which came into force on Jan. 1, 1862, dealt the real final blow at slavery in India.'—ED.

misery one must live amongst them, as I have been obliged to do. About half of my various congregations consisted of Pariah Christians. Wherever I went I was constantly called in to administer the last consolations of religion to people of this class. On reaching the hut to which my duty led me, I was often obliged to creep in on my hands and knees, so low was the entrance door to the wretched hovel. When once inside, I could only partially avoid the sickening smell by holding to my nose a handkerchief soaked in the strongest vinegar. I would find there a mere skeleton, perhaps lying on the bare ground, though more often crouching on a rotten piece of matting, with a stone or a block of wood as a pillow. The miserable creature would have for clothing a rag tied round the loins, and for covering a coarse and tattered blanket that left half the body naked. I would seat myself on the ground by his side, and the first words I heard would be: 'Father, I am dying of cold and hunger.' I would spend a quarter of an hour or so by him, and at last leave this sad spectacle with my heart torn asunder by the sadness and hopelessness of it all, and my body covered in every part with insects and vermin. Yet, after all, this was the least inconvenience that I suffered, for I could rid myself of them by changing my clothes and taking a hot bath. The only thing that really afflicted me was having to stand face to face with such a spectacle of utter misery and all its attendant horrors, and possessing no means of affording any save the most inadequate remedies.

Oh! if those who are blessed with this world's goods, and who are so inclined to create imaginary troubles for themselves because they have no real ones; if the discontented and ambitious who are always ready to grumble and complain of their fate, because perchance they have only the mere necessaries and are unable to procure the luxuries and pleasures of life; if they would only pause for a moment and contemplate this harrowing picture of want and misery, how much more gratefully would they appreciate the lot that Providence has assigned to them!

As for myself, for the first ten or twelve years that I was in India, I lived in such abject poverty that I had hardly sufficient means to procure the bare necessaries of life; but even then

I was as happy and contented as I am now that I am better off. Besides the consolations which my religion gave me under these trying circumstances, my reason found me others in the reflection that nineteen-twentieths of the people among whom I was living were bearing far greater trials of all kinds than any that I was called on to endure.

Besides the Pariahs, who are to be found all over the Peninsula, there are in certain provinces other classes composed of individuals who equal and even surpass them in depravity of mind and customs, and in the contempt in which they are held. Such, for instance, is the caste of *Pallers*, who are only found in Madura and in the neighbourhood of Cape Comorin. The *Pallers* consider themselves superior to the Pariahs, inasmuch as they do not eat the flesh of the cow; but the Pariahs look on them as altogether their inferiors, because they are the scum of the Left-hand faction, whilst they themselves are the mainstay of the Right-hand.

These two classes of degraded beings can never agree, and wherever they are found in fairly equal numbers, the disputes and quarrels amongst them are interminable. They lead the same sort of life, enjoy an equal share of public opprobrium, and both are obliged to live far apart from all other classes of the inhabitants.

Amongst the forests on the Malabar coast there lives a tribe which, incredible as it may seem, surpasses the two of which I have just spoken in degradation and squalid misery. They are called *Puliahs*, and are looked upon as below the level of the beasts which share this wild country with them. They are not even allowed to build themselves huts to protect themselves from the inclemencies of the weather. A sort of lean-to, supported by four bamboo poles and open at the sides, serves as a shelter for some of them, and keeps off the rain, though it does not screen them from the wind. Most of them, however, make for themselves what may be called nests in the branches of the thickest-foliaged trees, where they perch like birds of prey for the greater part of the twenty-four hours. They are not even allowed to walk peaceably along the high-roads. If they see any one coming towards them, they are bound to utter a certain cry and to go a long way round to avoid passing him. A hundred paces is the very nearest they may approach any one of a different caste. If a Nair, who always carries arms, meets one of these unhappy people on the road, he is entitled to stab him on the spot[1]. The *Puliahs* live an absolutely savage life, and have no communication whatever with the rest of the world.

The *Chucklers*, or cobblers, are also considered inferior to the Pariahs all over the Peninsula, and, as a matter of fact, they show that they are of a lower grade by their more debased ideas, their greater ignorance and brutality. They are also much more addicted to drunkenness and debauchery. Their orgies take place principally in the evening, and their villages resound, far into the night, with the yells and quarrels which result from their intoxication. Nothing will persuade them to work as long as they have anything to drink; they only return to their labour when they have absolutely no further means of satisfying their ruling passion. Thus they spend their time in alternate bouts of work and drunkenness. The women of this wretched class do not allow their husbands to outshine them in any vice, and are quite as much addicted to drunkenness as the men. Their modesty and general behaviour may therefore be easily imagined. The very Pariahs refuse to have anything to do with the *Chucklers*, and do not admit them to any of their feasts.

There is one class amongst the Pariahs which rules all the rest of the caste. These are the *Valluvas*[2], who are called *the Brahmins of the Pariahs* in mockery. They keep themselves quite distinct from the others, and only intermarry in their own class. They consider themselves as the *gurus*, or spiritual advisers, of the rest. It is they who preside at all the marriages and other religious ceremonies of the Pariahs. They predict all the absurdities mentioned in the Hindu almanac, such as lucky and unlucky days, favourable or unfavourable moments for beginning a fresh undertaking, and other prophecies of a like nature. But they are forbidden to meddle with anything pertaining to astronomy, such as the foretelling of eclipses, changes of the moon, &c., this prerogative belonging exclusively to the Brahmins.

There are other classes too, which, though a trifle higher in

[1] No native is nowadays allowed to carry arms without a licence. But even now the Puliahs are forbidden to approach a person of higher caste. They always stand at a distance of 20 to 30 yards.—ED.

[2] These are sometimes physicians and astrologers.—ED.

the Hindu social scale, are for all that not treated with much more respect. Firstly, amongst the Sudras there are those who follow servile occupations, or at least occupations dependent on the public; secondly, those who perform low and disgusting offices, which expose them to frequent defilements; and, thirdly, there are the nomadic tribes, who are always wandering about the country, having no fixed abode.

Amongst the first I place the barbers and the washermen. There are men belonging to these two employments in every village, and no one exercising the same profession can come from another village to work in theirs without their express permission. Their employments are transmitted from father to son, and those who pursue them form two distinct castes.

The barber's business is to trim the beard, shave the head, pare the nails on hands and feet, and clean the ears of all the inhabitants of his village. In several of the southern provinces the inhabitants have all the hair on different parts of their bodies shaved off, with the exception of the eye-brows; and this custom is always observed by Brahmins on marriage days and other solemn occasions[1]. The barbers are also the surgeons of the country. Whatever be the nature of the operation that they are called on to perform, their razor is their only instrument, if it is a question of amputation; or a sort of stiletto, which they use for paring nails, if they have to open an abscess, or the like. They are also the only accredited fiddlers; and they share with the Pariahs the exclusive right of playing wind instruments, as will be seen presently.

As to the washermen, their business is much the same here as everywhere else, except for the extreme filthiness of the rags that are entrusted to them to be cleaned.

Those engaged in these two occupations are in such a dependent position that they dare not refuse to work for any one who chooses to employ them. They are paid in kind at harvest time by each inhabitant of their village. No doubt the contempt in which they are held by men of other castes, who look upon them as menials, is due partly to this state of sub-

[1] This custom of shaving the hair from all parts of the body, for ceremonies where absolute purity is required, is not peculiar to the Brahmins; it was also common amongst the Jews, for the same reason, and was part of their ceremonial law (Numbers viii. 6, 7).—DUBOIS.

jection, and also to the uncleanness of the things which they are compelled to handle.

The potters also are a very low class, being absolutely uneducated.

The five castes of artisans, of which I have already spoken, and also, as a rule, all those employed in mechanical or ornamental arts, are very much looked down upon and despised.

The *Moochis*, or tanners, though better educated and more refined than any of the preceding classes, are not much higher in the social scale. The other Sudras never allow them to join in their feasts; indeed, they would hardly condescend to give them a drop of water to drink. This feeling of repulsion is caused by the defilement which ensues from their constantly handling the skins of dead animals.

As a rule, the mechanical and the liberal arts, such as music, painting, and sculpture, are placed on very much the same level, and those who follow these professions, which are left entirely to the lower castes of the Sudras, are looked upon with equal disfavour[1].

As far as I know, only the *Moochis* take up painting as a profession. Instrumental music, and particularly that of wind instruments, is left exclusively, as I have already mentioned, to the barbers and Pariahs[2]. The little progress that is made in these arts is no doubt due to the small amount of encouragement which they receive. As for painting, one never sees anything but daubs. The Hindus are quite satisfied if their artists can draw designs of striking figures painted in the most vivid colours. Our best engravings, if they are uncoloured, or our finest miniatures or landscapes, are quite valueless in their eyes.

Though the Hindus much enjoy listening to music, and introduce it freely into all their public and private ceremonies, both religious and social, yet it must be admitted that this charming art is here still in its infancy. I should say Hindus

[1] Those who follow these liberal arts are treated with more respect in these days. At all events, they are not looked upon with disfavour. There are now many Brahmins in Southern India who are professional musicians, though they play on certain instruments only.—ED.

[2] Classes superior to the barbers and Pariahs also play wind instruments at the present time.—ED.

are no further advanced in it now than they were two or three thousand years ago. They do not expect their musicians to produce harmonious tunes when they play at their feasts and ceremonies, for their dull ears would certainly not appreciate them. What they like is plenty of noise and plenty of shrill piercing sounds. Their musicians are certainly able to comply with their wishes in this respect. Such discordant noises are infinitely more pleasing to them than our melodious airs, which possess no charm whatever for them. Of all our various instruments, they care only for drums and trumpets. Their vocal music, too, is not a whit more pleasing to European ears than their instrumental. Their songs are chiefly remarkable for uninspiring monotony; and though they have a scale like ours, composed of seven notes, they have not tried to produce from it those harmonies and combinations which fall so deliciously on our ears.

Why is it, it may well be asked, that it should be considered shameful to play on wind instruments in India? I suppose it is on account of the defilement which the players contract by putting such instruments to their mouths after they have once been touched by saliva, which, as I shall show presently, is the one excretion from the human body for which Hindus display invincible horror. There is by no means the same feeling with regard to stringed instruments. In fact, you may often hear Brahmins singing and accompanying themselves on a sort of little harp which is known by the name of *vina*. This instrument has a rather agreeable tone, and would be still more pleasing if the sounds extracted from it were more varied. It has always been a favourite amongst the better classes; and its invention must date from an extremely remote period, for it is often mentioned in Hindu books, where the gods themselves are represented as playing on the *vina* to soothe themselves with its sweet melodies. It is generally taught by Brahmins; and as their lessons are very expensive, and they persuade their pupils that a great many are necessary in order to attain proficiency, it is obvious that none but the rich can afford themselves this pleasure.

The *vina* of the Hindus is probably the same as the *cithara*[1],

[1] The Mahomedans of Northern India have a stringed instrument known as *cithar*.—ED.

or harp, of the Jews, in playing which King David excelled, and with which he produced those melodies which soothed and calmed his unfortunate master Saul, after God had given Saul up as a prey to his evil passions.

Besides the *vina*, the Brahmins have another stringed instrument called *kinnahra*, which is something like a guitar, and the tone of which is not unpleasant.

The Hindus do not use gut for the strings of their instruments, as Europeans do. They would not dare to touch anything so impure, for if they did they would consider themselves defiled by the contact. To avoid such a serious impurity they use metal strings.

I will now turn to the nomadic castes, which swell the number of wretched and degraded beings amongst the nation I am describing. Without any fixed abode, wandering about from one country to another, the individuals of which these vagabond tribes are composed pay little or no attention to the various customs which are obligatory on every respectable Hindu ; and this is why they are so cordially detested.

One of the largest of these castes is that which is known in the south by the name of *Kuravers* or *Kurumarus*. This is subdivided into two branches, one of which carries on a trade in salt. Gangs of men bring this article from the coast and distribute it in the interior of the country, using asses, of which they possess considerable numbers, as their means of transport. As soon as they have sold or bartered this commodity, they reload the asses with different kinds of grain, for which there is a ready sale on the coast, and start off again at once. Thus their whole lives are spent in hurrying from one country to another without settling down in any place.

The occupation of the second branch of these *Kuravers* is to make baskets and mats of osier and bamboo, and other similar utensils which are used in Hindu households. They are obliged to be perpetually moving from one place to another to find work, and are without any fixed abode.

The *Kuravers* are also the fortune-tellers of the country. They speak a language peculiar to themselves, which is unintelligible to any other Hindu. Their manners and customs have much in common with those of the wandering tribes that are known in England as *Gypsies*, and in France as *Egyptians*, or Bohemians. Their women tell the fortunes of those who consult them and are willing to pay them. The person who wishes to learn his fate seats himself in front of the soothsayer and holds out his hand, while she beats a little drum, invokes all her gods or evil spirits, and gabbles aloud a succession of fantastic words. These preliminaries over, she studies with the most scrupulous attention the lines on the hand of the simple-minded person who is consulting her, and finally predicts the good or evil fortune that is in store for him. Many attempts have been made to trace the origin of these wandering tribes, who are to be found telling fortunes all over the world. The general opinion appears to be that they originally came from Egypt, but this view might possibly be changed if these *Kuravers* of India were to be closely examined, and their language, manners, and customs compared with those of the Gypsies and Bohemians.

The *Kuraver* women also tattoo the designs of flowers and animals which decorate the arms of most young Hindu women. The tattooing is done by first delicately tracing the desired objects on the skin, then pricking the outline gently with a needle, and immediately after rubbing in the juice of certain plants, whereby the design becomes indelible.

The *Kurumarus* are much addicted to stealing, and from this tribe come the professional thieves and pickpockets known by the name of *Kalla-bantrus*. These people make a study of the art of stealing, and all the dodges of their infamous profession are instilled into them from their youth. To this end their parents teach them to lie obstinately, and train them to suffer tortures rather than divulge what it is to their interest to hide. Far from being ashamed of their profession, the *Kalla-bantrus* glory in it, and when they have nothing to fear they take the greatest pleasure in boasting of the clever thefts they have committed in various places. Those who, caught in the act, have been badly hurt, or who have been deprived by the magistrates of nose, ears, or right hand, show their scars and mutilations with pride, as proofs of their courage and intrepidity; and these men are usually the chosen heads of their caste.

They always commit their depredations at night. Noiselessly entering a village, they place sentinels along the different roads, while they select the houses that can be entered with the least risk. These they creep into, and in a few minutes strip them of all the metal vessels and other valuables they can find, including the gold and silver ornaments which the sleeping women and children wear round their necks. They never break open the doors of the houses, for that would make too much noise and so lead to their detection. Their plan is to pierce the mud wall of the house with a sharp iron instrument specially made for the purpose, with which they can in a few moments easily make a hole large enough for a man to creep through. They are so clever that they generally manage to carry out their depredations without being either seen or heard by any one. But if they happen to be surprised, the *Kalla-bantrus* make a desperate resistance and do their best to escape. If one of their number is killed in the scrimmage, they will run any risk to obtain possession of the corpse. They then cut off the head and carry it away with them to avoid discovery.

In the provinces which are governed by native princes, these villains are, to a certain extent, protected by the authorities, who countenance their depredations in return for a stipulated sum, or on condition that they pay the value of half the booty that they steal to the revenue collector of the locality. But as such an understanding could not possibly be anything more than tacit in any civilized country, this infamous arrangement is kept secret. The culprits, therefore, can expect no compensation to be publicly awarded them by the magistrates for the wounds and mutilations which they may suffer in the course of their nocturnal raids; but these same magistrates will do their best to screen or palliate their offences, the profits of which they share, and will always protect their clients from well-deserved punishment when they appear before them in court.

The last Mussulman prince who governed Mysore had a regular regiment of *Kalla-bantrus* in his service, whom he employed, not to fight amongst his troops, but to despoil the enemy's camp during the night, to steal the horses, carry off any valuables they could find amongst the officers' baggage, spike the enemy's guns, and act as spies. They were paid according to their skill and success. In times of peace they were sent into neighbouring States to pilfer for the benefit of their master, and also to report on the proceedings of the rulers. The minor native princes called *Poligars* always employ a number of these ruffians for the same purposes.

In the provinces where these *Kalla-bantrus* are countenanced by the Government, the unfortunate inhabitants have no other means of protecting themselves from their depredations than by making an agreement with the head of the gang to pay him an annual tax of a quarter of a rupee and a fowl per house, in consideration of which he becomes responsible for all the thefts committed by his people in villages which are thus, so to say, insured[1].

Besides the *Kalla-bantrus* of the *Kurumaru* caste, the province of Mysore is infested by another caste of thieves, called *Kanojis*, who are no less dreaded than the others.

But of all the nomadic castes which wander about the country, the best known and most detested is the *Lambadis*, or *Sukalers*, or *Brinjaris*. No one knows the origin of this caste. The members of it have different manners and customs, and also a different religion and language from all the other castes of Hindus. Certain points of resemblance, however, which are to be found between them and the Mahrattas, lead one to believe that they must have sprung from these people in the first instance, and have inherited from them their propensities for rapine and theft, and their utter disregard for the rights of property when they think they are stronger than their victims and are safe from retributory justice. However, the severe sentences that the magistrates have latterly passed on them in several districts have exercised a salutary influence. They no longer dare to rob and steal openly. But the lonely traveller who meets them in some lonely spot had better beware, especially if they have reason to think that he would be worth plundering.

In time of war they attach themselves to the army where discipline is least strict. They come swarming in from all parts, hoping, in the general disorder and confusion, to be able to thieve with impunity. They make themselves very useful by keeping the market well supplied with the provisions that they have stolen on the march. They hire themselves and their large herds of cattle to whichever contending party will pay them best, acting as carriers of the supplies and baggage of the

[1] This, of course, is no longer allowed. The thieving classes have, under a more rigid system of police, been compelled to take to more lawful pursuits.—ED.

army. They were thus employed, to the number of several thousands, by the English in their last war with the Sultan of Mysore. The English, however, had occasion to regret having taken these untrustworthy and ill-disciplined people into their service, when they saw them ravaging the country through which they passed and causing more annoyance than the whole of the enemy's army. The frequent and severe punishments that were inflicted on their chiefs had no restraining effect whatever on the rest of the horde. They had been attracted solely by the hope of plunder, and thought little of the regular wages and other inducements which had been promised them.

In times of peace these professional brigands occupy themselves in trading in grain and salt, which they convey from one part of the country to the other on their bullocks; but at the least whisper of war, or the slightest sign of coming trouble, they are at once on the look-out, ready to take advantage in the first moment of confusion of any opportunity for pillaging. In fact, the unfortunate inhabitants of the country fear an invasion of a hostile army far less than they do a sudden irruption of these terrible *Lambadis*.

Of all the castes of the Hindus this particular one is acknowledged to be the most brutal. The natural proclivities of its members for evil are clearly indicated by their ill-favoured, wild appearance and their coarse, hard-featured countenances, these characteristics being as noticeable in the women as in the men. In all parts of India they are under the special supervision of the police, because there is only too much reason for mistrusting them.

Their women are, for the most part, very ugly and revoltingly dirty. Amongst other glaring vices they are supposed to be much addicted to incontinency; and they are reputed to sometimes band themselves together in search of men whom they compel by force to satisfy their lewd desires.

The *Lambadis* are accused of the still more atrocious crime of offering up human sacrifices. When they wish to perform this horrible act, it is said, they secretly carry off the first person they meet. Having conducted the victim to some lonely spot, they dig a hole in which they bury him up to the neck. While he is still alive they make a sort of lamp of dough made of flour, which they place on his head. This they fill with oil, and light four wicks in it. Having done this, the men and women join hands, and, forming a circle, dance round their victim, singing and making a great noise, till he expires.

Amongst other curious customs of this odious caste is one that obliges them to drink no water which is not drawn from springs or wells. The water from rivers or tanks being thus forbidden, they are obliged in a case of absolute necessity to dig a little hole by the side of a tank or river and take the water that filters through, which by this means is supposed to become spring water.

Another nomadic caste is that of the *Wuddars*, whose trade is to dig wells, tanks, and canals, and to repair dykes. They, too, have to travel about in search of work. This caste is also much despised. The manners of the individuals composing it are as low as their origin, and their minds as uncultivated as their manners. Their extreme uncouthness may, perhaps, account for the low estimation in which they are held.

In Mysore, and in the north-west of the Carnatic, another caste of nomads is to be met with, known as *Pakanattis*. They speak Telugu, and originally formed part of the caste of *Golla-varus*, or shepherds, and were agriculturists. They took to their present kind of life about a hundred and fifty years ago, and like it so much that it would be impossible to persuade them to change it for any regular occupation. The cause of their secession from the rest of their caste was that one of their headmen was grievously insulted by the governor of the province in which they lived. As they never received any redress at all commensurate with the affront, they determined to avenge themselves by deserting their homes in a body, and thus bringing all the agricultural work of the country to a stand-still. From that time to this they have never attempted to return to their former mode of life, but are always wandering from place to place without settling anywhere. Some of their headmen, with whom I have conversed, have told me that they number about two thousand families, half of whom wander through the Telugu country and the rest through Mysore. The headmen meet from time to time to settle the differences which frequently arise amongst the members. However, the *Pakanattis* are the quietest and best behaved of all the wandering tribes. They are kept in excellent order; and though they always go about in bands, theft and pillage are unknown amongst them, and if any of them are found guilty of either, they are severely punished by the rest. They are all most miserably poor; the better off possess a few buffaloes and cows, the milk of which they sell, but the greater number of them are professional herbalists. They collect plants, roots, and other things in the different countries that they wander through, such as are used for medicine or dyes, or for salves, &c., for horses and cattle. These they sell in the bazaars, and the little money that they thus earn helps them considerably. They supplement their livelihood by hunting, fishing, begging, and charlatanry.

All these tribes live entirely isolated from the rest of the world, with whom they hold no communication, except in order to obtain the bare necessaries of life. They lead for the most part a pastoral life, and their headmen occasionally possess considerable herds of cattle, consisting of bullocks, buffaloes, and asses. They travel in bands of ten, twenty, thirty, or more families. They shelter themselves under bamboo or osier mats, which they carry everywhere with them. Each family has its own mat tent, seven or eight feet long, four or five feet broad, and three or four feet high, in which father, mother, children, poultry, and sometimes even pigs, are housed, or rather huddled together, this being their only protection against bad weather. They always choose woods or lonely places as sites for their camps, so that no one can see what goes on amongst them. Besides their mat tents and the other necessaries for camping, they always take care to be provided with small stores of grain, as well as with the household utensils necessary for preparing and cooking their food. Those who possess beasts of burden make them carry the greater part of their goods and chattels, but the unfortunate wretches who have no other means of transport are compelled to carry all their worldly possessions, that is to say, the necessaries for housing and feeding themselves. I have seen the husband carrying on his head and shoulders the tent, the provisions, and some earthen vessels, whilst the wife, her body half uncovered, carried an infant on her back, hanging behind her in the upper part of her cotton garment; on her head was the mortar for husking the rice; while following her came a child bending under the weight of the rest of the household chattels.

I have often seen this sad spectacle, and always with deep feelings of pity. Such is the kind of life which many Hindus are accustomed to, and which they bear without murmuring or complaining, and without even appearing to envy those whose lives are spent in pleasanter places.

Each one of these nomadic tribes has its own habits, laws, and customs; and each forms a small and perfectly independent republic of its own, governed by such rules and regulations as seem best to them. Nothing is known by the outside world of what happens amongst them. The chiefs of each caste are elected or dismissed by a majority of votes. They are commissioned, during the time that their authority lasts, to enforce the caste rules, to settle disputes, and to punish all misdemeanour and crime. But however heinous offences may be, they never involve the penalty of death or mutilation. The guilty person has only either to pay a fine, or suffer a severe flogging or some other corporal punishment. Travelling ceaselessly from one country to another, these vagrant families pay no tax to any Government: the majority possess nothing, and they have consequently no need of the protection of a prince to guard them against spoliation. Further, they have no claims to take before the courts, since they administer justice themselves; and being without any ambition, they ask neither pardon nor favour from any prince. All these nomadic tribes stink in the nostrils of other Hindus, owing to the kind of life which they lead, to the small esteem in which they hold the religious practices observed by other castes, and, lastly, to the vulgar vices to which they are enslaved. But the heaviest indictment against them is their excessive intemperance in eating and drinking. With the exception of cow's flesh, they eat indiscriminately of every kind of food, even the most revolting, such as the flesh of foxes, cats, rats, snakes, crows, &c. Both men and women drink to excess toddy and arrack, i.e. the spirit of the country, and they will consume every kind of liquor and enervating drug which they can procure.

The majority of these vagabonds live in a state of extreme poverty. When no other resource remains to them they beg, or else send their women to earn their livelihood by prostitution.

Among the degraded beings who form the dregs of society in

India must be classed the jugglers, the charlatans, mountebanks, conjurers, acrobats, rope-dancers, &c. There are two or three castes which practise these professions, travelling from country to country to find patrons or dupes. It is not surprising, with a people so credulous and endued with such a love of the marvellous as the Hindus, that such impostors should abound. They are regarded as magicians and sorcerers, as men versed in witchcraft and all the occult sciences, and are viewed with fear and distrust; while the hatred in which they are held is much greater than is accorded in Europe to people of the same description. Some of these charlatans carry on a trade with a credulous public in quack medicines and universal panaceas. They may often be heard in the street haranguing the multitude and extolling their wares. They even surpass our own quacks in effrontery and barefaced imposture. Others are conjurers or acrobats; and both one and the other perform really astonishing feats of legerdemain and agility. European jugglers would certainly have to lower their colours before them.

The best known of these castes is that of the *Dombers* or *Dombarus*. To the earnings which the men make by their industry the women also add the sums that they gain by the most shameless immorality; their favours, if such a word be applicable, are accorded to any one who likes to pay for them. However, in spite of all this, the *Dombers* lead a wretched life; and their extreme poverty is caused by their boundless intemperance. They always spend in eating and drinking much more than they actually possess; and when all their means are exhausted they have recourse to begging.

Other troops of vagabonds of the same class adopt the profession of travelling actors. I once met a large party who were representing the ten *Avatars* (or incarnations) of Vishnu, on which subject they had composed as many sacred plays. The greater number of them, however, play obscene and ridiculous farces in the streets, with boards and trestles for their stage; or else they exhibit marionettes, which they place in disgusting postures, making them give utterance to the most pitiable and filthy nonsense. These shows are exactly suited to the taste and comprehension of the stupid crowd which forms the audience. Hindu players have learned from experience that they can never rivet the attention of the public except at the expense of decency, modesty, or good sense[1].

Some Hindu jugglers turn their attention to snake-charming, especially with cobras, the most poisonous of all. These they teach to dance, or to move in rhythm to music; and they perform what appear to be the most alarming tricks with these deadly reptiles. In spite of all their care and skill it sometimes happens that they are bitten; and this would infallibly cost them their lives, did they not take the precaution to excite the snake every morning, forcing it to bite several times through a thick piece of stuff so that it may rid itself of the venom that re-forms daily in its fangs. They also pose as possessors of the secret of enchanting snakes, pretending that they can attract them with the sound of their flutes. This craft was practised elsewhere in the very earliest times, as may be gathered from a passage in Holy Scripture, where the obstinacy of a hardened sinner is likened to that of a deaf adder that shuts its ears to the voice of the charmer. Be that as it may, I can vouch for it that the pretended power of Hindu snake-charmers is a mere imposture. They keep a few trained tame snakes, which are accustomed to come to them at the sound of a flute, and when they have settled the amount of their reward with the persons who think, or have been persuaded, that there are snakes in the vicinity of their houses, they place one of these tame reptiles in some corner, taking care not to be observed. One of the conditions on which they always insist is that any snake which they charm out of a hole shall not be killed, but shall be handed over to them. This point settled, the charmer seats himself on the ground and begins to play on his flute, turning first to one side, then to the other. The snake, on hearing these familiar sounds, comes out of its hiding-place, and crawls towards its master, gliding quietly into the basket in which it is usually shut up. The charmer then takes his reward and goes off in search of other dupes[2].

[1] At the present time there are many Indian theatrical companies formed somewhat after the fashion of European companies. Their performances, too, have improved a great deal since the Abbé's time.—ED.

[2] Even to this day there is a class of village servants called *Kudimis*, whose business it is to collect medicinal herbs and other plants that might be required by the people. These *Kudimis* are also professional snake-catchers, and are supposed to possess infallible antidotes against snake-poison.—ED.

I will now give some particulars about the wild tribes which inhabit the jungles and mountains in the south of India. They are divided into several castes, each of which is composed of various communities. They are fairly numerous in many places in the Malabar hills, or Western Ghauts, where they are known by the generic name of *Kadu-Kurumbars*. These savages live in the forests, but have no fixed abode. After staying a year or two in one place they move on to another. Having selected the spot for their temporary sojourn, they surround it with a kind of hedge, and each family chooses a little patch of ground, which is dug up with a sharp piece of wood hardened in the fire. There they sow small seeds, and a great many pumpkins, cucumbers, and other vegetables; and on these they live for two or three months in the year. They have little or no intercourse with the more civilized inhabitants of the neighbourhood. The latter indeed prefer to keep them at a distance from their houses, as they stand in considerable dread of them, looking upon them as sorcerers or mischievous people, whom it is unlucky even to meet. If they suspect a *Kadu-Kurumbar* of having brought about illness or any other mishap by his spells, they punish him severely, sometimes even putting him to death.

During the rains these savages take shelter in miserable huts. Some find refuge in caves, or holes in the rocks, or in the hollow trunks of old trees. In fine weather they camp out in the open. At night each clan assembles at a given spot, and enormous fires are lit to keep off the cold and to scare away wild beasts. Men, women, and children all sleep huddled together anyhow. The poor wretches wear no clothes, a woman's only covering being a few leaves sewn together and tied round the waist. Knowing only of the simple necessities of existence, they find enough to satisfy their wants in the forest. Roots and other natural products of the earth, snakes and animals that they can snare or catch, honey that they find on the rugged rocks or in the tops of trees, which they climb with the agility of monkeys; all these furnish them with the means of satisfying the cravings of hunger. Less intelligent even than the natives of Africa, these savages of India do not possess bows and arrows, which they do not know how to use.

It is to them that the dwellers in the plains apply when they require wood with which to build their houses. The jungle tribes supply them with all materials of this kind, in exchange for a few valueless objects, such as copper or brass bangles, small quantities of grain, or a little tobacco to smoke[1].

Both men and women occupy themselves in making reed or bamboo mats, baskets, hampers, and other household articles, which they exchange with the inhabitants of more civilized parts for salt, pepper, grain, &c.

According to the people of the plains, these savages can, by means of witchcraft and enchantments, charm all the tigers, elephants, and venomous snakes which share the forests with them, so that they need never fear their attacks.

Their children are accustomed from their earliest infancy to the hard life to which nature appears to have condemned them. The very day after their confinement the women are obliged to scour the woods with their husbands in order to find the day's food. Before starting they suckle the new-born child, and make a hole in the ground, in which they put a layer of teak leaves. The leaves are so rough that if they rub the skin ever so gently they draw blood. In this hard bed the poor little creature is laid, and there it remains till its mother returns in the evening. On the fifth or sixth day after birth they begin to accustom their infants to eat solid food; and in order to harden them at once to endure inclement weather, they wash them every morning in cold dew, which they collect from the trees and plants. Until the infants can walk, they are left by themselves from morning till night, quite naked, exposed to sun, wind, rain, and air, and buried in the holes which serve them for cradles.

The whole religion of these savages seems to consist in the worship of *bhootams*, or evil spirits, which worship they perform in a way peculiar to themselves. They pay no regard whatever to the rest of the Hindu deities.

Besides the *Kadu-Kurumbars* there is another tribe of savages living in the forests and mountains of the Carnatic, and known by the name of *Irulers*, or in some places *Soligurus*. Their habits are identical with those of the *Kadu-Kurumbars*. They lead the same kind of life, have the same religion, customs, and prejudices; in fact, one

[1] These transactions are now regulated by the forest laws.—ED.

may say that the difference between the two tribes exists only in name.

In several parts of Malabar a tribe is to be found called the *Malai-Kondigaru*, which, though as wild as those mentioned above, has perhaps a little more in common with civilized humanity. They live in the forests, and their principal occupation is to extract the juice of the palm-tree, part of which they drink, the rest they sell. The women climb the trees to obtain it, and they do so in a surprisingly agile manner. These people always go about naked. The women only wear a little rag, which flutters about in the wind and most imperfectly covers that portion of their bodies which it is supposed to hide. During one of the expeditions which the last Sultan of Mysore made into the mountains, he met a horde of these savages, and was much shocked at their state of nudity; for, however depraved Mahomedans may be in their private life, nothing can equal the decency and modesty of their conduct in public. They are horrified at word or look that even verges on indecency or immodesty, especially on the part of their women. The Sultan therefore caused the headmen of the *Malai-Kondigarus* to be brought before him, and asked them why they and their women did not cover their bodies more decently. They excused themselves on the plea of poverty, and that it was the custom of their caste. Tippu replied that he must require them to wear clothing like the other inhabitants of the country, and that if they had not the means wherewith to buy it, he would every year provide them gratuitously with the cotton cloths necessary for the purpose. The savages, however, though urged by the Sultan, made humble remonstrances, and begged hard to be allowed to dispense with the encumbrance of clothing. They finally told him that if they were forced to wear clothing, contrary to the rules of their caste, they would all leave the country rather than put up with so great an inconvenience; they preferred to go and live in some other distant forest, where they would be allowed to follow their customs unmolested. The Sultan was accordingly obliged to give way.

In and around Coorg is another tribe of savages known by the name of *Yeruvaru*. It is akin to the Pariah caste, and is composed of several communities scattered about in the jungles. These people, however, work for their living, and make themselves useful to the rest of the population. They leave their homes to get food from the more civilized inhabitants of the neighbourhood, who, in return for a small quantity of rice given as wages, make them work hard at agricultural pursuits. The indolence of these savages is such, however, that as long as there is a handful of rice in their huts they absolutely refuse to work, and will only return to it when their supply of grain is entirely exhausted. Nevertheless, the other inhabitants are obliged to keep on good terms with them, because they perform all the hardest manual labour, and because if one of them was affronted or thought himself ill-treated, all the rest of the clan would take his part, and leave their usual abode and hide in the forest. The civilized inhabitants, to whom they are thus indispensable, would not be able to persuade them to resume their work until they had made friendly overtures and agreed to pay damages. These wild yet simple-minded people find it so difficult to procure the bare necessaries of life that they never even think of small luxuries which most other Hindus are so fond of, such as betel, tobacco, oil to anoint their heads, &c. They do not even appear to envy those who enjoy them, and are satisfied if they can get a little salt and pepper to flavour the tasteless vegetables and roots which form the principal part of their food.

All these wild tribes are gentle and peaceable by nature. They do not understand the use of weapons of any sort, and the sight of a stranger is sometimes sufficient to put to flight a whole community. No doubt the climate in which they live is in a great measure responsible for their timid, lazy, and indolent character. They are very unlike the savages who people the vast forests of America or Africa, inasmuch as they do not know what war means, and appear to be quite incapable of returning evil for evil. For, of course, no sane person believes the accusation brought against them that they can injure their neighbours by means of spells and enchantments. Hidden in thick forests, or in dens and caves in the rocks, they fear nothing in the world so much as the approach of a civilized being, and far from envying the happiness which the latter boasts of having found in the society of his fellow-men, they shun any intercourse with him, fearing lest he should try to rob them of their liberty and independence, and lest they should be condemned to submit to a civilization which to them is only another term for bondage.

At the same time, these wild tribes of Hindus retain a few of the prejudices of their fellow-countrymen. For instance, they are divided into castes, they never eat beef, they have similar ideas about defilement and purification, and they keep the principal regulations relating to them.

CHAPTER VI

The Poverty of the Hindus.

INDIA has always been considered a most wealthy and opulent country, more favoured by nature than any other in the world, a land literally flowing with milk and honey, where the soil yields all that is necessary for the existence of its happy people almost without cultivation. The great wealth accumulated by a few of its native princes, the large fortunes so rapidly acquired by many Europeans, its valuable diamond mines, the quality and quantity of its pearls, the abundance of its spices and scented woods, the fertility of its soil, and the, at one time, unrivalled superiority of its various manufactures: all these have caused admiration and wonder from time immemorial. One would naturally suppose that a nation which could supply so many luxuries would surpass all others in wealth.

This estimation of the wealth of India has been commonly accepted in Europe up to the present day; and those who, after visiting the country and obtaining exact and authentic information about the real condition of its inhabitants, have dared to affirm that India is the poorest and most wretched of all the civilized countries of the world, have simply not been believed. Many people in Europe, after reading what various authors have to say about India's manufactures and about the factories which turn out the delicate muslins, fine cloths, and beautiful coloured cottons, &c., which are so much admired all the world over, have supposed that the establishments producing such magnificent stuffs must have supplied models for those which are to be found at Manchester, Birmingham, Lyons, and other towns in Europe. Well, the truth is (and most people are still unaware of the fact) all these beautiful fabrics are manufactured in wretched thatched huts built of mud, twenty to thirty feet long by seven or eight feet broad. In such a workroom the weaver stretches his frame, squats on the ground, and quietly plies his shuttle, surrounded by his family, his cow, and his fowls. The instruments he makes use of are extremely primitive, and his whole stock in trade could easily be carried about by one man. Such is, in very truth, an exact picture of an Indian factory. As to the manufacturer himself, his poverty corresponds to the simplicity of his workshop. There are in India two or three large classes whose only profession is that of weaving. The individuals comprising these classes are, for the most part, very poor, and are even destitute of the necessary means for working on their own account. Those who deal in the products of their industry have to go to them, money in hand, and after bargaining with them as to the price, quality, and quantity of the goods required, are obliged to pay them in advance. The weavers then go and buy the cotton and other necessaries with which to begin work. Their employers have to supervise their work and keep a sharp look-out lest they decamp with the money, especially if the advances happen to be in any way considerable.

As regards the condition of the Hindus generally, I think that the following account may make things plain. It is based on a long acquaintance with the inhabitants of a large tract of country. Still, the casual observer may find fault with it if he judges it by what he has noticed in large towns, more especially on the coast. There, at least, most of the natives possess houses of more or less value which they can dispose of if necessary, an advantage not shared by the rural classes. Besides, the towns are the rendezvous of the rich and industrious, and of those who intend to become so by fair means or foul, so it is not surprising to find a higher standard of comfort prevailing there. It is from experience of the masses of the population that I have been able to present this sketch of the different degrees of poverty or wealth amongst the people.

I should class the inhabitants of the Indian Peninsula in the following manner. The first and lowest class may be said to be composed of all those whose property is below the value of £5 sterling. This class appears to me to comprise nine-twentieths, or perhaps even a half, of the entire population. It includes most of the Pariah class and nearly all the *Chucklers* (leather-workers); and these together form at least a quarter of the population. To them must be added a considerable portion of the Sudras, all the poorest members of the other castes, and the multitude of vagrants, beggars, and impostors who are to be met with everywhere.

Most of the natives of this class hire themselves out as agricultural labourers, and are required to do the hardest manual labour for the smallest possible wage. In the places where they are paid in coin, they receive only just enough to buy the coarsest of food. Their wage varies from twelve to twenty rupees a year, according to locality. They are better paid along the coast. With this amount they are obliged to feed and clothe themselves. In some places they are paid half in coin and half in grain, or else they get their keep, and over and above that receive from four to eight rupees a year[1].

Some of the younger members of this class hire themselves out without wages, on condition that, after working faithfully for seven or eight years, their master will provide them with a wife of their own caste and defray all nuptial expenses. Married servants who are fed by their masters carry home their daily rations. This food is supposed to be sufficient for the wants of one person, or, to quote the native saying, 'to be enough to fill the belly'; but they have to share it with their wives and children, who also have to work and thus add to the provision. When they are in actual want, as often happens, they go and seek for food in the woods, or on the banks of the rivers and tanks, where they find leaves, shrubs, roots, and herbs. These they boil, as often as not without even salt or any kind of condiment; and this primitive food forms, for the greater part of the year, the most substantial part of their meals. Clumps of bamboo abound in the woods, and its shoots form, for two or three months of the year, a great resource to the poor people who live near the places where it grows.

As soon as the children belonging to the class living in a state of servitude have reached the age of eight or nine, they join the same master who employs their father, the boys

[1] The scale is higher everywhere nowadays, but so also is the cost of food-stuffs. Nowhere in India does the common labourer earn much more than a 'living wage.'—ED.

looking after the cattle and the girls sweeping out the byres, collecting the dung, grinding the grain, &c.

The well-to-do cultivators always employ men of this class; and, in order to keep them in perpetual bondage, they lend them money either on the occasion of a marriage or for other purposes. The poor wretches find themselves, on account of their small wages, quite unable to pay back the capital thus advanced, and in many cases even the interest, which soon exceeds the original loan, and are therefore reduced to the necessity of working, with their wives and children, until the end of their days. From the time this happens their masters look upon them as actual slaves, and refuse to grant them manumission until they have repaid both the principal and interest of the sum which they or their fathers borrowed perhaps twenty or thirty years before.

Those natives belonging to this class who are in a state of independence live by various industries. The greater number are carriers and coolies, or casual agricultural labourers in receipt of a small daily wage. The last-named are generally paid in grain, but when they receive money their wage varies from a penny to twopence a day, according to the district. However, they only work in proportion to their wage, and, whatever the task, a good European workman would, in most cases, do as much as four natives. But as the independent labourer is often out of work, and as the smallness of his wage or his improvidence does not allow of his putting by anything, his lot is no better, perhaps even worse, than that of his brother in slavery, and he is often in absolute want. Most of them have nothing of their own, or at the best only a wretched hut twelve or fifteen feet long by five or six broad, and from four to five feet high, which is full of insects and vermin and exhales an awful stench. Into this hovel they, with their wives and children, crowd higgledy-piggledy. Their belongings consist of a few earthen vessels, one or two sickles, and the rags in which they stand. Those who are a little less poverty-stricken have a brass lotah for drinking purposes, and another out of which they eat, a hoe, two or three sickles, a few silver bracelets, worth three or four rupees, belonging to the women, and two or three cows [1]. These people are agriculturists and

[1] Many Hindus own a few oxen and cattle, which are supposed to be the most valuable part of their property; in fact their degree of comfort

farm Government lands, on which they pay a tax varying from two to twenty-five shillings.

Such, in truth, is the state of misery in which half the population of India passes its life[1].

I place in the second class all those whose property ranges from £5 to £25 sterling. This class, I should say, includes about six-twentieths of the entire population and is composed chiefly of Sudras. Those included in it are mostly agriculturists on their own account. Their poverty does not allow of their hiring others to work under them. They cultivate Government land, and pay a yearly tax of from one to twenty pagodas, according to the value of the land. They sometimes require as many as three ploughs. Their entire property consists of a few cattle, a few small gold and silver trinkets, one or two copper vessels for drinking and a few more for eating purposes, and some iron farm implements. They live in thatched mud huts, rather more commodious and a little less filthy than those previously described. Weavers, barbers, washermen, and other workmen who cater for the wants of the public may also, for the most part, be included under this head.

The cultivators of this second class, although better off than those of the first, find it hard to make both ends meet even in the best seasons. They are obliged to sell at least half their crop beforehand at low prices, to enable them to pay their taxes, and the miserly usurers who profit by their poverty

is judged, more or less, by the number of these valuable animals which they possess. As soon as a Hindu has acquired a sufficient sum of money, he spends it as a rule on a pair of draught oxen and a cow. But the intrinsic value of these animals is small. The country oxen are, as a rule, stunted, weak, and incapable of enduring much fatigue. Four or five rupees is their outside value.—Dubois.

[1] In this connexion the reader will do well to refer to an excellent Blue Book entitled, *Progress of the Madras Presidency during the Forty Years from 1853 to 1892*, by Dewan Bahadur S. Srinivasa Raghavaiengar, C.I.E., a distinguished Government official, who clearly proves therein that a very great advance has been made by the country during the last four decades. Emigration also offers large fields of profitable employment to the Indian coolie nowadays—Ceylon, the Straits Settlements, Africa, the West Indies, Mauritius, &c., all competing for his services. The difficulty is to induce him to leave his miserable home. Those who do emigrate sometimes return with comparatively large savings, and become either petty shopkeepers or petty cultivators.—Ed.

leave them hardly sufficient for the wants of their family during six or eight months of the year; in fact, many of them have only food enough to last four months. Some never even gather the harvest from the field they have sown, for as soon as the corn has formed in the ear they are day by day driven by hunger to cut off some of the green ears, with which they make a sort of soup. Consequently, by harvest time there is nothing but stubble left to gather, and to save themselves the trouble of cutting it they merely turn three or four cows into the field to graze. If by dint of self-denial they allow their crops to grow up intact, it is not they who benefit by them, for as soon as the grain has been threshed the money-lenders step in and take their due, and afterwards come those who lent them grain when they had nothing to eat, and demand payment of the original quantity plus twenty-five per cent. interest; that is to say, a man borrowing twenty measures of corn has to repay twenty-five.

The grain takes about four months to ripen, and this period is called *the time of prosperity*, or *sukha kala*. It is about the only season in the year when the poor have enough of even the coarsest kinds of food, consisting of various sorts of small pulse, much the same as that which is used in Europe to fatten pigs and fowls, and in India to feed horses. Hence the well-known proverb, 'Do not approach a Pariah during the *sukha kala* season, nor go within range of an ox during the *Divuligai*[1].' This is because both become unmanageable then, from an unwonted state of prosperity.

In most provinces those who cultivate rice do not eat it, but sell it to pay their taxes. During the four months the *sukha kala* lasts, they live on the pulse and millet which they cultivate in their fields. During the rest of the year their only daily sustenance, in almost all cases, consists of a plateful of millet, seasoned with a little pounded salt and chillies. When after paying their taxes and debts they come to the end of their store of grain, supposing there has been any remnant, they are reduced to living from hand to mouth. Some of them borrow grain, which they promise to repay with interest after

[1] This feast will be specially mentioned later on. Its celebration takes place in November, when the country is clothed in verdure.—DUBOIS.

It is also called *Deepavali* and *Divali*.—ED.

the next harvest; others explore the woods and the banks of rivers and tanks in search of leaves, bamboo shoots, wild fruits, roots, and other substances which help them to exist, or rather, prevent them from dying of hunger.

Thus for about three months of the year almost three-quarters of the inhabitants of the Peninsula are on the verge of starvation. In the south these three months are July, August, and September; and the saying is that those who have grain to eat then are as happy as princes. The scarcity begins to be less felt by October, for then several of the smaller species of grain are ready for harvesting, and the rains have brought out in the fields quantities of edible herbs, which suffice to allay the pangs of hunger.

Nor are men alone exposed to want during a great part of the year; domestic animals have to bear the same privations. Most families own cattle, and each hamlet possesses considerable herds which can only graze within the narrow limits assigned to them. The small amount of straw which the crops produce does not last long, and the animals are then reduced to nibbling at the few plants scattered here and there in the barren fields. During the three or four months when the sun is especially hot, all vegetable life is scorched up, and the wretched animals can scarcely find enough fodder for their daily sustenance. They may then be seen searching for clayey soil, impregnated with salt, which they proceed to lick with avidity, and that, together with the water they drink, comprises almost all their food. This is why, throughout the hot weather, they are mere skeletons and can hardly stand. I have often, at this time of the year, been in villages where there were more than a hundred cows, and yet sometimes I could not procure so much as half a measure of milk for my breakfast[1].

Thirdly, I may reckon together those Hindus whose property varies in value from £25 to £50 sterling. They comprise about one-tenth of the population, and are principally agricultural. They farm lands large enough to require two, three, or even four ploughs, and their rental is from ten to thirty pagodas. This

[1] The fact is, the slaughter of cattle being forbidden by the Hindu religion, large herds of old and useless animals are maintained, which deprive the healthy and useful animals of their proper share of food.—ED.

class lives in fairly comfortable circumstances, and most of the people are able to lay in sufficient grain for the whole year after meeting their taxes. Many of them have even more than they require for their own consumption, and are able to sell or lend the surplus to those in their village who have run short of food. We have seen on what outrageous terms these loans are effected. The well-to-do amongst them employ as servants one or more of those who come under the first class. They have larger, more comfortable, and slightly cleaner thatched dwellings than the others, and they and their wives have at least a change of raiment, which is more than rare in the two preceding classes. But even their possessions are far from betokening wealth; they consist of a few gold and silver trinkets, some copper vessels, and a great many earthenware pots piled up in a corner of the house; and besides these they own ploughs and other farming implements, some cotton-spinning wheels, and various primitive tools of small value. Cattle are their chief source of wealth. As to their comfort, it is at best a relative term, for the contraction of debts is a custom common to all the Hindus we have hitherto spoken of. Most of them are debtors as well as creditors, but their assets seldom exceed their liabilities, and they are in no greater hurry to pay their creditors than their debtors are to pay them.

Besides tilling the land, many Hindus of this class keep goats and sheep, and their young, added to the one or two calves they are able to sell from time to time, bring in a small income. Two or three milch-kine and one or two buffaloes supply them with a certain quantity of butter for four or five months in the year, of which they make good use. The sale of pigs, fowls, eggs, &c., also contributes to their support, and even enables them to save for future needs, or to meet matrimonial expenses. Nevertheless, after a bad harvest numbers of these cultivators are reduced to the same state of want as those below them, and are obliged to have recourse to the same shifts.

In these times of distress the Hindus have only their wonderful constitutions to fall back upon. Accustomed from their earliest infancy to privations of every kind, they are able to keep body and soul together on the smallest pittance of food. A pound a day of millet flour, boiled in water and reduced to a thin gruel, is enough to prevent a family of five or six persons from dying of hunger. With no food besides this gruel and water the majority of the natives manage to keep hale and hearty for months together. Furthermore, they possess the no less valuable faculty of sleeping at will. An idle Hindu invariably goes to sleep, and so does the man who has nothing to eat. If the homely proverb 'he who sleeps dines' can be taken literally, the Hindus certainly find consolation in it in times of scarcity.

The fourth class comprises those whose property varies in value from £50 to £100 sterling, and I should say it forms three-fortieths of the population. These people live in comfort, being chiefly Brahmins or well-to-do Sudras. They all keep servants belonging to the lowest class to aid them in cultivation. Besides this, some of them are rich enough to embark on commercial speculations in connexion with grain or other commodities, while others lend small sums of money at high interest. This class provides the villages with their Sudra headmen, and these men are at the same time the largest holders of Government lands. They also exercise in their villages the functions of collectors of revenue, petty magistrates, and public arbitrators. As they are usually held responsible by Government for the due payment of all taxes levied on their villages, they are obliged to conciliate the villagers, to prevent their secretly migrating elsewhere, which would mean the non-cultivation of the land, and consequent inability on their part to furnish the revenue due to the State. These men have quite a patriarchal authority in their villages, but those who attempt to abuse their power are soon confronted with deserted homesteads, waste lands, and ruin staring them in the face.

A striking example of this happened when a new and detested system was established by the creation of Muttadars, or hereditary farmers of revenue, which caused the ruin of most of the districts where it was enforced. No sooner were these Muttadars raised to what they considered an exalted position than they began to give themselves great airs and tried to carry things with a high hand. Men who had formerly been in a low position, or in obscurity, now indulged in horses, palanquins, trumpeters, and peons; in fact they gave themselves up, without any justification, to such pomp and splendour as the native delights in. As the crops produced by the lands whose revenue they had farmed could not possibly defray the cost of this expensive mode of life, they had recourse to a system of black-mailing to increase their incomes. The consequence of this arbitrary and unprecedented behaviour was the flight of their victims, who left the lands uncultivated. The final result was the ruin of the Muttadars.

The Sudra headmen of the villages are usually sensible, polite, and well-educated men. Most of them know how to read and write. Although they have the failings, common to all natives, of cunning and deceit, they are far from being proud, intolerant, and haughty like the Brahmins. By nature they are gentle, shy, and insinuating, and they behave with marked respect and submission towards their superiors. Towards their equals they are polite and complaisant, and towards their inferiors affable and condescending. In fact, they know well how to adapt themselves to their surroundings.

The class occupying the fourth rung on the ladder which I have used to describe the various degrees of civilization in India is the one which, to my mind, is the most respectable and the most interesting. It is this class, chiefly, which influences public opinion amongst the Sudras, and maintains order throughout all ranks of society. One can tell at a glance that the natives of this class are all well-to-do and independent. As a rule, they are a more polite, better-educated, and better-mannered race, and they look happier and more contented than the members of the other three classes. Most of the latter have thin, drawn faces, a heavy carriage, coarse minds, low manners, and a melancholy and stupid appearance, all of which bespeak plainly enough the privations and sufferings of their lot. Just the reverse is noticeable amongst the natives of the fourth class.

In the fifth class I should include all those whose property varies in value from £100 to £200 sterling. It comprises about one-thirtieth of the whole population, and is composed chiefly of Brahmins or Vaisyas, and of the wealthiest among the Sudras. Agriculture, trading in grain or other commodities, money-lending on such usurious terms as twenty-five, thirty, and even fifty per cent.: such are the different forms of livelihood they thrive upon. Their cleanly appearance betokens comfort, and most of them live in tiled houses. They are also careful to conform to the rules of polite society. They perform daily ablutions, and their houses are kept ceremoniously clean by smearing the floors regularly with cow's dung. To appear more worthy in the eyes of the public the Sudras of this class usually abstain from all animal food, and, in imitation of the Brahmins, live entirely on milk and vegetables.

The natives belonging to this and the following classes constitute what may be called the gentlefolk of Hindu society, and some of the faults which characterize the Brahmins, such as pride and intolerance, are noticeable in them. Those amongst them who are agriculturists do not till their own lands, unless very urgent works are necessary; they employ servants from the lowest class to do it for them.

The sixth class may be said to comprise individuals whose tangible property varies in value from £200 to £500 sterling, and it represents, I should say, about one-fiftieth of the population. Brahmins form quite half of this class, and the remainder is made up of the best representatives of the other castes. Their wealth consists partly of *maniams*, or hereditary lands exempt from taxation, partly of gardens planted with arecas, cocoanut and other fruit trees, and partly also of trinkets, money, and cattle. Besides this, they speculate in the same way as the natives of the preceding class. Some of them occupy the position of assistant collectors of public revenue, magistrates' clerks, and other posts in the public service. They are proud of the comfort they enjoy, and their arrogance is unrivalled.

Properties valued at more than £500 sterling are rarely to be met with in the villages. Natives who possess more than this live in *agraharams*, or Brahmin villages, in towns, or in district boroughs, where they have more opportunity for commercial speculations, and for furthering their ambitious schemes to procure posts under Government.

The seventh class may be said to be composed of those whose property varies in value from £500 to £1,000 sterling. I should say only one-hundredth part of the population belongs to this class, and at least half of them are Brahmins. The rest are the wealthiest among the Vaisyas and Sudras.

The eighth class includes those whose properties range in

value from £1,000 to £2,000 sterling, and it comprises one two-hundredths of the population. It is almost entirely composed of Brahmins, with a small percentage of Vaisyas and Sudras, who live in towns and capitals where they devote themselves almost entirely to commerce or are employed under Government. Properties valued at five to ten thousand pagodas are extremely rare, even in the towns, and are confined to the richest merchants and to those who have held for a long time the highest offices under Government. Still, there are some which exceed even ten thousand pagodas, but these are so few that they can easily be counted in each province.

Speaking generally, the following proportion may be established between properties in India and properties in Great Britain:—

	India.		*Great Britain.*
Those of	£500 to £1,000	correspond to	£5,000 to £10,000
,,	£1,000 to £2,000	,,	£10,000 to £20,000
,,	£2,000 to £5,000	,,	£20,000 to £50,000
,,	£5,000 to £10,000	,,	£50,000 to £100,000
,,	£10,000 and above	,,	£100,000 and above.

But a difference, more essential even than that between the characters of the two nations, is observable in connexion with properties. In Europe they are preserved intact, and are, with but few exceptions, transmitted from father to son generation after generation. In India, on the other hand, there is nothing permanent about them, especially among the Sudras. The latter make their money either by their industry, talents, or cunning, and once it is made they do not know how to spend it wisely. Realizing that, do what they may, they will necessarily be looked down upon as parvenus, they soon acquire all the characteristic vices of the *nouveaux riches*. In time they become as proud and arrogant as any Brahmin, and their sole object seems to be to win a name for lordly extravagance. Money becomes no object to them, so long as it procures the gratification of their vanity. Immense fortunes seldom survive the second generation, owing to the manner in which the sons foolishly squander the wealth laboriously gained by their fathers. It is not uncommon to find sons who have inherited millions from their father end their days in beggary.

A native's house is besieged as soon as he is known to be a wealthy man, and this not only by his own relatives, but also by the indigent of his caste, and by a horde of parasites of every description, including poverty-stricken Brahmins, religious mendicants, ballad-mongers, and low flatterers, who feed his vanity by writing odes to his honour and glory, and by lavishing on him praise of the most fulsome nature. All these dependants stick to the wealthy native like leeches, fighting with each other as to who shall carry off the largest share of the prize, and never releasing their hold on their victim until they have stripped him of everything.

As to the general condition of the natives now, as compared with what it was thirty years ago, the question arises, has it improved or has it deteriorated? I have occasionally heard this important question discussed amongst thoughtful and well-informed Europeans, but they could rarely agree with one another on the subject. Some maintained that the masses are enjoying greater prosperity than ever they did before; others that they have never been in a more wretched state; while a few hold that things are practically where they were before the change of government took place. But it is evidently absurd to suppose that a well-meaning, just, and equitable Government, which has succeeded one that was arbitrary, oppressive, and tyrannical, has produced no amelioration in the condition of the people, whatever peculiarities of character and disposition the latter may possess, and however great an obstacle their institutions may be to the philanthropic endeavours of the new *régime* to make their lives more bearable, if not actually happier. This commonsense view of the case is borne out by my own observations. To me it seems undeniable that the condition of the people has improved in many important directions at least, and I have found that the most sensible natives themselves admit it. I do not mean to imply that the lowest classes in the land are better off, for in some provinces close observation will reveal an increase of misery: but where that is the case, I attribute it to causes beyond the power of any Government to prevent or put an end to; and further, I think that, given the same causes, the misery would have been more acute under the old *régime.*

Of these causes the chief one is the rapid increase of the population. Judging by my own personal knowledge of the poorer Christian populations in Mysore and in the districts of Baramahl and Coimbatore, I should say that they have increased by twenty-five per cent. in the last twenty-five years. During this period Southern India has been free from the wars and other decimating calamities which had been dealing havoc almost uninterruptedly for centuries before.

Some modern political economists have held that a progressive increase in the population is one of the most unequivocal signs of a country's prosperity and wealth. In Europe this argument may be logical enough, but I do not think that it can be applied to India; in fact, I am persuaded that as the population increases, so in proportion do want and misery. For this theory of the economists to hold good in all respects the resources and industries of the inhabitants ought to develop equally rapidly; but in a country where the inhabitants are notoriously apathetic and indolent, where customs and institutions are so many insurmountable barriers against a better order of things, and where it is more or less a sacred duty to let things remain as they are, I have every reason to feel convinced that a considerable increase in the population should be looked upon as a calamity rather than as a blessing.

It is in the nature of things that, in times of peace and tranquillity, when the protection of a just Government is afforded both to person and property, an increase in the population of India should take place at an alarming rate, since it is an indisputable fact that no women in the world are more fruitful than the women of India, and nowhere else is the propagation of the human race so much encouraged. In fact, a Hindu only marries to have children, and the more he has the richer and the happier he feels. All over India it is enough for a woman to know how to cook, pound rice, and give birth to children. These three things are expected of her, especially the last, but nothing more. It would even appear displeasing if she aspired to anything else. No Hindu would ever dream of complaining that his family was too large, however poor he might be, or however numerous his children. A barren woman is made to feel that there can be no worse fate, and barrenness in a wife is the most terrible curse that can possibly fall on a family.

Another serious cause of the poverty of modern India is the decrease in the demand for hand labour, resulting from the introduction of machinery and the spread of manufactures with improved methods in Europe. Indeed, Europe no longer depends on India for anything, having learnt to beat the Hindus on their own ground, even in their most characteristic industries and manufactures, for which from time immemorial we were dependent on them. In fact, the *rôles* have been reversed, and this revolution threatens to ruin India completely.

Just before returning to Europe I travelled through some of the manufacturing districts, and nothing could equal the state of desolation prevailing in them. All the work-rooms were closed, and hundreds of thousands of the inhabitants, composing the weaver caste, were dying of hunger; for through the prejudices of the country they could not adopt another profession without dishonouring themselves. I found countless widows and other women out of work, and consequently destitute, who used formerly to maintain their families by cotton-spinning. Wherever I went the same melancholy picture confronted me.

This collapse in the cotton industry has indirectly affected trade in all its branches by stopping the circulation of money, and the cultivators can no longer reckon on the manufacturers who, in the days of their prosperity, were wont to buy up their surplus grain, and even to lend them money when they were in arrears with their taxes. This has led the cultivators to the hard necessity of relinquishing their grain to, and thus becoming the prey of, remorseless usurers.

Such is the deplorable condition into which the poor Hindus have sunk; and it grows worse daily, thanks to the much-vaunted improvements in machinery which some nations glory in. Ah! if only the inventors of these industrial developments could hear the curses which this multitude of poor Hindus never tire of heaping upon them! If only, like me, they had seen the frightful misery which has overtaken whole provinces, owing entirely to them and their inventive genius, they would no doubt, unless they were entirely wanting in human pity, bitterly repent having carried their pernicious innovations so far, and having thereby enriched a handful of men at the expense of millions of poor people, to whom the very name of their competitors has become odious as the sole cause of their utter destitution!

And let no one venture to assert that the unfortunate Hindus can, if they choose, find a recompense in the fertility of their soil. The sight of vast plains lying fallow and waste may induce the superficial observer to accuse the natives of indolence or the Government of mismanagement, but he is not aware that the greater part, if not the whole, of these vast plains are sterile, bare, and incapable of cultivation through want of water during most of the year. In Southern India, at the present time, there are few lands in the neighbourhood of wells, tanks, and rivers which are not under cultivation, even on the summits of the highest hills; and if by any chance a few fields still lie unreclaimed, it is due to the hopeless sterility of the soil, which, even in the best seasons, would never repay the labourer for his trouble, or else because, to yield any profit at all, they would require more capital and more courage than most of the people possess.

It is, to my mind, a vain hope to suppose that we can really very much improve the condition of the Hindus, or raise their circumstances of life to the level prevailing in Europe. The efforts of a Government which is humane and generous, as well as just, may succeed up to a certain point in lessening some of their hardships; but as long as it is in the nature of the Hindus to cling to their civil and religious institutions, to their old customs and habits, they must remain what they have always been, for these are so many insurmountable obstacles in the path of progress and to the attainment of a new order of things better calculated to bring them happiness. They will continue to grovel in poverty as long as their physical and intellectual faculties continue in the same groove.

Therefore, to make a new race of the Hindus, one would have to begin by undermining the very foundations of their civilization, religion, and polity, and by turning them into atheists and barbarians. Having accomplished this terrible upheaval, we might then perhaps offer ourselves to them as law-givers and religious teachers. But even then our task would be only half accomplished. After dragging them out of the depths of barbarism, anarchy, and atheism into which we had plunged them, and after giving them new laws, a new polity, and a new religion, we should still have to give them new natures and different inclinations. Otherwise we should run the risk of seeing them soon relapse into their former state, which would be worse, if anything, than before.

Let our theoretical philanthropists, with their mistaken and superficial notions concerning the genius and character of the Hindus and the varied and multitudinous social links that bind them together, exclaim as much as they please in their unreflecting enthusiasm, that nothing has been done for the physical and spiritual improvement of the race. My reply is, 'Why do you expound your shallow theories in Europe? Come and study the question on the spot. Make personal inquiry into the manners and customs of the people; realize for yourselves whether all possible means have been tried with a view to gaining this desirable end. And then, but not till then, make up your minds on the question.'

Since our European ways, manners, and customs, so utterly different from theirs, do not allow of our winning their confidence, at least let us continue to earn their respect and admiration by humane examples of compassion, generosity, and well-doing. Let us leave them their cherished laws and prejudices, since no human effort will persuade them to give them up, even in their own interests, and let us not risk making the gentlest and most submissive people in the world furious and indomitable by thwarting them. Let us take care lest we bring about, by some hasty or imprudent course of action, catastrophes which would reduce the country to a state of anarchy, desolation, and ultimate ruin, for, in my humble opinion, the day when the Government attempts to interfere with any of the more important religious and civil usages of the Hindus will be the last of its existence as a political power.

CHAPTER VII

The Mythical Origin of the Brahmins.—Their Name and their Original Founders.—Conjectures on their True Origin.—Buddhists and Jains.

THE real origin of the Brahmins is wrapped in mystery, and one can only hazard conjectures on the subject, or put belief in myths. The story most generally accepted says that they were born from Brahma's head, which accounts for their name. One would suppose that as all castes were born from this same father they would be privileged to bear the same name; but as the Brahmins were the first-born, and issued from the noblest part of the common parent, they claimed special privileges from which all others were rigorously excluded. They have another theory to bear out the accepted belief that no one else is entitled to the illustrious name of Brahmin. They say that no one knows anything about Brahma's attributes and virtues beyond what they themselves choose to teach mankind, and that this knowledge in itself gives them the right to bear his name. Anyhow, their name is undoubtedly derived from Brahma's. The old writers call them 'Brahmanahas,' or 'Brahmahas,' which some of the Latin authors turned into 'Brachmanes.' The great difference between their caste and all others is that a Brahmin only becomes a Brahmin after the ceremony of the triple cord, which will be described hereafter. Until this essential ceremony has been performed he ranks only as a Sudra. By mere birth he is no different from the rest of his race; and it is for this reason that he is called *Dvija* (*Bis genitus*, or Twice-born). His first birth only gives him his manhood, whereas the second raises him to the exalted rank of Brahmin, and this by means of the ceremony of the triple cord. Indeed, two out of the seven famous Penitents, who are supposed to have been the original founders of the various sects of Brahmins of the present day, did not originally belong to this caste at all; but by reason of the length and austerity of their term of penance, they were rewarded by having their state of penitent Kshatriyas changed to that of penitent Brahmins by the investiture of the triple cord. These seven Penitents, or *Rishis*, or *Munis*, of Hindu history (I shall often refer to them in the pages of the present work) are the most celebrated personages recognized by the people of India. Their names are Kasyapa, Atri, Bharadwaja, Gautama, Viswamitra, Jamadagni, and Vasishta. The last-named and Viswamitra are those who were considered worthy of being admitted into the high caste of Brahmins. These far-famed Rishis must be of great antiquity, for they existed even before the Vedas, which allude to them in several places. They were the favoured of the gods, and more especially of Vishnu, who at the time of the Deluge made them embark on a vessel which he piloted, and thereby saved them from destruction. Even the gods were called to account for having offended these holy men, who did not hesitate to curse the deities who committed infamies.

The seven Penitents, after setting a virtuous example on earth, were finally translated to heaven, where they occupy a place amongst the most brilliant constellations. They are to be recognized in the seven stars that form the Great Bear, which, according to Hindu tradition, are neither more nor less than the seven famous Rishis themselves. They are, according to Hindu legend, the ancestors of the Brahmins in reality and not by metamorphosis, and it is believed that without ceasing to shine in the firmament they can, and occasionally do, revisit the earth to find out what is occurring there.

Are there any families in Europe which can, notwithstanding the mythical origins which heraldic science professes to discover, pride themselves on the possession of such ancestors? And seeing that in our own aristocracy a man with a noble lineage is not above assuming an air of extreme *hauteur* and exclusiveness, we ought not to be surprised at a Brahmin's vanity or at the contempt with which he treats any one belonging to an inferior caste. This idea of handing down to posterity the names of their great men by immortalizing them, and assigning to them a place among the constellations, appears to have been an almost universal practice amongst ancient races.

Astronomy has played an important part in the history of

almost all idolatrous nations; and of all false creeds it certainly is the least unreasonable, and has survived the longest. The religious and political lawgivers of these races were clever enough to perceive that the worship of the stars had taken a great hold upon mankind, and that the simplest and most effectual way of perpetuating the memory of their heroes would be to transform them into outward objects that were always before the eyes of the people. It was thus that the Greeks and Romans consecrated the memory of their divinities and demi-gods; and no doubt the Hindu lawgivers were prompted to immortalize their seven Rishis by means of the brightest stars in the sky because they realized that a Hindu imagination is only appealed to through the visible, and therefore that was the best way to perpetuate the veneration due to these illustrious beings. But whatever may have been the claims of Brahmins to a celestial origin, it is a well-authenticated fact that neither their caste nor any other existed in the countries to the north-east of Bengal four or five centuries ago. About that time the inhabitants of those parts, thinking that it might be to their advantage to adopt the customs of their neighbours, began to clamour for Brahmins. Accordingly, some were made to order out of the youths of the country, who, after conforming to the customs and rites of the Brahmins, were incorporated into their caste by the investiture of the triple cord. The descendants of these ready-made Brahmins have ever since been considered on an equality with the rest. The southern Brahmins do not care to be reminded of the fact; yet they are obliged to admit it, as well as that two of the Rishis were originally Kshatriyas. An objection which people often put to them is that if nothing but the investiture of the triple cord can make Brahmins of them, then their wives, who do not go through the ceremony, really belong to the Sudras; and this means that all Brahmins are obliged to marry out of their caste and by so doing violate their most sacred principles. The reply they invariably make to this, as to other embarrassing questions, is that they are but following time-honoured customs and institutions.

One is certainly justified in expressing doubt on the subject of the Brahmins' origin, but I, for one, should be sorry to oppose my conjectures to their absurd fables. Far be it from me to start any theories. My only desire is to collect materials which may help those who are trying to lift the veil which shrouds from view the cradle of the universe. It is practically admitted that India was inhabited very soon after the Deluge, which made a desert of the whole world. The fact that it was so close to the plains of Sennaar, where Noah's descendants remained stationary so long, as well as its good climate and the fertility of the country, soon led to its settlement. I will say nothing of the conquests of Hercules, Bacchus, and Osiris, as most learned men look upon them as fabulous beings, and those who admit an element of truth in the tales carefully denude them of all the extravagant details which tradition assigns to them[1]. The history of Sesostris, although equally full of impossibilities, has something more truthful and authenticated about it. The few ancient monuments which have been preserved make him out to have been the bravest, not to say the only, warrior that peaceful Egypt had to boast of for a period of more than sixteen centuries, and they also lead one to believe that he was the greatest of all conquerors, with an empire extending from the Danube to the Ganges. But his Indian conquests were as temporary and unstable as those of his illustrious rival Alexander the Great much later on in the world's history.

As to the settlements that the Arabs are supposed to have made in India, according to some authors, I think only superficial students will be found ready to believe in them. The fact that they are nomads, who have always lived a wandering life within reach of India, gives some appearance of reality to the theory. Some indeed believe that the caste system was borrowed from them, since it still exists in Arabia; but, as a matter of fact, it is a custom common to all the ancient races of the earth.

I do not trace the origin of the Brahmins either to Egypt or to Arabia, and I believe them to be the descendants not of Shem, as many argue, but of Japheth. According to my theory they reached India from the north, and I should place the first abode of their ancestors in the neighbourhood of the Caucasus.

Two famous mountains situated in Northern India, known

[1] See Plutarch's *Isis and Osiris*, chap. xxxv.

as Great Meru (Maha-Meru) and Mount Mandara (Mandara Parvata), are frequently mentioned in their old books and in their prayers, liturgies, and civil and religious ceremonies. These mountains, which I believe to be one and the same under slightly different names, are so far away that their precise whereabouts is unknown to the Brahmins of to-day[1]. And this is not surprising in a country where geographical science is confined to knowledge of the places situated between Benares and Cape Comorin. The Hindus themselves claim to be descended from the inhabitants of these distant northern regions, and they believe that it was there that the seven illustrious ancestors of the Brahmins were born, whose descendants have spread little by little throughout the length and breadth of the land. This opinion of the Hindus as to the origin of the Brahmins is confirmed by the Brahmins themselves, by the manner in which they treat one another. The northern Brahmin considers himself nobler and of higher rank than his southern brother, inasmuch as, having originated closer to the cradle of the race, there is less room for doubt concerning the fact of his direct descent from the Rishis. Surely these seven Hindu Penitents, or philosophers, must be the seven sons of Japheth, who, with their father at their head, led one-third of the human race towards the West, when men began to disperse after the Flood. They did not all reach Europe. Some of them on their way there turned northwards, under the guidance of Magog, second son of Japheth, and penetrated into Tartary as far as the Caucasian Range, in which vast tract of country they made several settlements.

I hazard no conjectures here which are not borne out by the Scriptures or by the commentaries of its wise interpreters, with whose aid I might easily pretend to much erudition; it would only be necessary to copy out *verbatim* what Bochart and the savant Dom Calmet have written on this subject.

Any one believing in the connexion between names and facts will be struck with the similarity existing between Magog's name and Gautama's, commonly called Gotama. *Ma*, or *maha*,

[1] There can be no doubt that these mountains, and others mentioned as lying around them, belong to the great ranges of Central Asia, from which flow the great rivers that water Siberia, China, Tartary, and Hindustan. —ED.

signifies great, so that Gotama must mean the Great Gog or Magog[1].

Furthermore, pagan history adds weight to these conjectures of mine on the origin and antiquity of the Brahmins. Learned men allude to more than one Prometheus. According to the Greeks the most celebrated of them all is a son of Japheth. He created man out of the soil, and instilled life into him with the fire stolen from heaven. This bold enterprise irritated Jupiter, who punished him by chaining him to one of the Caucasian Mountains, where a vulture devoured his liver as fast as it renewed itself. Hercules killed the vulture, and thereby put the son of Iapetus, or Japheth, out of his torture.

Why should not Brahma and Prometheus be one and the same person? The Hindu divinity is known also under the names of *Brema* and *Prumé* in some of their tongues. All these names bear resemblance to Promé-theos, or the god *Promé* of the Greeks. Brahma, like Prometheus, is looked upon as the creator of man, who is supposed to have issued from the various parts of Brahma's body. Brahma was also their great lawgiver, being the author of the Vedas, which he wrote with his own hand. He had more than once to appeal to Vishnu for help, just as Prometheus relied on Hercules to deliver him from his enemies.

This pretension on the part of the Hindu Prometheus to be regarded as the maker of man, and therefore a god, has been handed down in some part to his eldest sons, the Brahmins, who humbly call themselves the *Gods Brahma*, or *the Gods of the Earth.* At certain times the people prostrate themselves before them in adoration, and offer up sacrifices to them.

Again, several authors, both sacred and profane, have tried to prove that the Prometheus who wished to pass as the creator of man was no other than Magog himself. It is hardly likely that so near the time of the Deluge the real Creator should have been so completely forgotten that a son of Noah was able to pass himself off as a god; but it is quite possible that his descendants deified him, when the spirit of idolatry began to reign on earth. It was Magog who settled in Tartary with all those who elected to follow him, having decided to separate

[1] Much of this seems extremely fanciful. Max Müller and other modern authorities should be consulted.—ED.

from Japheth's other children. From thence he or his descendants spread over India and other countries, which had rightly fallen to Shem's lot. This verified Noah's prophecy that Japheth's domination would be far-reaching, and that his posterity would dwell in the tents of Shem (Gen. ix. 27). But admitting that Tartary or the neighbourhood of the Caucasus was the birthplace of the Brahmins, it is not easy to decide the precise date of their arrival in India. It appears certain, however, that they were already established there in a flourishing condition more than nine centuries before the Christian era, as that was about the time of Lycurgus's visit to them; and it is not likely that one of the wisest of the ancient philosophers would have undertaken such a long and tedious journey unless the reputation of the learned men he was going all that way to consult was an old and established fact.

The ancient Hindu works teach us that the Brahmins of those times differed essentially in matters of principle and conduct from their brethren of to-day. The original Brahmin is described as a penitent and a philosopher, living apart from the world and its temptations and entirely engrossed in the pursuit of knowledge, leading a life of introspection and practising a life of purity. At that period of their history the Brahmins were not such an intolerant and exclusive race that penitents belonging to other castes could not be initiated by the *Diksha* ceremony[1], or the investiture of the triple cord. There are many examples of this in their literature. The simple and blameless lives led by the primitive Brahmins, their contempt for wealth and honours, their disinterestedness, and, above all, their extreme sobriety, attracted the attention of the princes and the people. The greatest kings were not above rendering homage to them and treating them with more respect than they would have dared to demand for themselves from their own subjects. These philosophers, living secluded from the world with their wives and children, multiplied exceedingly.

Although the modern Brahmin has degenerated considerably, he still acts up to a great many of the customs and institutions of his ancestors. Like them, he prefers to live in retired places,

[1] *Diksha* means consecration; (undergoing) a religious observance for a particular purpose; solemn preparation.—ED.

far from the noisy haunts of man; and that is the reason why he settles in isolated villages, from which all natives belonging to other castes are excluded. There are numbers of these villages in the different provinces of the Indian Peninsula, and they are known by the name of *agraras* or *agraharas*[1]. Still more do the Brahmins resemble their ancestors in the way in which they fast frequently and wash themselves daily, and in all that concerns their sacrifices; but, perhaps, most of all in their scrupulous abstinence, not only from meat and all forms of living food, but even from anything with which superstition or prejudice may have connected any idea of pollution.

The religious system of the Brahmins and the absurd theogony which they have propagated in India seem to be the points on which they have gone most astray from the teachings of their predecessors. I cannot believe that the original lawgivers of the Hindus intended to introduce a creed so abominable and palpably absurd as that which at present exists amongst them. Their mythology originally consisted of allegories made intelligible by means of visible and material objects, so that religious knowledge should not die out of the minds of men who appeared to be little influenced by anything that failed to make a direct impression on their senses. But a coarse, ignorant, indolent, and superstitious race soon forgot the spirit of its creed, and ended by believing solely in the forms and emblems which had been employed; so that, before long, they quite lost sight of the spiritual beings of which these emblems were only symbolical. But I shall have occasion to refer to this question again, and so shall merely state here that the long tissue of fables on which the present religion of the Hindus is founded is not, to my mind, very ancient; at least, the greater part of it is not. Although some authors think differently, nothing will persuade me that their mythology is much older than that of the Greeks.

The primitive creed of the ancient Brahmins seems to have been utterly corrupted by their successors. The first form of idolatry into which all nations fall, after forgetting their traditions concerning the unity of God and the absolute and exclusive worship He expects from all His creatures, is the adoration of

[1] *Agrara* is merely a corruption of the word *agrahara*, which literally means 'land-grant to Brahmins.'—ED.

the stars and conspicuous elements, such as earth, fire, and water. Apparently the first Brahmins practised the purer cult, but afterwards their descendants reached the lowest stage of idolatry by adoring images and statues, which were intended only as the emblems of the objects of their worship. It was when this came to pass that India and the greater part of Asia probably split up into the two beliefs which still exist, one embracing the fables of the Trimurti and the other the religion of Buddha.

The creeds of these two sects probably sprang from the common source of Brahminism, and are only corruptions of it. Some modern authors believe that originally Buddhism reigned supreme throughout India, on either side of the Ganges, and, perhaps, even throughout the whole of Asia from Siberia to Cape Comorin and the Malacca Straits, and from the Caspian Sea to the Gulf of Kamtchatka. In any case, Buddhism appears to have been as ancient as the cult of the Trimurti. In both Tibets, in Tartary, and in China, we know that Buddhism still predominates. According to the historian La Loubère, it was introduced into China from Siam in bygone ages, and not, as is generally supposed, from Cape Comorin. In Burma, Siam, Laos, Cambodia, Cochin China, Japan, Corea, and in most of the kingdoms beyond the Ganges, Buddhism is the recognized religion. The Singalese inhabitants of Ceylon are also Buddhists, and the cult was introduced to them by missionaries and colonists, who a long time ago came over from Burma to settle there. In fact, this religion, with the immortal *Grand Lama*[1] of Tibet as its sovereign pontiff, is still beyond dispute of all existing creeds the one that embraces the greatest number of adherents.

If the last census published by order of the Chinese Government is correct, their vast empire numbers about 300,000,000 inhabitants, and if one estimates the populations of the remaining Asiatic dominions where Buddhism prevails at 150,000,000 only, which is a very moderate calculation, then about one-half of the human race has Buddhism for its religion.

[1] Like a second Phoenix the Grand Lama never dies. When he is about to divest himself of his earthly coil, the Bonzes choose a child of three or four into whose body they cause his soul to migrate, and this child is declared his successor. All faithful Buddhists believe implicitly in this miraculous rebirth.—DUBOIS.

Besides these two predominant creeds, there exists a third about which, until recently, little was known. I refer to the religion of the Jains. This sect stands quite aloof, hating equally both Brahminists and Buddhists, as well as their doctrines. They maintain that both the Trimurti and Buddhism are abominable modern inventions, and mere travesties of the true and primitive religion of India, which has remained pure and unimpaired amongst them only. They also hold that they alone are the real descendants of the old Brahmin Penitents, whose doctrines, customs, and usages they protect from universal degradation and from the monstrous innovations of Brahmins and Buddhists alike.

Brahminism underwent a hard struggle before it succeeded in establishing its dominion in India, owing to the opposition offered to it by the Jains; but after a long and bloody war the latter were crushed and had to submit to whatever conditions the Brahmins chose to dictate. The jealousy and animosity which these religious wars stirred up still prevail as strongly as ever, even after a lapse of two or three thousand years. Time, which generally softens the strongest hatreds and brings together the greatest enemies, has, in this case, failed to obliterate the traces of the ancient wrongs of which each sect mutually accuses the other. The daily prayer of a certain sect of Brahmins contains a curse levelled at the heads of the Jains, who retaliate by exclaiming, when they rise to pray, '*Brahma kshayam!*' 'May the Brahmin perish.' If either sect comes into power, it takes the opportunity of humiliating its adversaries and of punishing them without mercy whenever occasion offers.

But whatever may be the respective claims of Buddhists, Brahmins, and Jains with regard to the antiquity of their religions and the differences of doctrine that divide them, it appears highly probable that they all sprang originally from the same source. All three believe in the fundamental doctrine of metempsychosis. The images they worship bear a great likeness to one another, and most of these seem to be merely allegorical emblems invented to help them to remember their original divinities. All their religious establishments are alike composed of priests, monks, and hermits. All their sacrifices, and the ceremonies which accompany them, are nearly identical.

And, lastly, there is the resemblance of the languages used by the priests in their religious services; that is to say, the Sanskrit of the Brahmins and Jains on this side of the Ganges, and the Pali, which is evidently derived from the Sanskrit, of the Buddhists beyond the Ganges. All these help to prove incontestably the affinity existing between the three religions.

As very little is known about the Jain cult by Europeans, although it is to be found in all parts of the Peninsula, I shall give in an appendix a short account of their doctrines and of the principal controversial points between them and their sworn enemies, the Brahmins. I should like to be able to do the same with regard to the Buddhists, but I have not been able to procure authentic documents about their cult. Residents of Ceylon, where Buddhism predominates, ought to be able to supply the blank thus left in my work.

CHAPTER VIII

Different Kinds of Brahmins.— Outward Signs by which they are distinguishable.

Brahmins are subdivided into seven sects, each of which has for its patron one of the celebrated Penitents already mentioned. Besides this, they are split up into four classes, each class recognizing one of the four Vedas as its own. Thus there are Brahmins of the Yajur-Veda, of the Sama-Veda, of the Rig-Veda, and of the Atharva-Veda. Some are of opinion that this fourth class is extinct; but, as a matter of fact, it still exists, although there are but few representatives left, who are even more exoteric than the other castes, because they allow bloody sacrifices to be offered up, and do not even draw the line at human beings. Added to this, they teach a belief in witchcraft, and any one who is supposed to possess the art earns the odious reputation of being a sorcerer. When the *yagnam* sacrifice takes place, it is customary for Brahmins of all four Vedas to be present. The prayers which are offered up at the *sandhya* [1] are quoted from the four Vedas, each Brahmin repeating those of his own particular Veda, which accounts for the slight differences. Under ordinary circumstances the Brahmins do not appear to be very strict about these minor distinctions, or to prefer one Veda to another. Nor is this altogether surprising, considering that the author of the famous Indian poem *Bhagavata* declares that originally the four Vedas were one and the same. According to him it was the Penitent Vyasa who divided them into four books, and at the same time added introductions and commentaries to render them more intelligible. Indeed, owing to inherent faults, or to the mistakes

[1] Later on I shall explain in what the *yagnam* and *sandhya* consist.—Dubois. [*Yagnam* literally means worship (in prayer or praise); sacrificial rite, or sacrifice (to, of, by)].—Ed.

made by ignorant and inattentive copyists, the Vedas are so obscure that even men of learning find it hard to fathom them. I shall have more to say about the Vedas presently. To Vyasa is also attributed the authorship of the eighteen Puranas[1]. These are eighteen poems, all equally futile, containing most minute accounts of Hindu mythology with its gods and heroes. The fables contained in them are responsible for the gross forms of idolatry practised by the Hindus.

Brahmins are also distinguishable by their sect, by their names, by the marks which they trace on their foreheads and other parts of the body, and also by the high priest to whose jurisdiction they are subject. The four principal sects of Brahmins south of the Kistna are: the Vishnavites, the Smarthas, the Tatuvadis, and the Utrassas. The distinctive mark of the Vishnavite Brahmins is the *namam*[2]. Their Simhasana, that is, the place where their high priest resides and their chief school, is at Hobbala in the Northern Carnatic. The Smartha Brahmins trace three horizontal lines on the forehead with sandalwood paste. Their Simhasana is at Singeri in North-west Mysore. Besides these horizontal lines on the brow, the Tatuvadi Brahmins have ineffaceable marks branded on certain parts of their bodies with a red-hot iron. Their Simhasana is at Sravenur. The Utrassa Brahmins draw a perpendicular line from the top of the forehead to the base of the nose.

There are also Brahmins known as Cholias, who are more or less looked down upon by the rest. They appear to be conscious of their own inferiority, for they hold themselves aloof from other Brahmins. All menial work connected with the temples is performed by them, such as washing and decorating the idols, preparing lighted lamps, incense, flowers, fruits, rice, and other similar objects of which sacrifices are composed. In many temples even Sudras are allowed to exercise these functions, and men of this caste are always chosen for the office of sacrificer in pagodas where rams, pigs, cocks, and other living

[1] The names are Brahma-purana, Padma-purana, Vishnu-purana, Siva-purana, Bhagavata, Bavirhotara-purana, Naraddia, Markandeya-purana, Brahmakeyvréta-purana, Linga-purana, Varaha-purana, Skanda-purana, Vamana-purana, Vayu-purana, Kurma-purana, Matsia-purana, Garuda-purana, Brahmanda-purana.—DUBOIS.

[2] See following chapter.

victims are offered up. No Brahmin would ever consent to take part in a sacrifice where blood has to be shed. It is perhaps on account of the work they condescend to do that the Cholia Brahmins have fallen into such contempt. According to the general view of the Brahmins, to do any work which can be left to the lowest amongst the Sudras is to put themselves on their level, and consequently to degrade themselves. In any case the work of a *pujari* is not thought much of, and by some it is considered absolutely degrading. However, some Brahmins have to accept this task on account of their poverty, but they only do so with extreme reluctance. It is a common proverb amongst them that *for the sake of one's belly one must play many parts*[1].

There are other Brahmins who are derisively called *meat Brahmins* and *fish Brahmins.* For instance, there are the Konkani Brahmins, who come from Konkana, who eat fish and eggs without the slightest compunction, but will not touch meat. And there are many Brahmins from the northern provinces who make no secret of the fact that they eat meat. People tell me, though I can hardly believe it, that such conduct does not lessen the esteem in which they are held in their own country by those of their own caste who abstain from such forbidden food. Anyhow, when these degenerate Brahmins visit Southern India, and their ways become known, all the other Brahmins keep them at a distance and refuse to have any dealings with them. I wonder whether the first Hindu lawgivers forbade the eating of meat and of all other substances containing the germ of life. Do the southern Brahmins observe a rule strictly laid down, and do the northern Brahmins therefore break a law common to the whole caste? It is probable that the northern Brahmins, feeling the want of more substantial food, freed themselves from a custom which was not found irksome by their southern brethren in a hotter climate.

[1] In Sanskrit: *Udara nimittam bahu krita vesham*, which literally means, 'To get food many *rôles* are played.'—ED.

CHAPTER IX

The different Hindu Sects.—Vishnavites and Sivaites.—The Exterior Marks and Customs peculiar to each.—The *Pavadam*.—The Mutual Hátreds and Differences between the Sects.—Reason for the Dislike which ordinary Brahmins feel for Vishnavite Brahmins and those belonging to other Sects. —Subdivisions of the two Principal Sects.

THE Brahmins recognize six sects, which they designate by the generic name of *Shat Mata* (the Six Sects, or Six Schools); and each of these sects has a numerous following. They are composed entirely of Brahmins, and each has its own particular doctrine of metempsychosis. However, they do not carry these purely scholastic differences to the point of reciprocal hatred or persecution, and the subjects under dispute are pretty much the same as those which provoke polemical discussions amongst scholars and dialecticians in other countries. I shall refer again to this matter elsewhere, and will now speak about the two great sects of the Sudras. It will be seen that they are far from being as calm and tolerant over points of doctrine as the Brahmins. As a general rule, Hindus profess to pay equal honour to the two great divinities of the country, Vishnu and Siva, without showing preference for either, though there are a great many sectarians who devote themselves exclusively to the worship of one or the other.

The one sect is usually called *Vishnu-bhaktas*, which means votaries of Vishnu; the other is called *Siva-bhaktas*, or votaries of Siva. The latter sect is also called *Lingadaris*, and the former *Namadaris*. These names are derived from the distinguishing marks which the sectarians wear [1]. The followers

[1] It is impossible to conceive anything more obscene than the symbolical meaning of these two marks of Hindu worship, namely, the *lingam*

of Vishnu wear the emblem called *namam*, which they paint on their foreheads. It consists of three lines, one perpendicular and two oblique, meeting at the base, and thus forming a sign which resembles a trident. The centre line is red, the two outer lines are white and are painted on with a sort of clay called *namam*; hence the name given to this emblem. The distinctive sign of the Sivaites is, generally speaking, the *lingam*. They sometimes wear it fastened to the hair or round the arm, enclosed in a little silver tube; but more often they hang it round the neck, and the silver box containing it rests on the chest.

Instead of the *namam*, some devotees of Vishnu paint a single red perpendicular line in the middle of their foreheads in a distinctive manner; and instead of the *lingam* many of the votaries of Siva rub their foreheads and various parts of their bodies with the ashes of cow-dung by way of showing their devotion.

The special devotees of Vishnu are to be found in great numbers in the southern provinces of India, where they are known by various names, such as *Andi*, *Dasari*, *Ramanjogi*, *Bairagi*, and many others [1].

Besides the *namam*, which is an unmistakable sign of this sect, most of the devotees may also be distinguished by the extraordinary costume that they affect. The cloths which they wear are dyed a deep yellow, shading into red; many cover their shoulders with a coloured patchwork blanket, which they partly use as a cloak; their turbans, too, are composed of a motley of many hues. Some wear a tiger's skin on their shoulders instead of the blanket. Most of them have long necklaces of black seeds, the size of nuts. Besides this ridiculous costume, which vies with a jester's motley, the devotees of Vishnu always carry a bronze gong and a large shell called a *sangu* when they are travelling or begging. Both of these are used to make a noise and to announce their approach [2]. With one hand they strike the gong with

and the *namam*; obscene, that is, from the European point of view. From the Hindu point of view they symbolize spiritual and religious truths connected with the divine origin and generation of mankind.—ED.

[1] The Abbé is wrong in saying that an *Andi* is a devotee of Vishnu; he is always a devotee of Siva. Among *Bairagis*, too, there are devotees both of Vishnu and of Siva.—ED.

[2] Also devotees of Siva do this.—ED.

a little drumstick, producing a bell-like sound; with the other they hold the *sangu* to their mouth, and blow through it shrill and piercing sounds, which are very monotonous. These two objects are always to be seen in the hands of those followers of Vishnu who are beggars by profession, and who in some way resemble the mendicant friars of old. On their breasts they wear a sort of brass plate, on which is engraved a likeness of the monkey *Hanumanta*, or else one of the *Avatars*, or incarnations, of Vishnu. Some of them wear a number of little bells either hanging from their shoulders or on their legs, the tinkling of which warns people of their approach. To all the above paraphernalia some add an iron rod, at each end of which hangs a little brazier of the same metal containing the fire for burning the incense of which their sacrifices are composed.

To ask for alms is looked upon as a right, and even an inherent duty, in this sect. Indeed, as a rule in India any one who assumes the cloak of religion can practise begging as a profession.

It is principally when they are making pilgrimages to some sacred spot that these religious beggars make use of their privileges. Sometimes you meet as many as a thousand in one party. They scatter themselves through the various villages within reach of their route, and each inhabitant takes in a certain number of them, so that all travelling expenses are saved. This is the only occasion on which they travel in such large numbers, though they never wander about quite alone. Their manner when demanding alms is most insolent and audacious, and often threatening. If their demands are not instantly complied with, they will noisily repeat their request, striking their gongs and producing the most deafening sounds from their *sangus* all the time. If such methods are not successful, they have been known to force their way into a house, break all the household utensils, and damage everything they can find. These religious mendicants generally pursue their begging to an accompaniment of singing and dancing. Their songs are a species of hymns in honour of their deities; and they very often sing indecent ballads. The more freely the latter are interlarded with obscenities, the better are they calculated to attract offerings from the public.

The intemperance to which these religious beggars, and indeed all the devotees of Vishnu, are addicted, causes the better class of Hindus to regard them with great disfavour. In fact, such mendicants seem rather to pride themselves on their want of moderation in eating and drinking, from a feeling of opposition to the Lingayats, and in order to make the difference between themselves and their adversaries more apparent. The sobriety of the latter equals, if it does not surpass, that of the Brahmins. Vishnavites eat all kinds of meat ostentatiously, and drink arrack, toddy, or any other intoxicating liquors or drugs that they can procure, without scruple or shame. Excesses of all kinds are laid to their charge, and it is amongst them that that most abominable rite called *sakti-puja*[1] is practised, of which I shall speak at greater length further on.

The chief objects of veneration amongst the votaries of Vishnu are the monkey, the bird of prey called *garuda*, and the cobra. Should any one be so imprudent as to kill, or even injure, any one of these creatures in their presence, he might find the consequences very unpleasant, and he would only be able to expiate this supposed crime by offering the sacrifice called *pavadam*, which is only performed on very grave occasions, such as those just mentioned, or when it is a question of obtaining reparation for an injury done to some member of the sect, but felt to reflect on all the others. This expiatory sacrifice is a very serious affair; for it consists in immolating a human victim, and then resuscitating him!

When it is reported that any person has committed such an offence as renders the *pavadam* necessary, all the *Vishnu bhaktas* flock in crowds to the culprit's house, round which as many as 2,000 and more have been known to assemble, each of them provided with his gong and his *sangu*. They begin by arresting the person who is the cause of the assemblage; and then they erect at a short distance from the house a small tent, which is quickly surrounded by many rows of Vishnavites. The chiefs select some member of the sect who is willing to be sacrificed, and he is exhibited to the crowd who have come to witness the

[1] *Sakti-puja* is the worship of *Sakti*, which is the active power or female energy of a deity (especially of Siva). This *puja* is observed largely among the Sivaites, and to some extent among the Vishnavites.—ED.

spectacle. They make a slight incision in his arm from which blood flows, and the victim then appears to grow weaker and weaker, until he falls fainting to the ground, where he remains motionless. The victim, who of course is only feigning death, is then carried to the tent which has been erected for the purpose, and around which the *Vishnu-bhaktas* group themselves, taking great care that no one shall approach who does not belong to their sect. Others watch the house of him who has been the cause of the ceremony. All this time the whole multitude are shouting and screaming at the top of their voices, which, added to the banging of the gongs and the harsh and lugubrious notes of the *sangus*, produces a din and confusion of sounds as indescribable as they are unbearable. This fearful hubbub continues until the offending party has paid the fine imposed on him, which is generally far beyond his means. However, the inhabitants of the village and neighbourhood, exasperated beyond all measure, usually try and make some agreement with the leader of the fanatics, and, paying them part of the stipulated sum, entreat them to bring the ceremony of the *pavadam* to a speedy termination, and to return to their homes. When their demands have been satisfied the headmen retire to the tent, and restore the dead man to life. To bring about this miracle an incision is made in the thigh of somebody amongst them. The blood which flows from it is collected in a vessel, and then sprinkled over the body of the victim. By virtue of this simple ceremony the pretended dead man comes back to life, in the best possible health. He is then again shown to the spectators, who appear thoroughly convinced of the reality of this marvellous resurrection[1].

In order to consummate the expiation of the crime or offence which has given rise to the ceremony, they give a great feast with the money derived from the fine, and every one departs as soon as it is over.

I once saw the *pavadam* celebrated with much solemnity in a village near my house. The offence which provoked it arose from an inhabitant of the village having unintentionally felled

[1] The *pavadam* is probably called after Pavadammai, a minor deity of ferocious temper. The ceremony is not observed nowadays in any part of the country.—ED.

a tree called *kaka-mara*[1], which bears yellow flowers, and to which the followers of Vishnu offer sacrifices and worship.

The sect of Siva is just as numerous as that of Vishnu. It predominates altogether in several provinces. In the western parts of the Peninsula, along the whole length of the long chain of mountains which separates what are known in Europe as Malabar and Coromandel, the Lingayats, or followers of Siva, form at least half of the population for a distance extending for more than 100 miles from north to south.

Like the Brahmins they abstain from all animal food and from everything that has had even a germ of life, such as eggs, &c., some vegetable products being included under this head. Instead of burning their dead, as do most Hindus, they bury them. They do not recognize the laws relating to defilement which are generally accepted by other castes, such, for instance, as those occasioned by a woman's periodical ailments, and by the death and funeral of relations. They have also other rules and regulations which differ from those generally in force. Their indifference to all such prescriptive customs relating to defilement and cleanliness has given rise to a Hindu proverb which says: 'There is no river for a Lingayat'; meaning that the members of this sect do not recognize, at all events on many occasions, the virtues and merits of ablutions.

The point in the creed of the Sivaites which appears to me to be most remarkable is their entire rejection of that fundamental principle of the Hindu religion, *marujanma*, or metempsychosis. In consequence of their peculiar views on this point they have no *titis*, or anniversary festivals, to commemorate the dead and to afford them the benefit of the prayers, sacrifices, and intercessions of the living, of which festivals I shall speak more fully later on. A Lingayat is no sooner buried than he is forgotten.

Amongst the Sivaites there also exists a sect known by the name of *Vira-seiva*, which refuses to recognize any caste distinctions, maintaining that the *lingam* makes all men equal. If even a Pariah joins the sect he is considered in no way inferior to a Brahmin. Wherever the *lingam* is found, there, they say, is the throne of the deity, without distinction of class or rank.

[1] *Cassia fistula.*—ED.

The Pariah's humble hut containing this sacred emblem is far above the most magnificent palace where it is not.

The direct opposition of their religious tenets and rules of life to those of all other Hindus, and especially to those of Brahmins, renders the Lingayats peculiarly obnoxious in the eyes of the latter, who cannot endure the sight of the *Jangamas* and other headmen of the sect. Amongst the Lingayats, as amongst the Namadaris, are an immense number of religious beggars, called *Pandarams, Voderus, Jangamas,* &c. Many of these penitent Sivaites have no other means of subsistence except begging. They ply their trade systematically and in gangs. Some, however, live in retreat in the *mutts* or temples, which usually possess lands, the rents of which, added to the offerings of the faithful, are sufficient to maintain them.

The *gurus,* or priests of Siva, who are known in the western provinces by the name of *Jangamas,* are for the most part celibates. They have a custom which is peculiar to themselves, and curious enough to be worth remarking. When a *guru* travels about his district he lodges with some member of the sect, and the members contend amongst themselves for the honour of receiving him. When he has selected the house he wishes to stay in, the master and all the other male inmates are obliged, out of respect for him, to leave it, and go and stay elsewhere. The holy man remains there day and night with only the women of the house, whom he keeps to wait on him and cook for him, without creating any scandal or exciting the jealousy of the husbands. All the same, some scandal-mongers have remarked that the *Jangamas* always take care to choose a house where the women are young.

The costume worn by the devotees of Siva is very much the same as that of the Vishnavites. Both are equally peculiar in their attire. They always wear clothes of *kavi* colour, that is to say, dark yellow verging on red. This colour is obligatory, not only on the devotees of both Vishnu and Siva, but also on every one who is under a vow of penance. It is the colour affected by all *gurus* and Hindu priests of all denominations, by *fakirs,* also by all the priests and religious followers of Buddha who live on the other side of the Ganges.

Besides the *lingam,* there are several other outward signs by which the devotees of Siva may be recognized, such as the long necklaces of seeds called *rudrakshas*, which resemble a nutmeg in size, colour, and nearly in shape; also the cow-dung ashes with which they besmear their forehead, arms, and various other portions of the body. The two chief objects of their devotion are the *lingam* and the bull.

Though children usually follow the religion of their fathers, they do not become Vishnavites or Lingayats merely by right of birth. They are only admitted to the sect that their parents belong to when they have reached a certain age, and after being initiated by the *guru*. This ceremony of initiation is called *diksha*[1]. It consists in repeating certain appropriate *mantrams*, or prayers, over the neophyte, and whispering some secret instructions in his ear. But these are all spoken in a language which is seldom understood even by the person who presides at the ceremony.

By the *diksha* the new member acquires a perpetual right to all the privileges of the sect into which he has been admitted. Persons of all castes can become Vishnavites, and after their admission can wear the *namam* or distinctive mark on their foreheads. Neither Pariahs nor even *Chucklers* are excluded; and it has been noticed that the lower castes are particularly numerous in this sect.

I do not think there would be any greater difficulty in becoming a member of the Siva sect, but as on initiation the members undertake to entirely give up eating meat and drinking any intoxicating liquor, the lower castes, who do both unhesitatingly, find the conditions too hard. Consequently, only high-class Sudras and scarcely any Pariahs belong to this sect. It is no uncommon thing for people to change from one sect to the other, according as it suits their interest, or even out of spite or caprice. Either sect will take a convert from the other without asking any questions or making any difficulty. Sometimes one comes across missionaries scouring the country with written professions of faith in their hands, and using various means for gaining proselytes to their respective sects. In some parts a remarkable peculiarity is to be observed in reference to these two sects. Sometimes the husband is a Vishnavite and bears the *namam* on his forehead, while the wife is a follower of

[1] This word means 'initiation.' Native Christians often call Baptism *gniana diksha*, which means 'spiritual initiation.'—DUBOIS.

Siva and wears the *lingam.* The former eats meat, but the latter may not touch it. This divergence of religious opinion, however, in no way destroys the peace of the household. Each observes the practices of his or her own particular creed, and worships his or her god in the way that seems best, without any interference from the other. At the same time, each sect tries its best to magnify its own particular deity and to belittle that of its rivals. The devotees of Vishnu declare that the preservation of the universe is entirely due to him, and that to him Siva owes both his birth and existence, since Vishnu saved him several times under such circumstances that without his aid Siva must infallibly have perished. Therefore Vishnu is immeasurably above Siva in every respect, and to him alone should homage be offered.

The devotees of Siva, on their side, maintain obstinately that Vishnu is of no account, and has never committed any but the basest actions, which only disgrace him and make him hateful in the eyes of men. As proofs of their assertions they point to several facts in the life of this deity, which their adversaries cannot deny, and which certainly do not redound to his credit. Siva, according to them, is sovereign lord of all, and therefore the proper object of all worship.

According to the Vishnavites it is the height of all abomination to wear the *lingam.* According to their antagonists, whoever is decorated with the *namam* will be tormented in hell by a sort of fork similar in form to this emblem. These mutual recriminations often end in violent altercations and riots. The numerous bands of religious mendicants of both sects are specially apt to provoke strife. One may sometimes see these fanatics collected together in crowds to support their opinion of the superexcellence of their respective doctrines. They will overwhelm each other with torrents of abuse and obscene insults, and pour forth blasphemies and imprecations, on one side against Siva, on the other against Vishnu ; and finally they will come to blows. Fortunately blood is seldom shed on these battle-fields. They content themselves with dealing each other buffets with their fists, knocking off each other's turbans, and much tearing of garments. Having thus given vent to their feelings, the combatants separate by mutual consent.

That these religious dissensions do not set the whole country ablaze, or occasion those crimes of all kinds which were for centuries the result of religious fanaticism in Europe and elsewhere, is due no doubt to the naturally mild and timid character of the Hindus, and especially to the fact that the greater number compound with their consciences and pay equal honour to Vishnu and Siva. Being thus free from any bias towards either party, the latter serve as arbitrators in these religious combats, and often check incipient quarrels.

There is no doubt, however, that these controversies were wont to excite general ferment in several provinces at no very remote date. The agitation, excited in the first instance by fanatical devotees, was further fomented by the Rajahs and other princes, who became Vishnavites or Sivaites according as it suited their political interests.

Those who are acquainted with the character and disposition of the *Bairagis* and *Goshais* of the north, and of the *Dasari, Andis, Jangamas,* and *Pandarams* in the south, are fully persuaded that it would still be quite easy for two ambitious and hostile princes to arm these fanatics and persuade them to come to blows if they raised the standard of *Basava* (the bull) on one side, and of *Hanumanta* (the monkey) on the other.

In these religious squabbles, which still take place occasionally, the Vishnavites appear to be the more fanatical and fervent, and they are almost always the aggressors. The reason is, that this sect draws most of its members from the very dregs of society, and so takes a delight in creating troubles or disturbances. The followers of Siva, on the other hand, who belong to the upper classes of the Sudras, are much more peaceable and tolerant.

The majority of the Hindus, and particularly the Brahmins, take no part whatever in these religious squabbles. The latter act on the principle of paying equal honour to the two chief deities of the country, and though, as a rule, they appear to have a preference for Vishnu, they never let a day pass without offering in their own houses a sacrifice to the *lingam*, which is Siva's emblem.

It is very difficult to determine the origin of these two sects. Some authors have thought that they are quite a modern institution. Yet they are alluded to in several of the most ancient Puranas. One of the *Avatars*, or incarnations, of Vishnu, called

Narasimha that is to say, *half-man half-lion,* is the form under which this deity disguised himself when he came to deliver the earth from the giant Hiranniakashiapa, who was ravaging it. We learn in the *Bhâgavata* that this cruel monster had a good son called Prahlada, who belonged to the Vishnavite sect, and who made the greatest efforts to induce his father to embrace his special form of religion, but without success. However, the ill-feeling between the two sects seems not to have been so marked at the beginning.

Brahmins in general look upon the Vishnavite Brahmins (see Chapter VIII), who profess a special devotion for Vishnu if they do not worship him exclusively, as detestable schismatics. The preference that the latter show for a sect composed almost entirely of Sudras and the lowest of the people, and their practice of appearing in public with their foreheads decorated with the *namam,* just like common Pariahs or *Chucklers,* are all offences which degrade them in the eyes of their noble *confrères.*

No doubt the same contempt would be felt for Brahmins who wore the *lingam,* but I have never seen one thus decorated, and I doubt whether one could be found anywhere in the south, from the banks of the Kistna to Cape Comorin. I have been told, however, that there are some districts in the north where persons of this caste are to be found who devote themselves exclusively to the worship of Siva, and who always wear the emblem of this deity.

The sect of Vishnavite Brahmins appears to have originated in Dravida or Aravam (the Tamil country). From there they spread over the provinces up to the Kistna, where they have retained, to the present day, their own peculiar customs and language, as well as their own cult. The Brahmins who inhabit the country north of this river have never permitted these stubborn schismatics to settle amongst them.

The feeling of aversion which orthodox Brahmins entertain for the Vishnavite Brahmins is shared by Hindus of all castes. A stigma of reproach appears to cling to them. It cannot be the case, however, that the disfavour with which they are regarded is entirely due to their exclusive worship of Vishnu. I think it must be largely imputed to their excessive pride and arrogance, their extreme severity, and their supercilious manners; for though all Brahmins share these characteristics, it is generally acknowledged that the Vishnavites display them in an intensified form.

Be the reason what it may, there is no denying that the Vishnavites form a class by themselves in society. The antipathy which these two orders of Brahmins feel for each other is noticeable on all occasions. The members of one sect never invite members of the other to eat with them, or to participate in their civil or religious feasts; and when one of them is raised to a position of authority, it is on persons of his own sect that his patronage is bestowed.

The two sects of Vishnavites and Sivaites are each subdivided into several others, which are known under the general term of *Mattas* or *Mattancharas.* Amongst the Vishnavites, for instance, there are the *Vaishnavas,* the *Tatuvadis,* the *Ramojus,* the *Satanis,* &c., sub-sects which again are divided into a great many others. For instance, amongst the *Vaishnavas* there are the *Vaishnava-triamalas,* the *Kandalas,* the *Nallaris,* &c.

The *Jogis,* the *Jangamas,* the *Voderus,* the *Viraktas,* the *Bolu-Jangamas,* the *Vira-seivas,* &c., belong to the Sivaites.

Each of these sub-sects has its own peculiar tenets, mysteries, *mantrams,* sacrifices; in fact, some points of variation in rites as in doctrines. The heads of these sub-sects dislike and avoid each other. They often quarrel over the various points of doctrine which cause such divisions. But these are forgotten, or, at any rate, allowed to remain in abeyance, should it be necessary to make common cause in defending the interests of the sect as a whole, during the disputes which occasionally arise between the Vishnavites and Sivaites.

CHAPTER X

The *Gurus*, or Hindu Priests.—The Portrait of a true *Guru*.—Their Temporal and Spiritual Power.—The Fear and Respect that they inspire.—Ecclesiastical Hierarchy composed of the Superior and Inferior Priests.—The Honours paid to them.—Priestesses.

I SHALL begin this chapter by giving an accurate description of a true *guru* belonging to the sect of Siva. This picture is taken from the *Vedanta Sara*, to which it serves as an introduction. At the same time I must warn my readers that it would be difficult to find any points of resemblance between this picture and the *gurus* of the present day, who are very far from attaining to this pitch of perfection. The sketch will, however, prove that even the very highest moral virtues were not unknown to the Hindus, though now they regard them only as subjects for speculative discussion.

'A true *guru* is a man who is in the habit of practising all the virtues; who with the sword of wisdom has lopped off all the branches and torn out all the roots of sin, and who has dispersed, with the light of reason, the thick shadows in which sin is shrouded; who, though seated on a mountain of sins, yet confronts their attacks with a heart as hard as a diamond; who behaves with dignity and independence; who has the feelings of a father for all his disciples; who makes no difference in his conduct between his friends and his enemies, but shows equal kindness to both; who looks on gold and precious stones with the same indifference as on pieces of iron or potsherd, and values the one as highly as the other; whose chief care is to enlighten the ignorance in which the rest of mankind is plunged. He is a man who performs all the acts of worship of which Siva is the object, omitting none; who knows no other god than Siva, and reads no other history than his; who shines like the sun in the midst of the dark clouds of ignorance which surround him; who meditates unceasingly on the merits of the *lingam*, and proclaims everywhere the praises of Siva; who rejects, even in thought, every sinful action, and puts in practice all the virtues that he preaches; who, knowing all the paths which lead to sin, knows also the means of avoiding them; who observes with scrupulous exactitude all the rules of propriety which do honour to Siva. He should be deeply learned, and know the *Vedanta* perfectly. He is a man who has made pilgrimages to all the sacred places, and has seen with his own eyes Benares, Kedaram, Conjeeveram, Rámésvaram, Srírangam, Sringeri, Gokarnam, Kálahasti, and other spots which are consecrated to Siva. He must have performed his ablutions in all the sacred rivers, such as the Ganges, the Jumna, the Sarasvati, the Indus, the Gódávari, the Kistna, the Nerbudda, the Cauvery, &c., and have drunk of each of these sanctifying waters. He must have bathed in all the sacred springs and tanks, such as the Surya-pushkarani, the Chandra-pushkarani, the Indra-pushkarani, and others, wherever they may be situated. He must have visited all the sacred deserts and woods, such as Neimisha-aranya, Badari-aranya, Dandaka-aranya, Goch-aranya, &c., and have left his footprints in them. He must be acquainted with all the observances for penance or *asramas*, such as are enjoined by the most famous devotees, and which are known by the names of Narayana-asrama, Vamana-asrama, Gautama-asrama, Vasishta-asrama. He must be one who has practised these religious exercises, and who has derived benefit from them. He must be perfectly acquainted with the four Vedas, the *Tarka-sastram* (or logic), the *Bhoota-sastram*, the *Mimamsa-sastram*, &c. He must be well versed in the knowledge of the *Vedanga*, of the *Jyotisha-sastram* (astrology), of *Vaidya-sastram* (medicine), of *Dharma-sastram*, of *Kaviana-takam* (poetry), &c., and he must know by heart the eighteen Puranas and the sixty-four Kalais[1]. This is the character of a true *guru*; these are the qualities which he ought to possess, that he may be in a position to show others the path of virtue, and help them out of the slough of vice.'

This is what the Hindu *gurus* ought to be, but are not. What follows is a description of them as they really are.

The word *guru*, properly speaking, means 'master' or

[1] These include all kinds of worldly wisdom.—DUBOIS.

'guide,' and this is why parents are sometimes called the *maha-gurus* or grand masters of their families, and kings are called the *gurus* of their kingdoms, and masters the *gurus* of their servants.

The word is also used to designate persons of distinguished rank who are raised to a high position and invested with a character for sanctity, which confers both spiritual and temporal power upon them. The latter, which is exercised over the whole caste, consists in regulating its affairs, in keeping a strict watch to see that all its customs, both those for use in private as well as in public, are accurately observed, in punishing those who disregard them and expelling from caste those who have deserved this indignity, in reinstating the penitent, and several other no less important prerogatives. Besides this temporal authority, which no one disputes, they also exercise very extensive spiritual power. The *sashtanga* or prostration of the six members [1] when made before them and followed by their *asirvadam*, or blessing, will obtain the remission of all sins. The very sight even of *gurus* will produce the same effect. Any *prasadam* or gift from them, though usually some perfectly valueless object, such as a pinch of the ashes of cow-dung with which they besmear their foreheads, the fruits or flowers that have been offered to idols, the remains of their food, the water with which they have rinsed out their mouths or washed their face or feet, and which is highly prized and very often drunk by those who receive it; in short, any gift whatever from their sacred hands has the merit of cleansing both soul and body from all impurities.

On the other hand, while the beneficial effects of their blessings or their trivial presents excite so large an amount of respect and admiration from the dull-witted public, their maledictions, which are no less powerful, are as greatly feared. The Hindus are convinced that their curses never fail to produce effect, whether justly or unjustly incurred. Their books are full of fables which seem to have been invented expressly to exemplify and strengthen this idea. The attendants of the *guru*, who are interested in making the part which their master plays appear credible, are always recounting ridiculous stories

[1] It has already been pointed out in a note to a former chapter that *sashtanga* does not mean the prostration of six members but of eight members.—ED.

on this subject, of which they declare they have been eye-witnesses; and in order that the imposture may be the less easily discovered, they always place the scene in some distant country. Sometimes they relate that the person against whom the curse was fulminated died suddenly whilst the *guru* was still speaking; that another was seized with palsy in all his limbs, and that the affliction will remain until the anathema has been removed; or that the *guru's* malediction caused some woman to be prematurely confined; or that a labourer saw all his cattle die suddenly at the moment when the malediction was hurled at his head; or that one man was turned to stone and another became a pig; in fact, they will relate a thousand similar absurdities quite seriously[1].

If the foolish credulity of the Hindu will carry him to these lengths, can any one be surprised if his feelings of respect and fear for his *guru* are equally extravagant? He will take the greatest care to do nothing that might displease him. Hindus have been reduced to such terrible straits as to sell their wives or their children in order to procure the money to pay the imposts or procure the presents that their *gurus* remorselessly claimed from them, rather than run the risk of exposing themselves to their much-dreaded maledictions[2].

Each caste and each sect has its own particular *gurus*: but the latter are not all invested with equal authority; a sort of hierarchy exists amongst them. Besides the vast numbers of subordinate priests who are to be met with everywhere, each sect has a limited number of high priests who exercise authority over the inferior *gurus*, deputing to them their powers of spiritual jurisdiction. These high priests have also the right of degrading their inferiors from their position and of putting others in their

[1] The ideas of the Hindus on the subject of the blessings and curses of their *gurus* are analogous, at any rate in point of extravagance, to those which, according to Holy Scripture, were current in the time of the ancient Patriarchs. Noah's curse on his son Ham and his blessing on the other two, Shem and Japheth, bore fruit (Genesis ix). The value that Esau and Jacob set on their father Isaac's blessing is well known (Genesis xxvii); also the bitter regret of Esau when he found that he had been supplanted by Jacob.—DUBOIS.

[2] Times are changed since the days of the Abbé, and the *gurus* in most cases are the mere hangers-on of rich disciples. They may be able to exercise some influence over the illiterate and poor, but with the majority of the educated and well-to-do their influence is not very great.—ED.

places. The residences of Hindu high priests are generally known by the name of *simhasana*[1]. These *simhasanas* are to be found in various provinces of India. Each caste and each sect acknowledges one that specially belongs to it. For instance, the Brahmins who belong to the *Smartha* sect have a different *guru* from the *Tatuvadi* sect, and these again recognize a different one from the Vishnavite Brahmins.

The different branches of the sects of Vishnu and Siva have also their own particular *gurus* and high priests. The *Sri-Vaishnavas,* for instance, acknowledge four *simhasanas* and seventy-two *pitahs* or supplementary establishments, where the inferior *gurus* reside, besides a multitude of subordinate ministers who are also called *gurus.*

The high priests, as well as the inferior priests belonging to the sect of Siva, are drawn entirely from the Sudra caste; but the greater number of the head *gurus* belonging to the Vishnavites are Vishnavite Brahmins, and they appoint the inferior clergy of that sect. The most famous *simhasana* of the Vishnavites is in the sacred town of Tirupati in the Carnatic. There a kind of arch-pontiff resides, whose jurisdiction extends over almost the whole of the Peninsula.

Brahmins are also, as a rule, the *gurus* of the various sects of Hindus who are more tolerant than those just mentioned, that is to say, those who worship both Vishnu and Siva.

The high priest or the *guru* belonging to one sect has no authority over any other. Neither his *prasadam*[2], nor his curse, nor his blessing would carry any weight with them; and it is very rarely that you hear of priests overstepping the limits of their own jurisdiction.

People of very high rank, such as kings or princes, have a *guru* exclusively attached to their households who accompanies them everywhere. They prostrate themselves daily at the *guru's* feet and receive from him the *prasadam* or gift, and

[1] This word may be translated 'throne.' It is derived from the two words *simha,* which means *lion,* and *asana,* which means a *seat,* because a high priest's throne ought to be covered with a lion's skin. Custom, however, has changed this for that of a tiger.—DUBOIS. *Simhasana* is more correctly derived from the figure of a lion on the back of the seat.—ED.

[2] *Prasada* means literally serenity, cheerfulness, kindness, favour, &c., and it has come to mean 'food or anything offered to an idol.'—ED.

the *asirvadam*, or blessing. When they travel the *guru* is always is close attendance; but if they are going to take part in a war or any other dangerous expedition, the holy man takes care to remain prudently behind. He usually contents himself under these circumstances with bestowing his blessing and giving some small present or amulet, which he has consecrated, and which, if carefully preserved, possesses the infallible virtue of averting all misfortunes to which they might be exposed when far from their spiritual guide.

Princes, from motives of ostentation, affect to keep their *gurus* in great splendour, with the result that the latter's extravagant pomp often exceeds their own. Besides giving them many very valuable presents, they also endow them with land yielding large revenues. Hindu high priests never appear in public except in magnificent state. They like best to show off all their splendour when they are making a tour in their districts. They either ride on a richly caparisoned elephant or in a superb palanquin. Many have an escort of cavalry, and are surrounded by guards both mounted and on foot, armed with pikes and other weapons. Bands of musicians playing all sorts of instruments precede them, and numberless flags of all colours, on which are painted pictures of their gods, flutter in the midst of the cavalcade. The procession is headed by heralds, some of whom sing verses in the high priest's honour, while the rest go on ahead and warn the passers-by to clear the way and to pay the homage and respect that are his due[1]. All along the route incense and other perfumes are burnt in the high priest's honour; new cloths are perpetually spread for him to pass over; triumphal arches called *toranams*, made of branches of trees, are erected at short intervals; bevies of professional prostitutes and dancing-girls

[1] The custom amongst persons of high rank, such as *gurus*, kings, princes, and governors of provinces, of being preceded on their march by heralds, singing their praises, is very general in India. These heralds give a long account of their master's noble origin, of his exalted rank, of his boundless power, his virtues, and his many excellent qualities; and they admonish the public to pay the respect and homage which are due to so great a personage. This custom, though of Hindu origin, has been adopted by the Mahomedans. It appears, as may be seen from the writings of both sacred and secular authors, that the practice of being preceded by heralds dates from very ancient times—see Genesis xli. 43; Esther vi. 8; and there are several other passages in the Bible where such heralds are spoken of.—DUBOIS.

form part of the procession, and relieve each other at intervals, so that the obscene songs and lascivious dances may continue uninterruptedly[1]. This magnificent spectacle attracts great crowds of people, who prostrate themselves before the *guru*, and, after having offered him their respectful homage, join the rest of the crowd and make the air ring with their joyful shouts.

The *gurus* of inferior rank make a show in proportion to their means. Those who belong to the sect of Vishnu known by the name of *Vaishnavas* generally travel on some sorry steed. Some are even reduced to walking on foot. The *Pandarams* and *Jangamas*, priests of Siva, go on horseback or in a palanquin, but their favourite mode of progression is riding on an ox.

Gurus, as a rule, rank first in society. They often receive tokens of respect, or rather of adoration, that are not offered to the gods themselves. And this is not surprising when one remembers that every Hindu is fully persuaded that, under certain circumstances, the *gurus* have authority even over the celestial powers.

From time to time *gurus* make tours of inspection in those districts where their followers are most numerous. They sometimes go as much as a hundred miles from their habitual residence. The chief, if not the only, object of the expedition is to collect money. Besides the fines which they impose upon those who have committed some crime, or been guilty of breaking some rule of their caste or sect, they are merciless in extorting tribute money from their followers, which often greatly exceeds their means. They call this method of obtaining money *dakshina*[2] and *pada-kanikai*[3], and no one, however poor he may be, is exempt from paying it. There is no insult or indignity that *gurus* will not inflict upon any one who either cannot or will not submit to this tax. Deaf to all entreaties, they cause the defaulter to appear before them in an ignominious and

[1] This picture is greatly exaggerated. Nowhere do 'professional prostitutes and dancing-girls' form part of processions in honour of *gurus*. On the contrary, prostitutes are not allowed to approach these holy men. —ED.

[2] *Dakshina* literally means the sacrificial fee. It has now come to mean gift. The gift to the priest is enforced more or less among the Madhvas; but among the Sivaites and Vishnavites the priests are more lenient.—ED.

[3] This word means literally 'offering at the feet.' See Chapter III.—DUBOIS.

humiliating attitude, publicly overwhelm him with insults and reproaches, and order that mud or cow-dung shall be thrown in his face. If these means do not succeed, they force him to give up one of his children, who is obliged to work without wages until the tribute money is paid. Indeed, they have been known to take away a man's wife as compensation. Finally, as a last and infallible resource, they threaten him with their malediction; and such is the Hindu's credulity, and so great his dread of the evils which he foresees will fall upon him if the curse be spoken, that, if it is not absolutely impossible, he submits and pays the required sum [1].

The *gurus* also increase their revenue by means of taxes, called *guru-dakshina*, which are levied on the occasion of a birth, at the ceremony of the *diksha* (initiation), at a marriage, or at a death.

If these pastoral visits were of very frequent occurrence it is evident that the resources of the poor flock would soon be exhausted. Fortunately, those of the chief *gurus*, which are the most expensive, take place but seldom. Some make a tour of their districts once in five years, others once in ten only, and others, again, only once in a lifetime.

Some *gurus* are married, but most are celibates. The latter, however, do not appear to adhere very strictly to their vow of chastity. Their conduct on this head is the more open to misconstruction in that they can have one or two women in their houses as cooks. According to the customs and ideas of the country, for a man to keep a female servant and to have her as his mistress are one and the same thing. No Hindu can be persuaded of the possibility of free, and at the same time innocent, intercourse between a man and a woman.

But in spite of this, the common herd, who fancy that *gurus* are not made of the same clay as other mortals and are consequently impeccable, are in no wise shocked at these illicit connexions. Sensible people take no notice, but shut their eyes and say that allowances must be made for human weakness.

The Brahmins pretend that they are the *gurus* for all castes, and that they alone have a right to the rank and honours

[1] Nowadays *gurus* exercise less extensive powers over their disciples. —ED.

appertaining to that profession; but, as I have already mentioned, a number of common Sudras also contrive to raise themselves to that dignified position. The Brahmins, of course, look upon them as intruders, but this does not in the least prevent their enjoying all the honours and advantages which belong to their rank in the caste and sect by which they are acknowledged.

Except when they are making their tours of inspection, most *gurus* live in seclusion, shut up in isolated hermitages called *mutts*. They are rarely seen in public. Some of them live in the vicinity of the large pagodas. But the high priests, whose large households and daily hospitalities entail considerable expenditure, generally live in the large *agraharas* or towns inhabited principally by Brahmins, and for this reason called *punyasthalas*, or abodes of virtue. There they give audience to the numerous members of their flocks who come to perform worship, to receive their *asirvadam* (benediction) and their *prasadam* (gift), to offer presents, to bring complaints about the infraction of rules and customs, &c. Hindus, on presenting themselves before their *guru*, first perform the *sashtanga*, and then touch the ground with each side of the forehead. The holy man replies to this mark of respect by gravely pronouncing the word '*Asirvadam!*' On hearing this, his worshippers rise and receive the *prasadam* from him, which he gives, whispering the following words, if they belong to the Siva sect, in their ear: 'It is I who am thy *guru*, and whom thou art bound to worship.'

The followers of Siva, having thus done homage to their *Jangamas* and *Pandarams*, proceed to perform a very disgusting ceremony. They solemnly pour water over the feet of their *guru* and wash them, reciting *mantrams* the while; then carefully collecting the water so used in a copper vessel, they pour part of it over their head and face, and drink the rest.

The Vishnavites go through a similar ceremony with their *gurus*; and this is by no means the most revolting of the marks of respect which these idiotic fanatics delight in paying. A piece of food that a *guru* has already masticated, or the water with which he has rinsed out his mouth, at once becomes sacred in their eyes, and is swallowed with avidity.

About ten miles from the fort of Chinnerayapatam a hermitage is to be found, known by the name of Kudlu-gondur, where a Vishnavite *guru* has taken up his abode. This solitary *mutt*, though but a poor place to look at, is visited by a great number of devotees, who go there to offer their homage to the penitent, to receive his *asirvadam* and *prasadam*, and through them the remission of their sins. I have been informed by some of these pilgrims themselves, that the more enthusiastic amongst them watch for the moment when the old *guru* is about to expectorate, when they stretch out their hands, struggling as to who shall have the happiness and good luck to catch the superfluous fluid which the holy man ejects; the rest of the scene is indescribable.

Gurus sometimes authorize agents to collect the tributes and offerings of the faithful, and also give them power to impose fines on evil-doers.

After having discharged the duties to their followers which their position imposes, and performed their daily ablutions and sacrifices, both morning and evening, the *gurus* employ the rest of their time—or they ought to do so if they adhered to their rules—in the study and contemplation of their sacred books. In the case of married *gurus* the office descends from father to son. Successors to the unmarried *gurus* are nominated by their superiors, who generally choose one of their own creatures. A high priest is usually assisted by a coadjutor during his lifetime, who succeeds his chief as a matter of course.

To the sects both of Siva and Vishnu priestesses are attached, that is to say, women specially set apart, under the name of *wives of the gods*, for the service of one or other of these deities. They are quite a distinct class from the dancing-girls of the temples, but are equally depraved. They are generally the unfortunate victims of the immorality of the *Jangamas* or *Vaishnavas.* These priests, by way of keeping up a character for good behaviour, and conciliating the families upon whom they have brought dishonour, put the whole blame on Vishnu or Siva; and the poor gods, as is only fair, are forced to make amends. So the girls are given to the gods as wives, by the aid of a few ceremonies; and we know that these worthy *gurus* enjoy the privilege of representing in everything the gods whose ministers they are. The women who are thus consecrated to Vishnu are called *garuda-basavis* (wives of *garuda*), and have the image of this bird tattooed on their breasts[1] as the distinctive mark of their rank.

The priestesses of Siva are called *linga-basavis*, or *women of the lingam*, and bear this sign tattooed on their thighs.

Though these women are known to be the mistresses of the priests and other dignitaries, still, for all that, they are treated with a certain amount of consideration and respect amongst their own sect.

[1] This bird, which is consecrated to Vishnu, and of which I shall presently speak at greater length, is known by European ornithologists as the Malabar eagle.—DUBOIS.

CHAPTER XI

Purohitas, or Priests who officiate at Public and Private Ceremonies.—The Hindu Almanac as published by the *Purohitas*.

To settle which are lucky or unlucky days on which to begin or put off an undertaking or expedition; to avert, by *mantrams* and suitable prayers, the curses, spells, or other evil influences of the planets and elements; to purify persons who have become unclean; to give names to newly-born children and draw their horoscopes; to bless new houses, wells, and tanks; to purify dwellings and temples which have become polluted, and also to consecrate the latter; to animate idols and install in them their particular deities by the power of their *mantrams*: these are but a few of the duties which come within the province of the Brahmin *purohitas*, whose services are indispensable on such occasions. The most important of their duties, however, is the celebration of weddings and funerals. The ceremonies on these occasions are so numerous and complicated that an ordinary Brahmin would never be able to get through them all; they can only be learned by special study. Besides, there are *mantrams* and formulas connected with them which are known only to the *purohitas*, and which are described in books of ritual which they take great care to hide from the eyes of all persons outside their own sect. The father makes his son learn these formulas by heart, and thus they descend from generation to generation in the same family. The *purohitas* are not actuated by any pious motives in taking this jealous care of their knowledge and surrounding all their doings with so much mystery; their fear is that rivals may step in who would share the profits which these religious exercises yield.

The consequence is that there are very few Brahmin *purohitas*, and sometimes they have to be fetched from a great distance when their ministrations are needed[1]. If they have reason to expect a generous reward, they will start off at once, or at any rate they will send a son who is well versed in their ritual. Sometimes ordinary Brahmins pass themselves off as *purohitas*, especially amongst the Sudras, who are not very particular on this point. These interlopers are unacquainted with the formulas and correct *mantrams*, and so they mumble a few words of Sanskrit or some ridiculous and unintelligible sentences, believing that this is quite good enough for stupid Sudras. But if the real *purohitas*, who from self-interest are always on the alert, discover that their prerogatives have been invaded and their powers usurped, a violent quarrel ensues between them and their sacrilegious rivals.

One of the most valued privileges of the *purohitas* is the right of publishing the Hindu Almanac. The majority of them, being too ignorant to compile it, buy copies every year from those of their brethren who are sufficiently well versed in astronomy to be able to calculate the eclipses and variations of the moon. It must be admitted that these learned Hindus, unacquainted as they are with the analytical operations which in Europe facilitate the computation of the movements of the stars, and having only the most ancient tables wherewith to assist their calculations, require an enormous amount of patience and concentrated attention to produce results which are in any degree trustworthy.

This almanac is an absolute necessity to every *purohita*, since it tells him not only which are the lucky and unlucky constellations, and fortunate or inauspicious days, but also which are the propitious hours in each day; for it is only at these particular moments that the ceremonies can begin at which he is called on to preside. The Brahmins also draw inspiration

[1] A *purohita* is now to be found in almost every village where Brahmins live. He enjoys a *maniam* or free grant of land. In course of time the original family is divided into many families of cousins, who hold office and enjoy the *maniam* in turn. The *purohita* is a Brahmin whose business it is to fix auspicious days for marriages, journeys, and undertakings generally. He presides at the marriage and funeral ceremonies of Sudras, but not at the marriage ceremonies of Brahmins. The Brahmin who presides at the latter is called *upadhiaya*. A *purohita* is sometimes called a *panchangi*, or one who has charge of the *panchangam* or almanac, not a very dignified office.—ED.

from this book in predicting happy and unhappy events in life. Numbers of people come to consult them on points like these; and it is not the common people only on whom this superstition has such a strong hold, for princes and persons of the highest rank believe in it even more firmly, if that be possible. There is no one in high position who has not one or more official *purohitas* living in his palace; and these men act, so to speak, like rulers of the universe. They go every morning and with ludicrous gravity announce to the prince, to his state elephant, and to his idols, each in their turn, all that is written in the almanac relating to that particular day. Should the prince wish to hunt, walk, or receive visits from strangers, and the perspicacity of the *purohita* discovers in his infallible book that this is an unpropitious moment, the chase, the walk, or the visit is postponed. In large temples a *purohita* is specially retained to read to the idols every morning the predictions for that day contained in the almanac[1].

The Hindu calendar is known by the name of the *panchangam*, which means the five members, because it contains five leading subjects: to wit, the age of the moon in the month; the constellation near which the moon is situated on each particular day; the day of the week; the eclipses; and the positions of the planets. Lucky and unlucky days are also indicated; those, for instance, on which a person may travel towards one of the four cardinal points; for any one who could safely travel to-day towards the north would probably be overtaken by misfortune if he attempted to journey to the south. There are numberless other predictions of a similar nature in the almanac, which it would be tedious to give in detail.

[1] The *panchangam* Brahmin is one who, by studying the almanac, is able to state propitious or unpropitious times. He gets his livelihood by going certain rounds, day by day, from house to house, declaring the condition of things, as per the almanac, and receiving in return a dole consisting, usually, of grain. He is not held in much respect by his own caste people, but he is much looked up to by other castes. He is consulted by his constituents, from time to time, when they wish to know the propitious period for any undertaking, as starting on a journey, making an important purchase, putting on new clothes or new jewels, or when about to take up a new appointment, or when any other important event is contemplated. He is a Smartha by sect; that is, he is really a worshipper of Siva and wears the marks of that god, but at the same time he respects and worships Vishnu.—PADFIELD.

On the first day of the Hindu year, called *Ugadi*[1], which falls on the first day of the March moon, the *purohita* summons all the principal inhabitants of the neighbourhood to his residence, and there solemnly announces, amidst much music, singing, and dancing, who will be king of the gods and who king of the stars for the year, who will be their prime ministers, and who will command the army; who will be the god of the harvest, and what crops will be most plentiful. He foretells, too, whether the season will be wet or dry, and whether locusts or other insects will, or will not, attack and devour the young plants; whether the insects and vermin, which disturb the repose of the poor Hindu, will be more or less troublesome, more or less numerous; whether it is to be a healthy or unhealthy year; whether there will be more deaths than births; whether there will be peace or war; from what quarter the country will be invaded; who will be victorious, &c.

Those who ridicule the *purohita* and his predictions are the very first to have recourse to him if the country is threatened with any great calamity, such as war, famine, drought, &c. Thus powerful is the sway which superstition exercises over the whole land. It is not only the idolatrous Hindus who give credence to these absurdities; Mahomedans, Native Christians, half-castes, and sometimes even Europeans, are not ashamed to consult the astrologer or *purohita*.

The high-class *purohitas* only expound to Brahmins the oracles contained in the almanac, but many less fortunate Brahmins procure copies for themselves, and reap a rich harvest from the credulity of the lower classes. The *panchangam* serves as an excuse, but it is only another way of demanding alms. This method of earning a livelihood, however, causes them to be despised by persons of their own caste, and they only resort to it when other resources have failed. They always quote their favourite axiom: 'In order to fill one's belly one must play many parts.'

The *purohitas* appear to date back to very ancient times. Most Hindu writers mention them, and, if they are to be believed, the highest honours were paid to these Brahmins in times gone

[1] *Ugadi* is the Telugu New Year's Day. Nowadays there is no music or dancing on the occasion of the *purohita* reading the almanac.—ED.

by. They and the *gurus* share the duty of preserving intact the ancient customs, and it is they who are loudest in condemning those who violate them.

To them also is due the credit of having preserved from destruction all the books of history or of science that have survived the revolutions by which the country has been so often convulsed.

All the *purohitas* are married, and I believe this to be obligatory, in order that they may minister in Brahmins' houses. A widower would not be admitted, as his very presence would be considered sufficient to bring misfortune[1].

[1] This is only partially applicable nowadays.—ED.

CHAPTER XII

Mantrams.—Their Efficacy.—The *Gayatri.*—The word '*Aum.*'—Magic *Mantrams.*

THESE famous *mantrams*, which the Hindus think so much of, are nothing more than prayers or consecrated formulas, but they are considered so powerful that they can, as the Hindus say, *enchain the power of the gods themselves. Mantrams* are used for invocation, for evocation, or as spells. They may be either preservative or destructive, beneficent or maleficent, salutary or harmful. In fact, there is no effect that they are not capable of producing. Through them an evil spirit can be made to take possession of any one, or can be exorcised. They can inspire with love or hate, they can cause an illness or cure it, induce death or preserve life, or cause destruction to a whole army. There are *mantrams* which are infallible for all these and many other things besides. Fortunately one *mantram* can counteract the effect of another, the stronger neutralizing the weaker.

The *purohitas* are more familiar with these *mantrams* than any other class of Hindus; but all Brahmins are supposed to be acquainted at any rate with the principal ones, if this Sanskrit verse, which one often hears repeated, is to be believed:—

Devadhînam jagat sarvam,
Mantradhinam ta dêvata
Tan mantram brahmanadhînam
Brahmana mama dêvata.

which means, 'The universe is under the power of the gods; the gods are under the power of *mantrams*; the *mantrams* are under the power of the Brahmins; therefore the Brahmins are our gods.' The argument is plainly set out, as you may see, and these modest personages have no scruples about arrogating to themselves the sublime title of *Brahma gods,* or *gods of the earth.*

As an instance of the efficacy of *mantrams,* I will cite the following example, which is taken from the well-known Hindu poem *Brahmottara-Kanda,* composed in honour of Siva:—

'Dasarha, king of Madura, having married Kalavati, daughter of the king of Benares, was warned by the princess on their wedding-day that he must not take advantage of his rights as her husband, because the *mantram of the five letters,* which she had learned, had so purged and purified her that any man who ventured upon any familiarities with her would do so at the risk of his life, unless he had been previously cleansed from all defilements through the same medium. Being his wife she could not teach him this *mantram,* because by doing so she would become his *guru,* and consequently his superior. The next day the husband and wife both went in quest of the great *Rishi,* or penitent, Garga, who, on learning the object of their visit, bade them fast for one day and bathe the following day in the Ganges. Thus prepared the pair returned to the penitent, who made the husband sit down on the ground facing the east, and having seated himself by his side, but facing the west, he whispered these two words in his ear, "*Namah Sivaya*[1]!" Scarcely had the king Dasarha heard these marvellous words when a flight of crows was seen issuing from different parts of his body, which flew away and disappeared; these crows being nothing more or less than the sins which the prince had previously committed.'

'This story,' continues the author, 'is really true. I had it from my *guru* Veda-Vyasa, who learned it himself from the *Para-Brahma.* The king and his wife, thus purified, lived happily together for a great many years, and only quitted this world to join *Para-Brahma,* the Supreme Being, in the abode of bliss.'

When one points out to the Brahmins that these much-vaunted *mantrams* do not produce startling effects in the present day, they reply that this must be attributed to the *Kali-yuga,* that is to say, to the Fourth Age of the world, in which we are now living, a veritable age of iron, when everything has

[1] This means, 'All hail to Siva!' and is the *mantram* of the five letters.—Dubois.

degenerated; a period of calamities and disasters, when virtue has ceased to rule the earth. They maintain, nevertheless, that it is still not at all uncommon for *mantrams* to work miracles, and this they confirm by citing stories which are quite as authentic and credible as the one I have just related.

The most famous and the most efficacious *mantram* for taking away sins, whose power is so great that the very gods tremble at it, is that which is called the *gayatri*. It is so ancient that the Vedas themselves were born from it. Only a Brahmin has the right to recite it, and he must prepare himself beforehand by other prayers and by the most profound meditation. He must always repeat it in a low voice, and take the greatest care that he is not overheard by a Sudra, or even by his own wife, particularly at the time when she is in a state of uncleanness. The following are the words of this famous *mantram*[1]:—

Tat Savitru varenyam bhargo devasya
Dhimahi dhiyo yonah pracho dayat.

It is a prayer in honour of the Sun, one of whose names is *Savitru*. It is a great mystery. Each word, and indeed each syllable, is full of allusions which only a very few Brahmins understand. I have never met any one who was able to give me an intelligible translation or explanation of them. A Brahmin would be guilty of an unpardonable crime and the most terrible sacrilege if he imparted it to an unbeliever. There are several other *mantrams* which are called *gayatri*, but the one mentioned above is that which is most generally used.

After the *gayatri*, the most powerful *mantram* is the mysterious monosyllable *om* or *aum*. Though it is to the interest of the Brahmins to keep the real meaning of this sacred word a profound secret, and though the greater number of them do not

[1] Long after I had finished my first work, I found in No. 27 of the *Asiatic Journal* of 1818 two different English translations of the *gayatri*, the exactitude of which I in no way vouch for, nor can I give any preference to either translation. This, at any rate, is the sense of them:—

1. 'Let us worship the light of God, greater than you, O Sun, who can so well guide our understanding. The wise man always considers this (the Sun) the supreme manifestation of the divinity.'

2. 'Let us worship the supreme light of the Sun, the God of all things, who can so well guide our understanding, like an eye suspended in the vault of heaven.'—DUBOIS.

understand it themselves, there does not appear to be much doubt that it is the symbolic name of the Supreme Being, one and indivisible, like the word *aum*[1]. This mystic word, which is always pronounced with extreme reverence, suggests an obvious analogy to that ineffable and mysterious Hebrew word *Jehovah*.

Though the Brahmins are supposed to be the sole guardians of the *mantrams*, many others venture to recite them. In some professions they are absolutely indispensable. Doctors, for instance, even when not Brahmins, would be considered very ignorant, and, no matter how clever they might be in their profession, would inspire no confidence, if they were unable to recite the special *mantram* that suited each complaint; for a cure is attributed quite as much to *mantrams* as to medical treatment. One of the principal reasons why so little confidence is placed in European doctors by the Hindus is that, when administering their remedies, they recite neither *mantrams* nor prayers[2].

Midwives must also be acquainted with a good many; and they are sometimes called *mantradaris*, or women who repeat *mantrams*; for there is no moment, according to Hindu superstitions, when *mantrams* are more needed than at the birth of a child. Both the new-born infant and its mother are peculiarly susceptible to the influence of the evil eye, the inauspicious combination of unlucky planets or unlucky days, and a thousand other unpropitious elements. A good midwife, well primed with efficacious *mantrams*, foresees all these dangers and averts them by reciting the proper words at the proper moment.

But the cleverest *mantram* reciters, and at the same time the most feared, are the charlatans who profess to be thoroughly initiated in the occult sciences, such as sorcerers, necromancers, soothsayers, &c. They have in their possession, if they are

[1] The Hindu conception of the word *aum* is thus explained by one authority:—'As long as there has been a Hindu Faith the power of sound has been recognized in the Sacred Word. In that word lie all potencies, for the sacred word expresses the one and latent Being, every power of *generation*, of *preservation*, and of *destruction*. . . . Therefore was it never to be sounded save when the mind was pure, when the mind was tranquil, when the life was noble.'—ED.

[2] Failure to feel the pulse is also regarded by the Hindus as a sure proof of medical ignorance.—ED.

to be believed, *mantrams* which are capable of working all the wonders which I enumerated at the beginning of this chapter. They recite them for the purpose of discovering stolen property, thieves, hidden treasure, foretelling future events, &c. In a country where superstition, ignorance, and the most extravagant credulity reign supreme, it is no wonder that impostors abound and are able to make a large number of dupes.

The hatred which is felt for these mischievous sorcerers is only equalled by the fear that they inspire; and that is saying a great deal. Woe to any one who is accused of having injured another by his spells! The punishment that is usually inflicted consists in pulling out two front teeth from the upper jaw. When bereft of these two teeth, it is thought the sorcerer will no longer be able to pronounce his diabolical *mantrams* distinctly. If he mispronounces the words his familiar spirit will be angry, and the misfortune that he is trying to bring down upon some one else will, it is thought, fall on his own head.

One day a poor man who lived near me, and who had just undergone this painful punishment, came and threw himself at my feet, protesting his innocence and begging for protection and for advice as to how he could obtain justice. The unfortunate fellow certainly did not look like a sorcerer, but as I had neither the power nor the means of interfering in the affair, I could only offer him my sympathy and assure him how indignant I felt at the iniquitous treatment to which he had been subjected.

There are certain *mantrams* which have a very special signification. They are called *bija-aksharas*, or radical letters; such, for instance, as *hram, hrim, hrom, hroum, hraha,* &c. To those who have the key to the true pronunciation of them and know how to use and apply them, nothing is impossible; there is no limit to the miracles they can perform. The following is an example:—

Siva had initiated a little bastard boy into all the mysteries of these radical letters. The boy was the son of a Brahmin widow, and on account of the stain on his birth had experienced the mortification of being excluded from a wedding feast, to which many persons of his caste had been invited. He revenged himself by simply pronouncing two or three of these radical letters through a crack in the door of the room where the guests were assembled. Immediately, by virtue of these marvellous words, all the dishes that had been prepared for the feast were turned into frogs. This wonderful occurrence naturally caused great consternation amongst the guests. Every one was convinced it was due to the little bastard, and fearing worse might happen they all rushed with one accord to invite him to come in. After they had apologized humbly for what had happened he entered the room and merely pronounced the same words backwards, when the frogs suddenly disappeared, and they saw with great pleasure the cakes and other refreshments which had been on the table before.

I will leave it to some one else to find, if he can, anything amongst the numberless obscurations of the human mind that can equal the extravagance of this story, which a Hindu would nevertheless believe implicitly.

CHAPTER XIII

Explanation of the Principal Ceremonies of the Brahmins and of other Castes.—The *Sam-kalpa*.—*Puja*.—*Aratti*.—*Akshatas*.—*Pavitram*.—Sesamum and *Darbha* Grass.—*Puniaha-vachana*.—*Pancha-gavia*.—Purification of Places where Ceremonies take place.—*Pandals*, or Pavilions made of Leaves.

Before entering into more particular details with regard to the ceremonies of the Brahmins, it is necessary, in order to make the rest of this book intelligible, to begin by giving an explanation of certain terms pertaining to these ceremonies, and also a short summary of the chief objects aimed at. This sketch will suffice to indicate the peculiar tastes and inclinations of the Brahmins, and will no doubt cause my readers to inquire how these men were able to impose so many extravagant absurdities on a people whose civilization dates from such very ancient times, and yet to retain their full confidence.

The Sam-kalpa.

The chief preparatory ceremony amongst the Brahmins is the *sam-kalpa*, which means literally 'intensive contemplation[1].'

This method of mental preparation must in no instance be omitted before any religious ceremony of the Brahmins. When the *sam-kalpa* has been performed with due meditation, everything that they undertake will succeed; but its omission is alone sufficient to transform all the ceremonies that follow into so many acts of sacrilege which will not pass unpunished. The Brahmin must meditate preliminarily on the following points. He must think—

1. Of Vishnu, meditating upon him as the ruler and preserver of this vast universe, as the author and giver of all good things,

[1] *Sam-kalpa* literally means resolve of the mind, will, purpose, definite intention, determination, desire. It is no ceremony in itself, but is a prelude to every ceremony.—Ed.

and as he who brings all undertakings to a successful issue. With these thoughts in his mind he repeats thrice the name of Vishnu, and worships him.

2. He must think of Brahma. He must remember that there are nine Brahmas, who created the eight million four hundred thousand kinds of living creatures, of which the most important is man; that it is the first of these Brahmas who is ruling at the present time; that he will live for a hundred years of the gods[1]; that his life is divided into four parts, of which the first and half the second are already gone. He must then worship him.

3. He must think of the *Avatara*, or incarnation, of Vishnu in the form of a white pig, which was the shape in which that deity slew the giant Hirannyaksha. After having thoroughly realized the idea that this *Avatara* is the most celebrated of all in the *Kali-yuga*, he worships the pig god.

4. He must think of Manu. He reminds himself that there are fourteen Manus, of which the names are *Svarochisha, Tamasa, Svayambhuva, Raivata*, &c. &c., and that they reign over the fourteen worlds during the hundred gods' years that Brahma's life will last. As *Vaivaswata Manu* is now in power in the *Kali-yuga*, in which the Hindus are living at this present time, he offers him worship.

5. He must think of the *Kali-yuga*. He must recollect that we are at present in the early part of this *yuga*.

6. He must think of *Jambu-Dwipa*. This is the continent in which India is situated. He pictures it to himself as surrounded by a sea of salt water, having in the centre a mountain of gold sixteen thousand *yojanas*[2] high, called *Mahameru*, on the thousand summits of which the gods have fixed their abode. He must remember that at the foot of this mountain on the east side grows the *Jambu-vruksha*, a tree which is a thousand *yojanas* high and as many in circumference; that the juice of the fruits of this tree, which fall of their own accord when ripe, forms a large river which flows towards the west, where it

[1] Each day, according to the reckoning of the gods, is as long as several milliards of years.—DUBOIS.

[2] The ordinary *yojana* is about nine miles, but the sacred *yojana*, which is here mentioned, is very much longer.—DUBOIS.

Yojana literally means the distance driven at a yoking or stretch; equal to four *krosas*, or about nine English miles.—ED.

mingles its waters with those of the sea; that the water of this river possesses the power of converting everything it touches into gold, for which reason it has been called the *Bangaru-nadi* or Golden River. The Brahmin must not omit to think of this sacred tree, nor yet of the continent of *Jambu-Dwipa*, where it is situated.

7. He must think of the great king Bharata, who at one time governed *Jambu-Dwipa* and whose reign forms one of the Hindu eras.

8. He must think of the side of the *Mahameru* which faces him, that is to say, of the west side of this sacred mountain, if he lives to the west of it, of the east, if he lives to the east of it, &c.

9. He must think of the corner of the world called *Agni-diku*, or the Corner of Fire, over which the god *Agni-Iswara* presides, and which is that part of the world in which India is situated.

10. He must think of the Dravida country, where the Tamil (*Arava*) language is spoken.

11. He must think of the moon's pathway, and the change of one moon to another.

12. He must think of the year of the cycle in which he is living. The Hindu cycle is composed of sixty years, each of which has its own particular name. And he must say aloud the name of the particular year of the cycle in which he is living.

13. He must think of the *ayana* in which he is. There are two *ayanas* in the year, each of which lasts six months—one called the *dakshina-ayana* or southern *ayana*, which includes the time during which the sun is south of the equinoctial line, and the other called *uttara-ayana* or northern *ayana*, which comprises the rest of the year, during which the sun is north of this line. He must pronounce the name of the *ayana* which is then going on.

14. He must think of the *rutu*, or season of the year. There are six *rutus* in the year, each of which lasts two months. He must pronounce the name of the *rutu* in which he is performing the *sam-kalpa*.

15. He must think of the moon. Each moon is divided into two equal parts, one of which is called *Sukla-paksha* and the other *Krishna-paksha*. Each of these divisions lasts fourteen days, and each day has its own special name. He must call to

mind the division and day of the moon, and pronounce their names.

16. He must think of the day of the week and pronounce the name.

17. He must think of the star of the day. There are twenty-seven in each lunar month, each of which has a name. He must pronounce the name of the one which is in the ascendant on that day.

18. He must think of the *yoga*[1] of the day. There are twenty-seven of these, corresponding to the twenty-seven stars, each with its own name. He must pronounce the name of the *yoga*, as also that of the star.

19. He must think of the *karana*, of which there are eleven in each lunar month, each with its own name. The same formality must be gone through as with the star and the *yoga*.

All these divers objects to which the Brahmin must turn his thoughts when performing the *sam-kalpa* are so many personifications of Vishnu, or rather are Vishnu himself under different names. Besides this ordinary *sam-kalpa*, there is another more elaborate one, which is reserved for grand occasions, and which will be described further on.

This pious introduction to all their ceremonies averts, by virtue of its merits, every obstacle which the evil spirits and giants would put in the way. The name of Vishnu alone, it is true, is sufficient to put them to flight, but nothing can resist the power of the *sam-kalpa*.

PUJA, OR SACRIFICE[2].

Of all the Hindu rites, *puja* is the one that occurs most frequently in all their ceremonies, both public and private, in their temples and elsewhere. Every Brahmin is absolutely obliged to offer it at least once a day to his household gods. There are three kinds of *pujas*—the great, the intermediate, and the small.

The great sacrifice is composed of the following parts:—

1. *Avahana*. The evocation of the deity.
2. *Asana*. A seat is presented to him to sit on.

[1] *Yoga* means conjunction of stars. —ED.

[2] *Puja* means honour, respect, homage, worship.—ED.

3. *Swagata*. He is asked if he has arrived quite safely, and if he met with no accident on the way.

4. *Padya*. Water is offered to him for washing his feet.

5. *Arghya*. Water is presented to him in which flowers, saffron, and sandalwood powder have been placed.

6. *Achamania*. Water is offered that he may wash his mouth and face in the prescribed fashion.

7. *Madhu-parka*. He is offered in a metal vessel a beverage composed of honey, sugar, and milk.

8. *Snana-jala*. Water for his bath.

9. *Bhooshan-abharanasya*. He is presented with cloths, jewels, and ornaments.

10. *Gandha*. Sandalwood powder.

11. *Akshatas*. Grains of rice coloured with saffron.

12. *Pushpa*. Flowers.

13. *Dhupa*. Incense.

14. *Dipa*. A lighted lamp.

15. *Neiveddya*. This last offering is composed of cooked rice, fruit, liquefied butter, sugar and other eatables, and betel.

Before offering these gifts, care should be taken to sprinkle a little water over them with the tips of the fingers. The worshippers then prostrate themselves before the deity.

For the intermediate *puja* the last nine articles are offered; for the lesser, only the last six.

When sacrifices of blood are necessary to appease ill-disposed gods or evil spirits, the blood and the flesh of the animals that have been sacrificed are offered to them.

ARTI OR ARATTI.

This ceremony is performed only by married women and courtesans. Widows would not be allowed, under any circumstances, to participate in it[1].

A lamp made of kneaded rice-flour is placed on a metal dish or plate. It is then filled with oil or liquefied butter and lighted. The women each take hold of the plate in turn and raise it to the level of the person's head for whom the ceremony is being

[1] Widows are not allowed to take part in any of the domestic ceremonies of the Hindus. Their presence alone would be thought to bring misfortune, and if they dared to appear they would be rudely treated and sent away.—DUBOIS.

performed, describing a specified number of circles with it. Instead of using a lighted lamp they sometimes content themselves with filling a vessel with water coloured with saffron, vermilion, and other ingredients. The object of this ceremony is to counteract the influence of the evil eye and any ill-effects which, according to Hindu belief, may arise from the jealous and spiteful looks of ill-intentioned persons.

The *aratti* is one of the commonest of their religious practices, and is observed in public and private[1]. It is performed daily, and often several times a day, over persons of high rank, such as rajahs, governors of provinces, generals, and other distinguished members of society. Whenever people in these positions have been obliged to show themselves in public, or to speak to strangers, they invariably call for the courtesans or dancing-girls from the temples to perform this ceremony over them, and so avert any unpleasant consequences that might arise from the baleful glances to which they have been exposed. Kings and princes often have dancing-girls in their employ who do nothing else but perform this ceremony[2].

The *aratti* is also performed for idols. After the dancing-girls have finished all their other duties in the temple, they never fail to perform this ceremony twice daily over the images of the gods to whom their services are dedicated. It is performed with even more solemnity when these idols have been carried in procession through the streets, so as to turn aside malignant influences, to which the gods are as susceptible as any ordinary mortal.

Aratti is also performed for the same purpose over elephants, horses, and other domestic animals.

This superstition about the evil eye is common enough in many European countries. I have seen simple French peasants hastily draw their children away from some stranger or ill-looking person, for fear his glance might cast some spell over the little ones. The same notion was prevalent at the time of the ancient Romans, as Virgil, amongst others, bears witness in the following verse:—

'Nescio quis teneros oculus mihi fascinat agnos.'

[1] The word *aratti* itself means trouble, misfortune, pain.—ED.

[2] *Aratti* is performed also when people take children from one village to another, on visits to relations and friends.—ED.

The Romans too had their god Fascinus, and amulets of the same name were given to children to wear to preserve them from spells of this nature. The statue of the god, placed on the triumphal car, preserved returning conquerors from the malignity of the envious. Hindus call this spell *drishti-dosha*, or the influence of the eye. And they invented the *aratti* to avert and counteract it. Their credulity on this subject is boundless. According to them it is not only animate objects that come under the influence of the *drishti-dosha*; vegetable substances are equally susceptible to it. It is to avert this spell that they stick up a pole in all their gardens and fields that are under cultivation. On the top of this pole they fix a large earthen vessel, well whitened on the outside with lime. This is to attract the attention of malicious persons who may be passing, as it will be the first thing to catch their eye and will thus prevent their spells from producing any disastrous effects on the crops, which otherwise would certainly be affected by the evil influence.

Akshatas.

This is the name given to husked rice coloured with a mixture of saffron and vermilion. There are two kinds of *akshatas*, one specially consecrated by *mantrams*, the other simple coloured rice. The first is used when performing *puja* and in other great ceremonies; the other kind is only a toilet requisite, or is used as an offering of politeness. It is considered good manners to offer some in a metal cup to any one to whom a ceremonious invitation is sent. The latter in return takes a few grains and applies them to the forehead.

The Pavitram[1].

The object of the *pavitram* is to scare away giants, evil spirits, or devils, whose mission it is to bring disasters upon men and mar the ceremonies of the Brahmins. The very sight of the *pavitram* makes them tremble and take to flight.

This powerful amulet consists of three, five, or seven stalks of *darbha* grass plaited together in the form of a ring. Before

[1] The *pavitram* is made of stalks of *darbha* grass. It is worn simply as a mark of sanctification. Three stalks are generally used for funeral ceremonies; two for marriage ceremonies and other auspicious occasions.—Ed.

beginning any ceremony the presiding *purohita* takes the *pavitram*, and, after dipping it in sanctified water, places it on the ring finger of his right hand. The seeds and oil of sesamum are very nearly as efficacious as the *pavitram*; but the grass they call *darbha* is the most efficacious, for it possesses the virtue of purifying everything that it touches. The Brahmins can do nothing without it. It is the basis of all those pious and meritorious acts which are known by the generic term of *moksharthas*, or deeds which lead to everlasting felicity, and which consist of the *asva-medha* (sacrifice of the horse), the *vaja-peya*, the *raja-suya*, the *sattra-yaga*, and other kinds of *yagnas* which are particularly pleasing to Vishnu[1].

No important action in life can take place without it. That is to say, it is necessary in the *kamyarthas*, which include the *garbha-dana*, the *jata-karma*, the *nama-karma*, the *anna-prasana*, the *chaula*, the *upanayana*, the *simanta*, and marriage[2]. It is in frequent use in the various religious exercises of the Brahmins pertaining to their four states, namely, *Brahmachari*, *Grahastha*, *Vana-prastha*, and *Sannyasi*. In fact this sacred grass, the purity of which is considered unequalled, appears in every religious or civil ceremony.

PUNIAHA-VACHANA.

The literal translation of this word is 'the evocation of virtue,' and it is the name given to the ceremony by which the sacred water is consecrated. They proceed thus:—Having purified a place in the house in the ordinary manner, they sprinkle it with water. Then the officiating Brahmin *purohita* seats himself with his face to the east, and they place before him a banana leaf with a measure of rice on it. At one side is a copper vessel full of water, the outside of which has been whitened with lime; the mouth of the vessel is covered with mango leaves, and it is placed on the rice. Near the copper

[1] *Vaja-peya* = trial of strength; a kind of *soma* sacrifice. *Sattra-yaga* = another great *soma* sacrifice. *Raja-suya* = royal inaugural sacrifice.—ED.

[2] *Kamyarthas* = deeds which lead to worldly happiness. *Garbha-dana* = pregnancy. *Jata-karma* = horoscope writing. *Nama-karma* = naming ceremony. *Anna-prasana* = weaning or food-giving ceremony. *Chaula* = head-shaving ceremony. *Upanayana* = initiation of a pupil. *Simanta* = ceremony of parting the hair, in the case of women six or eight months in pregnancy.—ED.

vessel they put a little heap of saffron, which represents the god Vigneshwara, to whom they perform *puja*, and for *neiveddya* they offer jaggery (raw sugar) and betel. They then throw a little sandalwood powder and *akshatas* into the copper vessel, while reciting appropriate *mantrams*, with the intention of turning the water which it contains into the sacred water of the Ganges. Finally they offer a sacrifice to the vessel, and for *neiveddya* they offer bananas and betel. The water thus sanctified purifies places and persons that have become unclean.

PANCHA-GAVIA.

I have already explained[1] of what disgusting materials the mixture known by this name is composed. This is the way in which it is consecrated. The house is purified in the usual way. They then bring five little new earthen vessels, into one of which they put milk, into another curds, into a third liquefied butter, into a fourth cow-dung, and into the fifth the urine of a cow. These five little vessels are then placed in a row on the ground on some *darbha* grass, and they perform *puja* in the following manner:—First, they make a profound obeisance before the deity *pancha-gavia*, and they meditate for some time on his merits and good qualities. Some flowers are placed on the five vessels, and for *asana* they make the god an imaginary present of a golden seat or throne. They then offer to each vessel, as *arghya*, a little water, which is poured round them. For *padya*, a little more water is poured out for them to wash their feet, and *achamania* is offered immediately afterwards in the same way. The *snana-jala* is water in which a little *garika* grass has been steeped, which is presented to the god *pancha-gavia*, to enable him to perform his ablutions. The tops of the vessels are then covered with *akshatas*, while they are presented, in imagination of course, with jewels, rich garments, and sandalwood. In conclusion they offer them flowers, incense, a lighted lamp, bananas, and betel as *neiveddya*, and finally make another profound obeisance.

These preliminaries ended, the officiating priest addresses the following prayer to the god *pancha-gavia*, or, what is the same thing, to the substances contained in the five vessels: 'O god *pancha-gavia*, vouchsafe to pardon the sins of all the creatures in the world who offer sacrifice to you and drink

[1] Chapter III.

you, *pancha-gavia*. You have come proceeding from the body of the cow; therefore I offer you my prayers and sacrifices, in order that I may obtain the remission of my sins and the purification of my body, which are accorded to those who drink you. Vouchsafe also to absolve us, who have offered you *puja*, from all the sins that we have committed either inadvertently or deliberately. Forgive us and save us!'

After this prayer they make another profound obeisance and put the contents of the five vessels into one. Then taking this vessel into his hands, the *purohita* performs the *hari-smarana*[1], drinks a little of this precious liquid, pours a little into the hollow of the hands of all persons present, who also drink it, and keeps the rest for use during the ceremony. Betel is then presented to the Brahmins who are present, after which they disperse.

Nothing can equal the supposed purifying virtues of this mixture. Brahmins and other Hindus frequently drink it to remove both external and internal defilements.

There is also another lustral preparation called *pancha-amrita*, which is composed of milk, curds, liquefied butter, honey, and sugar mixed together. This is not filthy and disgusting like the one previously mentioned, but then it is much less efficacious. It however possesses a certain degree of merit under some circumstances.

The Purification of Places.

Before the performance of any ceremony the place where it is to take place must be previously purified. This is usually the duty of the women, and the principal ingredients required are cow-dung and *darbha* grass. They dilute the cow-dung with water and make a sort of plaster with it, which they spread over the floor with their hands, making zigzags and other patterns as they go on. They then draw wide lines of alternate red and white over this and sprinkle the whole with *darbha* grass, after which the place is perfectly pure. This is the way in which Hindus purify their houses day by day from the defilements caused by promiscuous goers and comers. It is the rule amongst the upper classes to have their houses rubbed over once a day with cow-dung, but in any class it would be considered an

[1] *Hari smarana* means meditating on *Hari*, or Vishnu.—Ed.

unpardonable and gross breach of good manners to omit this ceremony when they expected friends to call or were going to receive company.

This custom appears odd at first sight, but it brings this inestimable benefit in its train, that it cleanses the houses where it is in use from all the insects and vermin which would otherwise infest them.

PANDALS.

All the more important Hindu ceremonies, such as *upanayana*, marriages, &c., take place under canopies made of leaves and branches of trees which are erected with much pomp and care in the courtyard or in front of the principal entrance door of the house. The *pandal* is usually supported by twelve wooden posts[1] or pillars, and covered with foliage and branches of trees. The top or ceiling is ornamented with paintings or costly stuffs, while the whole is hung with garlands of flowers, foliage, and many other decorations. The pillars are painted in alternate bands of red and white. The *pandals* of rich people are often exquisitely decorated. A propitious day, hour, and star are always chosen on which to erect these canopies. Then the relations and friends all assemble to set up the centre pillar, which is called the *muhurta-kal*, and to which they offer *puja* to the accompaniment of music. Under this canopy all the ceremonies connected with the fête take place, and the guests remain underneath it till the end of the performance. The houses of Hindus are not as a rule sufficiently spacious, or in any way well adapted for receiving large numbers of guests, so necessity has suggested this picturesque alternative.

Besides these *pandals*, which are only used on grand occasions, upper-class people generally have a permanent one before their principal entrance door to protect from the sun persons who may come to visit them, and who could not with propriety and due regard to custom be invited to come inside.

[1] Amongst the Sudras it is only those who belong to the Right-hand faction who are allowed to have twelve pillars or posts to their *pandals*. If a Left-hand Sudra, who is only entitled to eleven, should take upon himself to put twelve, a frightful fracas would ensue.—DUBOIS.

CHAPTER XIV

Ceremonies to be observed after a Woman's Confinement.—Ceremonies performed over Infants.

JATA-KARMA.

WHEN a Brahmani begins to feel the pangs of child-birth her husband should be near her, so that he may carefully note the date of the month, the day, the star of the day, the *yoga*, the *karana*, the hour, and the moment when the child is born. And to prevent any of these details being forgotten, he puts them down in writing.

The house where a woman is confined, as well as all those who live in it, are unclean for ten days. Before this time is up they must have no intercourse with any one. On the eleventh day all the linen and clothes that have been used during this period are given to the washerman, and the house is purified in the manner I have already described. Then they call in a Brahmin *purohita*. The woman who has just been confined, holding the child in her arms, and with her husband by her side, seats herself on a sort of earthen platform, which is set up in the centre of the house and covered with a cloth. The *purohita* then approaches them, performs the *sam-kalpa*, offers *puja* to the god Vigneshwara, and goes through the ceremony of the *puniaha-vachana*, or consecration of the sacred water. He pours a small quantity of this water into the hands of the father and mother of the child, who drink a portion and pour the rest over their heads. He also sprinkles this water over the house and all who are living in it, and throws what remains down the well. The *purohita* is then presented with some betel and a small gift, after which he departs. This ceremony, which is called *jata-karma*, removes all uncleanness, but the woman who has been confined does not become perfectly pure before the end of a month. Until that time has elapsed she must live apart and have no communication with any one[1].

NAMA-KARMA.

On the twelfth day after the birth of the child they give it a name. This is the *nama-karma* ceremony. The house having been duly purified, the father of the child invites his relatives and friends to be present at the ceremonies and at the feast which follows them. The guests go all together to perform their ablutions. On their return they first of all offer the sacrifice to fire called *homam*, in honour of the nine planets. Then the father of the child, holding it in his arms, seats himself on the little raised platform of earth and performs the *sam-kalpa*. By his side is a copper dish full of rice. With the first finger of his right hand, in which he holds a gold ring, he writes on this rice the day of the moon, the name of the day, that of the constellation under which the child was born, and finally the name that he wishes to give him. He then calls the child three times by this name in a loud voice.

This ceremony ended, he gives a present to the presiding *purohita*, distributes betel to all the Brahmins present, and then all take their places at the feast which has been prepared. As soon as it is finished the master of the house again offers betel to his guests, and also presents, if he is rich enough.

The mother of the child does not appear at this ceremony for the reason mentioned at the end of the preceding section.

ANNA-PRASANA.

As soon as the child is six months old he is weaned. Then the *anna-prasana* takes place. The name of this ceremony expresses the idea of feeding the child on solid food for the first time. For this occasion they choose a month, a week, a day, and a star which all combine to give favourable auguries.

[1] This custom closely resembles that which Jewish women were obliged to follow under similar circumstances (Leviticus xii), but the Hindus pay no attention, as did the Israelites, to the difference in the sex of the child. As regards the time during which the uncleanness of the mother lasts, it is just the same with the Hindus whether a boy or a girl is born.—DUBOIS.

This is wrong. When a mother gives birth to a girl, pollution lasts for forty days; in the case of a boy, only thirty days.—ED.

A *pandal* is erected, which is ornamented all round with *toranams*[1], or wreaths of mango leaves, some of which are also hung over the entrance door of the house, the inside of which has been carefully purified by the women. The father of the child sallies forth, provided with a cup full of *akshatas*, to invite his relations and friends to the feast. All the guests, having purified themselves by bathing, assemble under the *pandal*. The mother, holding the child in her arms, and accompanied by her husband, seats herself beside him on the little platform of earth which has been set up in the centre. The *purohita* advances towards them, performs the *sam-kalpa*, offers, firstly, *homam* in honour of the nine planets, then a sacrifice to fire, to which he presents clarified butter and betel for *neiveddya*. When he has finished, the women sing verses expressing their good wishes for the future happiness of the child, and perform *aratti*[2] over him.

The father offers *puja* to his household gods, and a portion of the dishes prepared for the general feast is set apart as *neiveddya* for them.

Then the married women form a procession and sing, while they bring in a new dish of silver-plated copper, which is given by the maternal uncle of the child, and one of those cords made of cotton thread which all Hindus wear round their loins, and to which the little piece of calico is fastened which covers their private parts. They touch the child with these two articles, and then pour some *paramanna*, a mixture composed of rice, sugar, and other ingredients, into the vessel. Recommencing their song, they proceed in the same solemn order towards the household gods and place before them the dish, which is then known as the *dish god*. They make a profound obeisance all together to this new deity; then addressing it and the rest of the deities, they implore them to make the child grow, to give him strength, health, long life, and plenty of this world's goods. Then taking up again the *dish god*, they carry it back, still singing, to the child. They first of all fasten the little cord round its loins. Two of the women then make it open its mouth, while a third pours some of the mixture contained in the dish down its throat.

[1] These *toranams* are always used at times of rejoicing. They are an outward sign of rejoicing, and an announcement that a feast is going on, inviting people to come.—DUBOIS.

[2] See last chapter.

Instruments of music are playing and the women are singing during the whole of this ceremony. It is terminated by the *aratti*, after which all the Brahmins present are offered *akshatas* consecrated by *mantrams*. Each one takes a pinch of the coloured rice, part of which he puts on the child's head and the rest on his own.

Then they sit down to a feast, and the ceremony is ended by a distribution of betel and a few presents given by the master of the house to his guests.

THE CHAULA.

Three years after the birth of the child[1] the tonsure, or *chaula*, is made for the first time. The Brahmins who are invited assemble under the *pandal* after having performed their ablutions. The child is brought in by his father and mother, who seat him between them on the little earthen platform. The married women then proceed to perform his toilette. They begin by anointing him from head to foot with oil, after which they wash him with warm water. They then colour his forehead and sundry other parts of his body with powdered sandalwood and *akshatas*, deck him with ornaments, and finally put a long necklace of coral beads round his neck and two bracelets to match on his wrists.

The *purohita* then draws near the child thus adorned and performs the *sam-kalpa*, and also offers *homam* to the nine planets. He next traces on the floor in front of the child a square patch with red earth, which they cover with rice that has the husk on. The idol Vigneshwara is placed on one side, and to it they perform *puja*, offering brinjals[2], raw sugar, and betel for *neiveddya*.

The child is made to sit near the square patch, and the barber, after offering worship to his razor[3], proceeds to shave the child's head, leaving one lock at the top, which is never cut. While the barber is performing his part of the

[1] Only the male child.—ED.

[2] *Beringela* in Portuguese, a purple vegetable shaped something like a fig. —DUBOIS.

This is wrong. *Brinjals* are never offered to an idol.—ED.

[3] This act of worship, which the barber always performs before shaving any one, consists in putting the razor to his forehead.—DUBOIS.

The same practice is observed by all artisans.—ED.

ceremony, the women sing, musical instruments are played, and all the Brahmins present remain standing in perfect silence. As soon as the barber has finished, they throw him the money due to him. This he picks up, and before retiring he also carries off the rice that has been scattered over the square patch.

The child is immediately put into a bath to purify him from the defiling touch of the barber. Then his toilette is begun anew. The women perform the ceremony of *aratti*, and the *purohita* for the second time performs the *homam* to the nine planets. The entertainment generally ends with a feast and the distribution of presents to the Brahmins. The musicians are then paid, and receive besides their money a measure of rice each.

The ears of children of both sexes are pierced at about the same age. This is an occasion for another feast, very closely resembling the preceding ones. The goldsmith performs the operation with a very fine gold wire, and the size of the hole is gradually increased from time to time. The hole is generally made larger in the ears of girls, so that they may wear larger ornaments. In some provinces both men and women have the holes as large as a Spanish piastre.

However odd these customs may appear to us, at any rate they have the advantage of bringing the Brahmins often together and obliging them to fulfil their mutual obligations. And they certainly help to form a class of men who in tone and manners are infinitely superior to other Hindus.

PART II

THE FOUR STATES OF BRAHMINICAL LIFE

CHAPTER I

The *Brahmachari*.—Ceremony of the *Upanayana*, or Investiture of the Triple Cord.

In this Second Part I will bring to notice the most remarkable peculiarities of the Brahmin caste, the one of all others which clings most tenaciously to long established customs. Europeans have possessed up to the present time but very imperfect information on this subject, and what little information has been obtained has been taken as it were by stealth from the Brahmins, whose constant endeavour it is to veil their customs in mystery. I think that the details I am about to give will in consequence be found of considerable interest. These customs, however, do not belong exclusively to the Brahmin caste; some of them are common to other castes as well.

The life of a Brahmin has to be considered under four important aspects. The first is that of the young Brahmin who has been invested with the triple cord, and who is from that time called *Brahmachari*. The second is that of the Brahmin who has married, and who is thenceforward, but especially after he has become a father, called *Grahastha*. The third is that of the Brahmin who, renouncing the world, retires into the jungles with his wife, and who is then known as *Vana-prastha* (or dweller in the jungle). The fourth, and last, is the state of

Sannyasi, or that of the Brahmin who decides to live entirely in solitude, apart even from his wife, a mode of life considered even more edifying than *Vana-prastha.*

It is well known that all Brahmins wear a thin cord[1], hung from the left shoulder and falling on to the right hip. It is composed of three strands of cotton, each strand formed by nine threads. The cotton with which it is made must be gathered from the plant by the hand of a pure Brahmin, and carded and spun by persons of the same caste, so as to avoid the possibility of its being defiled by passing through unclean hands. After a Brahmin is married his cord must have nine and not three strands[2].

Brahmins, and all the other castes which have the right to wear this cord, prize it more highly and are certainly more proud of it than are many Europeans who by noble birth or great deeds possess the right to wear the *cordon* of the knightly orders.

Children from the age of five to nine are invested with this cord. March, April, May, and June are considered the most favourable months for the investiture. As the ceremony entails a considerable outlay, the poorer Brahmins go from house to house begging and collecting funds with which to defray the necessary expenses; and natives of all castes believe that in making such contributions they are performing a pious act.

This ceremony is called the *upanayana*, which means 'introduction to knowledge,' for by it a Brahmin acquires the right to study. Several of the rites performed on this occasion are also performed at the marriage ceremony, so I will only describe here those which are peculiar to the cord ceremony, and I will describe later on those common to both. The

[1] This cord is called *yagnopavitam* in Sanskrit, *jandemu* in Telugu, *punul* in Tamil, *janivara* in Canarese.—DUBOIS.

[2] The number three, adopted, and so to say consecrated, in this and in many other instances, is evidently used in an allegorical sense. I am rather inclined to believe that it refers to the three principal divinities of India—Brahma, Vishnu, and Siva.—DUBOIS.

The Abbé is incorrect as to the number of strands. After marriage a Brahmin *must* wear six, and *may* wear nine. The triple cord is thus explained by one authority: 'It symbolizes the body, speech, and mind. It symbolizes the control of each; and therefore when the knots are tied in it, it means that the man who wears the thread has gained control over body, speech, and mind.'—ED.

following details are extracts from the ritual of the *purohitas*, which bears the title of *Nittya Karma*.

To begin with, the father of the candidate must provide himself with many pieces of cotton cloth and plenty of small gold and silver coins, to be given as presents to the guests. He must also have a large supply of rice, flour, fresh and dried vegetables, fruit, oil of sesamum, clarified butter, and milk in various forms, &c., for the feast; sandalwood, vermilion, saffron; and, above all things, plenty of betel-leaf and areca-nut. Further, there must be in abundance earthen vessels of all kinds, shapes, and sizes, seeing that on each of the four days that the feast lasts new ones will be required; those which have been once used on this occasion, as on that of a marriage, being always broken into little pieces. When everything is ready, the father goes to consult the *purohita*, or family priest, to ascertain what day will be most propitious. The *purohita* having fixed a day, a *pandal*, or pavilion, is erected. The preliminary ceremonies and purifications are gone through, and the invitations issued in the customary manner. Meanwhile, the women decorate the walls of the house, both inside and out, with alternate broad bands of red and white paint. When the guests have arrived and are all assembled under the *pandal*, the *purohita* makes his appearance, bringing with him a cord and an antelope's skin [1].

Having performed the *sam-kalpa*, he offers *puja*, or adoration, to Vigneshwara, who is represented by a small conical heap of fresh cow-dung, placed in the centre of the *pandal*. He also makes to him offerings of *garika* [2], sandalwood, *akshatas*, or coloured rice, incense, and a lighted lamp.

This god Vigneshwara, or Pillayar, or Ganesa [3], &c., of whom we shall frequently have occasion to speak, is the god of obstacles, as his name denotes. He is of a morose and irascible disposition, and always ready to annoy and thwart those who fail to pay him sufficient respect. It is for this reason

[1] The antelope's skin is used as a mat on which the priest sits. The skins of both the antelope and the tiger are considered extremely pure; consequently one may sit on them without fear of defilement.—DUBOIS.

[2] *Garika* in Canarese, *arugu* in Tamil, *durva* in Sanskrit—a kind of millet-grass, *Panicum dactylon*.—ED.

[3] Ganesa literally means god of the inferior deities.—ED.

that so much deference is shown to him, and that on grand feast-days his good offices are the first to be invoked, his worshippers fearing lest he should take it into his head to disturb the feast and bring it to an untimely end.

The sacrifice to Vigneshwara ended, the master of the house presents betel-nut to the Brahmins, and then they all proceed to make their ablutions. On their return, the neophyte is made to sit on a raised platform of earth in the centre of the *pandal.* The married women chant sacred songs, while they proceed to adorn him as for the ceremony of the *chaula*, though on this occasion the garments are even richer and more costly; and finally they delicately pencil his eyelids with antimony[1].

His toilette finished, the father and mother of the candidate seat themselves by his side on the daïs, and the women perform the ceremony of the *aratti*. *Puja* is offered to the household gods, and for *neiveddya*, or votive offering, portions of all the dishes prepared for the feast are set aside. The guests then seat themselves on the ground, in rows, the women placing themselves so as not to be seen by the men. The women belonging to the household bring in the rice and the various dishes which have been prepared for the feast, helping everything with their fingers, the use of spoons being unknown amongst them. Each guest receives his portion on a banana leaf, or on other leaves sewn together, which are never used more than once. When the meal is over, betel and areca-nut are distributed, and the guests then separate.

The following day is called the *muhurta*, or great day; it is that on which the actual investiture takes place. The guests are invited to reassemble as on the preceding day.

The would-be recipient is seated on the daïs, between his father and mother, all three having their faces turned towards the east. His loins are girt with a 'pure' cotton cloth, that is to say, either a new one, or at least one that has been newly washed[2]. The married women perform his toilette, singing all the while.

[1] This is a kind of ointment formerly used by other nations. It is still a common practice amongst the people of India to ornament the faces of their children with it. Courtesans and beauties, too, often use it. It certainly enhances the brilliancy of the eyes, and is a pleasing addition to a handsome face.—DUBOIS.

[2] It is not only on this occasion that a 'pure' cloth is obligatory. Each time that a Brahmin bathes he washes his clothing, to purify it.—DUBOIS.

The *purohita* then approaches, holding in his hands an earthen chafing-dish full of hot embers. He performs the *sam-kalpa*, and then formally consecrates the pan of hot coals, which by virtue of his *mantram* becomes a god. To this he offers the sacrifice called *homam*, throwing on the fire some pieces of the *aswatta*, or sacred fig-tree, some cooked rice, and some melted butter. After this nine specially selected Brahmins offer the same sacrifice of the *homam* in honour of the nine planets. Then each having chosen a married woman, they all go off together, still singing, to convey the sacred fire to some place apart, where it must be carefully attended to and kept burning until the last day of the festival. It would be considered a very bad omen if, from inattention or any other cause, this fire were to be extinguished sooner.

The inauguration of the *ishta devata* (or tutelary deity) immediately follows. The married women provide themselves with a large copper vessel, which must be new and whitewashed outside. They take it, preceded by instruments of music, to be filled from a well or river. On returning to the house they place some mango leaves over the mouth of the vessel, and on the top of the leaves a cocoanut, coloured yellow with powdered saffron. The vessel is then wrapped in a woman's cloth which has been dyed the same colour, and is placed on the ground, on the top of a small heap of rice. Round its neck are then hung two palm leaves, rolled up and coloured red, and also a necklace of small black seeds, and a few other female ornaments. The *purohita* then invokes the tutelary deity and invites him to settle on the vessel, which becomes from that moment a female divinity, to whom the women promptly make an offering of flowers, incense, *akshatas*, a lighted lamp, and some betel-leaf. The mother of the young man then places the vessel, i. e. the new goddess, on her head, and accompanied by the other women, all singing in chorus, and preceded by the musicians, makes a solemn progress round the village, under a kind of canopy. On returning to the house she replaces the vessel, and, with the assistance of some of the other women, drapes round the two central pillars of the *pandal* two perfectly new cloths of the kind worn by women. The same procession then starts again to fetch some mould from ant-heaps raised by *karraiyan*[1]. With this

[1] These are the white ants so common in India, and so destructive.—DUBOIS.

they fill five small pots. These again are sown with nine kinds of seed, which are well sprinkled with milk and water, to make them sprout quickly. The *purohita* approaches the five pots, and by virtue of his *mantrams*, or incantations, turns them also into divinities. The women then perform the customary acts of *puja* before them, and after prostrating themselves place them close to the tutelary deity. Then comes the invocation of gods, planets, and ancestors. I shall give full particulars of this ceremony when describing a marriage.

During the invocation to the gods a piece of saffron-coloured thread is attached to the right wrist of the neophyte. A barber then cuts the nails of his fingers and toes and shaves his head, to the sound of instrumental music and the songs of the women.

The young Brahmin next proceeds to bathe, in order to purify himself after having been defiled by the barber's touch. After his ablutions the women again dress him in pure new cloths.

He is then purified by the *purohita's* incantations from all the sins committed through youthful ignorance since the day of his birth. The *purohita* also makes him a girdle of plaited *darbha*, or sacred grass (*Poa cynosuroides*), and winds it three times round his body, reciting *mantrams* all the time. At this juncture some small coins are distributed to all the Brahmins present. A *muduga*[1] stick, three cubits long, is then produced, and also ten pieces of rag such as are used by men in the East to cover their private parts[2]. These are dyed yellow in saffron water, and are hung in a row on the *muduga* stick, which the candidate puts over his shoulders. The *purohita* then recites the 'neck *mantram*' and invests the youth with the triple cord, which constitutes him a Brahmin. During this solemn performance the women sing, the musicians play, bells are rung, and to add to the uproar all present make as much noise as they can by striking gongs or anything else they can lay their hands on.

After his investiture the newly initiated member takes part in what is known as the *young men's feast*[3], which is prepared for

[1] *Butea frondosa*. In Sanskrit *palasa*. - Ed.

[2] Many natives only wear this diminutive covering. It is as small as is compatible with any regard to modesty.—Dubois.

[3] In Sanskrit *kumara bhojanam*. Only *Brahmacharis* partake of this feast, each being presented also with a new cloth.—Ed.

him and for other young Brahmins who have recently been invested with the cord.

At the termination of the repast the young man again seats himself on the raised platform of earth, facing the east. His father seats himself by his side, but with his face turned towards the west. A cloth is then thrown over them, hiding them from the eyes of the assembly. Again the women begin to sing, and the musicians to play. Meanwhile the father is whispering in his son's ear the secrets and *mantrams* which in his new position as a duly initiated Brahmin it is fitting for him to know. It is said that the following remarkable words form part of the discourse:—

'Remember, O my son, that there is only one God, who is the Creator, Lord, and Source of all things; whom every Brahmin should worship in secret. But know also that this is a great mystery that must never be revealed to the vulgar and ignorant people. Should you ever reveal it, surely great misfortune will fall upon you.'

These instructions, however, being given in Sanskrit, are not likely to be understood by the youth in whose ears they are uttered.

The Brahmins present then place *akshatas*, consecrated by *mantrams*, on the head of their new colleague, and the women perform the ceremony of *aratti*. Betel is afterwards served out to the guests, who, after bathing, return for the feast, which should on this day be on a particularly splendid and liberal scale.

The same evening, just when the lamps are being lighted, parents and friends again assemble under the *pandal*, and the newly initiated member seats himself on the earthen daïs once more. The married women then go and fetch the pan containing the sacred fire, which is solemnly placed beside him, much singing going on the while. The *purohita* performs the *samkalpa* and recites *mantrams* over this fire, while singers and musicians start afresh with renewed vigour. The young Brahmin, standing over the coals, offers for the first time in his life the sacrifice called *homam*, which, by his investiture with the cord, he has now acquired the right to do. After this sacrifice, and another, which the youth performs specially to the fire, the women make a procession and carry back the pan of coals to its place, returning to perform *aratti* to the young Brahmin. The day terminates with a further distribution of betel to the Brahmins, after which they all separate.

On the third day there is the same assembly again, and for the most part a repetition of the ceremonies of the preceding day, particularly that of the *homam*; while the day's proceedings are terminated as before by a feast.

The ceremonial of the fourth and last day has a few additional peculiarities. After a repetition of the usual preliminaries, the women of the party form a procession and, singing all the time, go and fetch the sacred fire, which they set down close to the newly initiated member, who, standing up, places a few stalks of *darbha* grass round the pan of hot embers. He then performs *homam* by throwing on to the brazier some twigs of the sacred fig-tree, some cooked rice, some liquefied butter, and some coarse sugar.

Thence they go to the tutelary deity, and having offered *puja* to him, they invite him to depart as he came. At the same time a little of the sacramental water from the deified vessel is poured into the hand of each person present, who forthwith drinks it, the remainder being thrown away. The deity is also despoiled of his yellow cloth and of the saffron thread with which he was decorated. After a few prayers have been addressed to these different objects, the divine essence is supposed to escape from them.

The saffron-coloured thread which was fastened round the wrist of the new member is now taken off and put to soak in some milk.

One large new earthen vessel and five smaller ones, all with lids, are then brought, smeared on the outside with lime. The five smaller vessels are filled with water to begin with, and are then all emptied into the larger one. The lid of the larger vessel is put on, and it is then placed against the central pillar of the *pandal*, to which is suspended a wreath of flowers falling exactly over the mouth of the vessel. An offering is made to it of sandalwood, coloured rice, and flowers, and for *neiveddya*, or votive offering, cakes and cooked rice. All those present are then sprinkled with the ceremonial water contained in the vessel. Then they go on to the five little vessels before mentioned, which are filled with earth. *Puja* is offered to them, and they are then placed in a row, receiving severally the name of one of the following five divinities: Brahma, Vishnu, Varuna, Rudra, and Devendra. They are then carried separately, and placed at the foot of five of the pillars supporting the *pandal*. They are invoked in the names which have just been given them, *puja* is offered to them, and the divinities are finally invited to return whence they came. *Puja* is offered to the five little pots, and the celestial beings they have been representing are also invited to retire. Then comes the turn of all the gods in general, the planets, and the ancestors whose presence was invoked at the beginning of the feast. Litanies are recited in their honour, and they too are politely invited to depart. Then the praises of the *mantapam* deity, that is to say, of the *pandal* itself, are sung; and he also is dismissed. Then the women, singing all the time, perform the *aratti* to the new member; and every one being seated for the feast, the new Brahmin takes his place amongst the elders of the caste. After the meal is over he is presented to each of the principal guests in succession, and does *sashtanga*, or prostration, to them; they, on their part, congratulate him on his promotion, and wish him every good fortune. In conclusion, the master of the house distributes money amongst his guests, also pieces of cloth, the value of which is in proportion to the wealth of the giver. A cow is occasionally added to the other gifts.

Brahmins everywhere are unsurpassed in the art of flattery; and on these occasions they laud to the very skies those who have been prodigal in their gifts. Their liberality is exalted in all directions, and the most exaggerated eulogies are lavished on them. The recipients of all this ridiculous flattery are generally sufficiently idiotic to be gratified by it, and consider that it amply repays them for the enormous outlay which their childish vanity has caused them to incur.

Before separating, all the guests, both men and women, accompany the new Brahmin, who is seated in an open palanquin, richly ornamented, on a solemn procession through the streets. On their return, the women, in songs, tell him of all the prayers that they have offered for his future happiness, and they wind up the feast by the ceremony of *aratti*. As for the new Brahmin, he must be careful to perform the *homam*, evening and morning, for the next thirty days.

Such are the formalities which accompany the most important

and solemn event in a Brahmin's life. As we have remarked already, it is not by birth alone that a Brahmin is superior to other men. It is this regenerating ceremony which gives him a new existence and makes him worthy to be elevated in his capacity as a *dvija*, or twice-born (*bis genitus*), to the sublime status of his ancestors.

All this long ceremonial, besides many other foolish trifles which I have not thought worth mentioning, is strictly obligatory. Were a single detail omitted, the whole community would raise a chorus of protest. It would be labour lost to endeavour to discover the origin of these ceremonies. Some few traces of it might be discovered in the old pagan times; but assuredly no other nation in the world has preserved so completely the minutest details of its ancient superstitions.

Some other Hindus share with the Brahmins the honour of wearing the triple cord. They are the Jains, the Kshatriyas or Rajahs, the Vaisyas, and even the Panchalas. Rajahs receive the cord from the hands of a Brahmin *purohita;* but the only ceremony necessary on this occasion is the sacrifice called *homam*. The new member then gives a great feast to the Brahmins to celebrate the event, but he is not allowed to be present himself; and further, he also distributes gifts amongst them. Before they depart he is admitted to their presence, and performs the *sashtanga*, perhaps in token of gratitude for the honour they have done him, or else merely to abase himself before these 'gods of the earth.'

If the Hindu books are to be believed, the Brahmins used formerly to exercise such supreme power over the kings and rulers of the country that they were looked upon by the latter as beings of a different order, and superior to other mortals; princes accounting it an honour to receive some mark of distinction from them. And the Brahmins, on their part, either to enhance their own dignity, or perhaps from gratitude for the favours they received from the Rajahs, granted them the special privilege of wearing, like themselves, the triple cord.

As for the Vaisyas, they do not receive it till the day of their marriage, when the officiating Brahmin presents it to them. The Panchalas are also decorated under similar circumstances, but it is conferred on them by the *guru*, or priest, of their own caste.

After a Brahmin has been invested, he is expected to keep the anniversary every year at the time of the full moon in the month of *Sravana*, or August. This anniversary is always celebrated by a feast, for which there are many prescribed ceremonies; but I will spare the reader any further wearisome details. Suffice it to say that the Brahmin has to change his cord, the small rag in front of his private parts, and the cloth with which his loins are girt, all of which is done with much solemnity. The performance of this periodical duty obtains for him the remission of all the sins committed during the year, and it is therefore called the Feast of the Annual Atonement.

The Kshatriyas and the Vaisyas also keep this annual feast like the Brahmins.

CHAPTER II

Conduct of the *Brahmachari*.—Rules to be followed.—Rights acquired by investiture with the Cord.—The Six Privileges of Brahmins.—The Vedas.

THE state of *Brahmachari* continues from the ceremony of the *upanayana* until marriage. This period of his life is looked upon as a time of study, of trial, of subordination, and of initiation into the rules and regulations of caste. To learn to read and write; to commit the Vedas and *mantrams* to memory; to study in those branches of knowledge for which he shows any aptitude, that is, if his parents are sufficiently wealthy to be able to give him masters; above all things, to learn arithmetic in its elementary forms, and to study the various idioms of the language: these are the occupations that fill up his days. The Brahmins have their separate schools, to which children of other castes, particularly Sudras, are never admitted. The nature of their studies, the discipline and mode of teaching, the very principles of education, are all totally different in the one and in the other. The *Brahmachari* must never chew betel; he must never put flowers in his turban or in his hair, or ornament his forehead with the paste of sandalwood[1]; and he must never look in a looking-glass. Every day, morning and evening, he must perform the *homam*, or sacrifice of fire. He must take the greatest pains to conform to the rules and customs of his caste; he must show the most absolute and prompt obedience to his parents and his teachers; he must be modest, deferential and respectful to his superiors, and affable to his equals. His family and his masters take particular care to instruct him in the art of lying and dissimulation, cunning and deceit[2], qualities which are fully developed in all Brahmins,

[1] This is incorrect. The use of this paste on the forehead is obligatory, though the smearing of it on the body is forbidden until after marriage.—ED.

[2] There is no truth in such an assertion. These evil qualities are never deliberately inculcated.—ED.

and form the principal traits in their character. There are, besides, hundreds of minute details most essential in a Brahmin's education, comprising rules of good manners and decorous conduct, the art of speaking and conversing in well-chosen language, the appropriate demeanour to assume on different occasions, how to hold oneself and how to use one's eyes, the different degrees of *hauteur* or humility which should be shown under various circumstances and at different times and places according to the people who are present.

Nevertheless, in spite of the stress which is laid upon these petty precepts governing the conduct of young Brahmins, there are few who conform to them in all essentials. Even of the rules of conduct many are merely matters of form. Nothing is more common than to see their foreheads ornamented with sandalwood paste and their mouths full of betel[1].

If, from want of means or other causes, a young Brahmin is still unmarried at the age of eighteen or twenty, he ceases to be a *Brahmachari*, but at the same time he does not become a *Grahastha*. For all that, be his age and condition what they may, from the time that he receives the cord, he obtains the right to the six privileges which are inherent in this status. These privileges are: (1) to read the Vedas, (2) to have them read to him, (3) to perform the sacrifice of the *yagnam*, (4) to cause the *yagnam* to be performed, (5) to give, and also (6) to receive, presents and alms. Three of these privileges, (2), (4), and (5), are also shared by the Kshatriyas or Rajahs. As to the despised Sudras, they possess only one of them, namely, that which allows them to give alms or presents to those Brahmins who will condescend to accept them from their impure hands.

To the Brahmins alone belongs the right of reading the Vedas, and they are so jealous of this, or rather it is so much to their interest to prevent other castes obtaining any insight into their contents, that the Brahmins have inculcated the absurd theory, which is implicitly believed, that should anybody of any other caste be so highly imprudent as even to read the titlepage, his head would immediately split in two. The very few Brahmins who are able to read these sacred books in the

[1] The chewing of betel by *Brahmacharis* is, nevertheless, an uncommon occurrence.—ED.

original only do so in secret and in a whisper. Expulsion from caste, without the smallest hope of re-entering it, would be the lightest punishment for a Brahmin who exposed these books to the eyes of the profane.

These four marvellous books are held to be the work of Brahma himself, who wrote them with his own hand on pages of gold. Brahma, it is said, explained their meaning to four famous *Munis*, or penitents, to whom the books were entrusted, and to whom was confided the task of explaining them to the Brahmins. Sumantu, the first of these celebrated personages, was given the *Yajur-Veda;* Pailada, the *Rig-Veda;* Jaimini, the *Sama-Veda;* and Angirasa, the *Atharva-Veda*[1].

But let it not be imagined for one moment that these books contain matter of much interest. Their antiquity alone, real or pretended, is their sole recommendation. A lengthy exposition of Hindu polytheism as it existed originally, the most contemptible and ridiculous stories concerning the fanciful penances to which their hermits subjected themselves, the metamorphosis of Vishnu, the disgusting *lingam*, &c.; such are, according to the evidence which I have acquired, more or less an epitome of the contents of these books, of which the Brahmins make such a great mystery[2].

The fourth of these books, the *Atharva-Veda*, is the most baneful work of all in the hands of a people already given over to the grossest superstition. It is a sort of conjuring book, professing to teach the magic art of injuring by means of spells and enchantments. Bloody sacrifices are also ordained in it.

It is from these books that the Brahmins have unearthed the greater number of those *mantrams* which bring them in so much money, and cause them to be held in such high

[1] Mahidhara, on the *Vajasaneyi Sanhita* (Weber's ed. p. 1), says in regard to the division of the Vedas: 'Veda-vyasa, having regard to men of dull understanding, in kindness to them, divided into four parts the Veda which had been originally handed down by tradition from Brahma, and taught the four Vedas, called Rig, Yajush, Saman, and Atharvan, in order, to Paila, Vaisampayana, Jaimini, and Sumantu; and they again to their disciples. In this way, by tradition, the Veda of a thousand Sakhas was produced.'—ED.

[2] The Vedas and other sacred Hindu writings are now, of course, available to any student. The Abbé's sweeping assertion would not now be endorsed.—ED.

esteem. This, in fact, is what renders the Vedas so precious to the Brahmins.

Such Brahmins as devote themselves to the higher branches of knowledge learn the Vedas by heart; and though the greater number do not understand the real meaning of what they have learnt, still they are looked upon in some sort as doctors of theology, and are given the name of *Veidikas.* It is true, nevertheless, that those who devote themselves to the study of these books cannot hope to extract any instruction from them, for they are written in ancient Sanskrit, which has become almost wholly unintelligible: and such numberless mistakes have been introduced by copyists, either through carelessness or ignorance, that the most learned find themselves quite unable to interpret the original text. Out of twenty thousand Brahmins I do not believe that one could be found who even partially understood the real Vedas.

The original text must not, as is often done, be confounded with the more modern introductions and commentaries written by the penitent Vyasa. These were interpolated with the view of rendering the text more intelligible. They are known under the general name of *Upanishads,* and are three in number—the *Upa-Veda,* the *Karma-Veda,* and the *Sakha-Veda.* It is not much more than these commentaries that the most learned of modern Brahmins are capable of explaining. Their meaning is unintelligible except to those who have a considerable acquaintance with Sanskrit, the language in which they are written. Many learn to read and recite them mechanically, without understanding a word of them.

In the *agraharas,* or Brahmin villages, and other places where Brahmins congregate in large numbers, you may perhaps come across some who are Sanskrit scholars, but even they would be unable to produce a good interpretation of the Vedas. Some Brahmins give gratuitous instruction in those parts of the Vedas which, thanks to the commentaries, have been made intelligible, while other Brahmins, too poor to forgo remuneration, hold classes in which the same instruction is given to paying pupils.

Rich Brahmins make a point of encouraging the study of the Vedas by offering prizes and other rewards, this being in the eyes of their fellows a work of the greatest merit.

The Brahmins have done the Rajahs the honour of allowing them also to encourage the study of the Vedas by founding schools for that purpose and paying the professors. And I am convinced that nowadays they would not refuse a similar honour even to a common Sudra. But be that as it may, there is not much eagerness displayed amongst the Brahmins for this tedious kind of study. Poverty prevents some from taking it up, while indifference and idleness prevent others.

In the *yagnam*, a name which comprises the third and fourth Brahminical privileges, the sacrifice called *homam* is apparently included, for the *homam* of the Rajahs is totally different. Every Brahmin must perform the *homam* at least once a day. It is a sacrifice offered to fire under various circumstances[1].

This sacrifice is made by lighting a brazier, which is then consecrated by *mantrams*. Into this are thrown small pieces of wood, gathered from one of the seven sacred trees, and afterwards a little melted butter and cooked rice; these offerings being accompanied by suitable *mantrams*. The *homam* is almost invariably followed by another sacrifice, which is specially offered to fire, but only the ordinary *puja* is performed. I think by the word *yagnam* may be understood all sacrifices which are accompanied by *mantrams*.

The fifth privilege of the Brahmins, namely, the giving of alms and presents, is much less to their taste than the sixth, in which the operation is reversed. It must, however, be admitted that rich Brahmins display a lavish hospitality, besides being charitable in other ways. But this is only to members of their own caste; the rest of the human race is, if not detested, at least absolutely of no account so far as they are concerned.

Amongst the gifts which Brahmins are willing to receive there are some which are more specially acceptable. They are called the *pancha-danas*, or the five gifts; and they are gold, land, clothes, grain, and cows. The last-mentioned gift causes them particular pleasure, seeing that milk in various forms is their principal food. Brahmins also possess large landed properties

[1] The sacrifice made to fire, or by means of fire, is a form of idolatry by no means peculiar to the Hindus. It is well known to what great lengths Persians, Chaldeans, and other ancient races carried superstition with respect to it.—DUBOIS.

originally given them by generous princes and on which they pay no taxes. These descend from father to son, and always retain their immunity from taxation. As a rule Brahmins do not cultivate their lands themselves, but lease them out to the Sudras, taking half the crops as rent.

The Brahmins generally live on their lands, which are called *agraharas*. Numbers of these estates are to be found in the various provinces of the Peninsula.

Then again, in their character as high priests, the Brahmins gather in the greater part of the revenue of the lands belonging to the different temples, and furthermore receive all the offerings brought by devotees to the various idols.

A Brahmin sees nothing humiliating in asking for or receiving alms. According to his ideas it is a right, of which he may make free use. His attitude when begging is also very unlike that of the poor wretch amongst ourselves, who fawns and grovels for the smallest trifle. The Brahmin asks for alms as for something that is his due, and not as if imploring a favour or benefit. At the same time he displays none of the importunity or impertinence to which people are subjected by the Mahomedan *fakirs*, or by the Sudra beggars who belong to the sects of Siva or Vishnu. The begging Brahmin boldly enters a house and states what he wants. Should he receive anything, he takes it without saying a word, goes away without any acknowledgement and without showing the smallest sign of gratitude. Should he meet with a refusal, however, he retires without any complaint or grumbling[1].

But woe betide any one who ventures to make the Brahmins promises which he subsequently fails to perform! That would

[1] Manu says: 'Let every man, according to his ability, give wealth to Brahmins, detached from the world and learned in Scripture; such a giver shall attain heaven after this life' (xi. 6). Very early in the statutes, a universal law is proclaimed, the spirit of which pervades the whole code. This law calmly lays down that whatever exists in the universe is all, in effect, though not in form, the wealth of the Brahmins; since the Brahmin is entitled to it all by his primogeniture and eminence of birth. 'The Brahmin eats but his own food; wears but his own apparel; and bestows but his own alms; through the benevolence of the Brahmin indeed other mortals enjoy life' (i. 100–101). This is a pretty broad principle to enunciate, so it is easy to see how there is nothing derogatory in a Brahmin receiving alms, since he takes but what is his own, besides leaving a blessing to the giver.—PADFIELD.

be a fearful sin, which could not fail to draw down the divine wrath upon the guilty person. A Hindu author gives the following example as a proof. 'Hata! Hata![1]' cried a monkey one day, seeing a fox devouring a rotten carcase. 'In a former state of existence you must have committed some atrocious crimes to be condemned in your present life to eat such disgusting food.' 'Alas!' replied the fox with a groan, 'it is only what I deserve. Once upon a time I was a man, and I then promised a Brahmin a present, and failed to keep my word; that is why I was born again in my present condition, which you find so revolting.'

Brahmins declare that he who fails to keep faith with them, or who injures them in any way, will be condemned after death to be born again as a devil. Such a person could live neither on the earth nor yet in the air, but would be reduced to dwelling in a thick forest, for ever hidden amongst the foliage of a leafy tree. Day and night he would groan and bewail his unhappy fate. His only food would be the filthy juice of the palm tree, mixed with the saliva of dogs; and he would have to use a human skull as a cup[2].

Brahmins, as a rule, are exempt from all taxes on houses and other personal property. In many districts they pay no customs duty[3]. They are, again, not liable to be impressed into compulsory service, or called upon for those requisitions which fall so heavily on the other inhabitants, who are obliged to labour at public works, such as the making and mending of the high-roads, the repairing of temples, tanks, canals, &c., and who also have to carry provisions for the troops when on the march, or for magistrates and other public servants, more often than not without any payment for their labour, or even sufficient food, and with no compensation for the losses which these requisitions cause them. Such general servants of the public as carpenters, blacksmiths, barbers, and washermen are often obliged, at least in many districts, to work gratuitously for the Brahmins[4].

[1] A kind of exclamation.—DUBOIS.

[2] Here and elsewhere the Abbé applies to Brahmins generally defects which are mostly noticeable in Brahmin priests.—ED.

[3] This, of course, is no longer the case under British rule.—ED.

[4] This, however, is not due to any actual pressure, but to the fact that these public servants enjoy grants of land (*maniams*), and they work gratuitously for the whole village.—ED.

In countries governed by native princes Brahmins are rarely condemned to any serious corporal punishment; and however heinous their crimes may be, they are never liable to the penalty of death. The murder of a Brahmin, no matter for what reason, would be considered absolutely unpardonable, for it is the greatest of all known crimes and would not fail to bring some terrible calamity to the whole country in which it had been committed.

However, in those countries which are under European or Mahomedan rule, where the sacred character of the Brahmin is held in much less reverence, they are liable like any other native to punishments proportioned to their misdemeanours. Sometimes the Mahomedans beat them to death, unless they pay considerable sums to buy themselves off, a process which suits their persecutors, who are much better pleased to have their money than their blood. But sometimes either from avarice, or because they are afraid that if they once let their oppressors fleece them in this manner they will never be rid of such persecutions until they are despoiled of all that they possess, they prefer to suffer all kinds of torture, even death itself, rather than part with their money. When Brahmins find themselves in this sorry plight there are no lies, no false statements, oaths, and protestations that they will not employ in the hope of extricating themselves. Such conduct can excite no surprise when one remembers that they do not hesitate to teach publicly that lies and perjury, if used to gain personal advantage, are virtuous and meritorious. This convenient doctrine has spread marvellously, for there is not a native of India who would scruple to make use of both, to serve his own ends[1].

[1] No respectable persons (Brahmins included) are known to preach such doctrines nowadays. And the Abbé's assertions are altogether too sweeping.—Ed.

CHAPTER III

External Defilements.—The care that a Brahmin should take to avoid them.—His Conduct in this respect.—Means of Purification.

All that pertains to external and internal defilement, bodily and spiritual, is the very beginning and foundation of a Hindu's education, both religious and civil. They have invented numberless minute and ridiculous precautions to prevent the possibility of coming in contact with anything which, according to their views, would defile their persons, their clothes, their furniture, their temples, &c., &c. It is principally this ineradicable prejudice which has raised such an insurmountable barrier between them and the rest of mankind. Obliged by their religious tenets to hold themselves aloof from every one who does not share their beliefs, they can never, under any circumstances, be on such friendly or confidential terms with any stranger as would arise from feelings of mutual esteem and respect. It is undoubtedly from the Brahmins that the other Hindus have picked up this absurd prejudice, for it is in strongest force amongst them (the Brahmins). The predominating idea in their general conduct, and in their every action in life, is what they call cleanness; and it is the enormous amount of care that they take to keep themselves 'clean,' to prevent any sort or kind of defilement, and to purify themselves from any uncleanness that they may have contracted, which gives them their ascendency over other castes. It is one of the special duties of the *Brahmachari* to be well versed, at an early age, in the customs and practices regulating this important branch of Hindu law.

In all countries the sight of a human corpse produces a thrill of horror. Every one has a strong aversion, amounting almost to repugnance, to touching a dead body. But Hindus consider that the mere fact of assisting at a funeral is sufficient to defile them. When the ceremony is over, they immediately hasten to plunge themselves into water, and no one would dare to return home without having thus purified himself. Even the news of the death of a relative, though it may have happened a hundred miles away, produces the same effect, and every member of the family who receives the news must purify himself. Friends and simple acquaintances, however, are not contaminated thereby.

The moment a Hindu has breathed his last the necessary preparations for his funeral begin, for as long as the body remains in the house, neither the inmates, nor even their neighbours, can eat or drink or attend to their usual occupations. I have seen the service in a temple, where a large congregation had assembled, entirely suspended until the body of a man who had died not far off had been removed. Neither incense nor any other perfume would purify a house where a death had taken place. A Brahmin *purohita* must come to remove the impurity with which all the inmates are contaminated. To this end he offers sacrifices, recites *mantrams* suitable to the occasion, and at frequent intervals makes copious libations of holy water [1].

The monthly period, and the after-effects of child-birth, as I have remarked before, render women for the time being unclean [2].

The mother of the newly-born child lives entirely apart for a whole month or more, during which time she may touch neither the vessels nor the furniture of the house, nor any clothes, and still less any person whatsoever. The time of her seclusion being over, she is immersed in a bath, or else a great quantity of water is poured over her head and body. Women

[1] According to the law of Moses, when an Israelite died in a house or in a tent, all the people living therein, and all the furniture it contained, were unclean for seven days (Numbers xix. 14, 15). Any one who touched the body, the bones, or the tomb of a dead man was also unclean for seven days. For purification, the ashes of a red heifer, which had been offered up as a sacrifice by the high priest on the Day of Atonement, were cast into a vessel full of pure water (Numbers xix. 3-6). And an undefiled person, free from all impurity, dipped a bunch of hyssop into this water, and besprinkled the furniture, the room, and the people who were defiled. On the seventh day these latter bathed themselves in water, and washed their clothes, after which they were considered perfectly cleansed.—DUBOIS.

[2] Jewish women were considered unclean under similar circumstances; and the law of Moses gives clear directions as to the manner in which they were to purify themselves.—DUBOIS.

are similarly isolated during the time of their periodical uncleanness. In all decent houses there is a sort of small gynaeceum set apart for them; but amongst the poor, in whose huts there is no such accommodation, the women are turned into the street, under a sort of shed or outhouse, or else they are allowed a corner of the cowshed.

When the time of uncleanness is passed, all the garments that the woman has worn are given to the washerman. Her clothes are not allowed inside the house; in fact, no one would even dare to look on them[1].

When the washerman brings the clothes back, the Brahmins never fail to put them into water again, inasmuch as the washerman, by the touch of his hand, has defiled them anew. The same thing happens with new cloths which come straight from the unclean hands of a Sudra weaver.

Wives of Lingayats, however, content themselves with rubbing their foreheads with the ashes of cow-dung to purify themselves on similar occasions; and by this simple act, which they call *bhasma snana*, or the bath of ashes, they consider that they are completely purified. In this way a precautionary measure most beneficial to health in this hot country becomes perverted by superstition. On the one hand it is minutely observed by those who do not in the least appreciate its real utility, while it is neglected by others who think it only a pious practice, to be replaced with equal advantage by another.

Earthen vessels, by reason of the material of which they are composed, can never be purified when once they become unclean, and in this they differ from metal ones. Washing will purify the latter, but should the former become defiled, they must be destroyed[2].

As long as earthen vessels are new, and in the hands of the potter, any one, even a Pariah, may handle them with impunity; but from the moment that they have contained water, they can only be used by the person who filled them, or by members of the same caste. Brahmins carry their scruples on this point

[1] The Jews shared the same views on this subject. Isaiah lxiv. 6. Esther xiv. 16.—DUBOIS.

[2] Beds, furniture, clothes, and vessels became, under the Jewish law, unclean by contact with anything that was impure, and often were the means of contaminating other objects (Leviticus xi. 32).—DUBOIS.

so far as never to allow strangers to enter their kitchens, the doors of which are always kept carefully shut, lest some profane and unclean person should cast an eye on the earthenware inside, which, rendered unclean by that one look, would be only fit to be immediately broken to pieces[1]. It is to avoid the risk of a similar disaster that their women never draw water in earthenware vessels, but always use those made of brass and copper.

It is just the same with their clothes as with their vessels. Some can be defiled, others cannot. Silk, for instance, remains always pure, also cloth made of the fibres of certain plants. For this reason the ancient Brahmin hermits always wore clothes made of either one or the other material. Brahmins at the present day, too, prefer to wear silk, particularly at meals. When a Brahmin doctor wishes to feel the pulse of a sick Sudra, he first wraps up the patient's wrist in a small piece of silk so that he may not be defiled by touching the man's skin[2]. The cotton clothes which are worn by most natives are peculiarly susceptible of defilement. It is quite sufficient to render them unclean if a person of an inferior caste, or, above all, a European or a Pariah, touch them. In the eyes of a Hindu, a Pariah and a European are on the same level. It is impossible to help laughing at the ridiculous care and perpetual pains which an orthodox Brahmin will take to preserve his person and his clothes from contact with anything unclean. But, whatever they may do, it is impossible for them to escape contamination in a populous town. Hence the more scrupulous are obliged to quit the towns and take up their abode in the villages. Others, however, from motives of self-interest, compound with their conscience, and disregard the rules. Exposed as they must be to continual contact with people of all sorts, in the busy haunts where their business takes them, they content themselves with changing their garments on their return home. These are immediately dipped into water, and the uncleanness is removed.

Leather and skins of all kinds, except those of the tiger and

[1] Brahmins and rich Sudras are gradually abandoning the use of earthenware vessels for cooking, and are using vessels of brass and bell-metal. These are even cleaned by Sudras nowadays.—ED.

[2] And so, too, when a Sudra doctor feels the pulse of a Brahmin patient. —ED.

the antelope, are considered particularly unclean. Caste Hindus must never touch with their hands the slippers or sandals that are worn on the feet. A person riding must always carefully cover with cloth any part of the harness or saddlery that is made of leather. So it is that caste Hindus do not understand how any one can possibly wear anything made, as they say, of the remains of dead animals, such as boots, gloves, or leather breeches, without a feeling of horror and repugnance. The ordinary costume of a European greatly contributes to increase the low opinion that Hindus have formed of the delicacy of our tastes. A scrupulous Brahmin must look very carefully where he puts his feet when walking. He would be defiled and obliged to bathe if by accident his feet should touch a bone, a piece of broken glass or earthenware, a rag, a leaf from which any one had eaten, a bit of skin or leather, hair, or any other unclean thing. The place where he sits must also be chosen with great care. Some penitents always carry with them the 'pure' skin of a tiger or antelope on which to sit; others use a common mat, while the rich have carpets; but any one may sit on the ground without fear of defilement, if the place has been recently rubbed over with cow-dung.

The way in which they take their food is also a matter of some moment. However many guests there may be, it would be considered very rude to speak to any one. They eat in silence, and conversation only begins at the end of the meal, after they have washed their hands and mouths[1]. Nothing must be touched with the left hand, for reasons to be given later on, unless it be the copper vessel which contains water. Hindus drink only once, that is when they have finished eating, and they do so by pouring the liquid into their mouths from a distance. To drink as we do, by putting the glass or cup to the lips, would in their eyes be the height of indecency. While eating great care must be taken that not a fragment falls into the leaf serving as a neighbour's plate. One single grain of rice, one crumb even, would effectually prevent the latter from continuing his meal; or at any rate he would have to take a fresh leaf and another portion of food.

[1] This is not now the case; conversation does go on during meals. Occasionally, however, an individual makes a resolve always to abstain from talking while at meals.—ED.

No doubt the same cause which makes Hindus of the higher castes so extremely particular about their manner of eating and drinking, accounts for their strong aversion to wind instruments of music. This cause is their insurmountable horror of saliva. They would look on a man who spat upon the floor as quite destitute of good manners. Spittoons are to be found in every house; but should none be provided and any one require to spit he would have to go outside[1]. However, from a sanitary point of view there is nothing astonishing in this excessive scrupulosity. No properly brought-up European would dream of expectorating on the floor of a room. But with a Hindu it is less from a due regard to cleanliness than from his ever-recurring fear of bodily defilement.

The remains of food are never put aside and kept after a meal, nor are they given to the servants. As has been already stated, to be a servant is no degradation. A servant generally eats with his master, and what he left could not be offered to the poor, unless they were Pariahs, who take anything. Food remnants, in fact, are thrown to the crows and the dogs. Rice that is to be given away to the poor of the same caste, or any other persons with whom it is allowable to eat, is boiled separately. Rice given to other castes is always uncooked; and it is thus that a Brahmin receives it from persons of an inferior caste, who make him a present.

High-caste Hindus, and particularly Brahmins, rarely use plates and dishes at their meals. Sometimes, but only when quite alone in their own houses, they may use a service of copper or other metal; but they are forbidden to use earthenware or china. Usually the rice and other dishes are served on a banana leaf, or on the leaves of some tree neatly sewn together in the form of a plate. To offer a Brahmin food on a metal plate which some one had already used, would be considered a deadly insult. Naturally the use of spoons and forks is also forbidden. Fingers are used instead, and Hindus cannot at all understand how we can use these implements a second time, after having once put them to our mouths, and allowed them to be touched with saliva. If Hindus should happen to eat dry food or fruits between meals, they break off pieces and

[1] Spittoons are not often found in Brahmin houses.—ED.

throw them into their mouths, fearing if they put them into their mouths with their fingers the latter might be tainted with saliva[1]. A European once wrote a letter to some friend of his, recommending a Brahmin acquaintance of mine to his notice. When he had finished his letter he sealed it with a wafer, which he moistened by placing it on the tip of his tongue. The Brahmin, who saw him do it, would not take or touch the letter, and left in anger, considering he had been grievously insulted. He preferred to lose any advantage he might have gained from this letter of recommendation, rather than be the bearer of a missive that had been thus defiled.

There are several kinds of animals, especially dogs[2], to touch which would defile a Brahmin. It is very interesting to watch their movements, and the care they will take to avoid the familiar caresses of these faithful companions of man. If, in spite of their efforts, the dog really does touch them, they are obliged to hurry off immediately and plunge, with all their clothes on, into water, and thus remove from both their person and their garments the stain which they had involuntarily acquired by the touch of one of these unclean animals.

There is an infinity of other kinds of exterior defilement to which Brahmins are exposed, but I think what has been already said is sufficient to make known their views on the subject.

It is obvious that so many external defilements necessitate endless ablutions. There are certain rivers and tanks which are held to possess peculiarly cleansing properties, and those Brahmins who live near them are perpetually bathing in their waters, while those who from living at a greater distance are deprived of this advantage, have to content themselves with whatever water or tank is nearest to their dwelling-place. In many places they do not allow Sudras to approach the place where they bathe, either for the purpose of drawing water or to

[1] This practice, like others, becomes mechanical. Hindus never give a thought to them.—ED.

[2] Amongst the many animals looked upon as unclean by Jews, the dog was particularly numbered. But it was only by eating the flesh, or touching the dead carcase of one, that they were defiled. The touch of a living dog did not matter. Furthermore, every commentator of the Holy Scriptures has agreed that these defilements were only figurative of other and far more important uncleannesses, namely, the sins and offences which we commit against God and our neighbour.—DUBOIS.

make their own ablutions. But they are obliged to be less exclusive in places where they are not supreme.

A Brahmin rarely passes a day without bathing at least once[1], while those who wish to call public attention to their minute observance of religious customs must bathe three times a day.

It is a common practice amongst natives to anoint themselves occasionally from head to foot with either oil of sesamum or sometimes castor oil. They remove the dirt which results from it by rubbing it off with certain herbs. They then have hot water poured over their bodies, and finally bathe in cold water. At their grand ceremonials Brahmins are in the habit of offering some such oily mixture to all their guests, who rub themselves over from head to foot with it, and then plunge into a bath. Dead bodies are similarly anointed before being conveyed to the funeral pile or burying ground; and this office is always performed by the nearest relatives.

[1] One bath every day is compulsory, and is invariably taken.—Ed.

CHAPTER IV

Internal Defilements.—Abstinence from all Intoxicating Liquors, and from everything that has had Life.—Particular Horror of the Brahmins for the Flesh of the Cow.—Their abhorrence of Europeans who eat it as Food.

BESIDES those external defilements which only affect the outer skin, there are others which Brahmins and other Hindus say insinuate themselves into the body, and which can only be got rid of by proper methods ordained by rule and custom. There is no doubt that it was for the sake of health and cleanliness, in the first instance, that Hindu lawgivers inculcated these principles of defilement and purification. The heat of the Indian climate, the profuse perspiration which is the natural result, and the diseases which are endemic in consequence of it, all help to impoverish the blood of the inhabitants; and from these causes doubtless originated those obligatory precautions which have since been strengthened by custom and superstition, and which are considered to be best calculated to counteract these deadly influences. If the salutary rules at first prescribed have in the course of ages become perverted into the present childish and puerile ceremonial, which common sense rejects, the fault must be attributed partly to popular superstition which exaggerates and distorts everything, partly to popular ignorance, and partly to the cunning and avarice of the hypocritical charlatans who mislead the people.

Water may be said to be a Brahmin's sole beverage. In order that it may be pure and may not defile the person who drinks it, it is indispensable that it should be drawn and carried by a member of his own caste; to drink water drawn by strange hands would be a great sin, the remission of which could only be obtained at the cost of elaborate and expensive ceremonies. In some places Brahmins and Sudras fetch their water from the same place, but if by chance the water-pot of the latter should touch that of the former, the Brahmin immediately breaks his, if it is made of earthenware, or, if of brass or copper, gives it a thorough scouring with sand and water. In those parts of the country which are under the rule of native princes, Brahmins forbid any one of another caste to approach their wells; but where Mahomedans are in power, and more particularly in the large towns under European rule, it is not unusual to see Brahmins, Sudras, and even Pariahs, all drawing water from the same source. But all the same, I once witnessed on the coast a violent disturbance caused by the inconceivable effrontery of a Pariah woman who had dared to draw water from the common well.

Curdled milk diluted with water is a very favourite drink with Hindus. It is usually Sudras who prepare and sell this refreshing beverage. Although, generally speaking, there is more water than milk in the mixture, Brahmins have no scruples in partaking of it, and if any one reproaches them with thus using water drawn and handled by Sudras, they reply that the curdled milk, which has come from the body of a cow, cleanses it from all impurities.

On the other hand, they have an invincible repugnance to the liquor which is obtained by tapping cocoanut and other palms and several other trees of the country. This juice is sweet and refreshing if drunk before it has begun to ferment, but if taken in excess it is intoxicating. A spirit called arrack is distilled from it, and for this also there is the same repugnance. As a rule, a respectable Hindu will not touch spirits or any intoxicating drink, considering that they cause one of the greatest internal defilements that it is possible to contract. In consequence of this praiseworthy opinion drunkenness is looked upon as a degrading and infamous vice, and any one would be promptly and ignominiously expelled from his caste were he found guilty of giving way to it. It is only Pariahs and men of the lowest classes who dare publicly to consume intoxicating drinks. Nevertheless, one does see occasionally in European settlements and in the large towns high-caste natives, and even Brahmins, breaking the law of temperance; but it is only in strict privacy, and after every precaution has been taken to conceal the unpardonable weakness.

The air one breathes may also be the means of internal defilement; for instance, it would mean defilement if the olfactory nerves of a Brahmin became sensible of the smoke arising from a funeral pyre where a body was being burned, or from the fire on a Pariah's hearth where food was being cooked.

In certain parts of the country, if Pariahs perceive that a Brahmin is coming their way, they make a long *détour*, in fear lest the effluvia which is given off by their unclean persons should defile the exterior and interior of this noble personage. When Sudras speak to a Brahmin etiquette obliges them to keep at a respectful distance, or at least that they should put the right hand before their mouths, so that the taint of their poisonous breath may not reach him. It were very desirable, for the peace and honour of Sudra husbands, that this excessive delicacy extended also to their wives; but Brahmins are far from feeling the same superb disdain towards them. As for the wives of Pariahs, the feeling of antipathy for everything connected with this class is so strong, and the defilement which results from even an innocent and accidental touch is so difficult to remove, that one very rarely hears of a Brahmin who has been so blinded by passion as to have had any intercourse with a woman of this class.

It is with regard to their food that Brahmins take the most excessive precautions. They are never allowed to touch meat, and this excludes not only anything that has had life, fish included, but also anything that has contained a germ of life, such as eggs of all sorts. Vegetables, which form their principal food, are also subject to numerous exceptions. Thus they reject any vegetable whose root or stem grows in the shape of a head, such as onions, garlic, mushrooms, &c. Is it because they have discovered some hurtful properties in these plants? I think not. The greater number of such vegetables are, on the contrary, considered by other people to possess, in that very hot climate, antiseptic and health-giving qualities.

I have often tried to find out the reason why these vegetables are avoided, but I have never been able to extract any other answer from those I have questioned than that it was the custom and rule to avoid them [1].

To adhere strictly to all these rules of abstinence is what

[1] Whatever the motive may be, there are no doubt some superstitions attached to it. Every one knows the extreme veneration in which the Egyp-

is called eating properly. Whoever eats of forbidden things cannot, according to Brahminical doctrine, keep his body really pure. However, I am quite satisfied by experience that there are some who occasionally relax the severity of these rules; but the extreme care which is taken to conceal the fact proves what a strong hold the rules have over the greater number.

These strict rules of abstinence are observed by all the respectable people of this large Hindu nation; they are most scrupulously obeyed in the family circle, without any one daring to think of violating them, even under the most pressing necessity. They appear to have existed from the time when the natives of India were formed into one nation; that is to say, at no very distant date from the Flood, and it seems to me they show a strong indication of the great antiquity of this people.

And this law of abstinence, far from losing force and falling into abeyance, has gained many additional adherents from among the better class of Sudras. Its minute observance is the surest way of gaining respect even amongst those who do not feel called upon to impose similar privations upon themselves. Only Sudras of the very lowest class eat meat openly; and many of these do not venture to cook it in their own houses, but in a secluded corner of their cowsheds. To ask a Hindu if he eats meat, even when it is a well-known fact that he does so, is to insult him deeply; while to offer meat at a meal to a guest with whom one is not intimate, would be the height of rudeness. Hindus who eat meat do so only in the privacy of their own families or in company with near relatives or intimate friends. Even the common Sudras do not offer meat at their festive gatherings such as wedding feasts. Were they to do so their guests would consider themselves insulted, and would leave immediately.

The Lingayats, or votaries of Siva, are strict abstainers from anything that has possessed the principle of life. But the careful manner in which they thereby try to maintain perfect internal purity does not profit them much, as they are credited

tians held onions and other vegetables of the same family. They even swore by the leeks and onions in their gardens. Juvenal (*Satires*, xv) laughs at them about it:

'Porrum et cepe nefas violare, et frangere morsu,
O sanctas gentes quibus haec nascuntur in hortis
Numina!'—DUBOIS.

at the same time with neglecting some of the precautions necessary to preserve their external purity. They are blamed, for instance, for allowing their women to come and go about the house during the time of their periodical uncleanness, and for not insisting on purifying ablutions afterwards; the same also during and after confinements. In fact, they neglect a great many cleanly customs which, putting superstition aside, are most beneficial to health in hot climates.

People who abstain entirely from animal food acquire such an acute sense of smell that they can perceive in a moment from a person's breath, or from the exudation of the skin, whether that person has eaten meat or not; and that even after a lapse of twenty-four hours.

In some parts there is a peculiar custom which allows men to eat meat, but strictly forbids it to women.

To eat the flesh of the cow is an ineffaceable defilement. The bare idea of tasting it would be abhorrent to any devout Hindu. This invincible repugnance, based as it is now solely on the superstition which places the cow among the principal Hindu deities, had most probably at first a much more sensible but not less forcible motive, namely self-interest. The Hindu lawgivers recognized, of course, that these animals, so useful to man in all places and under all circumstances, were particularly valuable in a country where there is no other beast available for tilling or for transporting agricultural and commercial products. Besides which, the milk was an indispensable addition to the food of the multitude of poor natives who would otherwise have no other food than insipid vegetables.

Perhaps we may also add another motive besides that of preserving the species of these valuable animals, and that is the indigestible nature of beef. Indeed, in a climate where the organs of the stomach are so much weakened by excessive perspiration, the habitual use of heavy food would have soon destroyed the health of the people. I have known many Europeans who entirely left off eating meat for this reason, because they found that they could not eat it without suffering afterwards from indigestion [1].

[1] Montesquieu says: 'There are many local laws peculiar to different religious beliefs. The tenet of metempsychosis is peculiarly suited to the Indian climate. The excessive heat burns up all the pasture, and

At the same time the Hindu lawgivers knew the character of their compatriots too well to imagine that simple prohibitions and punishments would suffice to save the lives of these precious animals. So, calling religion to their aid, they deified them. To kill a cow—according to the principles of Hindu law—is not only a crime, but an awful sacrilege, a deicide, which can only be expiated by the death of the offender; while to eat of the flesh of a cow is a defilement which cannot be purified. Pariahs, however, are tacitly allowed to feast on the flesh of those animals which die of old age or disease. In their case this is not looked upon exactly as a crime; but, as we have already seen, this privilege, of which these miserable outcasts avail themselves without scruple, contributes a good deal towards keeping up that sort of curse which overshadows them.

The flesh of the buffalo, camel, horse, elephant, &c., in fact everything that comes under the head of large meat, inspires all Hindus, Pariahs excepted, with almost as great an abhorrence as the flesh of the cow or ox. There is the same idea of defilement connected with it.

I have already pointed out that Europeans do not seem disposed to adopt the same rules of abstinence as are followed by the people among whom they live, and that, without paying any attention to the disgust which they cause, they continue to eat beef openly. It is certain that this conduct estranges them from all the better classes of Hindus, who, consequently, in this respect place them far below the Pariahs. It is true that the first

there is little left with which to feed the cattle. There is always a danger of there being too few beasts to till the ground. Cattle multiply but slowly in that country, and are subject to many diseases. Hence it is that a religious law which protects them is very necessary from an economical point of view. But while the pastures are all burnt up, rice and vegetables grow very well by the help of irrigation. Thus a religious law which only allows of this kind of food is useful to the people of the country. Furthermore, while meat is usually tasteless in hot climates, milk and butter, which are obtained from these animals, form the chief items of food. The law forbidding cows to be killed and eaten as food is therefore not without reason in India' (*Esprit des Lois*, book xxiv. ch. 24).—DUBOIS.

Sir M. Monier-Williams in his book on Hinduism says in a foot-note: 'Happily for the Hindus, the cow which supplies them with their only animal food—milk and butter—and the ox which helps to till their ground, were declared sacred at an early period. Had it not been so, this useful animal might have been exterminated in times of famine. What is now a superstition had its origin, like some other superstitions, in a wise forethought.'—ED.

conquerors of India, in defiance of the most sacred and long-established customs of the country, killed oxen and cows without exciting a general insurrection against such an insult as the slaughter of animals worshipped by Hindus as their gods; and it is also true that for several succeeding centuries the handful of foreigners established among them have been allowed to kill these sacred animals with impunity to satisfy their own appetites; but they have only to thank the mild, temperate, and indolent character of the nation which has spared them [1].

Amongst ancient nations there are few who would with so much patience have allowed their religious beliefs to be openly set at naught. The Israelites, when in captivity in Egypt, begged for permission from Pharaoh to make a pilgrimage into the desert, there to sacrifice to God without fear of interruption, because they would have been liable to be all massacred or stoned had they dared to perform such sacrifices in the sight of the idolatrous Egyptians, who worshipped as gods some of the very animals that they required for their sacrifices [2].

Cambyses made himself more execrable in the eyes of the Egyptians by killing the ox Apis, than by all the cruelties and acts of tyranny of which he was guilty in dealing with this peaceable people [3].

The Egyptians considered that to kill, even by accident, one of their sacred animals was the most heinous of crimes. Whoever was guilty of such an act was invariably put to death. A Roman soldier was torn in pieces by the populace, in spite of the terror that the name of Rome inspired, for having by

[1] This horror of cow-killing is as strong among Hindus throughout India to-day as it ever was. The remarkable revival of Hinduism during the last few years has been characterized by the formation of innumerable secret religious societies for the protection of the cow, and the riots among Hindus and Mahomedans in recent years are more or less directly traceable, it is asserted, to the propaganda of these societies. It may be mentioned that in Kashmir, until quite recently, cow-killing was punishable with death, and imprisonment for life is now the penalty.—ED.

[2] Exodus viii. 26.

[3] 'Did Cambyses do well,' asks Voltaire, 'when after conquering Egypt he killed the ox Apis with his own hand? Why not? He showed the idiots that their gods could be brought to the pit without nature rising in her wrath to avenge the sacrilege!' This is Voltaire's smart criticism, but I think few wise statesmen or sensible persons would share his opinion.—DUBOIS.

mischance killed a cat. Diodorus, who records this incident, also mentions that during a famine the Egyptians preferred to devour each other rather than touch the animals they held sacred.

The Hindus would also carry their scruples to the same point. In whatever straits they might be they would prefer to die rather than save their lives by killing cattle. From this we may conclude that, though they daily witness the slaughter of these sacred animals by Europeans, without uttering any loud complaint, they are far from being insensible to the insult. But restrained by the fear which these foreigners have always inspired in them, they content themselves with complaining in secret and storing up in their hearts all the indignation that they feel. Pious Lingayats have often come to me, imagining that my title of European priest gave me great influence over my fellow-countrymen, to implore me, in earnest terms, and often with tears in their eyes, to do everything in my power to put a stop to this sacrilege. In States which are still ruled by heathen princes on no pretext whatever is it permitted to kill a cow. In fact, this act of sacrilege, so hateful to Hindus, is only permitted in provinces where Europeans or Mahomedans hold sway.

To purify the body from any interior defilement that may have been contracted there is no more efficacious way than by the performance of the *pancha-gavia.*

As to other ordinary defilements, from which one can never quite escape, they may be removed in several ways, which I shall speak of in the next chapter. If these ceremonies can purify the soul from sin, so much the more will they be capable of purifying the body from all uncleanness, both external and internal.

CHAPTER V

Defilements of the Soul, and the Means of Purification.—Places of Purification.—Sins for which there is no Forgiveness.—Conjectures on the Origin of Brahmin Customs connected with Defilement and Purification.—Defilement by Europeans, and an Incident which happened to the Author from this Cause.

THE doctrine is laid down in Hindu books, is endorsed by the philosophers of the country, and is admitted also sometimes by Brahmins, that the only real defilement of the soul proceeds from sin, which is caused by perversity of the will. One Hindu poet, Vemana, expresses himself thus on this subject:—'It is water which causes mud, and it is water which removes it. It is your will that makes you commit sin, and it is by your will alone that you can be purified[1].' This doctrine, though imperfectly carried out in practice, certainly proves that Hindus acknowledge that it is only by an effort of the will and by a renunciation of sin that pardon and purification of the soul can be obtained.

But this enlightenment, which reason will never allow to be entirely extinguished even in the midst of the deep shadows of gross idolatry, has become, if not extinguished, at any rate entirely obscured by the religious formularization to which the Brahmins have become slaves. The Brahmins have allowed themselves to believe that without either the wish or the intention of renouncing evil it is possible for the soul to be purified by various means, which, through the extreme facility with which they can be employed, can only tend to lessen the real abhorrence of sin and give a false sense of security to the sinner. The *pancha-gavia*, for example, is sufficient to obtain the remission of any sin whatever, even when the sin has been committed deliberately; and that is really why the use

[1] This is not to be found among the verses of Vemana, but any Telugu verse of which the author is unknown is ascribed to him.—POPE.

of such a disgusting liquid (the urine of the cow) is so strongly upheld. Looking as they do upon sin as a material or bodily defilement, it is not surprising that they consider mere ablutions of the body sufficient to wipe it out. Ablutions performed in certain sacred rivers, such as the Ganges, the Indus, the Gódávari, the Cauvery, and others, purify both soul and body from any defilements they may ever have contracted. It is even possible for a person living at a distance to obtain the advantages conferred by their cleansing waters without leaving his house; he has only to transport himself thither *in intention*, and to think of the place while bathing.

There are several celebrated streams and tanks in India credited with the same purifying virtue; but some of them only possess this virtue at intervals more or less frequent. Thus the waters of the famous tank of Combaconum, in Tanjore, are only endowed with cleansing properties once in twelve years; while those of the spring which rises in the hill Tirutanimalai, in the Carnatic, are efficacious every three years. There are few provinces in India which do not possess sacred tanks. When the year and the day arrive for people to bathe in these sanctifying waters, a pilgrimage is made to the spot by enormous crowds of devotees, who have been warned beforehand by messengers sent in all directions by the Brahmins, who are interested in keeping up this holy fervour. On the appointed day they all stand round the tank, awaiting the propitious moment to plunge into it. Directly the *purohita* gives the signal, all present, men and women, rush into the water, shouting and screaming, and making an indescribable uproar. They soon find themselves heaped one on top of the other, so that they can hardly move. It almost always happens that in the midst of this frightful confusion several are drowned or suffocated, and many come out with broken or dislocated limbs[1]. Happy are those accounted who lose their lives on such an occasion! Their fate is more to be envied than lamented; for these victims of religious ardour go straight to the realms of bliss.

[1] This is the *Maha-makham* festival. A benevolent Government now takes the precaution of reducing the depth of the water to a few inches, to prevent such disasters. The festival was celebrated this year (1897) on Feb. 17, when 500,000 people were present.—ED.

The time of an eclipse is also considered a particularly opportune moment for purifying oneself from sin. Bathing at that time, wherever it may be possible, but especially in the sea, possesses the merit of cleansing the soul from all defilements. To bathe during the solstices or equinoxes, at the time of a new or of a full moon, or on the eleventh day of the moon, is also considered efficacious. The mouth of a river, the point where it joins another, or where in its windings its course runs from east to west, are also peculiarly propitious.

To read the Puranas and other sacred writings, to make pilgrimages to certain temples and holy places called *punyasthala*, to climb to the top of certain very high mountains, and even simply to gaze at them: all these procure the forgiveness of sins. There is one of these holy mountains in the Carnatic, in the district of Coimbatore. It is called *Nilagiri-malai*, and is believed to be the highest in the province[1]. For this reason alone the Hindus have made it a *punyasthala*, or place of virtue, their custom being to deify everything extraordinary in nature. As it is very difficult to reach the top of this mountain, a view of the summit alone (and it is visible a long way off) is considered sufficient to remove the burden of sin from the conscience of any person who looks at it; provided that he looks at it with that intention.

In connecting religious sentiment with everything which has any distinctive peculiarity or grandeur, they have not forgotten to include the magnificent waterfalls which surprise and charm the eye. Thus the Cauvery Falls, and several others, are supposed to be pre-eminently suitable for ablutions. In a word, one everywhere comes across places consecrated by superstition, where the greatest sinners can, with the most perfect ease, extinguish in a limpid and accommodating stream the burning fires of remorse by which they may be troubled.

To recite *mantrams*; to exercise the happy privilege of looking at the great ones of the earth, especially *gurus*; to think of Vishnu and the other principal deities: these are all most efficacious in purifying the soul. A Brahmin who happened to go three times round a temple of Siva merely in pursuit of a dog that he was beating to death, obtained the remission

[1] The Nilgiris, or Blue Mountains—now a sanitarium, the summer headquarters of the Madras Government.—ED.

of all his sins, and also the special favour of being transported immediately to Kailasa[1].

Admittance into Vaikuntha[2] was once granted to a great sinner simply for having pronounced, even in blasphemy, the name of Narayana and the name of Vishnu. All this is vouched for in the sacred Hindu books.

There are, however, some sins so heinous, according to Hindu ideas, that they cannot be expiated by any of the means before mentioned. These unpardonable sins are five in number:—

1. *Brahmahattya*, the murder of a Brahmin.
2. *Sisuhattya*, the destruction of an unborn child, i. e. wilfully causing an abortion.
3. *Surapana*, to drink toddy, the juice of the palm-tree.
4. *Swarna-Sněya*, to steal gold.
5. *Guru-talpa-gamana*, to have sexual intercourse with the wife of one's *guru* or of one's spiritual or temporal superior.

Some add a sixth, which consists in holding communication with any one guilty of any of these five sins, commonly called *pancha-patakas*, the five crimes. These fearful crimes cannot be wiped out in the lifetime of the offenders by any of the usual means employed for the purification of the soul. Those who are guilty of them expiate them after death, by one or more transmigrations of the soul into some vile animal, or by the torments of *Naraka*, i. e. hell.

Besides the sins committed during his present existence, from which a Brahmin must be constantly purifying himself, he must also think of expiating those committed in a former state. To become a Brahmin by reincarnation is the happiest destiny possible for a human being. It is a reward which is only granted for the accumulated merits of many successive generations. Yet the fact of the reincarnation is in itself a proof that there still remains in that person some fault to be expiated: otherwise the soul would have been transported to the Sattya-loka, or paradise of Brahma, and thereby would have been spared the trouble of animating another mortal body here below. Actual good deeds, such as giving alms to Brahmins, constructing wells or tanks, building temples, or contributing to the cost of religious services, and various other works of charity, are

[1] The paradise of Siva.

[2] The paradise of Vishnu.

held to add considerably to the efficacy of the various methods of purification which we have just spoken of, when performed in conjunction with them.

I will say nothing here of the many hindrances to the perfect purification of the soul caused by a man's wife or children, by his worldly possessions, by his caste, and by his passions. They will be referred to elsewhere.

Defilements and purifications form together one of the most important articles in Brahmin doctrine and the Hindu creed. The practices and opinions with regard to these subjects are so extraordinary and so unique that it would be most interesting to thoroughly investigate the motives which originally gave rise to them; but, either from prudence or from ignorance on their part, I have never been able to gather from Hindus any authentic information about them. Everything that I have been able to ascertain has been founded more or less on conjecture. But I have often had occasion to remark, that, after allowing for exaggeration, many Hindu rites bear a strong resemblance to those practised by other nations in bygone ages. Thus Jacob at Bethel, when preparing to offer up a sacrifice, commanded his household to purify themselves, and to change their garments[1]. When the Israelites were warned that God would appear to them in the desert of Sinai, God commanded them by Moses to wash their clothes, and not to touch their wives for three days beforehand[2]. Many passages in the Hindu sacred writings recall the rules which the law of Moses laid down for the children of Israel concerning the various kinds of defilements, real and technical[3].

It is, in fact, impossible to deny that there are many striking points of resemblance between Jewish and Hindu customs. Should one then conclude that the latter copied them from the former? I think not. If they are alike in some essentials, they display great dissimilarity in their outward forms. Besides, there is nothing that I know of in the history either of the Egyptians or of the Jews to show that these people existed as a nation prior to the Hindus. The peculiarity of the dogmas and rites of the Hindu religion, the strong antipathy which the Hindus feel for anything that savours of imitation, the

[1] Genesis xxxv. 2.
[2] Exodus xix. 10, 14.
[3] Leviticus xv. 11-15.

unshaken firmness with which they cling to ideas which originated at a date now lost in the darkness of antiquity, the intolerance, the pride, the presumption of the Brahmins, and above all their detestation and contempt for foreigners and foreign customs: all these make me confident that the Hindus never borrowed anything from other nations. Everything connected with the Hindus is stamped with the impress of originality and independence. Never could this vain and self-sufficient people, who are so filled with the idea of their own moral ascendency, have condescended to model their habits and customs on those of foreigners, whom they have always kept at the greatest possible distance. How, then, came the Hindus to originate these singular notions of defilement and purification? I feel that I possess neither the necessary learning nor the necessary talent to cope satisfactorily with this difficult question. I must therefore beg my readers' indulgence in briefly laying before them the conjectural opinions which I have formed on the subject.

Even before the Flood men were imbued with these notions of defilement and purification. Amongst animals there were the clean and the unclean. God recognized this distinction when He dictated to Noah the number of each species that was to go into the ark[1].

It is probable that the tradition of this classification of things clean and unclean was handed down by the descendants of the men who escaped the Flood. When they began to eat animal food, and noticed that the flesh of some beasts was not as wholesome or palatable as that of others, their opinions with regard to this tradition were strengthened; and, beginning by giving up what they found was deleterious to their health, they finally persuaded themselves that they could not even touch the unclean thing without being defiled.

These ideas about defilement were common to several other ancient nations. They, like the Hindus, had recourse to water and fire as means of purification. They also had their sacred rivers. At the time when the Hindus began to regard the waters of the Ganges, the Indus, and Gódávari as peculiarly sacred, and to attribute to them those cleansing properties which could purify both soul and body, the inhabitants of

[1] Genesis vii. 2.

Colchis and other peoples living near the Phasis credited the waters of that river with the same virtues, while those of the Nile were considered equally efficacious amongst the Egyptians.

Cleanliness is a most important factor in preserving public health. The luxury of clothes in those primitive times was reduced to just what was necessary to cover the body, or to protect it from atmospheric changes; and garments were rarely changed. The habits of the people therefore naturally tended to counteract the unhealthy consequences which would ensue from their prolonged use, by the frequent washing of these garments in pure water.

Everything in nature had deteriorated after the Flood. There were many more diseases, and in searching for the causes of them people thought that the unwholesome nature of certain kinds of food might be partly answerable for it. Therefore the use of such food was forbidden. They also realized that some of these diseases were contagious; therefore the persons who were attacked by them were isolated. The science of medicine was at that time in its infancy, but it was soon seen that the greater number of these maladies were caused by the unhealthy condition or poverty of the blood, owing to excessive perspiration; and the salutary effects of a bath being fully recognized, a bath was finally considered as a sovereign remedy for all complaints.

Men were at length obliged to disperse in different directions, and gradually peopled the various countries of the globe. India, being close to the plains of Sennaar and enjoying a good climate and a fertile soil, was doubtless one of the first countries thus inhabited. The very high temperature made those in authority feel that here, even more than in the country they had left, the rules of abstinence from certain meats, and attention to personal cleanliness, must be strictly enforced under pain of severe punishments.

In all probability, therefore, these Hindu notions about defilement and purification originated at some date anterior to the Flood, and after being handed down from generation to generation, undergoing various alterations and modifications either from superstition, the whim of some important person, or from motives of expediency to suit purely local conditions, they at length crystallized themselves into their present form, and still continue to have the strongest hold on the people.

Though the Hindus are fairly tolerant so far as the actual dogmas of their religion are concerned, they do not allow the smallest divergence of opinion on the subject referred to in the present chapter. If Europeans living in India, simply for the good of their health, would or could condescend so far as to make their mode of life conform to that of the higher classes of natives, at any rate in all essential matters, how much more cordial and friendly the relations between the two peoples would be! When I was travelling in districts where Europeans were as yet but little known I generally met with an agreeable welcome. Indeed, sometimes I was received with the most generous hospitality. Brahmins themselves have not disdained to offer me shelter in their own houses on seeing my long beard and my native costume[1]. I must own, however, that my attendants took care that people should be favourably disposed towards me by publishing abroad that though I was a European priest, a Feringhi *guru*, I was also the priest of all those castes of natives who had embraced the religion of Sarveswara[2], that I adhered strictly to all the Brahmin rules, made frequent ablutions, just as they did, abstained from meat and all intoxicating drinks, &c., &c.

These last assertions were pure falsehoods, which, on my honour, I had never sanctioned; but all the same they were made and repeated unknown to me, whenever my followers thought it to their interest or mine. Nevertheless, in spite of the greatest attention and circumspection on my part to avoid giving offence to my hosts, I occasionally found myself involved in a difficulty without its being in the least my fault. Here is a curious case in point. Travelling in South Mysore, I arrived one evening

[1] The influence thus acquired by the Abbé is testified to by Colonel Wilks, thus: 'Of the respect which his irreproachable conduct inspires, it may be sufficient to state that when travelling, on his approach to a village the house of a Brahmin is uniformly cleared for his reception without interference, and generally without communication to the officers of government, as a spontaneous mark of deference and respect.'—ED.

[2] A word which Native Christians employ to express God. It means literally, 'the Ruler of all things' (the Lord of all). Protestant missionaries have objected to the use of the word, because it is one of the titles of the god Siva.—DUBOIS.

at a village where I was obliged to pass the night. As there was no public lodging in the place, my people asked the village headman to provide some shelter. The headman was a Brahmin, and at first made some difficulties; but to gain his help my people told the usual falsehoods about myself. The Brahmin, before making any promise, came to the place where I was waiting, and after gazing at me from head to foot silently and attentively, asked me simply if I was accompanied by any Pariahs or dogs (for these both occupied the same level in his opinion). I told him that I allowed neither Pariahs nor dogs near me, and that all my followers were men of good caste. After a few moments' reflection, during which he fixed his eyes with evident predilection on my beard and my native costume, he said to me: 'You are a European, but out of respect for your dignity as *guru*, and in consideration of what your people tell me with regard to your strict conformity to the customs of the country, I will give you lodging in my own house. Take off your shoes and follow me.' I entered his house with my followers, and installed myself in a tidy part of the house which he assigned to me. Shortly afterwards my host, hearing me cough, ran to me in great haste, and with a very serious air expressed the hope that I would not defile the house by spitting in it. I did my best to calm his fears, assuring him that he had no reason to fear my transgressing any of the strict rules of Hindu custom. Despite my assurances, however, I noticed that he charged one of his sons to keep watch over me. Another spy was charged with observing the conduct of my servants. At sundown one of these latter left the village to answer a call of nature. Hardly had he returned when the person watching my servants, having seen him in the distance, ran to tell his master that his house had been polluted, that he had admitted into it people of low habits, for had he not seen with his own eyes one of my servants return from answering a call of nature without having washed himself and enter the house in this horrible state of defilement? On this my host rose in great wrath, and with gestures and looks of anger repeated to me what he had been told, ending by exclaiming: 'Is any sin equal to this! Behold the kind of gratitude which I ought to have foreseen in offering you hospitality. I had a presentiment that my good-nature would bring me trouble. To do such a thing without washing afterwards! What a crime! What a scandal! What an infamy! What shame for my house! . . . You must punish severely the low person who has so horribly defiled my house. You shall pay me all the cost of purification! And depart, quit my house at once!'

I let him vent his choler without interrupting him, and when he had ceased I answered him calmly that, if his complaints were well founded, reparation should be made him. But first of all he must prove that the offence had really been committed. My servant denied it strenuously, and indignantly demanded on his own part that his accuser should be punished. He had, he asserted, simply stooped down to answer a call of nature different from that alleged. His accuser nevertheless stuck to his assertion with horrible oaths. The Brahmin, believing him rather than my servant, insisted on my leaving the house. Thereupon, in a firm tone, I declared that I would neither punish my servant nor pay compensation for an injury which had not been proved. As to the order which he had given that I should leave his house, it was, I told him, an unreasonable violation of the laws of hospitality. I was ready to obey it, seeing that he was master of his own house, but he was also headman of the village, and he was therefore bound to find me another lodging for the night.

The Brahmin went out repeating his complaints for the hundredth time. Shortly afterwards he returned with a number of the villagers, who were even louder than himself in their protestations. They demanded that my servant should be delivered up to them for severe punishment, and that I should pay compensation, repeatedly exclaiming: 'What shame! What wickedness! What abomination!'

My servant, fearing the consequences that might ensue, racked his brains for some way of proving his innocence. At last he found one which would have been conclusive before less prejudiced judges. 'If I am guilty of what you say,' he exclaimed, 'let two of you come away with me and examine my person.' The Brahmin, anxious to prove him guilty, refused on unreasonable grounds to sanction such an unanswerable argument. Finally, after a long and useless discussion, we decided to adjourn the dispute until the morning. I left the Brahmin's house, and went and lodged, together with my people, in a cowshed outside the village, in which I was allowed as a great favour to pass the night. My people, even more alarmed than myself, left the cowshed to see what was happening in the village, and came and reported to me that a great disturbance was taking place: that everybody was talking about the incident; that everywhere punishment and compensation were demanded, and that if we stayed there until the morning my servant would run the risk of being severely beaten. To save myself such a vexation I was quite ready to sacrifice a few rupees, though I would never have consented to have my poor servant exposed to maltreatment for such an offence, whether guilty or not. Consequently I thought the most prudent thing to do was to flee. At one o'clock at night, when the cowherd was sleeping peacefully in a corner of the shed, we left quietly. I mounted my horse and we decamped in all haste. Before sunrise we had passed the borders of the district where this unfortunate occurrence took place, and were therefore out of danger.

CHAPTER VI

Marriage amongst Brahmins and other Hindus.—Celibacy.—Those who may remain unmarried.—Polygamy tolerated only amongst the Upper Classes. —The two Sexes nearly equal in numbers.—Indissolubility of the Marriage Tie.—How Marriages are arranged.—Preparatory Ceremonies.—Solemn Ceremonies for the first and following Days—Marriage amongst Sudras.— Marriage amongst Kshatriyas.—Duties after Marriage.

To a Hindu marriage is the most important and most engrossing event of his life; it is a subject of endless conversation and of the most prolonged preparations. An unmarried man is looked upon as having no social status and as being an almost useless member of society. He is not consulted on any important subject, and no work of any consequence may be given to him. A Hindu who becomes a widower finds himself in almost the same position as a bachelor, and speedily remarries.

Though marriage is considered the natural state for the generality of men, those who from pious motives remain unmarried are looked up to and treated with the utmost respect. But it is only those persons who have renounced the world, and have chosen to lead a life of contemplation, who can take vows of celibacy. In any other case marriage is the rule, and every one is under the obligation of discharging *the great debt to his ancestors*, namely, that of begetting a son[1]. No doubt it will be asked whether the Hindu devotees who take vows of celibacy do really remain as chaste as they are supposed to be. I should say without hesitation, No. Many have concubines under various pretexts, and many give themselves up in secret to vices which would disgust the most shameless libertine. Amongst this latter class are the greater number of the *gurus* and *sannyasis*, who wander about the country and live on the credulity of the public. Others shut themselves up in seclusion

[1] The Sanskrit word for son, *putra*, means literally, 'one who saves from *put* or hell'—the hell into which parents without sons fall.—Ed.

and lead idle and easy-going lives, their sole occupation being to receive the abundant offerings flowing in from the ignorant and foolish who believe in the false reputation for holiness which such people have acquired. But persons of sense are not taken in by their hypocrisy, and it is fairly notorious that these knaves, in the seclusion of their retreats, give themselves up to the grossest immoralities.

It must not be supposed, however, that I am accusing all unmarried Hindus without exception of leading dissolute lives. On the contrary, I have been credibly informed by those whose word may be relied on, and who know what they are talking about, that some few may be found who deny themselves all intercourse with women; but, on the other hand, one is led to believe that they allow themselves other infamous pleasures of such an abominable character that delicacy forbids one to accept the accusation except under strong proof; so I prefer to think that there are a few unmarried Hindus who are able to resist all sensual pleasures.

And why, after all, should one refuse to believe that some of these *sannyasis* or penitents are able to exercise such self-control, however difficult it may be to subdue one's passions in a country where the warm climate and the corrupt state of morality continually serve to arouse them[1]? Do not these men, either from ostentation or from fanaticism, subject their bodies to the most cruel ordeals? And the harsh, self-inflicted *tapasas*, or penances, do they not prove, as far as one can see, their wish and intention to subdue their sinful lusts? All the same, in spite of their hypocritical affectations of piety, the greater number of these *sannyasis* are looked upon as utter impostors, and that by the most enlightened of their fellow-countrymen.

But this privilege which men possess of remaining single, and giving themselves up to a life of contemplation, is not shared by women. They at all events cannot, under any circumstances, take vows of celibacy. Subjected on all sides to the moral

[1] Montesquieu says that our natural human tendency is to prefer in the cause of religion anything that presupposes effort. So in the matter of morality, we incline theoretically to anything that bears the impress of asceticism. Celibacy, for instance, has taken the greatest hold on those to whom it seems most unsuited, and on whom it might have the most disastrous results (*Esprit des Lois*, xxv. 4).

ascendency of man, the very idea that they could possibly place themselves in a state of independence and out of men's power is not allowed to cross their minds. The opinion is firmly established throughout the whole of India, that women were only created for the propagation of the species, and to satisfy men's desires. All women therefore are obliged to marry, and marriages are carefully arranged before they arrive at a marriageable age. If by that time they have not found a husband, they very rarely keep their innocence much longer. Experience has taught that young Hindu women do not possess sufficient firmness, and sufficient regard for their own honour, to resist the ardent solicitations of a seducer. Therefore measures cannot be taken too early to place them intact in their husbands' hands. Those who are unable to enter into any lawful union form a connexion as concubines with any man who cares to receive them as such.

Polygamy is tolerated amongst persons of high rank, such as rajahs, princes, statesmen, and others. Kings are allowed five legitimate wives, but never more. None the less this plurality of wives amongst the great is looked upon as an infraction of law and custom, in fact, as an abuse. But in every country in the world those in power have always been able to twist the law in their own favour, however definitely it may be laid down. The principal Hindu gods had only one wife. Brahma had only Sarasvati; Vishnu, Lakshmi; and Siva, Parvati. It is quite true that under their different forms these venerable personages committed frequent breaches of their marriage vow; but this only serves to prove that from the earliest times marriage was looked upon by the Hindus as a legal union between two persons of opposite sexes.

If in the present day any person of inferior rank cohabits with several women, one only of them bears the name and title of wife; the others are merely concubines. In several castes the children of the latter are illegitimate, and if the father dies without having previously settled some of his property upon them, they have no share when it comes to be divided. I only know of one case in which a man can legally marry a second wife, his first being still alive; and that is when, after he has lived for a long time with his wife, she is certified to be barren, or if she has only borne female children; for in the latter case *the debt to one's ancestors*—that is to say, the birth of a son—is considered to have been imperfectly paid. But even in this case, before a man contracts a second marriage it is necessary that he should obtain the consent of the first; and she is always regarded as the chief wife and retains all her prerogatives.

It may be remembered that for the same reason Abraham took Hagar to be his wife during the lifetime and with the consent of Sarah, his lawful wife. One may also remember what dissensions arose in the family of the holy patriarch as the result of this marriage with two women. It is exactly the same in Hindu families where there are two legal wives. Consequently the majority of Hindu husbands prefer, under such circumstances, to give up the hope of having a son, rather than be subjected to the numberless troubles which are the invariable result of the remedy permitted by law.

Some modern writers have hazarded the theory that in hot countries the number of women greatly exceeds that of men. It is Bruce, I think, who first advanced this opinion in his account of his travels in Arabia and Abyssinia. Even before my own experience had led me to a totally different conclusion on this point, it had always appeared to me that his deductions were wrong, or at any rate doubtful. If my memory does not deceive me, this author tried to prove the numerical excess of the female sex from the fact that in the families of some Arab princes, amongst a large number of children hardly one-sixth were males; and from this particular instance he drew a general conclusion. It is evident that the calculation is fundamentally wrong. To obtain a sound basis on which to found such a conclusion, a census must be taken of a large number of families of all classes, and upon that alone can such a rule of proportion be drawn. The proportion of births in the harems of a few Eastern princes, with many wives, cannot furnish any standard from which to determine what takes place amongst the people themselves, where conjugal union is restricted to what it ought to be according to the laws of healthy morality and true civilization.

Some sceptics, however, turning this pretended discovery of Bruce to account, have drawn from it what they consider an incontrovertible argument to prove that religion is merely a question of geography, and that Christianity cannot be suitable for all countries and all nations; for marriage being the natural state of all human beings, a religion that forbids polygamy would in hot countries reduce more than half of one sex to a state of enforced celibacy. But supposing the hypothesis on which this objection to the universality of Christianity is based to be as true as I believe it to be false, it seems to me that it would prove the existence of little or nothing contrary to Divine Providence, who in giving us the inestimable benefit of divine revelation, as manifested by the teaching of an Incarnate God, appears to have designed that this precious gift of Christianity should be shared by all the inhabitants of the terrestrial globe. It seems to me that, for this objection to have any weight, it is necessary to prove that amongst the whole of the human race, taken collectively, there is a much larger number of the female than of the male sex; for it is upon the whole human race, taken collectively, that the Creator looks as on one large family. In each individual member of this family He sees only the being created in His own image, without distinction of country, colour, language, or bodily form; and His intention was that all men should form one common brotherhood, united by all the ties of a common nature and common origin.

At the same time I have reason to believe, from my own personal observation, that the view is utterly wrong which holds that in hot climates the number of women far exceeds that of the men. For many years I exercised my religious calling in many parts of the Indian Peninsula, and I paid particular attention to the point in question. From exact registers which I kept of all baptisms, it may be seen that I yearly administered this sacrament to two or three hundred children of all castes; and I have been able to prove that during any single year the preponderance in births of one sex over the other never exceeded fifteen to twenty-five, and that it was sometimes one and sometimes the other sex which predominated within these narrow limits. These registers, which extended over a period of more than twenty-five years, are no longer within my reach; but I am convinced that out of perhaps 6,000 children baptized by me, one sex did not outnumber the other by more than 200. Another convincing proof that the proportion of the two sexes is about equal in India, is furnished by the Brahmins, who can only have one legitimate wife, and for whom marriage is obligatory. One hardly ever meets with a woman who is not, or has not been, married. Blind, dumb, deaf, or lame, all find husbands amongst poor Brahmins, whose low fortunes do not allow them to aspire to an alliance with any more attractive spouse.

It may, it is true, be retorted that amongst Brahmins a widow cannot remarry, whereas a widower may at once take to himself another wife. The consequence is, it may be urged, that the women of this caste must be more numerous than the men. But I reply that the age at which the two sexes marry compensates for this difference. Girls are married when seven or even five years old, whilst boys wait till they are sixteen, twenty, or even older. I am therefore decidedly of opinion that in hot as well as in temperate climates the births of the two sexes are nearly equal; and that polygamy is opposed to all laws, both natural and divine[1].

This unnatural custom of polygamy, which finds a place amongst some nations, may be attributed to sinful lust, to abuse of the power of the strong over the weak, and to the dominion of the one sex over the other. It is evidently altogether contrary to the intention of the Creator, who, when He created the father of mankind, gave him only one woman to wife, and indeed ordained that man and his one companion should form but one flesh[2].

A celebrated statesman of the last century (Burke), speaking on this subject from a political point of view, said that the Christian religion, by bringing marriage back to its primitive and only legitimate state, had contributed more by that alone to

[1] According to the Census Report of 1891, to every 1,000 males there are returned only 958 females; and the tables show that there are in the country fewer females than males to the number of, speaking roundly, 6¼ millions. The deficiency is greatest in the Punjab, N. W. Provinces, and Rajputana. In Bengal, Madras, and Upper Burma, however, females are in excess to the extent of something under three-quarters of a million. The conclusion arrived at with regard to the deficiency of females is that it is to a large extent due to deliberate concealment and deliberate omission from the Census returns. But the Report remarks: 'The subject of sex is a very intricate one, and the more one studies it the less inclined is a cautious statist to adopt any single explanation.' The Report examines the whole question at considerable length. —ED.

[2] Genesis ii. 24.

the general peace, happiness, stability, and civilization of the human race, than it would have been possible for it to do in any other department of divine providence.

The indissolubility of the marriage tie is also an essential principle which it seems to me is not less firmly established amongst the Hindus than that which limits this important act to the legal union of one man with one woman. A Hindu can only put away his legitimate wife for one cause, and that is adultery. If this rule is violated, it is only among the most degraded of the lower castes. A marriage can also be annulled if it has been contracted in violation of the prohibitory degrees which are laid down by custom, and which of themselves are sufficient to nullify the union.

I have never yet heard of a divorce being permitted on account of incompatibility of temper, nor have I ever heard of a man being allowed to put away his wife, however vicious she might be, simply in order to marry another woman. Hindus, as I shall presently show, put too serious a value on this solemn contract to allow it to be thus degraded to a state which would be nothing more or less than concubinage. A Hindu, and especially a Brahmin, would hardly be inclined to repudiate his wife even for adultery, unless her guilt were very notorious. As a general rule, when the wife of a Brahmin gives occasion, by injudicious behaviour, for remarks of a kind damaging to her character, her friends and relatives do their utmost to excuse her conduct and to hush up all scandal about her, so as to avoid the necessity of such an extreme measure as a divorce, the disgrace of which would reflect on the whole caste.

I will now give a detailed account of the principal ceremonies which take place both before and at the time of a wedding.

A young Brahmin should, ordinarily speaking, be married when he is about sixteen years of age, but the ceremony is often postponed till he is older than this. The wife chosen for him is generally five, seven, or at the utmost nine years old[1].

[1] The Jews also married their children at an early age. A youth who was not married before he was eighteen was considered by them to be sinning against the command of the Creator, which says: 'Increase and multiply.' He was free to marry as soon as he had attained the age of thirteen. Their daughters were betrothed in childhood, and were married as soon as they had arrived at a suitable age, which was usually fixed by them at twelve.—DUBOIS.

This custom of marrying girls in their early childhood, and as soon as possible, though common to all castes, is most strictly observed by the Brahmins. When once a girl has passed the marriageable age, it is very difficult for her to find a husband. In this caste there is often an enormous difference in age between the husband and the wife. It is no uncommon thing to see an old man of sixty or more, having lost his first wife, marry for the second time a little child five or six years old, and even prefer her to girls of mature age. What is the result of this? The husband generally dies long before his wife, and often even before she has attained the age which would allow him to exercise his rights as a husband. So the poor girl becomes a widow before she has even become a wife, and as by the custom of her caste she may not marry again, she is oftentimes tempted to lead a dissolute life, thereby reflecting discredit on the whole caste. Everybody recognizes these abuses, but the idea of remedying them, by allowing a young widow to break through the stern rule of custom and marry again, would never even enter the head of a Hindu, more especially of a Brahmin[1]. It is true that the strange preference which Brahmins have for children of very tender years would make such a permission almost nominal in the case of their widows[2].

The expenses of a wedding are so considerable that in all castes one often sees young men, who are without the necessary means, using the same expedient to procure a wife that Jacob employed with Laban. Just like the holy patriarch a Hindu without means will enter the service of one of his relations, or of some other person of the same caste who has daughters to marry, and will engage himself to serve for a certain number of years without wage, on condition that, at the end of that time, he is to receive one of the daughters in marriage. When the time agreed upon has expired the father fulfils his promise, undertakes the whole expense of the marriage, and then allows the young couple to go away and live where they please. At

[1] Hindu social reformers are now agitating for virgin-widow remarriages, and in a few instances such marriages have been brought about.—ED.

[2] Amongst the Jews it was permissible for widows to marry again; but those who voluntarily, out of respect and affection for their dead husbands, refrained from marrying again, were looked up to with very great respect. —DUBOIS.

their departure he gives them a cow, a pair of oxen, two copper vessels (one for drinking, the other for their food), and enough rice to feed them for the first year of their married life. It is very remarkable that in India the term which a man has to serve for his wife is the same as that for which Jacob bound himself to Laban, namely seven years (Genesis xxix. 20)[1].

The inclinations of the persons about to be married are never consulted. In fact, it would be ridiculous to do so amongst the Brahmins, seeing the age at which they marry their daughters. But even the Sudras, who often do not marry their daughters until they have attained full age, would never dream of consulting the tastes and feelings of their children under these circumstances. The choice is left entirely to the parents. That which chiefly concerns the young man's family is the purity of the caste of his future wife. Beauty and personal attractions of any kind count for nothing in their eyes. The girl's parents look more particularly to the fortune of their future son-in-law, and to the character of his mother, who after the marriage becomes the absolute mistress of the young wife[2].

The same months are chosen for a wedding as are selected for the ceremony of the *upanayana*, that is to say, the months of March, April, May, and June, and especially the two last[3].

However, it is possible in a case of urgency for a marriage to take place in November or February. But in both these months there are so many precautions to be observed, so many calculations to be made according to the signs of the Zodiac, the phase of the moon, and other ridiculous follies, that it is far from easy to find a day on which all the auspices are propitious.

There are four different ways of arranging the preliminaries of a marriage. The first, the most honoured and respected of all, is for the father of the bride not only to refuse to receive

[1] No such custom exists now.—ED.

[2] A Sanskrit verse, commonly quoted, says: 'The girl courts beauty; the mother, riches; the father, knowledge; relatives, good lineage; other people, sumptuous marriage-feasts.'—ED.

[3] It is probable that the original reason why the Hindus selected these four months as the most auspicious for marriages, is that during these months all agricultural work is either finished or suspended on account of the great heat, and also because the crops, which have just been gathered in, help to defray the expenses of the wedding. —DUBOIS.

the sum of money to which he is entitled from the young man's parents, but to undertake to bear all the expenses of the ceremony, to purchase all the jewels and other ornaments which it is customary to give a girl on this occasion, and also to make handsome presents to the son-in-law and his parents. But this can only be done by the rich and people of high position.

The second way is for the parents of both the contracting parties to agree to share all the expenses. The third method is that usually adopted by people of all castes who are not rich. The parents of the girl insist not only on the youth's parents bearing all the expenses of the wedding and of the jewels, but they also exact payment of a sum of money in return for their daughter, the amount of which is laid down by caste custom. This method is the commonest of all; for to marry and to buy a wife are synonymous expressions in India. Most parents make a regular traffic of their daughters. The wife is never given up to her husband until he has paid the whole of the sum agreed upon[1]. This custom is an endless source of quarrels and disputes. If a poor man, after the marriage has taken place, cannot pay the stipulated amount, his father-in-law sues him for it, and takes his daughter away hoping that the desire to have her back again will induce the man to find the money. Sometimes this succeeds, but it pretty often happens

[1] It was the custom also among the Jews for the husband to give the wife her dower. Genesis xxxiv. 8, 9, &c., xxxi. 15; 1 Samuel xviii. 25; Hosea iii. 2.—DUBOIS.

This is not true in the majority of instances, though there may be extreme cases of the kind. The following words were uttered recently by one of the speakers at an annual conference of the Kistna District Association: 'Gentlemen! The monstrous custom of selling girls needs no words of mine to make you try to root it out from our society. I will give you one particular case which will show you the advisability of taking proper steps to remove the evil. A certain gentleman, in a certain village, married his daughter, ten years old, to an old man of eighty-one, and received Rs. 2,000 for the bargain. In due course the girl matured, and the nuptial ceremony was performed. The girl was sent to her hated husband, much against her will. She escaped from the room in the dead of night and threw herself into a well. When the old man awoke in the morning he missed his young wife, and, on search being made, her dead body was found floating in a well. There are several instances of this sort. In some cases, if the ill-assorted pair be seen together, the bride will appear as a daughter, or even a grand-daughter. The young brides become widows even in a week after their marriages. These evils are too apparent to me, and I think you will enthusiastically carry this resolution.'—ED.

that the son-in-law, being always unable to pay the debt, leaves his wife for years as a pledge with his father-in-law, and at last the latter, convinced that by this means he will get nothing, and fearing lest his daughter should succumb to the temptations to which her youth exposes her, withdraws his demands. A compromise is effected and the husband at length regains his wife [1].

The fourth method, to which none but the very poorest have recourse, is very mortifying to the girl's parents, for they go themselves and hand her over to the tender mercies of the young man's parents, leaving it to them to do what they will with her, to marry her when and how they like, to spend as little or as much as they choose on the wedding, and begging them at the same time to pay them something for their daughter.

As soon as the parents have discovered a suitable girl, and have ascertained if the family are likely to assent, they choose a day when all the auguries are favourable, and go to formally ask for her. They provide themselves with a new cloth, such as is worn by women, a cocoanut, five bananas, some vermilion, and some powdered sandalwood. While on the way, they pay great attention to any omens that they may notice. If they consider them to be unfavourable they retrace their steps, and postpone the business till another day. Thus, for instance, if a snake cross their path, or a cat, or a jackal, or if they should happen to see anything that is regarded as an evil omen [2], they decide that the best thing to do is to return to their home.

If nothing of this sort has disturbed them on the way, they present themselves at the house of the girl's parents and make known the object of their visit. The latter, before giving any answer, look steadfastly towards the south, and wait till one of those little lizards which one sees running about the walls of a house has uttered a certain sharp cry, such as these reptiles often make. Then when *the Lizard of the South* has spoken,

[1] I do not believe that any Hindu father of respectability would take such a step.—ED.

[2] All Hindus are full of these superstitions. No matter how important the business may be that they are about to undertake, they will never hesitate for a moment to put it off, if they catch sight of one of these objects or one of these animals. I have several times seen labourers take their oxen back to their sheds, and remain idle all day, simply because when leaving the village in the morning, a snake had crossed their path.—DUBOIS.

the parents of the girl give their consent to the marriage, and accept the present which has been brought by the other parties.

In the evening of the same day, about dusk, they call together a few relatives and friends, and summon a *purohita* in order to consult him about the marriage. Whilst the men, seated on mats or carpets, are talking together, the women purify a part of the house; that is to say, they rub the floor well with cow-dung mixed with water, and then draw lines of red and white upon it. As soon as they have finished, they bring in the god Vigneshwara, to whom they do *puja*, and for *neiveddya* they offer peas, sugar, a cocoanut, and a sweet beverage called *paramanna*. All present worship this god, and pray him to remove any obstacles which might interfere with the projected marriage. If during this ceremony *the Lizard of the South* again utters his cry they think it a favourable omen.

After this ceremony, the *purohita* fixes on a lucky day on which to begin to celebrate the marriage. The parents of the girl then definitely give their permission, and in token of their promise they offer betel to all those who are present. These preliminaries ended, they begin to think of making preparations for the wedding. Gold and silver ornaments are ordered for the couple, and form the subject of endless discussion. The wedding garments are also got ready, a large number of cloths, such as are worn by both men and women, are bought to be given away as presents to relations and friends, a large store is laid in of rice, wheat flour, liquefied butter, oil of sesamum, peas of all kinds, dried and fresh vegetables[1], fruits, groceries, pickles, and in fact every sort of edible that a Brahmin is permitted to use. They also provide saffron, or turmeric, vermilion, antimony, sandalwood powder, incense, quantities of flowers, *akshatas*, or coloured rice, betel, areca-nut, &c., &c.; also a great quantity of small silver and copper coins. Further, they buy new baskets, and above all, plenty of new earthen vessels of all shapes and kinds; for these vessels may never be used a second time, and are immediately broken after being once used, no matter to what purpose they have been put.

[1] Amongst the many kinds of vegetables which Brahmins eat, there are three which are considered particularly choice; these are a species of small round pea, the *katri kai* (the *belingela* of the Portuguese, a sort of brinjal or egg-plant), and pumpkins. Among fruits they also have a preference for three—bananas, mangoes, and jack-fruit.—DUBOIS.

When everything is ready, they begin to put up a *pandal* or canopy. The god Vigneshwara is carried into it, and to him they do *puja*, entreating him to ward off any hindrance or misfortune which might happen during the celebration of the marriage.

The *purohita* who presides at the ceremony must be one of the first to take up his place under the *pandal*; he must be provided with some *darbha* grass, small pieces of wood from the seven sacred trees, and a few other indispensable objects for the sacrifices he is about to offer up.

In the first place, due honour is paid to the household gods. To this end all the Brahmins present, both men and women, anoint their heads with oil of sesamum, and then bathe. The women, after preparing the various dishes for the feast, take a portion from each, which they place on a metal dish, and proceed, singing songs and accompanied by all the guests, to offer it as *neiveddya* to these gods, having first, of course, done *puja* to them. They even go so far as to place to the right of them pickles, to give a relish to their rice, while on their left they place a cup full of the sweet drink called *para-manna*, with which to quench their thirst. The master of the house then performs the *sam-kalpa* and offers sandalwood, *akshatas*, flowers, and lustral water to his guests, who ought, when receiving all this, to think of the household gods, in whose honour the feast immediately following is spread, great pains having been taken to make it bountiful and magnificent. Betel is distributed at the termination of the repast, after which the guests disperse.

The second day, nine Brahmins specially chosen for the purpose perform the sacrifice of *homam* and another to fire, in honour of the nine planets, as at the ceremony of the *upanayana*. Two women take the consecrated fire and carry it, singing the while, to the centre of the *pandal*, placing it on the raised daïs of earth. Each of the women then receives a present of a new cloth, and a little bodice called *ravikai*. All present then walk round the brazier of hot coal reciting *mantrams*, scattering *darbha* grass and bowing to the ground. Presents are given to the nine Brahmins who have sacrificed to the planets, and, as usual, the meeting ends with a feast.

The third day the father of the bridegroom, having made his

ablutions, takes some *akshatas* in a cup, and goes out early to call together relatives and friends. As soon as all are assembled under the *pandal*, a pure cloth or carpet is spread on the raised earthen daïs, and the future husband and wife are seated thereon facing the east. The married women then approach them and rub their heads with oil, singing the while, and then proceed with the important ceremony known as *nalangu*, which consists in smearing the naked parts of their bodies with powdered saffron, and immediately after pouring a great quantity of warm water over their heads[1]. The women never cease singing the whole time, and are accompanied by musical instruments. After the *nalangu* is over the women array the young couple in new clothes, as has already been described in the chapter on the *upanayana*. The evening of the same day, at the moment when the lamps are being lighted, the guests return to assist at the following ceremony:—The married women, singing all the time, take a wooden cylinder which they cover with lime and then paint with red longitudinal stripes. On this they tie small twigs of the mango-tree. They next sprinkle a great quantity of powdered saffron over the cylinder, which they immediately afterwards dip into a new earthen vessel. This they carry with much solemnity, singing the while, to the centre of the *pandal*, where they offer it a sacrifice of incense, and offer some betel for *neiveddya*. Every person present makes a profound obeisance to the vessel. No other saffron but what is thus consecrated is used during the whole ceremony.

All these proceedings are merely preparatory to the marriage ceremony itself, which lasts for five days.

The first day is called *muhurta*, that is to say, the great day, or the happy and auspicious day. It is on this day that the most important and solemn ceremonies take place. The head of the family goes out early to invite his guests, while the women busy themselves with purifying the house and the *pandal*, which they decorate all round with wreaths of mango leaves. The guests having arrived stand in a row, and first adorn their foreheads with *akshatas* and sandalwood. They next anoint their heads with the oil of sesamum which is

[1] *Nalangu* is not a religious ceremony. The powdered saffron is mixed with quicklime, and made into a paste which is red in colour. It is rubbed only on the feet.—ED.

provided for them, and then they go and perform their ablutions. On their return the *purohita* performs the *sam-kalpa* and invokes all their gods, beginning with Brahma, Vishnu, Rudra, Devendra, and then the twelve Adityas, the eight Vasus, the nine Brahmas, the eleven Rudras, the Gandharvas, the Siddhas, the Saddhyas, the Naradas, the seven great Penitents, the nine planets; in fact, every deity whose name occurs to his memory. With low obeisances he invites them all to come to the marriage-feast, makes many flattering speeches to them, and begs them to remain under the *pandal*, and to preside over the ceremony during the five days that it lasts.

Then comes the invocation of ancestors. The couple about to be married are seated on the earthen daïs in the centre of the *pandal*, having on each side of them their fathers and mothers, all with their faces turned towards the East. The father of the bride rises, places the *pavitram* amulet on the ring-finger of his right hand, performs the *sam-kalpa*, and puts a certain quantity of rice in a metal dish, and on this rice a cocoanut dyed yellow, three areca-nuts in their shells, and five others without their shells[1].

Then, taking one of the nuts in one hand and the metal dish in the other, he repeats three times in a loud voice the names of his father, his grandfather, and his great-grandfather. Each time he pronounces their names he raps the copper dish three times with the areca-nut, and at last, again invoking them by name, he says: 'O my ancestors, you who dwell in the *pitra-loka* (or paradise of ancestors), deign to come to this *pandal*, bringing with you all the other ancestors who preceded you. Be present, I beseech you, during the five days of this marriage-feast, preside at the festivity, and grant to it a happy termination!' He then gives the rice, the cocoanut, and the areca-nut which were on the dish to the *purohita*.

This done, the married women bring some fire on a new earthen chafing-dish, and, singing, place it in the centre of the *pandal*. The *purohita* then consecrates it by scattering all round it some *darbha* grass. To the north of it he places some

[1] These various objects are an offering which he makes to his ancestors when inviting them to the wedding. It is always considered polite to offer a present to any distinguished guest whom you invite to any ceremony.—DUBOIS.

small pieces of the sacred fig-tree, by the side of which are placed three small earthen vessels and one of copper. The first contains milk, the second liquefied butter, the third curds, and the fourth a certain quantity of cooked and uncooked rice mixed together. To the south of the brazier are spread nine portions of rice on a large banana leaf. These are tastefully arranged in squares, each portion being destined for one of the nine planets. *Puja* is done to each of these nine planets individually, and offerings of bananas and betel are made to them as *neiveddya*, after which they receive the same invitation as the gods and the ancestors.

The *purohita* places on the east side of the brazier another banana leaf, on which he spreads *darbha* grass and *akshatas*. This is an offering to Brahma, to whom is presented a *neiveddya* of raw sugar and betel. Then follows the invocation of the *ashta-dik-palakas*, or the eight divine guardians of the eight corners of the world; and *puja* is offered them on the same banana leaf. Then comes the inauguration of the *ishta-devata* or tutelary deity, and the deification of the five little pots in the manner that has already been described for the *upanayana*.

These ceremonies ended, the father of the girl performs the *homam* in honour of Brahma, Vishnu, and Rudra, of the eight gods who guard the eight compass-points of the world, of the eight Vasus, and of Indra, taking care to mention all these gods by name, and also to repeat *mantrams* suitable to the occasion. He again does *homam* to the nine planets, makes a sacrifice to fire, and offers the latter some liquefied butter as *neiveddya*.

A new earthen chafing-dish is then brought, to which they fasten a piece of saffron thread, and on it is placed the consecrated fire. Women carry this fire away to a place apart, singing, of course, the while. Great care is taken not to let the fire go out till the end of the festivity. It would be considered a terribly bad omen if, through negligence or any other cause, it should be extinguished.

Now comes the *muhurta*, that is to say, the most essential ceremony of the marriage. To begin with, a sacrifice is offered to Vigneshwara. The bride and bridegroom are seated on the earthen dals, their faces towards the east, and the married women proceed, singing the while, with the young people's toilette, which is of the most elegant and sumptuous description.

When attired the bridegroom rises, performs the *sam-kalpa*, prays to the gods to pardon all the sins he has committed since he received the triple cord; and, to be the more sure of this pardon, he recites a *mantram*, and gives fifteen fanams to a Brahmin as alms. He then dresses himself up as a pilgrim, and makes all preparations as if he were really going to take a long journey, announcing that he is going to start on a holy pilgrimage to Kasi, that is Benares. He leaves the house accompanied by the married women singing in chorus, and by his parents and friends, and preceded by instruments of music. After passing the outskirts of the village he turns his steps to the east.

But here his future father-in-law meets him, and asks him where he is going, and on learning the object of his journey, begs him to give it up. He tells him that he has a young virgin daughter, and that if he wishes it he will give her to him in wedlock. The pilgrim accepts the proposal with joy, and returns with his escort to the place whence he set out. On his return the women perform the ceremony of the *aratti*.

The bride and bridegroom having again taken their places on the daïs, and the *sam-kalpa* having been performed, they then begin the important ceremony called *kankana*[1]. For this purpose they obtain two pieces of saffron or turmeric, round which they tie a double thread. They place on a metal dish two handfuls of rice, and on this rice a cocoanut painted yellow, and on the cocoanut the two pieces of saffron. Prayers are offered to all the gods collectively, who are implored to come and place themselves on this *kankana*, and to remain there till the five days of the marriage ceremony have been accomplished. The bridegroom then takes one of the pieces of saffron and ties it on his wife's left wrist, who in her turn ties the other piece on his right wrist. The rice and cocoanut on which the *kankana* has been lying are then given to the *purohita*.

Then follows the procession of the tutelary deity. The mother of the bride, accompanied by the other women and the Brahmins who are present, go and fetch the copper vase which represents the *ishta-devata*. The women begin to sing and the musicians to play, and forming a procession they march to the

[1] The ceremony is actually called *kankana-dharana*, that is, the tying or wearing of the *kankana*.—ED.

end of the street, where, after choosing a clean spot, they pour out some of the water contained in the vase. They do *puja* to the deity while it rests on the ground, and then it is taken back with the same pomp to the place whence it came. Then follows the most important ceremony of all, which is called *kania-dana*, or *the gift of the virgin*. This is what takes place. The bridegroom being seated facing the east, his father-in-law performs the *sam-kalpa*, places himself in front of him, and looks at him fixedly for some time without speaking. He is supposed to imagine that he sees in his son-in-law the great Vishnu; and with this in his mind, he offers him a sacrifice of *arghya*, *padya*, *achamania*, *akshatas*, sandalwood, and flowers. A new copper vessel is then brought. In this the young man places his feet, which his father-in-law washes first with water, then with milk, and then again for the third time with water, while reciting suitable *mantrams*.

He performs the great *sam-kalpa*, which consists in adding to the ordinary *sam-kalpa* (vide Part I, Chapter XIII) the names and attributes of the *Bharata Varsha*, the *Sali-vahana*, the seven islands, the seven seas, the seven *puras* or cities, the seven Penitents, the seven mountains, the sacred places (*punya-sthalas*), and the holy cities (*punya puras*).

He next thinks of his father, his grandfather, and great-grandfather. Pronouncing their names aloud, he prays that these and the twenty-one other ancestors who have preceded them, may attain *moksha* (or paradise). Then, holding betel in one hand and taking his daughter's hand in the other, he says a prayer to Vishnu, begging him to look with a gracious eye on this gift that he is making of his virgin daughter. He then places her hand in that of her future husband, pours a little water over it, and gives him some betel, the usual token of a gift.

The *gift of the virgin* is followed by three other gifts, namely, the *go-dana*, *bhu-dana*, and *salagrama-dana*, which mean the gift of cows, the gift of land, and the gift of *salagramas*, or small stones, to which they attach a superstitious value, and which will be spoken of later on.

Then follows the ceremony called *mangalashta*[1]. The bride

[1] This means 'the eight marriage blessings.' The ceremony concludes with the throwing of coloured rice over the couple by way of blessing them.—ED.

and bridegroom are seated facing each other, and a sheet of silk is suspended in front of them. This is held by twelve Brahmins, and hides them from the other guests, who successively invoke in a loud voice Vishnu and his wife Lakshmi, Brahma and Sarasvati, Siva and Parvati, the Sun and his wife Chhaya, the Moon and his wife Rohini, Indra and Sathi, Vasishta and Arundhati, Rama and Sita, Krishna and Rukmani, and several other pairs of gods and goddesses.

As soon as the *mangalashta* is finished they fasten on the *tali*, that is, the little gold ornament which all married women wear round their necks; the *tali* is strung on a little cord which is dyed yellow with saffron water, and composed of 108 very fine threads closely twisted together. Other little ornaments of gold are also added, round which are fastened flowers and fine black seeds. Two handfuls of rice are placed in a metal pot, on the rice is laid a cocoanut dyed yellow, and on the top of the cocoanut the *tali*, to which they offer a sacrifice of sweet perfumes. The *tali* is then taken round to all the guests, both men and women, who touch it and bless it [1].

Four large metal lamps, each with four wicks, are brought in and placed on a stand, which must also be of the same metal. Above are set other lamps fashioned out of a paste composed of ground rice, and these are filled with oil. They are lighted, and four women take them in their hands. At the same time all round the *pandal* a great number of other lamps are lighted. Then ensues a tremendous din. The women sing, the musicians play, bells are rung, cymbals are clashed, and anything and everything within reach from which sound can be extracted is seized on, each one striving to outdo the other in creating noise [2].

In the midst of this hubbub the husband advances towards his young wife, who is seated facing the east, and while reciting *mantrams* he fastens the *tali* round her neck, securing it with three knots.

The husband and wife, sitting side by side, then offer each other betel. Two married women approach them, give them

[1] Old ladies whose husbands are alive are specially requested to touch and bless the *tali*, to ensure the couple a long married life.—ED.

[2] This noise is intended to drown any sounds of weeping, sneezing quarrelling, &c., which are considered bad omens.—ED.

their blessing, and place *akshatas*, which have been consecrated by *mantrams*, on their heads, and finally perform the ceremony of *aratti*.

Fire is then brought on a new earthen brazier, and the *purohita* consecrates it with *mantrams*, surrounds it with *darbha* grass, and does *homam* to it. The fire is surrounded by lighted lamps, and near it is placed a small stone called the sandalwood stone, no doubt because it has been smeared with sandalwood oil. Then the husband, holding his wife's hand, walks three times round the sacred fire, and each time he makes the circuit he takes his wife's right foot in his right hand, and makes her touch the sandalwood stone with it, touching the stone with his own foot at the same time. Whilst performing this action the thoughts of both husband and wife should be directed to the great mountain of the North called *Sapta-kula parvata* or *the mountain of the seven castes*, the original home of their ancestors, the mountain being represented by this sandalwood stone.

These are the various ceremonies which compose the *muhurta*. As soon as they are finished, two bamboos are planted in the centre of the *pandal* side by side, and at the foot of each of them is placed a bamboo basket. The bride and bridegroom then stand up, each in a basket, and two other baskets full of rice are brought. They take handfuls of this rice and shower it over each other in turn. This they continue to do many times, until they are tired, or are told to stop[1].

In some castes the guests perform this ceremony, which is called *sesha*, for the newly married pair. Princes and very rich people have been known to use for the *sesha*, instead of rice, pearls and precious stones mixed together. After the *sesha* the couple return to their usual seat. *Akshatas* consecrated by *mantrams* are then distributed to the guests. The husband throws over his right shoulder a piece of new and clean cloth, one end of which he unfolds before the assembled Brahmins, from whom he receives a blessing, while they also recite a *mantram* and place a portion of the *akshatas* they have just

[1] In some countries the Jews of the present day observe a custom of throwing handfuls of wheat over a newly married couple, but especially over the wife, saying: 'Increase and multiply.' Sometimes pieces of money which are intended for the poor are mingled with the wheat.—DUBOIS.

received on the cloth. He takes these in his hand and puts one portion on his own head, and the rest on his wife's head, after which the women again perform *aratti* to the newly married couple.

It is easy to see the allegorical meaning of most of the ceremonies which have just been described, and which are the most solemn and important of the whole proceedings. The *kania-dana*, for instance, typifies the handing over of the girl by the father to the son-in-law and the renunciation of parental authority over her. The son-in-law for his part fastens the *tali* round his wife's neck to show that he accepts the gift, and that from henceforth she is his property. The sacrifice of the *homam* and the thrice-repeated circuit of the newly married couple round the fire are a mutual ratification of the contract they have just made with one another, for there is no more solemn engagement than that entered into in the presence of fire, which Hindus look upon as the purest of their gods, and which for this reason they always prefer to any other when they wish to make an oath specially binding. The ceremony of the *mangalashta* is to call down divine blessings on the newly married couple. That of the *sesha* is the outward expression of the wish that they may enjoy an abundance of this world's goods, or that their union may be fruitful, or perhaps both.

When all these ceremonies are ended sandalwood powder, *akshatas*, and betel are given to all the Brahmins present, both men and women. All must then go and perform their ablutions and return for the feast, which on this day must be specially magnificent.

Before sitting down to eat, they never fail to carry with due solemnity to the household gods their share of the food which has been prepared.

All the guests being seated in a row upon the ground, the men quite apart from the women, so that the latter are out of sight, a large banana leaf is placed before each person, and a helping of boiled rice is placed on it, and on one side two other leaves, folded in the form of cups, one containing melted butter and the other a strongly spiced sauce. The second course consists of dried peas, green vegetables, and roots of various kinds. The third course consists of fritters, puddings boiled in water, others fried in butter, others sweetened and spiced, curdled milk, and salt pickles. Bananas, jack, and other fruits make up the fourth course. Then follows the *kalavanta*, which consists of four different dishes all highly flavoured, and composed of various ingredients mixed with rice. To finish the repast a beverage is handed round composed of limejuice, sugar, cardamom, and aniseed mixed with water. The whole meal takes place in absolute silence.

When all the guests have feasted they turn their attention to the meal for the newly married couple, not forgetting the necessary ceremonies connected with it. First of all the sacred fire is brought and placed before the daïs on which they are sitting. The husband rises and does *homam* to the fire, whilst the *purohita* repeats *mantrams*. Then the women form a procession, and singing take the fire back to its original place. The young married couple, holding each other by the hand, go to the place where the tutelary deity is reposing, and make a deep obeisance to it. The husband then does *puja* to it, and offers as *neiveddia* some cakes and boiled rice. They make a similar obeisance to the five little earthen vases placed near the deity, in which are sown ten kinds of seeds, and sprinkle them with water.

It is only after having gone through all these preliminaries that the young married couple are allowed to partake of the meal which has been specially prepared for them. They sit down facing one another in the centre of the *pandal* on two little stools, the bridegroom facing east. Before them is spread a large banana leaf, and at each of its four corners are placed four lamps made of ground rice filled with oil, which are lighted, as well as many others all round the *pandal*. Then the married women bring in on two metal dishes the different viands which have been prepared for the young couple, much singing and music going on the while. After they have been helped, melted butter is poured three times on to their fingers, and after swallowing this they begin to eat their food together from the same leaf[1]. To eat in this manner is a sign of the most complete union, and is the most unmistakable proof of friendship that two

[1] This custom is not observed nowadays in Hindu marriages, but the bridegroom and bride exchange comestibles from each other's leaves. When they live together afterwards the wife may, and does, eat off her husband's leaf, after he has finished eating.—ED.

persons closely united could possibly give each other. Later on the wife will be allowed to eat what her husband leaves, but never again will she be permitted to eat in company with him. This is a favour which is only granted her on her wedding-day.

Their meal finished, the newly married couple go outside, preceded by music, and accompanied by the women singing, by all the guests, and by the *purohita*. The *purohita* points out to them a small star called *Arundhati*, the wife of the Penitent Vasishta, which is to be found near the pole-star. The couple make a deep reverence to the star and return to the house in the same procession[1]. There the women perform the ceremony of *aratti*. This terminates the ceremonies of the first day, called *muhurta*, or the great day.

I will spare my readers the details of the ceremonies which occupy the four following days, and which, as a rule, are merely a repetition of those just described. What little variety there is, is much in the same style. These ceremonies are interspersed with the most innocent games and amusements, which would appear to us utterly ridiculous, and only suitable for little children, but which afford them the greatest pleasure and infinite amusement.

Amongst the second day's ceremonies one of the most extraordinary is when they place a sort of ornament, called *bassinam*, on the forehead of both the husband and wife. This *bassinam* is covered with gold-leaf or gold paper, and flowers are entwined round it. The object of the *bassinam* is to avert the effects of the *drishti-dosha* or evil eye, the spell which is cast by the looks of jealous or ill-disposed people. Placed thus on the most conspicuous part of the body it is supposed to attract the eyes of the malevolent, and thus prevent them exercising their malign influence on the persons of the newly married couple.

Amongst the ceremonies which take place on the third day there is a peculiar one. The husband, as usual, performs the sacrifice of the *homam* and another to fire, and after him his wife comes up and performs the same sacrifice, only with this difference, that instead of using boiled rice, she uses parched rice. This is, I believe, the only occasion on which a woman

[1] Arundhati was the chaste and devoted wife of Vasishta Rishi; and when the couple look at this star they make a vow that they too will live like Vasishta and Arundhati.—ED.

can take an active part in any of these sacrifices, which the Brahmins hold to be most sacred and most solemn.

The only remarkable ceremony which takes place on the fourth day is the *nalangu*, in which the newly married couple rub each other's legs three times with powdered saffron. I do not in the least understand the meaning of this ceremony. I fancy its only object is to kill time. Europeans under similar circumstances would spend it in drinking, often to excess; or in gambling, dancing, singing songs in honour of love and wine, sometimes even in carrying on intrigues with the object of loosening the sacred marriage tie, which it is the object of marriage ceremonies to make secure. The Hindus spend their wedding-days more wisely in religious observances, of which the greater number are well calculated to leave a lasting impression on the minds of those attending them. The innocent and artless games with which they amuse themselves afford them none the less pleasure because they are so. In the domestic festivities of the Brahmins, decency, modesty, purity, and reserve are always conspicuous. This is the more remarkable as they obey a religion whose dogmas are for the most part saturated with immorality.

The fifth day is chiefly occupied in dismissing, with all the customary formalities, the gods, the planets, the great penitents, the ancestors, and all the other divinities who have been invited to the feast. They dismiss even the *kankanam*, that is to say, the two pieces of saffron attached to the wrists of the newly made husband and wife. Finally, the god of the *mantapam*, that is to say of the *pandal*, is himself dismissed. Then follows the distribution of presents, which vary in value according to the means of the host. The *purohita* who has taken the most prominent part, and after him the women who have been singing the whole time from beginning to end, carry off the lion's share of these bounties. I must just mention that the songs which are sung at these ceremonies contain nothing obscene or even erotic; they are either a sort of explanation of the aim and object of each ceremony or else a long rigmarole in praise of the bride and bridegroom, in which they also give expression to the most heartfelt wishes for their future happiness.

The festivity ends with a solemn procession through the streets, which generally takes place at night by torchlight in the midst of squibs and fireworks of all kinds. The newly married pair are seated face to face in an open palanquin highly decorated. Both of them are loaded, rather than adorned, with flowers, jewels, and other ornaments, for the most part borrowed for the occasion. The procession advances slowly. Relatives and friends before whose houses it passes, come out to meet it. The women perform the ceremony of *aratti* to the couple, and the men give presents of silver, fruits, sugar, betel, &c. These gifts are really only a loan, for those who receive them are expected to return them on similar occasions to the givers. I have sometimes seen wedding processions that were really beautiful, though perhaps not quite according to our taste.

Such are a Brahmin's wedding ceremonies, all of which, and many more minute observances which I have not thought it worth while to mention, are scrupulously performed with more or less magnificence by rich as well as by poor.

Sudras' marriage ceremonies are equally solemn, though much less elaborate. In every caste marriage is looked upon as the most important affair in a man's life. It is also the most expensive one, and brings many a Hindu to ruin. Some spend on it all that they possess, and a great deal more besides; while others, in order to fulfil what is expected of them, contract debts which they are never able to repay [1].

I shall say nothing of the feasts which are given by their relatives and friends to the newly married couple, of the presents they receive, or of the ceremonies in their honour. I will only add that for a whole month the feasting and rejoicings go on.

When all the festivities have at length come to an end, the bride returns home with her parents, who keep her shut up till such time as she shall be able to fulfil all the duties of a wife. This also is another occasion for festivities. There is the same gathering of friends and relatives, and almost the same ceremonies, with a few exceptions, that took place at the first wedding. The father and mother of the bridegroom, on being informed that their daughter-in-law has arrived at an age when the marriage can be consummated, go and fetch her, and conduct

[1] One of the planks of the Social Reform platform is the reduction of marriage expenses.—ED.

her home in triumph. And in order that she may become accustomed by degrees to married life, her own parents come at the end of a month and take her back to her own home, and for the first few years, or until she has children, she lives alternately in her parents' and in her husband's house. These mutual arrangements are at first a proof of the happy understanding existing between the two families. But unfortunately this harmony rarely lasts long, for very soon, finding herself ill-treated and even beaten by her husband, and tormented in a thousand ways by an exacting mother-in-law who treats her like a slave and vents upon her all her whims and ill-temper, the poor young wife is forced to a surreptitious flight, seeking shelter and protection under her father's roof. Then, relying on promises of better treatment in future, she consents to resume her fetters; but fresh outrages soon force her to escape again. In the end, resigning herself to the inevitable, or for the sake of her children, she gives up the struggle, and meekly bows to marital authority. A real union with sincere and mutual affection, or even peace, is very rare in Hindu households. The moral gulf which exists in this country between the sexes is so great that in the eyes of a native the woman is simply a passive object who must be abjectly submissive to her husband's will and fancy. She is never looked upon as a companion who can share her husband's thoughts and be the first object of his care and affection. The Hindu wife finds in her husband only a proud and overbearing master who regards her as a fortunate woman to be allowed the honour of sharing his bed and board. If there are some few women who are happy and beloved by those to whom they have been blindly chained by their family, this good fortune must be attributed to the naturally kind disposition of their husbands, and not in any way to the training the latter have received [1].

A Brahmin *purohita* does not usually preside at a Sudra marriage unless the contracting parties are very rich and of high position, and thus able to recompense him handsomely. Generally the ceremony is performed by one of the mendicant Brahmins who go about selling Hindu almanacs from door to door.

[1] The spread of education, though it has not extended far amongst Hindu women, is gradually changing many of these domestic evils.—ED.

In each caste custom differs as to the manner in which a bride is demanded, the sum of money paid for her, the quantity and the value of her jewels, the colour and price of the wedding garments, the arrangements as to who shall defray the expenses of the ceremony, the number of feasts provided for the guests, and the presents made to relatives and friends.

Amongst the Sudras the erection of the *pandal* is one of the most important and solemn of the ceremonies. It is set up in the street, opposite the entrance-door of the house, seven, five, or three days before the wedding festivities begin. As soon as it is put up a procession is formed, accompanied by music, to fetch the *ara-sani*, that is to say, a green branch of the sacred fig-tree with leaves on it. This is planted in the centre of the *pandal*; *puja* is offered to it and also votive offerings. All present walk round it in single file, making deep obeisance to it. It represents Vishnu, to whom the sacred fig-tree is specially dedicated, and it remains in the middle of the *pandal* during the whole of the ceremonies as the tutelary god of the festivity. Processions round it take place at intervals, always accompanied by the same marks of respect. Another peculiarity at a Sudra wedding is that a lamp is kept alight in a prominent part of the *pandal* during the three days' festivities, the wick of which is composed of 108 threads. Among the Sudras also the number of earthen cooking-pots is restricted to ten.

The Brahmin who presides at the marriage begins by breaking one or more cocoanuts before the *ara-sani*, and according as the nut breaks in this or that direction, favourable or unfavourable auguries of the future of the newly married pair are determined. Almost all the other ceremonies are identical with those of the Brahmins.

At the marriage of Kshatriyas or Rajahs, the ceremonial differs very little from that of the Brahmins. A *purohita* invariably presides and takes the leading part. All the Brahmins who live in the place and in the neighbourhood are invited, but as they cannot eat with people of this caste, they receive each day portions of rice, melted butter, curdled milk, peas, vegetables, and fruits, which they cook for themselves and feast upon apart.

At the termination of the ceremonies they receive more or

less valuable presents of cloths and other things according to their rank and in proportion to the means of the family who give the feast.

At the marriages of Kshatriyas, too, all the different kinds of weapons used in warfare are brought in with much solemnity, accompanied by the songs of the women and by instruments of music. These weapons remain hung up in the most conspicuous part of the *pandal* until the festivities are ended. The guests offer them sacrifices, and worship them from time to time, and similar processions are made round them to those of the Sudras round the sacred fig branch.

The work from which I have extracted these details gives particulars of a remarkable expedient for procuring a wife sometimes adopted by the noble caste of Kshatriyas. When a young man of this caste wishes to marry, instead of going through the usual prescribed forms and humiliating proceedings with the parents of the girl that he has in view, he exercises the right of carrying off the noble lady on whom he has set his affections. To ensure success in his enterprise he collects a numerous following, unexpectedly declares hostilities against the king whose son-in-law he hopes to be, and tries to wrest his daughter from him either by force or strategy. As soon as she is in his power he conducts her to his home in triumph, and celebrates the marriage with all due solemnity. This method of procuring a wife, says the author, is the most approved of all in the case of a Kshatriya; and, in fact, Hindu books often mention similar instances of rape, but always amongst the Rajah caste.

The ritual of the Brahmin *purohitas*, after describing in detail the ceremonies to be observed at a Kshatriya marriage, always terminates with a short sermon on the principal duties imposed on this noble caste.

'The real caste of Kshatriyas has ceased to exist,' says this same author, 'and the so-called Kshatriyas of the present time are a bastard race[1]. Whoever pretends to be a true Kshatriya

[1] This caste was almost entirely annihilated by Vishnu, who visited the earth in the person of Parasurama. The Kshatriyas, it is related, had increased to such an extent that they filled the whole earth, which they ruled with such unbearable tyranny, that Vishnu, with a view to deliver the world from their unjust oppression, began, as Parasurama, a long

ought to know that he can only be a soldier, and nothing else, and that his one object in life is to make war. During a war he should be careful not to injure a labourer, an artisan, any one who flees before him, who asks his assistance or who places himself under his protection, any one who during the battle or after it lays down his arms and with supplicating hands asks for quarter. In a word, he should conduct himself in these circumstances according to the rules laid down in the *Dharma-sastra*. The true Kshatriya when engaged in fighting an enemy should give up all desire to live. Far be it from him to think of retreating or taking to flight! On the contrary, let him advance bravely, resolved to conquer or to die! The happiest death for a Kshatriya, the one he should wish for most, is to die sword in hand, fighting. It procures for him the inestimable happiness of being admitted to *Swarga*[1]. Boundless ambition is the highest virtue a Kshatriya can possess. However vast his possessions may be already, he should never say that he has enough. All his thoughts should tend to enlarging and extending his territories and to making war on neighbouring princes with a view to appropriating their possessions by main force. He should show faith and piety towards the gods; he should respect Brahmins, placing the utmost confidence in them, and loading them with gifts. Truth and justice are the foundations on which all his actions should be based. His leisure moments should be given up to reading the *Dhanurveda*[2], and other sacred works which he has the right to study, and he should regulate his conduct by the customs of his caste. Humane and generous, he must never refuse to do good to any one, whoever he may be, and it should be said of no one that he left a Kshatriya's presence unsatisfied. The best and most honourable way in which he can spend his wealth is to give abundant alms to Brahmins, to build temples with *gopurams*, to erect rest-houses and other buildings for public use on the high-roads, to repair those that are falling into decay, to sink

and bloody war against them, in which all the men of the caste were exterminated. Only the women were spared, and they became the concubines of Brahmins. The Kshatriyas of the present day are descendants of the bastards who resulted from these illegitimate unions.—DUBOIS.

[1] Paradise of Indra.

[2] This Veda treats of the science of archery.—ED.

wells and make reservoirs and tanks, and to establish *chutrams* (almshouses for Brahmins) in many places. He should do his best to rule his country with equity, and should keep a careful watch lest he act unjustly. He must give to all his subjects their due, and never exact from them more than what rightfully belongs to him. In short, his duty is to model his conduct in everything on the rules laid down in the *Dharma-sastra*.'

CHAPTER VII

The second, or *Grahastha*, Status of Brahmin.—Rules of Life which the Brahmin *Grahastha* should daily follow.—Introduction.—Forms to be observed when relieving Nature and when Washing.—Manner of cleansing the Teeth.—*Sandhya*, Part I.—Rules relating to Ablutions.—The Correct Order of Daily Avocations.—Rules to be followed when Eating and when going to Bed.—*Sandhya*, Part II.—*Mantrams* of which the *Sandhya* is composed.—*Sandhya* for Morning, Noon, and Evening.—Conclusion.—General Remarks.

THE greater part of the matter contained in this chapter will not perhaps appear very interesting to some readers. However, the subject, considered from a philosophical point of view, seemed to me to be curious, and I think that many will forgive the prolix details that I am about to give for the sake of learning more exactly what the customs of the Brahmins really are. I have gleaned these details from the great book of Brahmin ritual called *Nittia-karma*. I shall classify them in parts and sections, as is usually done in works of this kind, and shall follow the divisions as they exist in the original. The name of *Grahastha* Brahmin is, strictly speaking, only given to those who are married, and who already have children. A young Brahmin after his marriage ceases virtually to be a *Brahmachari*, but as long as his wife by reason of her youth remains with her parents, he is not considered a real *Grahastha*. He only earns the right to this title after he has paid *the debt to his ancestors*, that is, by being the father of a son. Brahmins who have fulfilled this latter condition form the real bulk of the caste; it is they who uphold its rights and settle any differences that may arise. It is they who are expected to see that the customs are observed and to further them by precept and example.

INTRODUCTION.

The *Grahastha* should rise every day about an hour and a half before the sun appears above the horizon. On rising his first thoughts should be for Vishnu. He then calls upon the following gods to cause the sun to rise, saying: 'O Brahma, Vishnu, Siva, Sun, Moon, Mars, Mercury, Jupiter, Venus, Saturn, Rahu, Ketu, cause the dawn to appear'!

He pronounces the name of his *guru*, or spiritual teacher, and addresses the following prayer to him: 'I offer worship to you; to you who resemble the god whom I love most; it is by your wise advice that I am able to escape the dangers and perils of this world.'

He must then imagine himself to be the Supreme Being, and say: 'I am God! there is none other but me. I am Brahma; I enjoy perfect happiness, and am unchangeable.' He thinks deeply on this point with great complacency for some time, fully persuading himself that he is really Brahma. After this he addresses Vishnu thus: 'O god, who art a pure spirit, the giver of life to all things, the ruler of the universe, and the husband of Lakshmi, by your command I rise, and am about to occupy myself with the affairs of this world.'

He must then think of what work he has before him during the day, of the good deeds that he proposes to do, and of the best means of carrying out his intentions. He reminds himself that his daily tasks to be meritorious must be done zealously and piously, and not indifferently and perfunctorily. Whilst thus thinking he takes courage, and makes a resolution to do his best. After that he performs the *hari-smarana*, which consists in reciting aloud the litanies to Vishnu, and in repeating his thousand names[1].

These preliminaries ended, he must attend to the calls of nature, and the following are the rules which he must follow in this important matter:—

Section I.—*Rules to be observed by Brahmins when answering the calls of nature.*

I. Taking in his hand a big *chembu* (brass vessel) he will

[1] The *hari-smarana* consists in saying: 'Hail Govinda! Hail Kesava! Hail Narayana! Hail Hari!' &c., &c. It must not be supposed, however, that all the names and epithets by which this god is designated have any very flattering meanings attached to them. For instance, Govinda means cowherd; Kesava, 'he who has hair on his head'; Narayana, 'he who lives on the waters,' &c. Several other names of Vishnu are even more ridiculous than these.—Dubois.

proceed to the place set apart for this purpose, which should be at least a bowshot from his domicile [1].

II. Arrived at the place he will begin by taking off his slippers, which he deposits some distance away, and will then choose a clean spot on level ground.

III. The places to be avoided for such a purpose are: the enclosure of a temple; the edge of a river, pond, or well; a public thoroughfare or a place frequented by the public; a light-coloured soil; a ploughed field; and any spot close to a banian or any other sacred tree.

IV. A Brahmin must not at the time wear a new or newly washed cloth.

V. He will take care to hang his triple cord over his left ear and to cover his head with his loin-cloth.

VI. He will stoop down as low as possible. It would be a great offence to relieve oneself standing upright or only half stooping: it would be a still greater offence to do so sitting on the branch of a tree or upon a wall.

VII. While in this posture he should take particular care to avoid the great offence of looking at the sun or the moon, the stars, fire, a Brahmin, a temple, an image, or one of the sacred trees.

VIII. He will keep perfect silence.

IX. He must chew nothing, have nothing in his mouth, and hold nothing on his head.

X. He must do what he has to do as quickly as possible, and rise immediately.

XI. After rising he will commit a great offence if he looks behind his heels.

XII. If he neglects none of these precautions his act will be

[1] I have decided only after much hesitation to give these somewhat disgusting details. To a judicious and enlightened student, however, a knowledge of the common, everyday habits of a nation is not without its use; and overcoming my natural repugnance on this account, I have ventured to believe that my readers will pardon me for not excising so important a section of the Brahmin's *vade mecum*. I may remark at the same time that all these minute details pertaining to cleanliness and health belong to an elaborate system of hygiene which extends to other practices of the people of India, and which is certainly very beneficial in a hot country like theirs. The Hebrew lawgiver also did not forbear to insert rules similar to these in the Hebrew books of law (Deut. xxiii. 12, 13).—DUBOIS.

a virtuous one, and not without merit; but if he neglects any of them the offence will not go without punishment.

XIII. He will wash his feet and hands on the very spot with the water contained in the *chembu* which he brought. Then, taking the vessel in his right hand, and holding his private parts in his left hand, he will go to the stream to purify himself from the great defilement which he has contracted.

XIV. Arrived at the edge of the river or pond where he purposes to wash himself, he will first choose a suitable spot, and will then provide himself with some earth to be used along with the water in cleansing himself.

XV. He must be careful to provide himself with the proper kind of earth, and must remember that there are several kinds which cannot be used without committing an offence under these circumstances. Such are the earth of white-ant nests; salt-earth; potters' earth; road-dust; bleaching earth; earth taken from under trees, from temple enclosures, from cemeteries, from cattle pastures; earth that is almost white like ashes; earth thrown up from rat-holes and such like.

XVI. Provided with the proper kind of earth, he will approach the water but will not go into it. He will take some in his *chembu*. He will then go a little distance away and wash his feet and hands again. If he has not a brass vessel he will dig a little hole in the ground with his hands near the river-side and will fill it with water, which he will use in the same way, taking great care that this water shall not leak back into the river.

XVII. Taking a handful of earth in his left hand[1], he will

[1] It is only the left hand that may be used on these occasions. It would be thought unpardonably filthy to use the right hand. It is always the left hand that is used when anything dirty has to be done, such as blowing the nose, cleaning the ears, the eyes, &c. The right hand is generally used when any part of the body above the navel is touched, and the left hand below that. All Hindus are so habituated to this that one rarely sees them using the wrong hand. The custom of carefully washing the dirty part after answering a call of nature is strictly observed in every caste. The European habit of using paper is looked upon by all Hindus, without exception, as an utter abomination, and they never speak of it except with horror. There are some who even refuse to believe such a habit exists, and think it must be a libel invented out of hatred for Europeans. I am quite sure that when the natives talk amongst themselves of what they call our dirty, beastly habits, they never fail to put this at the head of them all, and to make it a subject of

pour water on it and rub it well on the dirty part of his body. He will repeat the operation, using only half the amount of earth, and so on three times more, the amount of earth being lessened each time.

XVIII. After cleansing himself thus he will wash each of his hands five times with earth and water, beginning with the left hand.

XIX. He will wash his private parts once with water and potters' earth mixed.

XX. The same performance for his two feet, repeated five times for each foot, beginning, under the penalty of eternal damnation, with the right foot.

XXI. Having thus scoured the different parts of his body with earth and water he will wash them a second time with water only.

XXII. After that he will wash his face and rinse his mouth out eight times[1]. When he is doing this last act he must take very great care to spit out the water on his left side, for if by carelessness or otherwise he unfortunately spits it out on the other side, he will assuredly go to hell.

XXIII. He will think three times on Vishnu and will swallow a little water three times in doing so[2].

SECTION II.—*Rules to be observed when cleaning the teeth*[3].

I. To clean his teeth a Hindu must use a small twig cut from either an *uduga*, a *rengu*, or a *neradu* tree, or from one of a dozen others of which the names are given by the author.

bitter sarcasm and mockery. The sight of a foreigner spitting or blowing his nose into a handkerchief and then putting it into his pocket is enough to make them feel sick. According to their notions it is the politest thing in the world to go outside and blow one's nose with one's fingers and then to wipe them on a wall.—DUBOIS

[1] It is necessary to rinse the mouth out after every action which is calculated to cause any defilement. The rule is to rinse the mouth out four times after making water, eight times after answering an ordinary call of nature, twelve times after taking food, and sixteen times after sexual intercourse. It is easy to recognize in this rule one of those wise ordinances of hygiene so appropriate to the climate and rendered obligatory by usage.—DUBOIS.

[2] This is called *achamania*.—ED.

[3] The practice of rinsing out the mouth and scrubbing the teeth well with a small piece of green wood freshly cut from the branch of a tree is very general, not only amongst Brahmins, but also amongst all other castes. Europeans, as a rule, are considered to neglect this practice so indispensable to cleanliness and comfort, and in consequence are still further de-

II. If such a twig is unobtainable, he may use a bit of wood cut from any thorny or milky shrub.

III. Before cutting the twig he must repeat the following prayer to the gods of the woods: 'O gods of the woods! I cut one of your small twigs to cleanse my teeth. Grant me, for this action, long life, strength, honours, wit, many cattle and much wealth, prudence, judgement, memory, and power.'

IV. This prayer ended, he cuts a twig a few inches in length, and softens one end into the form of a painter's brush.

V. Squatting on his heels and facing either east or north, he scrubs all his teeth well with this brush, after which he rinses his mouth with fresh water.

VI. He must not indulge in this cleanly habit every day. He must abstain on the sixth, the eighth, the ninth, the eleventh, the fourteenth, and the last day of the moon, on the days of new and full moon, on the Tuesday in every week, on the day of the constellation under which he was born, on the day of the week and on the day of the month which correspond with those of his birth, at an eclipse, at the conjunction of the planets, at the equinoxes, the solstices, and other unlucky epochs, and also on the anniversary of the death of his father or mother.

VII. Any one who cleans his teeth with his bit of stick on any of the above-mentioned days will have hell as his portion!

VIII. He may, however, except on the day of the new moon and on the *ekadasi* (eleventh day of the moon), substitute grass or the leaves of a tree for this piece of wood.

IX. On the day of the new moon and on the *ekadasi* he may only clean his teeth with the leaves of the mango, the *juvi*, or the *nere*.

After having cleaned his teeth the Brahmin must direct his steps to some water to go through the important act of the *sandhya*[1].

spised on that account; while those Europeans who do clean their teeth are held to do so in such an objectionable manner as rather to add to the disgust which Hindus feel for those who are neglectful of this custom, because they use for this purpose a brush made with the bristles of a dead animal, and therefore impure, and also because they use the same brush many times, though it has after the first time been defiled by saliva — DUBOIS.

[1] The word *sandhya* answers to our word 'twilight'; it indicates the moment in the day when the sun reaches its apogee. Thus the *sandhya* must be performed three times a day, morning, noon, and evening.—DUBOIS.

Sandhya literally means 'meeting,' between day and night, that is.—ED.

SECTION III.—*The First Part of the Sandhya. Rules to be observed by a Brahmin while washing.*

I. He performs the *sam-kalpa*, then calling to mind the gods of the waters, he worships them. He then thinks of the Ganges, and addresses the following prayer to the sacred river: 'O Ganges! who were born in Brahma's pitcher, whence you descended in streams on to Siva's hair, from Siva's hair to Vishnu's feet, and thence flowed on to the earth to wash out the sins of all men, to purify them and promote their happiness! You are the stay and support of all living creatures here below! I think of you, and it is in my mind to bathe in your sacred waters. Deign to blot out my sins and deliver me from all evil.'

II. This prayer ended, he must think of the seven sacred rivers (the Ganges, the Jumna, the Indus, the Gódávari, the Sarasvati, the Nerbudda, and the Cauvery). Then plunging into the water, he fixes his thoughts intently on the Ganges, and imagines that he is really bathing in that river.

III. His ablutions finished, he turns towards the sun, takes water in his hands three times, and makes a libation to the sun by letting the water run off the tips of his fingers.

IV. He then leaves the water, girds up his loins with a pure cloth, and puts another on his shoulders. He sits down with his face to the east, fills his brass vessel with water, which he places in front of him, rubs his forehead with the ashes of cow-dung or sandalwood, and traces on it the red mark called *tiloki* according to the custom of his caste. He ends by hanging either a wreath of flowers round his neck, or else a string of seeds called *rudrakshas*.

V. He thinks of Vishnu, and in honour of him drinks three times a little of the water contained in the vessel. He also makes three libations to the sun by pouring water on the ground.

VI. Similar libations are made in honour of the gods Vishnu, Siva, Brahma, Indra, Agni, Yama, Neiruta, Varuna, Vayu, Kubera, Isana, the air, the earth, and all the gods in general, mentioning those by name which occur to his memory.

VII. Then he rises, pronouncing aloud the name of the sun,

and worshipping him. He then meditates some time on Vishnu, and repeats the prescribed form of prayer in his honour [1].

VIII. He again repeats the names of the gods, turning round the while, and ends by making them a profound bow.

IX. Thinking once again of the sun, he addresses the following prayer to him:—

'O sun-god! You are Brahma at your rising, Rudra at noon, and Vishnu when setting. You are the jewel of the air, the king of the day, the witness of everything that takes place on earth; you are the eye of the world, the measurer of time; you order the day and night, the weeks, the months, the years, the cycles, the *kalpas*, the *yugas*, the seasons, the *ayanas*, the times of ablution and of prayer. You are lord of the nine planets; you absolve the sins of those who pray to you and offer you sacrifices. Darkness flies at your approach. In the space of sixty *ghatikas* (twenty-four minutes) you ride mounted in your chariot over the great mountain of the North, which is ninety million five hundred and ten thousand *yojanas* in extent. I worship you with all my strength; deign in your mercy to put away all my sins.'

X. Hereupon he turns round and round, twelve, twenty-four, or forty-eight times according as he is able, in honour of the sun.

XI. He then goes to a sacred fig-tree, and with his face towards the east makes it a profound inclination, repeating the following prayer the while: 'O *aswatta* tree! You are a god! You are the king of trees! Your roots represent Brahma, your trunk Siva, your branches Vishnu. Thus are you the emblem of the Trimurti. All those who honour you in this world by performing to you the ceremony of the *upanayana* or of marriage [2], by walking round about you, by adoring you and singing your praises, or by other similar acts, will obtain remission of their sins in this world and a home of bliss in the next. Penetrated with the consciousness of these truths I praise and adore you with all my strength. Deign to give me a proof of your goodness by vouchsafing the pardon of my sins in this world, and a place with the blessed after death.'

[1] Details of this will be found in the second part of the *sandhya*.

[2] It will be seen in the following pages that this tree is given in marriage with all due solemnity.—DUBOIS.

XII. He then walks round the tree seven, fourteen, twenty-one, twenty-eight, thirty-five, or more times, according as he has strength, always increasing the number by seven.

XIII. He then reads some devotional book for a certain time, and having finished he rises, clothes himself with pure cloths, plucks a few flowers to offer to his household gods, fills his copper vase with water, and returns to his house.

SECTION IV.—*A Brahmin's daily avocations.*

I. On returning to his house the Brahmin *Grahastha* makes the sacrifice of *homam*, and may then attend to his ordinary affairs.

II. Towards noon, after having ordered his meal, he returns to the river to perform the *sandhya* for the second time, just as he did in the morning, the prayers only being different.

III. He returns home, taking the greatest care to remain undefiled, and avoiding with scrupulous anxiety the touch of anything on the road that might defile him. For instance, he would have to return promptly to the river if by any accident he set foot on a piece of broken glass or pottery, a bit of rag, hair, or a piece of skin, &c., or if he was touched by a person of inferior caste. It is necessary for him to preserve the most absolute purity to be able to perform the sacrifice which he is about to make.

IV. On his return to his house he proceeds with the daily sacrifice due to his household gods. Everything being ready for this important ceremony, he turns towards the east or towards the north, and remains some time in deep meditation. Taking a position below the divinity, he places the flowers he brought as an offering to the right of the god to whom he is going to do *puja*. Before him is placed a vessel full of water, also incense, a lamp, sandalwood, cooked rice, and other things of which the sacrifice is to be composed.

V. He first drives away the giants and evil spirits by snapping his fingers ten times, and turning round and round. By these means he prevents their approach.

VI. He then sets to work to provide himself with a new body, beginning with these words: 'I myself am the divinity to whom I am about to offer sacrifice.' By virtue of these words he unites the individual soul which reposes in his navel with the supreme soul which reposes in his breast. In the same way he unites successively the different elements of which he is made, the earth to the water, the water to the fire, the fire to the wind, the wind to the air.

VII. He presses the right nostril with his thumb and repeats the monosyllable *jon* sixteen times, and breathing heavily through the left nostril he thereby dries up the body which forms his mortal tenement.

VIII. With his thumb and first finger he closes both nostrils, repeats the word *ron* six times, holds his breath, thinks of fire; and by this means burns his body.

IX. He repeats the word *lom* thirty-two times, blowing hard all the time through his right nostril. He thus blows away the body which has just been burned. He must think of a new set of senses, and the thought will of itself suffice to procure them for him.

X. Then thinking of water, he causes the *amrita* to fall from the moon by pronouncing the sacred word *aum*. He diffuses this *amrita* over the whole of his body, which then becomes resuscitated.

XI. Finally, while saying the word *jom* he thinks of the elements of which he is composed, and arranges them in order, in the place of those he has just got rid of.

XII. He again repeats: 'I am myself the divinity to whom I am about to do sacrifice.' He then brings back to his navel the individual soul which had been incorporated in the supreme soul, after which, putting his right hand on his head, he says: 'Glory to the Penitent Narada!' and he imagines that this Penitent is then resting on his head. Placing his hands on the vessel of water beside him he evokes upon it the *mantra gayatri*. Finally, he lays his hand on his chest, and Vishnu is at once there. He finishes by saying the letters of the alphabet over the new and perfectly pure body which he has just made for himself.

After this preparatory ceremony, called *santi-yoga*, he does *puja* to his household gods. He may also do it, over the little stone *salagrama*, to all kinds of gods. This is indeed the most perfect form of worship. But he may also do it over a vessel full of water.

XIII. He then sits down to his meal. If his means allow of it he should not fail to invite daily as many poor Brahmins as possible to this repast.

XIV. He eats in silence, but he does not begin until he has carefully put on one side for his departed ancestors a small portion of the rice and other dishes prepared for him.

The following are the principal rules which he is enjoined to observe while taking his meal; but for the most part they are neglected:—

After his food has been served the Brahmin pours a little water round the food, then traces a square patch with a thin stream of water, puts a little rice in the middle, and says: 'Glory to Narayana!' sprinkling over it a few drops of water. He also places a little rice on each of the corners of the square, saying successively: 'Glory to Vishnu! Glory to the god of evil spirits (Siva)! Glory to the god of the earth (Brahma)! Glory to the earth!' repeating each time, 'I offer him this rice.' On the rice that he is going to eat he places either some leaves of the *tulasi*[1], or a few of the flowers that he offered in the preceding sacrifice. He then traces a circular patch with a thin stream of water, and puts some rice in the centre. This is an offering to the evil spirits.

Pouring a little water into the hollow of his hand, he drinks it as a foundation for the meal he is about to make. He takes a little rice soaked in melted butter and puts it into his mouth, saying: 'Glory to the wind which dwells in the chest!' At the second mouthful, 'Glory to the wind which dwells in the face!' At the third, 'Glory to the wind which dwells in the throat!' At the fourth, 'Glory to the wind which dwells in the whole body!' At the fifth, 'Glory to those noisy ebullitions which escape above and below!'

Sannyasis, penitents, and widows may not eat anything in the evening. Should they do so they would be guilty of a crime equal to that of killing a Brahmin. The most minute attention must be paid to food; but the chief point, and the most laudable without doubt, is to see that the cooking is done with perfect cleanliness. This duty generally devolves on the women, though most Brahmins pride themselves on being good cooks. The room set apart for cooking operations is, as far as possible, the

[1] The basil plant, *Ocimum sanctum*.—ED.

most retired room in the house, so that strangers, and particularly Sudras, may not be able to look in, as that would defile the earthen vessels. The spot must be well purified to begin with by rubbing the floor over with cow-dung mixed with water. The clothing of the persons who do the work must have been freshly washed.

The Brahmin being seated on the ground, his wife places a banana leaf in front of him, or the leaves of other trees sewn together to serve as plates. She pours a few drops of water on them, and then helps the rice, putting the other dishes on each side. To flavour the rice they pour upon it melted butter, for which Brahmins have a particular fondness, or they flavour it with a kind of sauce so highly spiced that no European palate could stand its pungency. Everything is helped as well as eaten with the fingers only. Should however the dishes be very hot the wife may use a wooden spoon so as not to burn herself.

When a Brahmin or any other Hindu eats, those whom he has invited are allowed to be present. As a rule it is considered the height of rudeness to look at any one who is eating, and Hindus who are obliged when travelling to take their meals in rest-houses, or under trees, are very careful to hang up screens round the place where they eat so as not to be seen.

As soon as the husband has finished his meal the wife takes hers on the same plate, upon which, as a proof of his affection for her, the husband will leave a few scraps. She, for her part, will show no repugnance at eating the fragments that he has left. The following story, which I read in some Indian book, illustrates this:—

'An old Brahmin was so badly attacked by leprosy that one day a joint of one of his fingers dropped off while he was eating, and fell on his leaf-plate. When his wife's turn came to take her food, she contented herself with simply putting this piece of finger on one side, and ate up the remains that her husband had left without showing the smallest repugnance. The Brahmin, who was watching her, was so delighted with such a proof of her devotion that, after overwhelming her with praise, he asked her what she would like as a reward. 'Alas!' she said in a melancholy tone, 'what reward can I hope for? I am young and childless, and perhaps soon I may find myself one of the hated and despised class of widows!' 'No,' answered the Brahmin, 'you shall not go unrewarded. I will arrange for your happiness.' Accordingly the Brahmin, being a holy man and much beloved by the gods, in spite of his leprosy, was granted the favour of re-incarnation and was allowed to live with his wife as long as she and he desired. In the enjoyment of abundant riches, and of all the gifts that nature can bestow, they saw three generations pass away, being reborn each time they reached the ordinary term of human life. Moreover as a climax to their happiness they had numerous children with each new life. At last, tired of this life, they both died, and were transported to the *Sattya-loka* or paradise of Brahma.' But to return to our subject.

XV. His meal over, the Brahmin washes his hands and rinses his mouth. He must also gargle his throat twelve times.

XVI. He takes some leaves of the *tulasi* which he had offered before his meal to his household gods, and bringing to his mind the thought of either the penitent Agastya or the giant Kumbhakarna he swallows these leaves, by doing which he ensures a good digestion for the meal just eaten and wards off any illness[1].

XVII. He gives betel and areca-nut to the poor Brahmins invited to dinner and dismisses them. He then spends some time reading devotional books.

XVIII. His reading finished, he puts some betel into his mouth, and is then free to look after his ordinary business or to go and see his friends, taking care all the time not to covet either the goods or the wives of others.

XIX. Towards sunset he returns for the third time to the river and performs the evening *sandhya*, repeating the ceremonies of the morning and midday.

XX. On his return home he performs the *homam* for the second time, and reads some Puranas. He again goes through the *hari-smarana*, which, as we have already described, consists in reciting the litanies to Vishnu and pronouncing his thousand names aloud.

XXI. He then visits the temple nearest to his house, but he

[1] Agastya is the dwarf Rishi, who is said to have swallowed the ocean in three gulps. Kumbhakarna is a giant famous for his voracious appetite.—ED.

must never present himself there empty-handed. He must take as an offering either oil for the lamp, cocoanuts, bananas, camphor, or incense, &c., of which the sacrifices are composed. If he is very poor he must at least bring some betel leaves.

XXII. If the temple is dedicated to Vigneshwara (Pillayar) he walks round it once, after which, turning towards the god, he takes the lobe of his left ear in his right hand and the lobe of his right ear in his left hand, and in this position squats down on his heels three times; he then strikes himself gently on both his temples. If the shrine is dedicated to Siva he walks round it twice, and three times if it is consecrated to Vishnu.

XXIII. Having performed his religious duties he returns home, takes his evening meal, observing the usual ceremonies, and goes to bed soon afterwards. A Brahmin must purify the place where he is going to sleep by rubbing it over with cow-dung, and he must manage so that the place cannot be overlooked by any one.

A Brahmin must never sleep on a mountain, in a graveyard, in a temple, in any place where they do *puja*, in any place dedicated to evil spirits, under the shadow of a tree, on ground that has been tilled, in a cowshed, in the house of his *guru*, in any spot that is higher than that where the image of some god happens to be, any place where there happens to be ashes, holes made by rats, or where snakes generally live. He must also take care not to spend the night in houses where the servants are insolent, for fear of some accident.

A Brahmin puts a vessel full of water and a weapon near where he lays his head. He rubs his feet, washes his mouth twice, and then lies down.

A Brahmin must never go to bed with his feet wet, nor sleep under the beam which supports the roof of the house[1]. He must avoid sleeping with his face turned to the west or north. If it is impossible to arrange it otherwise it would be better to be turned towards the north than towards the west. When lying down he offers worship to the earth, to Vishnu, to Nandikeswara, one of the chief spirits who guard Siva, and to the bird *garuda* (Brahminy kite), to whom he makes the following prayers:—

[1] This is said to be a necessary precaution, as on these beams snakes are often to be found.—ED.

'Illustrious son of Kasyapa and Vinata! king of birds, with beauteous wings and sharp-pointed beak; you who are the enemy of snakes, preserve me from their poison!'

He who repeats this prayer when he goes to bed, when he rises, and after his ablutions, will never be bitten by a snake. Here is another and most efficacious prayer which they are supposed to make a rule of saying before going to bed. It bears the name of *kalasa*, and is addressed to those evil spirits, Siva's guardians. While repeating it the right hand must be placed over the various parts of the body as they are mentioned:—

'May my head be preserved from all accidents by Bhairava, my forehead by Bishana, my ears by Bhuta Karma, my face by Preta-Vahana, my thighs by Bhuta Karta, my shoulders by the Ditis who are endowed with supernatural strength, my hands by Kapalini who wears round his neck a chaplet of human skulls, my chest by Santa, my belly, lips, and two sides by Ketrika, the back of my body by Kadrupala, my navel by Kshetraja, my sexual organs by Vatu, my ankles by Siddha Vatu, and the rest of my body from my head to my feet by Surakara, my body to my waist by Vidatta, and from below my waist by Yama! May the fire which receives the worship of all the gods preserve me from all evil in whatever place I may happen to be! May the wives of the demons watch over my children, my cattle, my horses, my elephants! May Vishnu watch over my country, and may the God who takes care of all things also take care of me, particularly when I find myself in some place which is not under the protection of my divinity!'

Whoever recites this prayer every evening when going to bed will come to no harm. It suffices to wear it on the arm, to write it, and to read it, to become rich and live happily.

XXIV. Finally, the Brahmin must again think of Vishnu, and this should be his last thought before sleeping.

SECTION V.—*Second Part of the Sandhya. Mantrams or Prayers, according to the Yagur Veda ritual.*

If for any reason the Brahmin *Grahastha* is unable to perform the ablutions that form part of the first part of the *sandhya*, he must at any rate try to accomplish the second part by attentively and devoutly repeating the prayers that belong to it. He first stands with his face to the east or towards the sun. He begins by knotting the little lock of hair which grows on the top of his head, then he takes a little *darbha* grass in his left hand, and in his right hand a larger quantity which he cuts to the length of his palm.

THE MORNING SANDHYA.

He begins his religious exercises with the following prayer:—

Apavitraha pavitrova sarva vastam,
Gatopiva yassmareet pundareekaksham,
Sabahiabhian tara suchihy.

This means: 'Whether a man be pure or impure, or in whatsoever station in life he may find himself, if he thinks of him who has eyes like the lotus[1] he shall be pure within and without.'

He then prays to the water in the following words:—

'Water of the sea, of the rivers, of tanks, of wells, and of any other place whatsoever, hear favourably my prayers and vows! As the traveller, fatigued with the heat, finds rest and comfort under a tree's shade, so may I find in you solace and assistance in all my ills, and pardon for all my sins!

'O Water! you are the eye of sacrifice and battle! You have an agreeable flavour; you have the bowels of a mother for us, and all her feelings towards us! I call upon you with the same confidence with which a child at the approach of danger flies to the arms of a loving mother. Cleanse me from my sins, and all other men of their sins. O Water! at the time of the Flood Brahma the omniscient, whose name is spelt with one letter, existed alone, and existed under your form. This Brahma brooding over you and mingling with you[2] did penance, and by the merits of his penance created night. The waters which covered the earth were drawn into one place and formed the sea. Out of the sea were created the day, the years, the sun, the moon, and Brahma with his four countenances. Brahma created anew the firmament, the earth, the air, the

[1] That is, Vishnu.

[2] These words recall the words of the second verse of the first chapter of Genesis.—DUBOIS.

smaller worlds, and everything that was in existence before the Flood.'

This prayer ended, the Brahmin sprinkles a few drops of water on his head from three stalks of the sacred *darbha* grass.

Whoever in the morning shall address these prayers to water, and shall be duly impressed with their import, will surely receive remission of his sins.

Then clasping his hands, the Brahmin says:—

'Vishnu! your eyes are like a flower! I offer you my worship. Pardon my sins; I perform the *sandhya* to keep my good name and dignity as a Brahmin.' He then recalls to mind the names of the greater and lesser worlds and the divinities who inhabit them, particularly the fire, the wind, and the sun, also Brihaspati, Indra, and the gods of the earth.

After that he puts his right hand on his head, and recalls to his memory the names of Brahma, of the wind, and of the sun. He then shuts his eyes, and at the same time closing his right nostril with his thumb, he invokes the god Brahma in these words:—

'Come, Brahma, come to my navel, and stay, stay there a long time.'

He then fancies to himself that this powerful god is seated on his navel; that the deity is red in colour, having four faces and two arms, a cord round his waist, holding a pitcher in his hand, riding on a goose, and accompanied by a multitude of divinities. He then thinks of him as having had no beginning, as possessing the key to all knowledge and being able to grant all the desires of mankind, and especially as the head *guru* of Brahmins, endowed with the fullest power to purify and sanctify them; finally as the Creator of all things, and as an eternal being. After which he says:—

'Glory to the earth! Glory to the greater worlds[1]!' (These he mentions by name, and thinks of them as all lighted by the sun.) 'May my heart and my will be drawn to the path of virtue; may my desires be fulfilled in this life and in the next.

[1] There are seven greater worlds, the names of which are Bhu, Bhuvar, Svar, Mahar, Janar, Tapah, Sattya. The first is the earth, the last the paradise of Brahma. They always add the word *loka*, which means a place (*locus*).—ED.

To you, Brahma, who have created water, light, *amritam*, &c., to you I offer adoration.'

This prayer finished, he breathes heavily through his left nostril, and thereby puts to flight all the sins contained in his body. Then, closing the left nostril with either the thumb or the middle finger of the right hand, he thinks of Vishnu, whom he addresses in these terms:—

'Come, Vishnu, come to my chest, and stay there, stay there, stay there a long time.'

He then fancies Vishnu seated on his chest. This god is brown in colour, he has four arms, he carries a shell in one hand, the weapon called *sankha* in another, in the third a *chakra*, and in the fourth a lotus. He rides on the bird of prey *garuda*. The Brahmin thinks of him as omnipresent in the fourteen worlds and upholding everything by his power. Then he says:—

'Glory to the lesser worlds[1]!' (These he mentions by their names.) 'I think of them, of water, and of *amritam*.'

By virtue of this prayer all his sins are blotted out.

He then thinks of Siva, whom he invokes as follows:—

'Come, Siva, come to my forehead! Stay, stay, stay there a long time.'

He imagines Siva seated on his forehead. This god is white; he carries the *trisula* or trident in one hand, and a small drum in the other; on his forehead is a new moon. He has five faces, and each face has three eyes; he rides on an ox. He is represented further as the god self-creating and self-sufficient, as the universal destroyer. Then the Brahmin says:—

'Glory to all the lesser worlds!' (These he mentions by name.)

Then he adds, speaking to Siva: 'Destroyer of everything in the fourteen worlds, destroy my sins also.'

Whoever repeats this prayer, and makes the foregoing meditation, will assuredly obtain pardon of all his sins and be saved. However, as men are liable to fall into innumerable sins, they can hardly do too much to ensure their being

[1] There are seven lesser worlds, the names of which are Atala, Vitala, Sutala, Rasatala, Talatala, Mahatala, Patala. The last is the infernal regions, the lowest of all.—ED.

forgiven, and the stain of their wickedness removed. The Brahmin therefore addresses the following prayer to the sun:—

'O sun! who art prayer itself and the god of prayer: forgive me all the sins that I have committed while praying, all those that I have committed during the night by thought, word, and deed; forgive me all those that I have committed against my neighbour by slander or false witness, by violating or seducing another man's wife, by eating forbidden food, by receiving presents from a man of low caste, in a word, all sins of any kind into which I may have fallen by night or by day.'

Whoever addresses this prayer to the sun, and is filled with the conviction of what he is saying and performs the *achamania* at the same time, will be absolved from all his sins and will go after his death to the abode of the sun.

To perform the *achamania* he must hold some water in the hollow of his right hand, and put it three times to his mouth. He must touch the under part of his nose with the back of his thumb; then joining his thumb and first finger together he must touch both his eyes, then joining all the other fingers together to his thumb he must touch his ears, his navel, his chest, his head, and both shoulders. And before putting the water to his mouth he must always be careful to purify it by repeating over it the following prayer: 'Water! you are of a good taste,' &c., as mentioned before. Passing his hand three times above his head he lets fall a few drops of water on it, and then thrice pours a little on the ground. He draws a long breath, and thus ejects all the sins in his body. He must then recite the prayer which begins with the words: O water! at the time of the Flood,' &c., as cited above.

Water should be looked upon as the Supreme Being, and as such adoration is offered to it. Nothing is more efficacious than water to cleanse men from their sins. Therefore one cannot perform one's daily ablutions too often; or at least touch water and think of it, and so obtain a remission of sin. After having thus worshipped, the Brahmin draws a little water into his nostrils, and then shoots it out again. With this water the sinful man also falls to the ground and is crushed under the left heel. Then turning to the east, the Brahmin stands on tiptoe. Raising slightly his hands, the palms turned towards heaven, he makes the following prayer to the sun:—

'O Sun! fire is born of you, and from you the gods derive their splendour; you are the eye of the world and the light of it!'

Nothing is more efficacious than this prayer, accompanied by adorations, for turning aside anything that may bring sorrow, or sin, or pain, and for protection against untoward accident. He must add, still addressing the sun:—

'Glory to Brahma, Supreme Being! Glory to the Brahmins! Glory to the Penitents! Glory to the gods! Glory to the Vedas! Glory to Vishnu! Glory to the winds!'

While reciting this prayer he offers the *tarpana*, that is, a libation of water, to such of these gods as he names and to all the gods in general. He puts under his feet a stalk of *darbha* grass, and standing upright, on one foot if possible, he recites the famous *gayatri mantram*, which is as follows[1]:—

'Come, goddess, come and make me happy. You who are the voice of Brahma, whose name is formed of three letters; who are the mother of the Vedas, who are also the mother of Brahma; I offer you my adoration.' He who thus invokes the goddess *gayatri* three times a day will thereby be purified from all his sins.

He then pronounces the monosyllable *aum*, and cracks his fingers ten times while turning round. This is to scare away giants and evil spirits. He must then think again of the goddess *gayatri*. In the morning he must picture her to himself as a young girl of extraordinary beauty, resembling Brahma in appearance, riding on a goose, holding in her hand a stalk of *darbha* grass, dwelling in the sun's face and in the ritual of the Yajur Veda. Having thus pictured her in his mind, he prostrates himself before her.

He then addresses Vishnu in these words: 'Vishnu! your eyes are like a flower,' &c., as before.

To recite the *gayatri* without having previously offered homage to Vishnu would be labour lost. Such a lapse would indeed be a source of sin. They count on their fingers the

[1] The *gayatri mantram*, as we have already observed, is the most sacred, the most sublime, the most meritorious, and the most efficacious of all the *mantrams* of the Brahmins. They have deified this prayer, until they have come to look upon it not only as a *mantram* but as an actual goddess itself.—DUBOIS.

number of times that they recite the *gayatri*. The hands should be held aloft and covered over with a cloth, so that no one can see how many repetitions have been made. They say it in a low voice so that no one can hear them. The following is the text of this sublime prayer:—

'*Aum!* Glory to Patala! Glory to the Earth! Glory to Swarga! I think of the splendid light of the Sun. May he deign to turn my heart and my soul towards the path of virtue, and to the blessings of this world and of the next[1]!'

Every Brahmin ought to recite this *mantram* from a thousand to ten thousand times daily. He may, if self-indulgent, repeat it only a hundred or even only twenty times, but in no case less than eight times.

It is by virtue of this prayer that Brahmins become like Brahma, and after their death share his happiness. It is so extremely efficacious that its fervent repetition will blot out the most heinous sins, such for instance as having killed a Brahmin or a pregnant woman, drunk intoxicating liquors, or betrayed one's most intimate friend, &c. The Brahmin then dismisses the goddess in these terms:—

'I have prayed to you, O illustrious goddess, to obtain remission of my sins. Forgive me them, and grant that after my death I may enjoy the delights of Vaikuntha. You have Brahma's face; you are Brahma himself. It is you who have created, who preserve, and who destroy everything. Grant that I may be happy in this world, that joy, wealth, and prosperity may always be my portion, and that after my death my lot may be still happier and more lasting! Return, O goddess, after having granted me this favour, return to your usual dwelling-place!'

[1] This form does not seem to agree altogether with the original text given in the chapter on *mantrams*. I think the explanation is that there are several forms of *gayatri* which vary according to the Vedas from which they are taken.—DUBOIS.

One would think from the Abbé's description of the *gayatri* that it was a meaningless *mantram*, but the Hindus assert that in it is summed up their highest philosophy. The following is the text of the *gayatri*, with its translation:—

Aum, bhur, bhuvah, Suvah!
Aum, tat savitur Varenyam
Bhargo devasya dhimahi
Dhiyo yonah prachodayat.

Aum, earth, sky, heaven!
Aum, that excellent vivifier
The light divine, let us meditate upon.
Which (light) enlightens our understanding. ED.

He offers her *tarpana*, or the libation of water, as also to the sun and to the planet Venus, saying:—

'Glory to the sun and to the planet Venus! May the water that I now offer you find favour in your sight!'

He finally addresses this prayer to fire:—

'O Fire! listen to what I am about to say! Burn my enemies, and those who speak evil of the Vedas! The number of my sins is like a sea of fire, without bottom and without shore, ready to consume me. I implore your mercy, and may it be to me a means of salvation!'

He then evokes Rudra (Siva), whose countenance is like that of time and of fire, and says to him:—

'You are the Veda, you are the truth! You are the Supreme Being! Your face is marvellous! You are the face of the world! I offer you adoration.' Then he says:—

'Glory to Brahma! Glory to water! Glory to the god Varuna! Glory to Vishnu!'

He offers the *tarpana* to each of these gods, and then to the sun, to whom he says:—

'Illustrious son of Kasyapa, you resemble a lovely flower! You are the enemy of darkness; through you all our sins are forgiven. I offer you my worship as to the greatest of gods; deign to receive it graciously.' Finally, he turns round three times in honour of the sun, and makes him a profound bow.

THE NOONDAY SANDHYA[1].

The Brahmin, having performed his ablutions and tied up the little lock of hair on the top of his head, traces one of the usual marks on his forehead, and turning towards the east, says:—

'Vishnu! the gods delight to look on the beauties of your dwelling-place; the sight charms them, they are never tired of beholding it, they open wide their eyes, the better to be able to contemplate it!'

Then, addressing the sun, he says: 'God of light! God of the day! You are the god of the planets and of all that has life; you are the god who purifies men and blots out all their transgressions, accept the worship that I offer to you!'

[1] This is really called *Madhya-Vandana*.—ED.

He then says:—

'Glory to the lesser worlds! Glory to Swarga! Glory to the earth! Glory to Maha-loka! Glory to Tapo-loka! Glory to Yama-loka! Glory to Sattya-loka! It is by the almighty power of the sun, the Supreme Being, that water, light, *amrita*, Brahma with the four faces, and everything that exists, have been created.'

Putting his left thumb on his right hand, he says:—

'May everything in me, be it good or bad, commendable or blameworthy, be purified by the sun, the Supreme Being!'

By virtue of this prayer his sins are *dried up*. Then, closing up both his nostrils, he carries his thoughts back to Krishna, the son of Nanda. This thought causes sin to tremble. He must picture sin to himself under the form of a black man with a horrible face. Then, putting his thumb to his left nostril, he recalls Siva, and says:—

'Siva, who are the chief of evil spirits, save me from punishment and put my sins to flight with your trident!'

Breathing strongly through his left nostril, he performs the *achamania*, and says.—

'The water purifies the earth; may the earth which has been purified by the water take away all the sins which I may have committed—by eating after another person, by partaking of forbidden food, by receiving gifts from a man of low caste or from a sinful person. I pray that the water may purify me from all sin, whatsoever it may be.' He performs the *achamania* twice more, for nothing washes away sin more surely than water. Every Brahmin should therefore perform *achamania*; for by this act alone not only will all his sins be remitted, even to the murder of a Brahmin or of a pregnant woman, but further it also makes him sinless for all time to come. He then takes three stalks of *darbha* grass, and sprinkles some drops of water on his head with it; but he must first purify the water by reciting over it the *gayatri* and the following *mantrams*:— 'O water! who are spread on the bosom of the earth, grant that I may perform the *sandhya*, so that, being purified by it, I may perform *puja*!' 'O water! you have a good taste,' &c., and so on as before. He sprinkles some water with the three stalks of *darbha* grass, first on the earth and then on his head. He who in addition to the above recites the following prayer, may be assured that all his desires will be gratified, that he will live in the midst of plenty and be happy:—'O water! you are in everything that has life, in all quarters of the world, even on the tops of the highest mountains. You are of superlative excellence, you are the light, you are the *amrita*!' He then rises, and filling both his hands with water, pours it on the ground, saying:—

'Glory to Patala! Glory to the Earth! Glory to Swarga!' Then, turning to the sun, and raising his hands on high, he says:—

'O Sun! you are the will of the gods, you are the opposite of water! You are the eye of the gods Mitra, Varuna, and of Fire; you shine in Swarga, on the earth, and everywhere!' He then repeats the prayer which begins with these words:—

'Glory to Brahma, the Supreme Being!' &c., and so on as before.

He places one or two stalks of *darbha* grass under his feet, and evokes the *gayatri* in these words:—

'Come, goddess, come and shower your favours upon me! You are the word of Brahma, the mother of the Vedas: it is from you that Brahma was born. I offer you *puja*! You are the mother of Brahmins. It is you who bear the engine of the world, and carry the weight thereof. It is through your protection that men live peacefully in the world, for by your care all evil, fear, and danger are kept far from them. It is through you that men become virtuous, and it is from you that *puja* derives its efficacy. You are eternal! Hasten, great goddess, and answer my prayer!'

It is by virtue of this prayer that the gods have attained to Swarga; that snakes penetrate into the bowels of the earth, and float in the midst of the waters; that fire possesses the power of burning; that Brahmins, grown like to the gods, merit daily to receive worship and sacrifice from other men in acknowledgement of their surpassing knowledge and virtue. He repeats the invocation to the sun, and purifies himself in pronouncing the sacred word *aum*. Then he performs the *vyahriti* in the following manner:—

'Glory to Patala!' (he puts his hands to his head).

'Glory to the Earth!' (he puts his hands on the tuft of hair on the top of his head).

'Glory to Swarga!' (he touches himself all over his body).

Then he exclaims, '*Aum-bhatu!*' at the same time cracking his fingers ten times whilst turning round, and he stamps the ground with his left heel to scare away giants and evil spirits.

He evokes the *gayatri* afresh, whom now at noon he represents to himself under the image of Vishnu, in the prime of life, clothed in a golden robe, and dwelling in the sun's face. He then recites the *gayatri mantram* the proper number of times, exactly as before described, and then he dismisses the deity, saying:—

'You are born of Siva's face; you dwell in the bosom of Vishnu; you are known of Brahma; go, goddess, whither you will! You are Brahma, the Supreme Being; you receive the worship of Vishnu; you are the life of Brahmins; their fate is in your hands; it is in your power to give them happiness in this world and in the next; give me many children, and may I always have abundance of wealth. Illustrious mother! I have offered you *puja*; now depart whither it seemeth good!'

Nevertheless he says yet another prayer to her:—

'Divine wife of Narayana! preserve me from any pain in my head, face, tongue, nose, nostrils, ears, shoulders, thighs, feet, and in any part of my body; preserve me from pain day and night!'

He thus sings the *gayatri's* praises:—

'You are quick-witted; you are enlightenment itself; you are not subject to human passions; you are eternal; you are almighty; you are purity itself; you are the refuge and salvation of mankind; you are omniscient; you are the mother of all the Vedas, of which you are the emblem; you are also the emblem of prayer. It is to you that all sacrifices must be offered; all earthly blessings are at your disposal; in an instant you can destroy everything. Happiness and misery, joy and sorrow, hope and fear are in your hands; everything is dependent on you. All men pray to you, and at the same time your fascinations cast a spell over them. You fulfil all their desires, and overwhelm them with benefits; to you they owe success in all their undertakings; you put away their sins; you make them happy; you are present in all three worlds; you have three bodies and three faces, and the numeral three is of your very essence!'

He who thus sings the *gayatri's* praises will receive his reward; all his sins will be forgiven.

Casting his eyes on liquefied butter, he says: 'O butter! you are the light; by your power everything shines; you are the friend of the gods; you form part of the sacrifices that are offered to them, you are the essence of these sacrifices!'

Then, addressing the *gayatri* anew, he says: 'You can be divided into two, three, and four parts; nothing can equal your brilliancy; I offer you *puja*!' He adds:—

'O goddess, who dwell on the mountains of the North, you are known to Brahma! Go now whither you will, you are the sacrificer of the sacrifice. It is you who offer it, it is you who receive it. It is you who regulate the offerings, it is you who make them, it is you who receive them; you have yielded the north-east to Siva, and you have taken up your abode in the north-west. If we enjoy light, it is you to whom we owe it, to you who have granted it to us that we may by its aid fulfil our religious duties!'

He addresses the fire in these words:—

'O fire! come here; I have need of you for *puja*; offer it yourself, since you are the emblem of it!'

He says to the water:—

'O water! remain on the earth, for the use of us who require you: remain that we may drink you, and come down abundantly to fertilize our land!'

Whoever repeats all these prayers at the midday *sandhya* will have all his wishes gratified and obtain pardon for all his sins.

He again addresses the *gayatri* as follows:—'I worship you, O goddess, under the image of Brahma. You are the mother of the world; Brahmins offer you *puja*, and in return enjoy your favours. You have the outward appearance of a stone; but you are indeed the creator, preserver, and destroyer of everything!'

He offers *arghya* to the sun. To this end he puts water and red flowers, some *darbha* grass, some sandalwood powder, and some mustard seed into a plated copper vessel. While mixing all these together, he says:—

'O sun! you are the most brilliant of all the stars! Vishnu borrows his splendour from you! You are pure and you purify men; I offer you worship! Glory to the sun! I offer him this *arghya*!'

Such, then, is the noonday *sandhya*. It is a religious exercise which must never be omitted, but if for any reason one fails to perform it, one must do penance before performing the evening *sandhya*. This penance consists in repeating the *gayatri* ten times, and offering *arghya* to the sun.

A Brahmin who does not perform the *sandhya* regularly is not-permitted to fulfil any other act of religious worship. It would be quite fruitless for him to offer *puja*, or *sraddha* (the sacrifice for the dead), or to fast or to pray.

The inestimable advantages which the *gayatri mantram* procures are proportionate to the number of times it is repeated. Thus for a thousand repetitions you would obtain success in all your undertakings; for ten thousand, the forgiveness of sins and abundance of this world's goods; for twenty thousand, the spirit of wisdom and the gift of knowledge; for a hundred thousand, the supreme grace of becoming a Vishnu after death.

It is considered most meritorious to solemnly undertake to recite the *gayatri* for a certain fixed time daily, the credit gained thereby being graduated according to the length of time devoted to the exercise. It depends, that is to say, on the choice that one makes of the three following periods: (1) from sunrise to sunset; (2) from sunrise to noon; and (3) at intervals of about three hours.

Any Brahmin who makes such a vow calls together a certain number of his fellow-Brahmins, and says in their presence:—

'To-day being such and such a day of such and such a month, I, so-and-so Brahmin, of such and such country and family, being desirous of averting all danger from myself, of growing in virtue, and of obtaining the delights of Swarga after my death, hereby call all present to witness that I vow to recite the *gayatri* every day from such an hour till such an hour.'

The Evening Sandhya.

Brahmins begin this *sandhya* about sunset, but it must not be performed on the day of the *sankranti*, that is to say, on the day that the sun moves from one sign of the Zodiac to another, nor on the days of the new and full moon, nor on the twelfth day of the moon, nor yet on the day on which one has offered the sacrifice for the dead called *sraddha.* To perform the evening *sandhya* under these circumstances would be committing a crime equal to the murder of a Brahmin. If a Brahmin has just lost his father, his mother, or one of his children; if his gums bleed, or if through a wound or accident any part of his body above the navel has been bleeding, or in a word if he finds that he is impure, he would commit an unpardonable sin by performing the evening *sandhya.* Indeed, in the last case he would lose all his possessions and his children. Except under these special circumstances, he must never neglect this religious duty, and he must carefully observe the following rules:—

He makes the usual ablutions. Then, turning to the north, he recalls the memory of Vishnu. He then thinks of Brahma and addresses the following prayer to him:—

'Brahma, you have four faces, you are my creator! Forgive me all the sins that I have committed. I am now beginning the evening *sandhya.* Deign to be present, and repose on my chest, and deliver me from my sins.'

He then recites the *mantram* which begins with these words:—'Glory to the lesser worlds!' and so on as before. Closing up both nostrils, he thinks of Vishnu, and imagines that he is resting on his navel, and says: 'Oh, Vishnu! you are of great stature and black in colour. You have four arms, you are the preserver of all that exists; destroy my sins.' He offers worship to the seven greater worlds, as in the morning *sandhya,* and again addressing Vishnu, he says: 'You have created light, *amrita,* and all that is used for the food of mankind. Preserve me, and preserve all that lives in the world!' Closing the right nostril with his finger, he breathes strongly through the left, and by this means burns all the sins that are in his body. Then he ejects them by breathing forcibly through the right nostril. He then directs his thoughts to Siva, the destroyer of sin and of all things, and imagines that he is resting on his forehead. He says to him: 'O Siva! you are white and tall. You have the mark of a half-moon on your forehead; you have three eyes; you destroy all things; you are the god of gods; I implore your protection, and offer you worship!' He once more offers *puja* to the different worlds, and destroys his sins by virtue of the following prayer:—'Oh, may my sins be destroyed by the almighty power of the sun and the fire!' He adds: 'O fire! you are prayer and the god of prayer. Forgive me all the mistakes I have made in the different *mantrams* that I have recited; and forgive me, besides, all the sins that I have this day committed in thought, word, and deed. May this water, which I drink from my uplifted hand, destroy everything bad and sinful that may be in me.' He performs the *achamania* as at the morning *sandhya*. He also inhales some purified water into his nostrils, as he did before, and recites the *mantram* which begins with the words: 'O water! at the time of the Flood,' &c., and so on, as before mentioned.

Then he ejects by a forcible expiration the water in his nostrils, which carries away the sinful man, whom he crushes at once upon a stone. He represents this man of sin to himself as a powerful being, of extraordinary strength, with a red belly, white hair and beard, and a hideous and distorted face[1].

He evokes the *gayatri*, and turning to the west, he says:—

'O god of the day, on whom depends the happiness of mankind, I offer the evening *sandhya*: deign to honour me with your presence! O goddess *gayatri*, who are the emblem of the Vedas and the word of Brahma, whose name is composed of three letters! I offer you *puja*; hasten hither that I may be happy!'

Whilst making this prayer his hands are spread open and raised towards heaven. He then rubs his hands together and puts them to his breast, believing in imagination that the *gayatri* is reposing there. He cracks his finger-joints ten times, and turns round at the same moment; and by that he closes

[1] Here is another portrait of a man of sin, culled from the *Sama-Veda*: 'The murder of a Brahmin forms the head of the man of sin; drinking intoxicating liquors, the eyes; theft, particularly of gold, the face; the murder of a *guru*, the ears; the murder of a woman, the nose; the murder of a cow, the shoulders; the rape of another man's wife, the chest; the wilful production of abortion, the neck; oppression of the innocent and just, the belly; ill treatment of any one who has sought protection, the stomach; to slander your *guru*, violate a virgin, betray a secret confided to you, or to be false to any one who has relied on you, these are the private parts and the thighs; and the hairs of these are the smaller sins. This man of sin is of gigantic stature, and has a horrible face; he is black, and has wild bright eyes; he delights in torturing mankind.'—DUBOIS.

all places of egress, so that the goddess cannot depart. He pictures her to himself as an old woman, having Siva's face, riding on an ox, dwelling in the disk of the sun, and united to all the Vedas. Then he says:—

'Divine wife of Siva! you are the mother of all that is. I offer you *puja* at the approach of night, take me under your protection and save me! Come, *gayatri*, come and favourably hear my prayers!'

Whoever recites these words will obtain all that he asks for. Then, facing the north, with his arms hanging down, he recites the *gayatri mantram*, in the same manner and the same number of times as before. It is impossible to repeat this prayer too often in the evening, evening prayers being so much more efficacious than others. A Brahmin who daily recites this prayer uninterruptedly from sunset to midnight will by this pious exercise most assuredly place himself beyond the possibility of want or misery, and will ensure for himself a quiet and peaceful death, without sickness or pain, when his long and prosperous career shall draw to a close.

To dismiss the goddess *gayatri* he uses the same formulas as those of the noonday *sandhya*, and, after the *tarpana*, or libation of water, to the sun and the planet Venus, he addresses Siva in these words:—'O Rudra! protect me from all accident and danger as well by night as by day. You are the lord of the world; take me under your protection that nothing may hurt me or do me harm.' The prayer to fire follows; then he offers *tarpana* to the following gods, saying: 'Glory to Brahma! Glory to water! Glory to Varuna! Glory to Vishnu! Glory to Rudra!' While offering *arghya* to the sun, he says: 'God of light, god of the day! I offer you worship! Receive the *arghya* that I now present to you, and deliver me from the cares and dangers of the world!'

CONCLUSION.

'I will conclude,' the author goes on to say, 'by explaining what the *sandhya* is, and on what occasions it should be offered.

'Brahma, the author and father of the Vedas, wishing to extract the essence of them, composed the *sandhya*, which is in respect to the other Vedas what butter is to milk, or what gold is compared with the other metals. In short, as honey is the quintessence of flowers, so the *sandhya* is the quintessence of the Vedas.

'And as the *sandhya* is all that is most sublime in the Vedas, so is the *gayatri* all that is most sublime in the *sandhya*. This celebrated prayer obtains for mankind the remission of their sins, plenty, joy, wealth, health, and also ensures their happiness hereafter.

'They must beware of teaching this prayer to the degraded Sudras. Whoever dared to do so would assuredly go to the infernal regions—he, his father, and his children; and if a Sudra happened to overhear a Brahmin repeating it he would inevitably go to the same place and remain there for all eternity.

'I have said it, and I repeat it,' says the author, 'let them beware of making it known to the Sudras, under pain of eternal damnation.

'No meditation, penance, sacrifice, knowledge, prayer, can compare in efficacy to the *gayatri mantram*. Its merits are superexcellent, but it must also be kept a profound secret. It was Brahma himself who composed it expressly for Brahmins.

'This is the idea which must be formed of the goddess *gayatri*. Though she appears under the form of a prayer, it must be recognized that she is the Supreme Being, and she must be worshipped as such. Brahma, who composed this *mantram*, taught it to Indra, who taught it to Yama; he in turn instructed Siva, who taught it to the Brahmins.'

Such are the prayers and ceremonials used by Brahmins when performing the three *sandhyas*, and such are the extravagant absurdities to which they are bound to conform.

The intense and mysterious solemnity with which they perform all this ceremonial is intended to persuade others that its end and object must be of the highest and most vital importance; the inner meaning being quite beyond the reach of the vulgar and ignorant. Every care is taken to strengthen this opinion; and they use the greatest precautions to exclude the searching eyes of educated persons.

Though assured of the blind credulity of the ignorant masses over whom they hold sway, they are well aware that, if ever the spell should be broken, their charlatanism and cupidity would stand revealed, and they would then become the laughing-stock of the public.

If the *sandhya* really represents the cream of the Vedas, I do not think that any European will regret the want of a wider acquaintance with these famous books. As an excuse for the fantastic folly of many of their religious performances Brahmins assert that some, if not all, are only allegories, of which the inner meaning is more rational. This may very likely be true; but I am fully persuaded that the tradition of this inner meaning has been lost. There are beyond question very few Brahmins who would be able to give even the most imperfect idea of what their rites were originally intended to convey. It is an undoubted fact that the greater number of them have nothing in their minds beyond the material and literal fulfilment of the ridiculous ceremonies which they are in the habit of performing. Take, for instance, their celebrated mysterious *gayatri*, of which each word, they aver, contains a hidden meaning—a meaning, however, which is interpreted in as many different ways as there are castes and sects[1].

The first four sections of this chapter are taken from the *Nitya Karma*, or Brahminical ritual. I was acquainted with the second part of the *sandhya* when I first compiled this work; I had read a full description of its details in a little manuscript of M. Pons, formerly a Jesuit missionary in the Carnatic, who died about eighty years ago. He had travelled all over Southern India, and was a good Sanskrit scholar, having written a grammar of that language. But the particulars which this learned man gave appeared to me so extraordinary and so incredible, that I doubted their authenticity and did not venture to use them. I afterwards procured a book in Canara entitled *Purohita-Asrama-Karma*, or 'The Religious Observances of a Brahmin Purohita,' in which I found the same details in almost exactly the same words. I consulted some Brahmins on the subject, and they assured me that they were substantially correct, but that there were some *mantrams* and ceremonies mentioned which were not in use in the Southern Provinces, though they were

[1] A Hindu would contend that the fact of the hidden meaning of the *mantrams* having been lost does not make the *mantrams* absurd, but only those who perform the ceremonies without understanding their meaning. —ED.

used in the north. Indeed I was assured the ceremonial and *mantrams* vary slightly in different parts, according to the Veda and the sect of those that follow them. But, according to my informants, most Brahmins neglect and are even altogether ignorant of the greater part of them.

The Kshatriyas and the Vaisyas must also perform the *sandhya*; but it is not as obligatory for them, especially for Vaisyas, as it is for Brahmins. Furthermore, the *mantrams* and ceremonials of the latter are quite different, and not nearly so numerous.

The Jains also perform the *sandhya*. As for the Sudras, they can only make simple ablutions, without any prayers or ceremonies; but any one who wishes to be distinguished from the vulgar herd, and to be considered a more exalted person, rarely fails to perform the ablutions at least once a day. To see them one would never think that those who perform the *sandhya* are actuated in any way by a spirit of devotion. The Brahmin gets through all these ceremonies and repeats all these prayers as quickly as possible; he is like a schoolboy gabbling over a lesson he has learnt by heart; and this, like everything else, is all performed perfunctorily and as a duty to be discharged with all possible celerity.

CHAPTER VIII

Brahminical Fasts.—The Custom of Rubbing the Head and Body with Oil.—The Over-indulgence of Brahmins.—Their Scrupulous Observance of Custom.—Reflections on this Subject.—Their *Samaradhanas*, or Public Feasts.—Sudra Feasts.

BRAHMINS are obliged to keep frequent and often prolonged fasts[1]. They are expected to accustom themselves to them as indispensable adjuncts of their religion from the day they assume the triple cord. Even old age, infirmity, or sickness, unless it be very serious, is not held to exempt them from these fasts.

On ordinary days the Brahmin *Grahastha* may take two meals; one after midday, and one before going to bed. But this rule has many exceptions. There are many days on which he is allowed to take only one meal, about three o'clock in the afternoon; and there are others when he may neither eat nor drink.

The days of the new and full moon are fast-days, as also the tenth, eleventh, and twelfth days of each lunar month, which are called the *ekadasi vrata*; on the tenth and twelfth days one meal may be taken, on the eleventh day, called *ekadasi*, no meal at all is allowed. To fast on these three days has a special merit[2].

[1] One is perpetually struck by the numerous points of resemblance between the manners and customs of modern Brahmins and those of the Pharisees, with which we have become acquainted through the Holy Scriptures. Their lives are full of the same affectations, they share the same dread of defilement, there are the same continual ablutions and bathings, the same scrupulous attention to the outward observance of the law, the same frequent fasts, &c.; but all this is tainted by overweening pride, ostentation, and hypocrisy. What St. Matthew says of this sect (xxiii. 27) might certainly be applied without injustice to the Brahmins of India.—DUBOIS.

[2] The eleventh day is the only strict fast-day, and it is observed only by old and religiously disposed Brahmins and widows. The Madhva Brahmins observe the fast more scrupulously than others nowadays.—ED.

As the fast which is kept on the eleventh day of each lunar month is observed with particular solemnity, I will give a few details of it in an appendix [1].

The thirteenth day of the moon is an unlucky day. Brahmins must eat nothing on that day till sunset [2]. In the evening, before taking their food, they offer *puja* to Siva, to propitiate him, and then begin to eat.

The feast called *Sivaratri* (or 'Siva's Night') falls on the fourteenth day of the moon in the month of *Maga* (February), the origin and particulars of which will be seen in an appendix [3]. On that day no one must eat or drink, or even sleep, for the whole twenty-four hours. Every three hours during the day and night *puja* is offered to Siva, and not until the following day, after having performed the *sandhya*, are they at liberty to eat [4].

On the ninth day of the lunar month *Cheitra* (April), being the anniversary of the incarnation of the great god Vishnu in the person of Rama, Brahmins may take only one meal in the day, and that without rice; they may only eat peas, cakes, bananas, and cocoanuts [5].

On the eighth day of the month of *Sravana* (August), the day of Vishnu's incarnation in the person of Krishna, they are forbidden to take any food at all, and must give themselves up to works of piety. They make clay images of Krishna and his wife Rukmani, Satya Bhama, Bala-Badra, Rohini, Vasu-Deva, Nanda, Devaki. At midnight they offer *puja* to all these deities together, and for *neiveddya* they offer cocoanuts, bananas, coarse sugar, common peas, peaflour, milk, and cakes. The next day, after the *sandhya*, they can take their usual meals.

They must also fast on the anniversaries of the ten *Avatars* (incarnations) of Vishnu; on the days called *manuvadi*, *yugadi*, *sankranti*; on the days of eclipses; at the equinoxes, solstices, and the conjunction of planets, and other unlucky days; on the anniversary of the death of father or mother; on Sundays and several other days during the year.

[1] Appendix II.

[2] This fast is not generally observed nowadays.—ED.

[3] Appendix III.

[4] This festival is only observed by followers of Siva, and never by Vishnavites.—ED.

[5] This festival, though strictly speaking a Vishnavite festival, is also observed by ordinary Sivaites.—ED.

On fast-days a man is not allowed to have intercourse with his wife; the women are forbidden to rub their bodies with powdered saffron and the men to anoint their heads with oil. Wednesday and Saturday are the only days in the week on which this cosmetic process may be indulged in with advantage. To anoint yourself on other days might produce serious consequences. For instance, if you anoint yourself on Sunday, you run the risk of catching all sorts of complaints; if on Monday, that of losing your personal attractions; if on Tuesday, you will shorten your life; and if on Friday, you will probably become overwhelmed with debts. Nevertheless, when the case is one of urgent necessity, they may anoint themselves on one of these days after taking certain precautions [1].

Whenever any one wishes to perform this operation, it is necessary first to think of Asvatthama, of Bhali Chakravarti, of Veda-Vyasa, of Hanumanta, of Vibhishana, of Krupacharia, and of Parasu-Rama. Dipping the tips of his fingers in the oil, the anointer must let seven drops fall on the ground, as a libation in honour of these seven personages. After that he may anoint his head in the usual manner [2].

This libation is considered rather important. The seven personages whose names have been mentioned are supposed to require oil to anoint their heads; it is only fair, therefore, to give them a few drops. They, on their side, from feelings of gratitude, grant long life and riches to whoever shows them this mark of respect.

But to return to the fasts. The Brahmins do not appear to feel the least inconvenience from enforced abstinence from food. Neither is it a great hardship to them, for from their early youth they are accustomed to eat nothing till after

[1] These customs are not very strictly observed nowadays.—ED.

[2] The custom of oiling the body was very common among the Jews. They considered it a healthy and cleanly habit. They anointed the hair and beard (Psalm cxxxiii. 2). At festivals or on days of public rejoicing they anointed either their whole bodies or else only the head or feet with unguents (St. Matthew vi. 17; St. Luke vii. 38; St. John xii. 3). They also anointed the dead (St. Mark xiv. 8, xvi. 1; St. Luke xxiii. 56). Their kings and high priests were anointed at their consecration. The vessels of the Tabernacle were also consecrated with holy oil (Exodus xxx. 26–28).—DUBOIS.

These semi-divine personages are called *Chiranjivis* in Sanskrit, literally "the long lived."—ED.

midday. Besides, on these days of mortification they take care to make up for the lateness of their meal by the large quantity they eat when once they begin. Habit has enabled Brahmins to overload their stomachs with most indigestible food, without feeling any discomfort or inconvenience. One often sees a Brahmin, after making a hearty meal of rice and liquefied butter, eat the whole of a huge jack-fruit[1], which would be enough to give ten Europeans violent indigestion.

These frequent fasts appear to form part of a dietary system which has been misinterpreted in a religious sense; or more probably they are due to a desire on the part of the Brahmins to attract public attention and respect by an ostentatious display of moderation. Be that as it may, gluttony may certainly be included among the numerous vices of the Brahmins. There is no limit to their appetite when they get the opportunity of indulging it, and such opportunities frequently occur, seeing that their numberless ceremonies always end with a feast; and on these occasions they make a point of gorging themselves to the utmost extent. There is no doubt that, in spite of their being accustomed to it, this habit of eating to excess would in the end be productive of disastrous consequences in a climate where moderation in all things must be the rule of life, if fasts enforced by custom did not give their stomachs a little rest from time to time.

If Brahmins can with a certain amount of justice reproach Europeans for intemperance in drinking, with no less justice can Europeans retort that Brahmins show great want of moderation in eating. Besides, drunkenness is not an habitual vice among respectable Europeans, and those who frequently give way to it are looked upon with contempt by their own countrymen; whereas Brahmins, who are the cream of Hindu society, and 'the gods of the earth,' are perfect slaves to their stomachs. Indeed the most revolting gluttony does not horrify them, and they even justify it under the cloak of religion. It is by no means uncommon for them to gorge themselves to such repletion that they are unable to rise from the place where they have been eating.

Far from being ashamed of this, they pretend that it is

[1] The tree which produces this is the *tijaca-marum* of Malabar. It is the largest fruit known, and is extremely indigestible.—DUBOIS.

infinitely pleasing to the god Jivattma, that is to say, to *the principle of life*, which they have deified. The more liquefied butter and other food they can cram into their stomachs, the better the god Jivattma will be pleased. When they sit down to a feast it is curious to watch the preparations that are made so that nothing may hinder the full play of the appetite, and Jivattma be thoroughly satisfied. To prevent themselves from being inconvenienced in any way during this important operation of eating, they begin by taking off their turbans and clothes, sitting down to the feast almost naked. While eating they occasionally stroke their heads, their throats, their chests, and their stomachs, and rub these portions of their bodies in order, as it were, to help the food to descend more quickly into the abdominal regions. They never get up from a meal until it is absolutely impossible to swallow another morsel; and then, to alleviate the enormous amount of work their stomachs are put to, they swallow a piece of assafoetida, the aperient and sudorific qualities of which no doubt prevent the ill effects which would otherwise infallibly result from such excesses.

To fill one's stomach well is a very favourite expression amongst Hindus, and one you very often hear. Whenever they feast in another's house the host never fails to ask his guests if their stomachs are well filled. The first question that a Brahmin's wife and children ask on his return from a feast is, 'Have you filled your stomach well?' and it affords him the greatest pleasure to be able to answer, while he gently rubs that part of his person, 'My stomach is well filled.'

Hindus belonging to other castes which have the right to wear the triple cord also keep most of the Brahminical fasts, and so do even some Sudras who have not that privilege, but who wish to gain the respect and consideration of the public. When these days of mortification come round all manual labour is stopped, all outdoor work is suspended, the shops are closed, and workmen, artisans, and labourers give themselves and their cattle a rest. Fasts which recur so often naturally cause a considerable waste of time, but in a country where industry meets with so little encouragement this drawback is not much felt; and the indolent Hindu has generally more time on his hands than he requires to look after his business, which is never of a very pressing nature. It is indeed quite probable that their natural indolence and dislike for work of all kinds partly contributed to the institution of so many days of rest!

All these practices which the Hindu thinks himself called upon to observe are so overladen with fanciful and even ridiculous details that it is difficult to understand how any civilized people could have preserved them intact up to the present day. The Hindus, however, are so obstinately devoted to custom and precedent that no sensible person amongst them would think for a moment of trying to bring about a change. It is true that several of their modern philosophers, such as Vemana, Tiruvalluvar, Pattanattu-pillai, Agastya and others, have ridiculed such customs; yet they nevertheless recommend people to follow them, and themselves conform minutely to every observance[1].

Our Western religion, education, and manners are so diametrically opposed at all points to the religious and civil usages of the Hindus that they are naturally looked upon with a most unfavourable eye by the latter. In their opinion Europeans may almost be placed below the level of beasts, and even the more sensible among them cannot understand

[1] Amongst the few Hindu works which are written in a free philosophical vein, and in which the Hindu religion and its customs are openly criticized, not one that I know of has been written by a Brahmin. All the works of this kind that I have seen have emanated from authors who were not of this caste. Tiruvalluvar was a Pariah, Pattanattu-pillai and Agastya were both of the *Vellala* caste, and their poems are written in Tamil; Sarovignaimurti was a Lingayat, and his works are in Canarese. One of the most famous is Vemana, whose poems, originally written in Telugu, have since been translated into several other languages. We are told that this philosopher, who was of the *Reddy* caste, and was born in the district of Cuddapah, died towards the end of the seventeenth century. His writings, from which I have seen several extracts, appear to me to be most interesting, and are distinguished by much discernment and independence. It is to be noticed that the authors of all these satirical and revolutionary works belong to recent times. If in earlier days any enlightened writers published similar works, the Brahmins have taken care that not a trace of them shall remain. Nowadays they rage against the authors we have mentioned, and speak of their works with contempt. They cannot, of course, succeed in destroying them, but they do everything in their power to prevent the reading of them.—DUBOIS.

The last sentences of the Abbé's note are misleading, for these authors are held in great respect, and are much read by educated Brahmins. These latter must be distinguished from the purely priestly class of Brahmins, whose interest it may be to dissuade people from studying these works.—ED.

how people, possessed in other ways of so many superior qualities, can conform in their everyday life to manners and customs which differ so radically from their own, and which, as a natural consequence, they consider most coarse and degraded.

The Brahmin rule of life is in appearance intolerably severe, but it has become for them a mere matter of habit encouraged by vanity and self-interest. Their punctiliousness in the fulfilment of their religious duties day by day, their self-denials and their fasts, form part of the business of their lives and are looked upon in the light of pastimes. They know, too, full well, that the eyes of the multitude are always on them, and the smallest relaxation of their discipline or the least negligence in any particular would put an end to the almost boundless veneration and respect with which the common people regard them. I have however met with Brahmins who were sufficiently reasonable to admit that many of their customs were opposed to all common sense, and that they only practised them out of consideration for their co-religionists. I know also that most of them evade the rules and absolve themselves without hesitation from the performance of very many of their trifling ceremonies when they are quite certain that these lapses will remain a profound secret. Thus, for example, there are very few who perform their ablutions more than once a day, or who strictly observe the prescribed fasts. To keep up appearances, to dazzle the eyes of the public, to avoid scandal, such are the limits of their pious zeal. Although in public they affect the utmost strictness, they are very much less particular in private life; and a well-known saying confirms this assertion: 'A real Brahmin in the *agrahara*[1], half a Brahmin when seen afar off, and a Sudra when entirely out of sight[2].'

It must be acknowledged, however, that they are very tenacious of these long-established customs. Any one who is believed to openly neglect them incurs severe censure and contempt, and also lays himself open to serious insults and annoyances. The *gurus* of the Brahmins keep a very watchful eye over the others. Those found guilty of a breach of discipline are not

[1] The name of villages entirely peopled by Brahmins.

[2] This is even more true nowadays than it was in the time of the Abbé, at any rate among the Brahmins educated on Western lines.—ED.

always let off with severe reprimands publicly delivered. The saintly *gurus* rarely omit the imposition of a heavy fine, the amount of which is fixed by themselves.

The *purohitas* also are obliged, for the sake of example and to keep up appearances, to follow the Brahminical usages with the utmost strictness, even to the minutest details; but it is greatly to their interest to keep up all these practices, seeing that they form a never-failing source of profit.

The scrupulous exactitude of the Brahmins is particularly noticeable at the *samaradhanas*, or public feasts, to which they are often invited by persons of high degree, such as Rajahs, governors of provinces, and other high officials, or wealthy individuals who pride themselves on the enormous expense which their prodigality entails on these occasions. The dedication of a new temple, the inauguration of an idol, the celebration of a feast-day or of a marriage, the birth of an heir, &c., expiatory ceremonies for the sins of the departed to procure their admittance into the abode of bliss, votive ceremonies to ensure victory in time of war, to avert the evil effects of an unlucky constellation, or to obtain rain in time of drought, &c., &c.; one and all of these are opportunities for *samaradhanas*[1]. It is needless to add that the Brahmins who make their living out of these and similar practices insist very warmly on their being kept up, and place them in the foremost rank of meritorious actions. When a *samaradhana* is announced as about to take place, all, men and women, from seven or eight miles round, flock to it, sometimes to the number of over two thousand[2]. Each and all bring with them an appetite well calculated to do full justice to the hospitality of their entertainer. These gatherings are composed entirely of Brahmins, and as every one keeps his eye on his neighbour there is much rivalry as to who will show the greatest familiarity with the customs of their caste and the greatest zeal in carrying them out. An ancient Roman philosopher once said that he could not imagine how two augurs could meet without laughing in each other's faces. What would he have thought of the grave and serious

[1] The Jews had also their solemn feasts. Frequent mention is made of them in the Bible.—DUBOIS.

[2] There is a sarcastic Tamil proverb to the effect that 'a Brahmin will walk even a hundred miles for rice and dholl.'—ED.

mien which Hindu soothsayers and impostors preserve under similar circumstances?

Seated on the ground in long rows, the women entirely separated from the men, they sing in turn while waiting for their food, either Sanskrit hymns in honour of their deities or love-songs. All those who are listening cry out as a mark of approval, '*Hara! Hara! Govinda*[1]!' though the greater number have probably understood nothing of what has been sung.

The giver of the entertainment is not permitted to eat with his guests unless he is himself a Brahmin. If he is of another caste he appears after the feast is finished, and prostrates himself humbly before these *gods of the earth* who have done him the honour to devour the food he has provided, and who in return give him their *asirvada* or blessing. If their host crowns the feast by a distribution of presents of cloth or money, their fulsome compliments will know no bounds, and they will exalt him even above their own deities. At this the host feels excessively flattered, thoroughly convinced that such an honour cannot be too dearly bought. I have already remarked that all Hindus are particularly susceptible to flattery. There is an entire caste called *Battus*, who are in a way flatterers by profession. Their only occupation in life is to grovel before people of position or importance, and to recite or sing before them verses composed in their honour, which are full to overflowing of the most extravagant eulogies. The most astonishing thing is that, instead of wounding the modesty and susceptibilities of those to whom they are addressed, these songs are received with complacency and looked upon as sincere tributes to undoubted merit, the author being handsomely rewarded for them.

Those who belong to the sects of Siva and Vishnu also have their *samaradhanas*, or public feasts, which are given by the wealthy among them[2]. As all the guests who crowd to these entertainments are Sudras, and for the most part low, uneducated people, the festivities are generally very noisy and disorderly,

[1] A style of acclamation. They are the names of Siva and Vishnu.—DUBOIS.

[2] This is untrue of Vishnavite Brahmins, for no two Vishnavite Brahmins will eat together unless they be very closely related.—ED.

and frequently end in a quarrel. The various classes of common Sudras also get up feasts amongst themselves, but these have no resemblance to the *samaradhanas* of the Brahmins, the only motive of the feasters being to enjoy a festivity which usually ends in a debauch. At a Brahmin feast the greatest order and propriety prevail, but Sudra feasts differ in no wise from the orgies which take place in Europe in the low pot-houses frequented by the scum of the population. The Sudras generally postpone the discussion of their many and frequent differences until some occasion of this sort comes round. Every one, indeed, arrives with a firm determination to have a good fight and to make plenty of noise over it. The moment when the meal is ready and the giver of the feast has invited his guests to come in and partake of it, is generally the time that they consider most suitable for the discussion of their pretended grievances. They stop the whole assemblage by uttering the customary oath in the name of the prince or governor of the province, and declare that no one shall begin to eat until their grievances have been listened to, their wrongs redressed, and the culprits punished. And then the dispute begins. Some take one side and some another, but all participate in it, and the quarrel becomes general. They all scream at the top of their voices, without listening to a word any one else is saying; they hurl the most disgusting accusations at one another, mixed with horrible imprecations and insults, without pausing to give either party a chance of replying. Then their blood rises, and the quarrel waxes warmer and warmer. They proceed to threatening gestures and rush towards each other, their faces contorted with rage and fury. Any one who did not know the Hindu character would swear they were all going to fly at each other's throats. Their host, however, who generally maintains a strict neutrality on these occasions, continues to superintend his domestic arrangements with the utmost composure, or else retires to some peaceful corner and quietly smokes his pipe, a tranquil spectator of the scene around him, knowing full well that the belligerents must ultimately tire themselves out by the vehemence of their cries and gesticulations, and that they will calm down from sheer exhaustion. He then selects three or four to act as arbitrators, and, placing himself with them between the two parties, succeeds, after no little difficulty, in restoring peace. They then investigate the cause of the quarrel, and try to arrange the affair so as to satisfy both sides. If this is impossible, the final decision is put off till some future time, when the whole scene is re-enacted from the beginning. Promptly forgetting the epithets which they have been mutually heaping on each other, the guests at length seat themselves and begin the feast, which has had plenty of time to get cold. As a rule it would be waste of labour to try to arrange a difference of opinion between Sudras without first allowing them to quarrel and abuse each other, and even come to blows[1]. After these preliminaries, which they generally repeat several times, you may attempt the task of reconciliation with some hope of success.

The Pariahs also sometimes have feasts amongst themselves, but these are invariably disgusting orgies. Following the customs of their caste, they make a point of intoxicating themselves with the juice of the palm-tree, of which there is always a vast quantity drunk. The guests, who know that these orgies always end in a free fight, go ready armed with stout sticks, and the feast rarely concludes without bloodshed. Similar quarrels almost always form part of the wedding ceremonies of a Sudra. During the time that I lived in India, I celebrated over 2,000 marriages amongst Christian Sudras of all castes; and I only remember one such occasion on which there was not a violent altercation, which ended more often than not in a furious, if not sanguinary, battle. The principal cause of dissension is the marriage settlement. It is seldom that the bride's parents do not try to cheat those of the bridegroom over the quantity or value of the jewels, or over the colour and price of the wedding garments. At other times, perhaps, it is the friends and relations who feel themselves aggrieved. They complain bitterly that the respect and consideration which were their due have not been shown them, either in not consulting them before the marriage was arranged, or by a lack of due form and ceremony in their invitation.

[1] The truth is, a marriage or funeral ceremony is the only occasion when all the members of one family or members of one caste meet, and it therefore offers the best, if not the only, opportunity for an aggrieved member to lay his complaint before his caste-headmen. It is too much to say that they come 'determined to have a good fight,' with or without reason.—ED.

There are many small details which must be attended to when a feast is given amongst the various Sudra classes. The quality of the food, the method of preparing and serving it, and a thousand other minutiae, are all points which have long since been settled by immemorial custom, the non-observance of which would entail very serious consequences. Even involuntary mistakes of the most trivial kind are not overlooked or forgiven. The following story is an instance. I was once in a village where a man of the *Oopara* or gardener caste was giving a feast to his friends and to the headman of his caste. All the guests had seated themselves and begun their meal, when one of them, whilst eating, found a small stone in his rice, which hurt his teeth. He promptly spat out everything he had in his mouth on to his plate, found the tiny stone, and placing it in the hollow of his hand rose from his place, and thus addressed all the other guests. 'Sirs!' he said, pointing to the giver of the feast, 'here is a man who invites us to his house, and then gives us stones instead of rice!' And he then showed this little pebble to every person present. 'Shame! shame!' cried all the guests; 'our host must be punished.' Thereupon they all got up, leaving their meal unfinished, to deliberate as to the punishment that should be inflicted for so grave an offence. The poor fellow was mulcted in a heavy fine, and was also condemned to provide another feast on twice as sumptuous a scale for the heads of the caste.

It is considered good style amongst the Sudras never to appear pleased or satisfied with any entertainment that may be offered them. The host may spend large sums for the gratification of his guests, and may take every possible care that the food is nicely prepared and well served; but the greatest compliment that he can expect or hope for is that his feast is just fit for dogs. Hence the common saying, that if a Sudra invited to a feast can find fault with nothing else, he will be sure to complain that there was not enough salt.

The master of the house must not be annoyed at these incivilities; he must listen to the fault-finding patiently, and make what excuses he can for the inferiority of his repast. His only consolation is the thought of the revenge he will take when he, in his turn, is invited to a feast by his fastidious and too candid friends.

Intoxicating drinks are forbidden at these feasts, and it would be considered an insult of the deepest dye to even suggest them. When the meal is over, betel is handed round, and the guests retire at once.

CHAPTER IX

The Kinds of Food expressly forbidden to Brahmins.—Occult Rites.—The Disgusting Rite called *Sakti*.

THERE are as regards food three things which a Brahmin must avoid with the most scrupulous care: he must not eat anything that has had life or has even contained the principle of life; he must not drink intoxicating liquors; he must not touch food that has been prepared by persons of another caste. It is no greater privation to a Brahmin to abstain from eating meat, accustomed as he is from his earliest youth to go without it, and even to look upon it as abominable food, than it is for us to refrain from eating the flesh of certain domestic animals, for which, either from natural prejudice or from its unpleasant taste, we feel a strong repugnance. Thus, when a Hindu abstains from all animal food, he is only conforming to a feeling of unconquerable repulsion, the result partly of imagination and partly of long-established custom. I once met a Brahmin who, on seeing some eggs being broken and beaten up for an omelette, immediately complained of feeling unwell, and in the course of a few moments was violently sick.

The aversion which Brahmins feel for *sura-pana*, or the use of intoxicating beverages—an aversion to which I have several times had occasion to call attention—springs at any rate from most commendable principles. In places where Brahmins congregate in great numbers infractions of this rule of abstinence are extremely rare, and such a thing as a drunken Brahmin is unknown. They are not, however, quite so strict on this point when they live in some isolated spot, away from the watchful eyes of their *gurus*. A Brahmin's house, situated at some distance from a village in Tanjore, once caught fire, and the inhabitants of the village hastened to the spot to try and snatch what they could from the flames.

Amongst the things saved were a large earthen vessel of salt pork and another containing arrack, or native rum. The proprietor felt the loss of his house much less than he did this overwhelming disclosure. He became the laughing-stock of the neighbourhood, and felt the jeers and mockery of which he was the object so keenly that he was obliged to leave the country and hide his shame elsewhere. One may well conjecture, without doing them any injustice, that there are many other Brahmins whose delinquencies have not been brought to light by accidents of this kind. These lapses from strict adherence to the law are especially frequent in towns, where illicit pleasures are easily obtainable. More than once it has come to my knowledge that certain Brahmins were in the habit of meeting in small numbers in the houses of Sudras in whom they thought they could place confidence, there to partake in the strictest privacy of feasts from which neither intoxicating liquors nor meat were excluded. Furthermore, the Brahmins became so demoralized by these debauches that they allowed their hosts to eat with them, thus shamelessly committing a threefold breach of those laws of their caste which they are most especially enjoined to keep.

These little orgies sometimes entail very unpleasant consequences. The Sudras' wives are, of course, obliged to be in the secret, and as La Fontaine says:—

> 'Rien ne pèse tant qu'un secret ;
> Le porter loin est difficile aux dames.'

Hindu women are by no means exceptions to this rule. A Brahmin woman whom I knew, allowed herself to be persuaded by a Sudra woman, a friend of hers, to eat part of a stew which the latter had cooked, and she even went so far as to say she thought it excellent. A short time afterwards the two friends quarrelled, and at the end of a violent altercation the Sudra woman, to punish her adversary and silence her at the same time, publicly proclaimed the sin which the other in a moment of greediness had committed. Covered with shame and confusion at this unexpected revelation, which she found it impossible to refute, the poor Brahmin woman fled from the place in despair, vowing, too late, that she would never allow herself to be caught again.

The use of intoxicating liquors is more common than the eating of forbidden food, as it is so much less liable to detection. At the same time, it must be admitted, it is an unheard-of thing to see an intoxicated Brahmin in the public streets. The reproach of intemperance can only be levelled at a very small number of men of low reputation, who have lost all sense of shame. One could not, with any degree of justice, say that the reproach was generally applicable to Brahmins, who are in this matter beyond even the shafts of slander itself[1].

The duty of punishing offences of this kind devolves upon the *gurus*. When in the course of their peregrinations they hear that any one has misconducted himself in such a manner, they order the culprit to appear before them; and if after due investigation his delinquency is proved, he has to listen to a severe reprimand and occasionally undergo corporal punishment. Frequently also he has to pay a heavy fine; and if the offence is a very grave one, he is put out of caste. Nevertheless, for fear lest too many persons might be inculpated, or on account of the high position of a particular delinquent, or to avoid creating a scandal, or for other similar reasons, the *gurus* find it advisable to shut their eyes to many peccadilloes. The *gurus*, too, are not always impeccable in the matter of bribes, and will often find reasons for allowing a culprit to escape who has managed to ingratiate himself with them.

I was once at Dharmapuri, a small town in the Carnatic, just at the time when a Brahmin *guru* was visiting that district. A person of the Brahmin caste was accused before him of breaking the rules with regard to food, and even of publicly deriding them. The accusation was a very serious one, and well substantiated; so the culprit was cited to appear, and the evidence against him was heard. The *guru*, convinced of the guilt of the accused, had made up his mind to break his triple cord and turn him out of caste; but the accused, on hearing of this terrible determination, showed not the smallest emotion. Without displaying the least discomfiture he advanced boldly

[1] This applies equally well in the present day. Yet nobody can doubt that the number of Brahmins who infringe caste-customs in food and drink is increasing year by year.—ED.

into the midst of the assembly, and prostrating himself before the *guru*, made the following speech:—'So you have decided, you and your assessors, to break my cord! Well, that will not be a heavy loss, as for two farthings I can get another. But what is your motive for treating me with so much severity, and for dishonouring me thus publicly? Is it because I have eaten animal food? But then a *guru's* justice should be meted out impartially, and punishments should be awarded without respect of persons. Why am I the only one to be accused, the only one to be punished, when there are so many others who are quite as much to blame as myself, or even more so? If I turn my eyes on one side, I see two or three among my accusers who not long since partook with me of an excellent leg of mutton. If I look on the other side, I see several who have not disdained to accept the invitation of a common Sudra friend, who treated us to an admirable chicken stew; while there are others not less to blame on this score who have not dared to put in an appearance in this assembly. Have I your permission to mention their names? I am quite ready to produce witnesses, and to substantiate my accusation.'

Struck dumb by this speech, which was delivered with the utmost confidence and imperturbable assurance, the *guru* began to consider what the consequences of this affair would be, and how it would end if he persisted in carrying it to its proper termination; so he put a stop to all future complications by crying out, with great presence of mind: 'Who has brought this babbler here? Do you not see that he is mad? Turn him out of the assembly at once, and let me hear no more of him.'

If these slight and rare infractions of the law, which are, after all, only weaknesses inseparable from human nature, were the only sins, they would be undeniably small indeed; but occasionally one may also come across vice and wickedness in their most hideous forms. It once came to my knowledge that men calling themselves conjurers or magicians used to attend nocturnal gatherings, which were held in a deserted spot that I knew of, there to give themselves up to indescribable orgies of debauch and intemperance.

The leader of these orgies was a Vishnavite Brahmin, and several Sudras were initiated into the mysterious iniquities which were carried on there. They drank and ate to excess everything that is forbidden to a Hindu, not excepting even the flesh of the cow, and the abominations practised on these occasions are too disgusting to be described. They always finished up with sacrifices and displays of magic, the supposed effects of which spread fear and consternation amongst the peaceable inhabitants of the whole neighbourhood, for the superstitious terrors of the Hindu are easily awakened. People were on the point of appealing to the magistrates for protection against these diabolical assemblies, when the debauchees who composed them, seeing they were about to be discovered, left the province and never dared to appear there again.

Amongst the abominable rites practised in India is one which is only too well known; it is called *sakti-puja*; *sakti* meaning strength or power[1]. Sometimes it is the wife of Siva to whom this sacrifice is offered; sometimes they pretend that it is in honour of some invisible power. The ceremony takes place at night with more or less secrecy. The least disgusting of these orgies are those where they confine themselves to eating and drinking everything that the custom of the country forbids, and where men and women, huddled together in indiscriminate confusion, openly and shamelessly violate the commonest laws of decency and modesty.

The *Namadharis*, or followers of Vishnu, are the most frequent perpetrators of these disgusting sacrifices. People of all castes, from the Brahmin to the Pariah, are invited to attend. When the company are assembled, all kinds of meat, including beef, are placed before the idol of Vishnu. Ample provision is also made of arrack, toddy and opium, and any other intoxicating drug they can lay their hands on. The whole is then offered to Vishnu. Afterwards the *pujari*, or sacrificer, who is generally a Brahmin, first of all tastes the various kinds of meats and liquors himself, then gives the others permission to devour the rest. Men and women thereupon begin to eat greedily, the same piece of meat passing from mouth to mouth, each person taking a bite, until it is finished. Then they start afresh on

[1] It is more correctly described as 'the power or energy of the god as represented in some of the many female forms.' It has been estimated that of the Hindus in Bengal, about three-fourths are devoted to the worship of *sakti*, though the forms of worship vary greatly. In Bengal the *Vamacharis* observe the most disgusting rites of all.—ED.

another joint, which they gnaw in the same manner, tearing the meat out of each other's mouths. When all the meat has been consumed, intoxicating liquors are passed round, every one drinking without repugnance out of the same cup. Opium and other drugs disappear in a similar fashion. They persuade themselves that under these circumstances they do not contract impurity by eating and drinking in so revolting a manner. When they are all completely intoxicated, men and women no longer keep apart, but pass the rest of the night together, giving themselves up without restraint to the grossest immorality without any risk of disagreeable consequences. A husband who sees his wife in another man's arms cannot recall her, nor has he the right to complain; for at those times every woman becomes common property. Perfect equality exists among all castes, and the Brahmin is not of higher caste than the Pariah. The celebration of these mysterious rites may differ sometimes in outward forms, but in spirit they are always equally abominable. Under certain circumstances the principal objects which form the sacrifice to *sakti* are a large vessel full of native rum and a full-grown girl. The latter, stark naked, remains standing in a most indecent attitude. The goddess *Sakti* is evoked, and is supposed to respond to the invitation to come and take up her abode in the vessel full of rum, and also in the girl's body.

A sacrifice of flowers, incense, sandalwood, coloured rice, and a lighted lamp is then offered to these two objects; and for *neiveddya* a portion of all the viands that have been prepared. This done, Brahmins, Sudras, Pariahs, both men and women, intoxicate themselves with the rum which was offered to *sakti*, all drinking from the same cup in turn[1]. To exchange pieces of the food that they are in the act of eating, and to put into one's own mouth what has just been taken from another's, are under these conditions regarded as acts of virtue by the fanatics. As usual, the meeting winds up with the most revolting orgy.

Without the salutary restraint of a healthy tone of morality, how can these people be expected to fight successfully against the vehemence of their passions? And then, when they give way to unbridled licence, they think to stifle remorse by investing these horrible practices with a religious element, as if

[1] I have mentioned before that to a Hindu who has been decently brought up this mode of drinking is absolutely abhorrent.—DUBOIS.

sacrilege could disguise their moral turpitude. Strange to say, it is the Brahmins, and very often the women of this caste, who are frequently the most ardent promoters of these Bacchanalian orgies. However, debauches of this kind entail such heavy expenses as fortunately to prevent their frequent recurrence.

Of course it is well known that most ancient nations had their own peculiar mysterious rites, and that very few among them failed to worship profligacy in some shape or other. Greece might well feel ashamed of the depravity which pervaded the *cultus* of a large number of her deities. Many remains still exist, proving irrefutably that the grossest excesses defiled the temples of Venus, Ceres, Bacchus, &c., while the Persian Mitra and the Egyptian Osiris were the objects of equally impure worship.

Holy Scripture tells us something of the abominations practised by the Canaanites in honour of Baal, Baal-peor, and Moloch, which brought down upon them such terrible punishments. Thus we see that, all the world over, idolatry assumed much the same forms, for ignorance and fanaticism can have but one termination.

At the same time, the Hindus, accustomed as they are to carry everything to extremes, appear to have surpassed all the other nations of the world, both ancient and modern, in the unconscionable depravity with which so many of their religious rites are impregnated.

CHAPTER X

The Various Occupations of Brahmins.

If Brahmins kept strictly to the letter of the rules of their caste, they would live in isolated places, far from the haunts of men, where their whole lives would be spent in religious exercises. They would perform their ablutions regularly three times a day; they would offer the sacrifice called *sraddha* to their ancestors, a ceremony which they alone have the right to perform; they would look after their households, paying particular attention to the education of their children; and they would devote all their leisure moments to reading the Vedas and other sacred writings, to acquiring knowledge, and to meditation. But the poverty of many of their number, and the avarice and ambition which are the ruling passions of each and all, preclude the possibility of such a philosophical mode of existence.

Naturally cunning, wily, double-tongued, and servile, they turn these most undesirable qualities to account by insinuating themselves everywhere; their main object, upon which they expend the greatest ingenuity, being to gain access to the courts of princes or other people of high rank. This end achieved, they quickly gain, by their hypocritical conduct, the affection and confidence of those who have received them; and very soon the best and most lucrative posts are the reward of their pressing attentions. Thus it happens that the prime ministers of Asiatic princes are almost always Brahmins. Shut up in their palaces, and plunged in voluptuous idleness, the nominal rulers rarely give a thought to anything beyond the means of increasing their enjoyments, creating fresh amusements, and giving new zest to their passions by ever-varying means. The welfare of their people and the government of their country are very secondary considerations, if not matters of indifference. Women, baths, perfumes, obscene dances, filthy songs, each in turn excite their senses. Only flatterers of the lowest type and despicable procurers are allowed to come near them, and these are always ready to applaud the dissolute vagaries of their master.

That the Brahmins, thus raised to positions of importance at the courts of these slothful and useless princes, do not forget their relatives and friends, can well be imagined. Indeed they usually divide the most lucrative of the subordinate posts among them. Thus surrounded by creatures upon whom they can rely and who can also rely upon them, a tacit collusion is established, by means of which each one can, in his own department, enrich himself with remarkable rapidity, by carrying on unchecked a system of injustice, fraud, dishonesty, and oppression—qualities in which most individuals of this caste have been thoroughly well trained.

Better educated, more cunning, more keen-witted, with greater talents for intrigue than other Hindus, Brahmins become necessary even to the Mussulman princes themselves, who cannot govern without their assistance. The Mahomedan rulers generally make a Brahmin their secretary of state, through whose hands all the state correspondence must pass. Brahmins also frequently fill the positions of secretaries and writers to the governors of provinces and districts. Generally speaking, the Mahomedans of India are so ignorant of the first principles of public administration, and so utterly unacquainted with the simplest rules of arithmetic, that they are obliged to have recourse to the Brahmins for everything that requires enlightenment and knowledge. In return, the latter know how to copy only too faithfully the harsh and tyrannical methods of the Mahomedans. When it is a question of plundering the people or extorting money from them, they employ a thousand vexatious means, sometimes even going so far as to resort to torture. But they rarely obtain the same hold over the Mahomedan princes that they do over those of their own religion. With the former they remain at their posts until by endless peculation and extortion, either authorized or tacitly allowed, they contrive to amass large fortunes. But the moment their wealth becomes a notorious fact, that moment their disgrace is certain. They in their turn are imprisoned, tortured, and forced to disgorge the riches that they have so unjustly acquired. However, some of them, foreseeing the fate that must befall the servants of such masters, keep a sharp look-out, and place the fruit of their plunder in security, either by keeping a part of it in some secret hiding-place, or by sending it away to some country beyond the tyrant's reach.

The Brahmins have also been clever enough to work their way into favour with the great European Power that now governs India. They occupy the highest and most lucrative posts in the different administrative boards and Government offices, as well as in the judicial courts of the various districts. In fact there is no branch of public administration in which they have not made themselves indispensable. Thus it is nearly always Brahmins who hold the posts of sub-collectors of revenue, writers, copyists, translators, treasurers, book-keepers, &c. It is especially difficult to do without their assistance in all matters connected with accounts, as they have a remarkable talent for arithmetic. I have seen some men in the course of a few minutes work out, to the last fraction, long and complicated calculations, which would have taken the best accountants in Europe hours to get through[1].

Furthermore, their perfect knowledge of native opinion and of the ways in which it may be guided, to say nothing of the influence which they exercise over public feeling by the prerogatives of their birth, are quite sufficient reasons to account for the readiness with which their services are accepted. In fact, the veneration and respect with which their fellow-countrymen regard them shed, in the opinion of the vulgar, a kind of reflected glory and dignity on the different Government offices in which they occupy subordinate positions. But woe to the European head of the office, who does not keep the strictest watch over the conduct of these said subordinates, or places implicit confidence in them! He will soon find himself the victim of his own negligence, with his position seriously compromised. I have known many Europeans holding most distinguished and lucrative appointments end by losing their reputation, their honour, their position, and their fortune, all because they left too much in the hands of the Brahmins under them, for whose misdeeds

[1] The proportion of Brahmins in Government employ is higher than ever now; and it is the Brahmins who, more than any others, have availed themselves of the benefits of English education.—ED.

the Government held them responsible. In vain did these high officials exhaust all their resources against the authors of their ruin; imprisonment and punishment were equally ineffectual. Most of these peccant subordinates would rather die in irons than restore one farthing of their ill-gotten gains.

One can well imagine that when Brahmins are launched in the turmoil of public affairs they soon lose sight of the religious observances of their caste. Occupied with the government of a kingdom or a province, they have neither the time nor even the wish to give themselves up to the exercise of their interminable religious rites. As, however, they are in positions of authority and can dispense or withhold favours at their pleasure, no one dares to call attention to their negligence. It is sufficient if they conform in the more important matters. Their dignity releases them, without entailing disagreeable consequences, from the necessity of attending to minor details. Firmly convinced as they are of the truth of their favourite dictum that *to fill one's belly one must play many parts*, Brahmins are clever at turning their hands to many ways of earning a livelihood. Some take up medicine, and it is said with considerable success. Others become soldiers. In the Mahratta armies there are many Brahmins; but I cannot believe that a military force composed of men of this caste could ever be very formidable. Bravery and courage are foreign to their nature, and their education would not tend to foster these soldier-like qualities. Nevertheless, there have been several Brahmin generals whose military careers have not been without glory. Many Brahmins who are in trade, especially in the province of Gujerat, are considered excellent men of business. Those, however, who choose this walk in life are rather looked down upon by the rest of their caste, not so much on account of their profession as merchants or shopkeepers, but because of the very small amount of attention which they pay to their caste customs and observances. Trade in itself is not considered at all degrading to a Brahmin, and men of this caste who are engaged in it are to be met with everywhere; only there are many things which Brahmins are not allowed to sell, and which consequently they cannot include in their operations, such, for instance, as red cloths, the seeds and oil of sesamum, husked rice, liquids of every kind, salt, perfumes, fruits, vegetables, poisons, honey, butter, milk, sugar, &c.

One almost invariably finds that subordinate collectors of revenue, custom-house officers, writers, book-keepers, village schoolmasters, and astronomers are Brahmins. They are very useful as messengers, because they are never detained anywhere; and it is for this reason that many of the large merchants, living in provinces governed by native princes, employ them as coolies or porters, and pay them very highly, because custom-house officers have orders to let everything that they carry pass through free. This calling, though arduous, is by no means the least lucrative. Those who follow it travel almost free of expense, for along every main road there are numerous hostelries called *chuttrams*, where Brahmins alone have the right to lodge, and where they are fed gratuitously. The revenues which these establishments derive from their landed property, and the abundant alms which they receive, amply compensate the persons who manage them, and who are Brahmins also, for the expenses entailed by the hospitality which they extend to their brethren.

The great facility with which they can everywhere introduce themselves under all sorts of disguises, without exciting the smallest suspicion, and the adroitness with which they can play all sorts of parts and extricate themselves from the most difficult positions, render them peculiarly well fitted to act as spies in time of war, always supposing that you can be sure that they are not serving both parties, a circumstance which often happens without any one being the wiser. Poverty or self-interest sometimes reduces them to occupy positions which are very derogatory to their illustrious birth. Thus sometimes they are seen acting as dancing-masters to courtesans attached to the service of the temples. Others become cooks; but when they are reduced to this latter calling, and serve masters of inferior caste, these latter undertake never to touch the vessels which their cook uses in preparing the food. The cook will serve the food when it is ready, but will not remove what is left after the meal is over. What the Brahmin cook prepares and touches is pure for his master, but what the master touches is impure and would defile the cook. Some even demean themselves so far as to be washermen and water-carriers for persons of their own caste, and even undertake to perform the very meanest requirements of domestic service.

Superstition, which exercises such an important influence

throughout the whole of India, also affords great resources to those in search of a means of livelihood. An illness, a fall, a law-suit, a fresh undertaking, a newly built house, a bad omen, an unpleasant dream, and a thousand other similar things, are all occasions on which their credulous neighbours come running to them for advice, and for which they make them pay as dearly as possible. The Hindu Almanac, about the composition of which I have already spoken, has always an answer or a remedy for everything. Brahmins are never at a loss for an answer, no matter on what point they may be consulted. Clever charlatans that they are, they make their various calculations with the utmost gravity; and to give greater weight to their words they bewilder their clients with stories invented on the spur of the moment, which they tell with portentous emphasis. For, I repeat again, as arch-impostors they are absolutely unrivalled. Every Hindu is an adept at disguising the truth; but on this point the Brahmin far excels every other caste. Indeed, this vice has become so deeply engrained, that, far from being ashamed of it, they regard it on the contrary as a subject for exultation and vanity. I once had a long conversation with two of those Brahmins who gain their living at the expense of the credulous public, and they ended by agreeing with me as to the superiority of the Christian religion over the absurdities of their own theogony. 'All that you say is reasonable and true,' they repeated several times. 'But then,' I replied, 'if all that I say is reasonable and true, it follows that all that you say to the people must be false and ridiculous.' 'That also is true,' they admitted; 'but these lies comprise our livelihood. If we were to expound to the people only such truths as you have just been telling us, how should we obtain *the wherewithal to fill our stomachs?*'

Then again, flattery, in the art of which Brahmins are also past-masters, is also a great source of profit to them. However proud and haughty they may be, they never find any difficulty in grovelling, in the most humiliating manner, at the feet of any one from whom they think they can gain some advantage. They attach themselves like leeches to the great merchants or other rich individuals, and are never tired of playing the *rôle* of admirers and flatterers. They know full well that to appeal to a native's vanity is to attack him at his weakest point; and naturally they turn this knowledge to the best possible account. The grossest flattery, verging on the absurd, is what is most pleasing to the ears of their modest patrons, and is the surest way of loosening the latter's purse-strings. But the most inexhaustible mine of wealth to Brahmins is their religion. As chief priests they exercise the highest functions, and consequently derive almost all the profit. In certain famous temples, such as Tirupati, Rameswaram, Jaganath (Puri) and others, thousands of Brahmins live on the revenues with which these temples are endowed.

Those who cannot find means of existence in their native country go and seek their fortunes elsewhere, often journeying as much as two hundred miles from their families. Expatriation is a very small matter to them, and they never hesitate to accept it if there is anything to be gained by it.

CHAPTER XI

Religious Tolerance amongst the Brahmins.—Their Indifference with regard to their own Religion.—Their Sublime Ideas of the Deity.—A Comparison between them and the Greek Philosophers.—The State of Christianity.—The Political Intolerance and Ignorant Presumption of Brahmins.

I HAVE already said that the general feeling amongst Brahmins is that all the Hindu deities ought to receive an equal share of attention and worship, since they are not really antagonistic one to another. The quarrels and wars which erstwhile took place between these deities were never of long duration, and have in no wise prevented their living since then in perfect amity together. I have also remarked that in consequence of this the greater number of the Brahmins strongly disapprove of the numerous sectaries who devote themselves to the worship of one particular deity and pay little or no attention to the others, on the ground that they are inferior and subordinate to the special deity which they prefer. But are these self-same Brahmins really so devoted to the religion of their country and to the worship of these deities? Well, though this assertion may appear paradoxical, I should say that, of all Hindus, they care the least and have the smallest amount of faith in them. It is by no means uncommon to hear them speaking of their gods in terms of the most utter contempt. When they are displeased with their idols they do not scruple to upbraid them fiercely to their faces, at the same time heaping the grossest insults upon them, with every outward gesture and sign of anger and resentment. In fact, there is absolutely no limit to the blasphemies, curses, and abuse which they hurl at them under these circumstances[1].

[1] Any one who is familiar with the vernaculars of India knows that they contain an immense number of terms of abuse, which are so extraordinary,

There is a well-known Hindu proverb which says, 'A temple mouse fears not the gods.' This exactly applies to the Brahmins, who enter their temples without showing the slightest sign of serious thought or respect for the divinities who are enshrined in them. Indeed, they often seem to choose these particular places to quarrel and to fight in. Even while performing their numerous religious fooleries, their behaviour shows no indication of fervour or real devotion. As a matter of fact, their religious devotion increases or diminishes in proportion to the amount of profit they expect to make out of it, and it also depends on the amount of publicity surrounding them. Those deities who do not contribute towards the welfare of their votaries here below only receive very careless and perfunctory worship.

The histories of their gods are so ridiculous and so extravagant that it is not surprising that the Brahmins are at heart conscious of the absurdity of worshipping such beings. There is, therefore, very little danger incurred in ridiculing the gods in the presence of Brahmins. Very often they agree with the scoffer, and even enlarge upon what he has said. Many Brahmins can repeat by heart songs and verses that treat with very scanty respect the divinities which they worship so ostentatiously in public, while their audience listen without any sign of disapproval. Brahmins have no fear of such conduct calling forth either reproof or punishment. The Sudras, who are more simple and credulous than the Brahmins, would not be

and so abominably obscene, that it would be impossible to find their counterpart in any Billingsgate of Europe. However, disgusting expressions are so greatly to the taste of the Hindus, that, not content with their own well-endowed vocabulary, they carefully learn and appropriate all the bad language that they hear in their quarrels with the foreigners who live amongst them. When Hindus are angry with their gods, which is usually the case when they do not receive a favourable answer to their prayers, one may see them entering the temples with many outward expressions of rage and mortification, and exhausting their vocabulary in curses and reproaches hurled against their unhappy gods, whom they openly accuse of impotence and fraud. In their ordinary conversation they often use most irreverent expressions regarding their gods, one of the least obnoxious being, 'If I do not keep my word may the same punishment fall upon me as I should deserve if I had seduced the wife of my god.' If a person of high position has a grievance against the gods, he sometimes revenges himself by having the doors of their temples stopped up with thorns and brambles, so that no one can enter to worship or to offer sacrifices.—DUBOIS.

so indulgent under similar circumstances, and it would be particularly imprudent to ridicule any particular god of theirs in the presence of those who are specially devoted to him.

There is another factor which must be taken into account in estimating the scanty veneration which they pay their gods, to whom nevertheless self-interest, education, custom, and respect for public opinion oblige them to display outward respect; and that is the clear and precise knowledge which most of them must have gleaned from their books of a 'God who is the Author and Creator of all things; eternal, immaterial, omnipresent, independent, in all things blessed, exempt from pain and care; the spirit of truth, the source of all justice; governor, dispensator, and regulator of all things; perfect in wisdom and knowledge; without shape or countenance, without limit, without nature, without name, without caste, without parentage; of an absolute purity which excludes all passion, all bias, all compromise.'

All these qualifications and many others which are not less characteristic are translated literally from their books, and are used by Brahmins to explain the Supreme Being, to whom they sometimes give the name of *Parabrahma*, *Paramattma*, &c. Is it credible that, knowing this, they can seriously bestow the title of gods on the almost countless number of animate and inanimate things which form the chief objects of the vulgar cult? It follows, therefore, that they ought to confine their worship to this supreme and unique Being, of whom they still retain such a sublime perception. There appears to be no doubt whatever that their Brahmin ancestors worshipped only this one Supreme Being; but with the lapse of time they fell victims to idolatry and superstition, and, shutting their eyes to the light that they possessed, stifled the voice of conscience. Was it not for the same reason that God pronounced that condemnation of which the Apostle St. Paul speaks in the Epistle to the Romans against certain philosophers of his time, who knowingly rejected the truth? Is not this the reason why the Brahmins of to-day are given over, like those philosophers of old, to all the sins of a perverse will and to the many kinds of vice and corruption with which they are imbued, and from which other castes are more or less exempt, seeing that they possess stronger faith?

It is true that Brahmins are not the only philosophers who

have been induced by purely worldly considerations to hide the greatest and most important of truths from their fellow-men. They are only following in the steps of the philosophers of ancient Greece. Even Socrates, the greatest of them all, whose ideas on the subject of the Deity were almost as perfect as those which have been given us by revelation, never dared to avow them openly: and, although he thoroughly recognized all the absurdities of paganism, he maintained the principle that every one should follow the religion of his country.

Plato, his disciple, who was so distressed that Greece and all the other countries of the world should be given over to a false and dissolute religion, and who also, like Socrates, believed in the true God, said that these were truths which should not be disclosed to the common people.

The whole world, as Bossuet says, was plunged at that time in the same error; and truth, though known to a few, remained captive and dared not appear in the light of day. Those who knew and believed in the true God thought it sufficient to worship Him in secret, and held that there was no harm in paying outward respect to idols with the rest of the world. Revelation had not yet purified their ideas on this subject. The truth was known only in one very small corner of the world. The worshippers of the true God were only to be seen in small numbers in the temple of Jerusalem.

But there is one essential difference between these ancient philosophers and the modern Hindus: the former were few in number, and lacked the necessary means and influence which would have enabled them to make an impression on the multitude and successfully combat the errors into which it had fallen; whereas the Brahmins, owing to their numbers and to the high estimation in which they are held by the public, could easily, if they wished, and if their interests and their vices were not opposed thereto, overthrow the entire edifice of idolatry throughout the whole of India, and substitute the knowledge and worship of the true God, of whom they already possess so perfect an idea.

Brahmins do not confine themselves to professing devotion to all the Hindu deities. Though the rules of their caste forbid their indulging in any outward signs of worship to the gods of other nations, one of the principles taught in their books and recognized by them is that, among the many different religions to be found throughout the world, and which they call *Anantaveda*, there is not one that should be despised and condemned. They might even entertain some feeling of respect for Mahomedanism, encumbered though it is with so much outward form and ceremony, and with the many superstitions with which the Indian Mahomedans have invested it, had not the harsh and oppressive rule of the latter, as well as their open contempt for the civil and religious institutions of the rest of the inhabitants, made their persons and their religion equally odious to the Hindus.

The Christian religion commands the approbation of Brahmins in several respects. They admire its pure and holy morality; but, at the same time, they hold that some of its precepts are beyond man's power of fulfilment, and that its sublimely high standard of morality is only suitable for persons leading a contemplative life, who have retired from the world and are consequently sheltered from its temptations. On the other hand, as Christianity condemns most of their customs and superstitions, it has on that account become most hateful to them. The Hindu who embraces it is not considered to belong to the same nation as themselves, because his new religion forces him to reject those customs and practices which they regard as the link binding them all indissolubly together.

However, it must be confessed that if, in these latter days, idolatrous Hindus have shown a greater aversion to the Christian religion as they became better acquainted with Europeans, the result must be attributed solely to the bad conduct of the latter. How could the Hindus think well of this holy religion, when they see those who have been brought up in it, and who come from a country where it is the only one that is publicly professed, openly violating its precepts and often making its doctrines the subject of sarcasm and silly jests? It is curious to note that the Brahmin does not believe in his religion, and yet he outwardly observes it; while the Christian believes in his, and yet he does not outwardly observe it. What a sad and shameful contrast!

Before the character and behaviour of Europeans became well known to these people, it seemed possible that Christianity might take root amongst them. Little by little it was overcoming the numberless obstacles which the prejudices of the country continually placed in its way. Several missionaries, animated by a truly apostolic zeal, had penetrated into the interior of the country, and there, by conforming scrupulously to all the usages and customs of the Brahmins—in their clothing, food, conversation, and general conduct in life—had managed to win the attention of the people, and by dint of perseverance had succeeded in gaining a hearing. Their high character, talents, and virtues, and above all their perfect disinterestedness, obtained for them the countenance and support of even the native princes, who, agreeably surprised at the novelty of their teaching, took these extraordinary men under their protection, and gave them liberty to preach their religion and make what proselytes they could.

It is a well-known fact that Robert à Nobilibus, a nephew of the famous Cardinal Bellarmin, and founder of the Mission at Madura, where he died at the beginning of the last century, converted nearly 100,000 idolaters in that very kingdom. His contemporary, the Jesuit Brito, baptized 30,000 heathens in the country of the Maravas, where he finally gained the crown of martyrdom. The missionaries scattered about the other provinces of the Peninsula also laboured hard, and with the greatest success, to extend Christianity amongst the Hindus. The French Mission at Pondicherry numbered 60,000 native Christians in the province of Arcot, and was daily making further progress when the conquest of the country by Europeans took place—a disastrous event as far as the advance of Christianity was concerned. Having witnessed the immoral and disorderly conduct of the Europeans who then overran the whole country, the Hindus would hear no more of a religion which appeared to have so little influence over the behaviour of those professing it, and who had been brought up in its tenets; and their prejudice against Christianity has gone on increasing steadily day by day, as the people became more familiar with Europeans, until it finally received its death-blow. For it is certainly a fact that for the last sixty years very few converts have been made in India. Those still remaining (and their number is daily diminished by apostasy) are mostly the descendants of the original converts made by the Jesuit missionaries. About eighty years ago there must have been at least 1,200,000 native Christians in the Peninsula, while now, at the very utmost, they amount to but one-half of that number.

This holy religion, which, when it was first introduced into India about 300 years ago, had only such obstacles as indifference or deep-rooted superstition to contend with, is now looked upon with unconquerable aversion. A respectable Hindu who was asked to embrace the Christian religion, would look upon the suggestion either as a joke, or else as an insult of the deepest dye. To such an extreme is this hatred now carried in some parts, that were a Hindu of good repute to be on intimate terms with Christians, he would not dare own it in public.

A Hindu who embraces Christianity nowadays must make up his mind to lose everything that makes life pleasant. He is henceforth an outcast from society. He must renounce his patrimony, his right to inherit, his father, mother, wife, children, and friends[1]. He is abandoned and shunned by every one.

Europeans should indeed blush and take shame to themselves when they see to what depths of degradation and abasement the religion of their fathers has sunk in this country through the misconduct and bad example of their fellows[2].

But to return to the matter in hand: many people have attributed to narrowmindedness and intolerance the excessive care which Brahmins take to exclude strangers from their temples and religious ceremonies. For my part, I think that their only motive is to secure themselves from the approach of men who, from the way in which they live, and from the clothes which they wear, are in their eyes in a perpetual state of defilement. In the course of my travels, chance has sometimes brought me to the door, or into the enclosure, of one of their large temples, just when a crowd had assembled to witness some solemn ceremony or procession, and giving way

[1] The law now recognizes a convert's right to his share of the family property.—ED.

[2] In his *Letters on the State of Christianity in India* the Abbé goes into the whole of this question at great length; but he ascribes to Brahminical influence, rather than to Anglo-Indian immorality, the chief cause of 'the impossibility of making real converts to Christianity among the natives of India.'—ED.

to curiosity, I have stopped to look on at my leisure. On such occasions the Brahmins themselves have sometimes invited me to enter their temple, being satisfied as to my manner of living and conduct; an honour which, out of respect to my calling, I always felt bound to decline.

When I had to build or restore a church, it was very often from Brahmins that I obtained the site and the necessary materials; and when I did occasionally meet with opposition in the public discharge of my religious duties, it was never due to Brahmins, but to fanatical sectaries, to religious mendicants, and to other vagabonds who are always wandering about the country.

But if Brahmins cannot with any justice be accused of intolerance in the matter of religion, the same can certainly not be said in regard to their civil usages and customs. On these points they are utterly unreasonable. We have already seen many proofs of this in the preceding chapters, and what I am now about to add will form a fitting sequel. It is part of their principles to avoid and despise strangers. The signs of affection, friendship, and even respect which they sometimes show them are only hypocritical, their motive being entirely that of self-interest. If a European were to come and tell me that he had found amongst the Hindus a really disinterested friend, I should without hesitation predict, while pitying his simplicity and excess of confidence, that sooner or later his pretended friend would deceive and betray him.

Being fully persuaded of the superlative merits of their own manners and customs, the Hindus think those of other people barbarous and detestable, and quite incompatible with real civilization. This ridiculous pride and these absurd prejudices have always been so deeply ingrained in them, that not one of the great dynastic changes that have taken place in India in modern times has been able to effect the smallest change in their mode of thinking and acting. Though they have had to submit to various conquerors who have proved themselves to be their superiors in courage and bravery, yet, in spite of this, they have always considered themselves infinitely their superiors in the matter of civilization.

The Mahomedans, who can tolerate no laws, no customs, and no religion but their own, used every advantage which conquest gave them in a vain attempt to force their religion on the people who had succumbed to them almost without resistance. But these same Hindus, who did not dare to complain when they saw their wives, their children, and everything they held most dear carried off by these fierce conquerors, their country devastated by fire and sword, their temples destroyed, their idols demolished; these same Hindus, I say, only displayed some sparks of energy when it became a question of changing their customs for those of their oppressors. Ten centuries of Mahomedan rule, during which time the conquerors have tried alternately cajolery and violence in order to establish their own faith and their own customs amongst the conquered, have not sufficed to shake the steadfast constancy of the native inhabitants. Bribes of dignities and honours, and the fear of annoyance and loss of position, have had but a slight effect on them, and that confined to a few Brahmins. Indeed, the dominant race has had to yield, and has even been forced to adopt some of the religious and civil practices of the conquered people.

It is true that the tyrannical way in which the Mahomedans have always governed this mild and gentle people was not calculated to conciliate them; but perhaps the time is not far distant when the Hindus may see themselves delivered from the iron yoke which has weighed so long upon them. As a rule they care little for the troubles and ills of this life, but it would be difficult for them to forget all the miseries that their inhuman masters have heaped upon them.

The Brahmins in particular cherish an undying hatred against the Mahomedans. The reason of this is that the latter think so lightly of the pretensions of these so-called *gods of the earth*; and, above all, the Mahomedans do not scruple to display hearty contempt for their ceremonies and customs generally. Besides, the haughty Mussulmans can vie with them in pride and insolence. Yet there is this difference: the arrogance of a Mussulman is based only on the political authority with which he is invested, or on the eminence of the rank that he occupies; whereas the Brahmin's superiority is inherent in himself, and it remains intact, no matter what his condition in life may be. Rich or poor, unfortunate or prosperous, he always goes on the principle engrained in him that he is the most noble, the most excellent, and the most perfect of all created beings, that all the rest of mankind are infinitely beneath him, and that there is nothing in the world so sublime or so admirable as his customs and practices.

With regard to any special exhibitions of wisdom, particularly in the province of learning, it would be impossible to persuade Brahmins that there are men outside their caste who are capable of disputing the first place with them. As for the industrial or aesthetic arts, they look upon them as beneath their attention. Probably the gross ignorance of the greater number of the Mahomedan natives of India, who are not even capable of drawing up their own almanac, may have helped to contribute to the good opinion that Brahmins have of themselves; but, on the other hand, if the Mahomedans had any honesty of feeling at all, would they not drop some of this ridiculous boasting, considering the immense and incontestable superiority that the many Europeans who live in this country have over them? The Brahmins, on the other hand, far from accepting this superiority, scornfully repudiate anything that they hear in regard to the ingenious contrivances and useful discoveries which have made such giant strides in Europe of late years. Nothing that has not been discovered by Brahmins, and nothing that is not to be found in their books, would be considered worthy of one moment's attention on their part. You may often meet with men of the Brahmin caste who, from some interested motive or other, have learnt European languages and understand them thoroughly, but you never find in their hands a book written in one of these languages, and no one could ever persuade them that such a book contained anything useful which they did not already know, or which was not to be found in one of their books. No doubt frank and friendly relations between them and educated Europeans may in time overcome this absurd and inexplicable perverseness; but nothing leads one to hope that they will ever seek to establish such relations[1].

How, indeed, could a Brahmin or any other Hindu have any real feelings of friendship or esteem for Europeans so long as the latter continue to eat the flesh of the sacred cow, which a Hindu considers a much more heinous offence than eating

[1] The spread of English education during the last sixty years has certainly brought about an improvement in this direction.—ED.

human flesh, so long as he sees them with Pariahs as domestic servants, and so long as he knows that they have immoral relations with women of that despised caste? He, it must be remembered, considers himself defiled and obliged to purify himself by bathing if so much as the shadow of one of these Pariahs is thrown across him. How, indeed, could he feel well disposed towards Europeans when he sees them give way without shame or remorse to drunkenness, which to him is the most disgusting of vices, and which, were he to be but once publicly convicted of it, would bring upon him the most serious consequences? How can he respect Europeans when he sees their wives on terms of the most intimate familiarity with their husbands, being equally intemperate, and eating, drinking, laughing, and joking with other men, and, above all, dancing with them: he, in whose presence a wife dare not even sit, and to whom it is inconceivable that any woman, unless she be a concubine or a prostitute, could even think of indulging in such pastimes? How, again, could he mix with Europeans when he sees their clothing, which in shape alone seems to him to savour of indecency by showing too much of the human form, and of which so many articles, such as shoes, boots, gloves, are made from the skins of animals: he, who cannot understand how any decent man could handle, wear, or even touch these remains of dead animals without shuddering with disgust?

CHAPTER XII

The Morality of Brahmins.—Their Deceit and Dissimulation.—Their Want of Filial Devotion.—Their Incontinence.—Causes of their Depravity.—Unnatural Offences.—Outward Decency.—The Chastity of their Women.—Brahmin Methods of Revenge.—Brahmin Selfishness.

But are the Brahmins, who are so easily shocked at the sins and vices of others—are they themselves exempt from all human weaknesses? Are their morals irreproachable? Oh, far from it! My pen would refuse to describe all their wrong-doings; but, so far as is possible, I will try to give a clear and impartial sketch of them.

I think that we may take as their greatest vices the untrustworthiness, deceit, and double-dealing which I have so often had occasion to mention, and which are common to all Hindus. It is quite impossible to fathom their minds and discover what they really mean; more impossible, indeed, than with any other race. He would indeed be a fool who relied on their promises, protestations, or oaths, if it were to their interest to break them. All the same, I do not think that these vices are innate in them. It must be remembered that they have always been until quite recently under the yoke of masters who had recourse to all sorts of artifices to oppress and despoil them. The timid Hindu could think of no better expedient with which to defend himself than to meet ruse with ruse, dissimulation with dissimulation, and fraud with fraud. The prolonged use of weapons for which excuse may be found in their natural desire to resist the oppression of their rulers, ended by becoming a habit which it is now impossible for them to get rid of. An almost unconquerable propensity to theft is also to be noticed amongst the Hindus. They never let slip an opportunity of stealing, unless they think they are likely to be found out. With them honesty is always secondary to their own personal interest. The natural sentiments of filial respect and devotion, the foundation of all other virtues and the first link in the social chain, exercise very little influence over a Brahmin's children. The outward show of love and respect that they occasionally make is purely formal, and means nothing.

Young children will obey their father, because they fear punishment if they do not; but they will overwhelm their mother with abuse, and will insult her grossly, even going so far at times as to strike her. When they grow older they fail to respect even their father, and it often happens that he is obliged to give way to his sons, who have made themselves masters of the house. Strange to say, nowhere are parents fonder of their children than they are in India; but this fondness usually degenerates into weakness. If the children are good, they are extravagantly praised; if they are naughty, their parents show the utmost ingenuity in finding excuses for them. The mild punishments that their naughtiness or disobedience brings down upon them invariably err on the side of leniency. The parents do not dare to whip them or scold them sharply, or even inflict any punishment that they would be likely to feel. The father and mother content themselves with making feeble remonstrances about their bad behaviour, and if these produce no effect, they leave them to grow up in their evil ways. The few sensible parents who show more firmness and severity with their children are met with a show of temper. Sons do not hesitate to resist the parental authority, and threaten to escape it by running away and living elsewhere. This threat rarely fails to produce the desired effect; the parents' severity melts away and they become passive witnesses of the disorderly conduct of their sons, who, encouraged by this first victory, end by becoming absolute masters of the house. One must, however, do them the justice to say that, after having thus gained the mastery over their parents, they take great care of them, as a general rule, and see that they want for nothing in their old age. But I fancy that in acting thus they are moved less by filial affection than by considerations of what the world will say. In the case of such spoilt children, subjected as they are from their earliest youth to influences which prematurely develop the latent germs of passion and vice, the knowledge of evil always comes before the first dawnings of reason. At the time of their lives when, according to the laws of nature, the passions should remain unawakened, it is not at all unusual to find children of both sexes familiar with words and actions which are revolting to modesty. The instincts which are excited at an early age by the nudity in which they remain till they are seven or eight years old, the licentious conversation that they are always hearing around them, the lewd songs and obscene verses that their parents delight in teaching them as soon as they begin to talk, the disgusting expressions which they learn and use to the delight of those who hear them, and who applaud such expressions as witticisms; these are the foundations on which the young children's education is laid, and such are the earliest impressions which they receive.

Of course it is unnecessary to say that, as they get older, incontinence and all its attendant vices increase at the same time. It really seems as if most of the religious and civil institutions of India were only invented for the purpose of awakening and exciting passions towards which they have already such a strong natural tendency. The shameless stories about their deities, the frequent recurrence of special feast-days which are celebrated everywhere, the allegorical meaning of so many of their everyday customs and usages, the public and private buildings which are to be met with everywhere bearing on their walls some disgusting obscenity, the many religious services in which the principal part is played by prostitutes, who often make even the temples themselves the scenes of their abominable debauchery; all these things seem to be calculated to excite the lewd imagination of the inhabitants of this tropical country and give them a strong impetus towards libertinism.

In order to prevent the consequences of this precocious sensuality, parents must hasten to marry their children as early as possible. Yet marriage under these circumstances does not always prove a very powerful restraint. Nothing is more common than for a married man to keep one or more concubines away from his home, in a separate establishment, according as his pecuniary circumstances permit. This state of affairs is particularly common in large towns, where it is so much easier to keep it a secret from the legitimate wife, and thus avoid the domestic quarrels and dissensions which are the natural consequences. Nevertheless, even in the country, the jealousy of a wife is rarely a hindrance to a husband's profligacy. She may try in vain to bring him back by remonstrances and threats; in vain she may leave her home and take refuge with her parents. Her faithless husband recalls her and maybe swears to behave better in future. But she is soon deceived again! She soon finds herself deserted once more; and finally she must perforce resign herself to seeing, hearing, and suffering everything without making any further complaint.

And after all, is it surprising that libertinism and all its consequences prevail in a country where the passions have so many incentives and such ample opportunities of satisfaction? Look at the crowd of widows in the prime of life who are forbidden to remarry, and who are only too ready to yield to the temptations by which they are assailed. Modesty and virtue place no restrictions on them; their only fear is that their misconduct may be found out. Consequently, abortion is their invariable resource to prevent such a contingency, and they practise it without the slightest scruple or remorse. There is not a woman amongst them who does not know how to bring it about. This odious crime, so revolting to all natural feeling, is of no importance in the eyes of the Hindus. According to their view, to destroy a being that has never seen the light is a lesser evil than that a woman should be dishonoured. The crimes of these unnatural mothers do not always, however, go unpunished; many of them fall victims to the violent remedies which they employ to get rid of their shame. But should these remedies fail in having the desired effect, and the women be no longer able to conceal their condition, they give out that they are going to make a pilgrimage to Benares, which is a very favourite form of devotion amongst Brahmins of both sexes. Then having chosen a discreet companion in whom they can confide, they start on their journey; but the supposed pilgrimage comes to an end in a neighbouring village, at the house of some relative or friend, who helps them to live in seclusion until such time as the child shall be born. They then hand over the result of their misconduct to any one who will take charge of it, and return to the bosom of their family.

Besides these sources of depravity which are common to all castes, there are a great many others peculiar to the Brahmins. Many of them possess abominable books in which the most filthy and disgusting forms of debauchery are systematically described and taught. These books also treat of such matters as the art of giving variety to sensual pleasures, the decoction of beverages calculated to excite the passions, or renew them when exhausted. They also contain recipes for philtres, which are supposed to have the property of inspiring unholy love. The courtesans of the country often have recourse to these potions in the hope of retaining the affections of those whom they have enslaved, mixing them secretly in the food of their victims. I am told that the ingredients of which these potions are composed would inspire the greatest libertine with disgust and horror for his mistress if it ever came to his knowledge.

To have any connexion with a courtesan, or with an unmarried person, is not considered a form of wickedness in the eyes of the Brahmins. These men, who look upon the violation of any trivial custom as a heinous sin, see no harm in the most outrageous and licentious excesses. It was principally for their use that the dancers and prostitutes who are attached to the service of the temples were originally entertained, and they may often be heard to intone the following scandalous line:—

Vesya darisanam punyam papa nasanam!

which means, 'To have intercourse with a prostitute is a virtue which takes away sin[1].'

Adultery on the part of a woman, though it is considered shameful and is condemned in Brahminical law, is punished with much less severity in their caste than in many others. So long as it is kept a secret it is regarded as a matter of very small importance. It is the publicity of it which is the sin. If it becomes known the husbands are the first to contradict any gossip that may be current in order to avoid any scandal or disagreeable consequences.

However, the shame and dishonour which are the inevitable consequences of sins of this nature, and which are also reflected on the families of the culprits, serve as a check to a great many and keep them in the path of virtue. Those who succumb to an irresistible temptation are generally clever enough to invent

[1] The real translation is, 'Looking upon a prostitute,' &c. This line, it may be mentioned, is not a quotation from any book of Hindu religion, but is often quoted falsely as such.—ED.

expedients to hide their weakness from spiteful eyes. But woe to those who have been so imprudent or so careless as to fail to hide their misdeeds. There is no insult that charitable persons of their own sex will not heap upon them, and if the least quarrel arises amongst them this would be the first thing brought up against them. Their confusion under these circumstances proves a warning to others to be more circumspect, or, at any rate, to save appearances at all costs.

But the depravity of the Hindus does not end here. There are depths of wickedness a thousand times more horrible to which the greater number of them are not ashamed to descend.

In Europe, where the Christian religion has inspired a salutary horror for certain unnatural offences, one would find it difficult to believe the stories which show to what lengths these disgusting vices are carried by the greater number of heathens and Mahomedans, to whom they have become a sort of second nature. We all know how greatly the Arabs and their neighbouring tribes are addicted to them. Kaempfer says that in Japan there are public establishments for this purpose which are tolerated by Government; and very much the same thing is done in China.

The facility with which the Hindu can gratify his passions in a natural manner in a country where courtesans abound renders these disgusting practices less common; but it by no means prevents them altogether. In the larger towns in India there are generally houses to be found given over to this odious form of vice. One sometimes meets in the streets the degraded beings who adopt this infamous profession. They dress like women, let their hair grow in the same way, pluck out the hair on their faces, and copy the walk, gestures, manner of speaking, tone of voice, demeanour, and affectations of prostitutes. Other secret crimes are also carried on in India, and especially among the Mahomedans; but decency will not allow me to speak of them. They are the same as those which are mentioned in the Bible (Leviticus xviii and xx), and which brought down such terrible punishments on the inhabitants of Canaan who had been guilty of them.

Being hardly able to believe in the possibility of such abominable wickedness, I asked a Brahmin one day whether there was any truth in what I had heard. Far from denying the stories, he smilingly confirmed them; nor did he appear to be even shocked at such iniquity. Indeed he seemed to be quite amused at the confusion and embarrassment that I felt in asking him such questions. At last I said to him: 'How is it possible for one to believe that such depraved tastes exist, degrading men as they do to a far lower level than the beasts of the field, in a country where the union of the two sexes is so easy?' 'On that point there is no accounting for tastes,' he replied, bursting out into a laugh. Disgusted with this reply, and filled with contempt for the man who was not ashamed to speak thus, I turned on my heel and left him without another word.

From the earliest ages these unnatural offences have been common in the East amongst heathen nations. In the laws that God gave the Israelites, He warns them to be on their guard against these detestable vices, which were known to be very prevalent amongst the inhabitants of the countries they were going to take possession of, and which were one of the chief reasons for their total extermination.

If the Christian religion had done nothing more than render these iniquities revolting and execrable, that alone would be sufficient to ensure our love and respect for it.

It may seem incredible, after what I have just said, when I add that there is no country in the world where greater attention is paid to what may be described as outward propriety. What we call love-making is utterly unknown amongst the Hindus. The playful sallies, the silly jokes, the perpetual compliments, and the eager and unlimited display of attention in which our youths are so profuse would be looked upon as insults by any Hindu lady, even the least chaste, that is, if they were offered to her in public. Even if a husband indulged in any familiarities with his own wife it would be considered ridiculous and in bad taste. To inquire after a man's wife, too, is an unpardonable breach of good manners; and when one is visiting a friend one must be careful never to speak to the ladies of the house[1].

Thus it is that here below mankind seems incapable of preserving the happy medium. For our part we exceed in one direction by giving way to undue familiarity with persons of the opposite sex; while the Hindus for their part err on the side of

[1] In the case of relatives and intimate friends no such objection is taken.—ED.

reserve. The extreme susceptibility of the latter in this respect is due to the opinion they hold that no mark of affection between man and woman can be either innocent or disinterested. If a European lady is seen taking a gentleman's arm, even though he may profess the profoundest respect for her, nothing would persuade a Hindu that she was not his mistress.

These strict principles of etiquette are instilled into the mind of a Hindu woman from her early youth, and, owing to the severity with which lapses from them are treated in some castes, indiscretions are far less frequent than one would imagine to be the case, considering how early the licentious habits of Hindu men are formed. Whatever may be said to the contrary, Hindu women are naturally chaste. To cite a few examples of unseemly conduct, a few lapses attributable to human frailty, is no proof of their want of chastity as a body; just as it is no proof to cite the shameless conduct of those poor wretches, prostitutes by birth and profession, who follow the armies and live in concubinage with Europeans. I would even go so far as to say that Hindu women are more virtuous than the women of many other more civilized countries. Their temperament is outwardly calm and equable, and though a passionate fire may smoulder underneath, without the igniting spark it will remain quiescent. Is this dormant coldness of disposition to be attributed to the secluded way in which they are brought up, or to the reserved demeanour that is taught them from their infancy, or to the unbridgeable gulf that is fixed between them and their male relatives, with whom the least familiarity is not permissible; or, what is not very likely, can it be put down to climatic influence? I cannot say. But whoever studies their character and conduct from this particular standpoint as impartially and disinterestedly as I have done, will, I feel sure, be constrained to render the same tribute to their chastity.

Having thus spoken of the special power which sexual passion exercises in India, a power which unfortunately is only too strongly felt in other quarters of the globe, I will now say a few words on two other passions which are equally violent, and to which the Hindu is particularly susceptible, namely, the resentment of injury and the desire for revenge. The Brahmins are particularly rancorous. The bitter feeling caused by an injury or affront never leaves them. Feuds are perpetuated in families and become hereditary, and a perfect reconciliation is never effected. Self-interest sometimes brings two enemies together, but they only dissemble for the time being, and never conquer their feeling of hatred. It is not unusual to see a son or a grandson revenging wrongs done fifty years before to father or grandfather. Furthermore such vengeance takes a peculiar form. Duels seem to them foolish, and they rarely have recourse to assassination or violence. Timid and weak-minded as they are, they do not like to commit themselves to bold or murderous devices. Their favourite weapons are spells and enchantments. They think that by reciting maledictory *mantrams*, or calling to their aid the diabolical arts of some wicked magician, they will surely cause their enemy to be attacked by some incurable malady. To get up a quarrel and then overwhelm each other with the grossest insults is a common mode of revenge, and one in which Brahmins excel. But their most perfidious weapon, and one which they are especially clever at using, is slander. Sooner or later, by crooked ways or underhand intrigues, they contrive to deal their enemies some fatal blow by this means.

Murder and suicide occur occasionally amongst the Hindus, though such crimes are regarded by them with greater horror than by any other people. Poison is generally the means employed when a murder is committed. It is usually women who are guilty of suicide. Driven to despair by the ill-treatment of a brutal husband, or by the annoyances of a spiteful mother-in-law, or by any of those domestic worries which are so common in a Hindu household, they lay criminal hands on themselves and destroy the life which has become unbearable.

Intense selfishness is also a common characteristic of a Brahmin. Brought up in the idea that nothing is too good for him, and that he owes nothing in return to any one, he models the whole of his life on this principle. He would unhesitatingly sacrifice the public good, or his country itself, if it served his own interests; and he would stoop to treason, ingratitude, or any deed, however black, if it promoted his own welfare. He makes it a point of duty not only to hold himself aloof from all other human beings, but also to despise and hate from the bottom of his heart every one who happens not to be born of the same caste as himself. And further, he thinks himself absolved from any feelings of gratitude, pity, or consideration towards them. If he occasionally shows any kindliness, it is only to some one of his own caste. As for the rest of mankind, he has been taught from his earliest youth to look upon them all as infinitely beneath him. According to the principles in which he has been brought up, he ought even to treat them with contempt, hatred, and harshness, as beings created solely to serve him and minister to his wants without there being any necessity for him to make the smallest return. Such are the Brahmins[1]!

[1] It must be admitted that the Abbé paints the Brahmins in darker colours than, as a body, they deserve.—Ed.

CHAPTER XIII

The Outward Appearance of Brahmins and other Hindus.—Their Physical Defects.—Remarks on the *Kakrelaks* or Albinoes, as described by Naturalists, who are not allowed Burial after Death.—Other Hindus to whom the same Honour is denied.—Exhumation of Corpses.—The Feeble Physique of the Hindus.—The same Feebleness and Deterioration to be observed throughout the Animal and Vegetable Kingdoms.—Weakness of the Mental Faculties of Hindus.—The Language of the Brahmins.—Their Costume.—Their Houses.

HAVING given a sketch of the moral character of the Brahmins, I will now say a few words about their physical appearance. Many of the characteristics of this kind that I am to mention do not, however, specially pertain to them, but are common to Hindus of other castes. Faces and figures vary, as they do in every other caste; but there are certain physical deformities common enough in Europe which are much more rarely seen in India. Thus, for instance, one seldom meets persons who are humpbacked or lame, unless they have become so by accident. If a child is born with any bodily defect, it is attributed to the evil influence of two unlucky constellations which must have been in conjunction at the time of birth, or to some eclipse of the sun or moon that took place at that moment. On the other hand, blindness is very common. No doubt the chief cause of this is to be found in the habit that poor people have of going about in nature's garb, with their heads exposed to the burning rays of the sun; and it is doubtless in the hope of preventing, as far as possible, the terrible scourge of ophthalmia that they so frequently anoint their heads with castor oil or oil of sesamum.

The Hindus, like every other race, have certain physical characteristics which are peculiar to themselves. Except for their colour, however, they seem to me to be more like Europeans, especially in their physiognomy, than any other Asiatic race. Generally speaking, they have glossy black hair, narrow foreheads, and dark, or occasionally grey[1], eyes. Their stomachs are flat, and they rarely carry much flesh. Their legs are usually slightly bowed the wrong way and a little crooked, the result no doubt of their habit of squatting on the ground with their legs crossed under them like our tailors. Neither have they any calves, which are considered anything but a beauty. Men who work in the fields or who are always exposed to the sun are quite as black in colour as the inhabitants of Kaffraria or Guinea; but the complexion of those who, like the Brahmins, spend their days under cover, or lead a sedentary life, is many degrees lighter. A very dark Brahmin and a fair Pariah are looked upon as monstrosities. Hence no doubt the proverb 'Beware of a black Brahmin or a fair Pariah!' A Brahmin is generally the colour of brass, or perhaps of weak coffee. This is considered the most correct shade; and the women who are the colour of light gingerbread are most admired. I have seen Brahmins, and particularly Brahmin women, who were not as dark as the inhabitants of Southern Europe. Furthermore the palms of the hands and the soles of the feet of Hindus of both sexes are almost as white as our own[2].

On the mountains and in the dense jungles of the Malabar coast there are some savage tribes who are much lighter in colour. In Coorg there is a tribe known as the *Malai-Kondiaru* who in outward appearance closely resemble Spaniards and Portuguese. The cause of this phenomenon is no doubt due partly to the climatic influences of the country they live in, and partly to their habit of always living in dense forests where the rays of the sun cannot penetrate.

You may sometimes meet a few, but very few, individuals whose skin is even fairer than that of a European, and with hair of the same colour. Of course this extreme fairness is unnatural, and makes them very repulsive to look at. In fact, these unfortunate beings are objects of horror to every one, and even their parents desert them. They are looked upon as lepers[3].

[1] They do not at all admire the blue eyes of Europeans. They consider them a deformity, and call them 'cats' eyes.'—DUBOIS.

[2] They share this characteristic with the Negroes.—DUBOIS.

[3] Learned physiologists have thought that these men really are lepers, and

They are called *Kakrelaks*[1] as a term of reproach. This peculiarity does not prevent some of them from living to a great age. They cannot bear the light, neither can they look fixedly at anything so long as the sun is up. During the day they close their eyelids, leaving only a slit to look through; but as soon as night comes on they open wide their large pink eyes, and are able to go about quite easily, seeing as well as other people.

The question has been raised as to whether these degenerate individuals can produce children like themselves, and afflicted with nyctalopia. Such a child has never come under my observation; but I once baptized the child of a female *Kakrelak*, who owed its birth to a rash European soldier, though this circumstance does not afford any proof on the subject[2].

These unfortunate wretches are denied decent burial after death, and are cast into ditches. This custom arises from a native superstition which does not allow any person who has died while suffering from a cutaneous disease to be buried. The Hindus believe that were this done a drought or some other public calamity would befall the whole country.

that this whiteness is produced by some malady which dries up the skin. They also think that black people would be much more subject to this affliction if it were not for their habit of anointing themselves frequently with oil or some other fatty substance. At the same time it should be observed that these human anomalies are to be met with all over the world. Thus you find the *Bedas* in Ceylon, wild creatures with white skins and red hair. There are *Kakrelaks* in all the American Islands; then again there are the *Dondos* or albinoes of Southern Africa (*Aethiopes albicantes*). Lastly, these colourless people are particularly numerous in the Isthmus of Darien.—DUBOIS.

[1] The *kakrelaks* are horrible insects, disgustingly dirty, which give forth a loathsome odour. They are of the same species as our bugs, but much larger. These unpleasant and destructive insects shun the day and its light. They remain hidden in holes or crannies in walls, and come out at night to devour all the food they can find and to disturb sleepers.—DUBOIS.

[2] This fact disposes at any rate of the opinion which some have held that these people cannot bear children. It remains to be seen whether there would be any issue, supposing both parents were albinoes. The white Negroes of Africa are believed never to be able to produce children; but the *Kakrelaks* in Asia are supposed to be prolific, and their progeny are said to be of the same colour as the rest of the nation. Anyhow, no one has been able to discover for certain if albinoes have been born from other than Negroes or dark-coloured parents; and we may conclude that these ill-favoured children are not a special variety of the human species, any more than are the Cretins in the Canton of Valais.—DUBOIS.

Burial is also refused, at least in several provinces, to persons who die of wounds or eruptive diseases, such as small-pox or measles, &c.[1] Also to those whose bodies have white marks on them; to pregnant women who die before child-birth[2]; and above all to the many who fall victims to tigers. The tragic fate of these last is in a manner consecrated by those heaps of stones which the traveller sometimes comes across in his journeys, and which, on the very spot where they died, cover the remains of those who have perished so deplorably[3].

In consequence of this absurd superstition, when the country has been a long time without rain, the inhabitants think the drought is to be attributed to the fact that some one must have surreptitiously infringed this unwritten law. Accordingly the magistrates give immediate orders that all bodies that have been buried in the course of the year shall be exhumed, and become food for the birds of prey. I myself once had great difficulty in preventing a Christian cemetery being violated and the remains of the dead disturbed in this manner. Fortunately, at the critical moment, rain came down in torrents, and so the profanation of the dead was avoided. Otherwise I should have been forced to yield to the clamour of a senseless mob.

But to return to the subject in hand, which has been rather lost sight of during this long digression.

All Hindus, and particularly Brahmins, have weak constitutions, and in this respect they are greatly inferior to Europeans. They have not the strength, vigour, or activity of the latter. One European workman would, under any circumstances, do at least as much as two natives. This constitutional weakness, which is partly inherent, is greatly increased by the hardships

[1] Brahmins who die of small-pox are burnt in the usual way, at any rate in South India. The Sudras invariably bury such corpses.—ED.

[2] It is usual amongst Brahmins to take the foetus from the body of a dead pregnant woman, and the latter is burned separately.—ED.

[3] The bodies even of criminals and suicides were not deprived of burial by the Jews; yet there are examples in Holy Scripture which bear some resemblance to this Hindu custom. Thus Achan, after he had been stoned, was buried under a heap of stones (Joshua vii. 25, 26), and Absalom's case is mentioned in 2 Samuel xviii. 17. The king of Ai was treated in the same way (Joshua viii. 29). Finally, Jeremiah prophesies that the wicked Jehoiakim, son of Josiah, should have 'the burial of an ass' (Jeremiah xxii. 19).—DUBOIS.

and privations that they are condemned to bear all their lives.

The climate, which is the chief cause of the degeneration of the human race in these countries, exercises a no less fatal influence in the animal and vegetable kingdoms. Green stuff, roots, and fruits are for the most part insipid and tasteless, and do not possess half the nutritive value of those grown in Europe. A very few may be cited as exceptions to this rule. The vegetable products of India included in our list of groceries are pungent enough to destroy the membrane of one's throat. Again, the indigenous flowers, with two or three exceptions, have no scent. Lastly, the trees and shrubs to be found in the forests or in uncultivated places are generally covered with thorns and prickles. The elephant and tiger are strong and vigorous enough, but all the other animals, whether wild or domesticated, share in the universal debilitation. What we call butcher's meat has very little succulence in it, and there is nothing in the flavour of the game that would tempt the least fastidious European palate. Vainly would one search for a good hare or partridge. One is inclined to think that nature here has reduced the nutritive value of all animals and vegetables in proportion to the weakness of the human beings whose food they are to be.

But as a cruel compensation, nature is prodigal with creatures that are hurtful, and with many things that are useless, to man. The forests and jungles are inhabited by elephants, tigers, and other wild animals which are deadly foes to man and his flocks and herds. The country is overrun with snakes and other deadly reptiles, while birds of prey may be seen everywhere in large numbers. Every kind of irritating, destructive, and abominable insect swarms and multiplies in a manner that is equally surprising and annoying. Even poisonous plants are by no means uncommon, and their hurtful properties show no signs of deterioration.

It is true that the four elements seem to conspire together for the purpose of weakening everything that matures or vegetates in this portion of the globe. The soil itself is generally light, sandy, and wanting in substance; it requires a great deal of skilled labour to make it fertile. The air is almost everywhere unhealthy, damp, and enervating; the water in the wells and tanks is usually brackish and unpleasant to the taste: indeed, the excessive heat of the sun dries up everything, animal and vegetable. The mental faculties of the Hindus appear to be as feeble as their physique. I should say that no other nation in the world could boast of as many idiots and imbeciles. There are, of course, very many sensible, capable persons amongst the Hindus, who possess marked abilities and talents, and who by education have developed the gifts with which nature has endowed them; but during the three hundred years or so that Europeans have been established in the country no Hindu, so far as I know, has ever been found to possess really transcendent genius.

Their want of courage almost amounts to absolute cowardice. Neither have they that strength of character which resists temptation and leaves men unshaken by threats or seductive promises, content to pursue the course that reason dictates. Flatter them adroitly and take them on their weak side, and there is nothing you cannot get out of them.

The prudent forethought which prompts men to take heed to their future as well as to their present wants seems almost an unknown quality among the majority of Hindus. They take no thought for the morrow, and all they care about is to gratify their vanity and their extravagant whims for the moment. They are so taken up with the pleasures and enjoyments of the present that they never think of looking beyond to the possible misery and privations that may await them in the future.

This want of forethought is in a great measure responsible for those reverses of fortune which so frequently happen to them, and by which they pass from the greatest wealth and luxury to the bitterest poverty. It is true they bear these sudden transitions from comfort to misery with the most marvellous resignation; but then this resignation is not the outcome of principle or of dignified patience—it is due rather to their apathetic temperament, which makes them incapable of feeling any strong emotion. They enjoy their good fortune mechanically and without thought, and they take their losses with the same calm imperturbability[1].

I prefer to think that the ingratitude with which they are

[1] This imperturbability might more correctly be attributed to the prevailing belief in the doctrine of fatalism.—ED.

so often and so justly accused may be attributed to this phlegmatic disposition, and not to wilful wrong-headedness. Nowhere is a kindness so soon forgotten as among Hindus. Gratitude—which is a feeling that springs up spontaneously in all true hearts, which is a duty that bare justice prescribes, and which is a natural result of benefactions received—is a virtue to which the Hindu shuts his heart entirely.

But let us leave this picture, which does not represent a very pleasing side of their character, and let us return to the consideration of their physical peculiarities. It is easy to recognize a Brahmin by a sort of swagger and freedom in his gait and behaviour. Unconsciously, and apparently unaffectedly, he shows by his tone and manner the superiority that his birth, rank, and education have given him. Brahmins have also a peculiar way of talking and expressing themselves. They never make use of the common or vulgar expressions of other castes. Their language is generally concise, refined, and elegant; and they enrich their vocabulary with many Sanskrit words. They have also peculiar modes of expression which the Sudras never use; and their conversation is always interspersed with pedantic proverbs and allegories. Their idioms are so numerous and varied, that though you may think you know their language well, it often happens that you cannot understand them when they are talking familiarly amongst themselves. In speaking and writing they make use of endless polite and flattering terms, often very aptly; but they carry the practice *ad nauseam.* Their compliments are always exaggerated and high-flown. They think nothing of placing those whom they wish to flatter above the level of their deities; indeed, that is a very usual beginning to a congratulatory speech.

If the language of the Brahmins is rich in gracious and flattering expressions, it is even more so in terms of abuse and coarse, indecent invective. Though they pride themselves on their courtesy and knowledge of the world, when they lose their tempers they are no better than our lowest rag-pickers; and an incredible quantity of disgusting and obscene language pours from their mouths on such occasions.

Their clothing is of the most simple description. It is as nearly as possible just what it was in the earliest ages. Two pieces of cotton cloth without hem or stitch, one 10 or 12 feet long, the other 14 or 16, and 3 or 4 feet wide, are their only garments. With the first piece they cover their shoulders, with the second they gird their loins. Of the latter, one end is passed between their thighs and is tucked behind into the portion which goes round their bodies, while the other end forms a drapery in front, and hangs with a certain careless grace to their feet. Their loin-cloths are generally ornamented with a border of silk of a different colour from the rest of the cloth itself. This costume is very suitable for persons who, like them, are most particular about keeping themselves always in a state of purity and cleanliness, for, as one may imagine, it does not cost much to wash their cloths often. Many have also a kind of large sheet, with which they cover themselves up at night, or when the mornings are cold. Since European piece-goods have been procurable all over the country, those who have been able to afford them have bought cloths of brilliant scarlet, which are a source of great pride and pleasure to them. It appears that formerly the Hindus went about with bare heads, and their bodies naked to the waist; and even at the present day the natives on the Malabar coast go about in this fashion. So also do a great many others who live in the dense forests where the same customs have prevailed from time immemorial, and where no revolutionary changes have penetrated. Nowadays most Hindus wear a turban, an article of dress which they have copied from the Mahomedans. It is made of fine thin muslin, often as much as 60 or 70 feet long, but at most only 2 feet in width. They twist it artistically round their heads, but the manner of arranging it varies in different provinces and with different castes. Men who are in service with either Europeans or Mahomedans wear a long coat of fine muslin or calico, very full in the skirt, and made in a peculiar way. This also is a foreign fashion recently copied from the Mahomedans. Brahmins and Mahomedans may be distinguished from each other by the fact that the former fasten their coats on the left side, and the latter on the right. Both generally wear over this garment a belt, made of some fine material, and wound several times round the waist.

All Brahmins, rich or poor, dress alike; but the rich usually wear finer and more expensive materials.

Most Hindus wear more or less expensive ornaments either

in the middle or the upper part of the ears. These ornaments vary in size and pattern according to locality and caste. But I shall have occasion to speak of this kind of adornment later on.

The simplicity of their houses equals that of their costume. These are generally thatched with straw and have mud walls, particularly in the country. The houses in the towns are better built; but they are all arranged on the same plan, and are all equally simple. The interior resembles a little cloister, with a gallery round it, while in the centre there is a court of varying size. From this you enter the tiny, dark, windowless rooms, into which light and air can only penetrate by means of a door about 4 feet high by 3 feet wide. These little dens are absolutely uninhabitable during the hot weather. The kitchen is always placed in the furthest and darkest corner of the house, so as to be entirely beyond the reach of strangers' eyes. I have already explained the motive of this arrangement. The hearth is invariably placed on the south-west side, which they call 'the fire-god's quarter,' because the Hindus believe that there this deity resides.

As the men are not allowed to pay visits to the women of the family, who are always occupied with their domestic affairs and remain shut up in a part of the house to which outsiders, as a rule, are not admitted, large open seats or raised platforms are constructed both inside and outside the principal entrance door, on which the men sit cross-legged, while they talk about business, discuss religion, politics, or science, receive visits, and in fact kill time as best they can.

Besides the private houses, one or more public buildings are generally to be found in all villages of any size. These consist usually of a shed or long room, open down the whole length of one side. They are what Europeans call *choultries*, and they correspond to the *caravanserais* of other Eastern nations. These rest-houses, which are usually large and convenient, not only serve as a shelter for travellers, but are also used as council chambers, where the headmen assemble to consider the public affairs of the village, settle law-suits, put an end to quarrels, and pacify disputants. They are also used for the celebration of religious rites in places where there are no temples.

All the villages are built very irregularly, without any plan or symmetry. The houses are crowded closely together; the streets are very narrow, and excessively dirty, with the exception of the street in the larger villages where the market is held, which is kept cleaner, and in which a certain amount of order is maintained. A few steps from the entrance door of each house is a large ditch into which all the manure from the stable and the refuse from the house are thrown. During the rains these sewage pits become full of water and form cesspools, which give off the most disgusting effluvia. But this unpleasant arrangement, which is the same in all the villages, does not appear to affect the inhabitants in any way.

All the houses being covered with thatch and crowded together, when a fire breaks out—a by no means rare occurrence—a whole village is often burned down in less than half an hour.

Though in the larger towns the houses are tiled and not thatched, there is no more symmetry in their arrangement than in the villages, and the streets are so narrow that two persons can scarcely walk abreast. In the middle of each street there usually runs a sewer, which receives all the rubbish and filth from the houses. This forms a permanent open drain, and gives off a pestilential smell, which none but a Hindu could endure for a moment.

CHAPTER XIV

Rules of Etiquette amongst Brahmins and other Hindus.—Modes of Greeting.

It is unnecessary, and it would be tedious, to give a detailed list of the numberless rules governing Hindu etiquette. If I cite a few it will give a general idea of the rest.

Hindus have several ways of greeting each other. In some provinces they put the right hand on the heart; in others they simply stretch it out to the acquaintance they are meeting, for they never greet a person whom they do not know, unless he be of very high rank. When two Hindu acquaintances meet, they generally say a few meaningless words to each other, such as, 'You—So-and-so—you here? That's all right!' 'And I—So-and-so—here I am.' Then each goes on his way.

They have also borrowed the *salaam* from the Mahomedans; but this they never use except to strangers. The *salaam* consists in touching the forehead with the right hand, and bowing at the same time, with more or less emphasis, according to the rank of the person they are greeting. In the case of a person of very high rank they sometimes touch the ground with both hands and then raise them to their foreheads, or else they come close to him and touch his feet three times.

Hindus who do not belong to the Brahmin caste greet Brahmins by performing *namaskara*, which consists in joining both hands, touching the forehead, and then putting them above the head. This mode of salutation, which is only offered to a superior, is accompanied by these two words, '*Saranam, ayya*!' which means 'Respectful greeting, my lord'; upon which the Brahmin extends his right hand, partially open, as if he expects to receive something from the person who is paying him this mark of respect, and gravely answers with this one word, '*Asirvadam*!' which answers to the Latin '*Benefaxit tibi Deus*!'

or to our 'God bless you!' It is a mysterious compound expression, made up of three words which convey good wishes. Only Brahmins and *gurus* have the right to give the *asirvadam* or to pronounce the sacred word over those who treat them with respect or give them presents. Some persons, when saluting a Brahmin, content themselves with raising their clasped hands as far as their chest.

Another very respectful manner of greeting is to extend both hands towards the feet of him whom you wish to honour, or to seize his knees while you throw yourself at his feet. This is a very common mode of greeting between a son and a father, or between a younger and an elder brother, on meeting after a long separation. The same humble attitude is also adopted when asking for pardon or for a favour; and only when the object is attained does the postulant relax his hold on the feet of the person whom he is addressing.

But of all the modes of salutation the most solemn and the most reverential is the *sashtanga*, or prostration of the six members, of which mention has already been made elsewhere[1]. When a Hindu is about to make a ceremonious visit to members of his family who live at a distance, he makes a halt when he gets near the place and sends some one to warn his relatives that he is coming. The relatives then start at once to fetch him, and conduct him to their home, often with much ceremony, and accompanied by music. It is not customary either to shake hands or to kiss each other on these occasions. A man who publicly kisses a woman, even if she be his wife, commits the grossest breach of social decorum. A brother would not think of taking such a liberty with a sister, or a son with his mother. Only on a visit of condolence do they make a pretence of doing so to the person to whom the visit is paid; and this form of salute, in which the lips do not really touch the face, is only permissible between persons of the same sex.

Women bow respectfully to men without speaking or looking at them. Children salute their parents in the same manner and stand upright before them, with their arms crossed on their chests. Whenever relatives or very great friends meet after

[1] See Chapter III.

[2] It has already been pointed out in a note in a previous chapter that the Abbé is wrong in translating *sashtanga* as 'six members' instead of 'eight members.'—ED.

a long separation, they clasp each other in their arms and take hold of each other's chin, shedding tears of joy.

Hindus who visit or meet each other after a long absence have, like ourselves, a set of commonplace phrases which they make use of for want of anything better. But in most cases the ideas they express are diametrically opposed to ours. Thus, for instance, if we Europeans were speaking to a friend or acquaintance, we should think he would be pleased if we congratulated him on his appearance of good health, his increased stoutness, or his good complexion, &c. If we think him altered for the worse, we take care not to let him see that we notice it, for fear it might pain him.

A Hindu, on the contrary, when he meets a friend, no matter how strong and well he may be looking, never fails to offer him the following greeting: 'How sadly you have altered since I last saw you! How thin and worn you look! I fear you must be very ill,' and other equally consoling remarks. It would offend a Hindu deeply if you were to say he was looking well on first meeting him. Any one who was so ill advised as to make so indiscreet a remark would certainly be suspected of feeling jealous, envious, and regretful at the signs of health which were the theme of his unfortunate compliments.

In the same way, you must never congratulate a Hindu on his good luck; you must not say that he has pretty children, a lovely house, beautiful gardens, fine flocks and herds, or that everything that he undertakes turns out well, or that he is happy or lucky, &c.; he would be sure to think that envy prompted compliments of this kind. Long ago, before I knew anything about Hindu etiquette, I was walking one day at the edge of a large tank or lake, where some men were fishing with nets. I stood still to watch them, and seeing that they landed a quantity of fish each time the nets were let down, I thought I might congratulate them on their good luck. But my civility had a most unlooked-for result, for these worthy people gathered up their nets and their fish without a word, and looking at me very indignantly, promptly went off, grumbling to each other under their breath: 'What have we done to this Feringhi *guru* that he comes here and is so jealous of us?'

Just as we French and English do, but contrary to the Spanish and Portuguese custom, the Hindus, in quitting an apartment with a visitor, always allow him to walk first. The object is to avoid turning one's back upon a guest, and he, in turn, in order not to appear wanting in politeness, walks sideways until both have passed the threshold. When leaving the presence of a prince or any great personage, it is customary, for the same reason, to walk backwards until one is out of his presence; and this is also why a servant, when accompanying his master on foot or on horseback, never walks in front of him.

It is considered good manners in India to blow your nose with your fingers; and there is nothing impolite in audibly getting rid of flatulency. Persons of all ranks, indeed, seem to rather encourage this habit, as according to them it is a sure sign of a good digestion. It is certainly an original, if somewhat disgusting spectacle to a European, to see a large number of Brahmins coming away from a feast indulging in a sort of competition as to who shall give vent to the loudest eructations, calling out at the same time, with emphatic gravity, '*Narayana*!' as if to thank Vishnu for his favours.

After sneezing a Hindu never fails to exclaim, '*Rama*! *Rama*!' and no doubt there is some superstition attached to this pious ejaculation[1]. Again, when a Brahmin yawns, he snaps his fingers to the right and left to scare away evil spirits and giants.

To tread on any one's foot, even by accident, demands an immediate apology. This is done by stretching out both hands towards the feet of the offended person. A box on the ear is not considered a graver affront than a blow given with the fist, or a kick with the bare foot; but a blow on the head, should it knock off the turban, is a very gross insult. By far the greatest indignity of all, however, is to be struck with one of the shoes or sandals that Hindus wear. Whoever submitted to such an insult without insisting on receiving satisfaction, would be excluded from his caste. The mere threat of such an insult is often sufficient to provoke a criminal prosecution.

[1] One knows that amongst the old heathen nations a sneeze was supposed to contain a great mystery. Old writers mention many facts which prove what superstitious deductions credulous persons drew from it. The custom of uttering a prayer or good wish on behalf of a person who has sneezed has existed from time immemorial. The Greeks said to such a person ζῆθι; the Romans, '*Salve.*' Though with us the fashion of saying, 'May your wishes be granted!' or 'God bless you!' has rather gone out, politeness demands that at least you should make a bow.—DUBOIS.

It is a mark of respect when women turn their backs on men whom they hold in high esteem. At any rate, they must turn away their faces or cover them with their *saris*. Again, when they leave the house, propriety requires them to proceed on their way without paying any attention to the passers-by; and if they see a man they are expected to bow their heads and look in the opposite direction. There are a good many, however, who are not always quite so modest.

Any one who sees a person of high rank coming towards him, must go off the road, if he is on foot, so as to leave the way perfectly free, and if he is on horseback or in a palanquin he must get down and remain standing until the great person has passed and is some distance off. When speaking to a superior, politeness demands that an inferior should put his right hand before his mouth to prevent any particle of his breath or saliva reaching and defiling him. If an inferior meets a superior out of doors he must take off his shoes before greeting him. A Hindu, moreover, must never enter his own house, much less a stranger's, with leather shoes on his feet.

In several of the Southern Provinces the Sudras are in the habit of taking off the cloth which covers the upper part of their bodies, winding it round their waists, and standing with arms crossed on their chest while speaking to a superior. The women of certain castes do the same in the presence of their husbands, or, of any man to whom they wish to show respect. Their rules of propriety oblige them to appear before men stripped to the waist; and to omit to do so would show a great want of good breeding.

When Brahmins are talking to a man of another caste, or to a European from whom they have nothing to hope or to fear, they stand with their hands behind their backs—a position which signifies contempt for their interlocutor, and which they are always very pleased to assume, to show the sense of their own superiority. When they pay a visit, no matter what may be the rank or dignity of their host, they never wait till they are asked to take a seat, but do so the instant they enter the room. People of all castes, when visiting a superior, must wait until they are dismissed before they can take leave.

There are several ceremonious visits which must be paid, such as visits of condolence, visits at *pongul*, and several others of which I shall speak later on. The feast of *pongul* and the following days are mostly celebrated by presents which near relatives make to each other, and which consist of new earthen vessels on which certain designs are traced in lime, also ground rice, fruit, sugar, saffron, &c. Such gifts are conveyed with much solemnity and accompanied by instruments of music. These little attentions are indispensable in the case of certain individuals. For instance, a mother must not neglect giving presents to her married daughter; otherwise the mother-in-law would resent the omission to her dying day.

With them letters of condolence on occasions of mourning can never take the place of a visit, as they so often do with us. Some member of the family must go in person to wail and lament, and perform the other ridiculous ceremonies that are customary on such occasions, even though a journey of fifty miles or more has to be made.

When a Hindu visits a person of importance for the first time he must not omit to take presents with him, which he will offer as a mark of respect, and to show that he comes with friendly intentions. It is generally considered a lack of good manners to appear with empty hands before any one of superior position, or from whom a favour is expected. Those whose means do not permit of their offering presents of great value may bring such things as sugar, bananas, cocoanuts, betel, &c.

In conclusion, it must be admitted that the laws of etiquette and social politeness are much more clearly laid down, and much better observed by all classes of Hindus, even by the lowest, than they are by people of corresponding social position in Europe.

CHAPTER XV

The Ornaments worn by Hindus.—The Different Marks with which they adorn their Bodies.

EVERY Hindu, even including those who have made a profession of penitence and have renounced the world, wears earrings. The *sannyasis* or penitents, who are supposed to have given up the three things which most naturally tend to excite man's cupidity—that is to say, women, honours, and riches—wear copper earrings in token of humility. But generally such ornaments are made of gold, and are of different shapes, though most frequently oval. Occasionally these pendants are so large that one can easily pass one's hand through them. Some are made of copper wire, round which gold wire is so twisted as to cover the copper completely. Those who are fairly well off wear them with a large pearl or precious stone in the centre.

These ear ornaments, which are sometimes of enormous size, are another proof of the Hindu's strong attachment to his old customs. All writers, both sacred and profane, bear witness to the fact that similar ornaments have been worn from time immemorial. On grand occasions, such as marriage feasts, they put four or five pairs into their ears, and at the end or in the centre of each of these is added another small ornament set with some precious stone. In some parts of the country a gold ring is also attached to the cartilage which divides the nostrils. Poor people, Pariahs included, who cannot afford to buy such valuable ornaments, wear some small inexpensive trinket in their ears. But, no matter what their caste or circumstances, fashion decrees that no one shall be without this species of adornment.

Rich Hindus wear round their necks gold chains or strings of pearls with large medallions set with diamonds which reach to their chests; and you often see them wearing gold finger-rings set with precious stones of great value. They also frequently wear round their waists a girdle made of gold or silver thread woven with much taste and skill, and carry massive gold bracelets on their arms, which sometimes weigh as much as a pound each. Married men wear silver rings on their toes[1]. Many, again, tie above their elbows little hollow tubes of gold or silver containing magical *mantrams*, which they wear as charms to avert ill luck.

They have many other baubles of the same kind[2]. Even the private parts of the children have their own particular decorations. Little girls wear a gold or silver shield or codpiece on which is graven some indecent picture; while a boy's ornament, also of gold or silver, is an exact copy of that member which it is meant to decorate.

Then there is the custom of painting the forehead and other parts of the body with different figures and emblems in various colours, a custom unknown elsewhere, but which appears to have been common enough among ancient nations. The simplest of all and the most common is the one called *pottu*, which consists of a small circular mark about an inch in diameter, placed in the centre of the forehead. It is generally yellow, but sometimes red or black in colour, and the paint is mixed with a sweet-smelling paste made by rubbing sandalwood on a damp stone. Instead of the *pottu*, some paint two or three horizontal lines across their foreheads with the same mixture, and others a perpendicular line from the top of the forehead to the nose. Some Brahmins and some of the Hindus of Northern India apply this paste to their cheeks rather effectively. Others use it to decorate the neck,

[1] Brahmin men never wear such rings.—ED.

[2] The variety and number of ornaments is almost bewildering; but they all have their proper names and shapes. Indian artisans do not need to rack their brains to invent novelties. There are no changing fashions, either in dress or in ornaments. A woman can wear what once belonged to her grandmother, or to one removed very many degrees further back, for the matter of that, either clothes or jewels; and this without any incongruity, or exciting remark. There is a perpetual recurrence of old patterns, improved, it may be, but the design will be the same. Of course it is in jewels for females that the variety occurs most.—PADFIELD.

It is a common belief among Hindus that there must always be at least a speck of gold on one's person, in order to ensure personal ceremonial purity.—ED.

breast, belly, and arms with different designs, while others again smear their bodies all over with the mixture.

Vishnavite Brahmins, as well as those of other castes who are particularly devoted to the worship of Vishnu, paint their foreheads with the emblem *namam*[1], which gives their faces a most extraordinary, and sometimes even ferocious appearance. The most enthusiastic devotees of this sect paint the same design on their shoulders, arms, breast, and belly; and the *Bairagis*, a sect who go about stark naked, often draw it on their hinder parts.

The worshippers of Siva cover their foreheads and various parts of their bodies with the ashes of cow-dung, or with ashes taken from the places where the dead are burned[2]. Some of them smear themselves all over from head to foot; others content themselves with smearing broad bars across the arms, chest, and belly.

Many Hindus who do not belong to any sect in particular smear their foreheads with ashes. Brahmins, with the exception of a very few who belong to some special sect, do not follow this custom, though sometimes, after they have performed their morning ablutions, they draw a little horizontal line with ashes across their foreheads.

The Hindus also display on their bodies many other marks and devices of different colours and designs, which vary according to the different castes, sects, and provinces. It would be difficult to explain the origin and meaning of the greater number of these symbols; those who wear them are often themselves ignorant of their meaning. Some, the *pottu* amongst the number, appear to have been invented solely for ornament, but there is no doubt that, as a rule, some superstitious meaning is attached to them. Thus the ashes of cow-dung are used in memory of the long penance of Siva and of several other holy personages, who always covered themselves with these ashes in token of humility.

Anyway, the Hindu code of good breeding requires that the forehead shall be ornamented with a mark of some sort. To keep it quite bare is a sign of mourning. It is also a sign that the daily ablutions have not been performed, that a person is

[1] See Chapter IX.

[2] Ashes taken from burning-grounds are not usually employed nowadays.—ED.

still in a state of impurity, or that he is still fasting. If one meets an acquaintance after noon with his forehead still bare, one always asks if it is because he has not yet broken his fast. It would be rude to appear before decent people with no mark whatever on the forehead.

Women attach much less importance than men to this kind of decoration. As a rule, they are satisfied with making the little round *pottu* mark on the forehead in red, yellow, or black, or else a simple horizontal or perpendicular line in red. But they have another kind of decoration of which they are very fond. It consists in painting the face, neck, arms, legs, and every part of the body that is visible with a deep yellow cosmetic of saffron. Brahmin women imagine that they thereby greatly enhance their beauty, since it makes their skin appear less dusky. Love of admiration no doubt has taught them that this paint gives them an additional charm in the eyes of Hindus, but it produces quite the contrary effect on Europeans, who think them hideous and revolting when thus besmeared.

No doubt all these daubings appear very ridiculous in our eyes, and it is difficult to believe that it can render any one more attractive, at least according to our way of thinking. But amongst the many artificial means of adornment which caprice and fashion have forced upon us there are several which excite just as much ridicule amongst the Hindus. Thus, for instance, in the days when it was the custom to powder the hair, they could not understand how a young man with common sense could bring himself to appear as if he had the white head of an old man. As to wigs, Hindus are absolutely horrified at seeing a European, holding some important position, with his head dressed out in hair which may have been taken from a leper, or a corpse, or at best from a Pariah or prostitute. To defile one's head with anything so unclean and abominable is regarded by the Hindu as most horrible! It would be no great hardship to expose a bald head to free contact with the air in such a warm climate, but were they all doomed to severe colds, nothing would ever persuade the Hindus to adopt the fashion of wearing wigs. And so we laugh at them, and they at us. And this is the way of the world.

'*Vae tibi! vae nigrae! dicebat cacabus ollae.*'

CHAPTER XVI

Brahmin Wives.—The Education of Women.—Ceremonies which take place when they arrive at a Marriageable Age, and during Pregnancy.—The Low Estimation in which Women are held in Private Life.—The Respect that is paid to them in Public.—Their Clothing and Ornaments.

THE social condition of the *Brahmanis*, or wives of Brahmins, differs very little from that of the women of other castes, and I shall have little to say about it. This interesting half of the human race, which exercises such enormous power in other parts of the world, and often decides the fate of empires, occupies in India a position hardly better than that of slaves. Their only vocation in life being to minister to man's physical pleasures and wants, they are considered incapable of developing any of those higher mental qualities which would make them more worthy of consideration and also more capable of playing a useful part in life. Their intellect is thought to be of such a very low order, that when a man has done anything particularly foolish or thoughtless his friends say he has no more sense than a woman. And the women themselves, when they are reproved for any serious fault and find it difficult to make a good excuse, always end by saying, 'After all, I am only a woman!' This is always their last word, and one to which there is no possible retort. One of the principal precepts taught in Hindu books, and one that is everywhere recognized as true, is that women should be kept in a state of dependence and subjection all their lives, and under no circumstances should they be allowed to become their own mistresses. A woman must obey her parents as long as she is unmarried, and her husband and mother-in-law afterwards. Even when she becomes a widow she is not free, for her own sons become her masters and have the right to order her about!

As a natural consequence of these views, female education is altogether neglected. A young girl's mind remains totally uncultivated, though many of them have good abilities. In fact, of what use would learning or accomplishments be to women who are still in such a state of domestic degradation and servitude? All that a Hindu woman need know is how to grind and boil rice and look after her household affairs, which are neither numerous nor difficult to manage.

Courtesans, whose business in life is to dance in the temples and at public ceremonies, and prostitutes are the only women who are allowed to learn to read, sing, or dance. It would be thought a disgrace to a respectable woman to learn to read; and even if she had learnt she would be ashamed to own it. As for dancing, it is left absolutely to courtesans; and even they never dance with men. Respectable women sometimes amuse themselves by singing when they are alone, looking after their household duties, and also on the occasions of weddings or other family festivities; but they would never dare to sing in public or before strangers.

Such feminine occupations as knitting or needlework are quite unknown to them; and moreover any talents that they might develop in this direction would be wasted, as their clothing consists of one long piece of coloured calico, without any join or seam in it, though most of them know how to card and spin cotton, and very few houses are without one or more spinning-wheels[1].

I have already described what takes place when a young girl, who has been married in her early childhood, arrives at the age when she is fit to live with her husband (Chapter VI). These festivities are called *the consummation of the marriage.*

The young woman herself cannot appear, because she is, for the first time in her life, in a state of uncleanness, and for several days she is obliged to remain in a separate part of the house. But after she has gone through the usual rites of purification she returns to the family, and numberless other ceremonies are performed over her, amongst others several

[1] Many Hindu women and girls now do needlework of some kind, and it is taught in most of the girls' schools. The old-fashioned mothers-in-law complain that this new departure has proved detrimental to the performance of the more ordinary household duties. —ED.

which are supposed to counteract the effects of witchcraft or the evil eye. She is then conducted with much pomp to her husband's house.

The Sudras, and even the Pariahs, have grand festivities when their daughters, though still unmarried, arrive at a marriageable age. The event is announced to the public with all the outward show that accompanies the most solemn ceremonies. A *pandal* is erected; *toranams* or strings of mango-leaves are hung in front of the entrance door of the house; feasts are given; much music resounds. In fact, it is a kind of advertisement or invitation to young men in want of a wife.

When a Brahmin's wife becomes pregnant there are endless ceremonies to be performed, some indeed for each separate month. In any caste it would be considered a disgrace to the woman, and in a less degree to her parents, if her first child were born anywhere but under the paternal roof. Her mother accordingly comes and fetches her about the seventh month of her pregnancy, and she is not allowed to return to her own home till her health is entirely re-established. When she departs her mother is supposed to give her a new piece of cotton cloth and some more or less valuable ornaments according to her means and her caste. But in no case would the woman, to whatever caste she might belong, return from her parents' to her husband's house unless her mother-in-law or some equally near relation came to fetch her. Her husband has to conform to this custom when his wife chooses to leave him and takes refuge under the paternal roof, sometimes for a mere whim, or for some very trifling cause. But in any case, even when the fault is all on her side, the husband must go and fetch her back.

These domestic quarrels and separations occur frequently, and are generally the fault of the mother-in-law, who looks upon her son's wife as a slave that has been bought and paid for. The elder woman, indeed, lives in constant dread of her daughter-in-law obtaining too much ascendency over the husband, and by this means contriving her own emancipation; and accordingly seizes every opportunity of breeding discord between them. This fear is, as a rule, perfectly uncalled for; for the men themselves show very little inclination to be ruled by their wives, and condescend to very little of what we call conjugal tenderness in their relations with them.

The women, on the other hand, are so thoroughly accustomed to harsh and domineering treatment from their husbands that they would be quite annoyed if the husbands adopted a more familiar tone. I once knew a native lady who complained bitterly that her husband sometimes affected to be very devoted to her in public and allowed himself such little familiarities as are looked upon by us as marks of affection. 'Such behaviour,' said she, 'covers me with shame and confusion. I dare not show myself anywhere. Did any one ever see such bad manners amongst people of our caste? Has he become a Feringhi (European), and does he take me for one of their vile women[1]?'

As a rule a husband addresses his wife in terms which show how little he thinks of her. *Servant, slave,* &c., and other equally flattering appellations, fall quite naturally from his lips.

A woman, on the other hand, never addresses her husband except in terms of the greatest humility. She speaks to him as *my master, my lord,* and even sometimes *my god.* In her awe of him she does not venture to call him by his name; and should she forget herself in this way in a moment of anger, she would be thought a very low class of person, and would lay herself open to personal chastisement from her offended spouse. She must be just as particular in speaking of him to any one else: indeed, the Hindus are very careful never to put a woman under the necessity of mentioning her husband by name. If by chance a European, who is unacquainted with this point of etiquette, obliges her to do so, he will see her blush and hide her face behind her *sari* and turn away without answering, smiling at the same time with contemptuous pity at such ignorance.

Politeness also forbids you to address a person of higher rank by his name.

But if women enjoy very little consideration in private life, they are in some degree compensated by the respect which is paid to them in public. They do not, it is true, receive those insipid compliments which we have agreed to consider polite; but then, on the other hand, they are safe from the risk of

[1] It may be noted that at marriage feasts, &c., the males and females keep apart; and furthermore the usual personal invitations to such feasts are invariably conveyed to men by men, and to women by women.—ED.

insult. A Hindu woman can go anywhere alone, even in the most crowded places, and she need never fear the impertinent looks and jokes of idle loungers. This appears to me to be really remarkable in a country where the moral depravity of the inhabitants is carried to such lengths. A house inhabited solely by women is a sanctuary which the most shameless libertine would not dream of violating. To touch a respectable woman even with the end of your finger would be considered highly indecorous, and a man who meets a female acquaintance in the street does not venture to stop and speak to her.

When travelling the men walk in front and the women follow some distance behind. You very rarely see the men address a word to their humble followers. If they come to a river which has to be forded the women tuck up their cloths above the hips, and in this naked state they approach near enough to their travelling companions to permit of the latter stretching out a helping hand behind them to help them to withstand the force of the current; but never would you see any one under these circumstances commit an indiscretion like that which caused Orpheus to lose his Eurydice.

I have often spent the night in one of the common rest-houses, where the men and women lodging there were lying all huddled together anyhow and almost side by side; but I have never known or heard of any one disturbing the tranquillity of the night by indecent act or word. Should any person be so ill-advised as to attempt anything of the sort, the whole room would be up in arms against him in a moment, and prompt chastisement would follow the offence.

A woman's costume consists of a simple piece of cotton cloth, made all in one piece, and woven expressly for the purpose. It is from 30 to 40 feet long, and rather more than 4 feet wide. All sorts and kinds are made, in every shade and at every price, and they always have a border of a contrasting colour. The women wind part of this cloth two or three times round their waists, and it forms a sort of narrow petticoat which falls to the feet in front; it does not come so far down behind, as one of the ends of the cloth is tucked in at the waist after passing between the legs, which are thus left bare as far as, or even above, the calf. This arrangement is peculiar to Brahmin women; those of other castes arrange their draperies with more decency and modesty. The other end of the cloth covers the shoulders, head, and chest. Thus the clothing for both sexes is made without seams or sewing—an undeniable convenience, considering how often they have to bathe themselves and wash their garments; for Brahmin women have to observe the same rules of purification as the men, and are equally zealous in the performance of this duty. The custom of women veiling their faces has never been practised in India, though it has been in use among many other Asiatic nations from time immemorial. Here the women always go about with their faces uncovered, and in some parts of the country they also expose the upper half of their bodies [1].

Quiet and retired as is the life of a Hindu woman, it cannot be said to be one of complete and rigorous seclusion. Though all friendly intercourse with men is forbidden to them, still they may talk to those who come to the house as friends or acquaintances without fear of unpleasant consequences. Eunuchs—those deplorable victims of Oriental jealousy—are unknown in India, and the natives never dream of putting the virtue of their women under the care of these miserable beings. They are not to be found even in the palace of a prince, where women are always guarded and waited on by women.

In several parts of India young girls and married women wear a sort of little bodice under their cloth, which covers the breast, shoulders, and arms as far as the elbows; but this, I am told, is a modern innovation, and borrowed from the Mahomedans.

I have reason to believe that the custom of leaving all the upper part of the body uncovered as far as the waist was formerly common to both sexes in the southern parts of India. It still prevails on the Malabar coast, and in the neighbouring provinces.

The custom of tattooing the arms of young girls with indelible designs of figures or flowers is very general. I have already described how this tattooing is done. When their skin is not very dark they generally ornament their faces in the same way, by putting three or four spots on the cheeks and chin.

[1] This custom still prevails in Malabar and Travancore, but it is gradually dying out amongst the educated classes.—ED.

These marks produce very much the same effect as the black patches which were once the fashion with European ladies. I have already mentioned the habit which the beauties of India and Brahmin ladies observe of painting all the visible parts of their bodies with yellow saffron, and also of darkening their eyelids with antimony.

In order to make their hair more glossy and silky they frequently oil it. They part it exactly in the middle, and then roll it up behind into a sort of chignon, which is fastened behind the left ear. To make this chignon larger they often insert some tow, or else some cotton wool specially prepared for the purpose. Hindu women generally possess beautiful black hair, which is soft and straight. It is very rarely to be seen of any other colour. They are much given to wearing sweet-smelling flowers in their hair, and also ornaments of gold, none of any other metal being permissible, though they sometimes use a silver buckle to fasten the hair together at the back.

Silver ornaments may be worn on the arms, but are more frequently used to decorate the feet and ankles[1]. Some of their anklets are actual fetters, weighing as much as two or three pounds. There are special rings made for each toe, often entirely covering them.

Bracelets are sometimes made hollow, and are more than an inch in diameter. They are of different patterns, according to the country in which they are made and the caste of the person who wears them. They are worn either above the elbow or round the wrist, and are made of gold or silver, as the means of the wearer will allow. Quite poor women wear copper bracelets, and some have more than half their fore-arms covered with glass bangles.

Neck ornaments consist of gold or silver chains, or strings of large gold beads, pearls, or coral. In fact, beads of all kinds and of greater or less value are much in demand. Some women wear necklaces more than an inch wide, set with rubies, emeralds, and other precious stones. But to enumerate all the different kinds of ornaments worn by Hindu ladies would take

[1] It is remarkable that gold ornaments are never worn by Hindus on the feet, the reason being that it is a sacred metal, and would be thereby defiled.—ED.

a very long time. To give a single instance, I could mention eighteen or twenty different kinds of ornaments that are used for the ears alone.

Even the nose is considered a suitable object for decoration. The right nostril and the division between the two nostrils are sometimes weighted with an ornament that hangs down as far as the under lip. When the wearers are at meals, they are obliged to hold up this pendant with one hand, while feeding themselves with the other. At first this strange ornament, which varies with different castes, has a hideous effect in the eyes of Europeans, but after a time, when one becomes accustomed to it, it gradually seems less unbecoming, and at last one ends by thinking it quite an ornament to the face.

It is no uncommon sight to see a woman decked out in all her jewels drawing water, grinding rice, cooking food, and attending to all the menial domestic occupations, from which even the wives of Brahmins do not consider themselves exempt.

It is, of course, needless to remark that all this extravagant display is very often obtained only at the sacrifice of other more useful and necessary requirements in their homes.

When a girl marries, everything that she receives from her future father-in-law, or that she takes away with her from her old home, is most clearly and distinctly set down, item by item, in a kind of legal document. All these things are her own personal property, which she takes care to claim when she becomes a widow.

CHAPTER XVII

Rules of Conduct for Married Women.

NOTHING serves so well to illustrate the attitude and behaviour of Hindus towards their wives as the rules of conduct which are prescribed for the latter in the *Padma-purana*, one of their most valued books: rules which I will translate literally. They are reputed to be the work of the famous penitent Vasishta, who recommends their observance by every faithful wife. I cannot say that I altogether approve of them; some of them appear to me absurd; others there are which, from a social point of view, are harmful; all of them evidently have for their object the reduction of this interesting 'better half' of the human race to the lowest state of subjection. It is not to be wondered at, therefore, if we find many foolish examples of Hindu superstition, which is a necessary element in every institution of the country. Order and continuity are not so conspicuous as one might desire in the ideas of the great penitent Vasishta; but I give a passage closely following the original, as a specimen of the style of writing that prevails among the Hindus :—

'Give ear to me attentively, great King of Dilipa! I will expound to thee how a wife attached to her husband and devoted to her duties ought to behave.

'There is no other god on earth for a woman than her husband. The most excellent of all the good works that she can do is to seek to please him by manifesting perfect obedience to him. Therein should lie her sole rule of life.

'Be her husband deformed, aged, infirm, offensive in his manners; let him also be choleric, debauched, immoral, a drunkard, a gambler; let him frequent places of ill-repute, live in open sin with other women, have no affection whatever for his home; let him rave like a lunatic; let him live without honour; let him be blind, deaf, dumb, or crippled; in a word, let his defects be what they may, let his wickedness be what it may, a wife should always look upon him as her god, should lavish on him all her attention and care, paying no heed whatsoever to his character and giving him no cause whatsoever for displeasure.

'A woman is made to obey at every stage of her existence. As daughter, it is to her father and mother she owes submission; as wife, to her husband, to her father-in-law, and to her mother-in-law; as widow, to her sons. At no period of her life can she consider herself her own mistress.

'She must always be attentive and diligent in all her domestic duties; she should be ever watchful over her temper, never covetous of the goods of others, never quarrelsome with her neighbours, never neglectful of work without her husband's permission, and always calm in her conduct and deportment.

'Should she see anything which she is desirous of possessing, she must not seek to acquire it without the consent of her husband. If her husband receives the visit of a stranger, she shall retire with bent head and shall continue her work without paying the least attention to him. She must concentrate her thoughts on her husband only, and must never look another man in the face. In acting thus, she will win the praise of everybody.

'Should any man make proposals to her, and endeavour to seduce her by offering her rich clothes or jewels of great value, by the gods! let her take good care not to lend an ear to him, let her hasten to flee from him.

'If her husband laugh, she must laugh; if he be sad, she must be sad; if he weep, she must weep; if he ask questions, she must answer. Thus will she give proofs of her good disposition.

'She must take heed not to remark that another man is young, handsome, or well proportioned, and, above all, she must not speak to him. Such modest demeanour will secure for her the reputation of a faithful spouse.

'It shall even be the same with her who, seeing before her the most beautiful gods, shall regard them disdainfully and as though they were not worthy of comparison with her husband.

'A wife must eat only after her husband has had his fill. If the latter fast, she shall fast too; if he touch not food, she also shall not touch it; if he be in affliction, she shall be so too; if he be cheerful, she shall share his joy. A good wife should be less devoted to her sons, or to her grandsons, or to her jewels than to her husband. She must, on the death of her husband, allow herself to be burnt alive on the same funeral pyre; then everybody will praise her virtue.

'She cannot lavish too much affection on her father-in-law, her mother-in-law, and her husband; and should she perceive that they are squandering all the family substance in extravagance, she would be wrong to complain and still more wrong to oppose them.

'She should always be ready to perform the various duties of her house, and to perform them diligently.

'Let her bathe every day, rubbing saffron on her body. Let her attire be clean, her eyelids tinged with antimony, and her forehead marked with red pigment. Let her hair be well combed and adorned. Thus shall she be like unto the goddess Lakshmi.

'Before her husband let her words fall softly and sweetly from her mouth; and let her devote herself to pleasing him every day more and more.

'She must be careful to sweep her house every day, to smooth the floor with a layer of cow-dung, and to decorate it with white tracery. She must keep the cooking vessels clean, and must be ready with the meals at the proper hours.

'If her husband be gone out to fetch supplies of wood, leaves, or flowers to perform the *sandhya*, or for any other purpose, she shall watch for the moment of his return and shall go to meet him. She shall go before him into the house, shall hand him a stool to sit down upon, and shall serve up the food prepared to his taste.

'She shall inform him in time of what is wanted in the house, and shall manage with care what he brings home.

'Prudent in her conversation, she must be careful, in conversing with *gurus*, *sannyasis*, strangers, servants, and other persons, to adopt a tone suitable to the position of each.

'In exercising in her house the authority given to her by her husband, she must do so gently and intelligently.

'She must, as in duty bound, use for the expenses of her household all the money with which her husband entrusts her, not taking any of it surreptitiously for herself or for her parents, or even, without her husband's permission, for works of charity.

'She must never meddle with the affairs of others, nor lend ear to stories of the good luck or misfortune which has befallen others.

'Never let her yield to anger or malice.

'Let her abstain from all food that is not to her husband's taste. Let her not oil her head when her husband does not oil his own.

'If her husband go away anywhere and ask her to accompany him, let her follow him; if he tell her to remain at home, let her not leave the house during his absence. Until his return she shall not bathe, or anoint her head with oil, or clean her teeth, or pare her nails; she shall eat but once a day, shall not lie down on a bed, or wear new clothes, or adorn her forehead with any of the ordinary marks[1].

'A woman during her menstrual period shall retire for three days to a place apart. During this time, she shall not look at anybody, not even at her children, or at the light of the sun. On the fourth day she shall bathe, observing the proper rites for such occasions which were established before the *Kali-yuga*[2].

'A woman, when she is pregnant, must conform to all the rites prescribed for such occasions. She must then avoid the company of women of doubtful virtue and of those who have lost all their children; she must drive away from her mind all sad thoughts; she must be careful not to gaze at terrifying objects, or to listen to sad stories, or to eat anything indigestible[3]. By observing these rules, she will have beautiful children; by neglecting them she will risk a miscarriage.

'A wife, during the absence of her husband, should strictly conform to his parting counsels. She should be heedless of her attire, and should not devote herself, under the plea of devotion to the gods, to any special acts of piety.

'If a husband keep two wives, the one should not amuse

[1] These restrictions are not observed nowadays.—ED.

[2] The hermit Vasishta here describes these practices. I will explain them in Appendix IV.—DUBOIS.

Nowadays a woman in this condition is not forbidden communication with her children.—ED.

[3] It may be added that a cocoanut is never broken in the presence of a pregnant woman.—ED.

herself at the expense of the other, be it for good or for evil; neither should the one talk about the beauty or the ugliness of the children of the other. They must live on good terms, and must avoid addressing unpleasant and offensive remarks to each other.

'In the presence of her husband, a wife must not look about her, but must keep her eyes fixed on him, in readiness to receive his orders. When he speaks, she must not interrupt him, nor speak to anybody else; when he calls her, she must leave everything and run to him.

'If he sing, she must be in ecstasy; if he dance, she must look at him with delight; if he speak of learned things, she must listen to him with admiration. In his presence indeed she ought always to be cheerful, and never show signs of sadness or discontent.

'Let her carefully avoid creating domestic squabbles on the subject of her parents, or on account of another woman whom her husband may wish to keep, or on account of any unpleasant remark which may have been addressed to her. To leave the house for reasons such as these would expose her to public ridicule, and would give cause for much evil speaking.

'If her husband flies into a passion, threatens her, abuses her grossly, even beats her unjustly, she shall answer him meekly, shall lay hold of his hands, kiss them, and beg his pardon, instead of uttering loud cries and running away from the house.

'She must not say to her husband: "Thou hast hurt me, thou hast beaten me unjustly; I will no more speak to thee; hereafter the relations between ourselves will be no other than those between a father and his daughter, or a brother and his sister. I shall no more have anything to do with thy affairs; I will no longer have anything in common with thee." Such words ought never to fall from her lips.

'If any of her relatives or friends invite her to their house on the occasion of some feast or ceremony, she shall not go there without the permission of her husband, and unless accompanied by some elderly woman. She shall remain there for as short a time as possible, and on her return she shall render a faithful account to her husband of all that she has seen or heard; she shall then resume her domestic duties.

'While her husband is absent, she shall sleep with one of

her female relatives, and not alone. She shall make constant inquiries after the health of her husband. She shall send constant messages to him to return as soon as possible, and shall offer up prayers to the gods for him.

'Let all her words and actions give public proof that she looks upon her husband as her god. Honoured by everybody, she shall thus enjoy the reputation of a faithful and virtuous spouse.

'If, in the event of her husband dying, she resolves to die with him, glorious and happy will she be in the world to which her husband will lead her after his death. But whether she dies before or with her husband, or whether she survives him, a virtuous wife may rest assured that all sorts of blessings will await her in the other world.

'A wife can enjoy no true happiness unless she attains it through her husband; it is he who gives her children; it is he who provides her with clothes and jewels; it is he who supplies her with flowers, sandalwood, saffron, and all good things.

'It is also through his wife that a husband enjoys the pleasures of this world; that is a maxim taught in all our learned books. It is through his wife that he does good works, that he acquires riches and honour, and that he succeeds in his enterprises. A man without a wife is an imperfect being.'

These rules of conduct may seem extremely severe, yet they are faithfully observed, especially among the Brahmins.

Among certain sects of the Vishnavite Brahmins a peculiar custom exists. A daughter-in-law is never allowed to speak to her mother-in-law. When she wishes to communicate anything to her, she does it by signs; and when the mother-in-law gives orders to the daughter-in-law, the latter answers by an inclination of the head, thereby indicating that she has understood the orders given her. She, however, at times manages to make up for this enforced silence by having recourse to spirited and expressive gestures: so much so, that her dumb repartees often cause her mother-in-law to boil with rage.

CHAPTER XVIII

Mourning.—The Condition of Widowhood.—The General Contempt for Widows.—Remarriages forbidden.

THE happiest death for a woman is that which overtakes her while she is still in a wedded state. Such a death is looked upon as the reward of goodness extending back for many generations[1]; on the other hand, the greatest misfortune that can befall a wife is to survive her husband.

Should the husband die first, as soon as he breathes his last the widow attires herself in her best clothes and bedecks herself with all her jewels[2]. Then, with all the signs of the deepest grief, she throws herself on his body, embracing it and uttering loud cries. She holds the corpse tightly clasped in her arms until her parents, generally silent spectators of this scene, are satisfied that this first demonstration of grief is sufficient, when they restrain her from these sad embraces. She yields to their efforts with great reluctance, and with repeated pretences of escaping out of their hands and rushing once again to the lifeless remains of her husband. Then, finding her attempts useless, she rolls on the ground like one possessed, strikes her breast violently, tears out her hair, and manifests many other signs of the deepest despair. Now, are these noisy professions of grief and affliction to be attributed to an excess of conjugal affection, to real sorrow? The answer will appear rather perplexing, when we remark that it is the general custom to act in this manner, and that all these demonstrations are previously arranged as a part of the ceremonies of mourning.

After the first outbursts of grief, she rises, and, assuming

[1] Children are even consoled with the thought, when their mothers die in a wedded state.—ED.

[2] This is the last occasion on which she is allowed to wear ornaments of any kind.—ED.

a more composed look, approaches her husband's body. Then in one continuous strain, which would be hardly possible under real affliction, she apostrophizes her husband in a long series of questions, of which I give a summary below:—

'Why hast thou forsaken me? What wrong have I done thee, that thou shouldst thus leave me in the prime of my life? Had I not for thee all the fondness of a faithful wife? Have I not always been virtuous and pure? Have I not borne thee handsome children? Who will bring them up? Who will take care of them hereafter? Was I not diligent in all the duties of the household? Did I not sweep the house every day, and did I not make the floor smooth and clean? Did I not ornament the floor with white tracery? Did I not cook good food for thee? Didst thou find grit in the rice that I prepared for thee? Did I not serve up to thee food such as thou lovedst, well seasoned with garlic, mustard, pepper, cinnamon, and other spices? Did I not forestall thee in all thy wants and wishes? What didst thou lack whilst I was with thee? Who will take care of me hereafter?'

And so on. At the end of each sentence uttered in a plaintive chanting tone, she pauses to give free vent to her sobs and shrieks, which are also uttered in a kind of rhythm. The women that stand around join her in her lamentations, chanting in chorus with her. Afterwards, she addresses the gods, hurling against them torrents of blasphemies and imprecations. She accuses them openly of injustice in thus depriving her of her protector. This scene lasts till her eloquence becomes exhausted, or till her lungs are wearied out and she is no longer capable of giving utterance to her lamentations. She then retires to take rest for a while, and to prepare some new phrases against the time when the body is being prepared for the funeral pyre.

The more vehement the expression of a woman's grief, the more eloquent and demonstrative her phrases, the more apparently genuine her contortions on such occasions, so much the more is she esteemed a woman of intelligence and education. The young women who are present pay the most minute attention to all that she says or does; and if they observe anything particularly striking in her flights of rhetoric, in her attitudes, or in any of her efforts to excite the attention of the spectators, they carefully treasure it in their memory, to be made use of should a similar misfortune ever happen to themselves. If a wife who was really afflicted by the loss of her husband confined herself to shedding real tears and uttering real sobs, she would only be thoroughly despised and considered an idiot. The parents of a young widow once complained to me of her stupidity as follows: 'So foolish is she that, on the death of her husband, she did not utter a single word; she did nothing but cry, without saying anything[1].'

In several parts of India, as formerly among the Greeks and Romans, professional women mourners may be hired. When called in to attend the obsequies, these women arrive with dishevelled hair and only half clothed, wearing their scanty garments in a disordered fashion. Collecting in a group round the deceased, they commence by setting up in unison the most doleful cries, at the same time beating their breasts in measured time. They weep, sob, and shriek in turns. Then addressing themselves to the deceased, each in succession eulogizes his virtues and good qualities. Anon they apostrophize him, vehemently remonstrating with him for quitting life so soon. Finally, they point out to him, in the plainest possible terms, that he could not have committed a more foolish act. In discharging these duties, which are a curious mixture of tragedy and comedy, they take turn and turn about, and their affected sorrow lasts until the corpse is removed. As soon as the obsequies are over, they receive their wages, and their faces, which were so lugubrious a few moments before, once more assume their wonted calmness.

Widows, who in the learned tongue are called *vidhava*, a word akin to the Latin *vidua*, are held in much less respect than other women; and when they happen to have no children, they are generally looked upon with the utmost scorn. The very fact of meeting a widow is calculated to bring ill-luck.

[1] The Hebrews also, on the death of friends and relatives, made a great parade of all the external signs of sorrow. They cried, rent their garments, beat their breasts, tore out their hair or beards, or else had them cut, and even inflicted cuts on their bodies. See Leviticus xix. 28, xxi. 5; Jeremiah xvi. 6, &c.—DUBOIS.

They are called *moonda*, a reproachful term which means 'shorn-head,' because every widow is supposed to have her hair cut off. This rule, however, is not everywhere followed, especially among the Sudras[1]. When women quarrel, this opprobrious term, *moonda*, is generally the first abusive word that passes.

A widow has to be in mourning till her death. The signs of mourning are as follows:—She is expected to have her head shorn once a month; she is not allowed to chew betel; she is no longer permitted to wear jewels, with the exception of one very plain ornament round her neck; she must wear coloured clothes no longer, only pure white ones; she must not put saffron on her face or body, or mark her forehead[2]. Furthermore, she is forbidden to take part in any amusement or to attend family festivities, such as marriage feasts, the ceremony of *upanayana*, and others; for her very presence would be considered an evil omen.

A very few days after the death of her husband, a widow's house is invaded by female friends and relatives, who begin by eating a meal prepared for them. After this they surround the widow and exhort her to bear her miserable lot with fortitude. One after another they take her in their arms, shed tears with her, and end by pushing her violently to the ground. They next join together in lamenting her widowhood, and finally make her sit on a small stool. Then, one of her nearest female relatives, having previously muttered some religious formulae, cuts the thread of the *tali*, the gold ornament which every married woman in India wears round her neck. The barber is called in, and her head is clean shaved. This double ceremony sinks her instantly into the despised and hated class of widows. During the whole time that these curious and mournful rites are being performed, the unfortunate victim is making the whole house resound with her cries of woe, cursing her sad lot a thousand times.

The thread of the *tali* must be cut, not untied. This practice has given rise to a very common curse; two women when

[1] And also among the Tengalai Vaishnava Brahmins.—ED.

[2] She must, however, smear her forehead with sacred ashes if she is a widow of the Saiva sect, and mark her forehead with red powder if a Vaishnava.—ED.

quarrelling never forget to say to each other: 'May you have your *tali* cut!' which means, 'May you become a widow!'

The signs of sorrow manifested by a Hindu lady who loses her husband are of so exaggerated a description that one cannot help doubting their perfect sincerity; yet it is impossible that any Hindu widow could face the sad future awaiting her with tearless eyes. Doomed to perpetual widowhood, cast out of society, stamped with the seal of contumely, she has no consolation whatever, except maybe the recollection of hardships that she has had to endure during her married life.

I do not refer here to those unfortunate girls of five or six years of age, who, married to Brahmins of over sixty, very often become widows before they attain the age of puberty. Fortunately their youth and inexperience prevent their brooding over the sad condition in which they have been placed by such inhuman and iniquitous prejudices. But think of the numberless young widows in the prime of life and strength. How do they bear up against this cruel expulsion from the society of their fellow-creatures? The answer is, Better than one would be inclined to believe. The fact is, they must perforce be resigned to their fate; and however despised a widow may be, there is this consolation, that one who remarries is a hundred times more so, for she is shunned absolutely by every honest and respectable person. Thus there are few widows who would not look upon proposals to remarry as a downright insult, though in this respect they are seldom put to the test. Even an old gouty Brahmin, as poor as Irus, would feel indignant at the very suggestion of marrying a widow, though she were rich and endowed with all the charms of youth and beauty.

One result of this prejudice, which is firmly and irrevocably established in India, is that the country abounds with widows, especially among the Brahmins. Among this caste *shorn-heads* are to be seen everywhere. Of course a certain corruption of morals is the inevitable result of such a state of things, but it is not pushed to such an extent as might be expected. The natural modesty of Hindu women, the way in which they are brought up, their ordinarily chaste and circumspect demeanour, the calmness of their passions: all these go a great way towards providing as it were strong barriers against the attacks of the licentious, who, whatever may be said to the contrary by ill-informed writers, do not succeed in winning over women of the better class so easily as in many other countries where the lawful union of the two sexes is not beset with so many obstacles.

Besides, even if we refuse to believe that young widows possess in themselves sufficient strength of will to resist seduction, there are many other obstacles beyond their own control, which also serve as so many bulwarks to their modesty. Chief among such obstacles must be reckoned the diligent watchfulness exercised over them by their parents; the severity of the *convenances* which forbid any kind of familiar intercourse between men and women; the very heavy punishments which follow even the most trivial lapses; and, finally, the mere disgrace, which in India, above all countries of the world, entails the most tremendous penalties on the person detected in an indiscretion[1].

[1] The social reformers of the present day are doing all that they can to encourage the remarriage of *virgin* widows, those unhappy girls who, married before they come of age, become widows before cohabitation with their husbands is possible. So far, however, the success which these reformers have met with is extremely small, and those who brave caste custom in this respect are invariably outcasted.—Ed.

CHAPTER XIX

The Custom which at times obliges Widows to allow themselves to be burnt alive on the Funeral Pyre of their Deceased Husbands.

ALTHOUGH the ancient and barbarous custom which imposes the duty on widows of sacrificing themselves voluntarily on the funeral pyre of their husbands has not been expressly abolished, it is much more rare nowadays than formerly, especially in the southern parts of the Peninsula. In the North of India and in the provinces bordering on the Ganges, however, women are only too frequently seen offering themselves as victims of this horrid superstition, and, either through motives of vanity or through a spirit of blind enthusiasm, giving themselves up to a death which is as cruel as it is foolish.

The Mahomedan rulers never tolerated this horrible practice in the provinces subject to them; but, notwithstanding their prohibition, wretched fanatics have more than once succeeded in bribing the subordinate representatives of authority to give permission to commit the deed in violation of the laws of humanity and common sense.

The great European Power which nowadays exercises its sway all over the country has tried, by all possible means of persuasion, to put an end altogether to this barbarous custom; but its efforts have been only partially successful, and, generally speaking, it has been obliged to shut its eyes to this dreadful practice, since any attempt to remedy it by force would have exposed it to dangerous opposition.

Nobody is a greater admirer than myself of the wise spirit that animates this enlightened and liberal Government in manifesting to its Hindu subjects such a full and perfect tolerance in the practice of their civil and religious usages; and nobody is more fully alive than I am to the dangers and difficulties that an open defiance of these prejudices, which are looked upon as sacred and inviolable, would give rise to. But does the abominable custom in question form part of Hindu institutions? Are there any rules which prescribe its observance by certain castes? All the information which I have been able to gather on the subject tends to make me believe that there are no such rules. The infamous practice, although encouraged by the impostors who regulate religious worship, is nowhere prescribed in an imperative manner in the Hindu books. It is left entirely to the free will and pleasure of the victims who thus sacrifice themselves. No blame and no discredit are attached nowadays to the wife whose own honest judgement suggests that she ought not to be in such a hurry to rejoin in the other world the husband who so often made her wretched in this. It would be quite possible, therefore, by the display of firmness, combined with prudence, to strike, without any considerable danger, at the very root of this shocking practice. Certainly it reflects discredit on the Government which tolerates it and manifests no great indignation[1] with regard to it.

[1] During recent years, owing to the number of these abominable sacrifices being on the increase, especially in the Bengal Presidency and in the districts bordering on the Ganges, the Government has thought fit to interfere to check this inconceivable mania by adopting at least persuasive measures. It has, therefore, directed the different magistrates scattered about the country to examine very minutely all the circumstances attending the custom of *suttee* (this is the name by which these barbarous sacrifices are known), and never to sanction it except after exhausting all the means to oppose it which prudence may suggest to them. No woman can, therefore, now devote herself to a death of this kind without the sanction of the magistracy. When such permission is sought, the magistrates cause the victim to appear before them and question her carefully to assure themselves that her resolution is entirely voluntary, and that no outside influence has been brought to bear upon her. They then try by every possible exhortation and counsel to induce her to give up her horrible design. But should the widow remain firm in her resolution, they leave her mistress of her own fate. The Protestant missionaries, when they first arrived in the country, expressed a just horror of these abominable sacrifices, and strove to diminish their number; but being ill acquainted with the character of the Hindus and with their devoted attachment to custom, they used brusque and violent measures which only resulted in augmenting the evil. I have seen the lists of widows who had sacrificed themselves on the funeral pyre of their husbands from 1810 (the period at which the missionaries commenced their labours) up to the year 1820; and I have remarked that the number of these victims progressively increased every year during that space of time. In 1817 there were 706 *suttees* in the Bengal Presidency. It

It was principally in the noble caste of Rajahs that the *suttee* originated. It was looked upon as a highly honourable proof of wifely attachment and love, which enhanced the glory of the families of these wretched victims of blind zeal. Should a widow, by reason of a natural fondness for life or through lack of courage, endeavour to avoid the honour of being burnt alive on the funeral pyre of her deceased husband, she was considered to be offering a gross insult to his memory.

I was once able to thoroughly convince myself of the influence which this false point of honour still exercises over the minds of fanatical Hindus, and at the same time to discern that this act of devotion to which these wretched victims sacrificed themselves is not always the result of their own free will and resolution. The poligar or prince of Cangoondy in the Carnatic having died, neither entreaties nor threats were spared to induce his widow to allow herself to be burnt alive with him. It was urged that this honourable custom had been observed for a long time past in the family, and that it would be a great pity, indeed, to allow it to fall into disuse. The funeral ceremonies were delayed from day to day in the hope that the widow would at last make up her mind to prefer a glorious death to a remnant of life spent in contempt and opprobrium. It was a fruitless attempt! The obstinate princess turned a deaf ear to all the pressing entreaties of her relatives; and ultimately the deceased was obliged to depart alone to the other world.

It must, however, be confessed that some widows commit this folly readily enough, spurred on as they are by the thought of the wretchedness of widowhood, by vanity, by the hope of acquiring notoriety, perhaps also by a genuine feeling of enthusiasm. It should be remembered that they are awarded boundless honours, and are even deified after death. Vows are made and prayers addressed to them, and their intercession is sought in times of sickness and adversity. Such remnants of their

is true that this insane practice is much more in vogue on the banks of the Ganges than anywhere else. In the southern parts of the Peninsula of India *suttees* are seldom seen. I am convinced that in the Madras Presidency, which numbers at least thirty millions of inhabitants, not thirty widows allow themselves to be thus burnt during a year.—DUBOIS.

Suttee is now, of course, absolutely abolished. Its prohibition by law was effected during the Governor-Generalship of Lord William Bentinck (1825–1835), at the instance of the great Rajah Ram Mohun Roy.—ED.

bodies as have not been entirely consumed by the fire are most devoutly gathered together, and on the spot where they have sacrificed themselves small monumental pyramids are erected to transmit to posterity the memory of these brave victims of conjugal affection—a tribute all the more conspicuous, because the erection of tombs is almost unknown among the Hindus[1]. In a word, women who have had the courage to deliver themselves so heroically to the flames are numbered among the divinities, and crowds of devotees may be seen coming in from all sides to offer them sacrifices and to invoke their protection.

To these inducements of vain and empty glory—sufficient of themselves to make a deep impression on a feeble mind—must be added the entreaties of relatives, who, if they perceive the slightest inclination on the part of the widow to offer up her life, spare no means in order to convince her and force her to a final determination. At times they go so far as to administer drugs, which so far deprive her of her senses that under their influence she yields to their wishes. This inhuman and abominable method of wheedling a consent out of the unhappy woman is in their opinion justified, because her tragic end would bring great honour and glory to the whole of their family.

Some authors have maintained that this detestable practice originated primarily either from the jealousy of husbands, or rather, perhaps, from their fear that their discontented wives might seek to get rid of them by poison. As for myself, I have been unable, either in the writings of Hindu authors, or in my free and familiar intercourse with many persons well versed in the manners and customs of the country, to discover any justification for either of these two theories. And surely the lot of a wife, even when she is doomed to suffer wrong at the hands of a cruel and immoral husband, is far preferable to that of a widow, to whom all hope of a remarriage under happier conditions is forbidden. It is hardly likely, indeed, that Hindu women would go to the length of committing a crime which must render their lot much worse than before! At the same time I am by no means inclined to attri-

[1] In some old Hindu houses, even to this day, may be seen, impressed with turmeric paste on the walls, the marks of the hands of women who underwent *suttee*.—ED.

bute these voluntary sacrifices to an excess of conjugal affection. We should, for instance, be greatly mistaken were we to allow ourselves to be deceived by the noisy lamentations which wives are accustomed to raise on the death of their husbands, and which are no more than rank hypocrisy. During the long period of my stay in India, I do not recall two Hindu marriages characterized by a union of hearts and displaying true and mutual attachment[1].

When a woman, after mature deliberation, has once declared that she desires to be burnt alive with her deceased husband, her decision is considered irrevocable. She cannot afterwards retract; and should she refuse to proceed of her own free will to the funeral pyre, she would be dragged to it by force. The Brahmins who regulate all the proceedings of the tragedy, and also her relatives, come by turns to congratulate her on her heroic decision and on the immortal glory which she is about to acquire by such a death—a death which will exalt her to the dignity of the gods. All possible means which fanaticism and superstition can suggest are brought to bear upon her in order to keep up her courage, to exalt her enthusiasm, and to excite her imagination. When, at last, the fatal hour draws nigh, the victim is adorned with rare elegance: she is clothed in her richest apparel, is bedecked with all her jewels, and is thus led to the funeral pyre.

It is impossible for me to describe the finishing scenes of this dreadful ceremony without feelings of distress. But, in the meantime, I must solicit the indulgence of my readers for a short digression which is not wholly disconnected with my subject. When a husband has several lawful wives, as often happens in the caste of the Rajahs, the wives sometimes dispute as to who shall have the honour of accompanying their common husband to the funeral pyre, and the Brahmins who preside at the ceremony determine which shall have the preference. Here is an instance to the point extracted from the *Mahābhārata*, one of their most esteemed books:—

[1] It is impossible to regard the conclusion here drawn as anything but greatly exaggerated. The influence of women, ignorant and uneducated as they are, is in many Hindu households exceedingly strong, and it is an error to picture them as the mere slaves of the men, though the ascendency of the latter is still a marked feature of Hindu sociology.—ED.

'King Pandu had retired into the jungles with his two wives, there to devote himself to acts of penance. At the same time a curse was imposed upon him, which doomed him to instant death should he dare to have intercourse with either of them. The passion which he felt for the younger of his wives, who was extremely beautiful, overcame all fear of death; and, in spite of the fact that for several days she continued to represent to him the dire results that must necessarily follow his incontinency, he yielded at last to the violence of his love; and immediately the curse fell upon him. After his death, it was necessary to decide which of his two wives should follow him to the funeral pyre, and there arose a sharp altercation between them as to who should enjoy this honour.

'The elder of the two spoke first, and addressing the assembly of Brahmins who had gathered together for the purpose, she urged that the fact of her being the first wife placed her above the second. She should, therefore, be given the preference. Besides, she urged, her companion had children who were still young, and who required their mother's personal care and attention for their bringing up[1].

'The second wife admitted the seniority of the first; but she maintained that she alone, having been the immediate cause of the sad death of their common husband in allowing him to defy the curse which doomed him to perish, was thereby entitled to the honour of being burnt with him. "As regards the bringing up of my children," she added, addressing the other wife, "are they not yours just as much as they are mine? Do not they too call you mother? And by your age and experience are you not better fitted than I to attend to their bringing up?"'

In spite of the eloquence of the younger wife, it was, at last, unanimously agreed by the judges that the first wife should have the preference—a decision at which the latter lady was greatly delighted.

Most Sudras, as well as Hindus of the Siva sect, bury their dead instead of burning them, and there are several

[1] The custom of *suttee* does not require widows who have young children to burn themselves with the body of their husbands; they are even forbidden to do so. Does this exception proceed from a feeling of humanity? By no manner of means! It is actuated merely by the fear that a large number of orphans would become a burden to the community.—DUBOIS.

instances of wives having been buried alive with their deceased husbands. But the ceremonies in either case are nearly the same.

I will relate here two incidents which took place at no great distance from the place where I was living, and which will give a good idea of what these deplorable scenes of mad fanaticism are like:—

In 1794, in a village of the Tanjore district called Pudupettah, there died a man of some importance belonging to the *Komatty* (Vaisya) caste. His wife, aged about thirty years, announced her intention of accompanying her deceased husband to the funeral pyre. The news having rapidly spread abroad, a large concourse of people flocked together from all quarters to witness the spectacle. When everything was ready for the ceremony, and the widow had been richly clothed and adorned, the bearers stepped forward to remove the body of the deceased, which was placed in a sort of shrine, ornamented with costly stuffs, garlands of flowers, green foliage, &c., the corpse being seated in it with crossed legs, covered with jewels and clothed in the richest attire, and the mouth filled with betel. Immediately after the funeral car followed the widow, borne in a richly decorated palanquin. On the way to the burning-ground she was escorted by an immense crowd of eager sight-seers, lifting their hands towards her in token of admiration, and rending the air with cries of joy. She was looked upon as already translated to the paradise of Indra, and they seemed to envy her happy lot.

While the funeral procession moved slowly along, the spectators, especially the women, tried to draw near to her to congratulate her on her good fortune, at the same time expecting that, in virtue of the gift of prescience which such a meritorious attachment must confer upon her, she would be pleased to predict the happy things that might befall them here below. With gracious and amiable mien she declared to one that she would long enjoy the favours of fortune; to another, that she would be the mother of numerous children who would prosper in the world; to a third, that she would live long and happily with a husband who would love and cherish her; to a fourth, that her family was destined to attain much honour and dignity and so forth. She then distributed among them leaves of betel;

and the extraordinary eagerness with which these were received clearly proved that great value was attached to them as relics: Beaming with joy, these women then withdrew, each in the full hope that the promised blessings of wealth and happiness would be showered on her and hers.

During the whole procession, which was a very long one, the widow preserved a calm demeanour. Her looks were serene, even smiling[1]; but when she reached the fatal place where she was to yield up her life in so ghastly a manner, it was observed that her firmness suddenly gave way. Plunged, as it were, in gloomy thought, she seemed to pay no attention whatever to what was passing around her. Her looks became wildly fixed upon the pile. Her face grew deadly pale. Her very limbs were in a convulsive tremor. Her drawn features and haggard face betrayed the fright that had seized her, while a sudden weakening of her senses betokened that she was ready to faint away.

The Brahmins who conducted the ceremony, and also her near relatives, ran quickly to her, endeavouring to keep up her courage and to revive her drooping spirits. All was of no effect. The unfortunate woman, bewildered and distracted, turned a deaf ear to all their exhortations and preserved a deep silence.

She was then made to leave the palanquin, and as she was scarcely able to walk, her people helped her to drag herself to a pond near the pyre. She plunged into the water with all her clothes and ornaments on, and was immediately afterwards led to the pyre, on which the body of her husband was already laid. The pyre was surrounded by Brahmins, each with a lighted torch in one hand and a bowl of ghee in the other. Her relatives and friends, several of whom were armed with muskets, swords, and other weapons, stood closely round in a double line, and seemed to await impatiently the end of this shocking tragedy. This armed force, they told me, was intended not only to intimidate the unhappy victim in case the

[1] Several travellers have said, and I am inclined to believe it, that they force upon these wretched victims of superstition a kind of drink, which confuses the mind and prevents them from forming a correct notion of the dreadful torture to which they are being led. This beverage, they say, consists of a decoction of saffron. It is known that dried saffron pistils (*Crocus sativus*), taken in large quantities, cause violent and convulsive laughter, sometimes terminating in death.—DUBOIS.

terror of her approaching death might induce her to run away, but also to overawe any persons who might be moved by a natural feeling of compassion and sympathy, and so tempted to prevent the accomplishment of the homicidal sacrifice.

At length, the *purohita* Brahmin gave the fatal signal. The poor widow was instantly divested of all her jewels, and dragged, more dead than alive, to the pyre. There she was obliged, according to custom, to walk three times round the pile, two of her nearest relatives supporting her by the arms. She accomplished the first round with tottering steps; during the second her strength wholly forsook her, and she fainted away in the arms of her conductors, who were obliged to complete the ceremony by dragging her through the third round. Then, at last, senseless and unconscious, she was cast upon the corpse of her husband. At that moment the air resounded with noisy acclamations. The Brahmins, emptying the contents of their vessels on the dry wood, applied their torches, and in the twinkling of an eye the whole pile was ablaze. Three times was the unfortunate woman called by her name. But, alas! she made no answer.

The last king of Tanjore, who died in 1801, left behind him four lawful wives. The Brahmins decided that two of these should be burnt with the body of their husband, and selected the couple that should have the preference. It would have been an everlasting shame to them and the grossest insult to the memory of the deceased had they hesitated to accept this singular honour. Being fully convinced, moreover, that no means would be spared to induce them to sacrifice themselves either willingly or unwillingly, they made a virtue of necessity and seemed perfectly ready to yield to the terrible lot which awaited them.

The necessary preparations for the obsequies were completed in a single day.

Three or four leagues from the royal residence a square pit of no great depth, and about 12 to 15 feet square, was excavated. Within it was erected a pyramid of sandalwood, resting on a kind of scaffolding of the same wood. The posts which supported it were so arranged that they could easily be removed, and would thereby cause the whole structure to collapse suddenly. At the four corners of the pit were placed huge brass jars filled with ghee, to be thrown on the wood in order to hasten combustion.

The following was the order of the procession as it wended its way to the pyre. It was headed by a large force of armed soldiers. Then followed a crowd of musicians, chiefly trumpeters, who made the air ring with the dismal sound of their instruments. Next came the king's body borne in a splendid open palanquin, accompanied by his *guru*, his principal officers, and his nearest relatives, who were all on foot and wore no turbans in token of mourning. Among them was also a large number of Brahmins. Then came the two victims, each borne on a richly decorated palanquin. They were loaded, rather than decked, with jewels. Several ranks of soldiers surrounded them to preserve order and to keep back the great crowds that flocked in from every side. The two queens were accompanied by some of their favourite women, with whom they occasionally conversed. Then followed relatives of both sexes, to whom the victims had made valuable presents before leaving the palace. An innumerable multitude of Brahmins and persons of all castes followed in the rear.

On reaching the spot where their untimely fate awaited them, the victims were required to perform the ablutions and other ceremonies proper on such occasions; and they went through the whole of them without hesitation and without the least sign of fear. When, however, it came to walking round the pile, it was observed that their features underwent a sudden change. Their strength seemed wellnigh to forsake them in spite of their obvious efforts to suppress their natural feelings. During this interval the body of the king had been placed on the top of the pyramid of sandalwood. The two queens, still wearing their rich attire and ornaments, were next compelled to ascend the pile. Lying down beside the body of the deceased prince, one on the right and the other on the left, they joined hands across the corpse. The officiating Brahmins then recited in a loud tone several *mantrams*, sprinkled the pile with their *tirtam* or holy water, and emptied the jars of ghee over the wood, setting fire to it at the same moment. This was done on one side by the nearest relative of the king, on another by his *guru*, on others by leading Brahmins. The flames quickly spread, and the props being removed, the whole structure collapsed, and in its fall must have crushed to death the two unfortunate victims. Thereupon all the spectators shouted aloud for joy. The unhappy women's relatives standing around the pile then called to them several times by name, and it is said that, issuing from amidst the flames, the word *Yen*? (What?) was heard distinctly pronounced. A ridiculous illusion, no doubt, of minds blinded by fanaticism; for it could never be believed that the unfortunate victims were at that moment in a condition to hear and to speak.

Two days after, when the fire was completely extinguished, they removed from amidst the ashes the remnants of the bones that had not been entirely consumed, and put them into copper urns, which were carefully sealed with the signet of the new king. Some time afterwards, thirty Brahmins were selected to carry these relics to Kasi (Benares) and to throw them into the sacred waters of the Ganges. It was arranged that, on their return from that holy city, they should receive valuable presents, upon producing authenticated certificates to the effect that they had really accomplished the journey, and had faithfully executed the task entrusted to them. A portion of the bones was, however, reserved for the following purpose:—they were reduced to powder, mixed with some boiled rice, and eaten by twelve Brahmins. This revolting and unnatural act had for its object the expiation of the sins of the deceased—sins which, according to the popular opinion, were transmitted to the bodies of the persons who ate the ashes, and were tempted by money to overcome their repugnance for such disgusting food. At the same time, it is believed that the filthy lucre thus earned can never be attended with much advantage to the recipients. Amidst the ashes, too, were picked up small pieces of melted gold, the remains of the ornaments worn by the princesses.

Presents were given to the Brahmins who presided at the obsequies, and to those who had honoured the ceremonies with their presence. To the king's *guru* was given an elephant. The three palanquins which had served to carry the corpse of the king and the two victims to the pile were given away to the three leading Brahmins. The presents distributed among the other Brahmins consisted of cloths and of money amounting to nearly twenty-five thousand rupees. Several bags of small coin were also scattered among the crowds on the roadside as the funeral procession was on its way to the pyre. Finally, twelve houses were built and presented to the twelve Brahmins who had the courage to swallow the powdered bones of the deceased, and by that means to take upon themselves all their sins.

A few days after the funeral the new king made a pilgrimage to a temple a few leagues distant from his capital. He there took a bath in a sacred tank, and was thus purified of all the uncleanness that he had contracted during the various ceremonies of mourning. On this occasion also presents were given to the Brahmins and to the poor of other castes.

On the spot where the deceased king and his two unhappy companions had been consumed a circular mausoleum was erected, about 12 feet in diameter, surmounted by a dome. The reigning prince visits it from time to time, prostrates himself humbly before the tombs, and offers sacrifices to the manes of his predecessor and to those of his worthy and saintly spouses.

Crowds of devotees also repair thither to offer up vows and sacrifices to the new divinities, and to implore their help and protection in the various troubles of life.

In the year 1802 I heard accounts of a great number of so-called miracles performed through their intercession.

It is only after long and serious reflection on the many eccentricities and inconsistencies of the human mind that one can look without astonishment upon the deplorable scenes of which a few of the main features have just been described. It is indeed unaccountable how these Brahmins, who are so scrupulous and attach so much importance to the life of the most insignificant insect, and whose feelings are excited to pity and indignation at the very sight of a cow being slaughtered, can, with such savage cold-bloodedness and wicked satisfaction, look upon so many weak and innocent human beings, incited by hypocritical and barbarous inducements, being led with affected resignation to a punishment so cruel and undeserved. I leave to others the task of explaining these inconceivable contradictions, if, that is to say, it is possible to assign any reasons for such superstitious fanaticism, whose characteristic feature is to suppress all natural and rational sentiment.

CHAPTER XX

Adoption.—Rules regarding the Partition of Property.

When a Brahmin finds that he has no male issue, whether by reason of the barrenness of his wife or through the untimely death of all the sons he has had by her, he is permitted, nay bound, by the rules of his caste to procure a son by means of adoption, in order that he may, at least fictitiously, fulfil *the great debt to his ancestors,* namely, the propagation of a direct line of posterity. Although marriage constitutes the perfect state of man, this perfection is nevertheless deficient when a man does not leave a son behind him to perform his obsequies; and this defect alone, according to Hindu writers, is quite sufficient to deprive him of happiness in the next world.

This notion prevails so strongly among the Hindus that I have known barren women not only consenting to their husbands taking other wives, but even earnestly advising them to do so, and helping them in their quest. There is not one of them, however, who is not fully alive to the annoyances and discomforts to which she is exposing herself by thus introducing as her rival another woman, who must naturally, by her youthfulness and fecundity, soon become an object more beloved than herself by their common husband.

It has already been said that polygamy is tolerated among the ruling classes only; and when we find other women besides the lawful wife living in the families of private individuals of high caste, especially among the Brahmins, either they are living there, as already stated, with the consent of the lawful wife, or else they are merely hired concubines. However, a husband who has had no male issue by his wife, being fully alive to the unpleasant consequences arising from a second marriage, almost invariably prefers to have recourse to the system of adoption.

A Brahmin generally chooses from among his own relatives the child that he wishes to legally adopt as his son; and if perchance he finds nobody in his own family worthy of the honour, he applies to some poor fellow of his own caste who is burdened with many children. So long as the adoptive father is rich, he is sure not to meet with a refusal [1].

The adopted son renounces wholly and for ever all his claims to the property and succession of his natural father, and acquires the sole right to the heritage of his father by adoption. The latter is bound to bring him up, to feed him, and to treat him as his own son; to have the ceremony of *upanayana*, or the triple cord, performed for him, and to see him married. The adopted son, in his turn, is obliged to take care of his adoptive father in his old age and in sickness, just as if he were his natural father, and to *preside at his obsequies*. On the death of his adoptive father he enters into full possession of his inheritance—assets as well as liabilities. Should there be any property left, he enjoys it; but if, on the other hand, there are debts, he is bound to pay them. He is, moreover, by his adoption admitted into the *gothram* or family stock of the adopter, and is considered to have left that in which he was born [2].

It is only natural that, in a country where everything is performed with so much solemnity, an event of such importance should be attended with great ceremonies. The following are a few of the most important:—

The first thing to be done, as might be expected, is to select an auspicious day. They then adorn the portals of the house with *toranams* (garlands of leaves) and put up a temporary *pandal*. The festivities open with a sacrifice to Vigneshwara and the nine planets; and the other preparatory ceremonies already described are likewise gone through. The adoptive father and mother take their seats on the small daïs raised in the middle of the *pandal*.

[1] The strict rule is that the natural mother of the adopted son must be a marriageable relative of the adoptive father. Nowadays, however, a Hindu is allowed to adopt any boy provided he be of the same caste.—Ed.

[2] *Gothram* literally means 'cow-shed.'—Ed.

The mother of the child is presented with a new garment and with a hundred or a hundred and fifty pieces of silver as her *nursing wages*. Then, with her son in her arms, she approaches the adoptive father, who asks her in a loud and distinct voice, in presence of the whole assembly, whether she delivers over her child to be brought up. To this she answers in the same tone that she does deliver the child to be brought up. This utterance bears a comprehensive meaning. It is a formal intimation that she gives up her son not as a slave who is sold, but to be looked upon and treated as a child of the family into which he is about to enter[1].

They next bring in a dish filled with water into which some powdered saffron has been thrown. The *purohita* blesses this mixture by muttering *mantrams* and performing certain ceremonies. Then the mother of the child[2] hands the dish to the adoptive father, and at the same time, invoking fire to bear witness to the deed, she thrice repeats the following words:—'*I give up this child to you; I have no more right over him.*' The adoptive father then takes the child, and seating him on his knees, addresses the relatives present as follows:—'This child has been given to me, after fire has been invoked as a witness of the gift: and I, by this saffron water which I will now drink, promise to bring him up as my own son. From this moment he is entitled to the enjoyment of all his rights over my property, sharing, at the same time, the burden of my debts.'

After these words, he and his wife pour out a small quantity of the saffron water in the hollow of their right hands and drink it up. They then pour a little into the hand of the adopted child and make him also drink it, adding: 'We have admitted this child into our *gothram*, and we incorporate him into it.'

[1] Generally a boy is adopted when he is fit for the *upanayana* ceremony; and both ceremonies are performed simultaneously.—ED.

[2] It is the mother of the child who plays the most important part in this ceremony; the father being present there only as a mere formality. The reason is that in India all the children are supposed to belong by right to the mother. Should a married man, or a man living in concubinage, happen to separate himself, for some cause or other, from his wife or concubine, the latter would be entitled to take away all their children, without the possibility of the slightest opposition on the part of the father.—DUBOIS.

This is the last event in the ceremony of adoption. I have remarked that at the age of six months Hindu children are solemnly invested with the girdle or waist-string, to which, six or seven years later, is attached a small piece of cloth intended to cover the private parts. Should the adopted child be already wearing this string, they break it and supply him with a fresh one; but should he have none, they at once begin to invest him with it with all the usual ceremonies. It is by this act that his incorporation into the *gothram* or family clan of his new father is sanctified.

The festivities, as usual, wind up with a repast and the distribution of betel and presents to the guests.

The use of saffron water on this occasion accounts for the fact that an adopted child generally receives the appellation of the '*saffron-water child*' of such a one[1], a term which, it should be added, has nothing offensive about it.

The ceremony of adoption is almost identical among the Sudras and the Brahmins, with this one difference, that among the Sudras the adoptive father and his wife pour the saffron water on to the feet of the adopted child with one hand, and catch and drink it with the other.

An adoptive father may choose not only a child of tender years, but even an adult, should that suit his taste and purpose better.

Persons whose means do not permit them to perform the ceremony of adoption with so much pomp and circumstance, have a simpler and more expeditious mode of performing it. It is deemed sufficient if the mother of the child and the adopted father invoke fire to witness their mutual bargain. Dwellers on the banks of the Ganges need simply call to witness, in such a case, the waters of that sacred river.

In whatever fashion the ceremony of adoption be performed, the adopted child no longer retains any right either to the property or the heritage of his natural father, nor can he be held answerable for the debts which the latter may leave at his death.

[1] The Hindus take a pleasure in giving each other nicknames, some of which are very insulting indeed. They generally choose such names with reference to some mental or bodily defect of the person concerned, or on account of some dishonourable act imputed to him.—DUBOIS.

The adoption of girls is rare, although instances of it are not wanting.

The work from which I have extracted these particulars relating to adoption also furnishes a solution of some of the difficulties that arise in certain cases with regard to the division of property. The little that it contains on the subject seems to me sufficiently interesting.

We find there laid down the supposititious case of a man who, after adopting a son, has subsequently had, contrary to his expectation, six children by his legitimate wife, namely, four boys and two girls. The father and two of the boys die; one of the girls and the adopted son are married; there remain two boys and a girl who are unmarried; and provision must also be made for the subsistence of the widow. The question is, How, in such a case, ought the property devolved by succession to be divided?

The answer given is to the following effect:—*First*, the amount necessary for the funeral expenses of the deceased father ought to be set apart, and the money required for the marriage of the three unmarried children ought to be placed in the hands of a trustworthy executor.

Secondly, the property that remains after these amounts have been set aside shall be divided into six shares. The adopted son shall take for himself a share and a half, and the remainder shall be equally divided among the brothers and the mother. Should the mother be dead, the property is divided only into five shares and a half, unless all the brothers, with common accord, relinquish on behalf of their unmarried sister, with the object of providing her with jewels, that part of the inheritance which would have fallen to the mother, who is perfectly at liberty, before her death, to dispose of this share in favour of her daughters, without the slightest objection being raised thereto by the sons. If she has not done so, the brothers alone, independently of the sisters, set apart a reasonable amount for a decent funeral, and divide equally among themselves whatever remains of her property.

This decision of the Brahmins, while in accordance with the general custom of the country, which entitles sons to equal shares of the paternal property, and excludes the daughters by merely granting them a dowry, departs from it in so far as mothers have no share whatever in the property of their husbands, their sons being conjointly bound to provide for their maintenance during their lives.

Should a man, by reason of the barrenness of his first wife, marry a second, and the latter have a son, all the father's property belongs exclusively to this son; the first wife, after the death of the common husband, can claim nothing from the estate: but the son is bound to provide for her maintenance in a decent manner, and to meet all the expenses of her funeral. If the first wife does not choose to continue to live with the second, the relatives meet together and arrange for the allotment to her of a sufficient income according to her condition in life.

A certain man, finding that his first wife was barren, married a second, then a third; but it so happened that these two, like the first, were barren also, and the man, therefore, died without issue. The deceased had an elder and a younger brother, besides several cousins, sons of his paternal uncles. None of these, however, had been living with him. They had long before divided their family property, and each was living separately. The question arises, Who ought to be regarded as the rightful heir of the deceased? The answer given is, that the rightful heir is the younger brother, because, being the youngest of the family, to him, according to the custom of the country, belongs the right of presiding at the obsequies—a right which carries with it the heirship. He thereby becomes the head of the family and the master of the house. It is he, therefore, who is obliged to provide for the maintenance of the three widows left by his brother. Should any one of the three choose to return to her father's house, she would be at perfect liberty to do so, and even to take away with her all the jewels given to her by her deceased husband. Furthermore, the family council would determine upon the allowance which her brother-in-law, as the heir to her husband's property, would be bound to make to her to enable her to subsist. If she elected to remain in her deceased husband's house and to have an establishment of her own there, she could not be refused permission; but in that case her brother-in-law would not be under the necessity of assigning her any considerable income; and she would be obliged, at her own risk, to supplement such income with alms. It is well known, however, that such a mode of living has nothing disgraceful about it, since begging is one of the six privileges of the Brahmins. Finally, the brother-in-law is bound to bear all the expenses of the funerals of the three widows should they happen to die before him.

If the deceased husband be the youngest of the brothers, the elder brother would then become the sole inheritor, and on him would devolve all the rights and obligations connected with the heritage. In the absence of brothers, the nearest relative on the father's side becomes sole heir.

In cases where doubts arise as to the transmission of the property, the relatives are called in to decide the matter according to the prevailing custom of the country, or as justice may dictate to them. But very often the partiality prevailing in these family councils turns the scale in favour of the one who is able to purchase the support of the others. The collusions, intrigues, and acts of injustice practised on such occasions are without number, and tend to throw discredit on an institution which owes its origin to truly patriarchal principles.

It may be observed from what has been already said that the right of inheritance and the duty of presiding at the obsequies are inseparable one from the other. When, therefore, a wealthy man dies without direct descendants, a crowd of remote relatives appear to dispute with each other the honour of conducting the funeral rites. The contest is occasionally so tumultuous and prolonged that the body of the deceased is in a state of complete putrefaction before a definite settlement of these many pretensions is arrived at. On the other hand, on the death of a needy man burdened with debts, the survivors take every possible care to disprove near relationship.

There is another rule regarding succession among the Hindus, which will, doubtless, appear to us highly incompatible with the true principles of justice.

A father dies, leaving several male children, who, from carelessness or some other cause, do not trouble themselves about the legal partition of the paternal inheritance. One of them, by his industry and diligence, acquires wealth, while the others, leading a debauched and idle life, become seriously involved in debt. These, after a life of dissipation and wandering from place to place, learn at last that their brother, by his industry and good conduct, has amassed a brilliant fortune. They at once hasten to him and call upon him to share with them the property he has acquired by the sweat of his brow, and moreover render him jointly responsible for the debts resulting from their disorderly habits[1]. The creditors themselves, too, have the right to recover from him by law what is due to them from his brothers. More than this, should brothers, who neglect to divide their family property, die before such partition has been actually effected, the same community of property and of debts holds good among their children, and it descends from generation to generation so long as the property remains undivided. It is by no means rare to see cousins of the third and fourth degree engaged in lawsuits concerning rights of succession dating back from time immemorial. Neither is it an uncommon thing to see the richer members of a family coerced by the poorer ones to admit the latter to a share of their hard-earned fortune, while these burden them with their poverty and their debts.

In a country where nearly everything is regulated by custom, and where the usages are as many and as various as the different provinces, these lawsuits in connexion with the partition of properties are an endless source of chicanery. There is one advantage, however, from a social point of view, arising from this singular system, namely, that it gives such relatives as are liable to be affected by the law of partition the right to watch over each other's conduct, and to restrain the debauchery and extravagance of those whose misconduct might involve them all in distress.

The appointment of a single heir among the male children

[1] In Madras a proposal was recently made by a Hindu member of the local Legislature to introduce a Bill to secure for every individual of an 'undivided' Hindu family 'the gains of his learning.' The Bill, however, has not yet been passed. At present, when a claim is made to 'the gains of learning' of one of the members of an 'undivided' family, those who prefer the claim invariably attempt to prove that the member to whose gains they lay claim was educated out of the undivided family property, and that therefore the undivided members have a right to share his gains.—ED.

of a family is a thing unknown in India. The brothers divide the paternal property equally, to the exclusion of the sisters, who have no share whatever in it. The father does not even possess the privilege of treating one of his sons more generously than the rest[1]. The Hindus cannot conceive how a father could despoil several of his children in order to enrich one of them in particular; and they are simply astounded when they are told that this custom prevails in many countries of Europe. But what makes us still more ridiculous in their eyes is that this favoured heir should very often be, not the son who distinguishes himself above the rest by his filial devotion, his virtues, and his talents, but one who by chance happens to be the first-born, and who may perhaps be the most foolish and vicious of the whole family.

[1] There is nothing, however, to prevent a father from allotting the whole or any portion of his *self acquired*, as opposed to his *ancestral* property, to any one of his sons, or disposing of it in any other way he pleases.—ED.

CHAPTER XXI

The Learning of the Brahmins.—Their Colleges.—Astronomy.—Astrology.—Magic.

It is certain that from the earliest times learning was cultivated by the Hindus. The Brahmins have always been, as it were, its depositaries, and have always considered it as belonging exclusively to themselves. They saw well enough what a moral ascendency knowledge would give them over the other castes, and they therefore made a mystery of it by taking all possible precautions to prevent other classes from obtaining access to it.

The question arises, Have they themselves systematically cultivated learning? Have they made any appreciable progress in its pursuit? This we must answer in the negative, if at least we are to compare what has come down to us from their ancient authors with the present conditions of instruction and learning amongst them. I do not believe that the Brahmins of modern times are, in any degree, more learned than their ancestors of the times of Lycurgus and Pythagoras. During this long space of time many barbarous races have emerged from the darkness of ignorance, have attained the summit of civilization, and have extended their intellectual researches almost to the utmost limits of human intelligence; yet all this time the Hindus have been perfectly stationary. We do not find amongst them any trace of mental or moral improvement, any sign of advance in the arts and sciences. Every impartial observer must, indeed, admit that they are now very far behind the peoples who inscribed their names long after them on the roll of civilized nations.

The learning which won for them so much respect and reverence from their fellow-countrymen, and which rendered them so famous in the eyes of foreign nations, among whom ignorance and superstition then prevailed, was connected with astronomy, astrology, and magic. Several authors have given details of their astronomical system, and it is fully explained in the *Asiatic Researches.* Moreover, Father Pons, a former Jesuit missionary in the Carnatic, had, long before this, discussed it in a highly interesting treatise published in the *Mémoires de l'Académie des Sciences,* and likewise we find it discussed in the *Histoire Générale de Tous les Peuples* by the Abbé Lambert. It is from these sources that the famous astronomer Bailly derived almost all that he has written on Hindu Astronomy.

The accuracy of the investigations of the learned Jesuit missionary in this direction has been since confirmed; but in the same work he speaks of the schools and of what he calls the 'academies' of India. It seems to me that he is rather too favourably impressed with these latter institutions, and is far too profuse in his eulogies on the methods of teaching and the course of studies in vogue in the so-called academies.

As a matter of fact, no comparison whatever can be drawn between schools in India and those in Europe. The system pursued in the former of causing everything to be learnt by rote is, in my opinion, essentially wrong, and tends to prolong indefinitely the course of study. Moreover, there is no regular plan of instruction, and there is no public institution which is, properly speaking, devoted to the diffusion of knowledge. It is true that in certain large towns, or in the precincts of some of the more important temples, Brahmins who are really learned, or who pretend to be so, impart the knowledge which they possess—some gratuitously and others for payment; still, for all this, instruction is carried on without any definite system or any attempt at discipline—elements absolutely necessary to give to these studies a character of permanence and uniformity. Let a youth learn who has a mind to do so, and as long as he chooses: this seems to be their guiding principle. There is nothing in these institutions which is calculated to stimulate the teachers or to encourage the pupils. There are no public examinations to undergo, no degrees to aspire to, no prizes to be won; in fine, no special privilege or advantage of any importance is held out to students who distinguish themselves by their attainments. It is true that those who have a reputation for learning are esteemed by the public, but empty reputation without any substantial benefit is not a motive sufficiently powerful to stimulate a Brahmin. It would be well enough if learned Hindus were frequently encouraged by the liberality of their princes, but the latter are too deeply immersed in the enjoyment of material pleasures to be able to appreciate the real value of learning and to take the trouble to patronize it[1]. Accordingly one seldom comes across educated Brahmins who owe their knowledge to one of these public schools. They are, in fact, entirely beholden for it to the exertions of their parents and to private tuition. Thus it is that learning is almost always transmitted from family to family, from generation to generation, and becomes, so to say, hereditary.

So much, then, for the course of study, the universities, and the *littérateurs* of India.

The Hindu system of astronomy being, as I have said before, sufficiently well known, I shall refrain from repeating here what others have said on the subject. But I shall dwell at some length on the other two branches of their scientific knowledge, namely, astrology and magic.

ASTROLOGY.

Astrology, together with the silly notions which originate from it, has at all times exercised a great influence over the nations of the world, civilized as well as uncivilized. In Europe the appearance of a comet or a total eclipse formerly spread the greatest terror in the minds of the multitude, who looked upon these celestial phenomena as the forerunners of some public calamity; and even at the present day these chimerical fears still exercise some influence over the imagination of the ignorant and superstitious.

The influence of the stars, scrutinized with the eyes of reason, need not be looked upon altogether as an idle imagining; and there is doubtless a happy medium to be observed between the widely divergent opinions of authors concerning the action,

[1] Education on European lines is now widely extended, of course, but the diffusion of Hindu knowledge and the study of Sanskrit, its principal medium, is still pretty much as the Abbé describes it. It is only just to observe, however, that it has been, and is, more largely patronized by Hindu princes than the Abbé implies. —ED.

more or less direct, more or less limited, exercised by the stars over the vegetable and animal kingdoms of this earth of ours. Be this as it may, however, no other nation appears to have carried its astrological notions to such extremes of folly as the Hindus. With their wonted exaggeration in all things, it is only natural that they should entertain wild ideas about a science which opens so vast a sphere to the imagination. All the rubbish they have written on this subject would certainly be too tedious to read. I will, therefore, content myself with referring briefly to a few of the important principles on which their so-called science of astrology rests.

Each planet in turn is supposed to exercise its influence during the space of a year. The ruling planet is attended by another, which plays the part of a minister. The latter assumes in the following year the supreme functions of the former; and so on year after year.

Some of these planets are beneficent, others the reverse. The Moon, Mercury, Jupiter, and Venus are of the former order. Under their sway everything thrives: men live happily and are blessed with abundance; the fertile fields yield rich harvests, and the fruitful trees bear abundantly. The Sun, Mars, and Saturn, on the other hand, have a tendency to cause evil to animate as well as to inanimate nature. Their reign is, therefore, almost always disastrous. Men are oppressed with sickness; they attain success in nothing; they experience only troubles and disappointments: moreover, the rains hold off, the soil becomes unfruitful, famine and misery everywhere prevail. When, however, an unpropitious planet has for its attendant minister a planet of an opposite character, and vice versa, the good one counteracts and counterbalances, at least to a certain degree, the evil influence of the other. Thus one can expect to enjoy unalloyed happiness only during those years when two benign planets hold their sway at one and the same time. Similarly, one must dread continual misfortunes when both planets have an evil inclination to harass unfortunate mankind.

There are four principal clouds which yield rain, and each in its turn discharges this duty for the space of one year. Their names are *Samvarta, Avarta, Pushkala, Drona.* The first and the last are favourably disposed towards mankind, and yield copious showers. *Avarta* and *Pushkala*, on the other hand, produce nothing but storms and hurricanes, and are sparing of the rain which refreshes and fertilizes the soil.

The frequency of rain depends also to a great extent on the good or bad will of seven elephants. Each of these is known by its own name, and each in turn is charged with the annual duty of carrying water to the clouds. Four of them display great activity in the discharge of their duty, and supply the clouds with an ample provision of rain. But the other three acquit themselves very carelessly of their duty during their terms of service; consequently the ground remains parched up, and scarcity prevails.

Seven snakes, each also bearing a particular name, exercise in turn for the space of one year supreme authority over all species of snakes.

The snake *Ananta*, the first one, is the most powerful of all, and supports the earth on its head. The year of its reign is considered unhappy, inasmuch as snakes are then extremely venomous, and their bite invariably proves fatal.

The reign of the snake *Karkataka* is equally unhappy.

The remaining five are by no means equally mischievous. It is seldom that persons are bitten by snakes while these are in power; and should a person be bitten, the bite does not prove fatal. The snake *Maha-Padma* particularly is the friend of men; it not only prevents other snakes from harming them, but also comes to their aid by sending the physician *Dhanmantari* to cure such as may have been accidentally bitten.

By the combination of the twelve signs of the Zodiac with the planets and with the star which is in the ascendant on each day of the moon, Hindu astrologers believe themselves capable of telling the secrets as well as the future events of life.

The Sun remains thirty days in each of the signs of the Zodiac; the Moon, two days and a quarter; Mars and Mercury, a month and a half; Jupiter, one year; Venus, two years and a half; Saturn, one year and a half.

Each sign of the Zodiac has, besides, two stars and a quarter, which are assigned to it from among the twenty-seven constellations or stars of the lunar month.

By comparing all these phenomena, and by joining, in regular order, certain words with the different signs of the Zodiac, they are enabled to know the past, the present, and the future, and to recover things that have been lost or stolen. The coincidence of these words is, for this purpose, combined with the sign of the Zodiac, the planet, the star, and the time of the day or night at which the astrologer is consulted.

By the same means it is possible to find out, not only the place wherein a stolen object is secreted, but also the sex and the caste of the thief. They are also able to ascertain whether or not the stolen or lost article will be recovered, according as the sign, the planet, and the star which correspond to the time at which the consultation takes place are favourable or the reverse.

They discover in the same way whether a person who has been long absent is dead or alive; whether he is sick or in good health; whether he is at liberty or in prison; whether he will return or not.

But one of the most important combinations calculated is that relating to birth. In fact, according to the Hindus, the future lot of men is supposed to depend on the sign of the Zodiac and the star under which they are born. This is what they call *lagnam*. It is supposed that each of the twelve signs prevails over daily occurrences during a fixed interval of time. Thus, for instance, the sign Aries (the Ram) prevails for two hours; Taurus (the Bull) for two hours and a quarter; Gemini (the Twins) for two hours and a half; and so on. Again, the sign which corresponds to the moment of birth is termed *Jamma-lagnam*; and by combining it with the planet and the star of the day, they ascertain beyond a doubt whether the child is born to be happy or unhappy.

Of the seven days of the week, three are held to be unlucky, namely, Sunday, Tuesday, and Saturday. On these days no important business ought to be undertaken, no journey begun.

Of the twenty-seven stars of each lunar month, seven are reputed to be more or less unlucky; and everything undertaken on the days on which these appear is attended with disastrous results.

The rest of the science is based on similar considerations.

MAGIC.

Magic, that art which gives shrewd people such influence over fools, seems to have found a favourite abode in the

Peninsula of India. Certainly, in this respect, India has no reason to be envious of the ancient Thessaly or of the city of Colchis, famous for the enchantments of Circe and Medea. True, I am not aware that Hindu sorcerers have retained the power of causing the moon, whether willing or not, to come down from the height of the firmament; but short of this, there is nothing which Hindu magicians are incapable of doing. Thus there is not a single Hindu who does not, during the whole course of his life, dream about sorcery and witchcraft. Nothing in this country happens by chance or from natural causes. Obstacles of every kind, disappointments, unlucky incidents, diseases, premature deaths, barrenness of women, miscarriages, diseases among cattle; in fine, all the scourges to which human beings are exposed are attributed to the occult and diabolical machinations of some wicked enchanter hired by an enemy. Should a Hindu, at the time he is visited by any calamity, happen to be at variance with any one of his neighbours, the latter is immediately suspected and accused of having had recourse to magic to harm him. The accused, of course, never puts up patiently with an imputation so invidious. Anger is engendered, and the flame of discord grows hotter and hotter, until some serious consequences result from this new development.

If the immense progress in enlightenment made by the most civilized nations of Europe has not yet been able to completely eradicate these absurd prejudices, if the rural parts of Europe are still full of people who believe in sorcerers and in their magical charms, and if in the public places of our towns one still sees crowds of impostors in wretched garb professing to furnish those around them with the favours of fortune, is it to be wondered at that in a country like India, plunged as it is in the darkness of gross ignorance and superstition, the belief in magic is carried to the very last point? Thus it is that at every step one meets with batches of these soothsayers and sorcerers distributing good luck to all comers, and for a consideration unfolding to the view of the rich and of the poor the secrets of their destinies.

But these sorcerers of the lowest rank, whose whole stock-in-trade consists of a large fund of impudence, are not held in much dread. Others there are whose diabolical art knows no bounds, and who are initiated into the most profound secrets of magic. To inspire love or hatred; to introduce a devil into the body of any one, or to expel it; to cause the sudden death of an enemy, or to bring on him an incurable disease; to produce contagious diseases among cattle, or to preserve them against such contagion; to lay bare the closest secrets; to restore stolen or lost articles, &c.: all these are mere bagatelles to such men. The very sight of a person who is reputed to be gifted with such enormous power inspires terror.

These professors of magic are often consulted by persons who wish to avenge themselves on some enemy by means of witchcraft. Their help is also sought by sick folk who are persuaded that their disease has been caused by the casting of some magical spell upon them, and who wish to recover their health by throwing a counter-spell upon those who caused the disease by such means.

The Hindus have several books which treat *ex professo* of all these follies of the magic art. The principal and most ancient of them is the fourth Veda, called the *Atharva-Veda*[1]. The Brahmins would have it believed that this book has been lost; but it is known that it still exists, and that they keep it in concealment with even greater care than they do the other three. In fact, the magicians being everywhere dreaded and hated, the Brahmins have good reason to conceal everything that may lead to the suspicion of their being initiated in the secret dealings of these impostors. It is. however, certain that magic occupies one of the first places in the list of sciences of which these great men profess to be the sole inheritors[2]. There can be no doubt

[1] *Atharva-Veda* is a collection of formulae to avert the consequences of mistakes or mishaps in sacrifices. *Atharvan*, Brahmana's eldest son, identified with Angirasa, is the author of this Veda, which belongs to a later period than the other three Vedas. This Veda is a collection of original hymns mixed up with incantations. It has no direct relation to mere rituals or sacrifices. The recitation of this Veda is considered to confer longevity, to cure diseases, to obtain success in love or gaming, to effect the ruin of enemies, and to secure the reciter's own prosperity.—Ed.

[2] It should be remarked that if the Hebrews and the various other peoples, whom Holy Writ represents as being addicted to these abominable superstitions, did not actually borrow them from the Hindus, they must both at least have copied the system from the same sources. We are aware of the extensive reputation enjoyed by magicians and soothsayers among the children of Israel, who were strictly warned by God, through Moses, against

that their ancestors cultivated the art from time immemorial; and it is not likely that the successors would have neglected so good an example and allowed the practice to fall into disuse. Many Brahmins, moreover, in spite of the restrictions imposed upon them, are known to have made a special study of this mysterious book. Besides, do not their religious sacrifices and their *mantrams* bear a great resemblance to magical formulae and conjurings? Furthermore, do not the marvellous effects which they are supposed to produce, and the power ascribed to them of counteracting the will even of the gods themselves, place them on a par with the chimerical attributes which the vulgar mind ascribes to enchantments?

I happen to have come across a Hindu book treating of the subject in hand, which perhaps few Europeans have yet heard of. It is called the *Agrushada Parikshai.* The passages which I will here extract from it will never make anybody a sorcerer, but it strikes me that they may not be wholly uninteresting to those who like to meditate on the aberrations and follies of the human mind.

The author begins by investigating the extent of a magician's power. Such power is enormous. A magician is the dispenser of both good and evil; but is more frequently inclined by natural malevolence to do evil rather than good. Nothing is easier for him than to afflict anybody with sicknesses, such as fever, dropsy, epilepsy, stricture, palsy, madness; and, in fine, diseases of all species. But all this is a mere trifle compared with what his art can otherwise do! It is capable of completely destroying an army besieging a city, and also of causing the sudden death of the commander of a besieged fortress and of all its inhabitants, and so forth.

The Mahomedans in India, being quite as superstitious as the natives of the country, are no less infatuated with the power of magic. It is a well-known fact that the last Mussulman prince who reigned in Mysore, the fanatical and superstitious Tippu Sultan, during his last war, in which he lost his kingdom and his life, engaged the services of the most celebrated magicians of his own country and of neighbouring provinces,

consulting such men (Leviticus xix. 31, xx. 6). Saul, who had vainly tried to exterminate or expel them, was weak enough to have recourse to the enchantments of the witch of Endor.—DUBOIS.

in order that they might employ all the resources of their art in destroying by some efficacious operation the English army which was then advancing to besiege his capital, and which he found himself utterly incapable of repelling by force of arms. In this difficult and critical position the magicians very humbly acknowledged their powerlessness; and to save the reputation of their craft they were obliged to maintain that their magical operations, so potent when directed against every other enemy, were utterly ineffectual against Europeans[1].

But if magic teaches the means of doing evil, it also affords the means of counteracting its pernicious effects. There is no magician so skilful but that others can be found more skilful than he, to destroy the evil effects of his enchantments and cause them to recoil with all their force upon himself or upon his clients. Apart from the direct influence exercised by themselves, the magicians also possess an ample collection of amulets and talismans, which are looked upon as efficacious against all sorcery and spells, and which are largely distributed, not without payment of course, amongst those who consult them. For instance, there are certain glass beads made magical by *mantrams*, different kinds of roots, and thin plates of copper engraved with unknown characters, strange words and uncouth figures. These amulets are always worn by Hindus, who, when protected by such talismans, believe themselves quite safe from all kinds of evil.

Secret remedies for inspiring illicit passion, for rekindling the flame of extinct love, and for reviving impaired virility, also fall within the province of these professors of magic, and form by no means the least lucrative part of their trade. It is to such men that a wife always applies when she wishes to reclaim her faithless husband or to prevent him from becoming so. Debauched gallants and lewd women also seek the help of love philtres to seduce or captivate the object of their passion.

I was not a little surprised to find in the book which I am now describing mention made of *incubi*. But these demons of India are much more mischievous than those of whom

[1] It is generally believed by the Hindus that such sorcerers and magicians are powerless against Government—an ingenuous admission of *force majeure*!—ED.

the Jesuit Delrio speaks in his *Disquisitiones Magicae.* By the violence and persistence of their embraces they so tire out the women whom they visit at night under the form of a dog, a tiger, or some other animal, that the unfortunate creatures die of sheer lassitude and exhaustion.

Our author speaks at great length of the means best suited to enchant weapons. The effects which weapons so treated have the virtue of producing are in no way inferior to those caused by the famous *Durandal* (Orlando's enchanted sword) and by the spear of Argail, which in ancient times routed so many miscreants. The Hindu gods and giants in their wars against each other used no other weapons but these. Is there anything, for instance, that can be compared with the *Arrow of Brahma* or the *Arrow of the Serpent Capella?* The former is never shot without causing the destruction of a whole army; and the latter, launched in the midst of enemies, has the effect of causing them to drop down in a state of lethargy—an effect which, as one may well suppose, made singularly short work of those who were subjected to it.

There is not a secret of magic which this book does not teach us. It puts us in possession of the means of acquiring wealth and honour; of rendering barren women fruitful; of discovering, by merely rubbing the hands and eyes with some enchanted mixtures, treasures buried in the ground or hidden elsewhere; of acquiring invulnerability and the most formidable powers in war by means of bones carried on the person. Strange to say, the only thing which it does not reveal is the means of rendering oneself immortal.

It is not by entering into compact with the devil, as our magicians were erstwhile supposed to have done, that the magicians of India obtained the power of performing so many prodigies. These latter, indeed, are not the kind of people to run the risk of having their necks twisted in evil company of this sort. It is quite sufficient for a Hindu to become an expert in the black art if he receives a few private lessons from the *guru*, or master, of the adepts. It is this *guru* who guides him in the right way, who confers his powers upon him, and to whom he owes obedience. Should a god, a demon, or a spirit be so stubborn as to disregard the orders of the newly initiated disciple, the latter has simply to repeat his injunction *in the name and from the feet of his guru.*

Brahma, Vishnu, and Siva themselves are subject to the commands of the magicians. There are, however, certain divinities who are invoked by preference. Among these the planets occupy the first place. The term *graha*, by which they are designated, signifies the *act of seizing*, that is, of laying hold of those whom they are enjoined by magical enchantments to torment. The next in order are the *bhoothams*, or the elements, each of which contains a destructive principle. Then come the *pretas* or spirits of dead bodies, the *pisachas* or *pisasus*—a term by which the Native Christians designate the devil; the female deities called *sakti*; *Kali*, the goddess of destruction; and *Marana Devi*, the goddess of death.

In order to call all these spirits into action, the magician has recourse to various mysterious ceremonies, *mantrams* and sacrifices. The sacrifices are the same as those already described, with a few trifling differences. For instance, the magician must be stark naked while he offers up these sacrifices to Lakshmi, the wife of Vishnu; while, on the other hand, he must be decorously clad when such sacrifices are offered to Rama.

The flowers offered to the god invoked must be red; and, when the object is to produce the death of any person, the boiled rice offered up must be stained with blood, for which purpose a human victim, a young girl for choice, is sometimes slain[1].

We have already spoken of the grand virtue of *mantrams*; but it is especially in connexion with magic that they are most effective. *Mantrams* have such an influence over the gods, even of the very first rank, that they are quite unable to resist doing, either in the heavens, or in the air, or on earth, all that the magician requires of them.

Among the said *mantrams* there are some, called the fundamentals, whose effects are decisive and irresistible. They are composed of various strange monosyllables, harsh of sound and difficult to pronounce; such as *h'hom, h'rhum, sh'hrum, sho'rhim, ramaya, namaha.* This last word signifies 'respectful greeting.'

[1] Such a thing is unheard of nowadays.—ED.

The magician sometimes repeats these *mantrams* in a humble and supplicatory manner, loading with praises the god whom he invokes; but he quickly resumes his imperious tone, and exclaims as though in a vehement rage, 'Grasp it! Grasp it!' or 'Begone! Begone! If thou art willing to do what I ask of thee, well and good; if not, I command thee to do it in the name of such and such a god, in the name of the feet of my *guru*!' Whereupon the god cannot do otherwise than comply with the magician's demands without a murmur!

From the haughty and indecorous manner in which the Hindu magicians treat their good-natured deities, it may be judged that they are not the men to allow themselves to be frightened as easily as were the poor witches of Horace, Canidia and Sagana, who, it will be remembered, were put to terrified flight by a commonplace sound, resembling the bursting of an inflated bladder, made by the God of the Gardens, who had been troubled by the enchantments which they came to perform every night in the place entrusted to his keeping.

It is impossible to enumerate the various drugs, ingredients, and utensils that go to make up the stock-in-trade of an Indian magician. There are certain incantations, in the performance of which it is necessary to use the bones of sixty-four different animals—neither more nor less—and amongst them may be mentioned those of a man born on a Sunday which happens to be new-moon day, of a woman born on a Friday, the feet-bones of a Pariah, of a cobbler, of a Mahomedan, and of a European. If all these bones are mixed together, enchanted by *mantrams*, consecrated by sacrifices, and then buried in the house, or at the threshold of an enemy on a night that the stars show to be propitious, they will infallibly cause the enemy's death.

In the same way, should the magician, in the silence of the night, bury these bones at the four cardinal points of a hostile camp, and then, retiring to some distance, repeat seven times the *mantram* of defeat, the result will be that within seven days the whole encamped army will either disperse of itself or perish to the last man.

Thirty-two weapons, consecrated by the sacrifice of a human victim, will spread such dismay among a besieging army that a hundred of their opponents will appear to it as a thousand.

Sometimes a quantity of mud collected from sixty-four filthy places is kneaded together with hair, parings of nails, bits of leather, &c., and is then moulded into small figures, on the breasts of which the name of one's enemy is written. Certain words and *mantrams* are then repeated over these figures, which are also consecrated by sacrifices. No sooner is this done than the *grahas* or planets take possession of the person against whom such incantations are directed, and afflict him with a thousand ills.

These figures are sometimes pierced through and through with an awl, or are mutilated in various ways with the intention of killing or mutilating in the same manner the person who is the object of vengeance [1].

Sixty-four roots of different kinds of noxious plants are known among the magicians, and, when duly prepared with *mantrams* and sacrifices, become powerful weapons for covertly dealing fatal blows to obnoxious persons.

It must here be remarked that the profession of a magician is

[1] At all times and in all places the same ridiculous and barbarous means have sufficed to excite the imagination of the vulgar, the ignorant, and the superstitious. They were, are, and will be the same throughout the world. Thus Medea, in Ovid:—

'Per tumulos errat, passis discincta capillis,
Certaque de tepidis colligit ossa rogis;
Devovet absentes, simulacraque cerea fingit,
Et miserum tenues in iecur urget acus.'

The two witches of Horace who have just been mentioned also had, among their other magical apparatus, two figures, one of wool and the other of wax:

'. . . . . Maior
Lanea, quae poenis compesceret inferiorem:
Cerea suppliciter stabat, servilibus, utque
Iam peritura, modis.'

The fanatical Leaguers of France in the sixteenth century carried their superstitious practices to such extremes that they caused wax figures to be made representing Henry III and the King of Navarre. They pierced the different parts of these figures with thorns for the space of forty days, and on the fortieth day they struck them about the region of the heart, believing that they would thereby cause the death of the princes whom the images represented. In the year 1751 a pretended sorcerer named *Trois-échelles*, who was executed on the Place de Grève, declared during his examination that there existed in France three hundred thousand persons practising the same profession as himself. Possibly he exaggerated, but at all events, if historians eliminated from their records all the follies of men, they would certainly not have much left to relate.—DUBOIS.

not altogether free from danger. If the Hindus themselves are revengeful, their gods are also passably so. Again, the gods do not obey without some feeling of anger the orders given to them by a miserable mortal, and they sometimes punish in a very cruel and brutal manner the person who ventures to command them. Woe to him who commits the smallest error, or makes the slightest omission in the innumerable ceremonies that are obligatory under such circumstances! He is immediately crushed with the full weight of the mischief which he was preparing for others.

Then again, a magician is in constant danger from rivals who exercise the same trade, especially when his rivals are as skilful as himself, or maybe more so. For these may succeed in counteracting his charms, and in bringing upon his own head, or upon the heads of his clients, the whole weight of his evil machinations. Accordingly there exists, in appearance or in reality, an inveterate mutual hatred amongst this crowd of men who pretend to be the interpreters of destiny. Occasionally they are seen to bid defiance to each other, and to enter the lists in the presence of witnesses and arbitrators, whom they call upon to decide which of the two is the more skilful in his art. The test consists, for example, in having to lift from the ground a spell-bound object, such as a piece of straw, a wand, or a piece of money. The two antagonists, placing themselves at either side of and at an equal distance from the aforesaid object, pretend to approach it; but the *mantrams* which they utter, or the enchanted ashes which they sprinkle upon each other, have the effect of arresting their course. An invisible and irresistible force seems to drive them back; they try again and again to advance towards the object, but as often have to draw back. They redouble their efforts; convulsive movements agitate them; the sweat pours from them; they spit blood. At last one of them succeeds in getting hold of the spell-bound object, and he is proclaimed the victor.

Sometimes, again, one of the combatants is thrown violently upon the ground by the force of the *mantrams* of his antagonist. He then rolls about like one possessed, and finally remains for some time motionless, feigning unconsciousness. At last, however, he recovers the use of his senses, gets up apparently much fatigued and exhausted, and retires covered with shame and confusion. A sickness of several days' duration is supposed to be the immediate result of his strenuous yet futile efforts.

It will, doubtless, be easily guessed that these pitiable fooleries are the outcome of a premeditated understanding between the shameless charlatans who practise them. But the multitude who pay for being treated to a spectacle of this kind, and who look upon the actors with fear and admiration, are fully persuaded that all their contortions are due to supernatural causes. It must, however, be admitted that these men go through their parts with really admirable skill and precision. On many an occasion they have been seen to perform sleight-of-hand tricks with such rare skill as to astonish persons of a much less credulous turn of mind than the Hindus[1].

[1] The magic art is still firmly believed in throughout India. However, the rules whereby magical powers can be acquired are so rigorous and difficult, and the consequences of any violation or infringement of them supposed to be so dangerous to the man who attempts to practise them, that only a very few ever become adepts. In all parts of the country men are to be seen who are said to have become mad on account of some violation of the prescribed ceremonies for the acquisition of the black art.—ED.

CHAPTER XXII

The Poetry of the Hindus.

FROM the very earliest times poetry has been very much in vogue with the Hindus, and it is still held in high regard by them. One is even inclined to believe that at first they had no other written language. Not one of their original ancient books is written in prose, or in the vulgar tongue—not even the books on medicine, which are said to be very numerous in the Sanskrit language.

We may naturally infer that the practice of writing in a style and idiom beyond the comprehension of the vulgar was mainly due to the artful precaution of the Brahmins, who found in it a sure means of excluding all other castes from participating in a knowledge of which they wished to retain a monopoly.

It is quite certain that all the Hindu books in prose are of modern origin. It is in verse that the eighteen Puranas, and other similar works, have been translated from the Sanskrit into Tamil, Telugu, and Canarese, and, I think, into all the other vernaculars of India.

Tamil poetry seems to have been chiefly cultivated by the Sudras; and even Pariahs have been the authors of various poems in that language. The Tamil poets, however, while imitating the form and style of Sanskrit poetry, have added so many rules of their own that it is difficult to excel in the writing of it.

Telugu and Canarese poetry is chiefly the work of Brahmins.

Having acquired some knowledge of the most important rules of Hindu prosody, which, I think, are the same in all the vernaculars of the country, Sanskrit not excepted, I will try to describe them briefly here. The subject seems to me likely to interest philologists. I will, therefore, describe: (1) the different kinds of poetry; (2) the long and short quantities; (3) the different feet; (4) the different metres; (5) the method of rhyme; (6) the composition of verses; (7) the style of their poetry generally.

The Different Kinds of Poetry.

There are five kinds of poetry, namely, *padam*, *padyam*, *dwipada*, *dandaka*, *yakshakaram*. Some add to these another kind under the name of *padia*, but as this is, properly speaking, poetical prose, it is not generally considered as belonging to the province of poetry.

The *padam* includes not only the odes in honour of gods, princes, and other great personages, but also obscene and amorous ditties, sprightly dialogues between gods and goddesses, and other similar compositions, some of which are called *sringaram* (ornament), because they describe the beauty of women and their different methods of adornment.

The erotic songs are also called *sittinbam* (pleasures of the will). Of this sort there is an infinite variety. They are sung, for the most part, by religious mendicants when they go from house to house asking for alms. The more coarse and indecent they are, the better they suit the tastes of the hearers, whose generosity is manifested in proportion to the enjoyment derived from them.

The hymns in honour of the gods are called *kirthanam* (praise), a term which these compositions well deserve on account of the high-flown eulogies with which they are replete.

The word *padam* corresponds likewise to our strophe, stanza, or couplet.

Padyam includes the great poems composed in honour of gods and heroes. They are divided into stanzas. There are at least thirty different forms of these stanzas, which may be introduced and interspersed in the course of the same poem. The *padyams* are also used in compositions dealing with moral and satirical subjects. The Telugu poet Vemana and the Tamil poet Tiruvalluvar excelled in these two kinds of composition, of which I shall speak again at the end of the present chapter.

The species of poetry called *dwipada* (two feet) is not subject to very strict rules. It might be described as free improvisation, and is used in the recital of short stories and adventures.

It is unnecessary to enter into details about the other kinds of poetry; it is easy to conjecture what they are like from what has been already said.

LONG AND SHORT QUANTITIES.

Hindu verses, like those in Greek and Latin, are formed of feet, composed of letters long or short in quantity. From these long and short feet are formed hemistichs, or lines which, combined in their turn, form stanzas.

I have remarked that the feet are composed of *letters*, because in the Indian languages there are no such things as syllables. Every consonant carries its own vowel, which is incorporated with it. In several languages of India combinations such as *bra*, *pla*, &c., which we call syllables, are also written as one single letter.

The short letters are called *laghu-aksharam*, and the long ones *guru-aksharam*, in allusion, no doubt, to the slow and solemn gait of a Hindu *guru*. Even in ordinary writing they seldom fail to make a distinction between the long and short letters with their particular marks. This is scrupulously observed in pronunciation; and in verse it is quite indispensable.

In Hindu as well as in Greek and Latin poetry, a long letter is equivalent to two short, and two long to four short. Thus the word *mālā*, composed of two long letters, is equivalent to the word *iruvadu*, composed of four short ones. But there are letters which, though short in prose writing and in ordinary conversation, become long in verse by their position; thus the initial *a* in the word *aksharam*, though short generally, becomes long in versification, being placed before two consonants, *k* and *sha*. In the same manner the letter *ka*, though usually short, is long in such words as *karman*, *karnam*, &c., on account of the two consonants which follow it.

As I wished to know whether this rule admitted of that poetical licence of which we find some examples in the writings of the best Latin poets—that is, whether a final short letter could become long by position when the word which follows it begins with two consonants—I questioned a Brahmin whom I had asked to explain to me the structure of Hindu versification. He had already seemed somewhat surprised at the facility with which I understood his explanations, and I noticed that his professorial tone and arrogant self-conceit were gradually diminishing. But when I asked this question he stood dumbfounded, and for a while stared me in the face without uttering a word. At length he answered: 'I wonder how such a thought could have occurred to you, knowing as you do so little as yet even of the rudimentary elements of our poetry.' I told him that the different kinds of poetry which were studied in my own country bore many resemblances to the poetry of India, and that the knowledge I had previously derived from the former had led me to ask this particular question. But his astonishment, instead of decreasing, grew still greater. He found it very difficult to understand how such sublime things could ever have entered the minds of foreigners, and how poets could be found elsewhere than in India. This absurd prejudice on his part easily impressed him with the idea that I was a person of wonderful mental penetration. One advantage which resulted from our conversation was that in future his conduct towards me became much more respectful.

As in Latin, the last letter or vowel of a Hindu verse may be of any quantity at pleasure; but in such cases the distinction must always be marked in accentuation.

In an idolatrous country everything necessarily tends towards superstition. The poets of India, therefore, hold some letters to be of good and others of ill omen. The *ambrosial* letters (*amritam*) come under the head of the former, while the poisonous letters (*visham*) belong to the latter class. This distinction, however, is not observed in the poems in praise of the gods, who are supposed to be beyond such influences. But in verses which concern simple mortals the case is very different. Particular care must be taken never to begin any verse addressed to them with a *visham* or unlucky letter. In the Telugu and Canarese languages, the letters *ke*, *ki*, *pe*, *pi*, *te*, *ti*, &c., are of this number, because these letters when written have the point turned downwards. On the other hand, the letters *ko*, *po*, *to*, &c., are considered to be lucky letters (*amritam*), because they have the point turned upwards.

THE FEET IN VERSE.

The feet are called *ganams*, and there are two kinds, the simple *ganams* and the *upaganams*. The first are eight in number, and are expressed by the word *mahajasanarayala*, made up of the first letters of the following:—(1) *maganam*, (2) *haganam*, (3) *jaganam*, (4) *saganam*, (5) *naganam*, (6) *raganam*, (7) *yaganam*, (8) *laganam*.

The first consists of three longs; the second, of a long and two shorts; the third, of a long between two shorts; the fourth, of two shorts and a long; the fifth, of three shorts; the sixth, of a short between two longs; the seventh, of a short and two longs; the eighth, of two longs and a short.

There are eight *upaganams* expressed by the word *gavahana-gamanala*, made up likewise by the combination of the first letters of the following words:—(1) *gaganam*, composed of two longs; (2) *vaganam*, of a short and a long; (3) *haganam*, of a long and a short; (4) *nalam*, of four shorts; (5) *galam*, of two shorts; (6) *malagam*, of three longs and a short; (7) *nagam*, of three shorts and a long; (8) *latam*, of two longs and two shorts.

The Hindu poets discern a certain relation between the *ganams* and the *upaganams*, according to the effects which they are severally supposed to possess the faculty of producing. They are all under the protection of different planets; and according to the good or evil dispositions of these latter, they bring good or ill luck. Those under the auspices of the moon, which in India is the symbol of comfort and coolness, are favourable; but the case is just the reverse with those governed by the sun. It therefore follows that a piece of poetry must never begin with a malign *ganam*. The Hindu prosodies are very diffuse and wearisome on this subject.

THE DIFFERENT METRES.

The lines, properly speaking, of verses are formed of *ganams* and *upaganams*, and are called *padams* or *charanams*, words which signify literally *feet*. They may be compared to the hemistichs or lines of pentameter verse in Latin, or to the lines of ten and twelve syllables in French and English. The variety of *padams* depends on the number of *ganams* they contain; some having three, five, seven, or more.

In certain *padams* any of the *ganams* may be used, and these latter may be varied at pleasure, provided the requisite number of shorts and longs is preserved. This variety, however, must be managed with a certain amount of taste and be free from all affectation; when it is done with discretion, it enhances the beauty and force of the verses, which otherwise would become too monotonous. It is just the same with Latin hexameters, which would be wanting in grace if the poet were to put either all dactyls or all spondees in the first four feet.

The Hindu poets, however, cannot indulge in this interchange of *ganams* in all their compositions. There are cases in which it is absolutely necessary for them to use only such as the rules prescribe.

The various kinds of lines in Hindu verse have all special names. One is called the elephant, another the tiger, another the cobra; and so forth.

RHYME.

There are two kinds of rhymes in Hindu poetry. One occurs at the beginning of the line, and is called *yeti* or *vadi*. Thus, where one line begins with the word *kirti* and the other with *kirtana*, *ki* is the *yeti*. The other kind of rhyme occurs in the second letter or syllable of the line, and is called *prasam*. Thus, in two lines, one beginning with *gopagni* and the other with *dipantram*, *pa* is the *prasam*.

For the *yeti* rhyme the letters *ka*, *kaha*, *ksha*, *ga*, *gsha*, the simple *tsha*, and the aspirate *tshaha*, &c., may be used.

For the *prasam* rhyme attention is, strictly speaking, paid only to the consonant, which ought to be absolutely the same; the vowel does not matter so much. Thus *da*, *de*, *di*, *do*, *du* all rhyme together. These kinds of rhymes, however, are not considered fine.

Generally speaking, the more words there are in a line having the *yeti* and the *prasam* alike, the more beautiful they appear to the Hindus. For our part we should look upon them as mere childish alliterations, recalling to our minds the line of Ennius so often in the mouths of schoolboys:

'O Tite tute Tati tibi tanta, tyranne, tulisti!'

There are also other kinds of poetry, which, like ours, have their rhyme at the end of the lines. In these cases they end as a rule with the same consonant and sometimes with the same word.

Generally speaking, the difficulties of rhyme are simply hopeless, and often puzzle Hindu versifiers themselves.

VERSES.

With the *padams*, or lines, arranged symmetrically with regard to quantity and rhyme, are formed the *padyams*, sometimes called *slokams*. They are, properly speaking, stanzas or couplets, sometimes regular, sometimes irregular.

These *padyams* are of several kinds, and each has its special name.

In the simple *kanda-padyam* certain feet only can be introduced, in the same way as in Latin hexameters in which dactyls and spondees only are used. But a single *ganam*, or foot, may sometimes comprise a whole line, such as the following: *Devaki-Deviki-Kamsudu.*

The limits of this work hardly permit me to enter into more minute details concerning the numerous rules to which the structure and arrangement of Hindu poetry are subject; but it will appear from what has been already said that Hindu versification is by no means easy. There are nevertheless a great many people of all castes who dabble in rhymes, and amuse themselves by reading out publicly and ostentatiously the pieces they have composed. In India, as in Europe, poetasters abound, while good poets are very scarce. The Indian languages, however, being very rich in synonyms, afford a great advantage to the Hindu poet.

There are five principal authors who have written on the subject of Hindu prosody; and these have laid down fixed and unalterable laws for making verses. Their collected works are called *Chandas*. The Brahmin who taught me was guided in his instructions by a book whose author had so arranged that every rule was comprised in a verse which served at once the double purpose of an example of the rule as well as the rule itself.

OF TASTE AND STYLE IN HINDU POETRY.

The predominating features of Hindu poetry are emphasis, affectation, and bombast. Every Hindu poet would seem to be a prototype of him who, in Horace,

> 'Proicit ampullas et sesquipedalia verba,'

or of the Clitarchus compared by Longinus to a man who opens his mouth wide to blow through a tiny flute. The poetry of all nations has its peculiar turns of expression, its licences, its own vocabulary, &c., which render it difficult of understanding by foreigners; but in Hindu poetry the frequent use of elliptical phrases, of allegories, of metaphors, and of expressions not in vogue in ordinary language, renders the meaning so obscure that it is impossible to understand it properly unless one makes a special study of the subject. Even a thorough knowledge of Hindu prose works is of no avail.

Were Hindu literature better known to us, it is possible that we should find that we have borrowed from it the *romantic* style of our days, which some find so beautiful and others so silly. If the Hindu poet has occasion to describe any particular object, he seldom omits even the minutest details. He thinks it his duty to present it to the view in all its phases.

> 'S'il rencontre un palais, il m'en dépeint la face;
> Il me promène après de terrasse en terrasse:
> Ici s'offre un perron; là règne un corridor;
> Là ce balcon s'enferme en un balustre d'or,
> Il compte des plafonds les ronds et les ovales.'

If a Hindu poet has a beautiful woman for his theme, he will certainly never be content with merely stating, in a more or less flowery style, that she is endowed with all the charms of body and mind. Like the painter who reproduces on the canvas one feature after another of his model, so does our Hindu poet pass in review *a capite usque ad calcem* the various charms of the beauty he is describing. The colour of her skin, the expression of her face and eyes, in fine, everything connected with her, even her most secret charms, appear to him objects worthy of his praise. The finishing strokes of his brush are generally reserved for the touching up of all the moral and intellectual qualities which his imagination can impart to the fair subject of his verses. It may be easily imagined that these descriptive details, overloaded as they are with a vast display of epithets, become exceedingly diffuse; but we cannot deny to them at least the credit of exactitude.

Hindu poetry at first sounds harsh and inharmonious to a European ear, by reason of the frequent aspirations with which many of the letters at the beginning, in the middle, and at the end of the words are pronounced; but, on the other hand, this laboured pronunciation gives to the recital a stately and sonorous tone, which seldom fails to please one who has become used to it. At the same time it must be confessed that foreigners, and even natives who have not been well trained in it from infancy, find almost insurmountable difficulties in mastering this method of pronunciation.

The short pieces that I have seen have appeared to me generally weak and uninspiring. I know not whether the Hindus have any real dramatic works. I only know of a few productions of this nature, and these are mixed up with songs and dialogues. The *Dasa-avatara*, or the ten incarnations of Vishnu, is among the number. But I am not in a position to give any particulars as to their merit, or even of their contents, seeing that I have never taken the trouble to read any of them.

More fortunate than the French, who are never weary of repeating that no epic poem exists in their literature, the Hindus boast of a great number. The two most celebrated are the *Ramayana* and the *Bhagavata*. Both are of inordinate length. The former recounts the deeds and exploits of Vishnu under the incarnation of Rama; while the latter relates the adventures of Vishnu metamorphosed in the form of Krishna. Their authors have introduced into them the whole idolatrous system of the country—a system on which they are often at variance among themselves. It may be easily understood that the 'unities' prescribed by Aristotle have not been observed in these epics. The *Bhagavata* takes up its hero even before his birth, and does not quit him till after he is dead.

The fertile imagination of the ancient Greeks conceived nothing that can be compared with the incredible powers and wonderful achievements of the Hindu heroes, whose exploits are celebrated in these books. Even the colossal Enceladus and the giant Briareus, with his fifty heads and his hundred hands, were but pigmies compared with the wonderful giants who, according to the *Ramayana*, sometimes fought for Rama and sometimes against him.

CHAPTER XXIII

Brahmin Philosophy.—The Six Sects called *Shan Mata*.—The Doctrine of the Buddhists.

I HAVE previously shown (in Part II, Chapter XI) that the ancient Brahmins recognized one Supreme and Almighty Being, possessing all the attributes that reasonable man should ascribe to such a Being. It is impossible to believe that these sages, being thus impressed with the idea of so perfect a Godhead, could have countenanced the absurdities of polytheism and idolatry. It was their successors who adopted these absurdities, little by little, until they led the nation, whose oracles they were, into all the extravagant doctrines in which they are now involved. It must nevertheless be acknowledged that the speculative theories in which these ancient philosophers indulged in the first instance, and of which I shall have occasion to speak later on, were calculated to corrupt this pure conception of the Deity and of the worship due to Him. Indeed, it was not long before divided opinions arose regarding the nature of God and the creation of the Universe. Two principal sects were gradually developed, each of which possesses up to the present day numerous adherents among the modern Brahmins[1]. The first

[1] There are, as a matter of fact, three sects. The first is that of *Adwaita*, or non-dualism. 'The Universe exists, but merely as a form of the one eternal essence. All animate and inanimate things are but parts of the Deity, and have no real existence of their own.' Then comes the *Dwaita* doctrine, or dualism, which holds that 'God is supreme, yet essentially different from the human soul and from the material world, both of which have a real and eternally distinct existence.' A third and important section hold the doctrine of *Visishtadwaita*, or doctrine of unity with attributes. This doctrine is like that of *Adwaita*, holding that the Deity and the Universe are one, but it goes further in holding that the Deity is not void of form or quality; it regards Him as 'being endowed with all good qualities and a twofold form: the Supreme Spirit, *Paramatma* or Cause, and the gross one, the effect, the Universe or Matter.'—ED.

is called the *Dwaita* (twofold) sect, whose adherents recognize the existence of *two* beings, namely, God and Matter, which He created and which is one with Him. The other sect, called *Adwaita* (not twofold), comprises those who acknowledge but one Being, one Substance, one God. It has a more numerous following than the other, and includes in its ranks the majority of those Brahmins who profess to be exceptionally learned. Its adepts designate the leading principles of their doctrine by the technical words *Abhavena Bhavam Nasti*, meaning *de nihilo nihil fit* (from nothing nothing is made). They maintain that Creation is an impossibility, and at the same time they hold that pre-existing and eternal Matter is absolutely chimerical. From these premises they conclude that all that we call the universe, including all the various phenomena which we see to be comprised within it, has no real existence at all, but is merely the result of illusion, which is known among them as *Maya*. From the large number of stories which they have invented for the purpose of illustrating this doctrine I have selected the following:—

'A certain man, in a dream, imagined that he had been crowned king of a certain country with great pomp and circumstance. The next morning, on leaving his house, he met a traveller, who gave him a detailed account of festivities and ceremonies that had actually taken place on the occasion of the coronation of the king of the same country, and of which he was himself an eye-witness. The incidents related by the latter agreed in all particulars with what the former had dreamed. Illusion, *Maya*, was equally prevalent in both cases; and there was no more reality in what the one man had seen than in what the other man had dreamed. In a word, things that we take for realities are nothing but illusions emanating from the Deity, who is the sole Being with an actual existence. Our senses deceive us in presenting to us objects which do not really exist. These objects indeed are nothing but appearances or modifications of the Deity; that is to say, there is nothing real about them.'

I do not know whether these would-be philosophers deduce from this pernicious doctrine all the consequences which naturally result from it, and look upon God as the immediate author of all the evil as well as all the good that takes place on the earth. Several of them, at any rate, are not ashamed to express this opinion. The Brahmins with whom I have discussed the subject have candidly confessed to me that, in their opinion, neither good nor evil exists; that, in fact, all crimes, even parricide, adultery, fraud, and perjury, are but acts incited by the divine power; or rather, that these acts are imaginative and are simply the strange result of *Maya*, a delusion which deceives us and causes us to take the shadow for the reality[1].

The doctrine of *Dwaita* admits of two actual substances—God, and Matter created by God, with which He is inseparably united. God, according to this doctrine, is omnipresent. He pervades all Matter and incorporates Himself, so to speak, with it. He is present in every animate and inanimate thing. He does not, however, undergo the least change or the least modification by such coexistence, whatever may be the badness and imperfection of the things with which He is united. In support of this last contention, the adherents of the doctrine of *Dwaita* cite, for the purpose of comparison, fire and the rays of the sun. They say that fire can be incorporated in every substance, pure and impure, yet it never loses any of its own purity; so also with the rays of the sun, which are never polluted even when penetrating heaps of filth and mud.

According to these sectarians our souls emanate from God and form part of Him; just as light emanates from the sun, which illuminates the whole world with an infinite number of rays; just as numberless drops of water fall from the same cloud; and just as various trinkets are formed from the same ingot of gold. Whatever may be the number of these rays, of these drops of water, and of these trinkets, it is always to the same sun, to the same cloud, and to the same ingot of gold that they respectively belong.

However, from the very moment that a soul is united with a body it finds itself imprisoned in the darkness of ignorance and sin, just like a frog caught in the gullet of a snake from which it has no chance of escaping. Although the soul, thus imprisoned, continues to be one with God, it is, nevertheless, to

[1] The Abbé's opinion of the *Adwaita* doctrine is not supported by modern authorities, such as Professor Deussen and Professor Max Müller, who have written of it in the highest terms of praise.—ED.

a certain extent disunited and separated from Him. However great and good the soul may be which animates a human form, it becomes from that moment subject to all the sins, to all the errors, and to all the weaknesses which are the natural consequences of this union with a body. The vicissitudes that affect the soul while it is united with a body do not, however, affect that part of its nature which is divine. In this respect the soul may be compared to the moon, whose image is reflected in the water: if the water in which the image of the moon is reflected be disturbed, the image also becomes disturbed; but it cannot be said that the moon itself is disturbed. The changes and chances of the soul united with different bodies do not seriously concern God, from whom it emanates; and as to the soul itself, it is immutable, never undergoing the slightest change. Its union with the body lasts till such time as, by meditation and penance, it attains a degree of wisdom and perfection which permits it to reunite itself anew, and that inseparably and for ever, with God: that is to say, it ceases to migrate from one body to another.

The soul is said to be endowed with one of the following three *gunas*, or inherent qualities, viz. *sattva*, *rajas*, or *tamas*—*goodness*, *passion*, or *ignorance*. It frees itself at one time from one, at another time from another, of these inherent qualities, and it attains perfection only after it is entirely freed from all of them.

The five senses of the body play the part of councillors and slaves to the soul. For instance, should the soul perceive a desirable object, it immediately conceives the desire of possessing it. The feet are ordered to approach it, and when the object is in view, the eyes are commanded to behold it, and the hands to seize it, which orders are immediately executed. The nostrils are then commanded to smell it, the mouth to open, and the tongue to taste it; and these organs comply with its wishes. Thereupon the object passes into the body with which the soul is united, and the soul is then satisfied. Thus it is the soul that regulates the actions and the movements of the body. It may be compared, in this respect, with a magnet placed on a brass plate beneath which is an iron needle. If the magnet be moved round the plate, the needle follows in the same direction; but if the magnet be removed, the needle at once drops down and remains motionless. The magnet is therefore typical of the soul, and the needle of the body. As long as these two are united, the body is susceptible of motion; but no sooner does the soul quit the body to take up its abode elsewhere than the body becomes insensible, is dissolved, and returns to the five elements from which it was originally formed. The soul, on the other hand, like the magnet, loses nothing of its efficacy, and in whatever body it takes up its abode, always remains the same.

The two great sects of philosophers above mentioned were subsequently divided into six others, known by the general name of *Shan Mata* (the six sects, or schools). Their names are (1) *Saiva*, (2) *Sakta*, (3) *Charvaka*, (4) *Kapalika*, (5) *Vaishnava*, (6) *Bouddha*. To strive to purify the soul, to acquire wisdom and perfection, to dissipate the darkness of sin and ignorance, to free oneself from the thraldom of passion and from the wretchedness of life with a view to union with and absorption in the Great Being, the Universal Soul, the *Paramatma* or *Parabrahma*: such are the objects aimed at by these various sects. Each is distinguished from the others by differences of opinion on the nature of perfect happiness and on the means of attaining it.

The different forms of knowledge taught in these schools are known by the following names: (1) *Nyaya*[1], (2) *Vedanta*, (3) *Mimamsa*, (4) *Sankhya*, (5) *Patanjala*, (6) *Vaiseshika*.

The first of these schools, the *Saiva*, founded by Gautama[2], who came from Tirat, near Patna, on the borders of the Ganges, is held to surpass the others in *Tarka-sastra*, i. e. Logic. It recognizes four sources of knowledge, viz. (1) *Pratyaksha*, or the testimony of the senses rightly exercised; (2) *Anumana*, or natural and visible signs, as for instance smoke, which is proof of the presence of fire; (3) *Upamana*, or *Upama*, or the application of a known definition to an unknown object still to be defined; (4) *Aptha-sabdam*, or the authority of infallible texts, which authority they ascribe to the Vedas, so far as religion and the worship of the gods are concerned, and to

[1] *Nyaya* is a compound Sanskrit root, meaning literally 'that by which we enter into a thing and draw conclusions.'—ED.

[2] This Gautama is not to be confused with Gautama Buddha, the founder of Buddhism.—ED.

the maxims of Gautama, their founder, so far as other matters are concerned.

After the study of Logic, the professors of this school lead their disciples to the study of the visible world, and then to a knowledge of its Author, whose existence, although invisible, is demonstrable by the process of *Anumana*. They gather from the same source proofs of His understanding, and from His understanding they deduce His immateriality.

But although God in His essence is spiritual, they say that He possesses the power of rendering Himself perceptible, and has, in fact, exercised that power. From *nirakara*, or possessing no form, He has become *akara*, or possessing form, with a view to shape and animate the world, whose atoms, although eternal, are nevertheless, without His presence, motionless and lifeless.

Man, according to them, is composed of one body and two souls, the one *supreme*, called *Paramatma*, which is nothing else than God Himself; the other *animal* or *vital*, known by the name of *Jivatma*, which is in us the sentient principle of pleasure and pain. Some hold that this is spiritual, others that it is material.

In order to attain supreme wisdom and perfect happiness this sentient principle must be extinguished; its complete extinction leading to union with *Paramatma*. The various gradations by which this union is attained will be spoken of later on. It begins with contemplation of, and ends in perfect identity with, God Himself. The process of metempsychosis continues in the meantime, the soul never ceasing its transmigrations from one body to another.

It must here be remarked that by the word *Soul* the learned mean the *Will* or else the *Ego*, the consciousness of Self.

The *Vedanta* school, founded by the celebrated Sankara Acharya, is distinguished from the rest by its metaphysics, and, we may add, by the obscurity of its dogmas. Most of the Brahmins of the present day who wish to pass themselves off as learned men, blindly embrace its principles without understanding them. True *sannyasis* are nowadays not to be found except in this school, which is founded on the system of *Adwaita*.

The characteristic feature of this sect is the belief in the simple *unity* of the being, who is none other than the Ego, that is to say, the Soul. Nothing exists except the Ego, yet this Ego in its simple and absolute unity is, so to speak, a trinity (*trinus*) by (1) its existence, (2) its infinite wisdom, and (3) its supreme happiness.

But as the consciousness of Self is not at all in accordance with the sublime notions of this school, they admit another purely negative principle, which, in consequence, has no actual existence. This is the *Maya* of the Ego, i.e. error or illusion. For instance, I believe I am now writing to you about the *Vedanta*; but I am mistaken. It is true, indeed, I am Ego, I do actually exist; but you are not YOU, you do not exist. There is nothing existent in the world, except the Ego. There is neither *Vedanta*, nor doctrine, nor any being except the Ego. In imagining to myself that you exist, I am under the illusion of *Maya*. I am mistaken; that is all: the subject of my illusion does not in fact exist.

Maya, or illusion, makes men believe that they have wives and children, that they possess cattle, jewels, houses, and other temporal goods: but nothing of all this is real. Hindus explain the effects of this illusion very imperfectly by comparing them to a rope coiled on the ground and mistaken for a snake.

True wisdom consists in obtaining deliverance from this illusion by diligent contemplation of Self, by persuading oneself that one is the unique, eternal, and infinite Being, and so forth, without allowing one's attention to be diverted from this truth by the effects of *Maya*.

The key by which the soul may free itself from these illusions of *Maya* is contained in the following words, which these pretentious sages are bound to repeat without ceasing:—*Aham-Eva-Param-Brahma*, that is to say, *I am myself the Supreme Being*. The hypothetical conception of this idea, they say, should eventually result in actual conviction and lead to supreme blessedness.

The basic principle of the *Sankhya* school, founded by Kapila, is the doctrine of *Dwaita*; it rejects the *Upamana* of Logic, and seems generally less pretentious than the other schools. It also teaches that the soul is simply a part of God, and that the wisdom acquired by *yoga*, or contemplation, ends in either actual or spiritual unity with God.

Kapila recognized a spiritual nature and a material nature,

both of them real and eternal. The spiritual nature, by the exercise of the will, unites itself with the material nature outside itself From this union are born an infinite number of forms and a certain number of qualities. Amongst the forms is that of the Ego, by reason of which each being can say: *I am I, and not another.*

As stated above, the qualities are three in number, viz. *goodness, passion, ignorance.* One or other of these three qualities predominates in all animate beings and accounts for the differences to be observed amongst them.

Another union of spirit (together with its forms and qualities) with Matter produces the elements; and a third produces the world as it stands.

Such then, according to this doctrine, is the synthesis of the universe. Wisdom acquired through various stages of contemplation produces freedom of the spirit, which liberates itself at one time from one form or quality, at another time from another, by constantly meditating on these three truths:—

1. I exist not in any thing!
2. Nothing exists in me!
3. I myself exist not!

This is expressed by the combination of these three words:

Nasmeeha-namama-naham!

The time comes at last when the spirit has liberated itself from all its forms and qualities. This means the end of the world, when everything, returning to its primitive state, is lost in and identified with God.

Kapila maintains that every religion known to him serves but to draw together more closely the bonds in which the spirit is held, instead of helping it to free itself from them. For, says he, the worship of subordinate deities, who are in reality nothing but the offspring of the most degraded and latest conceived union of spirit with Matter, binds us more closely to the object of it instead of liberating us from it.

The worship also of superior deities, who are in reality only the offspring of the closest union of spirit with Matter, cannot but be in the same way an obstacle to complete spiritual freedom. Such is the contention of Kapila, and one can but conclude that he wished to sap to the very foundations the authority of the Vedas and of the Hindu religion. Indeed, the groundwork of his doctrine seems to bear a very close resemblance to that of Spinoza and other modern philosophers.

His doctrine gives us also to understand that the gods of the Vedas are merely allegorical figures relating to the world itself, as much in its first principles as in its component parts, which are but emanations from or modifications of these first principles.

Kapila rejects *in toto* the commonly accepted tenets of the Hindu religion, which, according to him, are founded on mythical, wicked, and impious stories.

He teaches that everything that tends to cherish the passions, to which one must necessarily yield if they are not surmounted, is calculated to bind the spirit anew to Matter and to prolong its captivity. It is only after having overcome all such passions, and especially those of lust, anger, and avarice, that one can aspire to complete freedom and the supreme blessedness known as *mukti*.

The *Mimamsa* school, which recognizes a blind and irresistible predestination, professes absolute toleration with regard to other sects. Its adepts scrutinize and discuss the dogmas of these sects, without condemning them or venturing on any decided opinion with regard to them. They commend the utmost tolerance in matters of opinion, and affirm that every sect—nay, every religion—pursues the same end, viz. happiness, although they may differ as to the means of attaining it.

I have already described[1] the abominable orgies of the *sakti-puja*, practised by the votaries of the *Sakta* sect[2]. Their

[1] See Part II, Chapter IX.

[2] The Saivas are all worshippers of Siva and Bhavani conjointly, and they adore the *linga* or compound type of this god and goddess, as the Vaishnavas do the image of Lakshminarayana. There are no exclusive worshippers of Siva besides the sect of naked Gymnosophists called *Lingis*; and the exclusive adorers of the goddess are the *Saktas*. In this last-mentioned sect, as in most others, there is a right-handed and decent path, and a left-handed and indecent mode of worship; but the indecent worship of this sect is most grossly so, and consists of unbridled debauchery with wine and women. This profligate sect is supposed to be numerous, though unavowed. In most parts of India, if not in all, they are held in deserved detestation; and even the decent *Saktas* do not make public profession of their tenets, nor wear on their foreheads the mark of the sect, lest they should be suspected of belonging to the other branch of it. The sacrifice of cattle before idols is peculiar to this sect.—H. T. COLEBROOK.

principal doctrine seems to be that happiness consists in the enjoyment of sensual pleasures.

There is another sect called *Bouddha Mata*, which has no Brahmin adherents at all, its followers being chiefly Buddhists, whose number at present is very small in Southern India. Their doctrine is pure materialism. Spinoza and his disciples endeavoured to palm it off as a new invention of their own; but the atheists of India recognized this doctrine many centuries before them and drew from it pretty much the same deductions which their European brethren afterwards drew, and which have been propagated in modern times with such deplorable success.

According to this odious doctrine there is no other god but Matter, which is divided into an infinite number of substances, forming as many deities according to some, and forming but one god according to others. They hold that there can be neither vice nor virtue during life; neither heaven nor hell after death. The truly wise man, according to them, is he who enjoys every kind of sensual pleasure, who believes in nothing that is not capable of being felt, and who looks upon everything else as chimerical.

God, that is to say Matter, remarks a philosopher of this abominable school, possesses four *saktis* or *faculties*, which are like so many wives to him. These are *Knowledge*, *Desire*, *Energy*, and *Maya*, or *Illusion*. The body, by applying all its senses at one and the same time to a particular object, enjoys unalloyed pleasure, which is said to be imperfect when the enjoyment is limited to a part only of the senses. It is also from this want of consciousness, or from its partial application, that pain and sleep originate. Death is merely the total failure of the application of bodily consciousness to the senses. The body thus becomes insensible and perishes.

It is, they say, simply to amuse and divert Himself with the pleasures of infancy that God, that is to say Matter, assumes the form of a child. Similarly He attains the respective stages of adolescence and old age. Such, briefly, according to this school, is the whole secret of birth, life, and death.

The second *sakti* or divine faculty is Desire, the effects of which are as varied as its impressions. God is man, horse, insect, &c., in fact, whatever He wishes to be. This Desire is, in different creatures, as varied as their inclinations. But each is satisfied when enjoying what pleases him most.

The *sakti* of Desire, however, obscures that of Knowledge: that is, it hinders one from knowing that there is no other deity but the body, and that birth, life and death, sin and virtue, and the successive re-births are purely chimerical. From this ignorance, occasioned by Desire, originate the inclinations of mankind; such as the affection of a mother for her children and the care she bestows in bringing them up. The truly wise man, who is anxious to acquire a clear perception of the truth, must, therefore, renounce all such Desire.

The third *sakti* is *Energy*, about which these pretentious philosophers speak still more foolishly. The universe, according to them, was in a state of chaos; men lived without laws and without caste, in a state of utter insubordination. To remedy this disorder, a general consultation of bodies was held. Energy spoke first: 'Collecting from all bodies whatever is found most excellent in each, I will form a perfect man, who, by his beauty, wisdom, and strength, shall make himself master of the whole earth and shall become its sovereign lord. I will be his spouse; and from our union shall be born bodies innumerable, each more perfect than another.'

The proposal of Energy was approved and carried into effect. It fully succeeded; and from the wife of a Brahmin called Suddhodana Energy begot the god Buddha, who was a man incomparable in all his perfections and the lawgiver of the human race. He promulgated laws, the transgression of which alone constituted sin. And the greatest sin of all is to deny Buddha to be what he is. He who acknowledges him is the true Buddhist, the genuine Brahmin, the *guru* among Brahmins. He knows no other god than his own body. To his body alone he offers up sacrifice, and procures for it all possible sensual pleasures. He has no dread of anything; he eats indiscriminately of all food; he scruples not to lie in order to attain the object of his wish; he acknowledges neither Vishnu nor Siva, nor any other god but himself.

But, seeing that all individual bodies are so many deities, why is it that they do not all possess the same feelings, the same inclinations, and the same knowledge? Why is there such a great number of them ignorant of so many beautiful things, of which the Buddhists make so much? Such were substantially the objections which a new proselyte of the sect addressed to one of its wise men. The latter replied that the evil was born of the fourth wife, or *sakti*, of the divinity, called *Maya* or Illusion, which fascinates and deceives mankind, making them look upon what is false as true. It, moreover, misleads them into the belief that there are gods; that there are such vicissitudes as living and dying, pollution and purification; and, finally, that there are sufferings and rewards after death. The only method of preserving oneself from *Maya* is to cling to the doctrine of Buddhism in acknowledging no other god but the material body.

The author from whose work I have extracted this very obscure account of the system undertakes to explain the theory of Creation, and to show how God, united to *Maya*, produced men differing so greatly in their inclinations. But all that he advances on this subject is merely the result of an extravagant imagination, and is no more worthy of attention than the talk of a sick man deprived of the use of his reason by delirium [1].

Returning to his doctrines, I may remark that he sneers at the Brahmins for their ablutions, fasts, penances, sacrifices, Vedas, &c. The true Veda, or rather the true religion, he declares, is for a man to procure for himself all sensual enjoyments; to gratify all his desires; to avenge himself on his enemies, even unto death; to renounce all feelings of humanity, and to live but for himself. Such sentiments as filial affection, kindness, gentleness, and pity are regarded in this infamous book, not as virtues, but (who would believe it?) as sins. As an illustration of this principle, mention is made, in terms of the highest praise, of a certain king who scarcely ever quitted the apartments of his wives, and who condemned to death a person whose only crime was to pity the sufferings of his fellow-creatures.

It is not, therefore, to be wondered at that human monsters who professed doctrines so detestable and so opposed to all considerations of social well-being, became objects of general execration, and that they were almost exterminated in India, where, it appears, they were once so powerful.

1 This description of Buddhism conveys an altogether false impression, and readers are recommended to consult more modern authorities on the subject.—ED.

Nevertheless, I doubt whether the genuine Buddhists, even in countries where their religion is predominant, would dare to avow publicly such terrible doctrines. I even suspect that the book which contains an exposition of this doctrine is the work of Brahmins themselves, who, for the purpose of bringing odium upon a sect for which their caste entertains the most implacable hátred, invented these opinions, the very mention of which makes one shudder. At any rate the book contains certain maxims which betray the influence of Hindu sophistry. The following are examples illustrating the foolish extremes to which they go :—

'One ought never to yield to taste or appetite in eating or drinking; one must habituate oneself to the most nauseous food.'

'One must elevate oneself above the prejudices of the vulgar, and one must always pursue, in one's conduct and mode of thinking, a course opposite to that of others.'

The Brahmins, in order to cast odium on the Jains, their enemies, accuse them also of professing the doctrines of Buddhism; but the Jains resent with indignation the false insinuations of their adversaries. I have myself heard several Jains speak very forcibly on the horror which such principles inspire in them, and complain most bitterly of the dubious methods of the Brahmins, who, actuated by hatred and jealousy, are not at all ashamed to resort to these false imputations.

There are also other sects, not so well known; and among them is the *Nastika* sect, whose fundamental doctrine consists in absolute pyrrhonism or scepticism; and also the *Lokayatha Sastra* sect, whose adherents recognize no differences of condition amongst mankind, no precepts relating to pollution and purification, and who are, moreover, accused of devoting themselves to witchcraft and enchantments.

Such, in brief, is what I have been able to understand of the numerous doctrines about which there exists such diversity of opinion amongst the Hindus. With the object of obtaining an insight into these various matters with greater facility, I engaged the services of a Brahmin, who was said to be learned, and who, in fact, was not wanting in intelligence or knowledge. But I soon perceived that he was himself completely lost in this labyrinth of metaphysics; and the various Commentaries to which he referred for some plausible explanations of my difficulties tended only to increase those difficulties. However, being very often too proud and presumptuous to acknowledge his inability to make me understand what he did not understand himself, he tried to get out of his difficulties by hums and haws. By gestures and pantomimic signs, which were truly laughable, he endeavoured to make up for the explanations which I in vain sought from him, and he often left me to myself to clear up my own difficulties.

CHAPTER XXIV

Chronology of the Brahmins.—The Epoch of the Flood.

The Hindus recognize four ages of the world, to which they give the name of *yugas*. They assign to each *yuga* a period of time which, when all the *yugas* are added together, would make the creation of the world date back several millions of years.

The first is called *Kritha-yuga*, to which they assign 1,728,000 years. The second, which they call *Tretha-yuga*, lasted about 1,296,000 years. The third, called *Dwapara-yuga*, lasted about 864,000 years. And the last, in which we are now living, is called *Kali-yuga*, or the Age of Misery. It should last about 432,000 years. The present year of the Christian era (1825) corresponds to the year 4,926 of the *Kali-yuga*.

According to this calculation the world has now been in existence for 3,892,926 years.

It is hardly necessary for me to waste time in proving that the first three ages are entirely mythical. The Hindus themselves seem to regard them in that light, since in ordinary life they make no mention of them. All their calculations and dates, as well as all the most ancient and authentic records at present to be found among them, are reckoned from the commencement of the *Kali-yuga*.

This pretension to remote antiquity is a favourite illusion amongst ancient civilized peoples, who, as they sank into idolatry, soon forgot the traditions of their ancestors regarding the creation of the world, and believed they could add to their own glory by assuming an origin which was, so to say, lost in the dim vista of mythical times. It is well known to what extremes the Chinese, the Egyptians, and the Greeks carried this mania, and it is characteristic of the Hindus that they far excel these nations in their pretensions.

At the close of each of the *yugas* there took place a universal upheaval in nature. No trace of the preceding *yuga* survived in that which followed. The gods themselves shared in the changes brought about by these great upheavals. Vishnu, for instance, who was white in the preceding *yuga*, became black in the present one.

But of all the *yugas* the most direful is the *Kali-yuga*, in which we now live. It is verily an Iron Age, an epoch of misrule and misery, during which everything on earth has deteriorated. The elements, the duration of life, the character of mankind: everything, in a word, has suffered, everything has undergone a change. Deceit has taken the place of justice, and falsehood that of truth. And this degeneration must continue and go on increasing till the end of the *yuga*.

From what I have just stated it will be seen that the commencement of the true era of the Hindus, that is to say, of their *Kali-yuga*, dates from about the same time as the epoch of the Deluge—an event clearly recognized by them and very distinctly mentioned by their authors, who give it the name of *Jala-pralayam*, or the Flood of Waters.

Their present era, indeed, dates specifically from the commencement of this *Jala-pralayam*. It is definitely stated in the *Markandeya-purana* and in the *Bhagavata* that this event caused the destruction of all mankind, with the exception of the seven famous *Rishis* or Penitents whom I have often had occasion to mention, and who were saved from the universal destruction by means of an ark, of which Vishnu himself was the pilot. Another great personage, called Manu, who, as I have tried elsewhere to show, was no other than the great Noah himself, was also saved along with the seven great Penitents. The universal flood is not, to my knowledge, more clearly referred to in the writings of any heathen nation that has preserved the tradition of this great event, or described in a manner more in keeping with the narrative of Moses, than it is in the Hindu books to which I have referred.

It is certainly remarkable that such testimony should be afforded us by a people whose antiquity has never been called in question; the only people, perhaps, who have never fallen into a state of barbarism; a people who, judging by the position, the climate, and the fertility of their country, must have been one of the first nations to be regularly constituted; a people who from time immemorial have suffered no considerable changes to be made in their primitive customs, which they have always held inviolable. And curiously enough, in all their ordinary transactions of life, in the promulgation of all their acts, in all their public monuments, the Hindus date everything from the subsidence of the Flood. They seem to tacitly acknowledge the other past ages to be purely chimerical and mythical, while they speak of the *Kali-yuga* as the only era recognized as authentic. Their public and private events are always reckoned by the year of the various cycles of sixty years which have elapsed since the Deluge. How many historical facts, looked upon as established truths. have a far less solid foundation than this!

Another very remarkable circumstance is that the Hindu method of reckoning the age of the world agrees essentially with what we have in Holy Scripture. In Genesis viii. 13, for example, we read: 'In the six hundredth and first year, in the first month, the first day of the month, the waters were dried up from off the earth.' We read in Hindu works: 'On such a day of such a month of such a year of such a cycle, reckoning from the commencement of the *Kali yuga*.'

It is true that in the passage just quoted from Holy Scripture the date is reckoned from Noah's birth. He was then entering on his six hundred and first year. But according to many chronologists, it appears that in times immediately succeeding the Deluge the Scriptures reckon time by this patriarch, and that the anniversary of his birth commemorated the day on which the earth was restored to mankind—a memorable epoch from which they henceforth dated the years of the newly-restored earth, that is, of the new era which they had just entered.

The mighty changes which nations underwent entirely upset their calculations relating to those remote times; but the Hindus, settled as they were in a country long exempt from the revolutionary troubles that agitated other countries, have been able to preserve intact the tradition of those events.

Their ordinary cycle is of sixty years, but they have also adopted another of ninety years, used in astronomical calculations. The latter is a much more recent invention, and was introduced at the time of the death of a famous king of India, named Salivahana, who reigned over a province then called Sagam, and who died at the end of the first century of the Christian era. It should be remarked that the use of these two different cycles could never occasion the least confusion in point of dates, since a period of three ordinary cycles corresponds to a period of two astronomical cycles, and they both start from the same epoch.

The Chinese, likewise, have an ordinary cycle of sixty years in common with the Hindus ; but there is this difference between the two : the Chinese, according to Du Halde, are ignorant as to when their era commenced, at least with reference to the epoch of the Flood. On the other hand, it is hardly likely that the two nations could have communicated with each other on this subject, seeing that they do not agree in their computations. According to the author just quoted, the birth of our Saviour falls on the fifty-eighth year of the Chinese cycle, while it coincides with the forty-second year of the Hindu cycle. But this coincidence, nevertheless, goes to confirm the high antiquity of the cycle of sixty years still in use with the two most ancient races on the face of the earth.

It would be quite useless to inquire whether this cycle was adopted before the Flood, and whether it was from Noah or his immediate descendants that the Hindus and Chinese learned its use. We do know for certain, however, that the weekly period was known prior to this remarkable event, and that the Hindu week agrees exactly with that of the Hebrews and with ours. Indeed, the days of their week correspond exactly with those of ours, and bear similar names.

One peculiar circumstance is that just as every day of the Hindu week has its own particular name, so has each of the sixty years of a cycle. Thus, they do not say like us that a certain event happened, say, on the twentieth or thirtieth year before or after such an era. But they give the year its particular name, and say, for example, that such an event happened in the year *Kilasa*, in the year *Bhava*, in the year *Vikary*, and so forth.

The only real difficulty is that the Hindu computation with regard to the epoch of the Flood does not appear to correspond with that of Holy Scripture.

But it should be remembered that there is a difference of more than nine hundred years between the period supposed to have elapsed between the Flood and the Birth of Christ according to the Septuagint on the one hand, and according to the Vulgate on the other hand. Yet neither of these calculations is wholly rejected, and both of them are supported by able chronologists. The Catholic Church, which adheres to the Vulgate for the Old Testament, adopts the calculation of the Septuagint for the Roman Martyrology, which forms part of its liturgy. The difference, therefore, between the Hindu calculation and ours does not appear a sufficient reason for rejecting it, or even for supposing that it does not proceed from the same source.

According to Hindu calculations, the time that elapsed between the Deluge and the Birth of Jesus Christ is 3,102 years. This period differs from that laid down in the Vulgate by about 770 years; but it approaches much nearer to the calculations made in the Septuagint, which gives 3,258 years between the Deluge and the commencement of the Christian era. If we accept this last calculation, the epoch of the Hindu *Jala-pralayam* does not differ from that of the Deluge of the Holy Scriptures by more than 156 years, a discrepancy of no great importance, considering the intricacy of a computation which dates from such remote times. I am, therefore, fully convinced that the Hindu computation serves to corroborate the accuracy of the event as narrated by Moses, and adds incontestable evidence to prove that most important event, the Universal Deluge.

Some modern chronologists, with the learned Tournemine at their head, who based their calculations on the Vulgate, have professed to reckon between the Deluge and the Christian era a period of 3,234 years, and they have supported their calculations with substantial arguments. Their learned investigations in this direction excited even in those days the admiration of competent critics. In relying, therefore, on this calculation, we have a difference of only 132 years between the Hindu computation and that of Holy Scripture as regards the Deluge.

Deucalion's Flood does not approach so near the Universal Deluge of Scripture as the *Jala-pralayam* of the Hindus. All the critics place the former so near the Birth of Jesus Christ that its comparative modernness alone is quite sufficient to prove that it has not even been borrowed from other ancient nations. The Flood of Ogyges, the occurrence of which is generally placed in the year 248 before that of Deucalion, is, however, posterior by more than twelve hundred years to the Universal Deluge, according to the Hindu calculations of the *Jala-pralayam*. We have, therefore, fresh evidence that the Flood of Ogyges and that of Deucalion were only partial inundations, if indeed they are not altogether mythical.

CHAPTER XXV

The Epistolary Style of the Brahmins.—Hindu Handwriting.

THE epistolary style of the Brahmins and of Hindus in general is in many respects so different from ours that a few specimens may be not uninteresting to many of my readers.

Letter to an Inferior.

'They, the Brahmin Soobayah, to him the Brahmin Lakshmana, who possesses all kinds of good qualities, who is graced with all the virtues, who is true to his word, who, by the services he renders to his relations and friends, resembles the *Chintamani*[1]. *Asirvadam*[2]!

'The year *Kilasa*, the fourth day of the month of *Phalguna*, I am at Dharmapuri and in good health. I am very anxious to have news of thee.

'As soon as this letter reaches thee, thou must go to that most excellent and most virtuous Brahmin Anantayah, and, prostrating thyself at full length at his feet, thou must offer him my most humble respects.

'And then, without delay, thou must present thyself before the *chetty* (merchant) Rangapah, and declare to him frankly on my behalf that if he will now place in thy hands the three thousand rupees which he owes me, with the interest due thereon at thirty per cent., I will forget all that has passed, and the matter shall be finally settled. But if, on the contrary, he makes excuses and puts off the payment of the said amount, including interest, tell him that I am acquainted with certain efficacious means of teaching him that no person shall with impunity break

[1] This is a mythical stone which is supposed to procure every blessing for those who possess it.—DUBOIS.

[2] The word *Asirvadam* means 'blessing.'—ED.

his word with a Brahmin such as I am. This is all I have to say to thee. *Asirvadam*!'

Letter to an Equal.

'To them, the lords, the lords Ramayah[1], who possess all those good qualities and virtues which render a man esteemed; who are worthy of all the favours which the gods can bestow; who are the particular favourites of the goddess Lakshmi; who are great as Mount Meru; who possess a perfect knowledge of the *Yajur-Veda*; they, the Brahmin Soobayah. *Namaskaram*[2]!

'The year *Durmati*, the fifteenth of the month of *Veishaka*, I and all the members of my family being in the enjoyment of good health. I shall learn with great pleasure that it is the same with you; and I trust you will let me know in detail all the matters which give you joy and contentment.

'The twenty-second of the above-mentioned month being a day on which all the good omens are combined, we have selected it for the commencement of the marriage festivities of my daughter Vijaya-Lakshmi. I beg you will be good enough to be present here before that day, and to bring with you all the members of your household without excepting any. I beg that you will place yourself at the head of the ceremony, and that you will be pleased to conduct it[3].

'Lastly, if there is anything in which I can be of service to you, I request you will be pleased to let me know. *Namaskaram*!'

Letter to a Superior.

'To them, the lords, the Brahmin lords, the great Brahmins Lakshmanayah, who are endowed with every virtue; who are great as Mount Meru; who possess a perfect knowledge of the four Vedas; who, by the splendour of their good works, shine forth like the sun; whose renown is known throughout the

[1] A superior and even an equal is always addressed in the plural, both in speaking and writing. This is a rule invariably observed among the well-bred.—DUBOIS.

[2] *Namaskaram* means 'respectful greeting.'—DUBOIS.

[3] This is an expression used merely out of politeness in the case of every one who is invited under similar circumstances.—DUBOIS.

fourteen worlds, and who are highly praised therein:—I, Krishnayah, their humble servant and slave, keeping myself at a respectful distance from them, with both hands joined, my mouth closed, my eyes cast down, my head bent—I wait in this humble posture, until they may vouchsafe to cast their eyes on one who is nothing in their presence. After obtaining their leave, approaching them with fear and respect, and prostrating myself on the ground at their feet, which are in reality *tamarasa* (lotus) flowers; after saluting those feet with profound respect and kissing them, I address to them the following humble supplication:—

'The year *Vikary*, the twentieth of the month *Pushya*, I, your most humble slave, whom you have deigned to look upon as some chattel, having received with both hands the letter which your excellency humbled yourself by writing to me, having kissed it and put it on my head, I afterwards read it with all possible attention and care. Your excellency may rest assured that I will execute punctually the orders contained in it, without departing from them by the breadth of a grain of sesamum. The business mentioned in the letter has already been fairly begun, and I hope that by the efficacy of your excellency's benediction it will soon terminate to your excellency's honour and advantage. As soon as it is finished, I, your most humble servant and slave, shall not fail to present myself at your excellency's feet to receive your orders.

'Lastly, I entreat your excellency to impart to me the commands and instructions necessary to enable me to act in a manner agreeable to your excellency, and to point out to me in what way I may render myself most acceptable to your sacred feet, which are real *tamarasa* flowers. For this purpose it will not be necessary for your excellency to humble yourself still more by writing to me a second time; but it will suffice if I receive from your excellency's bounty a leaf of betel indented with your nail, through some confidential person who can verbally explain to me the orders of your excellency[1].

'Such is my most humble prayer.'

The complimentary expressions used at the beginning of all

[1] This device frequently serves for credentials in conveying verbal messages.—DUBOIS.

these letters, and the humble and servile tone which pervades them, especially the third letter, present when translated sufficiently remarkable examples of epistolary style, yet I have by no means brought out the full force, or rather the extreme platitude, of all these expressions.

Our language has no equivalents for the expressions of base flattery and humility with which the Hindus are so lavish in their correspondence. These expressions are, moreover, used with a certain amount of moderation in the letters just quoted. I have seen some the complimentary preface alone of which would have filled two pages of this book. The eloquence of a writer is inexhaustible under this head, especially when there is any question of obtaining some boon or favour. A petitioner can, indeed, without fear of seeing it thrown back in his face,—

> 'A son héros, dans un bizarre ouvrage,
> Donner de l'encensoir au travers du visage.'

The thicker the smoke of the incense the more does it flatter him to whom it is offered.

In letters written by one Hindu to another, one never finds respectful assurances or compliments offered to a wife. The mere mention of her in a letter would be considered not simply as an indiscretion, but as a gross breach of politeness, at which the husband would have every reason to feel aggrieved.

When one Hindu has occasion to communicate to another the death of one of his relatives, the custom is to slightly burn the end of the palm-leaf on which the afflicting news is written; and this is similar to the black seal used by us in such cases. The same practice is observed as a sign of displeasure, when one has occasion to administer a severe reprimand in writing.

When a superior writes to an inferior, he puts his own name before that of the person to whom he writes. The reverse is the case when an inferior writes to a superior. Any breach of this token of civility on the part of an inferior would be considered a dire insult by the person to whom he owed respect. Politeness also requires that, when writing to an equal, you should place your own name last.

Having said this much on the epistolary style of the Hindus,

I will now offer some notes that I have collected on their handwriting.

Learned European scholars have made endless researches as to the origin of the art of writing, the manner in which it was transmitted by one people to another, the different characters used, and the various kinds of tablets and other materials employed. Many conjectures have been offered concerning the systems invented by the Chinese and the Egyptians to transmit their ideas otherwise than verbally. The languages of India, however, seem to have escaped the learned investigations of philologists. Nevertheless, a careful study of these languages would, if I am not mistaken, throw a good deal of light on questions still shrouded in uncertainty. I have not the slightest pretensions to having discovered any new origin of written language, nor have I the vain presumption of depriving the Phoenician Cadmus of the glory of having invented the elementary principles of—

> 'Cet art ingénieux
> De peindre la parole et de parler aux yeux
> Et par les traits divers de figures tracées
> Donner de la couleur et du corps aux pensées.'

I shall think myself fortunate enough if what I am about to say be considered worthy of the attention of the learned, and if it present some points of interest to those who are fond of discovering traces of primitive times in the usages that still exist.

The Hindu books attribute the credit of this invaluable invention to the great Brahma, the creator of men and the sovereign arbiter of their destinies. The serrated sutures to be seen on a skull are, they say, nothing less than the handwriting of Brahma himself; and these indelible characters, traced by his divine hand, contain the irrevocable decrees regulating the destiny of each individual of the human race. It may be urged that this Hindu belief is a mere myth, and, as such, cannot be regarded as the basis of any reasonable conjectures. I am of the same opinion; but it must also be admitted that it is one of the oldest myths of India, and it proves at any rate that when it was invented the knowledge of writing already existed. Otherwise how could the Hindus of those remote times have discovered traces of writing in these marks on skulls? Another fact, or another myth, if one prefers to call it so, may be said to corroborate this. The four Vedas are considered to be the work of the god Brahma, who wrote them with his own hand on leaves of gold. These books, which contain the ritual of the idolatrous ceremonies practised by these people, are held by them in great veneration, and their high antiquity is nowhere called into question. Other books, too, many of which are undoubtedly very old, speak of the Vedas as of a far earlier date. Moreover, the language in which they are written has become unintelligible in many places. The Vedas, indeed, by whomsoever they may have been written, conclusively prove that the origin of Hindu writing dates from a period which is lost in remote antiquity.

One of the principal articles of the Hindu faith is that relating to the ten *Avatars*, or incarnations, of Vishnu. The first and earliest is called the *Matsya-avatar*, that is, the incarnation of the god in the form of a fish. And what was the cause of it? It was the loss of the four books of the Vedas. Brahma, under whose care they were left, fell asleep, and a giant, his enemy, availed himself of the opportunity to steal the sacred volumes. Having escaped unperceived, the giant hid himself in the sea with his precious booty, which he swallowed, thinking it would be safer in his bowels. Vishnu, having been informed of what had happened, changed himself into a fish, and went in pursuit of this enemy of the gods. After a long search, he at length discovered the giant in the deepest abyss of the ocean. He attacked him, vanquished him, and tore him in pieces. He then plucked the hidden books from the giant's entrails, and restored them to the god who was their author and guardian.

Is there anything to be found in any books of ours whose unquestionable antiquity is recognized by European writers that might be said to compare with this fable, any indication of sources from which it could have been borrowed, thus proving its modern date? I think not.

Some of the Hindu authors ascribe the invention of writing to a famous Penitent called Agastya, who, it is said, was not taller than a hand's breadth. He is one of the most ancient persons recognized by the Hindus, inasmuch as they make him contemporary with the seven Penitents who were saved from the Flood in the ark, of which Vishnu himself was the pilot.

Again, the Gymnosophists, or naked penitents of India, have never been regarded as mythical personages. Even in the time of Lycurgus, that is to say, nearly nine hundred years before the Christian era, these philosophers enjoyed such a reputation for wisdom and learning that their fame had spread to countries far remote from their own. There is every reason to believe that their fame could only have been established gradually, and that their philosophy dated from a very remote period. True, some authors assert that their philosophy was handed down by oral tradition, and that they never committed anything to writing. It is, however, hard to believe that men who gave themselves up to the study of philosophy and astronomy could have done so without having recourse to written records.

Be this as it may, I will now briefly describe the present style of writing among the Hindus, mentioning (1) the written characters used, (2) the materials on which they are recorded, (3) the manner in which they are written, and (4) the shape of their books and of the communications which they address to each other.

It is generally stated that there are eighteen living languages in use in India; but as a matter of fact there are many more. All, or at any rate the majority of them, have their own distinct alphabetical characters. It is true that some of these characters, if carefully examined, bear a very close resemblance to each other; but in the majority of them one can distinguish no similarities. Yet, however diversified may be the characters employed in writing, there are many similarities to be observed in pronunciation and phraseology. In all these languages the arrangement of words admits of few changes or differences. In this particular they differ widely from the European languages, which, with a general resemblance in their alphabetical characters, admit of large variations in construction and phraseology.

What resemblance could, for instance, be found between the letters

அ	ஆ	த
(*a* short)	(*a* long)	(*tha*)

of the Tamil language and the letters

అ	ఆ	త
(*a* short)	(*a* long)	(*tha*)

of the Telugu language? And the difference is not less striking in the other letters of the alphabet. Yet these two languages are spoken in countries bordering on each other, which in other respects present many points of resemblance. The same diversity with regard to alphabets is noticeable in other Indian languages.

Other facts worthy of note are that in all the languages of India (1) the letters are arranged in the same order; (2) the short and long vowels are always placed at the beginning of the alphabet and before the consonants; (3) these vowels are purely initial letters, which are never written except at the beginning of a word, special inflections being assigned to them when used in the middle of a word or after a consonant; (4) each consonant must have a vowel inflection: thus, *b*, *c* are pronounced *ba*, *ca*, and their form is changed when other vowel inflections are substituted. For instance, in Canarese the following letters change their form according to the vowel inflections to which they are subject, thus:—

ಬ	ಬೆ	ಬಿ	ದ	ದೆ	ದಿ	ಧೊ	ಧು
ba	*be*	*bi*	*tha*	*they*	*thee*	*dho*	*dhu*

How is it that there is so much resemblance between the various idioms of these languages, and so much dissimilarity between the letters of their alphabets? Sanskrit appears to be the common type on which the other languages have modelled their phraseology; how comes it then that they have, in opposition to the mother-tongue, adopted letter formations so different from that of their common parent?

Similar variations are observable in the forms of their ciphers or symbols. Though they all use the decimal notation, they differ widely in the formation of their arithmetical figures. In the Tamil language, each decimal number is denoted by a different sign, thus:—

௧	௰	௱	௲
1	10	100	1000

In Telugu and in most of the other languages of the country, they follow exactly the system which we have adopted from the Arabs, the units being expressed by a single figure, the tens by two, the hundreds by three, the thousands by four, and so on.

This method, with the exception of a few slight differences in the shape of the figures, is the one most commonly used. The similarity which exists between this method and that of the Arabs can hardly have been the result of chance. If one nation did not borrow it from the other, it is at any rate probable that both borrowed it from the same source.

The Tamil arithmetical symbols seem, however, to bear a greater resemblance to the Roman than to the Arabic numerals. Like the Romans, the Tamils express the greater part of their arithmetical signs by letters of the alphabet, and use only a single letter to denote units, tens, hundreds, and thousands as stated above.

But, dissimilar as are the written characters of the various Hindu languages, they are still more dissimilar to the written characters known to us as used by other ancient nations, such as Syriac, Hebrew, Arabic, Greek, &c. Unlike the majority of Oriental languages, which are written from right to left, Sanskrit and the various dialects of India are written, like the European languages, from left to right.

Paper is not unknown to the Hindus. They manufacture it, not from cotton rags, as is generally believed, but from the fibre of the aloe. I am, however, inclined to believe that the use of this coarse paper is of comparatively recent date in India, subsequent, that is, to the invasion of the Moghuls, who must have introduced it. At any rate, following the example of the Moghuls, the Hindus living in the interior of the country, where palm leaves are not procurable, use paper instead. But more generally they use black tablets named *kadatta*, on which they write with a white pencil, called in Canarese *balapu*, made of a calcareous quarried stone which is very common in the country. And it is with these materials that children learn writing in the schools.

Nevertheless the ordinary practice almost everywhere is to write on palm leaves, of which there are two species, large and small. The latter are the commoner and are said to be the better; they are about three inches wide and two feet long. Seven or eight lines can be written on each leaf. They are thicker, stiffer, and stouter than double paper, so that one can easily write, or rather engrave, on both sides of them. The other kinds of leaves are broader, but not so strong. They are therefore used only in those places where the smaller kinds are not easily procurable. They are sometimes used specially as a mark of respect when writing to a person of rank. The island of Ceylon produces an enormous quantity of the smaller leaves, and they are so cheap that a halfpenny's worth of them would be sufficient for copying an entire folio vo'ume.

Quintus Curtius relates that the Hindus, at the time of the invasion of Alexander the Great, wrote with an iron *stilus* on the soft and smooth bark of trees. It is quite probable that palm leaves were mistaken for the bark of trees; for nowhere in India can any evidence be found to prove that the bark of trees has ever been used for the purpose of writing.

Aeneas, in Virgil's epic, implores the Cumaean Sibyl not to write her oracles on the leaves of trees, which the winds might speedily disperse:

> 'Foliis tantum ne carmina manda,
> Ne turbata volent rapidis ludibria ventis.'

All the commentators are of opinion that the reference here is to palm leaves. It is therefore to be presumed that these leaves were quite different from those now used in India, which, on account of their weight and thickness, could not be blown about by the wind.

The Hindus write with an iron *stilus*, or pencil, which is from eight to nine inches long. The handle of the instrument generally ends in a knife, which is used to trim the sides of the leaves so as to make them all of one size. In writing with the *stilus* neither chair nor table is required. The leaf is supported on the middle finger of the left hand, and is kept steady by being held firmly between the thumb and the forefinger. The *stilus*, in writing, does not glide along the leaf, as does our pen on paper; but the writer, after finishing a word or two, fixes the point of his instrument on the last letter, and pushes the leaf from right to left till the line of writing is finished. This is executed with such ease that it is by no means a rare sight to see Hindus writing as they walk along.

As the characters thus traced are only a sort of faint engraving, of the same colour as the leaf itself, and therefore not easily decipherable, it is the common practice to besmear the whole with fresh cow-dung. The leaf is afterwards wiped clean, but the new material fills up the engraved letters and gives them a darker colour, thus rendering them more distinct and readable.

This mode of writing is undoubtedly more convenient and more simple than ours, so far at least as writing on a small scale is concerned, for it does not require all the materials that we need on such occasions; but it will be readily understood that it is not equally convenient for writings of a somewhat voluminous nature.

As in our ancient manuscripts, the absence of every kind of punctuation, and the confusion arising from words and phrases not being sufficiently separated, render the perusal of the works of Hindu authors extremely difficult. The complicated rules of orthography pertaining to some of their languages, and especially to Tamil, tend to increase this difficulty still further. Very often the most experienced person is unable to read without difficulty, especially if the writer has adhered strictly to the rules of grammar, which are generally, however, either ignored or neglected.

When Hindus write on paper they do not use a quill pen. A Brahmin could not, without defilement, touch so impure an instrument. Consequently a thin reed is used, called *kalam*, a word evidently of modern origin borrowed from the Portuguese. The *kalam* is somewhat thicker than our quill pen, and is mended in the same manner. Hindus employed under Europeans, however, lay aside these scruples, and use the same materials as their masters.

When a Hindu wishes to make up a book of the palm leaves on which he has written, he has no need of a bookbinder. He merely bores a small hole at each extremity of the leaves, and fastens them all together by means of two small pegs or sticks of wood or iron. Two thin boards, of the same length and breadth as the leaves, are then placed at the top and bottom of them, and thus form the binding or covers of the book. A long string fastened to one of the covers serves to hold the leaves together. If this plan is simple, it certainly is not convenient; for whenever one wishes to consult the book, the string must be loosened, the pegs by means of which the leaves are strung together must be removed, and the whole volume taken to pieces.

It will thus be seen that the Hindu system of writing and of binding books closely resembles that of the ancient Romans, who wrote on extremely thin wooden boards, which they strung together and formed into a *codex.*

The following is the plan adopted by the Hindus in the transmission of letters:—They roll up the palm leaves on which they are written, and put them into an outer covering, upon which they write the address. At the junction of the two ends of the outer leaf, which are held together by means of a small incision in each, a kind of rough knot is made, serving as a seal. Due attention must be paid to the length and breadth of the leaves on which letters are written, which vary according to the rank and dignity of those to whom they are addressed.

To be the bearer of a letter denotes a kind of subordinate position. This duty cannot therefore be entrusted to superiors, or even to equals, unless they undertake it voluntarily. In the latter case, etiquette forbids the letter being given into the hands of the person who has offered to deliver it; the missive must be placed on the ground at his feet, and he picks it up and becomes responsible for its safe delivery.

The changes in the form of writing which time brings about in other countries do not offer a safe ground for conjecture in the case of Hindu manuscripts. I have seen a deed of gift written more than two hundred years ago on a plate of gold in Canarese characters, the letters of which were perfectly legible and exactly like those at present in use, the form of writing having undergone no change whatever during that long interval of time.

Nevertheless there are certain monuments in the country of very great antiquity, bearing inscriptions engraved in characters no longer in use. Some are also to be found in various places the characters of which are wholly unknown and evidently foreign. I must leave this matter to our learned philologists; as for myself, I admit that I am unable to explain the fact.

The remarks I have made above concerning the dissimilarity of the written characters and the resemblance of the grammatical style in the various Indian languages are equally applicable to Siamese. At least, so it has been pointed out to me by persons who are familiar with that language, and who have discovered in its alphabet an arrangement exactly similar to that of the Hindu alphabets. In some languages of India the sign or inflection denoting the vowel that always accompanies a consonant is placed before it; the same practice is followed with regard to several letters in Siamese writing. Like the Hindus, the Siamese write from left to right. This coincidence can hardly be alleged to be the result of chance; it rather indicates some common origin.

The investigations of modern authors with regard to this subject leave no doubt whatever that the *Pali* language, or the learned tongue of Siam, is a corrupt form of the Sanskrit. And this mother-tongue appears to have extended even still farther, since we find a large number of Sanskrit words in the Malay language.

However, in shape the Siamese letters as written appeared to me to bear no resemblance whatever to the Hindu alphabets with which I was acquainted.

CHAPTER XXVI

Hindu Fables.

THE Hindus are particularly fond of poetry and fiction, and their literature contains a large collection of interesting fables. Some of these fables possess a moral significance and are very popular; while others are merely stories, of no great value from a literary point of view. I have, however, selected a few stories which appeared to me calculated to interest my readers, and a collection of them will be found in the next chapter.

The fables are to be found in large numbers in various Hindu books. They are generally based on excellent moral principles, and contain some severe criticisms on the vices of men. The following I have heard related many times:—

'A traveller, having missed his way, was overtaken by darkness in the midst of a dense forest. In fear of wild beasts, he decided that the only means of escaping them would be to spend the night in the branches of one of the largest trees which he could find. He therefore climbed into a tree, and, without further thought of the dangers which might befall him, fell fast asleep, and awoke only when the rays of the morning sun warned him that it was time to continue his journey. As he was preparing to descend, he cast his eyes downwards, and espied at the foot of the tree a huge tiger eagerly and impatiently watching, as it were, for its prey. Struck with terror at the sight of the beast, the traveller remained for a while transfixed to the spot where he sat. At length, recovering himself a little and looking all round him, he observed that near the tree on which he sat were many others, with their branches so interlaced that he could easily pass from one to another, and thus escape the danger which threatened him below. He was on the point of making his escape in this way, when, raising his eyes, he saw a huge snake hanging to the branch immediately over him, with its head nearly touching his own. The snake was apparently fast asleep, but the slightest noise might rouse it. At the sight of this twofold danger to which he found himself exposed the poor traveller lost all courage. His mind wandered, his trembling limbs could hardly support him, and he was on the point of falling into the clutches of the tiger which was watching for him below. Chilled with fright, he remained motionless in face of the cruel death that awaited him, expecting every moment to be his last. The unfortunate man, however, having somewhat recovered his senses, once more raised his eyes, and perceived, on one of the topmost branches of the tree, a honeycomb, from which sweet drops of honey were trickling down at his side. Thereupon he stretched forward his head, opened his mouth, and put out his tongue to catch the drops of honey as they fell; and in this delicious enjoyment he thought no more of the awful dangers which surrounded him.'

Besides the detached apologues to be found in their books, which they are very fond of alluding to in their everyday conversations, the Hindus have a regular collection of old and popular fables called *Pancha-tantra* (the Five Tricks), which have been translated into all the languages of the country[1]. It

[1] Two volumes of these fables, translated by the Abbé, were published in Paris in 1872 and 1877, twenty years after his death.

The East, the land of myth and legend, is the natural home of the fable, and Hindustan was the birthplace, if not of the original of these tales, at least of the oldest shape in which they still exist. The *Pancha-tantra* have been translated into almost every language, and adapted by most modern fabulists The *Kalila wa Damna* (from the names of two jackals in the first story), or fables of Bidpai or Pilpay, is an Arab version made about 760 A.D. From the Hebrew version of Rabbi Joel, John of Capua produced a Latin translation about the end of the fifteenth century, whence all later imitations are derived. The *Hitopadesa*, or 'friendly instruction,' is a modernized form of the same work, and of it there are three translations into English by Dr. Charles Wilkins, Sir William Jones, and Professor F. Johnson.

From Hindustan the Sanskrit fables passed to China, Thibet, and Persia; and they must have reached Greece at an early date, for many of the fables which passed under the name of Aesop are identical with those of the East. Aesop to us is little more than a name, though, if we may trust a passing notice in Herodotus, he must have lived in the sixth century B.C. Probably his fables were never written

is perhaps the only literary work possessed by them which is instructive and worthy of attention. All castes, without any distinction whatever, are allowed to read it. The moral of some of these fables might possibly seem dangerous, because calculated to teach how to do evil rather than how to avoid it; but, speaking generally, their teachings are praiseworthy enough.

The first of these fables of the *Pancha-tantra* explains how impostors and clever knaves succeed by artifice and falsehood in causing harm to persons whom they wish to ruin, or in sowing dissension among the most intimate of friends. The object which the author has in view appears to be to warn princes and other great personages, for whose instruction, by the way, the work seems to be principally written, against the intrigues of mean parasites and hypocritical courtiers who throng their palaces, and who, by base flattery, calumny, deceit, and intrigue, succeed in ruining and supplanting their best friends and most faithful servants.

The following is a short *résumé* of the story:—

In the city of Patali-puram there reigned a king called Suka Darusha, who had a faithful minister named Amara-Sati. This good prince had three sons, who were noted for their stupidity and vulgarity, and who were viewed by their father with the most extreme dissatisfaction. The minister Amara-Sati, conscious of the sorrow which was preying on his master, advised him to convene a general meeting of all the Brahmins of his kingdom, in order to ascertain whether there was not one amongst them who would undertake the responsibility of educating the three young princes and instilling into them feelings more worthy of their high birth. The minister's advice was followed; but of all the assembled Brahmins there was only one, named Vishnu-Sarma[1], who felt himself capable of accomplishing so difficult a task.

Vishnu-Sarma, after carefully studying the characters and dispositions of his pupils, began the work of reformation; and in order to accomplish his task, related to them a large number

down, though several are ascribed to him by Xenophon, Aristotle, Plutarch, and other Greek writers, and Plato represents Socrates as beguiling his last days by versifying such as he remembered.—ED.

[1] In the Telugu copy he is called *Soma Jenma*.—DUBOIS.

of fables, the lessons of which he took great pains to instil into their minds.

The *dramatis personae* of the first of these fables are a lion holding sway in a vast forest, a bull named Sanjivaka, and two foxes, one called Damanaka and the other Karataka, both in the service of the lion king.

The bull Sanjivaka had been accidentally lost by his master in the lion king's forest, where he was leading a peaceful, harmless life. Now the two foxes, as it happened, had been disgraced and ignominiously expelled from the court of the lion. One day the lion was quenching his thirst in the river Jumna, which flowed through the forest, when suddenly, while returning to his cave, he heard a most frightful noise like thunder, the like of which he had never heard before. It was in fact the bellowing of the bull Sanjivaka. Seized with sudden fear, and believing that an animal which was able to utter such a dreadful noise must assuredly be vastly superior to himself, the lion was consumed with dread lest a rival had come to dispute his forest kingdom. Greatly troubled in his mind, he reflected how he might get rid of this imaginary danger. While in this dilemma, a happy thought struck him: it was to reconcile himself with his former ministers, the two foxes, who might possibly help him with their advice. He therefore sent messengers to them, beseeching them to resume their former posts in his court, and promising to honour them in future with unbounded confidence.

Karataka and Damanaka, aware of the real reason of their recall to the king's court, affected the greatest indifference with regard to the offers made to them. Before complying with the request of the monarch, they calculated all the possible consequences of such a reconciliation; and with this in view they related to each other a number of stories bearing on the advantages and inconveniences that might result from their return to the king's court. Suffice it to say they at last decided to accept the lion's offer, and accordingly waited upon him.

The monarch welcomed the two foxes with much cordiality, and confessed to them the alarming fears which assailed him and the cause thereof. Without further delay he deputed them, after giving them the necessary instructions, to wait upon the rival who had caused him such uneasiness. The object of their mission, they were informed, was to fathom the designs of this unknown personage, and, if he had come thither with hostile intentions, to inquire of him on what conditions he was willing to live in peace with the titular monarch.

The two foxes immediately went in search of the formidable Sanjivaka, and at last found him grazing peacefully on the borders of the river Jumna. At sight of him the two plenipotentiaries gazed at each other with astonishment and burst into loud fits of laughter, for they could not understand how the presence in the forest of a poor helpless bull, forsaken by his owner, could possibly cause so much anxiety to their master. After thinking the matter over, they decided to make the best of it by encouraging the lion in his fears, and thereby increasing the importance and value of their mediation. Their plan being well pondered over, they went up to the bull Sanjivaka and haughtily told him that the place he had chosen for his abode was the dominion of a lion, whose authority extended throughout the forest. They rated him severely for his daring conduct, and told him that he was running a great risk of falling a victim to the anger of the king of the forest. 'But,' added they, 'as the lion is of a generous disposition, we will persuade him to pardon you and to take you under his protection. Come along with us to him, and above all be very careful to show proper respect and humility in his presence.'

Returning to the lion, the two foxes began to make the most of their services. In their opinion the bull Sanjivaka was all that he was supposed to be; and moreover he had the reputation of being passionate, hot-tempered, distrustful, and obstinate. 'But,' added they, 'by dint of skill and persuasion we have succeeded in inducing him to be your intimate friend and faithful ally.' The bull was at this stage introduced to the lion, who deemed himself extremely fortunate in having, by the mediation of his two ministers the foxes, gained the alliance of so powerful a friend.

Sanjivaka was not long in gaining the favour of his royal master, whose full and unbounded confidence he soon won by his gentleness, obedience, and other good qualities.

Accordingly the two foxes were once more forsaken by their master, and found themselves obliged to live in obscurity and dishonour, as formerly. Sanjivaka, without even aspiring to any such honour, had become the channel and medium through whom all favours were bestowed by the king. Thereupon Karataka and Damanaka perceived that they had made a great mistake in introducing this stranger to the lion's court. The ruin of their rival was evidently the only means by which they could hope to regain their former influence. But finding themselves too weak to get rid of their enemy by force, they resolved to achieve their object by artifice and intrigue. Accordingly they prepared themselves for the task by telling each other a great many fables, the main purpose of which was to show what one could accomplish by bringing into play at the proper season the active powers of an intriguing mind.

Having skilfully devised a plan of attack, they succeeded in finding their way once again into the king's court; and concealing their wicked intentions under a guise of zeal and attachment to their master's interests, they succeeded by dint of slander and other machinations in poisoning the mind of the lion with a deep distrust of the bull Sanjivaka. At last the king, really persuaded that his quiet and well-behaved favourite cherished the design of secretly getting rid of him, in order that he might usurp the dominion of the forest, fell upon the unfortunate Sanjivaka and tore him to pieces.

The moral of the second fable of the *Pancha-tantra* is to show the advantages of union and friendship among the weak in times of trouble or danger. It tells the story of a dove, a rat, a raven, a gazelle, and a tortoise, who, by simply helping one another, escaped the greatest dangers.

The third fable tells the story of the crows and the owls. It sets forth the dangers to which a person is exposed by confiding his private affairs to those whose character he is not well acquainted with, or to those who, after having for a long time been avowed enemies, return under the deceitful mask of friendship. It relates how a crow, by his cunning and hypocrisy, succeeded in stealing his way into the society of owls, the declared enemies of his race, and in winning their entire confidence. Thereupon, the crow made the best of this opportunity to study their habits, their resources, and their strong and weak points, until he was able to devise a safe means of attacking and exterminating them. For instance, he soon found out that their common abode was a vast cave, which possessed only one entrance. He also discovered that his hated foes experienced insurmountable difficulty in facing the light of the sun. Furnished with this valuable information, he hastened to convene a general meeting of the crows. He counselled them all to take in their beaks as much straw, twigs, and other combustible material as they could carry and to follow him quietly. Accordingly some thousands of his fellows spread their wings and arrived at midday near the cave, where the owls, their enemies, were slumbering in fancied security. The crows heaped up before the entrance of the cave the inflammable material they had brought with them and set fire to it all. The majority of the owls were instantly suffocated by the smoke, while those which attempted to fly away perished in the flames.

A monkey and a crocodile are the characters represented in the fourth fable. It illustrates the dangers to which one is exposed by associating with wicked persons whose friendship and affection, however sincere they may appear to be to start with, result sooner or later in treachery, especially if their own interests are at stake. This is the attitude manifested by the crocodile towards his friend, the monkey, who had reposed the utmost confidence in him. The monkey, however, succeeds in evading by his cunning the treacherous plot which the crocodile devised for his destruction.

The fifth fable is about a Brahmin and his mongoose, and illustrates the imprudence of judging rashly by appearances. A Brahmin once possessed a mongoose, to which his wife and himself were very much attached. The same Brahmin had a child which was still in the cradle. One day, being obliged to leave the house on some very pressing business, and there being nobody to take care of the child, the Brahmin entrusted it to his mongoose, telling the little animal that it would have to answer with its life for any accident that might happen to the infant during his absence. As soon as the Brahmin had gone out, the mongoose took up its place quite close to the cradle, determined to perish rather than permit the slightest injury to the precious being entrusted to its care. Now it happened that a huge snake had, unobserved, found its way into the house by a crevice in the wall. Issuing from its hiding-place, it approached the cradle and prepared to attack the child. The mongoose no sooner perceived the frightful reptile than it rushed furiously upon it, and, after a long and painful struggle, seized it by the throat, strangled it, and in its rage tore it to pieces. Soon afterwards the Brahmin returned. The mongoose, recognizing the voice of its master, ran to him and tried to express its joy by rolling at his feet, playfully biting at his legs, showing indeed every manifestation of delight at having performed such a brave deed. The Brahmin, however, having carefully examined the mongoose, and finding it covered with the blood which had flowed from the wounds of the serpent, rashly concluded that the blood could only be that of his infant child, whom, as he thought, the mongoose had killed; and, in a fit of rage, he seized a thick stick which was close by and killed the poor animal on the spot.

However, what were his grief and despair when on entering the room where he had left his child, he found it calmly sleeping; while around the cradle were the scattered remains of the huge snake which the mongoose had just killed! He bitterly reproached himself for his imprudence and rashness, but, alas! too late; and was grieved sorely at the thought that he had inconsiderately sacrificed the poor animal, to whom alone he was indebted for the preservation of his beloved son[1].

The author of the *Pancha-tantra* has introduced into these five principal fables a large number of minor fables which are related by the respective characters to each other. Some of these latter resemble those of Aesop, but are far more prolix. The *Pancha-tantra* is so constructed that one fable, before it is finished, suggests another, which in its turn suggests a third, and so on. A great deal of ingenuity is displayed in this plan of narration; but the continuous dovetailing of one story into another is very wearisome to the reader, who sometimes loses sight altogether of the beginning of a story, which only ends later on in the work.

A literal translation of a few of these fables will give my readers a fair idea of the rest of them. The following are extracted from the first part of the *Pancha-tantra*:—

[1] A tale exactly similar to this has been long current in Europe. It has been told both in story-books and pictures. The circumstances are exactly the same, with the exception that the animal which fell a victim to the rashness of its master is a dog instead of a mongoose.—DUBOIS.

THE ADVENTURES OF THE BRAHMIN KALA-SARMA.

The Brahmin and the Crab.

Once upon a time, in the city of Soma-Puri, there lived a Brahmin named Kala-Sarma, who, after existing for a long time in penury, suddenly found himself raised to opulence by a happy combination of circumstances. He thereupon resolved to undertake a pilgrimage to the holy city of Benares, there to obtain pardon for all his sins by bathing in the waters of the sacred Ganges. On his way thither, he one day reached the river Sarasvati, flowing through a desert which he was crossing. He determined to perform his usual ablutions in it; and no sooner had he stepped into the water than he saw coming towards him a crab, which asked him where he was going. Learning that he was on a pilgrimage to the Ganges, the crab requested the Brahmin to carry it with him to this sacred river, promising in return for this service to remember his kindness all its life, and to do all that lay in its power to be of use to him should an opportunity offer itself. The Brahmin, astonished at the crab's promise, asked how a creature so weak and despicable as itself could possibly be of any service to a man, and especially to a Brahmin. To this the crab replied by the following fable :—

The King, the Elephant, and the Brahmin.

In the city of Prabavathi-Patna there lived a king named Adita-Varma. One day the king, when out hunting with a crowd of attendants in the midst of a dense forest, observed a huge elephant approaching, whose sudden appearance spread terror among his followers. The king, however, succeeded in calming the fears of his people, and told them that they must try to capture the animal and lead it away to his palace. Accordingly, they dug a deep pit, covering it with branches and leaves. This done, the whole company surrounded the elephant, leaving only one passage leading to the pit for him to escape, into which, in fact, the elephant eventually fell. The king was delighted at their success, and told them that before trying to release the elephant from the pit they must keep it starving there for eight days, when, having lost all its strength, it might be more easily made captive. Accordingly, everybody retired, leaving the elephant in the trap. Two days afterwards, a Brahmin who was travelling on the banks of the river Jumna happened to pass that way, and seeing the elephant in the pit, asked the animal by what unfortunate accident it found itself there. The elephant told him about its sad adventure, complaining at the same time of the torments which it was enduring, not only from the fall, but by hunger and thirst. It besought the Brahmin to have pity and to help it to regain its liberty. The Brahmin replied that it was quite beyond his physical powers to drag out from such a deep pit a body of such huge weight and bulk. But the elephant still further entreated him, and besought him at any rate to give it the benefit of his advice as to how it was possible to escape from the dangers which threatened it. To this the Brahmin replied that if it had formerly rendered service to anybody, it should now invoke that person's aid. 'I do not remember,' answered the elephant, 'to have rendered service to any one except to the rats, which I did in the following manner :—

The Elephant and the Rats.

'In the country of Kalinga-Desa there lived a king named Swarna-Bahu[1], who suddenly found his kingdom infested with myriads of rats, which destroyed every living plant and spread desolation everywhere. His subjects, unable to subsist in the midst of such a plague, waited upon the king and entreated him to devise some means of freeing the country from the ravages of these destructive creatures. The king immediately mustered all the hunters and trappers in his kingdom, who, furnished with nets and snares of all kinds, proceeded at once to make war on the rats. By dint of much labour and patience, they succeeded at last in drawing all the rats from their holes, every one of them being captured and shut up alive in large earthen vessels, where they were left to perish of hunger.

'Meanwhile,' continued the elephant, 'I happened to be passing by the spot where the rats were huddled up in confinement. Their chief, hearing me coming, called out to me and entreated me to have compassion on him and his com-

[1] Swarna-Bahu means 'golden-armed.'—ED.

panions and to save their lives, which, said he, was extremely easy, since all that was necessary was to kick to pieces the earthen vessels which held them captive. Touched with pity at the sad lot of these unfortunate creatures, I shattered their temporary prisons, and thus rescued them all from certain death. The chief of the rats, after thanking me profusely, promised that he and his companions would for ever remember the signal service I had rendered them, and swore that they would requite my kindness should I ever happen to get into any difficulty.'

When the elephant had finished its story, the Brahmin advised it to call to its aid the rats, whom it had so signally helped. He then wished it a speedy deliverance and proceeded on his journey.

The elephant, left to itself, concluded it could not do better than follow the advice given by the Brahmin. At the call of the elephant, the chief of the rats immediately ran to its aid. No sooner did the elephant perceive its little friend than it explained the misfortunes that had befallen it, as well as the troubles with which it was still threatened, and entreated the rat to help it somehow or other out of its prison.

'The service which thou standest in need of, my lord elephant,' answered the rat, 'presents no difficulties to me; be, therefore, of good courage, and I promise to effect thy deliverance very shortly.'

The chief of the rats immediately assembled several millions of its subjects, and led them to the pit where their liberator was buried. They set to work at once to burrow all round, throwing the earth into the pit, which gradually filled little by little until the elephant was able to reach the surface and shake itself free from all danger.

At the close of this fable the crab thus addressed the Brahmin: 'If a rat was able to render such a signal service to an elephant, is it not possible that an opportunity might occur when I might be in a position to oblige thee and to testify my gratitude to thee?'

The Brahmin Kala-Sarma, delighted at finding so much intelligence in such an insignificant creature, no longer hesitated to take the crab with him, and putting it in his travelling bag, proceeded on his journey. One day, while traversing a dense forest at midday, when the sun was hottest, he halted to rest beneath the shade of a thick tree, where he soon fell asleep; and this is what happened while he was buried in deep slumber:—

The Crow, the Serpent, the Brahmin, and the Crab.

Near the tree under which the Brahmin Kala-Sarma was enjoying his peaceful slumber, a huge snake had taken up its abode in a white-ant heap, and in the branches of the same tree a crow had built its nest. Now the crow and the serpent had, in the capacity of neighbours, contracted a close alliance. When any wearied traveller happened to rest under the shade of the tree, the crow by a certain cry gave notice immediately to its friend the snake, and the latter, forthwith emerging from its retreat, quietly approached the traveller and bit him, causing instantaneous death. Thereupon the crow would call its fellow-crows together, and the whole of them would fall upon the corpse and devour it.

No sooner had the crow perceived that the Brahmin pilgrim was sound asleep than it gave the serpent notice by the usual signal. The snake immediately issued from its retreat and bit the Brahmin, killing him instantly by its deadly venom. The crow hastened to summon its friends and relations, and the whole of them pounced together on the corpse. But as they were preparing to devour it, the head crow espied something moving in the bag of the traveller, and curious to know what it was, put its head into the bag. Thereupon the crab caught it by the neck with its claws and proceeded to strangle it to death. The crow cried aloud for mercy, but the crab swore that it would not let go, unless the Brahmin whose death the crow had just caused was restored to life. The crow made known to its companions the extremity in which it found itself and the conditions under which the crab agreed to spare its life. It besought its comrades to go in all haste and tell its friend the snake of its critical situation, and to request it to reanimate the body of the Brahmin without delay. The snake, informed of the misfortune that had befallen its friend, approached the deceased, applied its mouth to the spot where it had bitten him, sucked out all the venom with which it had poisoned him, and restored him to life.

When the Brahmin regained his senses he was not a little

surprised to see his crab holding a crow fast imprisoned in its claws. The crab gave him an account of what had just happened, at which the traveller, who had believed himself to be waking from a sweet slumber, was exceedingly amazed. 'However,' said he to the crab, 'since the crow has satisfied the conditions which thou didst ask of him, thou must also fulfil the promise which thou madest to him of sparing his life; let him, therefore, go now.'

But the crab, desiring to punish the wicked crow in a proper manner, and fearing to carry out its design in the neighbourhood of the snake, answered that it would set its captive free only at some distance from the spot where they were. The Brahmin, therefore, carried them both a little farther on, and then, opening his bag, told the crab to hesitate no longer in fulfilling his promise.

'Foolish man!' answered the crab, 'can we attach the least faith to the words of the wicked? Can we ever rely on their promises? Thou art, of course, ignorant of the fact that this treacherous crow has already caused the death of a host of innocent beings, and that if I now set him free he will cause a still greater number to perish. Wouldst thou like to know what good people gain by obliging the wicked? Wouldst thou like to learn how the latter ought to be treated when once they are in our power? The following fable will teach thee:—

The Brahmin, the Crocodile, the Tree, the Cow, and the Fox.

'Once upon a time, in the Brahmin village of Agni-sthala, situated on the banks of the river Jumna, there lived a Brahmin named Astika. While on a pilgrimage to the Ganges, he happened one day to reach a river in which he intended to perform his ablutions. No sooner had he stepped into the water than a crocodile approached him, and learning the purpose for which he had undertaken the journey, entreated him most earnestly to carry it with him to the waters of the sacred river, where it hoped to be able to live more at its ease than in that river, which frequently ran dry during the hot season and caused it the most terrible sufferings. The Brahmin, moved to compassion, allowed the crocodile to get into his bag, and, hoisting it on his shoulders, proceeded on his journey. On reaching the banks of the Ganges the pilgrim opened his bag, and pointing out to the crocodile the waters of the river, bade it crawl in. The crocodile, however, replied that it felt tired out by the long journey they had made together, and was not strong enough to reach the water by itself. It therefore requested the Brahmin to carry it in to a certain depth. The Brahmin, without the least suspicion of foul play, complied with this last request of the crocodile. He advanced as far as he could into the bed of the river and there deposited his travelling companion. Just as he was turning, however, the crocodile seized him by the leg and tried to drag him into deeper water. Filled with dismay, and incensed at such perfidy, the pilgrim exclaimed: "O deceitful and wicked villain! Is it thus that thou returnest evil for good? Is this the kind of honesty which thou practisest? Is this the gratitude which I have to expect from thee for the service I have rendered?"

'"Nonsense!" replied the crocodile. "Why dost thou talk to me of *honesty* and *gratitude*? The only honesty of our days is to ruin those who cherish us."

'"Be pleased, at any rate, to stay the execution of thy perfidious design for a little while," entreated the Brahmin, "and let us see if the morality which thou professest would be approved by anybody. Let us refer the matter to arbitrators; and should there be found only three who approve thy mode of acting and thinking, I consent to be devoured by thee."

'The crocodile yielded to the wishes of the Brahmin, and agreed to defer the sacrifice until it had secured the approbation of three arbitrators who saw nothing to blame in it.

'They applied first of all to a mango-tree planted on the river bank. The Brahmin asked the tree if it was right to do evil to those who had done us good.

'"I do not know," answered the mango-tree, "if that is permitted or not; but I know very well that it is just the kind of treatment which men like you mete out to me. I appease their hunger by nourishing them with my succulent fruits; and I shield them from the heat of the sun by sheltering them under my shade. Yet, as soon as old age or any accident makes me unfit to render them such services, they, forgetting my past kindness, cut my branches and lastly deprive me of life itself by digging up my very roots. Hence I conclude that honesty among men consists in destroying those who cherish them."

'The crocodile and the Brahmin then accosted an old cow which was grazing without a keeper on the banks of the river. The Brahmin asked if it was not an offence against honesty to do evil to those who had done good to us.

'"What dost thou mean by the word *honesty*?" answered the cow. "Honesty in our days consists in harming those who have rendered us service; I have learned this only too well from my own sad experience. Till recently I rendered most important services to man. I ploughed his fields; I gave him calves; I nourished him with my milk. But, alas! now that I am grown old and unfit to be of service to him, he has discarded me. Forsaken and helpless on the banks of this river, I find myself exposed at every moment to the fury of wild beasts."

'The opinion of a third arbitrator only was wanting to complete the ruin of the Brahmin. Perceiving a fox, he asked him the same question that he had asked the mango-tree and the cow. But before making an answer the fox wished to be better informed of the points at issue. So the Brahmin gave a detailed account of the services he had rendered to the crocodile and of the treacherous act that the latter was meditating. The fox laughed heartily, and seemed at first to be going to decide in favour of the crocodile. "However," said he, "before pronouncing a final judgement on your affair, I must see how you both travelled together."

'The crocodile, without the least suspicion as to what the fox intended to do, and without the least hesitation, got into the bag, which the Brahmin then hoisted upon his back. The fox told the Brahmin to follow him, and on reaching an isolated spot he made signs to the Brahmin to place his load on the ground. No sooner had the latter done so than the fox took a huge stone and smashed the head of the crocodile with it. Then turning to the Brahmin, the fox said: "Foolish man that thou art, may the dangers to which thou hast been exposing thyself teach thee to be more careful in future! Remember well that we should never make friends or associates of the wicked." The fox then called his family together and made an excellent meal of the dead crocodile; and the Brahmin, after accomplishing the object of his pilgrimage by bathing in the waters of the Ganges, returned home safe and sound.

'This fable,' said the crab to his benefactor the Brahmin, who was attentively listening to his narrative, 'ought to convince thee that no covenant should be made with the wicked, and that we may without the least scruple fail in our word to them. When we happen to have them in our power, we should ruthlessly destroy them.' Saying this, the crab tightened its clasp on the crow and strangled it to death.

After this exhibition of exemplary punishment the Brahmin Kala-Sarma, taking up the crab again, continued his journey; and when he reached the river Ganges, deposited his little benefactor there, as desired. After expressing his deep gratitude for the signal service the crab had rendered to him in saving his life, he performed his ablutions in the sacred river and returned to his own country, which he reached without further accident.

I will not relate any more of these fables, though most of them are very instructive. My intention has been merely to draw the attention of my readers to a work which, in my opinion, is the most interesting and useful in the whole range of Hindu literature.

It is impossible to determine the age of these fables, since no authentic evidence of their date is now extant. It is supposed that they were translated into Persian towards the middle of the sixth century, under the reign of the Emperor Nurjehan; and the fragments which have been published in Europe have, no doubt, been extracted from this Persian translation. Indeed, La Fontaine himself appears to have gone to it for some of his fables.

The Hindus themselves place the *Pancha-tantra* among their oldest literary productions; and the wide popularity which it enjoys may be said to be some proof in favour of this opinion. At any rate the fables contained in this work appear to be older than those of Aesop. It is uncertain what was the birthplace of that fabulist; whence we may suppose that he learnt from the Hindu philosophers the art of making animals and inanimate beings speak, with the view of teaching mankind their faults.

It is uncertain whether these fables were originally composed by the Brahmin Vishnu-Sarma in verse or in prose. They were most probably in verse, as that was the recognized mode of composition in ancient India. It is at any rate certain that copies exist of the *Pancha-tantra* written in Sanskrit verse. Thence they may have been translated into prose for the instruction and amusement of those to whom the poetic language was not familiar.

The five principal fables, together with the great number of minor tales interwoven in them, form a volume of considerable size.

It is not surprising that such a work should have an extensive popularity among a people like the Hindus, prone to fiction and admiring the marvellous. Nor is it necessary, in order to charm an imaginative people like the Hindus, to exhibit any particular wit or erudition. There are numbers of Hindus who make it their sole profession to wander from one place to another relating fables and stories which are very often utterly devoid even of common sense. Men of the shepherd caste in particular often earn a livelihood in this manner. Hence the saying, *It is a shepherd's tale,* which is frequently used by the Hindus to show that a story is incredible.

CHAPTER XXVII

Hindu Tales.

The Four Deaf Men.

ONCE upon a time a shepherd, who happened to be deaf, was tending his flock near his village. Though it was past midday, his wife had not yet brought him his breakfast. He was afraid to leave his sheep to fetch his food lest some accident should befall them; and so, after waiting some time longer, and being pressed by hunger, he adopted the following course. There chanced to be a *taliari*, or village watchman, cutting grass for his cow on the banks of a neighbouring stream, so the shepherd went up to him, though rather reluctantly, for men of this class, although placed as guardians over public and private property in the village and supposed to prevent any thefts being committed, are, generally speaking, great thieves themselves. The shepherd, nevertheless, requested him to keep an eye on his flock during the short time he would be absent, and assured him that on his return from breakfast he would reward him handsomely for his trouble.

Now the *taliari* happened to be as deaf as the shepherd himself, and not understanding a word of what was being spoken to him, answered angrily as follows:—

'What right hast thou to this grass, which I have been at such trouble to cut? Is my cow to starve, while thy sheep are being fattened at its expense? Go about thy business and let me alone!' As he finished speaking he made an expressive motion with his hand, which the shepherd understood as a signal of compliance with his request. The latter, therefore, immediately ran towards the village, fully determined to give his wife a good trouncing for her neglect. But he had no sooner reached his home than he saw his wife stretched in the doorway and rolling in the agonies of a violent colic, the result of eating a quantity of raw beans.

At the sight of the sufferings of his poor wife the anger of the shepherd vanished, although he saw to his chagrin that the necessity of rendering her help and of preparing his own breakfast would detain him longer than he had expected. Distrusting the honesty of the *taliari*, to whom he had confided the care of his flock, he made all possible haste, and finally returned. On reaching his sheep, which he found peacefully grazing at some distance from the spot where he had left them, his first thought was to count them; and overjoyed at finding that there was not a single one missing, he exclaimed: 'This *taliari* is a really honest fellow! He is the very jewel of his class. I promised him a reward, and he shall indeed have one.'

Now there was a lame sheep in the flock, which was however sound enough in other respects, and so he put it on his shoulders and carried it to the *taliari*, saying to him: 'Thou didst indeed watch my flock very carefully during my absence; well, here is a sheep which thou shalt have as a reward for thy trouble.' But the *taliari*, catching sight of the lame sheep, exclaimed angrily: 'What dost thou mean by accusing me of having broken thy sheep's leg? I swear that I have not stirred from the spot where thou now seest me; I have not gone near thy flock!'

'Yes,' answered the shepherd, 'it is nice and fat; it will furnish a good feast for thy family and friends.'

'Have I not told thee,' replied the *taliari* in a rage, 'that I never went near thy sheep? and yet thou accusest me of having broken the leg of one of them! Get away from here, or I will give thee a sound thrashing.' And he showed by his gestures that he was determined to put his threats into execution.

The shepherd, perceiving at last that his friend was getting into a passion, and unable to understand the cause of this unjust provocation, put himself into an attitude of defence. The pair were all but coming to blows, when a man on horseback happened to pass by. They thereupon stopped the rider; and the shepherd, laying hold of the bridle, said to him: 'Sir, kindly listen for a moment and say whether it is I who am in the wrong in this dispute. I want to present this man with a sheep as a reward for a small service which he has rendered me, and he falls upon me and wishes to fight me.'

The *taliari*, speaking in his turn, said: 'This dolt of a shepherd dares to accuse me of having broken the leg of one of his sheep, whereas I did not even go near his flock.'

Now the horseman to whom they had appealed as arbitrator was even more deaf than they were, and not understanding a word of what was spoken to him, replied: 'Yes, I confess that this horse does not really belong to me. I found him straying on the roadside; I was in a hurry, and I mounted him so that I might get along faster. If he belongs to you, take him by all means; but let me continue my way, for I have no time to lose.'

The shepherd and the *taliari*, each imagining that the rider had decided in favour of his adversary, became more violent than ever, cursing him whom they had chosen as their arbitrator, and accusing him roundly of partiality.

At this crisis an aged Brahmin chanced to pass by, and as he appeared more fit to settle their differences they stopped him and requested him to listen to them for a moment. Shepherd, *taliari*, and horseman all spoke together at the same time, each telling his own tale and explaining to the Brahmin the subject of the dispute, and requesting him to decide which of them was in the wrong.

The Brahmin, who was as deaf as the other three, replied: 'Yes, yes, I quite understand you. My wife has sent you all to prevent my going away, and to persuade me to return home; but I have quite made up my mind, and you will not succeed in your attempt. Now, do you all know my wife? She is a real shrew! It is impossible for me to live any longer with such a harridan! Ever since the time I had the misfortune to buy[1] her, she has made me commit more sins than it will be possible for me to expiate in a hundred regenerations. I am therefore going on a pilgrimage to Kasi (Benares), and on reaching the holy city I mean to wash myself in the sacred waters of the Ganges, in order that I may purify myself from the innumerable sins which her wickedness has caused me to commit. I have furthermore made up my mind to live henceforth by alms in a foreign country, and apart from her.'

[1] I have previously remarked that 'to marry' and 'to buy a woman' are synonymous terms among the Hindus. —DUBOIS.

While they were all four shouting thus at the top of their voices, without being able to understand each other, the rider perceived at a distance some people rapidly approaching them. Fearing lest they might be the owners of the horse which he had taken, he immediately dismounted and took to his heels.

The shepherd, finding suddenly that it was getting late, hastened back to his flock, which had strayed away some distance, uttering curses as he trudged along against all arbitrators, and complaining loudly that there was no more justice on the earth. Finally he attributed all the troubles and disappointments he had experienced that day to the fact that a snake had crossed his path[1] in the morning.

The *taliari* turned to his load of grass; and finding the lame sheep there, took it up on his shoulders and carried it away home, to punish the shepherd, as he thought, for the unjust quarrel he had fastened on him.

As for the aged Brahmin, he continued his way till he reached a neighbouring *choultry*, where he stopped to spend the night. Quiet rest and sound sleep dispelled the feelings of anger and ill-humour which he had cherished against his wife, and the next morning several Brahmins, relatives and friends of his, came in search of him, and having found him, succeeded at last in soothing his temper and persuading him to return home, promising to use their best endeavours to render his wife more obedient and less quarrelsome in future.

The Four Foolish Brahmins.

In a certain district proclamation had been made of a *samaradhanam*, one of those grand feasts given to Brahmins on divers occasions. Four individuals of this caste, having each set out from a different village to attend the feast, happened to meet each other on the road, and having discovered that they were all proceeding to the same place, agreed to travel together during the remainder of their journey. While thus walking along in company, they were met by a soldier going in the opposite direction, who, on passing them, greeted them with the saluta-

[1] This, as I have already pointed out, is one of the most evil omens.—DUBOIS.

tion generally made to Brahmins; that is, he joined his hands together, put them to his forehead, and said: '*Saranam ayya!*' ('Respectful greeting to you, my lord!') to which the four Brahmins replied at one and the same time: '*Asirvadam!*' ('Our blessing!').

Subsequently they reached a well by the roadside, and there they sat down to quench their thirst and to rest for a while under the shade of a neighbouring tree. While thus occupied, and finding no better subject of conversation, one of them took it into his head to break the silence by saying to the others: 'You will admit that the soldier whom we have just met was a man of exceptional politeness and discernment. Did you not remark how he singled me out, and how carefully he saluted me?'

'It was not you whom he saluted,' replied the Brahmin seated next to him, 'it was to me particularly that he addressed his greeting.'

'You are both mistaken,' exclaimed the third. 'I can assure you that the greeting was addressed to me alone; and the proof is that when the soldier said his "*Saranam ayya,*" he cast his eyes upon me!'

'Not at all,' replied the fourth. 'It was I only he saluted; otherwise, should I have answered him as I did, by saying "*Asirvadam*"?'

The altercation grew so warm that the four travellers were at last on the point of coming to blows, when one of them, the least stupid of the four, wishing to prevent so silly a quarrel proceeding to extremes, cried as follows:—'What fools we are to be thus quarrelling for no purpose! After heaping on each other all the insults we are capable of, and after fighting with each other like the Sudra rabble, shall we be any nearer to the solution of our differences? The fittest person to settle the controversy, I think, is he who occasioned it. The soldier cannot have gone very far. Let us, therefore, run after him as quickly as we can, and ascertain from him which of us four it was whom he intended to salute.'

This advice, appearing sound to all of them, was immediately followed. Accordingly, the four set off in pursuit of the soldier, and at last, quite out of breath, overtook him about a league beyond the place where he had saluted them. No sooner had they caught sight of him than they cried out to him to stop; and before they had quite reached him had put him in full possession of the points of their dispute, requesting him to settle it by saying to which of them he had directed his salutation.

The soldier, instantly perceiving the character of the people he had to deal with, and wishing to amuse himself a little at their expense, coolly replied that he intended his salutation for the greatest fool of the four, and then, turning his back on them, continued his journey.

The Brahmins, confounded with this answer, turned back and continued their journey for some time in perfect silence. But the greeting of the soldier had taken so strong a hold of them that at last they could remain silent no longer. The quarrel was therefore renewed with greater fury than before. The point at issue this time was as to which of the four was entitled to the distinction mentioned by the soldier, inasmuch as each claimed to be the greatest fool of the party.

The dispute as to who had the right to claim this extraordinary distinction grew so hot and strong that a hand-to-hand scuffle seemed inevitable. However, the one who had advised conciliation once before again wisely interposed with the view of making peace, and spoke as follows :—

'I think myself the greatest fool of us all, and each of you thinks the same thing of himself. Now, I ask you, is it by screaming at the top of our voices and by dealing each other blows that we shall arrive at a decision as to which of the four is the greatest fool? No, certainly not; let us therefore put an end to our quarrel for the time. Here we are within a short distance of Dharmapuri; let us go thither and present ourselves at the *choultry* (the court of justice), and request the authorities to settle our dispute[1].' As this advice seemed sensible enough, they all agreed to adopt it.

They could not have arrived at the *choultry* at a more opportune moment. The authorities of the village of Dharmapuri, consisting of Brahmins and others, were just then all assembled there; and as there was no other important case to be settled that day, they at once proceeded with the hearing of the cause of the strangers, who were asked to explain the facts of their case.

[1] Most Indian villages even to this day possess a *chavadi* or *choultry*, where the village authorities meet and dispense justice.—ED.

One of the four thereupon advanced into the middle of the assembly and related, without omitting the slightest detail, all that had happened in connexion with the greeting of the soldier and his ambiguous reply.

On hearing the details of the case the whole court burst into fits of laughter. The president, who was a man of humorous disposition, was delighted at having found so favourable an opportunity of amusing himself. Assuming, therefore, a grave demeanour and ordering every one to keep silent, he thus addressed the suitors: 'As you are strangers and quite unknown in this town, it is impossible that the point at issue, namely, who is the greatest fool, can be proved by the evidence of witnesses. There is only one way that I can see in which you can enlighten your judges. Let each of you in his turn disclose to us some incident of his life on which he considers he can best establish his claim to egregious folly. After hearing you all in turn, we can then decide as to which of the four has a right to superiority in this respect, and which of you can in consequence claim for himself exclusively the soldier's greeting.'

All the suitors having agreed to this proposal, one of the Brahmins obtained permission to speak, and addressed the assembly as follows:—'I am very poorly clad, as you doubtless see, and my ragged condition does not date from to-day. I will tell you how I came to be so shabbily attired. Many years ago a rich merchant of our neighbourhood, who was always very charitable towards Brahmins, presented me with two pieces of the finest cloth that had ever been seen in our *agraharam* (village). I showed them to all my friends, who never failed to admire them greatly. "A beautiful present like that," said they to me, "can only be the reward of good deeds performed in a previous birth." Before putting them on I washed them, according to the usual custom, in order to purify them from the defilement of the weaver's and merchant's touch. Now, they were hanging up to dry with the ends fastened to two branches of a tree, when a dog happening to come that way ran under them. I caught sight of the vile animal only after it had got some distance away, and I was therefore not quite sure whether it had touched my cloths and thus polluted them. I asked my children who were close by about it, but they said they had not noticed the dog. How, then, was I to make sure about the matter? Well, I decided to go down on all-fours till I was about the height of the dog; and in this posture I crawled under the cloths. "Did I touch them?" I asked my children, who were watching me. They answered, "No," and I leapt with joy at the happy result. Nevertheless, a moment later it struck me that the dog might possibly have touched them with his tail. So to be quite sure of this, I fastened an upturned sickle on my back, and then, again crawling along on all-fours, I passed a second time under the cloths. My children, whom I had asked to watch carefully, told me that this time the sickle had just touched the cloths. Not doubting in the least that the end of the dog's tail must have also touched the cloths in the same way, I laid hold of them, and, in a fit of thoughtless rage, tore them to pieces. The occurrence soon became known to everybody in the neighbourhood, and I was everywhere voted to be a fool. "Even if the dog really defiled thy cloths," said one, "couldst thou not have removed the defilement by washing them a second time?" Another asked why I had not given the cloths to some poor Sudra instead of tearing them to pieces. "Who would dream of giving you cloths again after such senseless folly on your part?" This last remark, I may add, has proved only too true; for ever since then, whenever I ventured to apply to anybody for a present of cloths, the usual reply has been that I simply wanted them to tear to pieces.'

When he had finished his story, one of the auditors remarked to him: 'You seem to be very clever at crawling about on all-fours.' 'Yes, I am indeed very clever at it,' answered the Brahmin, 'as you shall see.' And, suiting his action to his words, he went down on all-fours, and proceeded to run two or three times round the spectators, who were splitting their sides with laughter.

'Enough, enough!' cried the president. 'All that we have heard and seen furnishes evidence very much in your favour, but before coming to any decision we must hear what the others have to say for themselves.'

A second Brahmin accordingly spoke as follows:—

'One day, in order to present a decent appearance at a *samaradhanam* (treat to Brahmins), which had been announced in our neighbourhood, I called in the barber to shave my head and chin. When he had finished, I told my wife to give him a copper coin for his trouble; but by mistake she gave him two. In vain did I request the barber to return me the other coin. He was obstinate, and refused to do so; and the more I insisted on his returning it, the more stubborn did he become. The dispute was becoming very serious when the barber, assuming a milder tone, observed: "There is only one way of settling the difference between us. For the extra coin which you ask me to return I will shave your wife's head as well, if that suits you." "Certainly," answered I, after a moment's reflection; "your proposal will, doubtless, put an end to our quarrel without unfairness on either side."

'My wife, hearing what was about to happen to her, wished to run away; but I laid hold of her and made her sit down, while the barber, armed with his razor, completely shaved her head. My wife kept crying out most bitterly the whole time, abusing and cursing both of us; but I let her rave, for I preferred seeing her head clean shaven to giving this villain of a barber money which he had not rightly earned. My wife, deprived thus of her beautiful hair, immediately hid herself through sheer shame, and dared not appear again. The barber also decamped, and meeting my mother in the street, related to her with infinite gusto what had just taken place. She at once hastened to the house to assure herself of the fact, and when she saw her daughter-in-law completely shorn, she stood motionless and dumbfounded for a moment, and then, flying into a fit of anger, overwhelmed me with curses and insults, which I bore patiently without uttering a word, for I soon began to feel that I richly deserved them. The villain of a barber, in his turn, took a mischievous pleasure in telling everybody of the incident, until I became the general laughing-stock. Slanderous people, improving on his story, were not slow in insinuating that the object of my having my wife's head shaved was to punish her for her infidelity. Crowds gathered about the door of my house, and even an ass was brought to carry the supposed adulteress through the streets in the manner usual on such occasions.

'A report of the affair soon reached the ears of my wife's relatives, who hastened to inquire what was the matter. You can easily imagine the terrible hubbub and trouble they made at the sight of their unfortunate daughter. They immediately took her away with them, travelling at night that she might be spared the shame of being exposed to public view in so humiliating a condition, and they kept her for four years without coming to terms of any kind with me, though at length they restored her to me.

'This unfortunate incident made me miss the *samaradhanam*, for which I had been preparing by a three days' fast. I was all the more chagrined to find afterwards that it was a most sumptuous feast, and that ghee, among other good things, had been profusely served. A fortnight afterwards another *samaradhanam* was announced, which I had the imprudence to attend. I was greeted with howls from more than eight hundred Brahmins who had assembled there, and who, seizing me by force, insisted on my publishing the name of the accomplice of my wife's guilt, in order that he might be prosecuted and punished according to the rigid rules of the caste. I solemnly asserted that I was myself the guilty party, and explained to them all the true motive that induced me to act in such a manner. My hearers were immensely surprised at what I told them, and, looking at each other, at last exclaimed: "Is it possible that any married woman who has not violated the laws of honour should have her head shaved? This man must be either a downright impostor or the greatest fool on the face of the earth." And I hope, gentlemen,' said the narrator in conclusion, 'that you too will think the same, and that you will consider my folly to have been far superior to that of the Brahmin who tore his cloths to pieces.'

The assembly agreed that the speaker had put forward a very strong case; but justice required that the other two should also be heard.

The third claimant, who was burning with impatience to speak, addressed the court as follows:—

'My name was originally Anantayya, but I am now known everywhere as *Betel Anantayya*, and here follows the reason why this nickname was given me.

'My wife had been living with me for about a month, after having remained for a long time at her father's house on account of her youth, when one night on going to bed I told her—I know not for what reason—that all women were chatterboxes.

She at once angrily retorted that she knew some men who were as much chatterboxes as women. I saw at once that she was alluding to myself; and feeling extremely piqued at the sharpness of her retort, I said: "Now, just let us see which of us two will speak the first!" "Certainly," quoth she: "but what shall the loser forfeit?" "A betel-leaf[1]," answered I; and the wager being thus made, we both went to sleep without uttering another word.

'The next morning, when the sun was already pretty high, and there were no signs of our appearing, the other people in the house called out to each of us by name, but received no answer. They shouted louder still, and still there was silence. Then they knocked violently at the door of our room; but to no purpose. Finally, everybody in the house became thoroughly alarmed, suspecting that we had both died suddenly during the night. The carpenter of the village was accordingly sent for in hot haste. He was soon on the spot with his tools, and promptly broke open the door of our room.

'Judge of the surprise of all when they found both of us wide awake and in the apparent enjoyment of the best of health, but deprived of the use of speech. Various means were adopted to induce us to speak, but without success. My mother, who was greatly alarmed, gave loud vent to her grief, and all the Brahmins of the village, both men and women, flocked to our house to learn what all the noise was about. The house was soon filled with people, and each drew his own conclusions as to the accident which was supposed to have befallen us. The prevailing opinion was that it all resulted from the curse of some secret enemy. Accordingly, my relatives forthwith sent for a famous magician living in the neighbourhood to counteract the spell. As soon as he arrived he began by fixing his eyes on us for some moments. Then he walked round us several times, uttering strange words, felt different parts of our bodies, and did so many other strange things that the remembrance of them still makes me laugh whenever I think of them. At last he declared that we were really under the influence of a spell. He even named the evil spirit which, according to him, possessed us, and described it as very obstinate and uncontrollable. Considering the difficulties that he would have in expelling it, he stated that

[1] Thirty or forty of these leaves could be had for a farthing.—DUBOIS.

five pagodas at least would be required to meet the expenses of the sacrifices and other ceremonies that must be performed if he was to be successful.

'My relatives, who were by no means well-to-dò people, were utterly dismayed at the exorbitant sum demanded by the magician; but rather than allow us to remain dumb, they agreed to his terms, and promised moreover to give him a suitable present if he succeeded in restoring to us the use of our tongues.

'The magician was on the point of beginning his mystic ceremonies, when one of our Brahmin friends who was present maintained, in opposition to everybody else, that what we were suffering from was a simple malady enough, such as he had often seen before, and he undertook to cure us without any expense whatever. For this purpose all that he required was a plate of red-hot charcoal and a small bar of gold. As soon as these had been brought he heated the bar of gold almost to melting-point; then taking it up with pincers, he applied it red hot to the soles of my feet, below my elbows, on the pit of my stomach, and lastly on the top of my head. I endured these cruel tortures without showing the smallest symptom of pain or uttering the least complaint. Indeed, I would rather have died, if necessary, than lose the bet I had made. "Now let us try the remedy on the woman," said the shrewd operator, who was rather discouraged at my firmness. He then approached my wife and applied the red-hot bar of gold to the soles of her feet. But no sooner did she feel the effects of the burning than she quickly drew away her leg, and cried out, "*Appah*! *Appah*!" (Enough! Enough!). Then, turning towards me, she said: "I have lost the wager; here is your betel-leaf." "Did I not tell you," said I, taking the leaf, "that you would be the first to speak? You thus prove by your own conduct that I was right in saying last night, when we went to bed, that women are chatterboxes."

'The spectators, thoroughly astounded, were gazing at each other without understanding anything, until I explained to them the wager we had made overnight before going to sleep. "What downright folly!" they all exclaimed together. "What!" said they, "was it for a leaf of betel that you spread this alarm in your own house and through the whole village? Was it for a leaf of betel that you showed such courage in allowing yourself to be burnt from the feet to the head? Never in the whole world was there seen such stupid folly." And from that time I have always gone by the name of *Betel Anantayya.*'

This story appeared to the assembly remarkable enough as illustrating extraordinary foolishness; but it was only fair, they said, that they should hear the claims that the fourth suitor had to put forward. And he, having been granted permission to speak, thus addressed the assembly:—

'As the girl to whom I was married was too young to cohabit with me, she continued to remain for six or seven years in her father's house. At last, however, she attained the proper age, and I was duly apprised of the fact by her parents. My father-in-law's house was six or seven miles away from ours, and my mother, being unwell at the time we received this happy intelligence, was not in a fit state to undertake the journey. She therefore entrusted to me the duty of fetching my wife home. She counselled me so to conduct myself in word and deed that the girl's parents might not discover my natural stupidity. "Knowing as I do," said my mother as I took leave of her, "the shallowness of thy pate, I very much fear that thou wilt commit some foolish mistake or other." But I promised to conform to her instructions and to be on my best behaviour; and so departed.

'I was very well received by my father-in-law, who gave a grand feast to all the Brahmins of the village in honour of my visit. At length, the day appointed for our departure having arrived, my wife and I were permitted to start. On taking leave of us, my father-in-law poured out his blessings upon us both, but wept most bitterly, as if he had a presentiment of the misfortune that was about to befall his unfortunate daughter.

'It happened to be the hottest part of the year; and the heat, on the day of our departure, was something terrible. Moreover, we had to traverse a desert plain several miles across, and the sand, heated by the burning sun, soon began to scorch the feet of my young wife, who had been brought up in comfort in her father's house, and was not accustomed to such hardships. Unable to endure the fatigues of the journey, she burst into tears. I led her on by the hand, and tried my best to rally her spirits.

But it was in vain. She soon became so utterly tired that she could not move another step, and lay down on the ground, declaring that she was prepared to die on that very spot. My distress may easily be imagined. Seated by her side, I could not think what to do next, when suddenly I spied a merchant passing by, leading a number of bullocks laden with various kinds of goods. I accosted him at once, and, with tears in my eyes, told him the trouble I was in, and entreated him to help me with his good advice in my distressing position. The merchant approached my wife, and, looking at her attentively, informed me that, in consequence of the stifling heat then prevailing, the poor girl's life would be equally in danger, whether she remained where she was or proceeded farther on her journey. "Rather than that you should be subjected to the pain of seeing her perish before your very eyes, and perhaps also be exposed to the suspicion of having yourself killed her, I should advise you to give her up to me," he said. "I will put her on the back of one of my best bullocks, and will take her away with me, thus saving her from certain death. You will, it is true, lose her; but it is nevertheless far better that you should lose her with the satisfaction of having saved her life than that you should incur the suspicion of having killed her. As for her jewels, they cannot be worth more than twenty pagodas. See, here are twenty-five for them, and you shall give me your wife." The arguments of the man seemed to me quite unanswerable. I therefore took the money which he offered me, while he, lifting my wife in his arms, placed her on one of his bullocks, and made haste to continue his journey. I also continued mine, and reached home rather late, my feet all blistered by the hot sand over which I had to walk the whole way. "Where is thy wife?" my mother asked me, surprised to see me return alone. Thereupon I related to her all that had happened since I had left home, and finally told her of the sad accident that had happened to my youthful spouse, and how I had given her away to a passing merchant, rather than be a witness of her death, and be suspected moreover of having been the cause of it. At the same time I showed my mother the twenty-five pagodas that I had received from the merchant as compensation.

'Filled with rage at what I had told her, my mother was

utterly speechless for a while as if turned into stone. Then her suppressed feelings of indignation got the better of her, and she gave vent to the most violent imprecations and curses at my conduct. "Thou fool, thou wretch!" exclaimed she, "what hast thou done! Sold thy wife, hast thou? Delivered her up to another man! A Brahmin wife become the concubine of a low-caste merchant! What will people think of it? What will her relatives and ours say when they learn this disgraceful story? Is it possible to imagine a more egregious instance of folly and stupidity?" The sad occurrence which had happened to my wife soon reached the ears of her relatives, who hastened to my village, filled with rage and indignation, and fully resolved to beat me to death. And they certainly would have murdered both me and my innocent mother had we not been forewarned of their coming, and escaped from their furious vengeance by a speedy flight. Being themselves unable to avenge the wrong done, they laid the matter before the heads of the caste, who unanimously found me guilty, and sentenced me to pay a fine of two hundred pagodas as compensation for the injury done to the honour of my father-in-law. Moreover, a proclamation was issued by which everybody was forbidden, under pain of excommunication, ever to give any woman in marriage to such an idiot as myself. I was, therefore, condemned to remain a widower for the rest of my life. It was lucky for me, indeed, that I was not altogether outcasted, a favour which I owed to the great respect and esteem in which my father had been held.

'I must now leave you to judge if this instance of foolishness on my part is in any way inferior to those with which my rivals have been entertaining you, and if the honour of being the biggest fool is not justly due to me.'

The assembly, after mature deliberation, decided that all four suitors had given such absolute proofs of folly that each was justly entitled to claim superiority in his own way over the others; and that each was at liberty to call himself the greatest fool of all, and to attribute to himself the greeting of the soldier. 'Each of you has gained his suit,' remarked the president, 'so you may now continue your journey in peace, if that is possible.'

Delighted with so equitable a judgement, the travellers left the court, each shouting louder than the other: 'I have gained my suit, I have gained my suit!'

The Story of Appaji, Prime Minister of King Krishna Roya[1].

Before the invasion of the Mussulmans, at a time when the Hindus enjoyed the happiness of being ruled by princes of their own nation, one of these princes, named Krishna Roya, was holding sway over one of the most fertile provinces of Southern India. This benevolent ruler was ever anxious to gain the love and respect of his subjects by doing everything in his power to make them happy; and, in order to attain this end more readily, he always took the most particular care to employ as his ministers and confidential advisers those persons only who by their wisdom, experience, and prudence were capable of affording him wise counsel. His prime minister, Appaji, enjoyed more of his confidence than any other, because he possessed the happy knack of letting his master know the truth about things by means of the most entertaining and striking allegories. One day, when this wise minister was alone with his sovereign, the latter, having nothing particular to do at the moment, asked him to solve the following problem. 'Appaji,' said he, 'I have often heard it said that in their religious and social usages men simply follow a beaten track, blindly and indiscriminately, however absurd such usages may be. Can you prove to me the truth of this assertion and the justice of that famous proverb: *Jatra marula, Jana marula*[2]?'

Appaji, with his usual modesty, promised the king to apply

[1] I have included this little story in the collection of Hindu fiction, because I found it in the same book from which I extracted the others. However, well-informed Hindus have told me that the story has been clothed in the form of fiction simply in order to make it more popular, and that it is really founded on historical fact. The memory of the good King Krishna Roya, and of his faithful minister Appaji, is still cherished by the people of India, who speak of him as a prince whose sole care was to render his people happy, in which good work he was most powerfully seconded by his minister. The period of his reign is said to date a short time before the Mahomedan invasion. However, whether this little story be fact or fiction, it is none the less a most excellent satire on the credulity of the Hindus.—DUBOIS.

[2] The meaning of this is: 'Is it the customs that are ridiculous, or is it the persons who follow them who are ridiculous?' The answer being: 'It is the people who follow them who are ridiculous.'—DUBOIS.

himself to the solution of the question and to give his answer in a few days. Returning home with his mind full of the problem, the minister sent in search of his shepherd who was taking care of his sheep. This man was a simple country boor with a rustic's ordinary intelligence. When the shepherd arrived, Appaji addressed him as follows:—'Hear me, Kuruba[1]; you must instantly lay aside your shepherd's garb and put on that of a *sannyasi* or penitent, whom you must represent for a few days. You will begin by rubbing your whole body with ashes; you will then take in one hand a bamboo staff with seven knots, and in the other the gourd in which a penitent always carries water, while under your arm you will carry the antelope's skin on which persons of that class must always sit. Thus equipped, you must go without delay to the mountain just outside the town and enter the cave which is to be found on its slope. You must lay your antelope's skin on the floor of the cave, and then squat down on it like a *sannyasi*, your eyes firmly fixed on the ground, your nostrils tightly shut with one hand, and the other hand resting on the top of your head. Be very careful to play your part properly, and take good care not to betray me. It is possible that the king, accompanied by his whole court and by a great crowd of other people, will come to visit you in the cavern; but whoever presents himself, even though it be I or the king himself, remain perfectly motionless in the posture which I have described to you, looking at nobody, speaking to nobody. And whatever happens, even though they should tear out the hairs one by one from your body, show not the smallest sign of pain, and do not budge an inch. These, Kuruba, are my commands. If by any chance you deviate in the least degree from the instructions which I have given you, you will answer for it with your life; but if on the contrary you follow them punctiliously, you may count upon a magnificent reward.'

The poor shepherd, accustomed all his life simply to look after his sheep, was very diffident as to his ability to change his condition for that of a *sannyasi*; but the tone of his master was so imperative that he judged it prudent to waive all objections and to obey him blindly. Furnishing himself with

[1] This is a name common enough among persons belonging to the caste of shepherds. Those who take care of cows or goats form another caste called *Golla*.—DUBOIS.

all the necessary paraphernalia of his new profession, and thinking over all that he had been ordered to do, he departed for the cave. Meanwhile Appaji returned to the palace, where he found the king surrounded by his courtiers. Approaching the monarch with a serious air, Appaji addressed him in the following terms:—'Great king, pardon me if at this moment, when surrounded by your wise councillors you are considering the best means of making your people happy—pardon me, I say, if I interrupt you in order to announce to you that the day has come when the gods, pleased with your eminent virtues, have decided to give you a marked token of their favour and of their protection. At the very moment that I am speaking a most wonderful thing is happening in your kingdom and not very far from your royal residence. On the slope of the mountain that lies near to your capital there is a cave in which a holy penitent, who has descended without doubt from the very abode of the great Vishnu, has deigned to take up his dwelling. In profound meditation on the perfections of Parabrahma he is wholly insensible to all terrestrial objects; he partakes of no other nourishment than the air which he breathes; not one of the objects that affect the five senses make the slightest impression on him. In a word, it may with truth be said of him that his body alone dwells in this world below, while his soul, his thoughts, and all his feelings are already closely united to the Divinity. I have no hesitation in saying that the miraculous appearance of this holy personage in your kingdom is a manifest guarantee of the interest which the gods take in you and yours.'

These words of Appaji were listened to with astonishment and wonder by the king and his courtiers. The king at once decided to go without delay to visit this illustrious penitent, whose praises the prime minister had sung so highly. And in order that the visit might be made with a dignity worthy of the eminent virtues of him who was the object of it, the king announced that he would go accompanied by his whole court and escorted by his whole army. Furthermore, he caused to be proclaimed to all his subjects, by public criers, by the beating of drums, and by the blowing of trumpets, his reasons for making the visit to the mountain; and everybody was invited to follow him. The procession was soon on its way.

Never before had such a magnificent gathering been witnessed; never had such a huge multitude of people assembled together. Pleasure was depicted upon every countenance. The air rang with cries of joy; while every one congratulated himself on having lived to enjoy the happiness of looking upon one of the greatest personages that had ever appeared on earth. On his arrival at the cave the king, filled with awe at the sight of so sacred a spot, entered it with all the marks of the most profound respect. It was not long before he descried the form of the illustrious penitent, crouching in the strange manner enjoined upon him by the minister, and apparently as motionless as the rocks which formed his retreat. After gazing upon him for some time in silence, the king tremblingly approached, and prostrating himself before him, with his hands joined, addressed him humbly as follows:—'Illustrious penitent! happy is the destiny which allowed me to live until this day, so that I might enjoy the inestimable happiness of looking upon your sacred face. I know not what it is that has procured for me such a wonderful blessing. The little that I have done during my life cannot possibly have rendered me worthy of such a distinction; probably, therefore, it is to the good works of my ancestors or to some good work which I may have accomplished in preceding births that I now owe my good luck. However this may be, the day on which I have seen your sacred feet is certainly the most glorious and happy of my life. In future I have nothing more to desire in this world, for in seeing these sacred feet of yours I have obtained the greatest blessing which could happen to any mortal. The sight of your feet alone is sufficient to wash away all the sins which I have committed both in this generation and in the preceding one. Henceforth I am as pure as the water of the Ganges, and all my desires are accomplished[1].'

The supposed penitent heard this flattering discourse without evincing the slightest sign that he had heard it, and without change either of countenance or posture. The crowd surrounding him, astonished at this indifference, became perfectly convinced that he was a supernatural being, for in no other way could they account for his solemn silence and complete

[1] This is the stereotyped form of address used in all Hindu books when describing the respects paid to a holy personage.—ED.

immovability. 'It is evident,' they said, 'that only the body of this holy penitent inhabits this lower world, while his soul and his thoughts must be united to the Divinity whose image he is.' The king, Krishna Roya, in the ecstasy of his religious zeal, and unable to attract a single glance from the holy penitent, addressed him in still more flattering terms in the hope of winning at any rate one look from him. Vain hope, however! The penitent made not the slightest movement of the head, nor relaxed for one moment the imperturbable gravity of his demeanour.

The prince was just about to leave the cave, when Appaji addressed him as follows:—'Great king, having come so far to visit this grand personage, who will henceforth become an object of public veneration, you must not depart without having received his blessing, or at any rate some gift which will bring you happiness for the rest of your days. Absorbed in meditation, and insensible to the material objects which surround him, this penitent cannot break his silence; nevertheless you should try to obtain something from him, be it only one of the hairs of his body.' The king took the advice of his minister, and, approaching the *sannyasi*, he tore out with extreme care one of the hairs of his chest, put it to his lips, kissed it devoutly, and then, showing it to the spectators, he cried: 'I will preserve this all my life. I will cause it to be enclosed in a golden locket, which shall always hang about my neck and be the most precious of all my ornaments, thoroughly convinced as I am that so noble a relic will prove to be a talisman against all the untoward accidents of life.'

The ministers and courtiers, in imitation of their master and wishing to participate in the same blessings, surrounded the poor penitent, and each one of them tore a hair from his chest, promising at the same time to preserve it as carefully as the king had done and to honour it as a holy relic. Moreover, the escort of the prince and the huge multitude which had accompanied him, learning what the king and his courtiers had done, were determined to follow so good an example; and in a very short time the supposed *sannyasi* found himself deprived of every hair he possessed, from his feet to his head; for the more devout amongst the multitude did not content themselves with a single one of his hairs, but pulled them out by the handful.

The poor Kuruba bore this horrible torture without the slightest complaint or the smallest change of posture, and without even raising his eyes.

On his return to his palace the king hastened to inform his women of the wonderful person whom he had visited, and showed them the relic of which he had become the possessor. The royal ladies, filled with wonder, one by one took the hair between their fingers, kissed it devoutly, pressed it to their eyes, and expressed an eager longing to see this illustrious personage. But as etiquette forbade persons of their sex and rank to show themselves in public, they supplicated the king to accord them the favour of having the *sannyasi* brought to the palace, so that they too might enjoy the happiness of looking upon him and plucking out his hairs with their own hands. The king at first refused to grant their request, but, yielding at length to their repeated solicitations, and wishing also to show as much honour to the penitent as lay in his power, he dispatched his whole court and army on foot and on horseback to escort the holy man to the palace. The messengers arrived at the cave while the multitude were still scrambling for the hairs of the *sannyasi*. The foremost and most distinguished amongst them at once approached the holy penitent. After explaining to him most humbly the object of their mission, they took him in their arms and placed him in a superb palanquin, where he remained in the same posture that he had so carefully maintained. Thereupon he was conducted with the greatest pomp and circumstance through the streets of the town, followed by a multitude of spectators who filled the air with shouts of joy. The poor Kuruba, who had eaten nothing for two days, and who was moreover feeling extremely sore from the rough treatment which he had received, was very far from enjoying all these honours. However, in the hope that the farce would soon come to an end and that he would get his reward, and also fearing to incur the wrath of his master, he managed to keep up his courage and to restrain himself from declaring who he was. 'What have I done,' he nevertheless murmured to himself, 'that I should be made to play a part which so little suits me and which exposes me to so much suffering? I would a thousand times rather be in the midst of my flock listening to the roars of the tigers in the jungle than be deafened by the shouts and acclamations of this stupid crowd. If I were only with my sheep at the present time I should have had two meals already; but now for two days past I have had nothing to eat at all, and I am still quite in the dark as to when and how all this will end.'

The palace was reached while the supposed *sannyasi* was turning over all these things in his head. Carried into a superb apartment, he had not long to wait before he was visited by the princesses, who came one by one to prostrate themselves at his feet. Each of them, after gazing at him in wonder and silence for some time, was consumed with the desire of possessing one of his hairs as a relic to be kept in a locket of gold, and to be reckoned as the most precious of their jewels. But in vain they searched every visible part of his body. The crowd of devotees who had preceded them had not left a single hair to be seen. At length, after most careful search, they managed to discover here and there, in the wrinkles of his coarse skin, a few hairs which had escaped notice. With these they were perforce obliged to be content, and having religiously collected them they retired. Thereupon the king ordered that the penitent should be left alone during the night, in order that he might enjoy the repose of which he was so much in need, after the fatiguing and painful days which he had passed. Appaji, however, having slipped quietly into the apartment where the poor shepherd was languishing of hunger, fatigue, and anguish, addressed him in the following consoling manner:—'Kuruba, the time of thy trial is at an end. Thou hast played thy part most excellently, and I am very pleased with thee. I promised thee a reward. Rest assured that thou wilt get it. Meanwhile lay aside this costume of the penitent and put on thy shepherd's garments again. Go and refresh thyself by good food and peaceful slumber, and to-morrow morning thou shalt return to thy occupation.'

The poor fellow did not require to be told twice. He fled by a secret passage which his master pointed out to him, determined never to allow himself to be entrapped in the same way again.

The next morning the king, accompanied by his principal officials, returned to the apartment where the *sannyasi* had been left the night before, in order to offer him anew the homage due to his holiness. But what was their surprise to find that he had disappeared! This circumstance, of course, only contributed to strengthen the faith of the public; and none doubted that this holy *sannyasi* was really a divine being who under human form had deigned to pay a passing visit to their monarch, and during the silence of the night had returned to the abode of happiness from which he had descended. The appearance of the holy personage, as well as his miraculous disappearance, formed for many days afterwards the sole topic of conversation at the court, in the town, and throughout the entire kingdom, until at length people grew tired of always repeating the same story, and nothing more was heard of it.

A short time after the event Appaji was one day at the court of the king his master, when the latter reminded him of the question which he had asked him to solve, viz. Is it the customs which are ridiculous, or only the men who follow those customs? Appaji was only waiting for his opportunity of answering; and having obtained an assurance from the king that nothing he said would offend his majesty, if his explanation were sincere and full, he addressed the king as follows:—'Great king, your own conduct solved the question in a manner quite irrefutable, at the time when you visited the cave in the mountain to see the penitent. You will no doubt be astonished to hear that this famous personage is none other than the shepherd who for many years has been looking after my sheep, a stupid and uncouth man who is only capable of inspiring you with the most sovereign contempt! Yet it is to this very personage that you and your whole court rendered divine honours; and that, moreover, on my sole testimony. The multitude followed blindly in your steps, and without trying to get to the bottom of the matter, or to gain any knowledge of the object of their devotion, they gave themselves up in an access of religious zeal to honour as a god an unknown and miserable shepherd who has hardly sufficient intelligence to distinguish him from brute beasts. Does not all this afford a most striking proof that men in their religious and civil usages only follow a beaten track? Thus you yourself have justified the truth of the ancient proverb which says: *Jatra marula, Jana marula.*'

Krishna Roya, far from being angry with the liberty which Appaji had taken with him in order to bring home to him the truth on a point of such importance, evinced, on the contrary, more affection and confidence than ever towards his minister, and continued to regard him as the most faithful and stanch of all his adherents.

CHAPTER XXVIII

Niti Slokas, or Moral Stanzas.

THE *slokas*, or moral stanzas, of which I am about to give a translation, are familiar to all Hindus who are in any way educated. In most Hindu schools children are made to learn them by heart as a kind of catechism. They are written in Sanskrit verse, but as this classical language is not studied or understood by many people, each *sloka* is accompanied by a literal translation in the vulgar tongue. The Hindus take great delight in introducing these *slokas* into their ordinary conversations. I have tried in my translation to diverge as little as possible from the original text; but the difficulty of reproducing in a European language certain terms and expressions peculiar to the Indian languages has resulted in a few of these sentences being somewhat incoherent. This fault, of course, is not observable when they are read in the original. In translating them I have followed the order observed by the Indian author. The original collection contains a very large number of others, but I have restricted myself to reproducing the principal of them in order not to tire my readers.

I. He who feeds us is our father; he who helps us is our brother; he who places his confidence in us is our friend; those whose sentiments accord with ours are our kinsmen.

II. If a margosa seed be dropped into a beverage composed of sugar, honey, and ghee, the whole of it becomes so bitter, that although milk may rain upon it for a thousand years the mixture will lose nothing of its bitterness. This is symbolical of the wicked, who, however good people may be to them, never lose their natural tendency to do evil.

III. Beware of becoming attached to any country which is not your own, or of serving any master who is a foreigner;

renounce all relatives who are only so nominally; keep nothing which does not belong to you; and leave a *guru* who can do you no good.

IV. If you undertake to do anything which you find to be beyond your powers, give it up at once. If an individual dishonours a whole class, he should be excommunicated; if a single inhabitant causes ruin to a whole village, he should be expelled from it; if a village causes the ruin of a district, it should be destroyed; and if a district causes the ruin of the soul, it must be abandoned[1].

V. In the afflictions, misfortunes, and tribulations of life only he who actively helps us is our friend.

VI. Just as a plant of the forest becomes a friend of the body when by virtue of its medicinal properties it cures an illness which afflicts the body, however different the one may be from the other; similarly, he who renders us services should be considered our friend, however lowly may be his condition and however far he may be separated from us; whereas he who affects to be our friend should, if he attempts to hurt us, be regarded as our enemy.

VII. One may render good service to the wicked, yet whatever good one may do to them resembles characters written in water, which are effaced as soon as they are written; but services rendered to good people are like characters engraved on stone, which are never effaced.

VIII. One should keep oneself five yards distant from a carriage, ten yards from a horse, one hundred yards from an elephant; but the distance one should keep from a wicked man cannot be measured.

IX. If one ask which is the more dangerous venom, that of a wicked man or that of a serpent, the answer is, that however subtle the poison of a serpent may be, it can at any rate be counteracted by virtue of *mantrams*; but it is beyond all power to save a person from the venom of a wicked man.

[1] The first sentence appears to form part of another *sloka*. The correct rendering of this *sloka* is:—If an individual dishonours a family, he may be expelled from the family; if a family dishonours a village, it may be expelled from the village; if a village dishonours a district, it may be destroyed; if one's country is dangerous to one's personal safety, it may be abandoned.—Ed.

X. To attempt to change the character of a wicked man by being kind to him is like trying to make a hog clean. It is no use to mix water with milk and offer the same to an eagle, for the eagle knows the secret of separating the milk from the water[1]. This is symbolical of the wicked.

XI. The venom of a scorpion is to be found in its tail, that of a fly in its head, that of a serpent in its fangs; but the venom of a wicked man is to be found in all parts of his body.

XII. A wise man preserves an equal mind both in adversity and in prosperity. He allows himself neither to be crushed by the former, nor elated by the latter.

XIII. An intelligent man is he who knows when to speak and when to be silent, whose friendship is natural and sincere, and who never undertakes anything beyond his powers.

XIV. Virtue is the best of friends, vice is the worst of enemies, disappointment is the most cruel of illnesses, courage is the support of all.

XV. Just as the crow is the Pariah among birds, and the ass the Pariah among quadrupeds, so is an angry *sannyasi* the Pariah among penitents; but the vilest of Pariahs is the man who despises his fellows.

XVI. Just as the moon is the light of the night and the sun the light of the day, so are good children the light of their family.

XVII. Flies look for ulcers, kings for war, wicked men for quarrels; but good men look only for peace.

XVIII. The virtuous man may be compared to a large leafy tree which, while it is itself exposed to the heat of the sun, gives coolness and comfort to others by covering them with its shade.

XIX. When we die the money and jewels which we have taken such trouble to amass during our life remain in the house. Our relatives and friends accompany us only to the funeral pyre where our bodies are burnt; but our virtues and our vices follow us beyond the grave.

XX. Temporal blessings pass like a dream, beauty fades like a flower, the longest life disappears like a flash. Our existence may be likened to the bubble that forms on the surface of water.

[1] In the Hindu proverb it is the swan which is credited with this power, and not the eagle, as Dubois states it.—ED.

XXI. Take heed not to trust yourself to the current of a river, to the claws or the horns of an animal, or to the promises of kings.

XXII. Take heed to place no trust in a false friend; only disappointment will be experienced from a wicked woman; nothing good can be hoped for from a person who is forced to act against his inclinations; nothing but misfortune can be looked for in a country where injustice prevails.

XXIII. A man of courage is recognizable in a moment of danger, a good wife when one is reduced to misery, firm friends in times of adversity, and faithful relatives at the time of a marriage.

XXIV. A hypocrite who disguises his true character and wishes to pass for an honest man is comparable to strong vinegar which one tries to make sweet by mixing with it camphor, musk, and sandal. The attempt may well be made, but the vinegar will never altogether lose its sourness.

XXV. To show friendship for a man in his presence and to libel him in his absence is to mix nectar with poison.

XXVI. A mirror is of no use to a blind man; in the same way knowledge is of no use to a man without discernment.

XXVII. Take care to spend nothing without hope of profit; to undertake nothing without reflection; to begin no quarrel without good cause. He who does not follow these golden rules courts his own ruin.

XXVIII. He who works with diligence will never feel hunger; he who devoutly meditates will never commit any great sin; he who is vigilant will never feel fear; and he who knows when to speak and when to be silent will never be drawn into a quarrel.

XXIX. Truth is our mother, justice our father, pity our wife, respect for others our friend, clemency our children. Surrounded by such relatives we have nothing to fear.

XXX. It is easier to snatch a pearl from the jaws of a crocodile or to twist an angry serpent round one's head like a garland of flowers without incurring danger, than to make an ignorant and obstinate person change his ideas.

XXXI. The miser acknowledges neither god nor *guru*, neither parents nor friends. He who suffers from hunger pays no heed whether the viands be well or ill seasoned. He who loves and cultivates knowledge has no taste for idleness. The froward person has neither shame nor restraint.

XXXII. Temporal blessings are like foam upon the water; youth passes like a shadow; riches disappear like clouds before the wind. Therefore to virtue alone should we hold fast.

XXXIII. Let us realize well that death watches like a tiger to seize us unawares, sickness pursues us like a relentless enemy, earthly joys are like a leaky vessel from which water trickles ceaselessly until it is empty.

XXXIV. Before the existence of earth, water, air, wind, fire, Brahma, Vishnu, Siva, sun, stars, and other objects, God One and Eternal was in existence.

XXXV. Pride and arrogance suit no one; constancy, humanity, sweetness, compassion, truth, love for one's neighbour, conjugal fidelity, goodness, amiability, cleanliness, are all qualities that distinguish really virtuous people. He who possesses all these ten qualities is a true *guru*.

XXXVI. Unhappy is the son whose father contracts debts; unhappy is the father whose son bears a bad character; unhappy is the wife whose husband is unfaithful.

XXXVII. To show friendship to a man while he is prosperous and to turn one's back upon him when he is in distress, is to imitate the conduct of prostitutes, who evince affection for their protectors only so long as they are opulent and abandon them as soon as they are ruined.

XXXVIII. There are six things which almost invariably entail unhappy consequences—the service of kings, robbery, horsebreaking, the accumulation of wealth, sorcery, and anger.

XXXIX. Never make known one's condition, one's wealth, one's mistress, one's *mantrams*, one's remedies, the place where one has hidden his money, the good works which one does, the insults which one has received, or the debts which one has contracted.

XL. Knowledge is the health of the body, poverty is its plague, gaiety is its support, sadness makes it grow old.

XLI. A shameless man fears the maladies engendered by luxury, a man of honour fears contempt, a rich person fears the rapacity of kings, gentleness fears violence, beauty fears old age, the penitent fears the influence of the senses, the body fears Yama, the god of death; but the miser and the envious fear nothing.

XLII. Just as milk nourishes the body and intemperance causes it to sicken, so does meditation nourish the spirit, while dissipation enervates it.

XLIII. It is prudent to live on good terms with one's cook, with ballad-mongers, with doctors, with magicians, with the ruler of one's country, with rich people, and with obstinate folk.

XLIV. Birds do not perch on trees where there is no fruit; wild beasts leave the forests when the leaves of the trees have fallen and there is no more shade for them; insects leave plants where there are no longer flowers; leeches leave springs which no longer flow; women leave men who have become old or poverty-stricken; a minister leaves the service of an obstinate king; servants leave a master who has been reduced to poverty. Thus it is that self-interest is the motive of everything in this world.

XLV. Only the sea knows the depth of the sea, only the firmament knows the expanse of the firmament; the gods alone know the power of the gods.

XLVI. However learned one may be, there is always something more to be learnt; however much in favour one may be with kings, there is always something to fear; however affectionate women may be, it is always necessary to be wary of them.

XLVII. The meaning of a dream, the effects of clouds in autumn, the heart of a woman, and the character of kings are beyond the comprehension of anybody.

XLVIII. It is more easy to discover flowers on the sacred fig-tree, or a white crow, or the imprint of fishes' feet, than to know what a woman has in her heart.

XLIX. The quality of gold is known by means of the touchstone; the strength of a bull is known by the weight that it will carry; the character of a man is known by his sayings; but there is no means by which we can know the thoughts of a woman.

L. Place no confidence in a parasite, or in a miser, or in any one who meddles in affairs which do not concern him. Do nothing to damage your friend. Avoid all communications with your friend's wife when he is away.

LI. A prudent man will never divulge his thoughts to another before he knows that other's thoughts.

LII. Nothing is more seductive and, at the same time, more deceitful than wealth. It is extremely troublesome to acquire, to keep, to spend, and to lose.

LIII. Courage is the most splendid quality in an elephant; high-spiritedness is the most splendid quality in a horse; the moon is the most beautiful ornament of the night; the sun is the most beautiful ornament of the day; cleanliness is the most beautiful ornament of the house; gentleness in words is the most beautiful ornament of speech; virtuous children are the most beautiful ornaments of families; so too is modesty the most beautiful ornament in a woman, and justice the most beautiful quality in kings.

LIV. Just as rain brings an end to famine, the bearing of children an end to a woman's beauty, an illicit transaction an end to the wealth of him who permits it; so does the degradation into which great people may fall bring an end to their greatness.

LV. When one sees blades of *sahrabi*[1] grass on white-ant heaps one can tell at once that snakes are there; so when one sees anybody frequenting the company of wicked men one may feel sure that he is as wicked as the others.

LVI. Grêat rivers, shady trees, medicinal plants, and virtuous people are not born for themselves, but for the good of mankind in general.

LVII. The joy of a Brahmin invited to a good feast, of a famished cow to which fresh grass is offered, or of a virtuous woman[2] who goes to a feast where she meets her long-absent husband is not greater than that of a good soldier who goes to the wars

LVIII. Only death can cut short the affection of a faithful woman for her family, of a tiger and other wild animals for their claws, of a miser for his riches, of a warrior for his weapons.

LIX. Take care not to fix your abode in a place where there is no temple, no headman, no school, no river, no astrologer, and no doctor.

[1] Dubois evidently means *darbha* grass.—ED.

[2] If Hindu stories are to be believed, it was formerly a practice among Hindu women, who happened to become separated from their husbands by accident, to get up a feast on a very large scale, and to invite people of all sorts and conditions to it on the chance of coming across their long-lost husbands.—ED.

LX. We may descend into hell, establish our dwelling in the abode of Brahma or in the paradise of Indra, throw ourselves into the depths of the sea, ascend to the summit of the highest mountain, take up our habitation in the howling desert or in the town where Kubera reigns, take refuge with Yama, bury ourselves in the bowels of the earth, brave the dangers of battle, sojourn in the midst of venomous reptiles, or take up our abode in the moon; yet our destiny will none the less be accomplished. All that will happen to us will be such as it is not in our power to avoid[1].

LXI. Bad ministers cause the ruin of kings, evil opportunities that of young men, worldly communications that of penitents, good works done without discernment that of Brahmins.

LXII. The vice or virtue which prevails in a kingdom is attributed to the monarch; the faults of kings, to their ministers; the defects of women, to their husbands; those of children, to their parents; and those of disciples, to their *gurus*.

LXIII. Just as intoxicating liquors destroy our sense of taste, so does a son of bad character destroy a whole family. The society of wicked men dishonours those whose company they frequent. Self-interest destroys friendships that are most firmly cemented.

LXIV. He who boasts of knowing that which he does not know and he who affects not to know that which he does know are equally blameworthy.

LXV. There are three kinds of persons who are well received everywhere—a gallant warrior, a learned man, and a pretty woman.

LXVI. The favours of a prostitute appear like nectar at first, but they soon become poison. The pursuit of knowledge is troublesome at first, but knowledge is a source of great delight when it is acquired.

LXVII. A virtuous man ought to be like the sandal-tree, which perfumes the axe that destroys it.

[1] In order to understand clearly the sense of this stanza, one must remember that Hindus admit the doctrine of absolute predestination, and assert that the destiny of each man is irrevocably written on his forehead by the hand of Brahma himself.—DUBOIS.

CHAPTER XXIX

The Funeral Ceremonies of Brahmins

THE closing moments of a Brahmin's life are associated with a number of ridiculous ceremonies. One might suppose therefrom that Brahmins were eager to preserve after their death that superiority over their fellows which they boast about so much during their lifetime; and that their desire was to surpass everybody else in the foolishness of their practices at the period when the scythe of Father Time reduced *these gods of the earth* to the level of the humblest Pariah. For the rest, most Hindus observe very many formalities when their near relatives die. As soon as the symptoms of death become manifest in a Brahmin, a spot is chosen on the ground and smeared over with cow-dung. On this *darbha* grass is strewn, and over this again is placed a new and ceremonially pure cloth, upon which the dying man is then laid. His loins are next girded with another ceremonially pure cloth. Then, the dying man having given his permission, the ceremony called *sarva prayaschitta*, or perfect expiation, is performed by the *purohita* and the chief mourner—that is to say, the person who is most nearly related to the deceased or who by common usage has the right to perform this function. Then a few small coins of gold, silver, and copper are carried in on a metal salver, and in another *akshatas*, sandalwood, and *pancha-gavia*. The *purohita* pours a few drops of the *pancha-gavia* [1] into the mouth of the dying man, by virtue of which his body becomes perfectly purified. Then the general purification ceremonies are proceeded with. The *purohita* and the chief mourner invite the sick Brahmin to

[1] See Part I, Chapter XIII.

recite in spirit, if he cannot articulate distinctly, certain *mantrams*, by virtue of which he is delivered from all his sins. After this a cow is brought in along with her calf; her horns are ornamented with rings of gold or brass, her neck with garlands of flowers, while her body is covered with a new piece of cloth; and she is also decorated with various other ornaments. The cow is led up to the sick person, who takes her by the tail, and at the same time the *purohita* recites a *mantram* praying that the cow may lead the dying Brahmin by a happy road into the other world. The latter then makes a present of the animal to some other Brahmin, into whose hand he pours a few drops of water in token of the gift. This gift of a cow is called *godana*, and is indispensable if one wishes to arrive without mishap in Yama-loka, or the kingdom of Yama, the king of hell. Bordering Yama-loka there is a river of fire which all men must cross after they have ceased to live. Those who have made the *godana*, when they come to their last hour, will find on the banks of this river a cow which will help them to pass on to the opposite bank without being touched by the flame. After the *godana*, the coins placed on the metal salver are distributed to the Brahmins, and the sum total ought to equal the price of the cow. Afterwards the *dasa-dana*, or the ten gifts, are prepared. These are to be distributed at the obsequies which will subsequently take place. The gifts consist of cows, lands, gingelly seeds, gold, liquefied butter, cloth, various kinds of grains, sugar, silver, and salt. These ten articles, which are offered to the Brahmins, are supposed to be extremely acceptable to the gods, and procure for him who offers them a blessed sojourn in the Abode of Bliss after death.

A Brahmin must not be allowed to die on a bed or even on a mat, and for this reason: the soul in separating itself from the body in which it is incorporated enters into another body, which leads it to the Abode of Bliss destined for it, and if the dying Brahmin were to expire on a bed, he would be obliged to carry it with him wherever he went, which, it may easily be supposed, would be very inconvenient. Accordingly, it is necessary, in order to relieve the dying person of such a burden, to offer abundant alms and perform expensive ceremonies. This absurd custom has suggested a curse which is very common amongst the Brahmins when they quarrel with each other.

'Mayst thou,' they will say, 'have no person near thee to place thee on the ground in the hour of death!'

As soon as the dying person has breathed his last, it is a recognized custom that everybody present must at once burst into tears; and that in a fashion strictly laid down for the occasion. The chief mourner then proceeds to bathe without taking off his clothes, next has his head and face shaved, and lastly goes to bathe a second time in order to purify himself from the defilement of the barber's touch. On his return he causes to be brought to him *pancha-gavia*, gingelly oil, *darbha* grass, raw rice, and a few other things. He places on the ring finger of the right hand the *pavitram* [1]. Then he performs the *sam-kalpa*, and offers *homam* (sacrifice to fire) in order that the deceased may obtain a place in heaven.

Then the corpse is washed, and the barber shaves off all the hair. It is washed a second time, and after that sandalwood and *akshatas* are placed upon the forehead and garlands of flowers round the neck. The mouth is filled with betel-leaves and the body is apparelled in rich raiment and jewels. It is then placed on a kind of state bed, where it remains exposed to view during the time that the preparations for the obsequies are proceeding. When these have been finished, the person who is presiding at the ceremony brings a new piece of ceremonially pure cloth in which he wraps the corpse. A strip of this cloth is torn off, and a small piece of iron, on which a few drops of gingelly oil are poured, is tied up in it. This cloth is twisted into the form of a triple cord, and must be kept for twelve days, to be used in the various ceremonies of which I shall speak later on.

The litter on which the body is placed is constructed as follows. To two long parallel poles are fastened transversely seven pieces of wood with ropes of straw, and on this the body is placed. Then they bind the toes and the two thumbs together [2]. The shroud, which until then has been merely thrown over the body, is now wrapped around it, and is bound strongly with straw ropes. If the dead Brahmin happens to leave a wife behind, his face is left uncovered. The chief mourner then gives the signal to depart, and, carrying fire in

[1] See Part I, Chapter XIII.

[2] As soon as a person breathes his last his toes and thumbs are tied with a small piece of cloth.—ED.

an earthen vessel, puts himself at the head of the procession. After him comes the funeral litter, ornamented with flowers, green leaves, coloured cloths, and sometimes costly stuffs. Surrounding it are the parents and friends of the deceased, all of them without turbans, and having simply a piece of cloth thrown over their heads in token of mourning. The women are never allowed to attend the funeral ceremonies out of doors[1]. They remain in the house and utter most lamentable cries. On the way to the funeral pyre three halts are made. Each time the mouth of the dead person is opened, and a little raw and soaked rice is placed in it, so that hunger and thirst may at the same time be satisfied. These halts, however, have a more serious motive. Instances have been known, it is said, of persons believed to be dead having not been so in reality, or if really dead having come to life again[2]. Seeing that the spirits of the nether world or their emissaries have been known to make mistakes in their choice and to take one person for another, these halts are made to give plenty of time for the spirits to recognize any mistakes they may have made, so that no person may be thrown on the funeral pyre who is still destined to live. Each of these halts lasts about a quarter of an hour. On arrival at the burning-ground a shallow pit is first dug, about six feet in length and three in breadth. This is then consecrated by *mantrams* and sprinkled with ceremonial water, while several small pieces of money are thrown into it.

Then the funeral pyre is erected, and the corpse is placed upon it. The chief mourner next takes a small ball of dry cow-dung, sets fire to it, places it upon the hollow of the deceased's stomach, and performs on this lighted bratty the sacrifice of *homam*. Then follows a most extraordinary ceremony, which at the same time is certainly a very disgusting one, the chief mourner placing his lips successively to all the apertures of the

[1] This is not true of the Brahmins, whose women always follow the procession to the cremation ground.—ED.

[2] These halts are made to allow time for recovery, if the man is not dead, before reaching the cremation ground. For it is a firm belief that if by any chance the supposed corpse should revive after reaching the pyre, dire consequences would result to the village. He is not, under those circumstances, allowed to go back to the village, but is expelled altogether.—ED.

deceased's body, addressing to each a *mantram* appropriate to it, kissing it, and dropping on it a little ghee. By this ceremony the body is supposed to be completely purified. The chief mourner then places a small piece of gold money in the mouth, and everybody present in turn deposits in it a few grains of soaked rice. The near relatives then approach and deprive the corpse of all the jewels with which it is adorned, and even of its shroud; and then it is covered with small splinters of wood which are sprinkled with *pancha-gavia*. The chief mourner walks round the funeral pyre three times, and pours upon it some water that is allowed to trickle from an earthen vessel which he carries on his shoulder, and which he afterwards breaks on the head of the deceased.

This last act and that which follows formally constitute him the dead man's heir[1]. Then a lighted torch is brought to him. Before he takes it, however, it is customary for him to show his grief by uttering mournful cries. In displaying his grief he rolls upon the ground, strikes his breast fiercely with his hand, and makes the air resound with his cries. Following his example, all present also weep bitterly, or pretend to do so, holding themselves clasped one to another as a sign of grief. Then, taking hold of the torch, the chief mourner sets fire to the four corners of the pile. As soon as the flames have caught hold of it everybody retires, with the exception of the four Brahmins who have carried the corpse, and who must remain on the spot until the whole pyre has been consumed. Meanwhile the heir goes to bathe himself without taking off his

[1] 'The offering to deceased fathers at the *sraddha* is the key to the Hindu law of inheritance. It furnishes the principal evidence of kinship, on which the title to participate in the patrimony is founded, no power of making wills being recognized in Manu, or any other authoritative code of Hindu Jurisprudence. . . . The object of such *sraddhas* is two-fold, viz. first, the re-embodying of the soul of the deceased in some kind of form after cremation of the corpse, or simply the release of the subtile body which is to convey the soul away. Secondly, the raising him from the regions of the atmosphere, where he would have otherwise to roam for an indefinite period among demons and evil spirits to a particular heaven or region of bliss. There he is eventually half deified among the shades of departed kinsmen. Manu, however, is not clear as to the precise effect of the *sraddha*. He merely states that its performance by a son or the nearest male kinsman is necessary to deliver a father from a kind of hell called *Put*, and that the spirits of the departed (*Pitris*) feed on the offered food.'—MONIER-WILLIAMS.

clothes; while soaked in this way, he selects a clear spot on the ground and causes rice and pulse to be cooked there in a new earthenware vessel, which he must keep carefully for the ten days following. Then directing his thoughts to the deceased, he pours a libation of oil and water on the ground, strews *darbha* grass over it, which he also sprinkles with the same mixture of oil and water, and on this again he places the rice and pulse after moulding them in the form of balls. A third libation is then offered, *mantrams* are recited, and the balls are thrown to the crows, which, as every one knows, are very common in India. The Hindus believe these noisy and rapacious birds to be evil spirits, in fact, devils under the form of crows. This offering, therefore, is intended to render them kindly disposed towards the dead man. If they refuse to accept the food, which we are told sometimes happens, it is a very bad omen for him, and instead of being admitted into the Abode of Bliss he will find himself, despite all the *mantrams* and purifying ceremonies, made captive in the Yama-loka, that is to say, in hell.

After the corpse has been consumed, the four Brahmins who remained near the pyre return to the place where the other people present at the ceremonies have gathered together[1]. Three times they walk round the assembly, asking permission to take the *bath of the Ganges.* Then they proceed to perform their ablutions in order to purify themselves of the pollution of having carried a corpse. The chief mourner invites all present to take the *bath of the dead*, the *mritika-snana*, which is supposed to be on behalf of the deceased whose body has just been consumed by the flames. This bath, it is supposed, will refresh it after the fiery ordeal. Then a few small coins and some betel-leaves are distributed among those present, and every one who has a right to them is presented with the *dasa-dana*, after which all return to the door of the deceased's house, though no person enters the house because it is still defiled. Finally, everybody washes his feet and returns to his own house.

Nevertheless, for the heir another ceremony still remains, which consists in filling a little chatty with earth and sowing nine kinds of grain, namely rice, barley, gingelly seeds, and the five kinds of pulse. He waters them so that they may quickly sprout and be used for certain ceremonies which follow.

[1] These people always meet on the bank of a river or a tank.—ED.

A thing of the very highest importance that he must do that day is to place in the habitation of the deceased a small vessel full of water, over which he hangs a thread tied at one end to the ceiling[1]. This thread is intended to serve as a ladder to the *prana*, that is to say, to the life-breath which animated the body of the deceased, and which by this thread is enabled to descend and drink the water during the ten days which follow. And in order that the *prana* may have something to eat as well as to drink, a handful of rice is placed each morning by the side of the vessel.

It is not until all these ceremonies and formalities have been accomplished that the people of the house are allowed to take any food. For they have neither eaten nor drunk anything since the moment that the deceased gave up the ghost. All these practices and those which I will briefly detail in the following chapter are most rigorously observed. The omission of the most minute of them would cause no less scandal than the omission of the more important. Nevertheless poverty is allowed as an excuse for neglecting those which entail large expenditure. For instance, most Brahmins would be quite unable to make the *dasa-dana*, or ten gifts.

It is to be observed that these practices, however superstitious they may appear, clearly denote that the Hindus have preserved a most distinct idea of the immortality of the soul; that they recognize the corruption of human nature and the necessity of resorting to means of purification for enabling the soul to enter the blessed state and enjoy the rights which it has forfeited through sin. And the *prana*, for instance, which is regarded by the Hindus sometimes as the soul and sometimes as the breath of life, reminds us of the *spiraculum vitae* of the Holy Scriptures, by the aid of which the Creator gave life to the clay out of which He formed mankind.

[1] This is not done in some parts of South India.—ED.

CHAPTER XXX

The Various Ceremonies observed after Burial in honour of the Dead.

HINDU mourning lasts one year, during which a large number of ceremonies have to be observed. The principal are as follow:—

On the day after the funeral the chief mourner, accompanied by his relatives and friends, goes to the place consecrated to the burning of the dead. There he recommences the ceremonies of the previous evening, without forgetting the food for the crows, and places on the ground the strip of cloth which has been torn from the pall. The Brahmins present take *the bath of the dead* (*mritika-snana*), receive betel, and depart. The heir, however, keeps back one of them, and gives him two measures of rice, peas, and vegetables, wrapped in a new cloth, which he presents as well, so that he may make a good meal and be well clothed by proxy as it were for the deceased, in case the rice, the peas, the oil, and the water which have already been offered for the latter may not be sufficient to allay his hunger and quench his thirst, and so that he may not be without clothes to cover his nakedness in the next world.

On the third day, the heir again summons his relatives and friends. He erects a small *pandal* in a corner of his courtyard, and has rice, seven sorts of vegetables, cakes, &c., cooked there. When these viands have been prepared, he places them on a cloth folded in four, and covers them all with another cloth. Then five small earthen pots are brought filled with *pancha-gavia*, as also a measure of rice, some peas, vegetables, sandalwood, *akshatas*, three small pieces of cloth dyed yellow, some flour, a small stick two cubits in length, some betel, some gingelly oil, and the ten gifts (*dasa-dana*). Provided with all these and accompanied by his relatives, he returns to the burning-ground. There he performs his ablutions, puts on the ring *pavitram*, performs the *sam-kalpa*, and then fills a new earthen pot with water, which he sprinkles over the ashes of the deceased. After that he sprinkles them with milk. He squats on his heels with his face turned to the east, performs once more the *sam-kalpa*, stirs the ashes with the small stick above mentioned, looking for any bones that may have escaped the flames, and these he puts into an earthen pot, reciting a *mantram* meanwhile. Gathering up a portion of the ashes, he throws them into the water. The remainder he collects into a heap, to which he gives the rough semblance of a human figure, supposed to represent the deceased. He offers as sacrifice to it a portion of the things he has brought, sprinkles it with *pancha-gavia*, and puts the whole into an earthen pot. These sad mementoes of the deceased are destined to be thrown subsequently into one of the sacred rivers.

He then raises a mound of earth twelve inches high on the exact spot where the dead body has been burnt, and taking three small stones he places one in the middle of the mound, which receives the name of the deceased; the second, which he places at the south end, is named Yama; and the third, which he places at the north end, is called Rudra. Calling these three stones by the names which he has given them, he proceeds to rub them over with gingelly oil, bathes them while he continues to recite *mantrams*, and clothes them in the three pieces of yellow cloth with which he has provided himself. Afterwards, putting them back in their places, he offers them *puja* and *neiveddya*, and pours a libation of oil and water in honour of each particular one. Then all the Brahmins present file in one by one, embrace the chief mourner, and weep with him. The distribution of *dasa-danà* follows as on the first day.

The three stones are next placed in the earthen pot that is intended for cooking the rice and the peas, which are mixed with a fresh supply of these vegetables, and the heir carries it all to the border of the tank. After cooking the viands he offers them to the three stones, repeats his libations, and at last throws the rice and the peas to the crows. A meal and a cloth are again bestowed on a Brahmin by proxy as it were for the deceased; and the day ends in pretty much the same manner as those preceding it.

It is considered of great importance to preserve carefully for ten days the three little stones, as well as the pot used for the cooking of the crows' food. If by misfortune a single one of these articles were lost, all the ceremonies would have to be begun over again.

From the fourth to the ninth day inclusive, these foolish ceremonies are repeated daily. The objects are (1) to prevent the deceased suffering from hunger, thirst, and nakedness; (2) to enable him to divest himself as quickly as possible of his hideous and ghastly carcase and to assume a beautiful form, so that, in a new birth, he may be neither deaf, nor blind, nor dumb, nor lame, nor afflicted with any bodily infirmity.

On the tenth day the chief mourner rises early to make his ablutions, constructs a little *pandal* in his courtyard, causes rice, peas, and three sorts of vegetables to be cooked there, prepares the drink called *paramanna*, and some rice cakes cooked in water. He places the whole on a large plantain leaf, with three pieces of saffron on the top. In short, he prepares all the articles indispensable for the sacrifices and offerings which he is about to make.

When all is ready, the widow of the deceased, after performing her ablutions, paints her eyelids with antimony, her forehead with vermilion, her neck with sandalwood-paste, her arms and legs with saffron; she then puts on her richest garments, bedecks herself with all her jewels, twines red flowers in her hair, and hangs garlands of sweet-smelling flowers round her neck. The married women surround her, clasp her by turns in their arms, and weep with her.

The chief mourner, provided with all his sacrificial paraphernalia, and followed by his relatives and friends, as well as by the widow and her companions, returns once more to the burning-ground, where all the preparatory ceremonies are renewed just as those already described. This time he mixes some earth with water, and spreads three coats of the mud on the three stones, accompanied by *mantrams*, adjurations, sacrifices, offerings, &c.

The women present then surround the widow once more,

beating their heads and breasts in measured time and weeping and sobbing as loud as they can.

The chief mourner makes three little balls of boiled rice and peas, places them on the ground on *darbha* grass, pours a libation of oil and water, offers the little balls to the deceased, and then throws them to the crows.

He puts back the three stones into the earthen pot which has played so important a part during these ten days, carries them to the edge of the tank, performs *sam-kalpa*, puts the ring *pavitram* on his finger, walks into the water up to his neck, turns to the east, and looking towards the sun, says:—

'Till now, these stones have represented the dead body; may that dead body from this moment leave its hideous form and take that of the gods! May it be transported into *Swarga* to enjoy all its pleasures as long as the Ganges shall flow, as long as these stones shall last!'

At these words he throws the pot and the stones inside it over his head into the water. Then he performs his ablutions, returns to the bank, performs the *sam-kalpa*, and distributes the *dasa-dana*. Then, with the permission of the Brahmins, he and his near relatives are shaved; for during these ten days of mourning shaving is not allowed. Finally, after numberless foolish ceremonies, of which I have given only a short epitome, all repair to the edge of the tank. There a heap of earth four fingers high is made, on which is placed a little ball also of earth, which receives the name of the deceased. Then the widow, surrounded by her companions and showing no sign of grief, divests herself of her jewels and rich garments, wipes off the artificial pigments with which she had smeared different parts of her body, and finally takes off the *tali* which she wears round her neck. This discarded ornament she places near the ball of earth which represents her deceased husband, uttering these words the while: 'I abandon all these to prove to thee my love and my devotion.' Then ensue fresh wailings and weepings on the part of her companions.

The *purohita* appears on the scene at this moment to perform the *puniaha-vachana*, that is, the consecration of holy water[1]. He makes all the women who are participating in the mourning drink a little of this water, and sprinkles some drops on their

[1] See Part I, Chapter XIII.

heads. By this means they obtain purification from the defilement which they have contracted by taking part in the funeral ceremonies.

The heir gives to each person present an areca-nut and a betel-leaf, and to the widow a white cloth, which she immediately puts on.

Finally, all return to the house of the deceased, where, after having inspected the lamp, which ought to have been kept burning all this time on the spot where the deceased breathed his last, each one takes leave and does not enter his own house till he has washed his feet at the door.

Being now left alone, the heir takes the five little earthen pots in which he had sown some seeds on the first day, offers them *puja*, and then throws them into the water.

On the eleventh day, as soon as his ablutions are over, he goes to summon nineteen Brahmins, to whom he first of all offers a feast to be eaten by proxy for the deceased. Then he puts into a basket a large earthen chatty containing two measures of rice, and into another basket several more earthen pots of a smaller size. He provides himself with liquefied butter, gingelly oil, *darbha* grass, flowers, &c., and, accompanied by the Brahmins invited, goes to the edge of the tank. There he digs a small hole, blesses it with *mantrams*, places therein his little earthen pots, and lights a fire. At the four corners of the hole he places *darbha* grass and sprinkles oil all round it. He spreads some boiled rice on a plantain leaf, sprinkles it with ghee, and makes it into thirty-six little balls, which he throws subsequently into the fire one after the other. To this fire he makes profound obeisance, beseeching it to grant the deceased access into the Abode of Bliss. He then distributes *dasa-dana* and gives the Brahmins some betel. The latter then go to bathe themselves, and return to assist in the ceremony of *the deliverance of the bull*.

For this purpose a bull three years old is chosen. It must be all of one colour, either white, red, or black. After washing it they smear it with sandalwood-paste and *akshatas*, decorate it with garlands of flowers, and with a red-hot iron brand on the right haunch the figure of one of Siva's weapons called *sulah*. The chief mourner implores this god to consent to the *deliverance of the bull*, so that, as a reward for this good deed, the deceased may find a place in an Abode of Bliss. They then set loose the bull, which is allowed to wander about grazing without a keeper wherever it likes, and it is given as a present to some Brahmin[1].

The nineteen Brahmin guests seat themselves in a line on small stools. The heir spreads *darbha* grass before them, and gives a blade of it to each, while reciting a *mantram* and uttering the name of the deceased. He then sprinkles some drops of oil on their heads, presents them with sandalwood-paste, gives to each a present of two pieces of cloth, offers a libation of oil and water, and again serves them with food.

The repast over, he mixes some boiled rice, peas, and herbs together, rolling them all into three balls, which he puts into an earthen pot. After sundry libations, offerings, and other formalities, he throws these three balls to the cattle and dismisses the nineteen Brahmins, who, before returning home, take good care to bathe.

On the twelfth day the heir goes to summon eight Brahmins, and makes them sit down on as many stools in front of him. He chooses one of them to represent the corpse of the dead man, and gives him, as well as the seven others, a blade of *darbha* grass with the usual ceremony. He then traces three squares on the ground, over which he spreads cow-dung, which he blesses with *mantrams*, and over this again he pours oil and spreads *darbha* grass. In the middle square he places the Brahmin whom he has appointed to represent the corpse, sprinkles over his feet oil and *darbha* grass, and then washes them with water.

Two other Brahmins step into the second square, and the five others into the third. To each of them he performs the same office. Having made them sit down, he approaches the one who represents the corpse, sprinkles on his head and hands some drops of oil, while repeating a *mantram*, puts earrings in his ears and a gold ring on his finger, makes him a present of two pieces of cloth, a white blanket, a brass *chembu* (drinking bowl), and some betel, hangs round his neck one of the rosaries called *rudrakshas*, and smears him with sandalwood-paste. Each of the seven others also receives two pieces of cloth, a white

[1] These bulls are usually dedicated to a temple, and they are used for breeding purposes.—ED.

blanket, and a *chembu*. Then they all take part in the repast prepared for them. At its conclusion the heir puts some rice and oil in a dish, and moulds four balls, which he places on the ground after performing the necessary formalities. One of these balls is intended for the deceased, a second for the deceased's father, a third for his grandfather, and the last for his great-grandfather. Taking the deceased's ball, he says:—

'Till now thou hast preserved the hideous appearance of a corpse: from this moment thou shalt clothe thyself in the divine form of thy ancestors; thou shalt inhabit with them the *pitri-loka* (abode of the ancestors) and there enjoy every sort of happiness.'

He then divides this ball into three portions and mixes one portion with each of the remaining three balls.

In the same way he tears the little strip of cloth which represents the triple cord of the deceased into three pieces and puts one on each ball. To all of these he makes offerings and libations. After this, comes a further distribution of *dasa-dana*. Finally, the balls and offerings are thrown to the cattle.

When all this long and monotonous ceremony is ended, the chief mourner anoints his head with oil, takes a bath, and returns home well covered up in a cloth. He embraces his relatives and friends, addressing words of consolation to each in turn. He paints his forehead with sandalwood-paste and *akshatas*, resumes his turban and ordinary clothes, and distributes presents according to his means.

The *purohita* also recites a great many *mantrams*, and sprinkles all the corners of the house with holy water, by which means it is purified, together with all those who inhabit it[1].

On the thirteenth day the heir performs *homam* in the accustomed manner in honour of the nine planets.

A ceremony something like that of the twelfth day takes place on the twenty-seventh; but only three Brahmins take part in this, representing respectively the deceased, his father, and his grandfather. One is supposed to call himself Vasudeva,

[1] The same kind of ceremony took place amongst the Romans on the tenth day, named *denicales feriae*. As may have been observed, this is not the only feature of resemblance between the funeral ceremonies of the Romans and those of the Hindus.—DUBOIS.

the second calls himself Yama, and the third calls himself the Sun. The heir makes the usual offerings and libations to these personages, gives each of them a piece of cloth, and has a meal served up to them, at the end of which he kneads three balls composed of rice, peas, and herbs, which are solemnly offered to the deceased and his two ancestors.

The same ceremony is repeated on the 30th, 45th, 60th, 75th, 90th, 120th, 175th, 190th, 210th, 240th, 270th, 300th, and 330th day after the death of the deceased. Further, the anniversaries of the deaths of his father and mother must be celebrated by a Hindu all his life long without fail; and each time most of the formalities just mentioned must be observed and liberal gifts made to Brahmins.

At each new moon it is the indispensable duty of a man to offer a libation of oil and water to his deceased father, as well as to his grandfather and to his great-grandfather[1].

I have mentioned that the pecuniary circumstances of many Brahmins do not allow of their fulfilling to the letter the costly obligations imposed upon a chief mourner. But there are a great many which are obligatory and which entail considerable expense. Conceit and vanity, which are such strong incentives in the minds of Brahmins, induce many of them to contract debts infinitely beyond their means in order to make a show on such occasions.

The funeral ceremony for a woman is nearly the same as that for a man. Rather less attention, however, is paid to a widowed mother of a family. And much less still to a widow who dies without children; the flames of the funeral pile have scarcely consumed the mortal remains of such a one before she is forgotten. When a Brahmin woman dies, the married women, kinswomen, or friends of the family assist at her funeral ceremony, and it is they who receive the usual presents and distributions.

The obsequies of the Kshatriyas and Vaisyas are performed with nearly the same pomp as those of the Brahmins, the ceremonies which are observed lasting twelve days.

It is always a *purohita* who presides at the death-bed, and who

[1] And also to their wives. Libations are also sometimes offered to the maternal grandfather, great-grandfather, and great-great-grandfather and their wives.—ED.

directs the mourning ceremonies in both these castes. The chief mourner invites the Brahmins, to whom offerings and presents are made. These ceremonies are repeated every month during the first year; and after that it suffices if the *titi*, that is the anniversary, is celebrated regularly.

The last services which the Sudras render to their dead are accompanied by much less ceremony and formality. They have neither *mantrams* nor sacrifices. However, when a Sudra's last hour is come, it is customary to call a Brahmin to go through the ceremony of *prayaschitta* (expiation) for him. His family is also permitted to bestow on the Brahmins *godana* and *dasa-dana*, as well as the other customary gifts and presents. As soon as a Sudra dies, they wash his body and have him shaved by the barber. Then they pay attention to his toilet, which they strive to render as elegant as possible, and afterwards place him sitting cross-legged on a sort of bed of state. When all is ready for the obsequies, they remove him, still in the same position, to an open litter, or shrine, ornamented with flowers, green leaves, and valuable cloths, or else to an open palanquin splendidly decorated. The body is then carried to the funeral pyre by twelve bearers.

Musical instruments are employed in the funeral processions of the Sudras, but never in those of the higher castes. The two principal instruments are the long trumpet, called in Tamil *tarai*, and the *sankha*, or *sangu*, another no less lugubrious instrument made out of a large sea-shell (the conch). As soon as a Sudra has breathed his last, two of these *tarais* are blown to announce the sad news to all the neighbours. Their harsh and piercing sounds are audible at a great distance, and cannot fail to inspire a pious horror wherever they are heard. One trumpet will sound a B flat, droning on this note for the space of half a minute; then another trumpet answers in G sharp; and thus they respond by turns. This monotonous and ear-splitting noise continues without interruption from the moment of death until the end of the obsequies.

Mourning in the Sudra caste lasts only three days. The third day is called the *day of milk offering*. To perform this ceremony the chief mourner provides himself with three young cocoanuts, four cocoanut branches, a measure of raw rice, some boiled rice, herbs, fruits, &c. He fills an earthen pot with milk, places it in a new basket, and accompanied by the relatives and friends of the family, preceded by conch-players, goes to the place where the body of the deceased was burnt. On his arrival he draws some water in an earthen pot and sprinkles it over the ashes on the pyre. Above this he erects a small *pandal*, covered with palm leaves and supported by four pillars, the interior of which he drapes with a piece of cloth. He collects the bones which have escaped the flames, puts the largest one on a flat cake made of dried cow-dung, and gathers up the rest in a heap. He calls the deceased by name and pours milk over the bones. During this libation the conch-players make the air resound with their lugubrious noise.

The chief mourner then piles up the ashes over the bones. At the side he places half a cocoanut, and on the top pieces of another cocoanut which he breaks, sprinkling the milk over this pyramid of ashes. He places a third cocoanut close by on a plantain leaf and invokes Harischandra[1].

Finally, he kneads the rice and other eatables which he has brought with him into a round mass and throws the whole to the crows, calling meanwhile upon the name of the deceased.

Then the relatives and friends come in turn to embrace the chief mourner, holding him in their arms and weeping with him. He takes the large bone which was placed in reserve; and all the mourners, to the doleful notes of the conches, go and throw this bone into the neighbouring tank. After bathing, all accompany the chief mourner to his house. There with much ceremony they put a new turban on his head, and each hastens to do justice to the repast prepared for the occasion. Thus ends the funeral ceremony.

Wealthy Sudras do not stop here. They proceed on the thirtieth day to a new ceremony, on which occasion they strive to rival the Brahmins in magnificence. And the Brahmins, since they enjoy all the honour and profit of the feast, take care not to show any jealousy.

The funeral ceremonies of the Sudras vary much in different districts. In some places Hindus of this caste bury their dead instead of burning them. In other places they throw the body into the river, deliberately feigning the river to be the Ganges. This kind of burial, the most expeditious and least costly of any,

[1] One of the kings of Ayodhya, who was famous for speaking the truth.—ED.

is common enough among the sects of Siva and the poorer classes of Sudras.

The solemn occasion when man shuffles off his mortal coil naturally offers ample matter for speculation to the imaginative Hindus. They attribute to the moon a sort of Zodiac composed of twenty-seven constellations, each of which presides at one of the twenty-seven days of its periodical course. The last five are all more or less fatal. Woe to the relatives of him who dies in the period when the moon travels through them! The body of the deceased, in this case, cannot be removed from the house either by the door or the window. It is absolutely necessary to make an opening through the wall for this purpose. And this is not all. To escape the unfortunate accidents which would inevitably follow such an untimely death, the most prudent course is to abandon the house for six months, or at least three months, according to the degree of the malign influence of the constellation which was in the ascendant on the day of death[1]. At the end of this time they remove the bushes with which they stuffed up the front door of the ill-fated house where the death occurred. The remotest corners of the building are carefully purified, a purification which can be completed only by the intervention of a *purohita*, who has to be called in, and of course paid for. Finally, a meal must be given to the Brahmins and presents must be made to them; after that the occupants will have nothing else to fear.

A death happening on Saturday entails almost equally serious inconveniences. It is a hundred to one in that case that another member of the same household will die before the year is out[2]. The only way to stave it off is to sacrifice a living animal, such as a ram, a he-goat, a fowl, &c., as a burnt offering.

Thus superstition follows the Hindu even to the last days of his existence. We have already seen what silly fancies assail him from his cradle. The child born under an unlucky star is not only himself destined, according to common belief, to all sorts of troubles and accidents during the course of his life, but he brings bad luck to those with whom he is united by the ties of blood; and it is not uncommon to see parents, convinced

[1] Nowadays it is customary simply to shut up the room in which a man dies.—ED.

[2] It is also believed that a death on a Thursday entails two other deaths in the same family.—ED.

of the truth of these so-called malign influences, quietly abandoning on a high-road innocent babes who happened to be born on a certain day which the prognostications of the professional astrologer have signified to be unlucky, or else handing them over to any one who is bold enough to run the risk of assuming charge of such an ill-omened burden[1]. There are even unnatural parents of this kind who go the length of cruelly strangling or drowning these tiny victims of most stupid and at the same time most atrocious superstition[2].

[1] Nowadays this is not practised.—Ed.

[2] Cases of infanticide were in quite recent times witnessed daily, especially on the banks of the Ganges, until at last the Government of Lord Wellesley declared that any one guilty of such a crime would be tried in the courts and punished with all the rigour of the law. This measure has had the good effect of diminishing the evil, but has not rooted it out altogether.—Dubois.

CHAPTER XXXI

The Third Condition of Brahmins, viz. *Vanaprastha*, or Dweller in the Jungle. —The Respect paid to *Vanaprasthas.*—Conjectures as to their Origin.—Comparison between them and the Wise Men of Greece and other Philosophers.—The Rules of the *Vanaprasthas.*—Their Renunciation of the World and Pleasures of the Senses.—Their Moral Virtues.

THE third condition of Brahmins is that of *Vanaprastha*, that is to say, dweller in the jungle. I doubt if there are any of them left in the country watered by the Indus and the Ganges, where this sect of philosophers certainly flourished at one time in great numbers. The sect has entirely disappeared from the Peninsula of India[1]. In ancient times the desire of sanctifying themselves in solitude and of reaching a higher degree of spiritual perfection induced numerous Brahmins to abandon

[1] It is indeed wholly improbable that all Brahmins conformed to this rule, but the second verse of the sixth book of the Laws of Manu prescribes that when the father of a family perceives his hair to be turning grey, or as soon as his first grandchild is born, and after he has paid his three debts, he is to retire to a forest, and there to practise austerities as a hermit:—

Having taken up his sacred fire (*agnihotram*) and all the domestic utensils for making oblations to it, and having gone forth from the town to the forest, let him dwell there with all his organs of sense well restrained.

With many kinds of pure food let him perform the five *maha-yajnas* or 'devotional rites.'

Let him also offer the *vaitanika* oblations with the (three sacred) fires according to rule.

Let him roll backwards and forwards on the ground, or stand all day on tiptoe (*prapadaih*); let him move about by alternately standing up and sitting down, going to the waters to bathe at the three *savanas* (sunrise, sunset, and midday).

Let him practise the rules of the lunar penance.

In the hot weather let him be a *panca-tapas.*

Let him offer libations (*tarpayet*) to the gods and *Pitris*, performing ablutions at the three *savanas.*

Having consigned the three sacred fires (*vaitanan*) to his own person (by swallowing the ashes) according to prescribed rules, let him remain without fire, without habitation, feeding on roots and fruits, practising the vow of a *muni* (i. e. the *mauna-vrata* of perpetual silence).—ED.

their residence in towns and their intercourse with mankind, and to go and live in the jungle with their wives, whom they persuaded to follow them. They were favourably received by those who had originally conceived this praiseworthy resolution, and from them they learned the rules of their life of seclusion. These philosophers brought much distinction to the Brahmin caste; and it even seems likely that the Brahmin caste owed its origin to them. They are still revered as the first teachers of the human race and the first lawgivers of their country.

There can be no doubt that it was the fame of these *Vanaprastha* Brahmins that excited so lively a curiosity in Alexander the Great. They were in fact none other than those Brachmanes and Gymnosophists whose customs, doctrines, and learning have been described by several ancient historians.

Mention is often made of these hermit Brahmins in the ancient books of India. They are there represented as living in solitary cells, entirely cut off from all intercourse with mankind and from all the distractions of social life, and devoting their whole time to spiritual observances.

The most famous and ancient of all were the seven great Penitents whom I have already several times mentioned. Their successors, too, continued to enjoy the highest renown. Kings paid them honours which reached the point of worship, and attached the greatest value to their benedictions. Princes trembled at the mere idea of incurring their wrath, convinced that their curse would entail direful consequences. This is how the author of the *Padma-purana* describes the reception of some *Vanaprasthas* by the great King of Dilipa:—

'Filled with unutterable joy and respect, he bowed himself to the ground before them. Then making them sit down, he washed their feet, drank some of the water that he used for that purpose, and poured the rest over his head. Joining his two hands together and putting them to his forehead, he made a profound obeisance and addressed them in these words: "The happiness which I feel to-day on seeing you can only be the reward of the good works which I must have done in previous existences; at the sight of your sacred feet, which are verily lotus flowers, I possess all that heart can desire; my body is perfectly pure, now that I have had the honour of seeing you. You are the gods whom I worship; I know no other gods but you. I am henceforth as pure as the water of the Ganges."'

It is not surprising that kings humbled themselves in the presence of these sages, seeing that the great gods themselves paid respect to them; and considered themselves honoured by their visits. Indeed there is no mark of distinction and respect which the gods did not bestow upon the *Vanaprasthas*, who, on their part, treated the gods with scant courtesy and very often with insolence. For example, one *Vanaprastha*, who visited the three principal Hindu divinities in turn, began by giving each a kick to see how they endured such an affront, and to learn their character by their behaviour. In fact, these penitents were wont to assume a kind of superiority over the gods, and punished them severely when they found them to blame. The evil deeds, and especially the lasciviousness, of Brahma, Siva, and Devendra, brought upon them the curses of many penitents.

The mythologies which relate these adventures, however absurd they may be, at any rate prove in what high estimation these hermits were held, and how ancient is their origin. On this last point I wish to add certain considerations to those which I have already mentioned, and will then leave the subject to my reader's own judgement.

I start again with the very probable hypothesis that in the seven Hindu Penitents who escaped the catastrophe of the Flood, are to be recognized the seven sons of Japheth, some of whom at the time of the dispersion of mankind must have come by way of Tartary and established themselves in India, becoming the first founders of Brahminism and the lawgivers of the families whose descendants peopled this portion of the globe. As is the case with all ancient civilized nations, time wrought changes in the laws which they instituted, regulating religious worship, morality, and the maintenance of social order: indeed, in all the wise measures which they took to preserve the well-being of their fellow-men. This is the common fate of all institutions which do not bear the impress of God. They either collapse altogether or become disfigured under the ever-repeated attacks of prejudice, passion, and, above all, personal interest. The simple but wise maxims of the first Hindu lawgivers soon degenerated into an abstract and subtle system of metaphysics, quite beyond the comprehension of all but a few adepts; and these latter, moved by a common ambition to lord it over their fellows, gradually formed an exclusive community isolated from the rest of the nation. The privacy of their life, their frugality, their contempt of riches, the purity of their morals, could not fail to gain for these earliest Brahmins the respect and veneration of the common people.

There can be no doubt that philosophy flourished in India before it had been so much as thought of in Greece. Of what account, in truth, was the learning of Greece, of what account her system of polity, until Pythagoras, Lycurgus, and other famous Greek travellers, animated by the desire of educating themselves, studied the manners and customs of Asiatic peoples, and borrowed, from the Hindus especially, many precepts and doctrines?

But though the philosophy of the Greeks was of later origin than that of the *Vanaprasthas,* it soon surpassed the latter in the clearness of its principles and the soundness of its morality. Under the guidance of the Greek philosophers an immense impulse was given to the cultivation of learning; and the most profound and luminous investigations were made regarding the nature of the Deity, until the gods of paganism were shorn of all the false glory which had hitherto surrounded them. The *Vanaprasthas* had already, it is true, made great progress in this direction; but yielding to the impulses of an unbridled imagination, they soon buried their philosophy beneath a heap of false ideas and vain imaginings with regard to the means of purifying the soul and to the spiritual side of life generally. The ridiculous principles which they enunciated ended by becoming, in their eyes, divinely sanctioned obligations; and from that time forward the wisest Hindus really became the most foolish.

This chimera of soul-purification which they pursued, so to speak, beyond the range of their own reasoning powers, led them from error to error, from pitfall to pitfall, until they likewise dragged down with them the people whose oracles they were.

The question arises, was there ever any connexion between the Hindu Gymnosophists and Zoroaster, or the Magi of Persia? All that I can say in answer to this question is that, though some resemblances may be traced between the Ghebres, or descendants of the ancient Persian fire-worshippers, and the Hindus in the worship which they both render to this element and to the sun, their religious doctrines and customs are in every other respect entirely different. Indeed, so far as I can see, the Hindu religious and political system is *sui generis* in its very foundations, and contains special characteristics of which no trace can be found in that of any other nation.

Only minute examination can bring to light certain features of resemblance between the moral and religious principles professed by Hindus and those of other ancient schools of philosophy in other countries. Several of the Brahminical rules of conduct correspond closely with those followed by Zeno and the Stoics; their plan of making their pupils learn everything by heart resembles that of the Druids; their taste for a solitary life, like that of the *Vanaprasthas*, is also shared by the Rechabites, the Therapeutics, the Children of the Prophet, the Magi of Persia, the Essenes of Egypt. But what arguments can be drawn from these feeble analogies to disprove the antiquity and originality of Hindu philosophy? And possibly it was the Hindus that furnished the original models, while the others only imitated them.

The life of a *Vanaprastha* was founded on the rigorous observance of certain established rules to which he bound himself on initiation. Here are some of the principal, as found in Hindu books, together with a few remarks of my own on each:—

I. 'The *Vanaprastha* must renounce the society of other men, even of his own caste, and must take up his abode in the jungle far from towns and all habitations.'

He did not, however, renounce the world so entirely but that he was permitted to appear in it from time to time; and of this there are several instances in Hindu works. Besides, after he had passed thirty-seven years in solitude, the penitent might resume his place in society without losing any of the consideration which belonged to him as a *Vanaprastha*.

II. 'He must take his wife with him, who will subject herself to the same rule of life as himself.'

It is by this rule especially that the *Vanaprastha* is distinguished from the *Sannyasi*, who is obliged to live in celibacy and renounce his wife, if he is already married. But though complete continence is not enjoined on the *Vanaprastha*, he is directed to use the privileges of marriage with the greatest moderation.

III. 'He must live only in huts covered with leaves, more comfortable dwelling-places being forbidden to those who profess to renounce the world and all its pleasures.'

I may remark that houses thatched with palmyra or cocoanut leaves are very common in India.

IV. 'He must not wear cotton cloths; he must only wear materials made of vegetable fibres.'

This latter kind of cloth is not uncommon in Northern India. It is as soft as silk to the touch, and has the advantage, inestimable for a Hindu, of not being, like cotton, liable to pollution.

V. 'He must observe with the most scrupulous accuracy the rules prescribed for Brahmins, especially those regarding ablutions and the prayers accompanying them, which must be performed three times a day.'

VI. 'He must pay the greatest attention to the choice of his food. His usual diet should be the plants and fruits which grow wild in the jungle. He must abstain from all those whose root or stem grows in the form of a bulb.'

I have already remarked that the Brahmins of the present day retain this rule of diet.

VII. 'Meditation and the contemplation of Parabrahma must occupy all his leisure. He must strive by this means to attain to union with the Supreme Deity.'

I will detail elsewhere the different steps by which this union is achieved.

VIII. 'Sacrifice, and above all that of the *yagnam*, should be reckoned one of the principal religious exercises.'

It will be seen in the following chapter of what this famous *yagnam* sacrifice consists.

The acquisition of knowledge was another of the principal occupations of these hermits. Theology, metaphysics, and astronomy were what they cultivated by choice. Many of them devoted themselves to the vain study of astrology; and it is to them that the Hindus are indebted for the majority of their books of magic, from which magicians even at the present day learn the tricks which cause them to be so much in request.

According to these *Vanaprastha* philosophers, three principal desires are innate in man, viz. land, gold, and women; or, in other words, ambition, wealth, and luxury[1].

By the *desire of land*, they understood ancestral estates and the landed properties that a man can acquire in the course of his life, the possession of a whole kingdom not excepted. They had so completely severed themselves from the temporal blessings of this world, and had showed themselves so entirely disinterested, that their exhortations and example sometimes induced even kings to leave their dominions in contempt for the pomp and circumstance by which they were surrounded, and to join with them in leading an ascetic life in the jungle. Hindu books mention with approbation several cases of this sort. These anchorite princes sometimes outdid the *Vanaprasthas* themselves in fervour and austerity; and the latter, far from showing themselves jealous, as a reward for such great zeal granted the princes the signal favour of allowing them to become penitent Brahmins, thus enrolling them in their own caste.

By the *desire of gold* the *Vanaprasthas* understood not this metal alone, but also all the honours and luxuries of life which can be procured with money, such as lucrative employments, valuable household goods, fine houses, rich apparel, dainty fare, &c. They displayed a complete aversion from all these false blessings. The furniture of their huts was confined to a few brass and earthenware vessels. They considered themselves passing rich when they possessed a few cows to furnish the milk which formed their chief diet; and it was the gift of one of these animals that pleased them most. Hindu books relate extravagant stories about the cows of these ascetics. For instance, one of them furnished not only the milk but all the victuals necessary for an entire army[2]. A neighbouring prince heard of this wonderful beast, and conceived the plan of carrying her off by force from the *Vanaprastha*, who had received her from the gods as a reward for his great piety; but the cow, as brave as she was fruitful, charged the prince's army and completely routed it!

As these devotees lived very frugally, their expenditure

[1] These three great desires are expressed by the words *loka-vanchana*, *artha-vanchana*, *sthree-vanchana*.—DUBOIS.

[2] This is the cow *Kamadhenu* mentioned in a previous chapter.—ED.

was but small. The offerings brought to them by their numerous admirers were not only sufficient to keep them in food, but also placed them in a position to make doles to the poor, and to entertain other devotees who visited them. They ate only one meal a day. The use of intoxicating liquors was strictly forbidden, though this deprivation troubled them but little. Accustomed from infancy to look on such beverages with horror, they regarded drunkenness as the most degrading of vices.

By the *desire of women* the *Vanaprasthas* understood all the sensual pleasures which are not rendered lawful by the sacred bonds of marriage; and even in the exercise of the privileges of married life they were enjoined to exercise extreme moderation. Thus they preserved the tradition of those divine words which were spoken to our first ancestors, 'Increase, and multiply, and cover the earth.' They recognized no other end or object in the union of the sexes than the propagation of the human species, and beyond this saw nothing but intemperance and fornication. Moreover they were persuaded that a man could not acquire wisdom, and the happiness which results from it, except by subduing the passions, and especially the one which holds the greatest sway over mankind and has the most enervating effects on the mental faculties. They believed that a single act of incontinence was sufficient to destroy the virtue of many years passed in the most austere penance. Hindu books relate innumerable examples of the praiseworthy and unceasing efforts which they made to bridle the lust of the flesh. But by one of those contradictions which abound in Hindu books, side by side with the account of the punishments inflicted on a hermit for his inability to conquer his sensual passions, we find, related with expressions of enthusiasm and admiration, the feats of debauchery ascribed to some of their *munis*—feats that lasted without interruption for thousands of years; and (burlesque idea!) it is to their pious asceticism that they are said to owe this unquenchable virility.

Be all this as it may, if the moral virtues of the *Vanaprasthas* were neither real nor lasting, seeing that they were based, not on humility, but on ostentatious pride, we must nevertheless admit that, whatever motives influenced them, they at any rate were not inferior to the ancient philosophers of Greece. They practised hospitality and enjoined it on others. The founder of their sect directed them to look out of doors before every meal to see if there was anybody near who was hungry; and it was their duty to invite such a person to eat with them, whether he was a friend or an enemy. It was a sublime and admirable precept; but I will not commit myself to assert that it was strictly observed in practice. They were above all enjoined to restrain their anger, and greatly prided themselves on their patience and moderation under the insults to which they were sometimes exposed. Nevertheless, in spite of such admirable philosophy, it seems certain that it took very little to rouse their spleen. A wholesome dread of provoking their resentment was generally felt; for they were on such occasions unsparing with their curses, which, as we know, had terrible consequences.

Justice, humanity, honesty, compassion, disinterestedness, in fact all the virtues, were recognized by them; and they taught them to others by precept and example. Hence it is that the Hindus profess, at least in theory, almost the same principles of morality as ourselves; and if they do not practise all the obligations which one man owes to another in civilized society, it is not because they are ignorant of them.

CHAPTER XXXII

Sacrifices of the *Vanaprastha* Brahmins.—Sacrifice of the *Yagnam.*—The Lesser *Yagnam.*—The Greater *Yagnam.*—The Giants, Enemies of the *Vanaprasthas.*

THE most common sacrifice among the *Vanaprasthas* was that of *homam.* They performed it, as I have already mentioned, by kindling a fire, throwing into it some grains of rice soaked in ghee, and reciting *mantrams.* Fire seems to have been the object worshipped, and it was offered sometimes specially to the sun, sometimes to all the planets. These hermits also offered other daily sacrifices to the gods, consisting of simple products of nature, such as flowers, incense, rice, vegetables, and fruits. Their whole time was occupied in such sacrifices, repeated several times every day, in ablutions, and in meditation on the perfections of Parabrahma. Though it is certain that sacrifices of blood have been common in India from the remotest ages, we have no evidence that the Brahmins ever participated in them in the character of sacrificers. Such functions were always entrusted to people of other castes; and even Rajahs did not disdain to perform them. In the present day, the Brahmins do not officiate in temples where it is the custom to sacrifice living victims.

There was only one occasion on which the *Vanaprasthas* could, without scruple, deprive a living creature of existence; it was when they made the famous sacrifice of *yagnam,* which is still held in great honour among modern Brahmins. A ram is the victim usually offered: but such is the horror with which they regard the shedding of blood, that they either beat the animal to death or strangle it, instead of slaughtering it[1]. Latter-day Brahmins, however, are not all agreed about the lawfulness of this sacrifice. The Vaishnavas regard it as an abominable practice, in which they obstinately refuse to participate. They maintain that it is an innovation of much more recent date than their ancient religious laws, and that it is contrary to the most sacred and inviolable rule which forbids murder under any form and for any reason whatever. This doctrine of the Vaishnavas is one of the chief reasons why they are accused of heresy by other Brahmins[2].

The sacrifice of *yagnam* is, in the opinion of its advocates, the most meritorious sacrifice of any[3]. It is considered extremely acceptable to the gods; and the person who offers it, or causes it to be offered, may count on abundant temporal blessings and on the entire remission of the sins which he has committed for a hundred generations. Nothing less than such advantages was necessary to determine the Brahmins to overcome the horror with which the destruction of a living creature inspired them. Furthermore, Brahmins possess the exclusive privilege of performing this sacrifice. Other castes may not even be present at it, though by a special grace they are authorized to provide the means of carrying it out. The expenses that it necessitates are very considerable, for crowds of Brahmins attend the solemnity, and each one must receive a present from the person who offers the *yagnam*—a circumstance which suggests that it is not so much devotion as interest that takes them there.

1 This operation is usually performed by men of the potter caste.—Ed.

2 Nevertheless the sacrifice of *yagnam* is performed by the *Vadakalais* among the Vishnavites in Southern India.—Ed.

3 *The Indian Mirror*, the leading native newspaper of Calcutta, quite recently (1896) remarked: 'What are the Hindus doing to mitigate the rigour of the water-famine and the cholera epidemic? How many of them have even recollected the injunctions of the Vedas, so far as the *yagnas* are concerned? A *yagna* on a large scale, which not only means the feeding of the sacred fire with ghee, and the burning of incense, but also the feeding of the poor in large numbers daily for months together, will cost a hundred thousand rupees or more. If the Vedas are to be relied on, such a *yagna* does good always both to the rulers and the ruled. Vedic *yagnas* have not been performed in India for many and many a year. Is there no true Hindu among the millions of India who would come forward and support us in our proposal? Are there not among the Maharajahs and Rajahs of the land a few still who would be found ready and willing to bear the expense of such a *yagna*!'—Ed.

However, this sacrifice is rarely offered, few people being able or willing to bear the great cost which it entails. The following are the principal ceremonies which are observed :—

The person who is going to preside at the *yagnam* announces the day fixed for the sacrifice throughout the whole district, and invites all Brahmins to attend. It is necessary that Brahmins of each of the four Vedas should be present; if a representative of each of these classes does not appear, the solemnity must be put off. Neither Sudras, whatever their rank may be, nor Brahmins who are infirm or diseased, or blind or lame, &c., nor Brahmins who are widowers, may be present at it.

A ram is chosen after undergoing the most minute inspection. It must be perfectly white, about three years of age, in good condition and well proportioned in every respect[1]. A *purohita* proclaims the favourable moment when the ceremony can begin, and the assembled Brahmins, who sometimes number over two thousand, hasten to the appointed spot. A hole is first dug; and after the *homam* and other ordinary preliminaries, a large fire is lighted and is kept burning by logs of wood cut from the sacred trees *aswatta, alai, icham, porasu,* and by a great quantity of *darbha* grass. The whole is drenched with ghee, which causes the flames to rise to a great height. In the meanwhile the *purohita* recites *mantrams* in a loud voice, scraps of which are loudly repeated by the spectators. The ram is then brought into the midst of the assembly, rubbed with oil, put in a bath, and then stained with *akshatas.* The body and horns are garlanded with flowers, and cords made of *darbha* grass are tied, or rather tightly bound, round the animal. All the time the *purohita* is repeating *mantrams,* the supposed object of which is to kill the victim. This obviously inadequate proceeding, however, is supplemented by closing the nostrils, ears, and mouth of the animal while the Brahmins present deal heavy blows on the beast, and finally one of them suffocates it by pressing his knee on its throat. The *purohita* and his attendants meanwhile repeat *mantrams* in a loud voice, and these are supposed to ensure a quick and painless death for the victim. It would be a very inauspicious

[1] This is incorrect, inasmuch as the victim must be perfectly black. It is usually presented by the goatherds as a free gift.—ED.

omen if the ram uttered the slightest cry while it was enduring these tortures[1].

As soon as the animal is dead, the Brahmin who presides at the ceremony cuts open the stomach and tears out the entrails along with the fat. These he holds suspended over the fire, the fat dropping into it as it melts. At the same time liquefied butter is poured over the fire as a libation.

The victim is skinned and hacked in pieces, which are then fried in butter. A portion is thrown into the fire as an oblation, while the rest is divided between the Brahmin who has presided at the sacrifice and the person who bears the expense of it. These in their turn distribute their portions to the Brahmins present, who scramble wildly for the scraps and devour them as something sacred and auspicious. This is particularly remarkable, because it is the only occasion on which the Brahmins may, without committing sin, eat of that which has had life or the germ of life.

They then offer to the fire, as *neiveddya,* boiled and raw rice, the latter husked and well washed.

All these ceremonies and a great number of others being over, betel, which has previously been placed all round the fire, is distributed to the Brahmins. Finally, the person who has borne the expense of the sacrifice makes gifts, in money and clothes, to all present, according to the rank and dignity of each; a costly munificence, considering the multitude of those who take part in the ceremony.

The Brahmin who has presided at the *yagnam* is henceforth considered an important personage. He has acquired, for instance, the right of keeping up a perpetual fire in his house. If this fire, by some accident, were to be extinguished, he would be forced to rekindle it, not with light procured from a flint, but with that produced by rubbing two pieces of dry wood together. When a Brahmin honoured in this way dies, his funeral pile must be lighted with this fire. After that the fire is allowed to die out of itself.

I have never been able to discover whether this sacrifice has any particular divinity for its object. It would appear, however, that the Brahmin who offers it is free to dedicate it to any god

[1] If the victim utters any sound it is believed that the family of the Brahmin who offers the *yagnam* will gradually become extinct.—ED.

that he chooses, provided the deity be one of the first rank. Be this as it may, the fire of the *yagnam* bears the name of *agni-iswara*, which means the *god of fire*, as if it were offered to this element alone.

Hindu books testify that this sacrifice was much more frequent in the time of the old *Vanaprasthas*; but then it was performed in a much simpler manner, and was not accompanied with the foolish ostentation that was afterwards associated with it.

Yet; after all, this sacrifice is a mere nothing compared with the grand *yagnam*, the enormous cost of which has now caused it to fall into disuse. Trustworthy persons have assured me, however, that at the beginning of the last century the King of Amber (Jeypore), in Upper India, had it performed with the utmost magnificence. The gift which he made to his high priest alone is said to have cost a lakh of rupees, while the Brahmins who attended it, to the number of several thousands, all received presents proportionate to their rank[1].

The mythical stories of the Hindus make frequent mention of this splendid sacrifice, and the blessings which it procured for those who caused it to be performed. The gods themselves, and also the giants, during the wars which they waged against each other, seldom failed to perform this religious ceremony, of which one of the least remarkable results was to procure a certain victory over the enemy. It was usual, when the solemnities of the *yagnam* were over, for the prince on whose behalf it had been celebrated to seat himself on a high throne for the space of forty-eight minutes, and during that time the Brahmins present were permitted to ask him for anything they pleased. And the prince, on his part, was bound to satisfy their demands, however extravagant, even had they extended to demanding his kingdom, his wife, and everything he most highly esteemed. If he failed to satisfy a single one of these numerous requests, the sacrifice would have been of no avail.

A king of the olden times, says a Hindu chronicler, having caused the grand *yagnam* to be performed before setting out for a war which he was planning against a neighbouring potentate, presented a bushel of pearls to each of the Brahmins present, who were thirty thousand in number.

[1] *Yagnam* sacrifices on a smaller scale are performed nowadays in Southern India.—ED.

Four kinds of victims might be offered in sacrifice, namely, a horse, a cow, an elephant, or a man. The first was called *asvamedha,* the second *gomedha,* the third *rajasuya,* and the fourth *naramedha.* But they commonly sacrificed a horse; and hence the sacrifice is generally designated by the name of *asvamedha* (sacrifice of a horse).

The victim was chosen before its birth; and when the mare, its mother, had foaled, her offspring was reared for three years with extraordinary care and trouble. Continual sacrifices were made to Indra, that he might watch over the young animal; to Yama, that he might preserve it from death and every accident; to Varuna, the god of water, and also to the clouds, that they might cause a fertilizing rain to fall and plenty of grass to grow for its nourishment. Similar requests were also made to a number of other gods.

The victim was afterwards let loose and allowed to roam freely over a wide stretch of country, though it was followed everywhere by numerous attendants to prevent its being stolen. The gods, or the giants, or the princes against whom the sacrifice was to be directed would come with all their armies in search of this valuable animal, and try to seize it by force or stratagem. If they succeeded, the sacrifice was averted, and they were thereby delivered from the disasters which its accomplishment would have brought upon them. Indeed, the wonders wrought by this grand sacrifice were so mighty as to render the prince who had it performed invulnerable and certain of victory, for amongst other things it furnished him with enchanted weapons, a single one of which was sufficient to overthrow a whole army.

I will spare the reader long and wearisome details of the innumerable ceremonies which took place during the celebration of the *asvamedha,* and will content myself with giving a short extract from a story which refers to this famous sacrifice, and which at the same time describes one of the ten *Avatars* of Vishnu:—

'The giant-emperor Bali caused to be performed the grand sacrifice of the horse, the irresistible effect of which was to secure for him the overthrow of all other sovereigns and the conquest of the whole world. To counteract such fatal consequences, Vishnu the Preserver presented himself in the form of a Brahmin dwarf before the tyrant, and supplicated him humbly for the grant of a plot of ground only three soles of his own feet in area to enable him to offer sacrifices. The Brahmin's request appeared comical to the giant, and was granted without hesitation. Then Vishnu changed his shape, and with one of his feet he covered the whole earth, and with the other occupied all the space between earth and heaven. Then addressing the giant, he said: "Where shall I find room for the third sole?" "On my head," answered the enemy of the gods, who then recognized, but too late, with whom he had to deal. The giant thought he might save his life by thus placing himself at the mercy of Vishnu the Preserver. But it happened otherwise. Vishnu placed his foot on the head of the giant and precipitated the monster into *Patalam* (hell), and delivered the world of that great scourge.'

But let us return to the *Vanaprastha* Brahmins. It appears, according to the Hindu books, that they experienced great difficulties in the accomplishment of their sacrifices. Their declared enemies, the giants, and the gods themselves, were continually playing evil pranks with them. For instance, their enemies made themselves invisible, and, flying in the air, defiled the offerings by letting fall upon them pieces of meat or other impure substances, so that these pious acts were of no avail.

I should have written at less length about these famous giants, if they had not seemed to me to be grotesque representations of those of Holy Scripture[1], whose crimes in a great measure caused the Flood. This race of men again flourished after that great catastrophe, and were not entirely destroyed until the time of Joshua[2].

The Hindu giants are represented as being of such colossal stature that on one occasion, in order to wake one of them, it was necessary for several elephants to walk over his body. Even then the giant hardly felt the discomfort of this enormous weight; but, by dint of stamping on him, the huge animals at last produced a slight sensation, resembling the tickling which an ordinary man feels when an ant or a fly crawls over him. It was this tickling, rather than the weight of the elephants, which roused the giant, the hairs of whose body were like the

[1] Genesis vi. 4.

[2] Numbers xiii.; Joshua xi.

trunks of full-grown forest trees. During one of his wars with certain gods, this same giant fastened a huge rock to each of his hairs, and thus equipped, he advanced into the middle of the enemy's army, gave himself a good shake, and thus hurled off the rocks, which falling right and left crushed his enemies to the last man.

The giant Ravana, who carried off Seeta, Rama's wife, had ten heads. His palace in the Island of Ceylon, of which he was king, was of such an enormous height that at midday the sun passed under one of its arcades.

These giants were all of an extremely mischievous disposition, especially the Brahmin giants. A great number of this caste had, by the way, been turned into giants as a punishment for former crimes. In fact, there were whole armies of them, and sometimes there was civil war between them, though more often they joined forces in fighting against the gods. Occasionally they adopted a hermit's life, without thereby changing their character, or becoming better disposed. The penance performed by the giant Bhasmasura was so long and severe, that he thereby induced Siva to grant him the power of reducing to ashes all those on whose heads he placed his hands. The favour thus obtained, the ungrateful wretch decided to let Siva himself, his benefactor, have some experience of the power newly conferred upon him. Siva was at his wits' end to know how to escape from his enemy, when fortunately he was saved by a stratagem of Vishnu. The latter persuaded the giant to put his hand on his own head, which he did without thinking, and reduced himself to ashes.

The above is a sample of Hindu mythology.

It may be presumed that these giant enemies of the *Vanaprasthas* were merely the chiefs of the countries in which the hermits had taken up their abode. These chiefs, frightened by the continual sacrifices and mystic rites of the formidable strangers, tried to get rid of them by stirring up quarrels among them and otherwise interfering with their religious practices. Except the first of these hermit *Vanaprasthas*, most of those who embraced this kind of life gave themselves up entirely to the cultivation of magic and astrology, and, impotent though their mysterious practices were in reality, they were easily able, with the help of their false prestige, to spread terror in feeble and credulous minds. Some enthusiastic poet, in relating the history of the quarrels between these hermit Brahmins and the mighty princes who hated them, no doubt turned the latter into giants. Certainly no more than this was required to make the legend credible among a people so addicted to the marvellous. Be this as it may, it appears certain that the attacks made on the *Vanaprasthas* finally sapped their power to its very foundations, for the sect no longer exists in India.

CHAPTER XXXIII

Penance as a Means of purifying the Soul.—The Penance of the *Vanaprasthas*. —Modern Gymnosophists, or Naked Penitents.—Purification by Fire

The ancient hermit-philosophers of India maintained that it was necessary to perform divers acts of penance in order to disperse the phantoms of illusion, or *Maya*, by which men are seduced and led astray. It was only by penances, they contended, that man could break through the trammels of his personal passions and everyday surroundings, which held the soul enthralled. The right degree of excellence and spirituality necessary for the emancipation of the soul, they urged, could only be obtained, little by little, by the exercise of continuous penances. By these means alone could the soul be reunited for ever to the Supreme Divinity, to Parabrahma; and it was only when he had achieved this state of perfection that the penitent had the right to cry: '*Aham Brahma*!' I am Brahma! I am the Supreme Being!

Is it to be wondered at that men who, in this pursuit of spiritual perfection, were actuated only by motives of pride and self-conceit, when once they attained, according to their own vain presumption, the state of perfection at which they aimed—is it to be wondered at, I say, that these men looked down upon all the rest of their fellow-men with ineffable disdain, whatever their social rank might be, and considered them as degraded beings still wallowing in the mire of vice, slaves to their own passions[1]?

[1] The Abbé is hardly just in placing such a low value on this pride of righteousness. The sacred Hindu books are unanimous in describing these saintly men as gentle, quiet, and loving. The ignorant and narrow-minded Brahmin priests, however, cannot be said to have ever realized this high state of spiritual perfection. —Ed.

This spiritual pride was still further encouraged by the tokens of respect, and even adoration, which the very greatest princes showered upon them. The apparent coldness with which they received such homage was certainly not the outcome of humility; it was rather caused by the firm conviction that they were only receiving what was their just due. Alexander the Great, who bent every one to his will, tried in vain to persuade one of the most celebrated of these *Vanaprasthas*, called Dindime or Dandamis, to visit him. However, the Hindu philosopher condescended to write to the conqueror, though the letter attributed to him by the Greek historians is evidently apocryphal, or at any rate interpolated with many embellishments and ideas which would never have occurred to a Gymnosophist. Be that as it may, some report that the Macedonian hero saw in it nothing but impious pride, while others maintain that he admired the writer's noble and philosophic courage.

And how, it may be asked, did these recluses obtain, through penance, perfect wisdom and perfect purity? The answer is, by three means: by the repression of their animal passions, by meditation, and by the mortification of the flesh and of all the senses; in fact, by complete self-abnegation.

By the first of these means they strove to destroy the three strongest passions to which man is subject, namely, wealth, land, and women; and to free themselves completely from all prejudices in respect of caste, rank, and honours. They further aimed at the repression of the most ordinary and natural impulses, even that of self-preservation. They insisted on their disciples being insensible to cold or heat, wind or rain, pain or sickness. They called this *moksha-sadhaka*, or the *practice of deliverance.* It may, therefore, be said that in many respects they were greater stoics than Zeno himself and greater cynics than Diogenes. At the same time it is more than probable that the majority of these *Vanaprasthas*, while applauding these strict doctrines, left the practice of them to the more enthusiastic.

There are penitents professing the principles of *moksha-sadhaka* even at the present day. Some of them go about quite naked, the object of this indecent practice being to convince the admiring public that they are no longer susceptible to the temptations of lust. There is also a class of religious mendicants, called *Bairagis*, to be met with everywhere, who show themselves in public in a state of nature[1].

The people evince the greatest admiration for these unclothed devotees, and express the utmost wonder as to how they succeed in controlling a passion which is generally regarded as beyond control. Some say that the *Bairagis* owe this impotence to extreme sobriety in eating and drinking, while others assert that it is the result of the use of certain drugs. As to their alleged sobriety it is a mere fable. Generally speaking, they eat all kinds of meat and drink all kinds of intoxicating liquors without any shame, the practice of *moksha-sadhaka* and their status as *Sannyasi* acquitting them of all blame in this respect[2]. According to other authorities, the *Bairagis* attain this condition by purely mechanical means, that is, they attach to their generative organs a heavy weight which they drag about until the power of muscles and nerves is completely destroyed.

Some of these fanatics profess to conquer every feeling of disgust that is innate in a human being. They will even go so far as to eat human ordure without evincing any dislike. Instead of treating these degraded practices with the horror and contempt that they merit, the Hindus regard them with respect and honour, true to their custom of admiring everything that astonishes them.

Meditation, the second means of achieving spiritual perfection, accomplishes what the repression of the passions has only begun. It fills the soul with the thought of God and identifies it with the Divine Being, of which it is an emanation. This union with God is not brought about instantaneously, but gradually, as will be explained elsewhere. It was with the object of accomplishing, little by little, this blessed union with God that the *Vanaprastha* devoted a considerable portion of each day to meditation, combining this devout exercise with the ordinary sacrifices, particularly the sacrifice to fire, called *homam*.

The third means of arriving at spiritual perfection—mortification of the flesh—consists in leading a hard and austere life in rigorous and almost continuous fasting, and in voluntary

[1] This would now be punishable by law.—ED.

[2] This is only true of the lower types of *Bairagis*.—ED.

and self-inflicted punishments, and above all in never omitting the indispensable duty of frequent ablutions.

These *Vanaprastha* recluses were fully persuaded that the defilements of the soul were communicated to the body, and those of the body to the soul. They held that ablutions, while cleansing the body, also possessed the virtue of purifying the soul, especially if they were performed in the Ganges or in some other waters bearing an equal reputation for sanctity.

The purification of the soul was completed by fire; and that is the reason why the bodies of these penitents were burned after death.

Only their fellow Brahmin *Vanaprasthas* assisted at their funeral ceremonies, which, though fundamentally the same as those of the modern Brahmins, were much simpler and less elaborate. It was thought that the extreme care which the deceased had paid to the purification of himself during life rendered excessive care after death unnecessary and superfluous.

There was one sure and certain way by which the *Vanaprasthas* might attain to extreme perfection and gain inestimable happiness, and that was in cutting short their lives by throwing themselves into the fire. I do not mean to say that there have been many instances of this violation of the laws of nature amongst the *Vanaprasthas*. Only a single one has come to my own personal knowledge. I have read in a Hindu book that one of these recluses and his wife, having lived in retirement for a long time, and arrived at a very advanced age, and both of them being equally tired of this world, arranged their own funeral pile, quietly lay down upon it, then set fire to it with their own hands, and were thus consumed together. Having by this act of devotion arrived at the highest state of perfection, their souls were instantly united to the Divinity, and were exempted from reappearing on earth to undergo the successive transmigrations from one body to another which would have been their fate in the ordinary course of events.

There are still fanatics to be found who solemnly bind themselves to commit suicide, under the conviction that by the performance of this mad act they will ensure for themselves the immediate enjoyment of supreme blessedness.

The temple of Jagannath (Puri), and other places which superstition has rendered equally famous, have often been the scenes of self-inflicted death. From time to time, too, one comes across lunatics travelling through the country, loudly proclaiming their intention of destroying themselves, and at the same time collecting the money with which to defray the expenses attendant on the solemn execution of their wicked vow. I knew one of these wretches to be the recipient of very considerable sums. He was received with the greatest enthusiasm and respect wherever he went. He was nicknamed 'Sava[1],' or 'the corpse,' and he always carried upraised in his hand the dagger with which he was going to kill himself; on the point of it was stuck a small lemon. Everything was in readiness for the horrible sacrifice, the victim himself having fixed the day on which it was to be consummated. Immense crowds had assembled out of curiosity, greatly pleased to think they were to witness a horrid sight; but the magistrate of the district, who was a humane and sensible man, caused the hero of the tragedy to be brought before him, took away his dagger, and ordered him to be conducted out of the district, absolutely forbidding him to re-enter the country. A few months afterwards, I learned that the maniac had carried out his dreadful vow on the banks of the Tungabudra, to the delight of an enormous crowd which had collected to enjoy the revolting spectacle. There is nothing improbable, therefore, in the story told by Diodorus Siculus of the Brahmin Calanus, who terminated his life by allowing himself to be burnt alive in the presence of Alexander's army.

The above are a few examples of the deplorable and fatal effects of Hindu superstition. Such are the natural results of the foolish theories of ancient philosophers, the most enlightened men of their times, as to the best means of purifying the soul and ensuring certain and everlasting happiness.

[1] A corrupt form of the Sanskrit word *sapam*.—ED.

CHAPTER XXXIV

The Fourth State of the Brahmins, that of the *Sannyasi*.—Preparation for this Holy State.—Ceremonies of Initiation.—Rules to be followed by the *Sannyasi*.

THE fourth state to which a Brahmin can attain is that of a *sannyasi*, a state so sublime, according to the Hindu authors, that it ensures, even during the short space of a single lifetime, more spiritual blessedness than an ordinary man could attain in ten millions of regenerations [1].

The *sannyasi* is superior to the *vanaprastha*, inasmuch as the latter does not wholly renounce the world, being still connected with it to a certain extent by family ties; whilst the *sannyasi* imposes upon himself the painful sacrifice of leaving his wife and children. Like the *vanaprastha* he submits to severe privations, and furthermore takes a vow of poverty and resigns himself to living entirely on alms. Every Brahmin, before becoming a *sannyasi*, must have been a *grahastha*; that

[1] Book VI of the Laws of Manu directs him for the fourth period of his life to wander about as a *Bhikshu* or *Parivrajaka*, 'religious mendicant.' Here are a few rules for the regulation of this final stage of his existence, when he is sometimes called a *sannyasi*, 'one who has given up the world'; sometimes a *yati*, 'one who has suppressed his passions':—

Let him remain without fire, without habitation; let him resort once a day to the town for food, regardless of hardships, resolute, keeping a vow of silence, fixing his mind in meditation.

With hair, nails, and beard well clipped, carrying a bowl, a staff, and a pitcher, let him wander about continually, intent on meditation and avoiding injury to any being.

In this manner, having little by little abandoned all worldly attachments, and freed himself from all concern about pairs of opposites, he obtains absorption into the universal Spirit.—ED.

is to say, he must have been married and have acquitted himself of 'the great debt to his ancestors,' the first and most indispensable of duties in the eyes of a Hindu, that of perpetuating his species.

There are, however, a few examples of Brahmins who have become *sannyasis* while still young and unmarried. There are also, it is true, many penitents who have always been celibates; but they do not belong to the Brahmin caste.

A Brahmin is not allowed to become a *sannyasi* in a moment of remorse or from a sudden feeling of enthusiasm. His decision must be the result of calm and deliberate self-examination and reflection, and must be based on a sense of disgust for the world and its pleasures, and on an ardent desire to attain spiritual perfection. He must feel himself capable of complete severance from all earthly affairs. If he experiences the slightest inclination or longing for those things which the rest of mankind struggle for, he will thereby lose all the benefits of his life of penance.

When a Brahmin who aspires to the state of *sannyasi* has duly reflected on the step he is about to take, he calls together all the leading Brahmins of the neighbourhood, announces his intention, and begs them to be ready to receive his solemn vows with all the customary formalities and ceremonies.

On the day appointed for this important act, the candidate first purifies himself by bathing. He procures ten pieces of cotton cloth such as are worn on the shoulders, four of them, dyed a dark yellow (*kavi*), being destined for his own use, the other six being given as presents to men of his own caste. He also provides himself with a bamboo staff that has seven knots or joints, some small silver and copper coins, flowers, *akshatas*, sandalwood, and, above all, some *pancha-gavia*. He drinks a little of the last-named beverage, and then repairs to the spot where the ceremony is to take place.

The officiating *guru* performs the ordinary *homam* and *puja*, and then proceeds to whisper into the candidate's ear such *mantrams* and instructions as are prescribed for the state he is about to enter. He next commands him, first, to don one of the yellow cloths that he has brought, and then, in token of his renunciation of his caste as well as of the pomps and vanities of this world, to break his triple cord and to allow the tuft of hair which grows on every Brahmin's head to be shaved off. All this is accompanied by *mantrams* and other absurdities which it is unnecessary to describe in detail.

The ceremony ended, the candidate takes his seven-knotted bamboo in one hand[1] and a gourd full of water in the other, while under his arm he carries an antelope's skin. These three things are all that he is now allowed to call his own. Then he thrice drinks a little *pancha-gavia,* and also some of the water in his gourd; he repeats the *mantrams* which his *guru* has taught him; and he is then a *sannyasi* for life. All that remains for him to do is to present to the attendant Brahmins the cloths and money which he has brought with him.

The newly initiated must conform strictly to the instructions that he has received from his *guru,* and must follow minutely all the rules laid down for persons of his profession. The following

[1] One cannot fail to recognize in the Hindu *sannyasis* a class of men similar to those of the Jews who were imbued with Rabbinical doctrines in connexion with cabala and numbers, and to the Greeks who held the wild theories of Pythagoras—idiotic dreamers who crammed the minds of their fellow-countrymen with foolish notions. We know that the cabala believes the world to be full of spirits, which one can in the course of time resemble, by practising purity of life and meditation. The *sannyasi's* staff with its seven knots is not merely intended to aid him in walking. It is, like Aaron's rod, an instrument of divination. The seven knots are also not without a mysterious significance. Who has not heard of the perfection of the number seven? The high esteem in which it is held by the Hindus is clearly proved by the numerous sacred places and objects which are always spoken of in groups of seven, such as the Seven Penitents (*sapta rishis*), the Seven Holy Cities (*sapta pura*), the Seven Sacred Islands (*sapta dwipa*), the Seven Seas (*sapta samudra*), the Seven Sacred Rivers (*sapta nadi*), the Seven Sacred Mountains (*sapta parvata*), the Seven Sacred Jungles (*sapta arania*), the Seven Sacred Trees (*sapta vruksha*), the Seven Castes (*sapta kula*), the Seven Inferior and Superior Worlds (*sapta loka*), &c. Seven too is an uneven number, and all the uneven numbers are considered lucky. For example, take the famous *Trimurti* (Brahma, Vishnu, and Siva). Virgil also says:—

'Terna tibi haec primum triplici diversa colore
Licia circumdo, terque haec altaria circum
Effigiem duco: *numero Deus impare gaudet* . . .
Necte tribus nodis ternos, Amarylli, colores.'

While on the subject of the *sannyasi's* staff I might refer to the rods of Moses, of Elisha, and of all the prophets; the augur's staff, the pastoral staffs of the Fauns and sylvan deities, and those of the Cynics; but I will leave to the intelligent reader the task of making what comparisons he thinks proper.—DUBOIS.

are the chief of these, to which I have added a few remarks of my own :—

I. 'Every morning, after he has performed his ablutions, a *sannyasi* must smear ashes on his body[1].'

The majority of Hindus only smear them over their foreheads.

II. 'He must take only one meal every day.'

This rule of fasting is followed not only by the Brahmin *sannyasis*, but by many others who by severe abstinence seek to attract public attention and respect.

III. 'They must forgo the use of betel leaves.'

These are the leaves of a plant of the convolvulus species, which grows in the maritime districts of India. They have a slightly bitter taste, are mixed with calcined shells or lime, and are eaten with areca-nut and other spices according to taste. The Hindus are perpetually chewing this preparation. To give it up, when one is accustomed to it, would be a greater privation than it would be for any one among us to give up tobacco.

IV. 'Not only must he avoid all female society, but he must not even look at a woman.'

V. 'Once a month his head and face must be shaved.'

To save this trouble many *sannyasis* cause their disciples to pull out the hairs of their head and beard one by one. Some *sannyasis* neither cut their hair nor shave their beards, but plait them up in some ridiculous way. These, however, do not belong to the Brahmin caste.

VI. 'He may only wear wooden sandals on his feet.'

This is a most uncomfortable style of foot-gear ; it is held to the foot by a wooden peg, which comes between the big and second toes. The *sannyasis* use these clogs to avoid defilement, which could not be avoided if they went barefoot, or if they wore leather shoes.

[1] In times of great tribulation the Jews used to cover themselves with sackcloth and ashes in token of their sorrow and deep repentance for their sins. This was the way in which the Ninevites showed their repentance. In France, in several religious houses, it was a duty to lie on ashes when at the point of death. The Council of Benevento in 1091 ordained that the faithful should put ashes on their heads on the first day of Lent to promote a spirit of humiliation and penance during that holy season, by bringing to their recollection the words of Holy Scripture: '*Memento, homo, quia pulvis es, et in pulverem reverteris.*'—DUBOIS.

VII. 'When a *sannyasi* travels, he must carry his seven-knotted staff in one hand, his gourd in the other, and an antelope's skin under his arm.'

Provided with these three articles the *sannyasi* can say, *Omnia mecum porto.* The staff must be exactly his own height. The antelope's skin serves both for a seat and for a bed.

VIII. 'He must live entirely by alms, which he has the right to ask wherever he goes.'

Many collect considerable sums by this means; but they are obliged to spend any surplus in charity or other good works. Some spend it in the erection of rest-houses, pagodas, &c., or in digging wells and constructing reservoirs for water for the use of the public. They also dispense hospitality to persons who pass near their huts, or who come to visit them.

IX. 'Though a *sannyasi* has the right to ask for alms, it is more proper for him to receive them without asking. For instance, if he feel hungry, he should go to some house where people are living, but he must not say anything to them or even hint at his wants. If they give him anything voluntarily, he must take it as if it were of no consequence to him, and without expressing any thanks. If he receives nothing, he must go away without either feeling or showing any annoyance. Neither must he complain if he does not like the taste of what is given him.'

X. 'He must not sit down to eat.'

XI. 'He must build his hut near a river or a tank.'

The reason of this is that he may be able to make frequent ablutions, one of the first duties of a *sannyasi.*

XII. 'When travelling he must make no stay anywhere, and he must only pass through inhabited districts.'

XIII. 'He must regard all men as equals. He must not be influenced by anything that happens, and must be able to view with perfect equanimity even revolutions which overthrow empires.'

XIV. 'His one object in life must be to acquire that measure of wisdom and degree of spirituality which shall finally reunite him to the Supreme Divinity, from whom we are separated by our passions and material surroundings. To achieve this end he must keep his senses under perfect control, and entirely subdue any tendency to anger, envy, avarice, sensuality: in fact, to any unholy impulses. Otherwise his penance will bear no fruit.'

There are no doubt other general rules which these devotees are bound to follow; but I have only been able to ascertain the above.

Of all the *sannyasis*, those called *Bikshukas* are considered the most perfect of all. They are under no restrictions in regard to food; nothing that they eat or drink, no matter how impure it may be, has power to defile them.

CHAPTER XXXV

A *Sannyasi's* Principal Duties.—Meditation.—Its Various Stages.—What it consists of, and how Hindu Devotees practise it.—General Remarks.—Comparisons between the Hindu *Sannyasis* and those who lead Similar Lives among Christians.

A *SANNYASI'S* first and most important duty is to destroy, root and branch, any feeling of attachment that may still linger in his heart for the world and its vain pleasures. Wife, children, parents, friends, caste privileges, cattle, lands, jewels and other temporal possessions, animal passions, sensual pleasures—all these are but so many obstacles standing in the way of his soul's perfection. In Hindu books they are likened variously to thick clouds which, until they are dispersed, obscure the light of the sun, or to violent winds that disturb the surface of the water and prevent the reflection of this luminary in all its splendour; to the coils which caterpillars and other insects form, and of which they cannot rid themselves; or again to the kernels of certain fruits in which grubs and maggots are imprisoned.

Such are the similes which Hindu authors make use of when trying to give some idea of the hindrances which earthly passions oppose to spirituality, and which must be overcome before perfection can be attained and the soul reunited to the Divine Being. Nevertheless, these same authors add, the tenements in which caterpillars and grubs confine themselves do not hold them captive for ever. Neither do the insects cease to exist. After remaining for some time in a state of torpor and quiescence, the feeble spark of life which they still retain rekindles and gradually increases in strength till the insects are able to destroy the covering in which they are enclosed, and, by dint of persevering labour, at last open out a passage to the region of light and liberty. So it is with the soul. The body in which it is imprisoned, and which is a prey to worldly cares and tumultuous passions, will not hold it for ever. After many re-incarnations the spark of perfect wisdom, which is latent in every man, will burn more brightly, until the soul at last succeeds, after a long course of penance and meditation, in breaking asunder, little by little, all the ties which bind it to the world, and will so grow in virtue and strength that it will finally attain that degree of spiritual perfection which will render it fit to be incorporated with the Divinity. Then, leaving the body which has so long held it captive, it will soar upwards and be united for ever with the Supreme Soul from which it originally sprang.

The course which a *sannyasi* should pursue to arrive at this point of perfection differs somewhat according to the sect to which he belongs. His period of emancipation begins from the day on which he entered the holy state of *sannyasi*. By this single act he is supposed to have freed himself from those ties which bind other men to the world and its pleasures. All that he has to do to attain perfection is to make frequent ablutions, to drink *pancha-gavia* constantly, to offer daily sacrifices, and to live a life of asceticism and penance, but above all of meditation, to which he must devote all his leisure time.

This duty of meditation, to which Hindus attach so much importance, appears to me to be so remarkable a practice for idolaters, that I have thought it incumbent on me to call special attention to it. The details that I am about to relate will show to what extremes superstition and fanaticism will pervert men's minds, especially when they are connected with self-conceit and a longing for notoriety.

The doctrine of meditation is called *yogam*, and from it the word *yogi* is derived, which is the name usually given to a tribe of vagabonds who are erroneously supposed to devote themselves entirely to this practice [1].

According to the Hindu doctrine the practice of *yogam* has a peculiarly spiritualizing and purifying effect on a *sannyasi*, for he thereby passes through four different stages, each one more perfect than the last.

The first is called *salokyam*, or unity of place. In this state

[1] This is too sweeping an assertion. All *yogis* are not vagabonds.—Ed.

the soul inhabits, as it were, the same place as the Divinity; it is as though it were in the presence of God. After practising for a long time the duties of *salokyam*, the soul passes on to the second stage, called *samipyam* (proximity). In this stage, by practising meditation and keeping all earthly objects out of the mental pale, the knowledge and perception of God become more and more acute, and the soul seems to be drawn nearer and nearer to Him.

After having spent many generations in this stage, the soul passes on to the third, the *sarupyam* (resemblance). Once arrived at this point, the soul gradually acquires a perfect resemblance to the Divinity, and shares to a certain extent in His attributes. Finally, this stage leads on to the fourth, the *sayujyam* (identity), and then the perfect and inseparable union of the soul with the Deity becomes complete.

But the soul requires long periods of time to pass through these four stages of perfection; it must undergo a great number of re-incarnations, during which it gradually acquires the degree of perfection which is essential to its incorporation with the Godhead. In order to explain all these indispensable transmigrations of the soul, the Hindu books make use of various analogies, such as the following:—If one wished to extract gold from a mass composed of the five metals [1], one could not do so by melting it once for all. Only by putting it through the fire several times could one separate the different alloys of which it was composed and extract the gold in all its purity.

They illustrate the same truth by various other similes; for instance, that which may be drawn from the process of making clarified butter, an article of food which, as we already know, the Brahmins are particularly fond of, and which they consider the purest of all manufactured substances.

The majority of these analogies, and the principles deduced from them, might, if looked at from a non-controversial point of view, be not altogether repugnant to our learned metaphysicians, or at any rate to those among us who have given themselves up to a life of meditation. We may at any rate conclude that these ancient Hindu penitents spent more time and thought on spiritual matters than we might have expected. Originally, no doubt, this spiritual side of their religion was much purer and

[1] We Europeans recognize a greater number of metals than five.—DUBOIS.

less fanciful than it is now, when it has become corrupted by gross idolatry. Now it merely tends to increase the pride of the recluses who practise it. The latter indeed set up a claim to unity and equality with the Supreme Being himself; while they look down upon their fellow-creatures as objects of supreme contempt, as beings who are still wallowing in the mire of materialism and passion.

And how did these so-called penitents carry out their doctrine of meditation, concerning which they made such proud boasting? Before idolatry had gained a hold on the country, and while the tradition of the outward forms as well as of the inward meaning of the religion with which men worshipped the Deity after the Flood still lingered, this doctrine of meditation, prompted as it was by lofty motives, was doubtless capable of maintaining the soul in a constant state of fervent piety towards God; but at the present time this religious exercise is undertaken with an object very different and much less estimable.

I cannot better explain wherein this practice of meditation consists for a modern *sannyasi* than by repeating what I was told by two Hindus who had passed a long novitiate under the direction of two celebrated recluses.

'I was a novice for four months,' said one of them, 'under a *sannyasi* who had built himself a hermitage in a lonely spot not very far from the town of Bellapuram. Following his instructions, I spent the greater part of each night awake, occupied in keeping my mind an absolute blank and thinking of nothing. I made superhuman efforts to hold my breath as long as possible, and only breathed when I was on the point of fainting. This suffocating exercise made me perspire profusely. One day, at high noon, I thought I saw a bright moon, which seemed to move and sway from side to side. Another time I imagined myself enveloped in thick darkness at midday. My director, the *sannyasi*, who had warned me that while going through this course of penance I should see many marvels, was greatly pleased when I mentioned these visions to him. He congratulated me on the progress that I was making, and prescribed fresh exercises which were even more severe than the first. The time was not far distant, he assured me, when I should experience much more surprising results from my penance. At last, worn out by these foolish and fatiguing practices, and fearing lest my brain might really be turned, I left the *sannyasi* and his meditative penances, and returned to my former state of life.'

The second, an old man of a very cheerful disposition, told me the following story of his novitiate:—

'The *sannyasi* under whose direction I placed myself had built his hermitage at some distance from the fort of Namakal, in a desert spot. Amongst other exercises which he laid down for me, he obliged me to stare at the sky every day without blinking my eyes or changing my position. This prolonged effort inflamed my eyes terribly and often gave me dreadful headaches. Sometimes I thought I saw sparks of fire in the air; at others I seemed to see fiery globes and other meteors. My teacher was much pleased with the success of my efforts and with the progress I was making. He had only one eye, and I knew that he had lost the other in following out this practice, which he assured me was indispensable if I wished to attain to perfect spirituality. But at last I could bear it no longer, and fearing that I might lose the sight of both eyes, I bade farewell to meditation and the celestial firmament. I also tried another kind of exercise for a time. My master told me that an infallible means for making rapid progress towards spirituality was to keep all the apertures of my body completely closed, so that none of the five *pranams* (winds) which are in it could escape. To do this I had to place a thumb in each ear, close my lips with the fourth and little fingers of each hand, my eyes with the two forefingers, and my nostrils with the two middle fingers; and to close the lower orifice I had to cross my legs and sit very tightly on one of my heels. While in this attitude I had to keep one nostril tightly shut, and leaving the other open I had to draw in a long deep breath; then, immediately closing that nostril, I had to open the other and thoroughly exhale the air that I had just inhaled. It was of the greatest importance that the inhalation and exhalation should not be performed through the same nostril. I continued this exercise until I lost consciousness and fainted away.'

In order to make his description more intelligible the renegade *sannyasi* insisted on going through the performance in my presence. It is impossible to imagine a more ridiculous scene. But he took care to change his exhausting position as soon as possible, bursting into shouts of laughter at the recollection of the absurd things that he had been compelled to do.

I will now give some other examples of meditative exercises gathered from Hindu books, which will show how they were practised in former days. One of the most famous and edifying of the *yogams* is that called *sabda-brahma* (the word of Brahma) or *pranava*; that is to say, meditation on the sacred and mysterious word *aum*—*aum* being Brahma himself[1].

As this word *aum* is composed of three letters, which in writing form only one, we may consider that the *a* is Brahma, the *u* Vishnu, and the *m* Siva. The sign representing these three letters, which in combination form the *sabda-brahma*, ends with a semicircle with a dot in the centre, which is called *bindu*, and is the emblem of the purely spiritual being.

Those who desire to obtain salvation must be always meditating on this word and constantly repeating it.

But to make this meditation effectual one must begin by obtaining complete mastery over oneself and by entirely subduing all bodily senses and passions. One must, therefore, gradually withdraw one's thoughts and affections from all material objects and fix them on the dot, or *bindu*, mentioned above. This point once reached, a single moment of meditation is sufficient to ensure the most perfect happiness.

Vishnu always looks favourably on such meditations, and from the moment that one is able to bring oneself to believe firmly that the *pranava*, or the word *aum*, is the Divine Being, one sees Vishnu in everything. In fact, one sees, hears, and thinks of nothing but him; and, finally, one believes that there is nothing existing except him.

Just as there is nothing worth knowing that is not to be found in the Vedas, so no meditation is equal in merit to that of the *pranava*, or the word *aum*.

Another kind of meditation, which is quite as efficacious as that which I have just described, is the *ashta-yoga* (the eight *yogas*). The following is a short analysis of it, compiled from the *Saka* of the Rig-Veda:—

The *ashta-yoga* is peculiarly efficacious. By its means Siva himself obtained forgiveness for his sins[2] and the kingdom of

[1] It would be more correct to say Brāhman—the Supreme Spirit itself.—ED.

[2] See Part I, Chapter VII.

Kailasa. There are no sins that it will not wipe out! To kill a Brahmin or a cow, to steal gold, to drink intoxicating liquors, to violate the wife of one's *guru*, to bring about abortion, are all most heinous crimes. To slander or deceive a Brahmin, or break a promise made to a Brahmin; to look upon a poor man or a stranger when one is eating and not to have pity on him, but to repulse him and send him away hungry; to prevent cows from drinking when they are thirsty; to try to pass oneself off as learned when one knows nothing; to attempt to dogmatize on the practice of meditation while ignorant of the subject; to give medicines without being a doctor; to predict the future when one is no astrologer; for a Brahmin to offer sacrifices to the *lingam* or to an image of Vishnu after a Sudra has previously sacrificed to them:—all these are indeed terrible sins. But the *ashta-yoga* will wipe them all out. It is thus described:—First of all, one must fast for three consecutive days; after which one must repair to a temple dedicated to Siva, or to a cemetery, or to a *bilva* tree. There one must perform the *achamania* and paint the little circular mark called *tilaka* on one's forehead. Having prepared a clean spot on the ground, the devotee must stand upon it on his head with his feet in the air. In this position he must six times perform the *pranayama*, which consists in inhaling through one nostril and forcibly expelling the air through the other[1]. By this means the Man of Sin will be destroyed, for this Man of Sin resides in the nerve which is found on the left side of the head. While expelling the air from the body by the *pranayama*, one must say: 'Nerve, you are a goddess! In you resides the Man of Sin. I am about to wash you to rid you of him. So begone!' A violent exhalation through the left nostril having expelled this nerve where the Man of Sin dwelt, the devotee must then wash it in warm water and offer *puja* to it. Then it must be made to return to its proper place. To effect this a long inhalation must be made through the right nostril, accompanied by the following words:—'Behold, great goddess, freed from sin, you are the mother of the world! A sacrifice has been offered in your honour. Return now to the place that you occupied before.'

This is the exercise of the *ashta-yoga*. It was by practising

[1] *Pranayama* literally means suppression of breath.—ED.

this, the author asserts, that Siva became the ruler of the world; Indra, the lord of the *Swarga*; Durga, the mother of all living creatures; and Vishnu, the preserver of all things.

There are many other *yogams*. In the chapter on the *sandhya*, I gave a description of the *santi-yoga*, which serves as a kind of preparation to the Brahmin's daily sacrifice. But enough has perhaps been said to show how puerile are the religious exercises of the Hindu ascetics.

They have, by way of supererogation, eighteen kinds of *tapasas* or corporal penances, of increasing degrees of severity. A recluse selects the one for which he feels most inclination. Among the most painful may be mentioned that which consists in being exposed, stark naked, to the sun for the whole day in the hottest weather, and surrounded on all sides by huge fires; and that in which the devotee remains for a whole day immersed up to the neck in cold water, with a wet cloth round the head, during the coldest season of the year. These are called *pancha-tapasas* (the five penances).

One often sees devotees holding their arms folded above their heads, in which position they remain till the nerves become so strained and benumbed by the prolonged tension that they cannot regain their normal position.

Others, again, stand on one foot, holding the other foot in the air until the leg swells and inflames and breaks out all over into sores.

Hindu books are full of the merits of these *yogams* and *tapasas*. Amongst other self-inflicted tortures they give an honourable place to one which is in fact the *ne plus ultra* of its kind. It consists in holding the breath for such a length of time that the soul, forced to depart from the body, makes a passage for itself through the top of the head and flies off to reunite itself to Parabrahma.

But let no one carry away the idea that the majority of modern recluses feel any inclination to subject their bodies to such rough usage. Most of them rest content with sitting motionless, their eyes closed and their heads bent, spending their whole time and energy in thinking of nothing, and keeping their minds an utter blank. Others remain squatting imperturbably in the attitude which the minister Appaji recommended to his shepherd, as already described[1].

[1] See Part II, Chapter XXVII.

One of these meditative devotees, who lived near me, had a mania for imagining that he saw an image of Vishnu always before him, to which he offered, still in imagination, garments, jewels, and all sorts of food, the god in exchange giving him all that he asked for. He used to spend two hours every day in this occupation, but at the end of it all he invariably found himself, as before, with empty hands and an equally empty stomach.

No doubt there were men after the Flood who still retained the precious gift of a knowledge of the true God, and gave themselves up to the contemplation of His infinite perfections as a means of keeping alive in their hearts a proper sense of the worship that it was their duty to pay Him. Isaac most probably was only continuing the custom of his father Abraham in going out, at the close of the day, to meditate in the fields (Genesis xxiv. 63). Moses also commanded the children of Israel to meditate continually on the duty of loving God with all their hearts; and he enjoined them to meditate on this when in their houses, or when travelling, so that God might be always present to their minds. David, who had himself experienced the benefit of meditation, recommends the practice in almost all his Psalms; and this advice his son Solomon repeats. The pious habit has thus descended from generation to generation from the time of the Flood to the establishment of Christianity, and the religion of Christ likewise regards meditation on the precepts of God as an indispensable duty.

The first Hindu lawgivers, who, though separating themselves from the rest of mankind, preserved their knowledge of the true God, were fully impressed with the necessity of frequent meditation on His greatness, fearing that otherwise they might insensibly allow the recollection of the Deity to fade from their minds; but these just ideas were soon warped by human passions and corrupted by the spirit of idolatry, so that they quickly degenerated into ridiculous and meaningless practices. The pious men who in early ages gave up a few moments in each day to serious thought and meditation were succeeded by fanatics, who, retaining only the mere outward forms of their predecessors' inward piety, gave themselves up in their mad enthusiasm to the wildest extravagance, and in fact to any folly that they thought likely to attract the fancy of a people so devoted to exaggerations of all kinds as the Hindus. Modern authors, confusing religious practices which originate in sincere love for and devotion to God with those emanating from vainglory, hypocrisy, and superstition, have tried to throw discredit on the life of asceticism and contemplation which was advocated both by the old and the new dispensation, and have presumed to trace a similarity between it and the absurd *yogams* of the Hindu *sannyasis*. But it seems to me that a small amount of honest thought would have shown them what an immense difference there was both in the objects aimed at and in the means used to attain those objects. Let them compare the tenets and practices of the two great founders of the ascetic and contemplative life in Holy Writ with those of the so-called *sannyasi* philosophers amongst the Hindus. Can Elijah and John the Baptist be compared for one moment with the *sannyasis* Vasishta and Narada? Is there any sort of resemblance between the teachings and maxims of the former and of the latter? The *Padma-purana* and the *Vishnu-purana*, supposed to have been dictated by these two *sannyasis*, are a mass of exaggerations and absurdities. Could the same charge be brought against the doctrines of the holy prophet of Israel and those of the forerunner of the Messiah?

The penances of John the Baptist, for example, have certainly nothing in common with the exaggerations and hypocritical follies of the Hindu *sannyasis*, whose sole aim and object is to attract public attention to themselves[1]. The actuating motive of John the Baptist was the deepest humility. He hid himself from the world. He shunned, despised, and rejected its honours, and wished to be considered the least and humblest among men. Nevertheless, in his solitude he did not forget the duties laid upon him of instructing and preparing the world for the great event which was about to be accomplished. Attracted by the fame of his virtues, men of all ages and all classes flocked to hear the pure and holy doctrine which he taught. Labourers, soldiers, publicans, masters, servants—all desired to hear his preaching, and all received wise advice and counsel for the regulation of their conduct according to their various conditions.

[1] This can hardly be called an impartial and correct picture of the *sannyasi*.—ED.

If he left his desert home for a moment, it was only, like his predecessor Elijah, to extend yet further the word of God and to reprove with dauntless courage the criminal conduct of an incestuous king.

It was not by such unmeaning and ridiculous practices as the *moksha-sadhaka*, the *pranava*, the *santi-yoga*, the *homam*, the *pancha-gavia*, or the disgusting sacrifices to the *lingam*, that these saintly hermits and their disciples sought to arrive at perfection. They never aimed at gaining popular applause by excessive and unnatural penances. Their actions, on the contrary, were based on profound humility and on a sincere desire to live unhonoured by the world, with only their God as a witness to the purity of their lives and motives.

CHAPTER XXXVI

The Funeral Ceremonies of Brahmin *Sannyasis*.

THE ceremonies which accompany the funerals of *sannyasis* differ in many respects from those of ordinary Brahmins. *Vanaprasthas*, like ordinary Brahmins, are burned after death; but *sannyasis* are invariably buried, no matter what their rank or sect may be.

The son of a *sannyasi* (should the deceased have had one born to him before he embraced this state) must preside at the funeral. In default of a son, there is always some pious Brahmin who will take on himself the duty and bear the cost. There is often, indeed, much rivalry as to who shall have the honour of filling this office, as it is considered a most meritorious one. After the corpse has been washed in the usual manner, it is wrapped in two cloths dyed yellow with *kavi*. It is then rubbed all over with ashes, and a chaplet of large seeds called *rudrakshas*[1] is fastened round the neck. While all this is going on the other Brahmins play on bronze castanets, which make an ear-splitting noise.

Everything being in readiness for the obsequies, the body is placed, with its legs crossed, in a large bamboo basket, which is hung from a strong bamboo pole by ropes of straw. This basket is borne by four Brahmins. The grave must be dug near a river or a tank, and must be about six feet deep and circular in form. When they reach the spot the Brahmins deposit at the bottom of the grave a thick layer of salt, on which they place the deceased, with the legs still crossed. They then fill the hole with salt till it reaches the *sannyasi's* neck, pressing it well down so that the head may remain immovable. On the head, thus left exposed, they break innumerable cocoanuts until the

[1] This word *rudraksha* means the eye of Siva, because these seeds are, according to Hindu legend, formed by his tears.—DUBOIS.

N n 2

skull is completely fractured[1]. They then, for the third time, throw in salt in sufficient quantities to entirely cover the remains of the head. Over the grave they erect a kind of platform, or mound, three feet in height, on the top of which they place a *lingam* of earth about two feet high. This obscene object is immediately consecrated by the Brahmins, who offer to it a sacrifice of lighted lamps, flowers, and incense, and for *neiveddya*, bananas and *paramannam*, a dish to which the Brahmins are particularly partial, and which is composed of rice, cocoanut, and sugar. While these offerings are being made, hymns are sung in honour of Vishnu, all present screaming at the top of their voices.

This discordant music over, the presiding Brahmin walks round the *lingam* three times, makes a profound obeisance to it, expresses the hope that by virtue of the sacrifice offered to the image the deceased may be fully satisfied, that Siva may look favourably on him, that Brahma may receive him into his abode, and that thus he may escape another re-incarnation in this world. He then pours a little rice and a few drops of water on the ground, picks up all the fragments of the cocoanut shells that have been broken on the head of the deceased, and distributes them to those present, who scramble for the pieces, so eager are they to possess these relics, which are supposed to bring good luck. The *paramannam* is then divided among those who have no children, for when acquired under these circumstances it possesses the power of making barren women fruitful. The ceremonies of the day end with ablutions: not that the mourners need to purify themselves from any defilement, because none is contracted in attending the funeral of a *sannyasi*; but these ablutions serve instead of the bath which all Brahmins must take three times a day.

For ten successive days after the funeral the person who has presided thereat, and several other Brahmins in his company, meet every morning at the grave of the deceased to renew the offerings to the *lingam*. A similar ceremony takes place on the anniversary of his death.

On the conclusion of the ceremonies, the presiding Brahmin contents himself with giving a very frugal repast to all those

[1] The object of this is to free the *prana* (life), which is believed to be imprisoned in the skull.—ED.

who have attended the function, after which he walks thrice round the assembly, bows to them, and dismisses them without giving them any presents. They, in their turn, before their departure, congratulate him on the good deed that he has performed and on the reward that he has earned thereby.

The tombs of these *sannyasis* sometimes become famous, and crowds of devotees flock to them, bringing offerings and sacrifices as if to divine beings. The strange custom of breaking the heads of these dead hermits with cocoanuts at their burial has no doubt some connexion with the similar practice in regard to the *lingam* stones which may often be seen on the high-roads or in much-frequented places, the passers-by being in the habit of breaking on the top of these *lingams* the cocoanuts which they are about to offer as sacrifices.

All the prayers, oblations, and ceremonies which are offered up for the *sannyasis* after their death would seem to indicate an opinion that these hermits still have some sins to expiate, and that their perfect happiness remains doubtful[1]. This is not the only point on which Hindu beliefs contradict each other.

I have already said that it is a mistake to confuse Brahmin *sannyasis* with those Sudra penitents belonging to the sects of Siva and Vishnu, who live apart in solitary hermitages. These latter are not obliged to fulfil the condition of having previously been fathers of families. They are supposed to have always been absolutely continent, but I should be very sorry to be compelled to guarantee the fact.

A Brahmin can become a *sannyasi* at any age. Many are to be met with who, tormented by remorseful consciences, devote the last days of their lives to this profession, and even embrace it on their death-beds, convinced as they are that to have merely become a penitent is a sure safe-conduct to the other world. The same formalities as those which I have already described are used for the admission of these hoary old sinners to a tardy penitence; and be their repentance sincere or not, they can safely count on receiving after death all the advantages and all the happiness that the most persevering *sannyasis* have a right to expect who have grown old in the exercise of the most rigorous austerities.

[1] These ceremonies would appear to be observed more as a matter of ritual than of expiation.—ED.

PART III

RELIGION

CHAPTER I

Origin of the *Trimurti* and the Primitive Idolatry of the Hindus.—Comparison between the Greek and Indian Divinities.—Peculiar Idolatry of the Hindus.—Worship of the Elements represented by the *Trimurti*.

THE Hindus understand by the word *Trimurti* the three principal divinities whom they acknowledge. These are Brahma, Vishnu, and Siva. The word properly signifies '*the three powers*,' viz. *Creation*, the special attribute of Brahma; *Preservation*, the attribute of Vishnu; and *Destruction*, the attribute of Siva[1].

These three divinities are represented sometimes singly with their special emblems, and sometimes joined together in a single body with three heads. It is under the latter form that they obtain the name of *Trimurti*, which means, at once, both *the three bodies* and *the three powers*. This union of persons is the allegorical symbol of the existence of things created, which can neither be produced nor preserved without the agreement and the sanction of these three powers.

[1] The first is the religion of activity and works; the second, that of faith and love; the third, that of austerity, contemplation, and spiritual knowledge. This last is regarded as the highest, because it aims at entire cessation of action and total effacement of all personal entity and identity by absorption into simple Soul.—MONIER-WILLIAMS.

The *Trimurti* is recognized and worshipped generally by all Hindus except the Jains. Although many Hindus are specially devoted, some to Siva and others to Vishnu, nevertheless when these two divinities are united with Brahma in a single body with three heads they all pay equal worship to the three without regard to the particular points of doctrine which otherwise separate them.

It is very difficult to trace the origin of the *Trimurti*, inasmuch as the accounts of it do not agree. In some Puranas it is related that the *Trimurti* sprang from a female source called *Adi-Sakti* (the original power), who gave birth to these three divinities united in a single body; and it is added that after having brought them into the world she fell so desperately in love with them that she married them.

In some other Puranas we read that *Adi-Sakti* produced a seed from which was born Siva, the father of Vishnu.

Elsewhere we are told that a flower of the *tamarasa* plant (water-lily) sprang from the navel of Vishnu, and that from this flower Brahma was born.

In short, we find in the Hindu books a mere tissue of contradictions relating to the *Trimurti*, and the absurd details which are related in connexion with each are even more inconsistent. The point on which they agree to a certain extent is that which relates to the excesses and abominable amours of the three divinities composing it.

In spite of the great power which these divinities enjoyed, they were nevertheless often compelled to feel the terrible vengeance of virtuous persons, who, shocked at the sight of their infamous proceedings, found means of reducing them to subjection and inflicting on them severe punishment. Thus, for example, there was a certain virgin, named Anusooya, who was as much renowned for her inviolable chastity as for her devotion to the gods and for her tender compassion for the unfortunate. The divinities of the *Trimurti*, having heard of her, became so greatly enamoured that they resolved upon robbing her of her virginity, which she had till then treasured with so much care. To attain their object the three seducers disguised themselves as religious mendicants, and under this guise went to ask alms of her. The virgin came to them, and with her wonted kindness showered gifts upon them. The sham beggars, after being loaded with her gifts, told her that they expected from her another favour, which was to strip herself naked before them and to satisfy their impure desires. Surprised and frightened by this shameful proposal, she repulsed them by pronouncing against them certain *mantrams*. These, together with some holy water which she poured upon them, had the effect of converting them into a calf. After they had been thus transformed, Anusooya took upon herself to bring up this calf by feeding it with her own milk. The *Trimurti* remained in this humiliating position till all the female deities combined together and, fearing lest some great misfortune might befall them in the absence of their three principal gods, after consulting one another, went in a body to Anusooya and begged her most humbly to give up the *Trimurti* and to restore them to their former state. It was with great difficulty that Anusooya was persuaded to yield to their prayers, and even then she imposed a condition that they should first of all be ravished (by whom the fable does not say). The female deities, convinced that they could not otherwise rescue the *Trimurti*, consented to undergo the penalty required of them, choosing rather to lose their honour than their gods. The conditions being fulfilled, Anusooya restored the *Trimurti* to their former state, and they returned to the place whence they came[1].

This scandalous adventure of the mighty divinities of the *Trimurti* is one of the least indecent of the kind related in the Hindu books.

But whatever may be the confusion pervading the contradictory accounts of the different Puranas, I am inclined to believe that all that is said about the three divinities of the *Trimurti*, and of the follies which are ascribed to them, is a mere mass of disgusting allegory.

At the commencement of their idolatry the Hindus confined their worship to visible objects, such as the sun, the moon, the stars, and the elements. In those early times they felt no need of making idols of stone, wood, or metal. But as paganism extended its dominion, and when, in imitation of other idolatrous nations, the Hindus went so far as to deify simple mortals, they had

[1] Hindus would say that these stories were not intended to illustrate the immorality of their gods, but to affirm that a chaste woman is proof even against divine temptation.—ED.

recourse to statues and images in order to perpetuate the memory of their celebrated men and to transmit their virtues to posterity. By degrees, with the same object in view, they gave a bodily form to all the objects of their worship. The origin of the *Trimurti* dates, I believe, from a period long after the establishment of idolatry in India.

It may justly be presumed that this symbolic representation of the three divinities united in a single body denotes merely the three elements which are most perceptible to all, viz. earth, water, and fire. In course of time the original notion vanished, and an ignorant people, guided solely by the impression of the senses, gradually converted what was at first a simple allegory into three distinct and real divinities.

Before pushing my inquiries further upon this subject, I would make a few remarks on the origin which many modern writers have assigned to this triple divinity of India. They have asserted that these three gods are nothing else but the three principal deities of the Greeks and the Romans under different names. Brahma, according to them, is Jupiter, Vishnu is Neptune, and Siva is Pluto. In fact, according to the mythology of the Greeks, Jupiter is the author and the creator of all things; he is the father, the master, and the king of gods and men. Now, all these attributes belong equally to Brahma. The Hindus say that the universe is *the egg of Brahma*, and that after laying it, he hatched it. He also particularly resembles Jupiter in his incestuous alliances. Jupiter had for his wife Juno, his sister; Brahma is, at the same time, the father and the husband of Sarasvati: and it would be easy to enumerate many more points of resemblance between these two divinities.

The resemblance between Neptune and Vishnu is no less striking. Neptune makes the waters his abode; the sea is his empire; there he reigns, mounted on his chariot in the form of a shell drawn by sea-horses, and armed with his formidable trident. He is attended by Tritons, who make the whole sea re-echo with the sound of their conches. One of the most common names for Vishnu is *Narayana*, which signifies *one that sojourns in the waters*. He is represented as quietly sleeping on the surface of the ocean. It is true he has neither trident in his hand nor Tritons around him; but his devotees bear on their forehead a symbolic figure which closely resembles a trident, and in imitation of the companions of Neptune they are always provided with a conch, or *sangu*, from which they blow ear-splitting blasts, and the figure of which is also stamped on their shoulders with hot iron.

Siva, again, is a perfect prototype of Pluto, the gloomy god of hell, the lord of the shades and of night. To Siva belongs the power of destruction. He it is who reduces everything to dust; he takes delight in giving vent to his sobs and groans in places of burial, whence he derives the name of *Rudra* commonly given him. It signifies *one who causes lamentation.*

Pluto, unable to find a woman willing to dwell with him in his dismal abode, carried off Proserpine, and concealed her so well that for a long while she escaped the search of her mother Ceres. In like manner, Siva found a wife in a remote quarter. Unable to get one elsewhere, he obtained one at last from the mountain Mandra, who gave him in marriage his daughter Parvati, in consideration of a long and severe penance which Siva endured for her sake in the deserts. For fear lest she should escape from him, he carries her always on his head, concealed in his enormously thick hair[1].

But though some features of resemblance lead us to believe in the identity of the fabulous deities of India with those of Greece and Rome, we find ourselves disconcerted at every step. As a matter of fact both Vishnu and Siva, as well as Brahma, possess many traits of likeness to the Olympian king. It was Vishnu who cleared the earth of a multitude of giants that overran it—giants who far exceeded in stature Enceladus, Briareus, and the other Titans who were destroyed by Jupiter. Jupiter is borne by an eagle; Vishnu likewise rides a pretty eagle called *Garuda*, which, though the smallest of the birds of its own species, became enormously large when it carried the god under the designation of *Jagannatha*, i.e. Master of the World, an attribute which he shares with the most powerful of the sons of Saturn.

Juno is the goddess of wealth. The name of Lakshmi, the

[1] The Abbé is evidently confusing Parvati with Ganga (the Ganges), who according to Hindu mythology is always carried on Siva's head. Parvati is always said to be carried on Siva's left hip.—ED.

wife of Vishnu, also signifies *one who gives riches.* Jealous like Juno, Lakshmi had a good deal to suffer, as well as her prototype, on account of the numberless infidelities of her husband, the consequences of which were the same, namely, perpetual domestic quarrels. The Romans, in the feasts which they celebrated in honour of their gods, always represented Jupiter in company with his wife; and the Hindus do the same in the case of Vishnu and Lakshmi.

There are other divinities, such as *Devendra, Varuna,* and *Yama,* who display still greater resemblances to the three most powerful deities of Greek mythology. Devendra, whose name is equivalent to that of *master of the deities,* is the 'monarch of the sky.' He exercises his sovereignty over the deities of the second rank, who inhabit with him a place called *Swarga,* where they enjoy all kinds of carnal pleasures. He distributes among them the *amrita,* which has the virtue of rendering them immortal[1]. Like Jupiter, he is armed with lightning and launches it against the giants.

Varuna is really the Hindu Neptune. He is the god of water, the lord of the ocean, and is worshipped as such over the whole Peninsula.

We recognize Pluto in Yama. Yama exercises his sovereignty in *Naraka* (hell), as Pluto does in Tartarus. He presides at men's death-beds, and determines their subsequent destiny according to the deeds, good or bad, which they have done during their lifetime. I might prolong this comparison, without however drawing the conclusion that the Hindus ever borrowed their system of theogony from the Greeks, or the Greeks from the Hindus.

But if it is not from other ancient peoples that the Hindus derived their three principal divinities, whence have they derived them? I shall attempt some reflections on this point with all the reserve imposed upon me by a subject so difficult of explanation. Let us first observe that Hindu idolatry differs in one essential point from that which prevailed formerly in Athens and in Rome. In Greece and Rome it was not the sea that was worshipped, but its monarch, the god Neptune. All his attendants, the Nereids and the Tritons, had a share in the

[1] *Mrita* signifies death, and *amrita* immortality. The *amrita* does not appear to differ from the ambrosia of the Greeks.—DUBOIS.

worship offered to him. It was not to the forests, to the rivers, or to the fountains that prayers were offered, but to the Fauns and to the Naiads who presided over them.

The idolatry of India, which is of a much grosser kind, has for the object of its worship the material substance itself. It is to water, to fire, to the most common household implements; in a word, to everything which they understand to be useful or hurtful, that the Hindus pay direct worship.

It is true that they admit another kind of idolatry which is a little more refined. There are images of deities of the first rank which are exposed to public veneration only after a Brahmin has invoked and incorporated in them these actual divinities. In these cases, it is really the divinity that resides in the idol, and not the idol itself, that is worshipped.

But the one kind of worship does not exclude the other; and that which has for its object the actual substance itself is the most common.

The Hindus hold, as an invariable principle, that every object, animate or inanimate, which has the power of doing good or evil, should be worshipped.

'My god,' a respectable Hindu said to me one day, 'is the headman amongst my field labourers; for as they work under his orders, he can, by using his influence, do me much good or much evil.'

I have somewhere read a conversation between the wives of the seven famous *Rishis*, in which they agreed in the principle that the chief god of a woman is her husband, by reason of the good or evil he can do her; and we have already seen that the rules of conduct drawn up for Hindu ladies continually remind us of this idea. It is this same notion which makes the Hindus attach so much importance to the blessing or the curse of persons reputed to be saints; it is on the same principle also that they are so easily persuaded to give the name of god to princes and great personages, and, in short, to every one from whom they have something to hope or to fear.

There is one phrase which among the civilized nations of Europe has at all times been a metaphorical exaggeration, but which is taken literally in India. *To make a god of one's belly* bears quite a different meaning for a Brahmin and for a European.

The rage for deifying everything has spread even to the mountains and to the forests. The savage tribes who inhabit these places do not worship any of the gods of the country; they have one special deity of their own: it is a big root, a sort of potato, which grows abundantly in the forests, and forms their principal staple of food. Knowing nothing more useful than this vegetable, they make it the object of their worship. In its presence they celebrate their marriages, and in its name they take their oaths.

Probably the *Trimurti* owed its origin to this mode of viewing objects. Earth, water, and fire were the types of the three divinities which compose it. The earth is the common mother of all things, animate and inanimate. Either they spring from her bosom, or they live upon her productions. It is through her that everything subsists in nature. She has, therefore, been regarded as the divine creator, and holds the first rank in the opinion of the Hindus, who have made her their Brahma.

But what could the earth do without the help of water? Without the dews and the rains which develop the seeds of her fertility she would remain barren, and would soon find herself bereft of every living creature. It is water which gives life, preserves, and causes to grow everything that has life or vegetates. It was, therefore, regarded as the divine preserver, that is to say, Vishnu.

Fire, in penetrating the other two elements, communicates to them a portion of its energy, develops their properties, and brings everything in nature to that state of growth, maturity, and perfection which would never be arrived at without it. But, should it cease to act upon created things, every one of them perishes. When it is in its free and visible state, this active agent of reproduction destroys by its irresistible power the bodies to whose composition it had before contributed; and it is to this formidable power that it owed its title of god-destroyer, that is to say, Siva.

By uniting the three elements in a single body with three heads the founders of the Hindu theogony wished it to be understood that the harmony of these three primal elements was indispensable to the production and reproduction of all secondary bodies.

This is not a theory of my own invented merely for the purpose of explaining the original idolatry of the Hindus; it is their own peculiar doctrine, observed by them in daily practice. It is even one of the fundamental tenets of the religion of the Brahmins. To convince themselves of this, let my readers reperuse the chapter about *sandhya*, which so formally enjoins the special and direct worship of the three elements, while the two others, air and ether, are almost forgotten.

The Brahmins offer worship and address mystical prayers to the seven inferior worlds, of which the first and the most important is the earth. 'Glory to thee, O earth, mother most great,' are the words of the *Yajur-Veda*; and immediately after is added, 'Glory to thee, O fire, who art god.'

There is no surer proof that they attach to fire itself the idea of divine essence than their perpetual sacrifices of *homam* and of *yagnam*, in which no other object of worship than this element is observable.

The divinity of water is also incontestably recognized as an article of their belief. The Brahmins worship it and offer prayers to it when they make their daily ablutions. It is then that they invoke the holy rivers, among others the Ganges, and all its sacred branches. Often too they offer oblations to water by casting into the rivers and tanks, especially at the places where they bathe, small pieces of gold and silver, and sometimes pearls and other valuable jewels.

Furthermore, sailors, fishermen, and all who frequent the sea, visit the shore from time to time to pay their worship and to offer up their sacrifices to it.

When, after a long drought, an abundant rain brings hope to the despairing husbandman by filling the great reservoirs for the irrigation of the rice-fields, the inhabitants at once flock to them and with signs of joy exclaim, 'The lady is arrived'; and they bow with their hands clasped towards the water which fills the reservoirs, while he-goats or rams are sacrificed in its honour.

At the season of the year when the Cauvery inundates the barren and scorched fields on its banks and spreads freshness and fertility far and wide—which generally takes place in the middle of July—the inhabitants of that part of the Peninsula crowd to its banks, many of them coming from a great distance, in order to congratulate *the lady* (the water) on her arrival and to offer her sacrifices of all sorts, such as pieces of money, which they throw to her that she may have something to defray her expenses; pieces of linen to clothe herself; jewels to adorn herself; rice, cakes, fruits, and other eatables, lest she should suffer from hunger; household utensils such as baskets, earthen vessels, &c., in order that she may conveniently cook and store her provisions and have everything which may procure her an easy subsistence.

The homage which the Brahmins in the *sandhya* ceremonies pay to the water contained in the copper vessel, the frequent performance of *achamania*[1] or purification by water, and many other similar acts, attest the reality of the special worship which they pay to water. Hence no doubt arises the great veneration which they have for Vishnu, who represents this element in the *Trimurti*; a veneration far superior to that which they show to Siva, the representative of fire.

As far as one can see, in ancient times the elements had temples specially dedicated to their worship; but I confess that I have not been able to discover any vestiges of such buildings still remaining. Nevertheless, if we may believe the evidence of a Brahmin who was consulted on the subject by Abraham Rogers, there was, when this traveller visited India, in a district not far from the Coromandel Coast, a temple dedicated to *the five elements.* Be this as it may, however, one may not unfrequently see upon the door or in the interior of the temples existing at the present day the symbols of these elements represented either by five *lingams* arranged in a line, or by only three which are symbols of the material *Trimurti*—earth, water, and fire.

It may be remarked, perhaps, that the Hindus are not the only ancient nation which has adored the elements without attaching to the worship the idea of the divinities who subsequently became identified with it. Most idolatrous nations have, I am quite aware, made the elements the actual objects of their worship. But this confirms rather than contradicts the opinion that the Hindus gave themselves up to this absurd material idolatry, and that they invented their *Trimurti* in order to perpetuate it by symbols. For I persist in my belief that the

[1] Described in the chapter on *sandhya*.

three great divinities, Brahma, Vishnu, and Siva, were originally nothing else but the three elements personified.

The *Trimurti*, as we have seen, signifies at the same time the *three bodies* and the *three powers*. These three bodies, symbolical of the three great agents of Nature, were at first simply allegorical, just as are most of the religious and political institutions of India. This decided taste for allegory, which is characteristic of the founders of the Hindu religion and polity, has proved the source of many errors in the case of a people who are invariably guided simply by the impression of their senses, and who, accustomed to judge things only by their outward appearance, have taken literally that which was represented to them under symbols, and have thus come to adore the actual image itself instead of the reality.

This system of explanatory symbolism has always been, and is even now, so familiar to Hindu writers, that they often describe their three great divinities by the allegorical designations peculiar to each. We have seen, too, that they recognize in men three sorts of dispositions or qualities which they call *satva, rajas, tamas*. *Satva* is the gentle and insinuating disposition; *rajas*, the irascible, furious, passionate; *tamas*, the dull, heavy, and lethargic.

They attribute one of these qualities to each of the divinities which compose the *Trimurti*. Thus Vishnu is endowed with *satva*, Siva with *rajas*, and Brahma with *tamas*. Again, these same qualities are also applied to the three elements. The earth, like Brahma, is heavy and indifferent by nature; the water, like Vishnu, is insinuating and penetrating; the fire, like Siva, is capable of destroying everything by its violence.

The quality *tamas* is so inherent in the earth that Hindu astronomers often confound the two. Thus in a lunar eclipse, when the darkness of the earth intercepts the rays of the sun, they say that the *tamas-bimbam*, or the disk *tamas*, obscures *by its shadow* the disk of the moon.

The quality *rajas*, characteristic of fire and represented under the form of Siva, is ascribed in a special manner to that deity by the Hindu poets; and although the name of Siva, which is most commonly used, signifies *joy*, the deity bears many other names which seem to show that he is no other than fire personified.

Such, for instance, is the name *Jwala* (the inflamed), under which he is well known.

I shall here relate a strange practice which seems to me to support the opinion I hold regarding the origin of the *Trimurti.* Sometimes during the periods of excessive heat the Hindus suppose that Siva, from whom it emanates, is more than usually inflamed. Consequently, fearing lest he should set everything on fire, they place over the head of his idol a vessel filled with water. In this vessel a little hole is pierced, so that the water may, by falling on him drop by drop, refresh him and abate the burning heat that consumes him.

The quality *satva,* ascribed to Vishnu, applies also to water, which penetrates and insinuates itself into the earth, rendering it fertile; for the name of Vishnu signifies *one who penetrates everywhere. Appu* (water) is a common enough name for this deity; but the commonest of all is *Narayana,* that is to say, *one who moves upon the waters.*

Furthermore, the idea that the three principal divinities of India are the elements personified is admitted by a great number of Vishnavite Brahmins, and I am indebted to some of these for a portion of the arguments on which I have based my own view. They have at the same time told me that they themselves regard all that is commonly related of the *Trimurti* as mere fables; but as the disclosure of such a sentiment, which tends to nothing less than the undermining of one of the principal foundations of the popular religion, would stop the sources of their emoluments, and would at the same time expose them to public indignation, they are careful never to publish their private opinion on the matter.

This theory once admitted, it will be easy to find a very clear and natural meaning for certain expressions contained in the Hindu books—expressions which have led many authors to believe that the people of India possessed from the earliest times some knowledge of the Trinity. 'These three gods,' say those books, 'are but one; Siva is the heart of Vishnu, and Vishnu the heart of Brahma; it is one lamp with three lighted wicks.' At first sight these expressions would appear to indicate one god in three persons. But, even granted it were true that the primitive Hindus intended to transmit to their posterity the idea of the Trinity under the form and attributes of the *Trimurti,* it must be confessed that the result has been a sadly distorted presentation of this great mystery. On the other hand, I believe there is another explanation which is more simple and more reasonable. I cannot indeed doubt that the Hindu writers, in using the expressions just quoted, and many others of the same kind, wished them to be understood to mean that the co-operation of the three elements in question was indispensable for the production and reproduction of everything that exists in nature, a co-operation so necessary that the absence of one would reduce the others to a state of complete inertness and impotence.

The early Fathers of the Christian Church, such as St. Justin, St. Clement, Theodoret, St. Augustine, and others, proved the truth of the mystery of the Trinity to the heathens of their time by the authority of the ancient Greek philosophers, and particularly by that of Plato and his principal disciples, such as Plotinus and Porphyry. They gained at that time considerable advantage by laying stress on those authorities in whose works were to be found the words *Father, Son, Word, Spirit*; *the Father* comprehending perfection, *the Son* perfectly resembling *the Father*, and *the Word* by whom all things were created; these three Persons being but one God. Such expressions were not the chance creations of those philosophers; they formed the foundation of the system of Plato, who did not, however, venture to 'teach 'their meaning to a people steeped in the follies of polytheism, lest he should be treated in the same manner as his master Socrates.

Nevertheless, I doubt whether the illustrious Fathers of the Christian Church would have laid so much stress upon such authorities had they not found in the writings of these Platonic philosophers expressions more precise, less inconsistent, and less tainted with materialism than those to be found in the Hindu books relating to *Trimurti*.

My readers have, no doubt, been astonished to find that air, the element which some ancient Greek philosophers considered to be the beginning and ending of everything created, has so far not figured in this discussion. As a matter of fact, the Hindus go farther than the Greeks. They recognize five elements, and the air is divided by them into *ether* and *wind*, or, properly speaking, air, which is personified under the name of Indra, the chief of the inferior deities and the king of the ethereal regions, where he dwells. The word Indra signifies *the air*; in his domains the winds blow according to his commands. In the *Indra-purana* we find these words: 'Indra is nothing else than the wind, and the wind is nothing else than Indra.' The wind by condensing the clouds produces lightning, which is the weapon of this deity. He launches it against the giants, with whom he is often at war; and he is sometimes victorious, sometimes vanquished. The clouds, whose various forms represent the giants, sometimes stop the wind; sometimes, on the other hand, the latter disperses the clouds and rids the air of them.

This taste for allegory, which is inherent amongst all people in rudimentary stages of civilization, has become in the case of the Hindus an inexhaustible source of errors in matters of religion. In the earlier ages would-be commentators, by interpreting in their own way ideas whose original meaning had become obscured by lapse of time, confused everything instead of making everything clear; and later their successors, wearied by attempts to explain what seemed to them inexplicable, stuck to the literal meaning, and thus revived the extravagant and barbarous idolatry which forms the religious system of the modern Hindus.

CHAPTER II

Metempsychosis.—Explanation of this Religious Doctrine.—Penalties for Different Sins.—The Hindus as Authors of the Doctrine of Metempsychosis.—Difference between them and the Greeks in this Respect.—*Naraka*, or Hell; Punishments endured there.—Abodes of Bliss.

THERE are few Hindu books in which the doctrine of metempsychosis is not explained and expounded. This doctrine is, as is generally known, one of the fundamental principles of the Hindu religion. The following is an extract from the *Bhagavata*:—'Vishnu, the Supreme Being, before creating anything which now exists, began by creating souls[1], which at first animated bodies of fantastic shapes. During their union with these bodies they either committed sin or practised virtue. After a long abode in these provisional dwelling-places, they were withdrawn and summoned before the tribunal of Yama, who judges the dead. This divinity admitted into *Swarga* (paradise) those souls which had led virtuous lives; and he shut up in *Naraka* (hell) those souls which had given themselves up to sin. Souls which had been partly virtuous and partly sinful were sent to earth to animate other bodies, and so to endure proportionately the pain due for their sins and to receive the reward of their virtues. Thus every new birth, whether happy or unhappy, is the result of deeds practised in previous generations, and is either the reward or punishment for them. We may thus judge

[1] The philosophers of the School of Pythagoras held that these souls were not only immortal but eternal; that is to say, they existed before they entered the bodies of living creatures. The soul, they said, cannot be born of anything mortal; otherwise all things might become immortal. Nor can the soul be reborn of anything immortal, because that which is immortal cannot be reproduced. They held, therefore, that the soul is part of God Himself.—DUBOIS.

by the condition of a person in an existing generation what he has been in the previous one.

'Nevertheless, those who die in holiness are no longer exposed to new births; they go straight to *Swarga*.

'The souls of men, after death, go to animate other bodies. Sometimes it is the body of an insect, of a reptile, of a bird, or of a quadruped, and sometimes it is the body of another man. Nevertheless, the most perfect are admitted into *Swarga*, and the most guilty are plunged into *Naraka*. It is solely according to their good or bad deeds that their transmigration, advantageous or otherwise, is determined; and the good or evil they will have to experience in the various states through which they pass is determined in the same manner.

'The distinctions and differences which are to be observed amongst mankind must be attributed to the same causes. Some are rich, and others poor; some are weakly, others enjoy good health; some are handsome, others ugly; some are of low birth, others highly born; some are happy, others unhappy. These differences are not the result of mere chance, but of goodness or wickedness, as the case may be, in preceding existences.

'Man is the highest form of all the creatures on earth. To be born a man, in whatever caste it may be, always presupposes a certain degree of merit.

'Among men the Brahmins hold the first rank. The honour of giving a soul to a Brahmin is the reward only of the accumulated merits of many previous generations.

'To practise virtue in the hope of some reward is always a good thing; but to practise it with entire disinterestedness and without expecting any return or recompense, this is the most perfect. Those who thus practise it are certain of the happiness of *Swarga*, and are no more subject to change.

'This then is the fruit of our deeds. This is the reason why the same soul lives sometimes in the body of a man, at other times in that of an animal. This is why it is at one time happy, at another time unhappy, in this world and in the other.'

I will not follow the author in his detailed enumeration of the penalties which are reserved for various sins. I shall confine myself to the most important of them.

'He who kills the cow of a Brahmin will go after death to

hell, where he will for ever be the prey of serpents, and tormented by hunger and thirst. After thousands of years of horrible sufferings he will return to the world to animate the body of a cow, and will remain in this state as many years as the cow has hairs on its body. At length he will be born a Pariah, and will be afflicted with leprosy for a period of ten thousand years.

'The murder of a Brahmin, for any cause whatsoever, is a sin four times more heinous than the former. Whoever is guilty of it will be condemned at his death to take the form of one of those insects which feed on filth. Being reborn long afterwards a Pariah, he will belong to this caste, and will be blind for more than four times as many years as there are hairs on the body of a cow. He can, nevertheless, expiate his crime by feeding forty thousand Brahmins.

'If a Brahmin kills a Sudra, it will suffice to efface the sin altogether if he recites the *gayatri* a hundred times.

'He who kills an insect will himself become an insect after death. Then he will be reborn a Sudra, but he will be subject to all sorts of infirmities.

'Every Brahmin who cooks for a Sudra or who travels mounted on an ox will go to hell after death. He will be plunged there into boiling oil and be bitten continuously by venomous snakes. He will be reborn afterwards under the form of one of those birds of prey which devour corpses, and will remain a thousand years under this form, and also a hundred years under the form of a dog.

'Whoever fells a sacred fig-tree commits a crime four times greater than the murder of a Brahmin, and will be exposed after his death to penalties proportionate to a sin so heinous.'

Several modern philosophers have maintained that Pythagoras attached only an allegorical sense to the doctrine of metempsychosis. The most general opinion is that he taught it merely as an abstract religious doctrine. He is said to have borrowed it from the Egyptians, who, if we are to believe Herodotus, were its inventors. But the communications between Pythagoras and the Brahmins and Gymnosophists of India lead one to suppose with quite as much reason that he borrowed it from these Indian philosophers, for we know that the Hindus have never copied anything from contemporaneous nations. If it be true that at the time of the travels of Pythagoras the doctrine of metempsychosis was professed by the Egyptians, they had probably taken their ideas from the same sources as the people of India, if indeed they had not actually borrowed them from the latter. It is certain, furthermore, that it is not in this alone that the metaphysics of Pythagoras present some features of resemblance to those of the Gymnosophists. Again, we know that Pythagoras travelled for his own instruction, and it has never been contended that he taught anything to the peoples of Asia whom he visited. Besides, various Hindu books, which undoubtedly existed before the time of Pythagoras, are filled with this doctrine of metempsychosis and treat of it as an article of their primitive faith, which had been well established before his time. Anyhow, whoever the originator of it may be, it is none the less wonderful that such a chimerical system was not only acknowledged in almost the whole of Asia, but has even found credence in various other parts of the world. It is well known that Caesar found it in full force amongst the Gauls[1]; and one is astonished to find that enlightened men like Socrates and Plato made these fantastic theories the object of their serious speculations. Have we not seen modern writers, too, contending that the doctrine of metempsychosis is a masterpiece of genius? They have indeed maintained that Aristotle admitted the transmigration of the soul of one man into another, though it is proved that he rejected as absurd the idea of the transmigration of human souls into the bodies of beasts.

In consequence of his belief Pythagoras deprecated the eating of the flesh of any living creature, lest perchance a son might feed on the body of his father and thus repeat the horrible feast of Thyestes. The most zealous of his disciples ate only vegetables; and they even excluded beans from their meals. In the same way the Brahmins still refuse to eat onions, mushrooms, and certain other vegetables. Still, the example of these more rigorous disciples of Pythagoras found few imitators among the rest.

[1] 'Druides in primis hoc volunt persuadere, non interire animas sed ab aliis post mortem transire ad alios; atque hoc maxime ad virtutem excitari putant, metu mortis neglecto' (*De Bello Gallico*, vi. 14). Most heretics of the primitive Church, to say nothing of the Jews of later times, believed in this monstrous superstition, which was recognized also by Origen.—DUBOIS.

Either Pythagoras conceived a false impression of the motives of the abstinence which he had seen practised by the Hindus, or else he wished to excel them and to exaggerate their system according to his own manner.

As a matter of fact, everything induces us to believe that the Hindus, though foolish enough in many respects, are not so foolish as to believe, when they show repugnance to feeding on anything which has had life, that they might be swallowing the limbs of their ancestors. In proof of this I may remark that the Lingayats, that is to say, the followers of Siva, reject *in toto* the doctrine of metempsychosis, yet they abstain from all animal food more religiously perhaps than the Brahmins themselves.

The fear of pollution and the horror of murder are in fact the principal causes of the antipathy of Hindus to this kind of food. Their primitive teachers, as I have already remarked, simply had in view, when counselling such abstinence, the preservation of useful animals, and also the preservation of health. It was superstition, impetuous as a flood, that always tended to overflow the banks of reason.

We have already seen how susceptible and fastidious a respectable Hindu is in the matter of pollution. How then could a meat diet agree with his principles in this respect? The putrefaction of animals, which in a hot country manifests itself so quickly and in so disagreeable a manner; the comparative facility, on the other hand, with which products of the earth and other inorganic substances can be kept from the putrefying influence of the sun; the horror, so strongly felt, of feeding on the remains of a dead body; and a number of other prejudices which the leaders of the Hindu religion have been interested in fostering, are reasons sufficiently powerful to act upon minds prepared for them by custom and education. Let us add to these considerations the horror inspired by murder among Hindus in general—a horror which is so great in the case of many that it induces them to spare even the lives of filthy and troublesome insects; for the Brahmins are persuaded that there is no difference between the souls of men and those of the vilest of living things. Hence they hold that there is, morally speaking, as much crime in crushing an ant as in committing a murder.

The majority of the Sudras feel no scruples, it is true, in killing animals and eating their flesh, the cow alone excepted. They even include in their ranks butchers and professional hunters, such as the *Boyas* or *Baiders* who inhabit the jungles and mountains and live on the products of the chase. But it is also proper to remark that it is this violation of a respected usage which in a great measure brings upon them the contempt of the higher castes.

At first the doctrine of metempsychosis appears to have been limited to the successive transmigrations of souls into various human bodies. Later on, however, it received a new expansion, viz. that the souls could migrate to the bodies of beasts and to all material objects. The Platonic philosophers, who were ridiculed for assuming that the soul of a king might enter the body of a monkey, or that of a queen the body of a grasshopper, tried to evade the difficulty by reducing the doctrine to its primitive simplicity, that is to say, by limiting the transmigration of the souls of men to human bodies and those of beasts to their own species. Plotinus and Porphyry even ventured to assert that it was thus that their master had intended it to be understood. But their retractation was too late. It is always a mistake to endeavour to restore a building which is not solid in its foundations. The Hindus, who are more persevering and less exposed to the contradictions of enlightened men, have religiously preserved their own doctrine of metempsychosis in all its entirety.

After all, the doctrine seems to have been invented merely to justify, under a gross allegory, the ways of the Supreme Being in the dispensation of rewards and punishments. The first doctrinal article admitted by the Hindus is common to the Pythagoreans; namely, that sin ought to be punished and virtue rewarded. This of course does not usually take place in the present life, since very often vice is triumphant and virtue crushed. In order to remedy this the gods, who hold the destinies of men in their hands, have decreed that he who during his lifetime has been an unbeliever, a thief, a murderer, &c., shall be born again a creeping insect, a wild animal, an outcaste, blind, poor, &c.

Their notions of pollution pervade everything; so the Hindus believe that a soul after death retains some of the stains and impurities contracted in preceding generations, just as an earthen vessel retains for a long time the odour of any strong liquor which it has contained. This article of belief is illustrated by the example of a woman who had been a fish in an earlier generation, and who, though really a woman in the present, still retained, it is said, an odour which betrayed her first origin. It is necessary therefore that a long succession of generations should cleanse the soul from all the impurities which have polluted it in generations preceding—impurities which will increase indefinitely if people continue to lead dissolute lives.

When the Hindus are asked what is the limit of these transmigrations, they are unable to give any positive answer. Nevertheless their sacred books affirm that a soul only succeeds in getting rid of continual transformations when by long penance and contemplation it has raised itself to that high degree of wisdom and perfection which identifies it with the Supreme Being, that is, with Parabrahma. Before reaching such sublime heights, it must pass through all the trials and temptations to which human weakness has been condemned, and must acquire by its own experience a complete knowledge of good and evil. It begins its transmigrations under the form of the vilest insects, and rises little by little to the condition of man, in which state the spark of wisdom concealed in it, after having remained stationary for millions of years, is at length developed and imperceptibly leads to that state of perfection and purity which puts an end to changeful existence. In not assigning definite periods to each transmigration of the soul the Hindu philosophers seem to be wiser than the followers of Plato, who, with absurd presumption, have seen fit to assign fixed and definite periods—in some cases three thousand, and in others ten thousand years. Further, according to the latter, the transmigration is not left to chance; each soul has its choice of abode according to the inclinations of the man in whose body it has sojourned. Thus the soul of Agamemnon passed into the body of an eagle; that of Orpheus animated a swan; that of Ajax, a lion; that of Thersites, an ape, &c.

All this is simply ridiculous. But the stumbling-block of the system is recollection of the past. Since the body is only a prison, a shell, how is it that the soul, as soon as it has quitted its abode, loses all remembrance of what has befallen it? Pythagoras, it is true, used to relate to his disciples what he had successively been since the siege of Troy[1]. But the merest caviller among them might have offered the following objection: 'Since you so well remember what you have been before your present actual existence, why do I not remember in the same manner?' Pythagoras would no doubt have answered just as the Hindus answer, namely, that the gift of remembrance is granted only to certain privileged souls, and that they obtain it by reciting certain appropriate *mantrams*. Unfortunately, these *mantrams* are not unlike the waters of the Fountain of Youth, of which every one boasts to be the owner, but the whereabouts of which nobody knows. Plato, who was too enlightened not to recognize this weak side of the system, invented the river Lethe. The souls were obliged to drink its waters before returning to the world, and thereby entirely forgot the past. The invention of this fiction required neither ingenuity nor wit. The Hindus cut the knot more freely. They say that the act of regeneration suffices to make one forget all that has been seen or done before. A child under two or three years of age does not remember one day what he did the day before; still more therefore will he forget what he was and what he did before his new birth.

This explanation is at least more simple than that of Plato, if it is not equally ingenious.

NARAKA, OR HELL.

Through the tissue of vain fancies which the Hindus have woven over their system of metempsychosis, ostensibly to explain it but in practice to obscure it, we may catch a few faint gleams of the true religion, the principles of which were inculcated by the patriarchs of old. Apart from the rewards and punishments which they regard as the due retribution in this world of the good or evil which a man has done in a preceding generation, it is certain that they acknowledge a future life, and a Supreme Being, who is the rewarder of the good and the terror of the wicked. In a word, they recognize a paradise and a hell.

But how grievously have these sacred truths been distorted in

[1] See Ovid's *Metam.* xv. 3.

the mouths of these ministers of idolatry and falsehood! It is difficult to discover a single trace of such fundamental truths amid the mass of extravagant fables under which superstition has concealed them.

The Hindus agree that a place of punishment is set apart for those souls which have given themselves up entirely to sin during their life on earth. This they call *Naraka* or *Patala*. It is divided into seven principal sections, destined to contain the different kinds of sinful souls; and here they undergo torments more or less severe, according to the gravity of their crimes.

Yama, the judge of the dead, is the king of hell. He has servants to carry out his decrees, who are charged with tormenting the inhabitants of *Naraka*. His emissaries are constantly on the watch throughout the world. They await the moment of death, and then arrest the dead and bring them before Yama's tribunal. Yama consults his records, kept by many scribes working under his orders, and containing an exact account of all the good and evil which is done on earth. According to the report submitted to him, this sovereign judge pronounces the fate of the souls which appear before him for judgement, and awards punishments proportionate to their guilt.

Yama, however, is not the only deity possessing agents on earth for seizing upon the souls of the dead. Vishnu and Siva have also their agents, who know perfectly well the devotees of their respective patrons. When such souls die the emissaries of the two gods contend for them with Yama, and the result is a keen conflict and often a bloody battle. The special devotion to Siva or to Vishnu, however lukewarm it may have been, possesses so much merit that the emissaries of the two gods usually gain the victory over those of Yama.

As for the torments of *Naraka*, the punishments which the wicked have to endure there are truly terrible. I will here give an abstract of what the *Padma-purana* says of it:—

They are buried there in eternal darkness: only groans and frightful lamentations are heard; the sharpest pains that steel and fire can cause are inflicted without respite. There are punishments fitted to each kind of sin, to each sense, to each member of the body. Fire, steel, serpents, venomous insects, savage beasts, birds of prey, gall, poison, stenches; in a word, everything possible is employed to torment the damned. Some have a cord run through their nostrils, by which they are for ever dragged over the edges of extremely sharp knives; others are condemned to pass through the eye of a needle; others are placed between two flat rocks, which meet, and crush without killing them; others have their eyes pecked incessantly by famished vultures; while millions of them continually swim and paddle in a pool filled with the urine of dogs or with the mucus from men's nostrils, &c.

The damned do not succumb under these terrible penalties, but rend the air continually with their screams and groans, which echo throughout the whole abyss of hell and add still greater horror to this frightful dwelling-place.

The pains of hell do not endure for ever; they last proportionately to the gravity of the crimes committed. The Hindu sacred writers say nothing of eternal punishment. At the end of every *yuga*, they say, there takes place a universal revolution —a total change in nature. When the *Kali-yuga*, in which we now live, has filled its allotted span, all souls will return to the divine essence from which they were originally separated, and, the world having come to an end, the sufferings of the damned will cease also. I have before mentioned how many years of the *Kali-yuga* have already elapsed, and how many millions of years it has still to run.

When the souls in hell have expiated their sins, they are sent back to the earth in order to undergo new transmigrations. Their return to the world always takes place under the form of some vile animal; and proceeding from one metamorphosis to another, after millions of years they are able to acquire the degree of virtue and perfection necessary to admit of their being again united inseparably with the Supreme Being, the Universal Soul of the world.

The Abodes of Bliss.

The Hindus recognize several Abodes of Bliss for the souls of those who have expiated their sins by repeated transmigrations and by the practice of virtue. There are four principal abodes: The first is *Swarga*, where Indra the divinity presides, and where all virtuous souls, without distinction of caste or sex, are to be found.

The second is *Vaikuntha,* the paradise of Vishnu, where dwell his particular followers, Brahmins and others.

The third is *Kailasa,* the paradise of Siva, which is reserved for the devout worshippers of the *lingam.*

The fourth is *Sattya-loka* (the Place of Truth), the paradise of Brahma, where only virtuous Brahmins have the right to enter.

The pleasures enjoyed in these several abodes are all corporal and sensual.

The souls sojourning in them, having been indulged for periods of time more or less considerable according to their respective merits, are obliged to return to the earth, there to begin their transmigrations anew. This takes place until the soul is perfectly purified—a consummation, as we have seen, which is not the affair of a few days. However, with perseverance they eventually attain it. When a soul, by virtue and penances, has become as pure as gold and has freed itself entirely from the allurements of this world, it is re-united with Parabrahma, with God, with the Universal Soul, just as a drop of water returns to the sea from whence it came. This is the Supreme Happiness, to which the Hindus give the names of *Moksham* (Deliverance) and *Mukti* (the Last End).

Thus idolatry, whatever tendency it may have to corrupt all things, has at least respected some of the fundamental truths graven on the hearts of men, the knowledge of which is indispensable to the stability of all civilized society. The people of India, sunk from time immemorial in the darkness of error by reason of the avarice and ambition of their religious teachers, still preserve some positive ideas of a Supreme Being, and foresee rightly enough the immortality of the soul, and the necessity and existence of another life in which the good shall be rewarded and the wicked punished.

What other conclusion can we draw from this than that such sacred truths will never perish from off the earth? The atheist and the materialist may heap up sophistry on sophistry in order to obscure these truths and conceal them from the eyes of nations; but their efforts are in vain. Graven on the hearts of men in indelible characters by the hand of the Almighty Himself, these truths must continue to grow and to bear fruit so long as there are reasonable creatures and civilized peoples in the world.

CHAPTER III

Hindu Feasts.—The New-Year Feast.—The Feast of the Household Gods.—Commemoration of the Dead.—Feast of the Schools.—Feasts in Honour of Serpents.—Military Feasts.—The Feast of Lamps.—Sacrifices to Plants.—The Feast of the Lingayats.—The *Pongul* Ceremonies.—General Remarks.

EACH district and each temple of the least importance has its own particular feasts, recurring at intervals during the course of the year; and besides these local feasts there are many others that are generally observed everywhere, taking place at fixed periods. Feast-days are given up to rejoicings and diversions of all kinds; work is entirely suspended; relatives and friends meet together and feast each other in turn; the houses are decorated, the best jewels and apparel are worn, and the time is spent in games, which for the most part are very artless and innocent. Family feasts, however, have not the smallest resemblance to those celebrated in temples, to which the people flock from every side, and which often give rise to the most scandalous scenes.

There are in all eighteen obligatory Hindu feasts in the year, but I will mention only the principal ones. First, there is the feast which is celebrated on the first day of the year, called *Ugadi*[1], and which falls on the day of the new moon in the month of March. On this occasion Hindus are expected to pay each other visits of ceremony. The feast lasts for three days, during which they give themselves up to enjoyment. Fireworks are let off, and cannon, rockets, and guns are heard on every side. It is about this time, also, that the officers of Government prepare their revenue accounts for the year, and that the cultivators renew the leases of the lands which they farm.

[1] This is the name given to the Telugu New Year's Day.—ED.

At the time of the new moon in the month of February the Lingayats, or followers of Siva, celebrate with great pomp their feast *Siva-ratri* (Night of Siva). This lasts three days, and during the course of it the Lingayats wash and purify their *lingam*, cover it with a new cloth, and offer to it sacrifices of a special character. They also visit their *jangamas* or *gurus*, and present them with gifts[1].

The festival of *Gauri* takes place at the time of the new moon in the month of September, and lasts many days. Gauri is another name for Parvati, the wife of Siva, who is the object of peculiar worship on this occasion. On the last day of the feast they mould a figure of the goddess in rice dough; this is placed in a shrine beautifully adorned, and is then carried with great pomp through the streets. The *Gauri* feast, however, is also specially dedicated to the household gods, which are represented by the implements, tools, and utensils in common use amongst the people. Thus, the farmer collects his ploughs, his spades, and his sickles, and places them in a heap on a spot carefully purified by a layer of cow-dung. He prostrates himself at full length before the various implements of husbandry, and offers them *puja* and *neiveddya* according to the usual manner. He then puts them back in their places. The mason offers similar homage to his trowel, his square, &c.; the carpenter to his axe, his saw, and his plane; the barber to his razor; the writer to his pen or *stilus*; the tailor to his scissors and needles; the huntsman to his gun; the fisherman to his nets; the weaver to his loom; the butcher to his cleaver; and so on in the case of all artisans. The women, too, collect their baskets, winnows, rice-mills—in short, all their household implements, and prostrate themselves before them, offering them homage in like manner. In a word, there is not a person who, during this solemn time, does not regard as so many deities the instruments with which he gains his livelihood. The prayers which are addressed and the honours which are paid to them are intended to persuade them to continue to be useful to their possessors. In fact, the whole ceremony is based on the Hindu principle, that it is necessary to pay honour to everything which may be either useful or hurtful.

A month later, at the new moon of October, comes the

[1] Vide Appendix III.

feast of *Maha-navami*, known also under the name of *Dasara*, specially dedicated to the memory of ancestors. This feast is considered to be so obligatory that it has become a proverb that anybody who has not the means of celebrating it should sell one of his children in order to do so. Each family offers the usual sacrifices to its deceased ancestors, and also presents them with new cloths such as are usually worn by men and women, in order that they may be properly clothed. The feast lasts nine days. This is also the special festival of universities and schools. The students, dressed in gay apparel, parade through the streets every day, singing verses composed by their professors, who march at their head. They also recite these verses before the doors of their relatives and the principal inhabitants of the place. At the same time they dance and play in a simple fashion, marking time by striking sticks together. At the end of it all the professors receive small presents of money from the people before whom their students have performed. A portion of the sum collected is given to the students for a feast on the last day of the ceremonies, and the remainder the professors keep for themselves.

The *Dasara* is likewise the soldiers' feast. Princes and soldiers offer the most solemn sacrifices to the arms which are made use of in battle. Collecting all their weapons together, they call a Brahmin *purohita*, who sprinkles them with *tirtham* (holy water) and converts them into so many divinities by virtue of his *mantrams*. He then makes *puja* to them and retires. Thereupon, amidst the beat of drums, the blare of trumpets and other instruments, a ram is brought in with much pomp and sacrificed in honour of the various weapons of destruction. This ceremony is observed with the greatest solemnity throughout the whole Peninsula, not only by the Hindu princes and soldiers, but also by the Mahomedans, who have unreservedly adopted this idolatrous practice of the Hindus. It is known by the special name of *ayuda-puja* (sacrifice to arms), and is entirely military; no native belonging to the profession of arms, be he Pagan, Mahomedan, or Christian, makes any scruple of joining in it.

In order to increase the solemnity of the feast, the princes are in the habit of giving public entertainments, to which immense crowds of people resort. These entertainments resemble very much the gladiatorial combats of the ancient Romans, consisting as they do of contests between animals, or between animals and men, and above all between men. Athletes sometimes come from long distances to contend for the prizes. They belong mostly to a caste called *Jetti*, and are trained from their youth in contests of the kind. Their profession is to injure one another in the presence of persons who are able to pay them for the satisfaction to be derived from this horrible sport, in which both princes and people take infinite delight. Ordinary blows with the fist, however vigorously applied, would not cause sufficient bloodshed, so before entering the lists the champions put on gloves studded with sharp pieces of horn. They fight almost naked, and before coming to close quarters dance about in threatening attitudes. Then they close furiously, and deal heavy blows on each other's heads with their murderous gloves. Needless to say, blood flows freely. When they have had enough of this, they seize each other round the body and fall struggling to the ground, where they tear at each other like wild beasts. At intervals they cease fighting to regain breath; but they soon begin again, and the combat does not end until the umpires separate them and one of the two is declared victor. Covered with wounds and literally bathed in blood, they retire and make room for new combatants, who fight with the same ferocity. This disgusting spectacle sometimes lasts for hours together, to the great satisfaction of the spectators, who mark their enthusiasm by constant applause. When all is over, the prince distributes among the champions prizes proportionate to the skill and strength which each of them has displayed. The wounds and dislocations of the injured are attended to by men of their own caste, the *Jettis* being generally very clever in surgery.

At the end of November or the beginning of December the *Deepavali* (feast of lamps) is celebrated. It occupies several days. Every evening while it lasts the Hindus place lighted lamps at the doors of their houses or hang paper lanterns on long poles in the street. This feast appears to be specially dedicated to fire. But as it is held at a time when most of the cereal crops are ready for harvesting, the cultivators in many places are then in the habit of going together in procession to their fields, and there offering up to their crops prayers and sacrifices of rams or goats, in order, as it were, to give thanks to their crops for having ripened and become fit for the food of man. Every husbandman also, on three days in succession, proceeds to the dungheap which he has collected for manuring his fields and prostrates himself before it, presenting to it offerings of flowers, lighted tapers, boiled rice and fruits, and begging it humbly to fertilize his lands and to procure him abundant harvests. This worship, it may be remarked, very much resembles that which the Romans used to pay to their god Sterculius.

The *Nagara-panchami* is another great feast. It is celebrated in the beginning of February in honour of snakes, and especially of the most venomous species, such as the cobra, called *naga* or *nagara* by the Hindus. This reptile, which is very common and the most dangerous of all, is honoured in a very special manner on this occasion. The people pay visits to the holes where snakes of this sort are generally known to remain concealed, and make offerings to them of milk, plantains, &c. I shall have something more to say about this strange cult later on.

But the most solemn of all feasts, at any rate in the south of India, is the *Pongul*, which is also known in some places as the *Maha-sankranti*[1]. This feast is the occasion of great rejoicing; and the Hindus have two good reasons for regarding it with joy. One is because the month preceding the *Pongul*, which is entirely made up of unlucky days, has at last passed; the other is because the month which follows it must invariably consist of lucky days.

During the inauspicious month which preceded the *Pongul*, *sannyasis*, or mendicants[2], go from door to door about four o'clock in the morning, waking all sleepers by beating their gongs, warning them to be on their guard and to take every precaution against the evil influences of this unlucky period, by appeasing, by means of prayers and sacrifices, the god Siva, who presides over it. With this purpose in view, the women of the

[1] *Sankranti* is the name given to the first day of the solar month; that is to say, to the day on which the sun passes from one sign of the Zodiac to another. It refers here to its entrance into the sign of Capricorn, a period which the ancients celebrated as that of the *re-birth* of this bright luminary. —DUBOIS.

[2] These are *pandarams*, not *sannyasis*.—ED.

house every morning prepare a small patch about a yard square outside the door, smearing it with cow-dung, and tracing several white lines upon it with rice-flour. They then place within this square several pellets of cow-dung, each adorned with a pumpkin flower. I believe these pellets are supposed to represent Vigneshwara, the god of obstacles, whom they seek to appease by offering him a bouquet. But I do not know why it is that the pumpkin flower is chosen in this case. Every evening these little balls of cow-dung, together with their flowers, are carefully collected, to be kept till the last day of the month. When this day arrives the women, who alone are charged with this ceremony, put them into a new basket, and accompanied by musical instruments and clapping of hands, they solemnly carry them away beyond the precincts of their dwellings and throw them into a tank or some other retired but clean spot.

The *Pongul*, or *Maha-sankranti*, always takes place during the winter solstice, the period when the sun, having finished its course towards the southern hemisphere, turns to the north again and comes back to visit the people of India. The feast lasts three days; the first is called *Bhoghi-pongul* (*Pongul* of joy). On this day visits are exchanged between relatives and friends, who make presents and give entertainments to each other; the day passes in diversions and amusements of all sorts.

The second day is called *Surya-pongul* (*Pongul* of the sun). In fact the feast appears to be specially dedicated to the sun. The married women first of all bathe with their clothes on, and while still dripping wet put rice to boil in milk on a fire in the open air. As soon as it begins to simmer, they all cry out together, *Pongul, Pongul*! *Pongul, Pongul*! Almost immediately afterwards they remove the vessel from the fire and place it before the idol of Vigneshwara, to whom they offer a portion of the rice; another portion is given to the cows, and the rest is eaten by the people of the house.

On this day Hindus again exchange visits. On meeting each other the first words they say are: 'Has the rice boiled?' to which the answer is: 'It has boiled.' It is for this reason that the feast is called *Pongul* in the south of India, the word being derived from *pongedi* in Telugu, and *pongaradu* in Tamil, both signifying *to boil*.

The third day is called the *Pongul* of the cows. On this day they put into a big vessel filled with water some saffron powder, some seeds of the tree called *parati*, and some leaves of the margosa-tree. After mixing the ingredients well together, they sprinkle the cows and the oxen with the liquid, walking round them three times. All the men of the house (for the women are excluded from this ceremony) then turn successively towards the four points of the compass and perform the *sashtanga*, or prostration of the six members, four times before the animals [1].

The horns of the cows are painted in various colours, and round their necks are hung garlands of green leaves interlaced with flowers. On these garlands are hung cakes, cocoanuts, and fruits, which, as they are shaken off by the animals, are eagerly scrambled for and devoured, as though they were sacred things, by the crowd following.

The cows are then driven together outside the town or village, and are then made to scatter in all directions by the aid of drums and noisy instruments. On this day cattle are allowed to graze everywhere without restraint; and no matter what damage they may do in the fields, they are never driven away.

The idols are afterwards taken from the temples and carried in procession, to the sound of music, to the place where the cattle have again been collected. The temple dancing-girls, who are to be found at all feasts and public ceremonies, are not absent on this occasion; they march at the head of the large concourse of people, and from time to time pause to delight the spectators with their lascivious dances and obscene songs.

The feast terminates with a performance which, I believe, has no other object than simple amusement. The crowd forms itself into a big circle, in the middle of which a hare is let loose, which in its efforts to escape runs round and round, from side to side, exciting much laughter amongst the spectators, till at last it is caught.

The idols are then carried back to the temples, the cows are led back to the sheds, and thus ends the most popular of all Hindu feasts.

The *Pongul*, as I have said, is intended to celebrate the period when the sun is about to recommence its course. There would have been nothing blameworthy, nothing astonishing in the

[1] As already explained, it is prostration of the *eight*, not *six* members.—ED.

people hailing with joy the appearance of this great fertilizing luminary in their hemisphere, and rendering praise and thanks to the Almighty as the Creator of it; but when we see a nation which professes to occupy the first place amongst the civilized races of the world treating this as an occasion for the most idle ceremonies, surely we ought not to attribute it simply to the weakness of the human mind. Ought we not rather to recognize in it the prompting of some evil spirit seeking to seduce men by the empty pomp that accompanies these insane practices? We should not hesitate to regard them as folly in a single individual; are they therefore less unreasonable or more excusable when an entire nation practises them? Our astonishment ceases when we carefully consider the causes that keep the Hindus enchained to degraded forms of worship like these. The fact is, the laws and customs, both religious and civil, of the Hindu people are so closely bound together, that it is impossible to attack the one without equally injuring the other. Custom, prejudice, and national predilection have all served to establish their belief that religion and polity are inseparable; and they are thoroughly convinced that neither the one nor the other can be changed without exposing the nation to the danger of sinking into a state of barbarism and anarchy. This rigorous observance of their religious rites on the part of the Hindus is rendered yet more inviolable by reason of the pride, sensuality, and moral laxity which constitute the national character. Everything presented to them by their religion contributes to the encouragement of the national vices. Passion, predilection, and self-interest all combine in fostering the forms of idolatry to which they are enslaved. Even their games, dances, and entertainments are all conducted with a licence which derives force from the fact that it is sanctioned by religion. How, it may well be asked, can a people so credulous, so easily influenced by sensual impressions and all the pleasures resulting from them—how can they help being devoted to a religious cult which accords so well with their natural inclinations?

Self-interest, again, that powerful motive of human actions, is not the feeblest support of Hindu idolatry. The priests of the Hindu religion, although too enlightened to be blinded by the follies which they instil into the minds of their weak fellow-countrymen, are none the less zealous in maintaining and encouraging the absurd errors which procure their livelihood, and which keep them in that high estimation which they have wrongfully usurped.

Their deceitful tactics are specially noticeable in connexion with the feasts that are celebrated at the more important temples. The Brahmins who have charge of these enrich themselves by the offerings which the credulous and stupid worshippers periodically bring; therefore they take infinite pains to foster superstition and curry favour with the votaries. The triumphal cars, splendidly ornamented, on which the idols are exposed to public veneration in all the brilliant finery peculiar to India; the unceasing round of songs, dances, games, entertainments, and fireworks; the limitless crowd of devotees, the more wealthy among whom vie with each other in luxurious display and extravagant profusion; above all, the extreme licence which prevails on such occasions, and the facility with which every one can satisfy his depraved desires;—all these give infinite pleasure to a people who know nothing higher than such material enjoyments. Thus it is that crowds gather at these feasts from all parts; and the poor husbandman, whose whole harvest hardly affords subsistence for himself and family for six months during the year, will sell a part of it in order to contribute to the expenses incurred at the feasts, and to enrich the clever impostors who manage them [1]. But apart from the pomp and ceremony displayed for the purpose of dazzling the eyes of the people, the Hindu priests have recourse to another kind of deception. According to them nothing can equal the miracles which are daily wrought by the god of their particular temple in favour of those persons who put their trust in him and make him presents. Sometimes it is a barren woman who has ceased to be so, a blind man to whom the faculty of sight has been restored, a leper who has been cured, a cripple who has recovered the use of his legs, &c. There is not a single

[1] 'Une religion,' says Montesquieu, 'chargée de beaucoup de pratiques attache plus à elle qu'une autre qui l'est moins. On tient beaucoup des choses dont on est continuellement occupé; témoin l'obstination tenace des mahométans et des juifs et la facilité qu'ont de changer de religion les peuples barbares et sauvages qui, uniquement occupés de la chasse ou de la guerre, ne se chargent guère de pratiques religieuses.'—*Esprit des Lois*, xxv. 2.

Hindu who would dare to raise the shadow of a doubt concerning such miracles.

As depositaries of a religion to which they assign an origin that is lost in the darkness of ages, the Brahmins know very well how to make use of the fables and traditions which are at the bottom of it all, such as the wonderful adventures of the gods, giants, and ancient kings, the miraculous proceedings of the ancient Hindu sages; and the spiritual seclusion and sanctity of the ancient Hindu hermits. The austerity, however extravagant it may seem, of Brahmin penitents; the rigorous abstinence which ordinary Brahmins impose upon themselves; their frequent fasts; their daily ablutions; their excessive carefulness regarding external and internal cleanliness; their prayers; their long periods of meditation and absorption; the impenetrable secrecy and air of mystery which accompany their *sandhya*, their sacrifices, and the majority of their ceremonies; the sacred books, of which they are the sole interpreters;—all these contribute to support the influence which they have gained over minds that apparently will recognize as true only what dazzles the imagination, or what is contrary to common sense. So true it is, that mere reason is totally unable to raise mankind to a knowledge of God; in fact, no real religious cult can spring from man's reason alone. The more one reflects upon the gross absurdities pertaining to the idolatry of the Hindus, the more convinced one becomes of the inestimable benefit of Revelation, whereby the Supreme Ruler of the Universe, in Himself incomprehensible, reveals Himself to His creatures.

CHAPTER IV

Hindu Temples.—Ceremonies performed in them.—Temples built on Mountains.—Pyramids.—The Architecture of Pagodas.—The Shape and Ornaments of the Idols.—Their Consecration.—Sacred Pillars.—Temple Priests and Servants.—Sacrificers.—Dancing-girls.—Musicians.—Hindu Music.—Brahmin Tricks and Artifices for attracting Worshippers.—The Hindu Desire for Children.—The Revolting Practices to which they submit to obtain them.—Remarkable Ceremonies and Vows.—Prostitution in Certain Temples.—Religious Tortures.—The Rape of Women.—Famous Temples.—Tirupati.—Jagannath.—Public Processions.—General Remarks.

BUILDINGS dedicated to religious worship are extremely numerous in India. There are few villages or hamlets which have not at least one. It is even a generally received opinion that no place should be inhabited where there is no temple, for otherwise the inhabitants would run grave risks of misfortune.

Among the good works expected of the rich, one of the most honourable and most meritorious consists in spending a part of their fortune in the construction and endowment of these sacred buildings. Such munificence, it is argued, is an infallible means of obtaining the protection of the gods, remission of one's sins, and admission into an Abode of Bliss after death. But vanity, ostentation, and desire to attract attention are much more powerful factors, if indeed they are not the only ones that excite beneficence on the part of the wealthy.

Besides the temples with which all villages are provided, one finds many erected in isolated spots, in woods, on the highways, in the middle of rivers, on the borders of tanks and other large reservoirs, and especially on the summits of steep rocks, mountains, and hills. This practice of constructing buildings consecrated to religious worship upon elevated sites must have struck all persons who have travelled in India. In fact there are few mountains, where a well or a spring is to be found, that are not surmounted by a building of this sort. The choice of sites like these does not appear to be a matter of caprice. We know that the same practice exists among the majority of Asiatic nations. Not only the ancient heathen peoples, but even the children of Israel, always chose elevated sites for purposes of religious worship. When God ordered the Israelites to take possession of the land of Canaan, He commanded them above all things to destroy the heathen temples erected on mountains and other lofty spots, to break in pieces the idols, and to destroy the sacred groves with which those buildings were surrounded, as are those of the Hindus to this day. Holy Scripture refers often to these high places and sacred groves.

One can only offer conjectures regarding this custom of placing on elevated sites the temples dedicated to the sacrifices and vows which the people addressed to their gods. Some authors have remarked that the worship of the stars having always been more or less a part of pagan ritual, the heathen constructed their temples so as to face the east at a certain elevation, in order that the rising sun might flood the interior of the temples with its light and cast its rays upon the religious ceremonies which take place at that time of day[1]. No doubt, too, they thought they were thereby approaching as near as possible to the heavenly powers whom they invoked. Furthermore, the duties of the soothsayers often necessitated such elevated positions, in order that they might see the heavens clearly.

Besides the temples of idols which one meets with at every step in India, statues of stone, of baked earth, and especially of granite, representing objects of popular worship, may be seen on the high-roads, at the entrances of villages, near the *choultries*, on the borders of tanks, near rivers, in the market-places, and elsewhere. The Hindus also delight in placing these idols of stone under the shade of leafy trees, especially of those reputed sacred, such as the *aswatta*, the *alai*, the *vepu*, &c.[2]

[1] The ceremonies performed in honour of the infernal deities took place at sunset; and it is believed that the entrances of the temples of these divinities faced towards the west.—DUBOIS.

[2] The *Ficus religiosa*, the *Ficus indica*, and the *Melia Azadirachta*.—ED.

Some of these idols are placed in shrines, and others in the open air.

Most Hindu temples present a very wretched appearance, being more like barns or stables than buildings consecrated to the gods. Some of them are used as places of public assembly, courts of justice, or rest-houses for travellers. There are many, however, which as seen from a distance have an imposing effect and excite the admiration of the traveller. They recall to mind those ancient times when architects had an eye for posterity as well as for their contemporaries, and were much more intent on making their works durable than on securing elegance at the cost of solidity.

The structure of the large temples, both ancient and modern, is everywhere the same. The Hindus, devoted as they are to ancestral customs, have never introduced innovations in the construction of their public edifices. Their architectural monuments, such as they exist to-day, are probably better examples of building as practised by ancient civilized nations than the ruins of Egyptians and Greeks, concerning which European scholars have so much to say.

The entrance gate of the great pagodas opens through a high, massive pyramidal tower, the summit of which is ordinarily topped by a crescent or half-moon. This gate faces the east, a position which is observed in all their temples, great and small. The pyramid or tower is called the *gopuram.*

Beyond the tower is a large court, at the farther end of which is another gate, opening like the first through a pyramid of the same form, but smaller. Through this you pass to a second and smaller court, which is in front of the shrine containing the principal idol.

In the middle of this second court and facing the entrance to the shrine, you generally see upon a large pedestal, or within a kind of pavilion open on all sides and supported by four pillars, a coarsely sculptured stone figure, either of a bull lying flat on its belly, or of a *lingam,* if the temple is dedicated to Siva; or of the monkey Hanuman, or of the serpent *Capella,* if it is a temple of Vishnu; or of the god Vigneshwara; or maybe of some other symbol of Hindu worship. This is the first object which the natives worship before entering the shrine itself.

The door of the shrine is generally low and narrow, and it is the only opening which allows a free passage of air and light from outside, for the use of windows is entirely unknown in the Peninsula. The interior of the shrine is habitually shrouded in darkness, or is lighted only by the feeble flicker of a lamp which burns day and night by the side of the idol. One experiences a sort of involuntary shock on entering one of these dark recesses. The interior of the shrine is generally divided into two parts, sometimes into three. The first, which may be called the nave, is the largest, and it is here that the worshippers assemble. The second is called the *adytum*, or sanctuary, where the idol to whom the shrine is consecrated is placed. This chamber is smaller and much darker than the first. It is generally kept shut, and the door can be opened only by the officiating priest, who, with some of his acolytes, has alone a right to enter its mysterious precincts for the purpose of washing and dressing the idol and presenting the offerings of the faithful, such as flowers, incense of sandalwood, lighted lamps, fruit, butter-milk, rich apparel, and jewels.

Some of the modern Hindu temples are vaulted, but most of them have flat roofs supported by several rows of massive stone pillars, the capitals of which are composed of two heavy stones crossed, on which are placed the beams, also of stone, which extend through the length and breadth of the building. The beams again are covered horizontally with slabs of stone strongly cemented to prevent leakage. Whether the object be to make these buildings more imposing and solid, or to preserve them from the danger of fire, wood is never employed except for the doors.

The *adytum*, or sanctuary, is often constructed with a dome, but the building as a whole is generally very low, and this destroys the effect of its proportions in a striking degree. The low elevation; the difficulty with which the air finds a way through a single narrow and habitually closed passage; the unhealthy odours rising from the mass of fresh and decaying flowers; the burning lamps; the oil and butter spilt in libations; the excrements of the bats that take up their abode in these dark places; finally, and above all, the fetid perspiration of a multitude of unclean and malodorous people;—all contribute to render these sacred shrines excessively unhealthy. Only a Hindu could remain for any length of time in their heated and pestilential precincts without suffocation[1].

The principal idol is generally placed in a niche. It is clothed with garments more or less magnificent, and on great festivals is sometimes adorned with rare vestments and rich jewels. A crown of gold set with precious stones often adorns its head. For the most part, however, the idols of stone wear a cap like a sugar-loaf, which imparts to the whole figure the appearance of a pyramid. The Hindus, by the way, appear to have a special fancy for the form of a pyramid, which perhaps is due to some symbolical notion. We know that various nations of antiquity, among others the Egyptians, regarded the pyramid as the symbol of immortality and of life, the beginning of which was represented by the base and the end or death by the summit. The pyramid was also the emblem of fire.

In vain are Hindu idols decked with rich ornaments; they are not rendered thereby less disagreeable in appearance. Their physiognomy is generally of frightful ugliness, which is carefully enhanced by daubing the images from time to time with a coating of dark paint. Some of the idols, thanks to the generous piety of rich votaries, have their eyes, mouth, and ears of gold or silver; but this makes them, if possible, yet more hideous. The attitudes in which they are represented are either ridiculous, grotesque, or obscene. In short, everything is done to make them objects of disgust to any one not familiar with the sight of these strange monsters.

The idols exposed to public veneration in the temples are of stone, while those carried in procession through the streets are of metal, as are also the domestic gods which every Brahmin keeps and worships in his house. It is forbidden to make idols of wood or other easily destructible material. I know only one, that of the goddess Mari-amma, which is of wood. For this image the wood of a certain tree is employed, the trunk of which is red inside, and which, when cut, exudes a sap the colour of blood, a characteristic which accords well with the merciless nature of this cruel divinity. It is true, one also often

[1] The Abbé nowhere remarks on the burning of camphor, which plays so conspicuous a part in all Hindu worship, and which acts at the same time as a disinfectant.—ED.

sees statues of clay or of masonry, but these are not of much account, and inspire very little veneration.

No idol can become an object of worship until it has been duly consecrated by a number of ceremonies. It is necessary first of all that the deity should be invoked, in order that it may fix its abode in the idol, and be incorporated with it; and this must be done by a Brahmin *purohita*. New temples are also subjected to a solemn inauguration, and all objects destined for their service must be formally consecrated. Both temples and idols are liable to be desecrated on many occasions. If, for example, a European, a Mahomedan, or a Pariah unfortunately entered a sanctuary or touched an idol, that very instant the divinity would take its departure. And in order to induce it to return, all the ceremonies would have to be begun over again, and performed more elaborately and at greater cost than before.

Besides the idols which are to be found inside every temple, the walls and four sides of the supporting pillars are covered with various figures. On the *façade* of the building niches are arranged, to contain symbolical figures representing men and animals, for the most part in indecent attitudes. Furthermore, the walls of the temple enclosure, which are no less thick and solid than the actual buildings, are also sometimes covered with these obscene or grotesque images. Outside the shrine, opposite and close to the entrance door, and sometimes in the middle of one of the courts, there is commonly seen a granite pillar, from forty to fifty feet high, octagonal in shape, and square at the base of the shaft; on each side of the lower part figures are sculptured. The pedestal is a solid mass of hewn stone. The capital of the column ends in a square cornice, at the four angles of which small bells are usually suspended.. Above this, again, is a chafing dish in which incense is burned at certain times, or else lighted lamps are placed there.

The traveller often sees on the roads, and even in remote spots, lofty columns of this kind, on which certain devotees place lamps from time to time. During the feast of *Deepavali*, of which mention has been made above, and which is apparently held in honour of fire, lamps are to be seen burning every evening on such columns. Sometimes the pillars are wreathed with pieces of new cloth, which are finally set on fire. These details favour the view that the pillars, constructed as they always are in places exposed to the east, are consecrated to the sun or to the element of fire.

Temple offices are held by persons of various castes. Nevertheless all posts of any importance, and especially those which confer profit and dignity, are always held by Brahmins.

Among the numerous officials in Hindu worship the sacrificers occupy first rank; then come the consultative committees, the directors of ceremonies, the collectors of temple revenues, and the treasurers. Besides these, there are hosts of subordinates who assist in the administration of the temple funds, and in the supervision and direction of religious observances.

Sometimes, but not frequently, the high functions of sacrificers are performed by common Sudras and even Pariahs. At one of the most famous temples of Mysore, called Melkota, during the great festival which is there celebrated annually, the Pariahs are the first to enter the sanctuary and to offer sacrifices to the idol, and it is only after they have finished that the Brahmins begin their sacrifices. I have already remarked that the Sudras are the only persons holding this office in temples where it is usual to immolate living victims.

A fact worthy of remark is that the officiating priests wear no special costume in the exercise of their sacerdotal functions; they are dressed in their ordinary clothes, which are, however, newly washed for the purpose.

In most of the temples the oblations and sacrifices are confined to the simple products of nature. The offering of lamps is also specially in vogue. Sometimes thousands may be seen burning around the idol and in the enclosure of the temple; they are filled with butter, which is a much more acceptable offering to the gods than oil.

Hindu priests offer up sacrifices regularly twice a day, morning and evening. The idol to which the sacrifice is offered is first thoroughly washed, and the water used for this purpose is brought from the river with much pomp and ceremony. In some of the great pagodas it is brought on the backs of elephants, preceded by dancing-girls and musicians, and escorted by a great number of Brahmins and various attendants. In other temples the Brahmins themselves go with a similar show of ceremony to fetch the water morning and evening, bringing it on their heads in large brass vessels. The water that remains after the idol has been washed is called *tirtham* (holy water).

As soon as the task of washing the idol is over, the priest performs its toilet, which consists in putting on its clothes and tracing on its forehead one of the signs which the Hindus are accustomed to wear on their own foreheads. *Puja* is then offered to it. During these ceremonies the officiating priest tinkles a little bell, which is held in his left hand, the object no doubt being to call the attention of the worshippers to each stage in the ceremonial which is taking place inside the shrine and out of sight.

After completing his mysterious duties, which must be concealed from profane eyes[1], the priest appears and distributes to the people who are assembled in the hall of the temple fragments of the offerings made to the idol. This *prasadam* (sacred gift) is received with eagerness. If it is fruit or some other nutritious substance, it is eaten; if it is flowers, the men stick them in their turbans, while the women entwine them in their hair. Last of all, the priest pours into the hollow of each person's hand a little *tirtham*, which is drunk immediately. After this all the worshippers retire.

The courtesans or dancing-girls attached to each temple take their place in the second rank; they are called *deva-dasis* (servants or slaves of the gods), but the public call them by the more vulgar name of prostitutes. And in fact they are bound by their profession to grant their favours, if such they be, to anybody demanding them in return for ready money. It appears that at first they were reserved exclusively for the enjoyment of the Brahmins. And these lewd women, who make a public traffic of their charms, are consecrated in a special manner to the worship of the divinities of India. Every temple of any importance has in its service a band of eight, twelve, or more. Their official duties consist in dancing and singing within the temple twice a day, morning and evening, and also at all public ceremonies. The first they execute with sufficient grace,

[1] In Vishnu temples these 'mysterious duties' are performed behind a curtain drawn between the worshippers and the idol.—ED.

although their attitudes are lascivious and their gestures indecorous. As regards their singing, it is almost always confined to obscene verses describing some licentious episode in the history of their gods. Their duties, however, are not confined to religious ceremonies. Ordinary politeness (and this is one of the characteristic features of Hindu morality) requires that when persons of any distinction make formal visits to each other they must be accompanied by a certain number of these courtesans. To dispense with them would show a want of respect towards the persons visited, whether the visit was one of duty or of politeness[1].

These women are also present at marriages and other solemn family meetings. All the time which they have to spare in the intervals of the various ceremonies is devoted to infinitely more shameful practices; and it is not an uncommon thing to see even sacred temples converted into mere brothels. They are brought up in this shameful licentiousness from infancy, and are recruited from various castes, some among them belonging to respectable families. It is not unusual for pregnant women, with the object of obtaining a safe delivery, to make a vow, with the consent of their husbands, to devote the child that they carry in their womb, if it should turn out a girl, to the temple service. They are far from thinking that this infamous vow offends in any way the laws of decency, or is contrary to the duties of motherhood. In fact no shame whatever is attached to parents whose daughters adopt this career.

The courtesans are the only women in India who enjoy the privilege of learning to read, to dance, and to sing. A well-bred and respectable woman would for this reason blush to acquire any one of these accomplishments[2].

The *deva-dasis* receive a fixed salary for the religious duties which they perform; but as the amount is small they supplement it by selling their favours in as profitable a manner as possible. In the attainment of this object they are probably more skilful than similar women in other countries. They

[1] This custom is certainly not observed at the present day.—ED.

[2] In these days female education is slowly extending to all classes, and the prejudice which formerly existed no longer applies to women learning to read and sing, though dancing is still restricted to the professional dancing-girls, and is not considered respectable.—ED.

employ all the resources and artifices of coquetry. Perfumes, elegant costumes, coiffures best suited to set off the beauty of their hair, which they entwine with sweet-scented flowers; a profusion of jewels worn with much taste on different parts of the body; graceful and voluptuous attitudes: such are the snares with which these sirens allure the Hindus, who, it must be confessed, rarely display in such cases the prudence and constancy of a Ulysses.

Nevertheless, to the discredit of Europeans it must be confessed that the quiet seductions which Hindu prostitutes know how to exercise with so much skill resemble in no way the disgraceful methods of the wretched beings who give themselves up to a similar profession in Europe, and whose indecent behaviour, cynical impudence, obscene and filthy words of invitation are enough to make any sensible man who is not utterly depraved shrink from them with horror. Of all the women in India it is the courtesans, and especially those attached to the temples, who are the most decently clothed. Indeed they are particularly careful not to expose any part of the body. I do not deny, however, that this is merely a refinement of seduction. Experience has no doubt taught them that for a woman to display her charms damps sensual ardour instead of exciting it, and that the imagination is more easily captivated than the eye.

God forbid, however, that any one should believe me to wish to say a word in defence of the comparative modesty and reserve of the dancing-girls of India! Actions can only be judged by their motives; and certainly, if these Indian women are more reserved in public than their sisters in other countries which call themselves more civilized, the credit is due not to their innate modesty but to national prejudice. In fact, however loose the Hindus may be in their morals, they strictly maintain an outward appearance of decency, and attach great importance to the observance of strict decorum in public. The most shameless prostitute would never dare to stop a man in the streets; and she in her turn would indignantly repulse any man who ventured to take any indecent liberty with her. The man who behaved familiarly with one of these women in public would be censured and despised by everybody who witnessed the scandal. Is it the same among ourselves?

After the dancing-girls come the players of musical instruments attached to the service of the temples. Every pagoda of any importance always has a more or less numerous band of them. They, as well as the dancing-girls, are obliged to attend the temple twice a day, and to fill it with discordant sounds. Their presence at all feasts and ceremonies is likewise obligatory. Moreover, they cannot be dispensed with during the great family feasts and ceremonies. The Hindu taste for music is so marked that there is not a single gathering, however small, which has not some musicians at its head.

Those who are regularly attached to a pagoda receive a fixed salary. The instruments on which they play are for the most part clarionets and trumpets; they have also cymbals and several kinds of small drums. The sounds produced by these instruments are far from pleasing, and may even appear hideous to European ears. The Hindus recognize a kind of harmony, however, in two parts: they have always a bass and a high counter-tenor or alto. The latter is produced by a wind instrument in the form of a tube widened at its base, the sounds of which have some resemblance to those of the bagpipe.

The vocal part is executed by a second band of musicians, who take turns with the dancing-girls in singing hymns in honour of the gods. Sometimes the Brahmins and other worshippers form the chorus, or sing separately sacred poems of their own composition.

The *nattuva*, or conductor, is the most remarkable of all the musicians. In beating time he taps with his fingers on a narrow drum. As he beats, his head, shoulders, arms, thighs, and in fact all the parts of his body perform successive movements; and simultaneously he utters inarticulate cries, thus animating the musicians both by voice and gesture. At times one would think he was agitated by violent convulsions.

The dancing-women, the chorus, and the orchestra take turn and turn about during a religious ceremony, which often terminates with a procession round the temple.

Morning and evening the courtesans before leaving never fail to perform for the idol, singing the while, the ceremony of the *aratti*, for the purpose of averting the fatal influence caused by the looks of evil-minded persons, an influence from which the gods themselves, as I have already said, are not exempt.

The whole musical *répertoire* of the Hindus is reduced to thirty-six airs, which are called *ragas*; but most of the musicians hardly know half of them.

Hindu music, whether vocal or instrumental, may be pleasing to the natives, but I do not think it can give the slightest pleasure to any one else, however little sensitive be his ear. Hindu musicians learn to play and sing methodically; they keep excellent time; and they have, as we have, a variety of keys. In spite of all this, however, their songs have always appeared to me uninspiring and monotonous, while from their instruments I have never heard anything but harsh, high, and ear-splitting sounds.

However, I admit that the chief reason why a European forms an unfavourable opinion of Hindu music is because he judges it by comparison with his own. To appreciate it rightly, we must go back two or three thousand years and imagine ourselves in those ancient times when the Druids and other priests used in their civil and religious ceremonies no other music but dismal cries and noisy sounds, produced by striking two metal plates together, by beating tightly-stretched skins, or by blowing horns of different kinds.

We must remember that Hindu music at the present day is the same as it has always been; and that, as in the case of their other arts, it has undergone no alteration and has not been improved in any way. We shall then feel obliged to be more indulgent; indeed, we may even feel astonished that Hindu music attained such perfection at the very beginning. For it is almost certain that the scale used at present by the Hindus has existed from the earliest times. It bears moreover a striking resemblance to ours, being composed of the same number of notes, arranged in the same way, as follows:—

Sa ri ga ma pa da ni sa
Do re mi fa sol la si do.

Are we then to deny the merit of this invention to Guy of Arezzo? And is John de Meurs, or whoever it was that perfected the system of the learned Benedictine, to have no other credit than that of having borrowed with discernment from the same source? We know that Vossius maintained that the Egyptians had a musical scale similar to ours many centuries before Guy of Arezzo published his own. This question I must leave for others to solve.

There is nothing, as I have already shown, into which the Hindus do not introduce some superstitious notions, and it would have been a miracle if music—a diversion of the gods themselves—had not furnished them with means of satisfying their taste in this direction. Every note of the Hindu scale has a mark characteristic of some divinity, and includes several hidden meanings deduced from its particular sound or from something similar to it. There are also notes expressing joy, sadness, sweetness, anger, &c. And Hindu musicians take great care not to confound notes intended to express these varying passions of the human soul.

All the musicians who play wind instruments are taken, as I have already remarked, from the low barber caste, the profession being handed down from father to son.

Heathen worship being very expensive, the priests and servants of the temples have, necessarily, various sources of unfailing revenue. In some districts a kind of tithe is collected out of the whole produce of the harvest; in others, every temple has in its absolute possession extensive lands which are exempt from all taxation, and the produce of which is exclusively assigned to the maintenance of the temple and of its numerous staff. I have mentioned that in the case of these persons perquisites are of no small importance. The offerings of rich devotees, which are divided among them in proportion to their rank and dignity, are sometimes so considerable, in the principal temples, that they have aroused the cupidity of the princes of the country, particularly of Mahomedans. These latter, as a sort of compensation for tolerating a religion which they abhorred, thought fit to take possession of more than half of these offerings.

There is no trick which the Brahmins will not employ in order to excite the fervour of the worshippers, and thus to enrich themselves by their offerings. The most obvious means generally produce the best results. In the foremost rank we must place the oracles, a rich mine of wealth which pagan priests of other countries worked long ago with great success, and which the lapse of ages has not yet exhausted for the heathen priests of India. Here it is the idol itself which addresses the dull and profoundly attentive crowd of worshippers, who are unable to understand that some cunning rogue, concealed inside or close by the god of stone, is speaking through the mouth of the idol. The idol, or its interpreter, also undertakes to foretell the future; but these oracles, like those of ancient Greece, contain some ambiguous or double meaning. Consequently, whatever the issue may be, the Brahmins always find some way of making it agree with their predictions [1].

If the flow of offerings by any chance decreases, the idol will inveigh vehemently against the indifference and meanness of the inhabitants of the district, proclaiming once for all that if this state of things continues, it will withdraw its protection from them, and will even resort to the expedient of decamping in search of other more grateful, and especially more generous worshippers [2].

Or perhaps the devout mob will some day find the hands and feet of their cherished idol bound with chains. Cruel creditors, it is announced, have brought it to this humiliating condition because it could not pay certain sums of money which it had borrowed in times of need; and they have sworn not to restore it to liberty until the whole sum, capital and interest, which is due to them shall have been repaid. Touched with compassion, the devotees will hasten to consult together and exact contributions from all possible sources until the sum necessary to liquidate the liabilities of their deity has been furnished to the Brahmins. As soon as the money is secured, the chains of the idol fall off, to the great satisfaction of everybody. In some famous temples, such as that of Tirupati, they use silver instead of iron chains to bind the sacred limbs of the idol.

There is another expedient to which the Brahmins frequently have recourse. All of a sudden it is proclaimed abroad that the idol has been attacked by a dangerous disease caused by the grief it experiences on seeing the devotion of the people abating from day to day. The idol is taken down from its pedestal and carried to the entrance of the temple, where it is exposed to the

[1] These false oracles are confined to temples dedicated to the inferior deities.—ED.

[2] This remark also applies only to the temples dedicated to the inferior deities.—ED.

public gaze. Its head and temples are rubbed with sundry lotions; drugs and medicines are placed before it; the priests from time to time feel its pulse with a display of the gravest uneasiness. Still the symptoms of the disease develop from day to day, and the priests begin to despair of the recovery of the idol. This alarming intelligence is bruited abroad, and presents and offerings soon arrive from all sides. At sight of these the idol's strength begins to return little by little; then it becomes convalescent; and finally it is cured and restored to its place.

Fear and awe are also means which the Brahmins turn to good account in order to renew the wavering faith of the people. They engage certain confederates, into whose bodies they affirm the angry god has sent a *pisacha*, or demon, in order to avenge some outrage which it has received from wicked men. One frequently meets with charlatans who fall into dreadful convulsions and make contortions and grimaces calculated to frighten the stoutest heart. In their calmer moments they give a piteous and detailed account of their misfortunes, which they attribute to the just resentment of the god, who is punishing them for their indifference towards himself and his ministers. They gabble phrases in many dialects, asserting that it is the demon who inspires them, and who has imparted to them the gift of languages. They eat all sorts of meat, drink intoxicating liquors, and observe none of the rules of caste.

But this is not imputed to them as a crime; it is all laid to the charge of the devil that possesses them. The multitude are filled with fear at the sight of one of these impostors, and prostrate themselves before him, worshipping the demon who has taken up its abode in him, and offering him oblations and sacrifices, in order to propitiate him and prevent him from injuring them. The demoniac is given his fill of meat and drink; and when he departs he is accompanied with much pomp and music to the next village, where he plays the same trick and finds just as many dupes. When he is pleased to come to his senses again, he exhorts his sympathetic audience to profit by the terrible example which he affords them, to show more faith in their god than he did, and to ensure the god's favour and protection by numerous gifts and offerings.

Miracles, again, are a most profitable branch of business for

Brahmins. They have all kinds, and suitable for every disease. The blind recover their sight, the lame walk, the dead come to life again. But the most popular miracle is that which gives fecundity to women. One continually hears of women whose pious devotion has obtained for them the signal favour of bearing children. I have already remarked that barrenness is the greatest possible curse to a woman in India, and the most dreaded of all the misfortunes that can befall a Hindu family.

Other nations which are very proud of their enlightenment and morality suppress the natural desire of seeing oneself born again in one's numerous progeny from considerations of personal interest and ambition, and regard the fruitfulness of their women with aversion. They are moreover not ashamed of resorting to wicked and disgusting means of reducing or destroying it altogether, thus outraging the most holy instincts of nature in order that they may not deprive themselves of the means of satisfying their ambition or of procuring the luxuries of life, as if the love of a father for his children were not the greatest of all pleasures. Animated in this respect by the noblest and purest sentiments, the Hindus consider a man happy in proportion to the number of children he possesses. Among them, indeed, children are considered to be the blessing of a house. However numerous a man's family may be, he never ceases to offer prayers for its increase.

The children, it is true, soon become useful to their parents. At five or six years old they begin to tend the calves, while those a little older take care of the cows and oxen. And as soon as they are strong enough they assist their fathers in tilling the fields or help in some other way to maintain the family.

There is a superstition, admirable enough in its way, which is a powerful factor in keeping up in the mind of a Hindu this ardent desire of seeing his race prolonged. In his eyes there is no misfortune equal to that of not leaving a son or a grandson behind to perform the last duties in connexion with his funeral. Such a deprivation is regarded as capable of preventing all access to an Abode of Bliss after death.

Hence it is that we see women who are slower in conceiving children than they would wish, hastening from temple to temple, and sometimes ruining themselves in the extravagant gifts which they offer in order to obtain from the gods the inestimable favour of becoming mothers. Expert at reaping profit from the virtues as well as the vices of their countrymen, the Brahmins see in these touching impulses of nature merely a means of gaining wealth, and also at the same time an opportunity of satisfying their carnal lusts with impunity. There are few temples where the presiding deity does not claim the power of curing barrenness in women. And there are some whose renown in this respect is unrivalled, such, for example, as that of Tirupati in the Carnatic, to which women flock in crowds to obtain children from the god Venkateswara[1]. On their arrival, the women hasten to disclose the object of their pilgrimage to the Brahmins, the managers of the temple. The latter advise them to pass the night in the temple, where, they say, the great Venkateswara, touched by their devotion, will perhaps visit them in the spirit and accomplish that which until then has been denied to them through human power. I must draw a curtain over the sequel of this deceitful suggestion. The reader already guesses at it. The following morning these detestable hypocrites, pretending complete ignorance of what has passed, make due inquiries into all the details; and after having congratulated the women upon the reception they met with from the god, receive the gifts with which they have provided themselves and take leave of them, after flattering them with the hope that they have not taken their journey in vain. Fully convinced that the god has deigned to have intercourse with them, the poor creatures return home enchanted, flattering themselves that they will soon procure for their husbands the honour of paternity.

People who have not sufficiently reflected upon the extremes to which the superstitious and fanatical credulity of a people may be carried, have regarded as untrue the stories which Father Gerbillon, Tavernier, and other travellers have told of the Dalai-Lama. His excrements are carefully preserved, dried, and distributed as relics to pious Tibetans, who, when they fall ill, make use of them as an internal medicine, which is considered to be a sovereign remedy for all diseases. The fact I am about to relate, which, although even more revolting, is

[1] One of the names of Vishnu.

nevertheless quite true, will render any similar stories credible enough. It is not without shame that I enter upon an account of the disgusting incidents which I am here to describe. I would have passed them over in silence if the very nature of this work had not imposed upon me the painful duty of telling everything.

At Nanjangud, a village situated about ten leagues south of Seringapatam, there is a temple famous throughout Mysore. Among the numerous votaries who flock to it are many women, who go to implore the help of the idol in curing their sterility. Offerings and prayers are not the only ceremonies which have to be gone through. On leaving the temple the woman, accompanied by her husband, has to go to a place where all the pilgrims are accustomed to resort to answer the calls of nature. There the husband and the wife collect with their hands a certain quantity of ordure and form it into a small pyramid, which they are careful to mark with a sign that will enable them to recognize it. Then they go to the neighbouring tank and mix in the hollow of their hands the filth which has soiled their fingers. (But I will spare my readers the rest.) After having performed their ablutions they retire. Two or three days afterwards they visit their pyramid, and, still using their hands, turn the filthy mass over and over and examine it as carefully and as seriously as the Roman augurs scrutinized the entrails of sacrificed animals, in order to see if any insects have been engendered in it. In this case it would be a very good omen, showing that the woman would soon be pregnant. But if, after careful search, not even the smallest insect is visible, the poor couple, sad and discouraged, return home in the full conviction that the expenses they have been put to and the pains they have taken have been of no avail[1].

At Mogur, another village situated a short distance from the former (Nanjangud), there is a small temple dedicated to Tipamma, a female divinity, in whose honour a great festival is celebrated every year. The goddess, placed in a beautifully ornamented palanquin, is carried in procession through the streets. In front of her there is another divinity, a male. These two idols, which are entirely nude, are placed in

[1] We believe that no such disgusting practice exists nowadays.—ED.

immodest postures, and by help of a piece of mechanism a disgusting movement is imparted to them as long as the procession continues. This disgusting spectacle, which is worthy of the depraved persons who look upon it, excites transports of mirth, manifested by shouts and bursts of laughter. Nor is this all. A Pariah, who has made a special study of all the obscene and filthy expressions to be found in the Hindu language, is chosen; the goddess Tipamma is then evoked and takes up her abode in his person. Then any one who wishes to hear foul expressions stands before the man, and he is certain to be satisfied. As it is supposed to be Tipamma who speaks through the mouth of the Pariah, the devotees, far from being offended with him, are quite pleased with the goddess for having deigned to overwhelm them with insults. Even high-caste Hindus are to be seen at this festival seeking to obtain the coveted honour.

The goddess Tipamma of Mogur is not the only member of her family. She has six sisters, who are not in any way inferior to her in point of decency and politeness. Each one of them has her own temple, in which like ceremonies are performed. In the whole of Southern Mysore, from Alambadi as far as Wynaad, for a distance of more than thirty leagues, these abominable revels are held in the highest esteem.

There are temples in certain isolated places, too, where the most disgusting debauchery is the only service agreeable to the presiding deity. There children are promised to women who, laying aside all shame, grant their favours to all persons indiscriminately. At such places a feast is celebrated every year in the month of January, at which both sexes, the scum of the country-side, meet. Barren women, in the hope that they will cease to be so, visit them after binding themselves by a vow to grant their favours to a fixed number of libertines. Others, who have entirely lost all sense of decency, go there in order to testify their reverence for the deity of the place by prostituting themselves, openly and without shame, even at the very gates of the temple.

There is one of these sinks of iniquity five or six leagues from the village where I am writing these pages, on the banks of the Cauvery, in a lonely place called Junginagatta. The temple is not striking to look at; but the January feast is celebrated there with the utmost refinements of vice.

People have also pointed out to me a temple of the same description near Kara-madai, in the district of Coimbatore, and another not far from Mudu-dorai, in Eastern Mysore. I have before remarked that these dens of debauchery are always situated in places far removed from all habitations.

According to Herodotus and Strabo, every woman among the Assyrians and Babylonians was obliged to prostitute herself once in her life in the temple of the goddess Mylitta, the Aphrodite of the Greeks. This tradition so flagrantly defied the principles of modesty with which nature seems to have endowed even the majority of brute beasts that many modern writers, and among them Voltaire, have called its truth in question. What would they say of the infamous festivals of which I have just drawn a sketch? The authority of husbands in India is moreover such that it is impossible for debauchery of this kind to be carried on without their consent. But does superstition know any bounds? Many Hindu religious practices afford irrefutable proofs of the truth of similar incredible details which ancient historians have handed down to us.

Here the scene changes. It is no longer a question of licentious libertines profiting by the vicious tendencies or the stupid credulity of women in order to satisfy their passions. It is concerning the silly fanatics who make it their task to torture themselves and to mutilate their bodies in a hundred different ways. It is not uncommon to hear of Hindus, in case of a serious illness or of some imminent danger, making a vow to mortify some important part of their bodies, on condition of recovery. The most common penance of this sort consists in stamping upon the shoulders, chest, and other parts of the body, with a red-hot iron, the marks symbolical of their gods—brandings which are never effaced, and which they display with as much ostentation as a warrior does the wounds he has received in battle.

Devotees are often seen stretched at full length on the ground and rolling in that posture all round the temples, or, during solemn processions, before the cars which carry the idols. It is a remarkable sight to see a crowd of fanatics rolling in this manner, quite regardless of stones, thorns, and other obstacles. Others, inspired by extreme fanaticism, voluntarily throw themselves down to be crushed under the wheels of the car on which the idol is borne[1]. And the crowds that witness these acts of madness, far from preventing them, applaud them heartily and regard them as the very acme of devotion.

Chidi-mari is another torture to which devotees submit themselves in honour of the goddess Mari-amma, one of the most evil-minded and bloodthirsty of all the deities of India. At many of the temples consecrated to this cruel goddess there is a sort of gibbet erected opposite the door. At the extremity of the crosspiece, or arm, a pulley is suspended, through which a cord passes with a hook at the end. The man who has made a vow to undergo this cruel penance places himself under the gibbet, and a priest then beats the fleshy part of the back until it is quite benumbed. After that the hook is fixed into the flesh thus prepared, and in this way the unhappy wretch is raised in the air. While suspended he is careful not to show any sign of pain; indeed he continues to laugh, jest, and gesticulate like a buffoon in order to amuse the spectators, who applaud and shout with laughter. After swinging in the air for the prescribed time the victim is let down again, and, as soon as his wounds are dressed, he returns home in triumph[2].

Some votaries, again, are to be met with who make a vow to walk with bare feet on burning coals. For this purpose they kindle a large pile of wood; and when the flames are extinguished and all the wood consumed, they place the glowing embers in a space about twenty feet in length. The victim stands at one extremity with his feet in a puddle expressly prepared for the purpose, takes a spring, and runs quickly over the burning embers till he reaches another puddle on the other side. In spite of these precautions very few, as one can imagine, escape from the ordeal with their feet uninjured. Others, whose weak limbs do not permit of their running over the hot embers, cover the upper part of the body with a wet cloth, and holding a chafing-dish filled with burning

[1] This has now been prohibited by law.—ED.

[2] 'Hook-swinging,' as this is called, is still practised in the Madura district (Madras). Though the magistracy have orders to do all they can to prevent it, by dissuading men from offering themselves as victims, still, as it is not under ordinary circumstances a criminal offence, it cannot be prevented by legal process.—ED.

coals, pour the contents over their heads. This feat of devotion is called the *Fire-bath*.

Another kind of torture consists in piercing both cheeks and passing a wire of silver or some other metal through the two jaws between the teeth. Thus bridled, the mouth cannot be opened without acute pain. Many fanatics have been known to travel a distance of twenty miles with their jaws thus maimed, and remain several days in this state, taking only liquid nourishment, or some clear broth poured into the mouth. I have seen whole companies of them, men and women, condemned by their self-inflicted torture to enforced silence, going on a pilgrimage to some temple where this form of penance is especially recommended. There are others, again, who pierce their nostrils or the skin of their throats in the same way.

I could not help shuddering one day at seeing one of these imbeciles with his lips pierced by two long nails; which crossed each other so that the point of one reached to the right eye and the point of the other to the left. I saw him thus disfigured at the gate of a temple consecrated to the cruel goddess Mari-amma. The blood was still trickling down his chin; yet the pain he must have been enduring did not prevent him from dancing and performing every kind of buffoonery before a crowd of spectators, who showed their admiration by giving him abundant alms.

There are a great many ordinary forms of penance, which elsewhere would appear more than sufficiently painful; but devout Hindus do not rest satisfied with these; they try unceasingly to invent new methods of self-torture. Thus, for example, a fanatic self-torturer makes a vow to cut half his tongue off, executes it coolly with his own hands, puts the amputated portion in an open cocoanut shell, and offers it on his knees to the divinity.

Then, again, there are others who, apparently having nothing better to do, bind themselves to go on a pilgrimage to some distant shrine by measuring their length along the ground throughout the whole distance. Beginning at their very doors, pilgrims of this description stretch themselves on the ground, rise again, advance two steps, again lie down, again rise, and continue thus till they reach their destination. Considering the length of their journeys and the fatigue of such exercise, it is easy to imagine that the pilgrims do not go far off the route to sleep at the end of the day. Persons have been seen attempting to measure their length in this way along the entire road which runs between the sacred town of Benares and the temple of Jagannath (Puri), a distance of more than two hundred leagues. I should not like to swear, however, that they really accomplished such a feat.

This tendency of Hindus to submit their bodies to severe and often cruel tortures, or to spend their means in costly offerings, is manifested whenever they find themselves in critical circumstances, and particularly in times of sickness.

There is not a single Hindu who does not in such cases make a vow to perform something more or less onerous on condition that he is delivered safe and sound from his unfortunate predicament. The rich make vows either to celebrate solemn festivals at certain temples, or to present to the pagoda some gift, such as a cow, a buffalo, pieces of cloth or other stuffs, gold or silver ornaments, &c. If the eye, nose, ear, or any other organ be afflicted, they offer to the idols an image of it in gold or silver.

Among the numerous offerings which this superstitious mania causes to flow into the temples of the Hindu gods, there is one common enough, but which, without the perquisites which accompany it, would contribute very little to increase the wealth of the Brahmin priests. It consists in offering one's nails and hair to some divinity. It is well known that men in India are in the habit of shaving the head and leaving only a single small tuft of hair to grow on the crown. Those who make the particular vow referred to refrain, for many years together, from cutting their nails and hair. Then, at a certain fixed time, they proceed in state to the temple, and there, with great ceremony, get rid of the superfluous growth of hair and nails, which they lay at the feet of the divinity whom they wish to honour. This custom is practised only by men; it is chiefly recommended to those who believe themselves to be possessed with a devil[1].

We must do justice to the Brahmins by remarking that they are never so silly as to impose on themselves vows of self-

[1] This custom is also practised among Sudra women.—ED.

torture. They leave these pious pastimes to the stupid Sudras. And even the Sudras who practise such penances are for the most part men of low birth who do so to gain their livelihood; or else fanatical sectaries of Siva or Vishnu, actuated by religious mania, or more often by an inordinate desire of securing the applause and admiration of the public.

Apart from ordinary superstitious practices which flourish everywhere, there are certain temples which, in this respect, enjoy special privileges; such, for example, as that of Tirupati in the south of the Peninsula. This temple, which is in the Carnatic, is dedicated to Vishnu under the name of Venkateswara. Immense multitudes of pilgrims flock to it from all parts of India, bringing offerings of all sorts, in food, stuffs, gold, silver, jewels, costly cloths, horses, cows, &c., which are so considerable that they suffice to maintain several thousands of persons employed in the various offices of worship, which is there conducted with extraordinary magnificence.

Among the noticeable peculiarities which distinguish the great feasts of this temple there is one which I must not pass over in silence. At a certain time of the year a grand procession is formed, which attracts an immense crowd of persons of both sexes. While the image of Venkateswara is borne through the streets on a magnificent car, the Brahmins who preside at the ceremony go about among the crowd and select the most beautiful women they can find, demanding them of their husbands or parents in the name of Venkateswara, for whose service, it is asserted, they are destined. Those husbands who have not lost all common sense, understanding, or at least suspecting, that a god of stone has no need of wives, indignantly refuse to deliver up theirs, and bluntly speak their mind to the hypocritical rogues. The latter, far from being disconcerted, proceed to apply to others who are better disposed, for some of the men are delighted at the honour conferred upon them by so great a god in condescending to ally himself with their family, and do not hesitate to deliver their wives and even their daughters into the hands of his priests[1].

It is thus that the seraglio of Tirupati is recruited. When the god takes it into his head that some of his wives are beginning to grow old or are no longer pleasing to him, he signifies

[1] Such proceedings would hardly be tolerated in the present day.—ED.

through the priests his intention of divorcing them. A mark is branded on their thighs or breasts with a red-hot iron, representing the god Venkateswara, and they receive a certificate showing that they have faithfully served a certain number of years as legitimate wives of the god, and are therefore recommended to the charitable public. Then they are dismissed, and provided with their certificate of good conduct they go about the country under the name of *Kali-yuga-Lakshmis* the Lakshmis[1] of *Kali-yuga*). Wherever they go their wants are abundantly supplied.

This system of procuring wives for their idols is not a peculiarity of the temple of Tirupati. The priests of many other temples have found it convenient to have recourse to it, as for instance those in charge of the temple of Jagannath, which is even more famous than the temple of Tirupati. Religious ceremonies are conducted in this temple with the greatest magnificence. It is situated near the sea on the coast of Orissa. The principal divinity worshipped there is represented under a monstrous shape without arms or head. What particularly distinguishes this pagoda is that it is a centre of union among the Hindus. Although it is specially consecrated to Vishnu, there are no distinctions between sects and castes. Everybody is admitted, and may offer worship in his own way to the presiding deity. Accordingly pilgrims resort thither from all parts of India; the disciples of Vishnu and of Siva frequenting it with equal zeal. The *Bairagis* and the *Goshais* from the North, the *Dasarus* and the *Jangamas* from the South, lay aside their mutual animosities when they approach this sacred place, and it is perhaps the only spot in India where they do so[2]. While sojourning there they seem to form but one brotherhood. It is at this temple especially that one sees the religious fanatics, of whom I have already spoken above, throwing themselves before the car of the idol and allowing themselves to be crushed beneath its wheels.

Several thousands of persons, chiefly Brahmins, are employed in the performance of the religious ceremonies of the temple. The crowd of pilgrims never abates. Those from the South who go on a pilgrimage to Kasi, or Benares, always take the

[1] Lakshmi is the name of the wife of Vishnu.—DUBOIS.

[2] Tirupati is the same in this respect. —ED.

Jagannath (Puri) road up the coast in order to offer *en route* their respectful homage to its presiding deity. Those from the North who go to the temple of Rameswaram, which is situated on a small island near Cape Comorin, also take this road[1].

I have made mention elsewhere of a tank or reservoir of sacred water which is found at Kumbakónam in Tanjore, and which possesses the virtue once in every twelve years of purifying all those who bathe in it from all spiritual and corporal infirmities and from all sins committed during many generations. When the time for this easy means of absolution draws nigh, an almost incredible number of pilgrims flock to the spot from all parts of India.

At Palni, in Madura, there is a famous temple consecrated to the god Velayuda, whose devotees bring offerings of a peculiar kind, namely large sandals, beautifully ornamented and similar in shape to those worn by the Hindus on their feet. The god is addicted to hunting, and these shoes are intended for his use when he traverses the jungles and deserts in pursuit of his favourite sport. Such shabby gifts, one might think, would go very little way towards filling the coffers of the priests of Velayuda. Nothing of the sort: Brahmins always know how to reap profit from anything. Accordingly the new sandals are rubbed on the ground and rolled a little in the dust, and are then exposed to the eyes of the pilgrims who visit the temple. It is clear enough that the sandals must have been worn on the divine feet of Velayuda; and they become the property of whosoever pays the highest price for such holy relics.

It does not enter into my calculations to offer a complete account of all the extravagant absurdities which abound in the idolatrous worship of the Hindus, or of all the tricks and subterfuges, more or less clumsy, by means of which the hypocritical and crafty priests foster the faith of the people while they increase their own comfort. A subject of this nature would be inexhaustible, and in order to treat it fully I should require many volumes. I believe I have said enough, however, to give a fairly good idea of the rest. But I must add

[1] The temple of Jagannath being one of the most celebrated in India, I have given in Appendix VI some details about the myths and traditions relating to its origin.—DUBOIS.

a few words concerning the religious processions of the Hindus, which in their eyes are a matter of no small importance.

There is not a single temple of any note which has not one or two processions every year. On such occasions the idols are placed on huge massive cars supported on four large solid wheels, not made, like our wheels, with spokes and felloes. A big beam serves as the axle, and supports the car proper, which is sometimes fifty feet in height. The thick blocks which form the base are carved with images of men and women in the most indecent attitudes. Several stages of carved planking are raised upon this basement, gradually diminishing in width until the whole fabric has the form of a pyramid.

On the days of procession the car is adorned with coloured calicoes, costly cloths, green foliage, garlands of flowers, &c. The idol, clothed in the richest apparel and adorned with its most precious jewels, is placed in the middle of the car, beneath an elegant canopy. Thick cables are attached to the car, and sometimes more than a thousand persons are harnessed to it. A party of dancing-girls are seated on the car and surround the idol. Some of them fan the idol with fans made of peacocks' feathers; others wave yâk tails gracefully from side to side. Many other persons are also mounted on the car for the purpose of directing its movements and inciting the multitude that drags it to continued efforts. All this is done in the midst of tremendous tumult and confusion. In the crowd following the procession men and women are indiscriminately mixed up, and liberties may be taken without entailing any consequences. Decency and modesty are at a discount during car festivals. I have been told that it is common enough for clandestine lovers, who at other times are subject to vexatious suspicion, to choose the day of procession for their rendezvous in order to gratify their desires without restraint.

The procession advances slowly. From time to time a halt is made, during which a most frightful uproar of shouts and cries and whistlings is kept up. The courtesans, who are present in great numbers on these solemn occasions, perform obscene dances; while, as long as the procession continues, the drums, trumpets, and all sorts of musical instruments give forth their discordant sounds. On one side sham combatants armed with naked sabres are to be seen fencing with one another;

on another side, one sees men dancing in groups and beating time with small sticks; and somewhere else people are seen wrestling. Finally, a great number of devotees crawl slowly before the car on hands and knees. Those who have nothing else to do shriek and shout so that even the thunder of the great Indra striking the giants would not be heard by them. But in order to form a proper idea of the terrible uproar and confusion that reigns among this crowd of demoniacs one must witness such a scene. As for myself, I never see a Hindu procession without being reminded of a picture of hell.

The above is only a slight sketch of the religious ceremonies of the Hindus. Such is the spirit of piety which animates them! Whatever may have been the shameful mysteries, the revolting extravagances of paganism, could any religion be filled with more insane, ignoble, obscene, and even cruel practices?

It is true that human sacrifices are no longer openly tolerated in India. But what matters it? If the female victim does not fall under the sword of the sacrificer, she is so misled by the perfidious suggestions of the priests that she perishes of her own free will and accord on the funeral pyre, or, what is more horrible, by the very hands of those who have given her existence! Are not they also human victims, those unhappy widows on whom superstition has imposed the obligation of burning themselves alive? And what name shall we apply to the destruction of a number of innocent girls condemned to death at their very birth?

These self-same Brahmins, who are afraid of breaking an egg for fear of destroying the germ of a chicken, have they ever expressed the slightest indignation when they have seen parents, more ferocious than tigers, sacrificing all their daughters and preserving only their sons[1]?

[1] This execrable custom is prevalent among certain castes of Rajputs and Jats in the North of India. Happily, the efforts made by the Government nowadays to extirpate it have succeeded in making these infanticides less frequent.—DUBOIS.

The Census Report for 1891 states: 'It is pretty certain that the deliberate putting to death of female infants is a practice that in the present day, at all events, is confined to exceedingly narrow limits. . . . On the whole, even in Rajputana, the Census returns show that the practice must be very restricted in its operation. . . . But

Others, again, with feelings no less unnatural, either drown or expose to wild beasts children who happen to be born under unlucky stars. Furthermore, have they ever, these Brahmins, represented to the people over whom they exercise such paramount influence, how shamelessly they violate nature by placing the sick, whose recovery is despaired of, on the banks of the Ganges, or of some other so-called holy river, so that they may be drowned by the floods or devoured by crocodiles? Have they ever attempted to restrain the frenzy of those fanatics who, in their mistaken devotion, foolishly allow themselves to be crushed under the wheels of the cars of their idols, or throw themselves headlong into the stream at the junction of the Ganges and the Jumna[1]?

What a consoling contrast does the sublime religion of Jesus Christ offer to him who knows how to appreciate its blessings! How inestimable do its holy precepts, its sweet and pure morality, appear in comparison with the hideous and degraded doctrines which I have here so reluctantly sketched! Of a truth, it is God Himself who has not permitted His Divine attributes to be attached to a false religion.

But some will say that the iniquities which have roused my indignation are due far more to vicious conditions of civilization than to perversity of religious principle. But I may reply, what is then the object of true religion, if it is not to correct such vices? The priests of a religion who advise, encourage, or permit crimes to be committed which they could prevent, take upon themselves the whole responsibility for the evil. And in this the modern Brahmins are so much the more to blame because they have done their best to distort and render unrecognizable the primitive religion of which they constituted themselves the guardians, and which, however imperfect it may have been, was far from possessing the monstrous character which it acquired later in the hands of its avaricious and hypocritical interpreters. The Hindu system of religion is nothing more than a lever of which the Brahmins make use habitually for influencing the passions of a credulous people, and turning them to their own advantage. Instead of bending

many a girl is allowed to die unattended where medical aid would be at once called in if the son were attacked.'—ED.

[1] Attempts at suicide are now punishable by law.—ED.

the moral character of the nation under the yoke of the primitive creed, they have invented a sham religion suited to the natural propensities of the people. Quick to recognize the special predilections of their fellow-countrymen, they know that everything which is strange and extraordinary, everything which exceeds the bounds of reason, is calculated to please them; and they have omitted no opportunity of using this knowledge to their own profit.

It must be confessed that the imagination of the Hindus is such that it cannot be excited except by what is monstrous and extravagant. Ordinary objects produce not the slightest impression upon their blunted intellects; it needs giants or pygmies to attract their attention. However little one may be acquainted with them, it is easy to convince oneself of this truism. If you attempt to amuse or instruct them, they will listen to you with distracted indifference unless you intermingle with your discourse some extravagant story, some absurd fable, or some fiction that would overturn the whole economy of the universe. During the conversations which I have frequently held with Brahmins on the subject of religion, if I spoke to them of miracles wrought by the power of God, they saw nothing extraordinary in them. If I related to them the exploits of Joshua and his army and the wonders they performed through the intervention of God in the conquest of the land of Canaan, they would reply with an air of triumph by citing the prowess of their Rama, and the wonders, marvellous in quite another fashion, which attended his conquest of the island of Ceylon. According to them, Samson had no more strength than a child as compared with Bali, Ravana, and other giants. The resurrection of Lazarus was, in their opinion, quite unworthy of remark; for, they said, the Vishnavites daily perform similar miracles during the ceremony of *pavadam*.

What conclusion must be drawn from all this? It is that a wise and reasonable religious belief cannot be evolved by human agency alone. God alone is the Supreme Lawgiver. God alone can interpret His mysterious will to His Prophets and His Church. Without His grace reason is at fault, and is lost in the uncertainty of idle imaginings. False teachers of idolatry may invent dogmas and systems, but they can never reconcile them or build upon them any stable structure of religion.

If, for inscrutable reasons, which it is not given to us to know, God has not been pleased to reveal Himself till now to a people whose civilization dates back to the darkest ages, we at any rate should congratulate ourselves on having been chosen as the objects of His favour.

Many Europeans who visit India are struck by the incoherency of ideas that prevails in the religion professed by its inhabitants, and by the variety of its doctrines and ceremonies; and being far from robust in their own faith, they end by endorsing one of the favourite axioms of modern philosophy, namely, that 'all religions are equally agreeable to God and lead to the same good end.' But to me the strange and disquieting picture of Hindu religion has always presented itself in quite a different aspect. The sight of such an extraordinary religious cult, far from shaking my faith, has on the contrary greatly contributed to confirm it[1].

Certainly, every time that I compare the grand simplicity of our Holy Scriptures, the sublime teachings of our Gospel, the solemn splendour of our religious services, with the inconsistent and disgusting myths contained in the Hindu Puranas and with the extravagant, barbarous, and often terrible religious ceremonies to which the Hindus are addicted, I cannot help feeling that the Christian religion shines with new splendour. I cannot help experiencing an irresistible feeling of gratitude for the blessing of having been born in a part of the globe to which God's divine light has penetrated. It is then that I echo the words of the holy Lawgiver of the Hebrews contained in Deuteronomy iv. 8. Some so-called philosophers of modern times have maintained that the mind of man alone is able to conceive

[1] A Tartar king, recently converted, having communicated to Louis IX his intention of prostrating himself at the feet of the Pope, who was then at Lyons, the saintly monarch dissuaded him, for fear that the dissolute manners of the Christians might weaken the belief of this stranger in the sanctity of the Catholic religion. This precaution was no doubt wise. Nevertheless, another traveller, who was a witness of the immorality of the Roman people, felt his faith strengthened, and came to the conclusion that there could be only one true religion that could be upheld by God's omnipotence amidst such terrible corruption. For my part, I cannot conceive how any Christian can consistently ignore his religious duties when he becomes closely acquainted with an idolatrous people and with the perverse infatuation and extravagant unreasonableness which distinguish an idolatrous cult.—DUBOIS.

a just notion of the divinity. They have dared to attribute that which they themselves have conceived it to be to the efforts of their own critical faculties, as if this power itself had not been imprinted on their minds in the first instance by the Christian education which they received in early youth.

Where, indeed, are there to be found any philosophers, ancient or modern, who have arrived without the assistance of Revelation at trustworthy notions of God and of the worship due to Him? Socrates, the most renowned of all, spoke of the Supreme Being in a manner worthy of Him. Yet even he was unable to shake off entirely the fetters of pagan superstition. After drinking the cup of hemlock and addressing to his friends a sublime discourse upon the immortality of the soul, he again returned to the vain imaginings of pagan worship, and addressing Crito, told him he had vowed the sacrifice of a cock to Aesculapius and begged him to accomplish this vow on his behalf.

The Hindus, like all idolatrous nations, originally possessed a conception, imperfect though it was, of the true God; but this knowledge, deprived of the light of Revelation, grew more and more dim, until at last it became extinguished in the darkness of error, of ignorance, and of corruption. Confounding the Creator with His creatures, they set up gods who were merely myths and monstrosities, and to them they addressed their prayers and directed their worship, both of which were as false as the attributes which they assigned to these divinities.

Nevertheless, such is the moral obliquity of this people that nothing even to this day has been capable of shaking their faith in their idols, or of persuading them to believe in the more reasonable religion of their conquerors. The Christians have vainly endeavoured to introduce their creed by persuasion. And if the Mahomedans have succeeded in making a fairly large number of proselytes, it is only by employing here as elsewhere bribery or violence. But in spite of the honours and dignities offered by the latter to those who, renouncing their national religion, embraced the Moslem faith, Mahomedan missionaries have obtained only partial success and Mahomedanism has not become predominant in any single province of India.

The Christian religion, to which Europe owes its civilization—

that blessed and humane religion, so well adapted to alleviate and improve the condition of a wretched people crushed under the yoke of oppression: that religion whose manifest truths have softened the hard hearts of so many barbarous nations—has been preached without success to the Hindus for more than three hundred years. It is even losing day by day the little ground which it had once gained, against a thousand obstacles, through the zeal and persevering efforts of many virtuous and zealous missionaries. The seed sown by them has, in fact, fallen on stony ground. It must be acknowledged that the conduct of the Europeans who have been brought up in the profession of Christianity, and who are now to be found all over India, is too often unworthy of the faith which they are supposed to profess; and this scandalous state of affairs, which the natives of India can in no way explain, is a powerful factor in increasing the dislike of the latter for a religion which apparently its own followers do not themselves respect.

As a matter of course, the taint of corruption which characterizes all the religious institutions of the Hindus has duly left its mark on their social morality. How, indeed, could virtue prevail in a country where all the vices of mankind are justified by those of their gods? It naturally follows that their religion and their morality are equally corrupt, and this confirms in a certain sense the reflection of Montesquieu, that, 'in a country which has the misfortune to possess a religion that does not proceed from God, it necessarily follows that the religion is identical with the system of morality which prevails there, because religion, even when it is false, is the best guarantee that men can have of the honesty of other men.'

Some few articles of the Hindu faith, if freed from the absurd trammels with which Brahmin deceit has surrounded them, would be capable of offering successful resistance to the inroads of corrupt influences. For instance, the fear of the punishments reserved for the wicked in hell, the hope of the reward apportioned to the blessed in the Abodes of Bliss, and even the strange doctrine of metempsychosis which grants to the man who is neither altogether virtuous nor altogether vicious the prospect of a new birth more or less advantageous and proportionate to his deeds, would be so many incentives, which, if inculcated in the minds of the people by disinterested teachers and men of good faith, would contribute powerfully towards bringing them back into the paths of righteousness. But how different is this way of looking at things from that of the Brahmins! The punishments of hell, exclusion from the Abodes of Bliss, and regenerations in vile bodies are reserved only for those who have done some injury to these hypocritical and selfish persons, or who have not helped to enrich them. Robbers, liars, murderers—indeed the greatest criminals—are sure of immunity after death, provided they give presents to the Brahmins, or contribute in some way to their worldly comfort.

The only real good which the Hindu religion does is to unite in one body under its banner the various castes and tribes of India, the differences between which are such as would otherwise constitute them, so to speak, different nations. Without this common tie it may reasonably be presumed that only disorder and anarchy would prevail.

It is quite true, therefore, that a religion, however bad and absurd it may be, is still preferable to the absence of any religion at all. Unquestionably, in my opinion, the worshipper of the *Trimurti* is much less contemptible than the free-thinker who presumes to deny the existence of God[1]. A Hindu who professes the doctrine of metempsychosis proves that he has infinitely more common sense than those vain philosophers who utilize all their logic in proving that they are merely brute beasts, and that 'death is merely an eternal sleep' for the reasoning man as well as for the animal which cannot reason. But whatever I might say on this subject could in no way excel the logical conclusions which I might quote from Montesquieu, who refutes a paradox expressed by a man more celebrated for his genius than for the purity of his religious principles[2].

And I may fitly terminate these remarks by drawing attention to the testimony of Voltaire, a man whom nobody can accuse of too much partiality in the matter of religion[3].

[1] I say '*who presumes*,' because there cannot be an atheist by conviction. This would mean a man who, by making use of the reason which he can obtain only from God, concludes that there is no God; a conclusion which is evidently contradictory. Only a fool, then, can be an atheist. '*The fool hath said in his heart, There is no God.*'—DUBOIS.

[2] *Esprit des Lois*, xxiv. 2.

[3] *Traité de la Tolérance*, xx.

CHAPTER V

The Principal Gods of the Hindus.—Brahma.—Vishnu.—Rama.—Krishna.—Siva.—The *Lingam*.—Vigneshwara.—Indra.—The Abodes of Bliss of these Different Gods.—*Swarga*.—*Kailasa*.—*Vaikuntha*.—*Sattya-loka*.

SURELY no one will expect me to relate here the histories of all the inferior deities which swarm in Hindu mythology; a mere catalogue of them would fill a large volume; and much more numerous still are the strange stories that Hindu legends contain about them. Only the gods of the first order, *di majorum gentium*, can find a place here. Among those of the highest rank are first of all Brahma, Vishnu, and Siva. Sometimes, under the name of the *Trimurti*, these three gods receive the homage of their devotees in common; at other times each one is the object of particular worship. From these again have sprung a multitude of others, whom the Hindus, faithful to their practice of exaggeration, reckon up to the astounding total of three hundred and thirty millions. I will only refer to the most renowned of these, and I believe that my readers will thank me for sparing them the greater part of the foolish and disgusting details which the people of India attach to these gods, and which amount with them to articles of faith. Let us begin with the deity occupying the first rank in this extensive hierarchy.

BRAHMA[1].

According to tradition, Brahma issued originally from a *tama-*

[1] 'The more common name for the one Spirit is Atman or Paramatman, and in the later system, *Brahman*, neut. (nom. Brahmā), derived from root *brih*, "to expand," and denoting the universally expanding essence or universally diffused substance of the universe. It was thus that the later creed became not so much monotheistic (by which I mean the belief in one

rasa[1] flower. He was born with five heads; but he outraged Parvati, the wife of Siva, and Siva avenged himself by striking off one of the heads of the adulterous god in single combat. Consequently, Brahma is now represented with only four heads, and he is often called the *four-faced god.*

He rides on a swan, and his emblem is a water-lily. His own daughter, Sarasvati, is his wife. Having conceived for her an incestuous passion, and not daring to satisfy it under the human form, he assumed that of a stag, and changed his daughter into a hind. It is for having thus violated the laws of nature that he has, so they say, neither temple nor worship nor sacrifice. Some Pundits maintain, however, that the feeling of indifference evinced towards Brahma is caused by the malediction cast upon him by a certain penitent named Bunumi, who, on presenting himself for admission to the Abode of Bliss, was received with irreverence by the god. But whatever may be the motive, it is an accepted fact that Brahma does not anywhere receive public worship.

They allow him, however, three attributes of high importance: for he is (1) the author and creator of all things; (2) the dispenser of all gifts and favours; (3) the sovereign disposer of the destiny of man.

At the creation of mankind the Brahmins, the most noble of all men, sprang from his head, as I have stated elsewhere; the Kshatriyas issued from his shoulders, the Vaisyas from his stomach, the Sudras from his feet. This, at any rate, is the version most commonly recognized; but it is denied by some authors, who say that Brahma created a first man, who was the father of all the rest. Brahma made him first of all with only

God, regarded as a Personal Being external to the universe, though creating and governing it) as pantheistic; Brahman in the neuter being "simple infinite being"—the only real eternal essence—which, when it passes into universal *manifested* existence, is called Brahma, when it manifests itself on the earth, is called Vishnu, and when it again dissolves itself into simple being, is called Siva; all the other innumerable gods and demigods being also mere manifestations of the neuter Brahman, who alone is eternal. This, at any rate, appears to be the genuine pantheistic creed of India at the present day.'—MONIER-WILLIAMS.

[1] A species of lotus, or water-lily, *Nymphaea lotus*. It is well known how greatly this plant, which grows extensively in Egypt, in the canals that serve to conduct the waters of the Nile for watering and fertilizing the land, was held in veneration by the ancient Egyptians.—DUBOIS.

one foot; but seeing that he had difficulty in moving about in this form, Brahma destroyed his work, and made another with three feet: at last, perceiving that this third foot was like a fifth wheel to a coach, Brahma began his labour over again, and made man with two feet.

It is through Brahma in his quality of supreme disposer that the other gods, the giants, and certain other privileged creatures, have obtained the privileges and prerogatives which they enjoy. Brahma can even confer immortality, as he has done in the case of some famous personages, such as the giants Ravana, Hirannya, and several others.

By reason of the sovereignty which Brahma exercises over the destinies of mankind, all men are born with their fates written on their foreheads by the hand of the god himself. This destiny is absolute and irrevocable. It embraces five principal objects, namely, length of life, disposition, intelligence, worldly condition, and virtuous or vicious inclination. What Brahma has predestined in all these is inevitable and must be strictly fulfilled. The Hindus are so fully convinced of this that in all adversities and troubles of life they are heard to exclaim: *Thus was it written on my forehead*! If they are called upon to sympathize in the troubles of relative or friend, they never omit to utter this consolatory saying: *No being can escape that which is written on his forehead*! Thus, in all cases where a Christian would exclaim with humble resignation, *God's will be done*, they say with an equal resignation, *What is written on the forehead must be fulfilled.* It is also upon this irrevocable and irresistible destiny that Hindus lay the faults and crimes committed by them. Instances of this are constantly occurring in the European courts of justice now established in the country. Thus, when judges ask criminals what has brought them to commit the crimes for which they are convicted, they invariably respond, *Thus it was written on my forehead, and it was not in my power to avoid it*[1].

Each man is also endowed with one of the three qualities of which mention has been made before, namely, goodness or truth (*satva*), passion (*rajas*), ignorance (*tamas*). Whichever of these

[1] This was the excuse offered by a Hindu who was recently (1896) charged with the murder of his mistress at the Mazagon Police Court, Bombay, for the sake of her jewels. —ED.

qualities has fallen to a man's lot is inherent in his being, and is in conformity with his deeds in previous existences; it influences him in all the actions of his life.

This doctrine of fate or destiny was recognized in heathen antiquity from the earliest times. It was the subject of speculation among Greek and Roman philosophers; and, as we all know, there are philosophers of modern times who have felt no shame in adopting it. However, the wisest of the Greek and Roman philosophers correctly gauged the consequences of attributing such an influence to destiny, an influence which, by depriving men of all liberty, destroys both virtue and vice, and constitutes God the Author of all crime. In other terms, that is to say, it disturbs the basis of all morality and of all religion.

VISHNU.

One of the commonest names of Vishnu in the southern part of the Peninsula is Perumal. His devotees are fond of invoking him under the name of Narayana: and he has a thousand other names, of which the Brahmins have composed a species of litany which they call *Hari-smarana.*

I have said elsewhere, concerning the worship rendered to Vishnu, that the sign of the *namam,* which his followers trace on their forehead, is the distinctive symbol of that worship. His cult is more general than that of Siva, especially among the Brahmins, whose favourite god appears to be Vishnu.

He is represented with four arms, and hence is sometimes named the *four-armed god.* The bird *garuda* is his vehicle. He bears the title of redeemer and preserver of all that exists. The other gods, not excepting Brahma himself, have often had need of his help in escaping from perils which threatened them. In his quality of preserver he has found himself obliged to take different forms, which the Hindus designate under the name of *Avatars* (incarnations). Of these they count ten principal ones, the nomenclature of which is contained in the following verses:—

> *Adau matsyas tatah kurma Varahascha param tatah*
> *Narasimha maha saktir vamanascha param tatah*
> *Ramascha Balaramascha parasustadanantaram*
> *Kalkirupas:ha baudhascha hyavatara dasa smitah.*

1. *Matsya-avatar*, in the form of a fish;
2. *Varaha-avatar*, in the form of a pig;
3. *Kurma-avatar*, in the form of a tortoise;
4. *Narasimha-avatar*, in the form of a monster, half man and half lion.
5. *Vamana-avatar*, in the form of a Brahmin dwarf, named Vamana;
6. *Parasurama-avatar*, in the form of Parasurama;
7. *Rama-avatar*, in the form of the famous hero known as Rama;
8. In the form of Bala-rama;
9. *Bouddha-avatar*, in the form of Buddha;
10. *Kalki-avatar*, in the form of a horse.

There is yet another famous incarnation, which is that of Vishnu in the person of Krishna, without counting many others; and all these, if I am not mistaken, originally possessed an allegorical meaning, the object being to prove the all-pervading presence of the divinity. For instance, one reads in the *Bhagavata*:

One day, the penitent Arjuna having invoked Vishnu with fervour and devotion, and having prayed him to reveal himself to him, this powerful god, who has deigned to manifest himself to man under all kinds of forms, answered him thus: 'These, Arjuna, are the forms in which thou must above all invoke me, acknowledging them as part of my divine essence:—

'In prayer, I am the *Gayatri*.

'In speech, I am the word *Aum*.

'Among the gods, I am *Indra*.

'Among the stars, I am the *Sun*.

'Among the hills, I am *Mount Meru*.

'Among the Rudras, I am *Sankara*.

'Among the rich, I am *Kubhera*.

'Among the elements, I am *Fire*.

'Among the *purohitas*, I am *Bruhaspati*.

'Among the generals of armies, I am *Kartika*.

'Among the penitents, I am *Bhrigu*.

'Among the sages, I am *Kapila-Muni*.

'Among the Gandharvas, I am *Chitrarata*.

'Among the weapons, I am the *Thunderbolt*.

'Among the birds, I am the *Garuda*.

'Among the elephants, I am *Airavata*.
'Among the cows, I am *Surabhi*.
'Among the monkeys, I am *Hanuman*.
'Among the serpents, I am *Ananta*.
'Among the waters, I am the *Sea*.
'Among the rivers, I am the *Ganges*.
'Among the trees, I am the *Aswatta*.
'Among the shrubs, I am the *Tulasi*.
'Among the grasses, I am the *Darbha*.
'Among the stones, I am the *Salagrama*.
'Among the giants, I am *Prahlada*.
'Among the months, I am *Margasirsha*.
'Among the learned books, I am the *Sama-Veda*.

'In short, I am the spirit of all that exists; I permeate the universe.'

The *Kalki-avatar*, or horse incarnation, has not yet occurred, but it is expected, although the time and place where it will happen are not known. It will put an end to the kingdom of sin, which began with the *Kali-yuga*.

Vishnu will then appear in the form of a horse; he will be of gigantic stature; he will be armed with a huge axe; his voice will resemble the rolling of thunder, the noise of which will spread terror everywhere. First he will destroy all kings, then all other men. Finally, seeing that his father and mother are but sinners like the rest of mankind, he will sacrifice them also to appease his anger. After this a New Age will begin, when virtue and happiness will reign on the earth.

If one may believe certain learned Brahmins whom I have had an opportunity of consulting on this subject, it would appear that the incarnation of Buddha has also not yet taken place. It ought to have occurred at the beginning of the *Kali-yuga* in the country called Kitoki. This Buddha will preach pure atheism to mankind: he will lead even the gods themselves into sin and error. In these unhappy times Sudras will be seen wearing red cloths, a colour which is only meet for Brahmins, and acquiring knowledge, the Vedas not excepted. So little virtue will then be practised on the earth that what there is will not suffice to render man happy in this world or the next. The Brahmins will no longer fulfil the duties of their calling, will hold in no esteem the rules concerning defilement and cleanliness.

Children will no longer obey their parents; there will be no more caste distinctions; even kings will practise all that is most vile and contemptible among men. Earth itself and the other elements will feel the effects of the universal disorder which will then prevail in nature; the former will lose, at any rate partially, its fertility; little rain will fall from the clouds; the cows will yield but little milk, and that, moreover, will not be fit for making butter.

In the opinion of most Brahmins, however, the *Avatar* in question has already taken place. They cannot exactly fix its date, but they maintain that it is this *Avatar* which put an end to the bloody sacrifices formerly in vogue.

It is probable the same epoch witnessed the establishment of Buddhism, which prevails throughout the greater part of Asia, but has been almost entirely destroyed by the Brahmins in India. Be this as it may, it is certain that under this *Avatar* the Brahmins render no homage to Buddha or to Vishnu.

I must mention in conclusion the famous incarnation of Vishnu in the person of Rama, which forms the subject of the celebrated epic poem known as the *Ramayana*, the most famous of all Indian books, and read by persons of all castes.

RAMA.

Rama, or the incarnation of Vishnu under this name, was the son of Dasaradha, King of Ayodhya or Ayodhi[1]; his mother was Kousalya. He spent the first years of his life in the jungles under the guidance of the penitent Gautama[2]. It was there that, touching with his feet Ahalya, who had previously been turned into stone by a penitent's curse[3], he restored her to life and to her original form.

Subsequently he went to the court of Janaka, King of Mithila. This prince, having witnessed several of his deeds of prowess, proposed to him that he should break the bow of Siva, which until then none of the kings of the earth had been able to do. Rama accomplished this task with ease, and won Sita,

[1] Ayodhya literally means 'unconquerable.'—ED.

[2] The name of the penitent is not Gautama, but Viswamitra.—ED.

[3] It was Gautama, the husband of Ahalya, who was the penitent in this case.—ED.

daughter of the King of Mithila, as the reward of his strength and valour. Hardly had the marriage been celebrated when Rama's father recalled him, and entrusted him with the reins of government. After returning to his paternal home he was one day practising with his bow, and shot an arrow with such force that its twang as it left the bow caused an abortion in a Brahmin woman who was present. The husband, in a transport of rage, uttered this curse:—'May Rama henceforth possess no more knowledge than the rest of men!' The curse had its effect, and from that time Rama was deprived of the divine knowledge inherent in him. Shortly after this event, Kaikeyi, the fourth wife of Dasaradha, earnestly desiring to obtain the crown for her own son, visited Rama and implored him with the most urgent entreaties to forgo his claims. This Rama consented to do, and after abdicating he retired once more into the jungles, accompanied by his brother Lakshmana and his wife Sita.

One day, while Rama was afar off in the forests, Lakshmana cut off the ears of Surpanakha, sister of the ten headed giant Ravana, King of Lankah (Ceylon), who, indignant at the insult offered to his sister, avenged himself by carrying off Sita. Rama, learning on his return of the misfortune which had befallen him in his absence, was prostrated with grief, and could think of nothing but the means of rescuing his beloved Sita from the clutches of her ravisher. In order to succeed in his design, he began by making an alliance with Sugriva[1], king of the monkeys, to whom he rendered great service by killing Vali, his brother, who had long contested the empire with him and was then in possession of it.

Impatient for news of his wife, Rama determined to send some one to Lankah without further delay, to obtain information. The undertaking was not easy, as there was an arm of the sea to cross. But Hanuman, son of the Wind and commander-in-chief of the army of monkeys, whom Sugriva had sent to help his ally Rama, was endowed with extraordinary agility, which seemed to render him the most appropriate person for such an embassy. He was therefore appointed to the task. He started, crossed the straits, walking dry-shod over the surface of the waters, and arrived at Lankah. After a long and unsuccessful

[1] Sugriva literally means 'beautiful necked.'—ED.

search, Hanuman at last discovered Sita sitting in a solitary spot under a shady tree, plunged in the deepest grief, and watering the ground with her tears, while her sobs alternated with curses at her sad fate. At one time she would load Ravana with maledictions, at another she would utter the most poignant regrets at the separation from her beloved Rama, to whom she swore inviolable fidelity, whatever efforts her treacherous ravisher might employ to seduce her.

Hanuman hurried back and told Rama all he had seen and heard. Rama at once conceived the idea of constructing a dam across the straits to make a passage for his army. The monkey Hanuman, entrusted with this great undertaking, set to work to uproot mountains and rocks. At each journey to the straits he carried as many stones as he had hairs on his body, and piling them up on one another, had soon achieved his task of joining the island of Lankah to the continent.

Rama, however, thinking himself hardly strong enough to attack his formidable enemy with the army of monkeys, formed a second army of bears, and with this reinforcement he prepared to cross the straits. Before setting out he placed a *lingam* on the dam, and offered a solemn sacrifice to it. Then, turning towards his armies of bears and monkeys, he addressed them as follows:—

'Brave soldiers, do not let yourselves be frightened by the giants against whom you are to wage war; their strength is useless, since the gods are not on their side. Let us advance, then, without fear and without delay. We march to certain victory, since we go to fight the enemies of the gods.'

At these words the whole force moved forward, crossed the straits, invaded Lankah, engaged in several battles with the giant Ravana, and after many vicissitudes of victory and defeat at last gained the upper hand for Rama. Ravana was vanquished and killed; and Sita, the cause of this terrible war, was rescued and carried off in triumph to her own country of Ayodhya.

On leaving Lankah, Rama placed on the vacant throne Vibhishana, Ravana's eldest brother[1], in recognition of the great services which he had rendered during the war, and before

[1] Vibhishana was a younger brother of Ravana. He was a noble-minded *rakshasa*, or giant, unlike the other giants.—ED.

departing promised he should wear the crown as long as the world lasted, that is, as long as the name of Rama should exist.

Some time after his return to Ayodhya, Rama, having one night left his palace in disguise to find out what was doing in the city, overheard at a street corner some words uttered by a washerman quarrelling with his wife, of whose faithfulness he seemed to have conceived strong suspicions. In his anger the washerman declared that he would drive her from his house, telling her that he was not the man to keep a wife—*as Rama did*—who had been in the power of another. These words fell like a thunderbolt on Rama, who, full of rage and grief, hastened back to his palace. He at once sent for his brother Lakshmana, told him what he had heard, and ordered him to seize Sita, take her far away into the jungles, and put her to death.

Lakshmana immediately set about executing his brother's orders. However, as Sita was far advanced in pregnancy, he had scruples about killing her in this condition, and resolved to save her life. The difficulty was to invent some stratagem in order to persuade Rama that he had executed the task entrusted to him. Now it happened that in the jungles to which Sita had been taken there were several trees which, as soon as an incision was made in the bark, emitted a juice the colour of blood. Lakshmana accordingly bent his bow, and taking the arrow which had been destined to pierce Sita's heart, shot it into one of these trees, staining it with the juice, and then abandoned Sita to her unhappy fate. He at once returned and announced to Rama that his vengeance had been satisfied, and for proof of it showed him the arrow stained with Sita's blood [1].

Alone and abandoned in this deserted place, poor Sita proclaimed her despair in mournful cries and torrents of tears. It happened that Vasishta the penitent had made his dwelling-place not far off [2]. Attracted by the weeping and wailing which struck his ear, he approached Sita, and asked her who she was and what was the cause of her trouble. The unfortunate woman

[1] In memory of this event it is customary on the last day of the military feast of the *Dasara* for princes to go with great ceremony into the open country and there shoot off arrows.—DUBOIS.

[2] It was not Vasishta, but Valmiki, the author of the *Ramayana*.—ED.

thereupon stopped her sobs, and, assuming an air of dignity which filled the penitent with respectful fear, answered him thus: 'I am Sita! The king Janaka is my father, the Earth is my mother, and Rama is my husband.'

At these words the penitent, filled with the most profound feelings of veneration, prostrated himself before the goddess; then, rising and clasping his hands, he said to her—

'Illustrious goddess, why give yourself up thus to grief and despair? Have you forgotten that you are the queen and mistress of the world, and that on you the salvation of all creatures depends?'

He spoke a few more words of consolation, and then led her to his hermitage, where he offered sacrifices to her.

A few days afterwards Sita brought forth twins, which the penitent Vasishta[1] reared with as much care as if they had been his own children.

Now it came to pass subsequently that Rama resolved to perform the great sacrifice of *yagnam*, and let loose the horse which was intended for the victim. The animal, after passing through many countries, came to the place where the two sons of Sita dwelt; and they, full of strength and courage, though at that time only five years of age, intercepted and stopped him.

The monkey Hanuman, general of Rama's armies, was accordingly sent with a considerable force to fight against the sons of Sita and to recover the horse; but Hanuman was vanquished by them, and compelled to seek safety in flight.

Rama, at the news of this disaster, placed himself at the head of his whole forces, and went in person to attack his new enemies. But he in his turn was defeated by the sons of Sita, and he and his soldiers were cut to pieces, not one escaping. Vasishta[1] was informed of this occurrence, and proceeded to the field of battle, which he found literally strewn with the dead. Touched with compassion for Rama and his troops, he pronounced over them the *mantram* which restores life, and raised them all from the dead.

Rama returned home, and determined to perform once more the great sacrifice of the *yagnam*, to which he invited all the neighbouring kings and all the illustrious Brahmins of the country. But the latter, on being consulted as to the best

[1] See note 2 on p. 628.

means of making the sacrifice complete, answered that it could not be so unless Rama's wife was beside him. After raising many difficulties, Rama at last consented to recall her, and to all appearances gave her a hearty welcome. Consequently the sacrifice of the horse was a complete success. But Rama thereupon wished to repudiate his wife anew, and to send her back to the jungles. All the kings present interceded in her behalf. Still Rama would not yield to their entreaties, except on the condition that she proved, by subjecting herself to the ordeal of fire, that her virtue had not suffered any taint.

Sita, conscious of her innocence, issued from the ordeal with honour and glory, and from many others not less searching; yet, in spite of all, she could not cure her husband of his odious suspicions and unjust jealousy.

Overwhelmed at last with confusion and shame, she burst into a flood of tears, and in the extremity of her despair she addressed the following prayer to her mother:—

'O Earth! thou to whom I owe my existence, justify me this day in the sight of the universe; and if it is true that I have never ceased to be a virtuous woman, accord me an indisputable proof of my chastity by opening thyself under my feet and swallowing me up!'

No sooner had she uttered these words than the Earth, in response to her prayer, opened and swallowed her up alive within her bosom.

Rama did not tarry long before following his spouse. Having divided his kingdom between his two sons, he retired to the banks of the Ganges, where he lived for some time in retirement and penance, and then closed his mortal career.

KRISHNA.

The history of Krishna, or of Vishnu under this name, is told in many Puranas. The eighteenth, the *Bhagavata*, deals with him almost exclusively. I will give a very short analysis of this.

In the Jambu-Dwipa is a country called Bharata-Varsha. In this country is *Brinda-Vana*, or paradise of Krishna, which is the supreme paradise, where untold delights are to be enjoyed. It is larger than *Swarga*, and the beauty of it is beyond all description.

It is inhabited by an infinite number of shepherds, the chief of whom is Nanda, Krishna's foster-father. On the north of *Brinda-Vana* is the town of Mathura[1], where Ugrasena reigned. He was expelled from his kingdom by his son Kamsa, who seized the throne and indulged for a long while in innumerable acts of injustice and unheard-of cruelty.

The Earth, unable to bear this tyrant's violence any longer, took the form of a cow, went in search of the four-faced Brahma, and having done him homage, spoke as follows:—

'O Creator of all things, it is to you that I owe my being; it is your duty therefore to protect me. The king Kamsa, who has given himself up altogether to sin, holds me in the most cruel oppression. I can bear his tyranny no longer. This wicked man is your creature. Therefore issue orders to him and forbid his injuring me further.'

Brahma, angered at this report, went with the supplicant to Siva, and told him what he had learnt. All these next went together to Vishnu, the Supreme Being; and after they had offered their respectful salutations, the cow—that is, the Earth still in this form—spoke thus:—

'Great god, you always listen graciously to the prayers addressed to you. I come, then, in my unhappiness to implore your protection. Kamsa, the cruel Kamsa, is committing the most unheard-of cruelties against me. I prostrate myself at your feet, and beg of you to put an end to them by slaying this evildoer.'

After listening to these complaints, Vishnu asked Brahma whether he had not formerly granted some special favour to this Kamsa, and what was its nature.

'The favour which I granted him,' answered Brahma, 'is that he can only be deprived of life by his own nephew. Enter, therefore, into the womb of Devaki, his sister; for there is no other way of getting rid of this tyrant.'

So Vishnu followed Brahma's advice, and became incarnate in the womb of Devaki, sister of Kamsa and wife of Vassu-Deva, one of the most celebrated merchants of the country.

Kamsa, on learning all that was going on, placed guards and spies everywhere, thrust Vassu-Deva and his wife into close confinement, and loaded them with fetters. However, Devaki

[1] The modern Muttra.—ED.

was not long in giving birth to Krishna, and the day of his birth was the eighth of the moon of the month *Badra* (September)[1]. Being informed that Kamsa had resolved to kill the child, Devaki managed to escape the vigilance of the guards and had him secretly carried away into the town of Gokulam.

At the same time Yasoda, wife of the shepherd Nanda, had given birth to a daughter. To prevent this cruel design of Kamsa, the two children were interchanged. Yasoda, who had sunk into a deep slumber during the birth of her child, had been unable to ascertain whether she had given birth to a boy or a girl; she did not therefore detect the substitution, and always looked upon Krishna as her own son.

As soon as the tyrant Kamsa had learnt of his sister's safe delivery, he ordered the child to be brought to him that it might be put to death. But the child, an incarnation of the Supreme Being, was already in safety at Gokulam, in the house of the shepherd Nanda. Kamsa wished, but in vain, to vent his rage on the little girl, who was no less than the Supreme Being himself, under the name of Badra-Kali, whose adventures are to be found written in the history of the goddesses.

Little Krishna spent his earlier years in games and amusements suitable to his age. His ordinary pastime was to steal milk and butter, which he divided afterwards with his friends the shepherdesses. His youth was thus spent in the midst of a pastoral life, and he is often represented playing on a flute, the favourite instrument of shepherds.

On reaching manhood he gave himself up entirely to a life of dissipation and most unbridled debauchery. He did not even respect the virtue of his sisters or of his own mother. He carried them all off by force, and treated them as if they had been his legitimate wives.

In the meanwhile he declared war against the tyrant Kamsa, his uncle, routed and slew him, and gave back the crown to Ugrasena.

Having resolved to marry, he carried off the maiden Rukmani and very many other virtuous girls. The number of his wives amounted to sixteen thousand, and they bore him a prodigious number of children.

[1] It was the month of *Sravana* (eighth day after full moon), not the month of *Badra*.—ED.

He waged several wars against Vacharada, against the king Banasura, and even against Siva himself, who had sided with the latter monarch. It was Aniruddha, Krishna's son, who caused the dispute between his father and Banasura, whose daughter Balaramma[1] he (Aniruddha) had attempted to carry off. The ravisher was kept prisoner for a long time, and was only given back to his father after several long and bloody battles. Krishna, after rescuing his son, began to build in the middle of the sea the town called Dwaraka, and took his innumerable family thither.

At length, having seen all his children die before his eyes, he himself paid tribute to nature. The victim of a curse, which a penitent in his wrath had pronounced against him, he fell pierced by a huntsman's arrow.

The following are some of the principal blessings which the world gained from this incarnation of Vishnu in the person of Krishna:—

He put to death Poothana, a woman celebrated for her extraordinary size, strength, and ferocity.

He effaced from the earth a great number of giants.

He uprooted two trees of such tremendous size that they covered one-half of the earth with their shade.

He chastised the serpent Kaliya.

He suspended a mountain in the air to serve as an umbrella for forty thousand shepherds who had been overtaken by a storm[2].

Besides all this, he cut to pieces Kamsa and all his followers.

However, this is enough about the incarnations of Vishnu. Others before me have spoken at great length about him. I will merely repeat that, judging by the outward worship paid to him, this god must be considered as disputing the highest rank with Brahma; and in fact many Hindu pundits look upon Brahma merely as the chief of the inferior gods.

To Vishnu are attributed five weapons called by the common name of *panchayuda*. But the two principal ones are the *sankha*, which he holds in his left hand, and the *chakra*, which he holds in his right.

[1] The daughter's name was Usha.—ED.

[2] The mountain on that account was called 'Govardhanagiri.'—ED.

SIVA.

This god is also called Ishwara, Rudra, Sadasiva, Mahadeva, Parameswara, and a host of other names. He is represented under a horrible form, in allusion no doubt to the power which he possesses of destroying everything. He is made to appear still more frightful by having his body covered with ashes. His long hair is plaited in a strange manner ; his eyes of huge size make him appear to be in a constant state of fury. Instead of jewels his ears are adorned with snakes, which are likewise twined round his body. There are some colossal idols representing Siva which are calculated to inspire genuine terror.

The principal attitude of this god, as I have already mentioned more than once, is the power of destruction. Some Hindu authors attribute to him also the power of creation.

His vehicle is a bull, and his principal weapon is the trident or *trisula*.

The history of Siva, like that of the other Hindu deities, is a tissue of the most extravagant fables. It consists of endless wars waged by him against the giants, of his hatred and jealousy towards the other gods, and, above all, of his shameless intrigues.

In one of his wars, wishing by an unexpected attack to accomplish the ruin of all his enemies, the giants, and to take possession of the *tripuram* in which they had entrenched themselves, he split the earth into two equal parts, and took one-half as a weapon. He made Brahma the general of his army; the four Vedas served him for horses. Vishnu was used as an arrow, while Mandra Parvata served as a bow. In place of a bow-string he tied to his bow a monstrous serpent. With this formidable equipment Siva led his army against the enemies of the gods, took from them the three fortresses which they had constructed, and exterminated them all without sparing a single one.

Siva had much trouble in finding a wife; but having done a long and austere penance in the deserts bordering on Mandra Parvata, Parvata was so touched that he finally consented to give him in marriage his daughter Parvati.

THE LINGAM.

The *lingam*, an object of deep veneration throughout India, is the symbol of Siva, and it is under this obscene form that the god is principally honoured. I have described elsewhere what this infamous figure represents. One finds in several Puranas details of the origin of the superstitious worship of which it is the object. However much these details may vary, as to the main point the story is everywhere the same. Here, in abridged form, is what the *Linga-purana* says:—Brahma, Vishnu, and Vasishta, accompanied by a numerous following of illustrious penitents, went one day to *Kailasa* (the paradise of Siva) to pay a visit to the god, and surprised him in the act of intercourse with his wife. He was not in the least disconcerted by the presence of the illustrious visitors, and so far from showing any shame at being discovered in such a position, continued to indulge in the gratification of his sensual desires.

The fact was that the shameless god was greatly excited by the intoxicating liquors which he had drunk, and with his reason obscured by passion and drunkenness, he was no longer in a state to appreciate the indecency of his conduct.

At sight of him some of the gods, and especially Vishnu, began to laugh; while the rest displayed great indignation and anger, and loaded the shameless Siva with insults and curses.

They said to him, 'Behold, thou art but a devil, thou art worse even than a devil! thou hast the form of one, and dost possess all the wickedness! We came here in a spirit of friendliness to pay thee a visit, and thou dost not blush to make us spectators of thy brutal sensuality! Be accursed! Let no virtuous person from henceforth have any dealings with thee! Let all those who approach thee be regarded as brutes, and be banished from the society of honest folk!'

After pronouncing these curses, the gods and the penitents retired, covered with shame.

When Siva had recovered his senses a little, he asked his guards who it was that had come to visit him. They told him everything that had taken place, and described to him the angry attitude that his illustrious friends had assumed.

The words of the guards fell on Siva and his wife Durga like a clap of thunder, and they both died of grief in the same position in which the gods and the penitents had surprised them. Siva desired that the act which had covered him with shame, and which had been the cause of his death, should be celebrated among mankind.

'My shame,' said he, 'has killed me; but it has also given me new life, and a new shape, which is that of the *lingam!* You, evil spirits, my subjects, regard it as my double self! Yes, the *lingam* is I myself, and I ordain that men shall offer to it henceforth their sacrifices and worship. Those who honour me under the symbol of the *lingam* shall obtain, without fail, the object of all their desires, and a place in *Kailasa*. I am the Supreme Being, and so is my *lingam*. To render to it the honours due to a god is an action of the highest merit. The margosa-tree is, of all trees, the one I love the best. If any one wish to obtain my favours, he must offer me the leaves, the flowers, and the fruit thereof. Hear once more, evil spirits, my subjects. Those who fast on the fourteenth day of the moon of the month *Makha* (February) in honour of my *lingam*, and those who, on the following night, do *puja*, and present to me leaves of the margosa-tree, shall be certain of a place in *Kailasa*[1].

'Hear yet again, evil spirits, my subjects. If you desire to become virtuous, learn what are the benefits to be derived from honour rendered to my *lingam*. Those who make images of it with earth or cow-dung, or do *puja* to it under this form, shall be rewarded; those who make it in stone shall receive seven times more reward, and shall never behold the Prince of Darkness; those who make it in silver shall receive seven times more reward than the last named; and those who make it in gold shall be seven times more meritorious still.

'Let my priests go and teach these truths to men, and compel them to embrace the worship of my *lingam!* The *lingam* is Siva himself; it is white; it has three eyes and five faces; it is arrayed in a tiger's skin. It existed before the world, and it is the origin and the beginning of all beings. It disperses our terrors and our fears, and grants us the object of all our desires.'

It is incredible, it is impossible to believe, that in inventing this vile superstition the religious teachers of India intended that the people should render direct worship to objects the very names of which, among civilized nations, are an insult to decency. Without any doubt the obscene symbol contained an allegorical meaning, and was a type, in the first instance, of the

[1] It is the *bilva* (*Aegle Marmelos*), not the *margosa*, which is sacred to Siva. —ED.

reproductive forces of nature, the generative source of all living beings. For the rest, the *lingam* offers an incontestable analogy to the *priapus* of the Romans and the *phallus* of the Egyptians. The fact is, all the founders of false religions had need to appeal to the baser senses, and to flatter the passions of their proselytes in order to attract them to their foolish doctrines and blind them to their impostures.

What I have just said about the *lingam* applies also to the *namam* [1], another emblematic and not less abominable symbol, which is not unlike the *Baal-peor* or *Belphegor* of the Moabites.

One sees figures of the *lingam*, not only in the temples dedicated to Siva, but also on the high-roads, in public places, and other frequented spots.

VIGNESHWARA.

This divinity bears also the names of Ganesa, Pillayar, Vinayaka, &c. He is venerated by Hindus of all sects, and his cult is universal. One comes across his idol everywhere—in temples, schools, *chuttrams*, public places, forts, on the high-roads, near wells, fountains, tanks; in short, in all frequented places. It is taken into houses, and in all public ceremonies Ganesa is always the first god to be worshipped. He is, as I have said before, and as his name implies, the god of obstacles, and by reason of this a Hindu begins every serious undertaking by seeking to propitiate him.

He is represented under a hideous form, with an elephant's head, an enormous stomach, and disproportioned limbs, and with a rat at his feet. Siva was his father, and Badra-Kali, or Durga, his mother. He is said to have given himself up entirely to a life of meditation, and to have never married.

The first time that his mother Badra-Kali saw him, she reduced his head to ashes by the brilliancy of her look. Siva, on learning this misfortune, and being sorely grieved at having a son without a head, considered earnestly how he might provide him with this eminently useful member. With this intent he sent his servants with orders to cut off the head of the first living creature they met sleeping with the face turned towards the north, and to bring it to him. An elephant happened to be the first creature they perceived in this position, and following

[1] Part I, Chapter IX.

Siva's instructions they cut off the animal's head, and hurried back with it to their master. Siva took it and fitted it on his son's neck, and since then Ganesa has preserved the shape under which he is still represented.

The elephant's head, and also the rat, are probably emblems of the prudence, sagacity, and forethought which the Hindus attribute to this divinity.

INDRA, OR DEVENDRA.

Indra is the king of the gods of the second rank, who live with him in *Swarga*. He is the son of Kasyapa and Aditi. The inferior gods and the virtuous persons who inhabit his happy domains are without number.

To make them happy Indra distributes *amrita* (nectar) to them, and allows them to enjoy all the pleasures of the senses, to which he also gives himself up without restraint; there is no kind of sensual enjoyment that cannot be indulged in, without satiety, in *Swarga*.

Indra's vehicle is an elephant, and his weapon the *vajra*, a kind of sharp knife. Lightning is also his weapon in his wars against the giants.

THE ASHTA-DIK-PALAKAS.

Indra occupies the first rank among the eight Dik-Palakas, who preside over and guard the eight principal divisions of the world. The following table will explain all that is interesting about these divinities, who are placed by the Hindus after the gods of the first rank:—

Names.	Position of their kingdoms.	Their chargers.	Their weapons.[1]	Colour of their garments.
Indra	East	An elephant	The *vajra*	Red
Agni	South-east	A ram	The *sakti*	Violet
Yama	South	A buffalo	The *danda*	Orange
Neiruta	South-west	A man	The *kunta*	Dark yellow
Varuna	West	A crocodile	The *pasa*	White
Vayu	North-west	An antelope	The *dwaja*	Blue
Kubera	North	A horse	The *khadga*	Pink
Isana	North-east	A bull	The *trisula*	Grey

[1] The names of these weapons cannot be translated into any European language; each one of them has a particular shape, and in no way resembles any of ours.—DUBOIS.

Those who seek for analogies between the gods of India and those of Greece may remark certain striking similarities. Like the Greek gods, each Hindu god has a particular weapon, and also a particular animal sacred to him.

ABODES OF BLISS.

There are four Abodes of Bliss: *Swarga, Kailasa, Vaikuntha,* and *Sattya-loka.* The first is Indra's paradise, the second Siva's, the third Vishnu's, and the fourth Brahma's.

In describing these pleasant retreats, the Hindu books represent Mount Maha-Meru, on the slopes of which they are situated, as being in the form of a cone, convoluted like a snail's shell and divided into stages. On the first, on the north side, is *Swarga,* Indra's paradise; to the left, on the east side and at the next stage, is *Kailasa,* Siva's paradise; at a still higher stage, on the south side, is *Vaikuntha,* Vishnu's paradise; and, finally, on the summit of the mountain is *Sattya-loka,* Brahma's paradise.

SWARGA.

Indra's paradise is inhabited by the gods of the second rank, who are all children of Kasyapa, and of his first wife Aditi. The palace of Indra, their eldest son, and king of this realm of delight, is in the centre, sparkling with gold and precious stones. There is also another palace of equal splendour for Sati, his wife, Puloma's daughter. Their son is Jayanta. In this paradise grows the famous *kalpa*-tree, the golden fruit of which has an exquisite flavour; and there also is the cow *Kamadhenu,* which gives delicious milk. This fruit and milk form the nourishment of the gods.

The *kalpa*-tree and *Kamadhenu* the cow are held in high esteem by the Hindus, and are referred to on almost every page of their books. This *tree of life* of the Hindus, and their *Swarga* itself, may well be but a gross imitation of the *arbor vitae* and of the earthly paradise of Genesis. Be this as it may, however, the *kalpa*-tree, which grows to the height of ten *yojanas,* has the power of satisfying all the desires of men who put their trust in it. As for *Kamadhenu* the cow, she is not less prodigal of her bounties, and can, among other things, grant milk and butter in abundance to anybody who invokes her with sincere faith and devotion. Many other trees are to be found in *Swarga*, while the limpid waters of many rivers meander there in all directions, the principal one being the Mandakini. The eyes of the inhabitants of this happy abode are refreshed by the rhythmical and voluptuous movements of throngs of dancing-girls; while the sweet notes of the *vina* and *kanohra*[1], which the Gandharvas, famous musicians, play in accompaniment to their melodious songs, charm the ear without ceasing. Innumerable courtesans, too, are always ready to satisfy the passions which they excite. Bruhaspati performs the office of *guru* to the gods in *Swarga*, and explains the Vedas to them. Finally, strangely enough, two duly appointed physicians are to be found there, Chonata and Kumara[2]. The Ashta-Dik-Palakas, mentioned above, hold the first rank, as is natural, among the inhabitants of this Abode of Bliss. The nine planets also have their abode there, and it is from thence that they shine upon us. The seven famous penitents, or *munis*, and an infinite number of other saints are the habitual guests of Indra.

Entrance to *Swarga* is granted to all virtuous persons, without exception, of whatever rank or caste, provided they have attained on earth the required degree of sanctity.

Kailasa.

Above *Swarga* is a city constructed on a triangular plan. It is called *Kailasa*, and sometimes *Parvata* (mountain). It is a charming place. Siva rules over it, and it is here that he resides with his wife Parvati. They are both depicted as giving themselves up continually to carnal pleasures. Ganesa and Kartika are their sons, both of whom are endowed with extraordinary strength. Ganesa, the elder, devotes himself exclusively to meditation; Kartika cares for nothing but weapons, and thinks of nothing but war.

Siva's courtiers are a band of evil spirits, of whom Nandi is the chief. His lieutenants are Bringi, Bhima, and Kadurgita, all of whom have terrible countenances.

[1] We cannot trace this word. The Abbé probably means the Tamil *Kinnaram*.—Ed.

[2] The Abbé has made a mistake here. Apparently he refers to the twins Asvini Kumaras, divine physicians.—Ed.

Bhairava, Bhima, and Darshana are charged with the care of the city, which is peopled with various kinds of evil spirits, horrible to behold, which spread terror everywhere. They go about naked, and are continually drinking, quarrelling, and fighting.

Siva, who consumes intoxicating liquors only, is always drunk. He abandons himself to unlimited and shameless excesses of sensuality. He is clothed in a tiger's skin covered with ashes, and his body is entwined with serpents. Seated on his ox, he rides occasionally on the neighbouring mountains with his wife Parvati. The demons who form their escort utter piercing cries, terminating with a shriek like *kil! kil!* and it is from this that *Kailasa* takes its name. The paradise of *Kailasa* is reserved for the followers of Siva, the worshippers of the disgusting *lingam.*

VAIKUNTHA.

Vaikuntha is the paradise of Vishnu, reserved for those who are specially devoted to the worship of this god. It is above *Kailasa,* and occupies a most charming site; hence the name *Vaikuntha,* signifying 'Pleasant.' Gold and precious objects of all sorts sparkle on every side. In the midst of this enchanting abode rises a superb palace inhabited by Vishnu and his wife Lakshmi; close to them are Pradyumna, their eldest son, and a host of other children, their grandson Aniruddha, son of Pradyumna, Usha, his wife, and their daughter Bana. In this abode, as in the rest, there are flowers, trees, quadrupeds, birds, and especially peacocks in great numbers.

The river Karona flows below the royal residence[1]. Many penitents live on its banks and there spend happy, peaceful days; their food consists of fruits and vegetables, which grow without cultivation; their leisure is divided between reading the Vedas and meditating.

SATTYA-LOKA.

The name of *Sattya-loka* signifies 'The Place of Truth,' or 'The Abode of Virtue.' *Sattya-loka* is the highest of the Abodes of Bliss. It is the paradise of Brahma, where he lives with his

[1] The name of the river is Viraja and not Karona.—ED.

wife Sarasvati. The Ganges waters this divine retreat, and it is hence that some of its purifying waters have reached the earth. It is reserved for those Brahmins only who, by the practice of virtue on earth, have arrived at the degree of sanctity necessary to gain admittance thereto. Persons of any other caste, however edifying and pure their lives may have been, are irrevocably excluded from it.

CHAPTER VI

The Worship of Animals.—The Worship of Monkeys.—Of Bulls.—Of the *Garuda* Bird.—Of Snakes.—Of Fishes.—The Worship of *Bhootams*, or Evil Spirits.—Human Sacrifices.

Of all the different kinds of idolatry the worship of animals is certainly one of the lowest forms, and the one which most unmistakably reveals the weakness of human nature; for man thus shows himself incapable of recognizing in His works the great Creator of the universe. What a sad spectacle it is when man, created in God's own image, with a countenance so formed that he might always be *looking heavenwards*[1], so forgets his sublime origin as to dare to bow the knee to animals! It is almost incredible that human beings should so debase themselves. But we must not lament over facts without inquiring into their causes. The worship of animals becomes more comprehensible when one considers the foundations on which all idolatrous religions are based; namely, self-interest and fear. In the eyes of a heathen anything that can be useful to him seems worthy of being worshipped; and this feeling is much stronger in regard to anything that can harm him. Thus the Egyptians, though they were so highly cultivated in the arts and sciences, worshipped the bull Apis, the ibis, the crocodile, beetles, snakes, &c., on account either of the good they hoped for or of the harm they feared from them. As for the Hindus, they appear to be firmly convinced that as all living creatures are either useful or hurtful to man, it is better to worship them all, paying them more or less attention in proportion to the advantages they offer or the fear which their qualities inspire.

[1] 'Os homini sublime dedit, caelumque tueri
Jussit, et erectos ad sidera tollere vultus.'
Ovid, *Metamorphoses*, i. 85 sq.—Dubois.

First on their list of sacred creatures are the monkey, the bull, the bird called *garuda*, and snakes.

THE MONKEY, OR HANUMAN.

The great reverence in which the monkey is held by Hindus is no doubt due to its likeness to man, both in its outward appearance and in many of its habits. Perhaps also its thievish and destructive propensities may be partly accountable for the consideration which it enjoys. At any rate Hindu books are full of marvellous tales of monkeys. In my remarks in the preceding chapter on Rama I have already described some of the deeds of valour wrought by this hero at the head of his army of monkeys. Indeed, the greater part of the *Ramayana*, the favourite epic of the Hindus, is devoted to the achievements of these valiant monkey soldiers and their illustrious general.

The cult of the monkey Hanuman extends over the whole of India. The followers of Vishnu are specially devoted to this deity, but all are ready to give him a share of their homage. Images of Hanuman are to be seen in most temples and in many public places. They are also to be found in forests and desert spots. Indeed, in those provinces where there are many followers of Vishnu, you can scarcely move a yard without coming across an image of this beloved god. The offerings made to him consist solely of natural products, never of a sacrifice of blood. Wherever monkeys are to be found in a wild state, their devotees daily bring them offerings of boiled rice, fruit, and various other kinds of food to which they are partial. This is considered a most meritorious act.

BASAVA, OR THE BULL.

This is the favourite deity of the Sivaites, or followers of Siva. Many conjectures have been offered as to the origin of bull-worship among so many idolatrous peoples. It seems to me, however, that the reason is simple enough. Was it not most natural that those who worshipped so many different objects should offer homage to animals which were so pre-eminently valuable to them, which were their companions in labour, on which they relied to carry on all their agricultural work, which in primitive times constituted their one source of wealth, and which even at the present day form the basis of material wealth all over the world? The nations which did not actually worship them as gods were always careful to show the high value they set upon them. For instance, amongst the Romans to kill a bull was accounted a no less crime than to kill a fellow-citizen[1]; and it was a long time before the Athenians could bring themselves to offer up one of these animals in their sacrifices. There is every reason therefore why the Hindus should regard their cattle with extraordinary veneration, for as a matter of fact oxen and cows are so absolutely necessary to them that one may safely say it would be quite impossible for them to exist without their help. For this reason, therefore, these animals are reckoned among the most sacred objects of their religion. Their images are to be found in almost every temple, particularly in those dedicated to Siva, and are to be seen in great numbers in those districts where the sect of the Lingayats predominates. The sacred bull is usually represented as lying down on a pedestal, with three of his legs doubled under him, and the right forefoot extended straight out beyond his head[2].

Live bulls are also regarded as objects of public worship by Hindu devotees. By way of investing them with an appearance of sanctity these sacred beasts are branded on the right hind quarter with a design representing Siva's special weapon. They are allowed perfect liberty, are never tied up in a shed, and may graze wherever they please. They are often to be seen in the streets, where their devotees worship them publicly and at the same time bring them rice and different kinds of grain to eat. They are all under the safeguard of superstition, and though they wander hither and thither night and day, I have never heard of one being stolen. When they die, even the Pariahs dare not eat their flesh, the bodies being buried with much pomp and ceremony.

Priests of Siva sometimes travel from district to district with these sacred bulls, whose horns and bodies are decorated with much taste. Large crowds accompany them, carrying flags of various colours and headed by bands of music. The real object

[1] 'Bovis tanta fuit apud antiquos veneratio, ut tam capitale esset bovem occidere quam civem.'—Columella, Book VI.

[2] There is an enormous specimen in the Tanjore temple.—ED.

of all this display is to collect alms from the faithful, an object which is invariably attained; for multitudes flock to worship the venerated animal, prostrating themselves before it with every absurd demonstration of devotion that superstition can suggest, and one and all never forget to recompense the leader of the procession, who, when he thinks that he has collected sufficient contributions, sets the sacred beast at liberty again.

THE BIRD GARUDA.

The kite *garuda* is held in great honour, especially by the followers of Vishnu. Brahmins, after finishing their morning ablutions, will wait till they have seen one of these birds before returning to their homes. They call this a *lucky meeting*, and go back fully convinced that it will bring them good luck for the rest of the day. It is a common bird enough. Naturalists classify it among the eagles (the Malabar eagle), but it is the smallest of the species. It measures barely a foot from its beak to the tip of its tail, and about two feet and a half across its outspread wings. Its body is covered with glossy feathers of a bright chestnut colour; its head, neck, and breast are whitish; the ends of its wings are a glossy black; its feet are yellow, with black claws. It is a pretty and graceful bird to look at; but its offensive odour renders a near acquaintance unpleasant. It utters a harsh, shrill, quavering cry like *kra*! *kra*! the last note of which is prolonged into a mournful wail. Though apparently strong and vigorous, it never attacks any bird larger than itself that would be likely to offer resistance. Indeed its timid and cowardly nature makes one doubt whether it really does belong to the same species as the king of the feathered tribe. It wages perpetual war upon lizards, rats, and especially snakes. When it espies one of the last-named, it swoops down upon it, seizes it in its talons, carries it up an enormous height, and then lets it drop. Following swiftly, it picks it up again, killed of course by its fall, and flies off with it to some neighbouring tree where it may be devoured at leisure. Probably out of gratitude for the services rendered by this bird in ridding the country of reptiles, the Hindus have erected shrines in its honour, just as the Egyptians, from a similar motive, placed the ibis amongst their tutelary deities.

The *garuda* also feeds on frogs and any small fish that it can seize in shallow water. Moreover, it does not show much consideration for the poultry-yards of its worshippers, on which it often makes a raid. But its cowardice is such that an angry hen defending her chickens can easily put it to flight, and only the chickens which have imprudently wandered from their mother's side are likely to fall into its clutches. Protected by superstition, the bird has no fear of man; it may often be seen on the roof of a house, or in some frequented place. Sunday is the day specially devoted to *garuda*-worship. I have often seen Vishnavites assembled together on that day for the express purpose of paying it homage. They call the birds around them by throwing pieces of meat into the air, which the birds catch very cleverly with their claws.

To kill one of these birds would be considered as heinous a crime as homicide, especially in the eyes of the followers of Vishnu. If they come across one that has been accidentally killed, they give it a splendid funeral. And they pay the same respect to the dead remains of a monkey or a snake, performing in each case various ridiculous ceremonies, in order to expiate the wickedness of the unknown author of this dreadful crime.

SNAKES.

Among the many dangerous animals which infest India snakes are certainly the most to be dreaded. Though tigers are no doubt very formidable enemies, they are not answerable for nearly so many deaths as snakes. During my stay in India hardly a month passed without my hearing that some person had been killed, close to where I happened to be living, by the bite of a poisonous snake. One of the commonest snakes, and at the same time the most venomous, is the cobra, the bite of which causes almost immediate death. It is accordingly held in peculiar veneration.

Snake-worship, which is a common form of idolatry among almost every heathen nation, no doubt owes its origin to men's natural fear of these reptiles. They try to propitiate the poisonous species with offerings and sacrifices, and they treat those which do not possess deadly fangs with the same amount of respect, because in their ignorance they attribute to a benevolent instinct what is really only due to want of power.

As if the actual presence of these dangerous reptiles were not sufficient to terrify the native mind, Hindu books are filled with stories and fables about them, and pictures or images of them meet you at every turn.

Snake-worshippers search for the holes where they are likely to be found, and which more often than not are in the little mounds raised by the *kariahs,* or white ants. When they have found one, they visit it from time to time, placing before it milk, bananas, and other food which the snake is likely to fancy. If a snake happens to get into a house, far from turning out the inconvenient guest and killing it on the spot, they feed it plentifully and offer sacrifices to it daily. Hindus have been known to keep deadly snakes for years in their houses, feeding and petting them. Even if a whole family were in danger of losing their lives, no one member of it would be bold enough to lay sacrilegious hands on such an honoured inmate.

Temples have also been erected in their special honour. There is a particularly famous one in Eastern Mysore, at a place called Subramaniah, which is also the name of the great snake so often mentioned in Hindu fables[1]. Every year in the month of December a solemn feast is held in this temple. Innumerable devotees flock to the sacred spot from all parts, to worship and offer sacrifices to the snakes. An enormous number of the reptiles have taken up their abode inside the building, where they are fed and looked after by the officiating Brahmins. The special protection thus afforded has allowed them to increase to such an extent that they may be met with at every turn all over the neighbourhood. Many of their worshippers take the trouble to bring them food. And woe to him who should have the audacity to kill one of these gruesome deities. He would get himself into terrible trouble[2].

The denizens of water also come in for their share of Hindu worship. It is quite a common thing to see Brahmins throwing

[1] It is also called *Ananta* and *Mahasesha*. It is on this snake that Vishnu reclines while sleeping on the sea.—DUBOIS.

[2] There are many temples of this description still existing, to which pilgrimages are made.—ED.

rice or other food to the fishes in rivers and tanks. Where the Brahmins exercise undisputed authority, fishing is strictly prohibited, as, for instance, near the large *agraharas*, or Brahmin villages; and in those parts of the rivers where they are in the habit of bathing I have often seen huge shoals of large fish swimming about near the surface, waiting for their food. At the slightest sound they will rush in hundreds towards the bank, and they are so tame that they will actually feed out of a man's hand[1].

What I have said so far gives but a feeble notion of the superstitious feelings with which Hindus regard animals. Ought these feelings, as some writers think, to be attributed to their extreme tender-heartedness, to their gentle and compassionate natures? I should say decidedly not. Such childish, yet shameful, forgetfulness of the superiority of man over all other created beings cannot surely arise from any noble sentiments. I only see in it the foolish errors of a cowardly and weak-minded people, who are slaves to the idle fancies of their own imaginations, and whose reason has become so obscured that they are incapable of recognizing the just and natural laws governing the safety of mankind[2]. The most irreconcilable superstitions[3] and the most ill-conceived considerations of self-interest are the only motives which actuate Hindus in this absurd idolatry of birds and beasts. Any one who has made a careful study of the character of Brahmins, who display so much care and tenderness for monkeys, snakes, and birds of prey, will soon perceive that these same men show the most utter callousness and indifference for the misfortunes and wants of their fellow-men. Food that they bestow so lavishly on all sorts of animals would be pitilessly withheld from an unfortunate

[1] Fish-worship is connected with the fish *Avatar* or *Matsya-avatar* of Vishnu.—ED.

[2] In India we see the grossest forms of superstition side by side with the most wonderfully refined systems of philosophy. The philosophic Brahmin contends that it is ridiculous to try to inculcate into the common and uneducated herd the subtler forms of doctrine. Hence the various forms of idolatrous worship.—ED.

[3] People have been surprised that the crocodile was worshipped in one part of Egypt, while the ichneumon, the mortal enemy of its young, was worshipped in another. What would they say to the Hindus who might be found worshipping the deity *garuda* at the very moment that the latter was in the act of tearing to pieces and devouring their other deity, the snake?—DUBOIS.

man who was not of their own caste, though he were dying of hunger at their very doors. Instead of the kindly precept of Christian charity, 'Thou shalt love thy neighbour as thyself,' a precept which should draw together the whole human race in the bonds of brotherhood, the Brahmins have substituted, 'Thou shalt love all animals as thyself.' I will not go so far as to say that Hindus are unacquainted with those moral precepts which are more or less common to all civilized nations; but prejudice and superstition have so perverted their judgement that they are incapable of regulating their conduct with due regard to what is right and proper from a human point of view. More than this: in cases where these precepts are practised with a praiseworthy object, all the merit is spoilt by the evidently self-interested motives which influence them. To perform a virtuous action simply for the sake of enjoying the feeling of having done right, is a sentiment entirely beyond their comprehension. If you were to ask a rich Hindu why he spent part of his fortune in erecting buildings consecrated to religious worship, in establishing rest-houses for the accommodation of travellers, or in planting trees along the high-road to shelter wayfarers from the burning sun, he would frankly tell you that such munificence was calculated to raise him in public esteem during his lifetime, and to transmit his name to posterity after his death.

BHOOTAMS, OR EVIL SPIRITS.

Almost all ancient philosophers, among them Pythagoras and the followers of Plato, have agreed in saying that each human being is under the influence of a good spirit or an evil spirit; some even go so far as to allow him both a good and a bad spirit. Our own revealed religion can suggest more reasonable ideas on this subject; but superstition, the creature of ignorance and fear, was obliged to fall back on the imagination to find plausible reasons for the alternations of good and evil to which mankind is subject. Incapable of a just appreciation of the workings of Providence, and unable to fathom that which is inscrutable, these heathen people imagine that the sorrows and troubles which befall them are all the work of invisible and malicious spirits, to whom they must offer prayers and sacrifices by way of propitiation. Hindus carry their credulity on this point to a ridiculous excess. The worship of evil spirits is in fact firmly established and very generally practised among them[1]. These spirits are called by the generic name of *bhootams,* which also means elements, as if the elements were nothing else but evil spirits materialized and were the primary cause of all natural disturbances and troubles. Such demons are also called *pisachas, dehias,* &c.

There are temples specially dedicated to the worship of evil spirits; and there are some districts where this particular form of idolatry holds almost exclusive sway. Most of the inhabitants of the long range of hills which bounds Mysore on the west acknowledge no other deity than the devil. Each family has its own *bhootam,* to which it offers daily prayers and sacrifices in order that he may preserve its members from the ills which the *bhootams* of their enemies might bring upon them. *Bhootam* images are to be found all over these hills. Sometimes they are idols with hideous faces, but more often they are merely shapeless blackened stones. Every *bhootam* has his own particular name. Some are thought to be more powerful and more spiteful than others, and these are naturally most widely worshipped.

All these evil spirits delight in sacrifices of blood. Buffaloes, pigs, goats, cocks, and other living animals are frequently slain in their honour; and when rice is offered to them it must be dyed with blood. They do not disdain to accept offerings of intoxicating liquors and drugs, or even flowers, provided they are red.

I have noticed that the worship of evil spirits is most prevalent in mountainous regions and in sparsely populated rural tracts. The inhabitants of these out-of-the-way districts have little communication with more civilized parts, and are more ignorant, more cowardly, and consequently more superstitious even than their more civilized fellow-countrymen. All the troubles and misfortunes that happen to them are put down to their *bhootams,*

[1] The system of demon-worship seems to have been that of the tribes whom the Hindus supplanted and drove into the mountains or into the extreme south. The Brahmins have given a place to those demons in their system, and represent them as attendants of Siva (*Bhutesa* = lord of demons). The method of worship, the ceremonies and observances of this ancient system, are foreign to the genius of Hinduism.—POPE.

whose anger they think they have somehow incurred; and it is for the purpose of disarming this malevolence that they are so prodigal in their worship of them.

The wild tribes scattered through the forests of Malabar, on the Carnatic Hills, and elsewhere, where they are known as *Kadu-Kurumbars, Sholigars, Irulers,* &c., worship no other gods but these *bhootams.*

HUMAN SACRIFICES.

In vain has the attempt been made, for the credit of humanity, to throw doubt upon the many evidences of human sacrifices; but unfortunately the proofs are too strong: they are written in blood in the history of many nations, and can be only too clearly proved. Man, overwhelmed with infirmities and misfortunes, and fully convinced that they were the punishment of his sins, imagined that he would appease and propitiate the gods by offering them the noblest and most perfect sacrifice that he could find. Firmly imbued with this horrible idea, he considered himself justified in shedding the blood of human victims as well as that of animals. If such an atrocious custom needed confirmation, recent instances of it could be quoted among the Hindus, who, in common with other heathen nations, have not scrupled to drench the altars of their gods with the blood of their fellow-men.

I will say nothing of the abominable teachings of their magicians in this respect. Criminal abuses committed by a few are no proof of the absence of religion and morality in a nation as a whole. If an infamous charlatan ventures to assure powerful patrons who are so weak as to have recourse to his arts, that it is necessary to shed human blood in order to ensure success in his mysterious operations, and if it is only too certain that unfortunate virgins have been sacrificed at the *satkis* of these magicians, the disgrace of it all must rest on the heads of those who are responsible for the maintenance of social order.

A similar sacrifice, however, is recommended when the grand *yagnam* is performed; and though a horse is most often offered, still the *nara-medha,* or sacrifice of a human victim, is held to be infinitely more pleasing to the deity who is the object of the ceremony, and is consequently to be preferred. There is, furthermore, not a single province in India where the inhabitants do not still point out to the traveller places where their Rajahs used to offer up to their idols unfortunate prisoners captured in war. These horrible sacrifices were performed with a view to securing success to their campaigns through the intervention of the gods. I have visited several places where these scenes of carnage used to be enacted. They are generally situated on the top of a mountain or in some isolated spot; and there you find a mean-looking temple, or sometimes only a little shrine containing the idol in whose honour all this human blood was spilt. The victims were beheaded, and their heads were then hung up as trophies before the bloodthirsty deity. Sometimes the sacrificers contented themselves with cutting off the nose and ears of a prisoner, a very common form of punishment in India, and then sent him away thus mutilated. A little pagoda still exists, perched on the mountain at the foot of which lies the town of Mysore, not far from Seringapatam, which enjoyed a wide notoriety owing to the number of executions which took place there when heathen princes still ruled the country.

Old men have told me that this horrible custom was still practised when they were young. There was nothing in it, according to their views, contrary to law or to the rights of the people as understood by the then reigning princes. It was based on the principle that reprisals were fair and legitimate in war; and it was accepted by the people without any feelings of horror. In fact, the old men spoke of it with the utmost indifference, as if it were the most natural thing in the world. However, the advent of Mahomedans and Europeans, and the just indignation manifested by both at these abominable sacrifices, at last resulted in their abolition. But if the general opinion is to be believed, there are still several small independent princes who, if they had their own way, would still sanction these horrible massacres.

It is, I fear, indisputable that human sacrifices have been offered, both in ancient and modern times, on the altars of Hindu divinities. If any additional proof be needed it may be found in the *Kali-purana*. Abominable rites of this kind are there expressly enjoined. The ceremonies which should accompany them are described in the minutest detail, as also the results which will ensue. The same book contains rules of procedure in sacrificing animals, and mentions the kinds and qualities of those which are suitable as victims. Lastly, it specifies those deities to whom these bloody offerings are acceptable. Among them are Bahirava, Yama, Nandi, and, above all, the bloodthirsty goddess Kali.

To offer human sacrifices is regarded as the exclusive right of princes, and they are even enjoined to offer them. Neither a Brahmin nor a Kshatriya may ever be sacrificed. Every human victim must be free from all bodily blemish, and must not have been guilty of any serious crime. All animals that are offered as sacrifices must be at least three years old, and must be healthy and free from all defects. Under no circumstances can Brahmins preside or assist in any way at a sacrifice of blood.

CHAPTER VII

Inanimate Objects of Worship.—The *Salagrama* Stone.—The *Tulasi.—Darbha* Grass.—The Sacred Fig-Tree.

VOLTAIRE thought it incredible that the Egyptians could ever have worshipped onions and other products of their gardens. He always jeered at this tradition, and looked upon it as a mere fable. But the fact is, in matters of superstition truth is sometimes stranger than fiction. What I have already said and what I am now about to say respecting the Hindus will show incontestably that there are absolutely no limits to the follies of idolatry. The Brahmins, indeed, must needs borrow objects from all three kingdoms of nature in order to arrive at the magnificent total of three hundred and thirty millions of deities which they recognize[1]. Amongst the inanimate substances which they worship, there are four which they consider especially sacred, namely, the *salagrama* stone, *darbha* grass, the plant *tulasi*, and the *aswatta* or sacred fig-tree.

THE SALAGRAMA[2].

This little stone is held in great honour throughout India. Brahmins consider it to be a metamorphosis of Vishnu, and for this reason they offer daily sacrifices to it. It is a sort of fossilized shell, ammonite or nautilus, oval, striated, umbilicated, and ornamented with 'arborizations' or tree-like markings on the outside. The more there are of these tree-like markings, the more highly they are revered.

[1] These are properly speaking *devas* or divine beings, not deities in the strict sense of the term.—ED.

[2] The *salagram* or ammonite found in the Gundick and other rivers flowing through Nepal is said to be a form of Vishnu. The account of its origin given in the *Skanda-purana* is most monstrously and incredibly abominable.—POPE.

It is obligatory for every Brahmin to have one of these stones in his possession. They are handed down from father to son, and are regarded as precious heirlooms which must never pass out of the family. It is written in the *Atharva-Veda* that any Brahmin's house in which there is no *salagrama* is to be considered as impure as a cemetery, and the food which is prepared in it as unclean as a dog's vomit.

Though the *salagrama* is looked upon as one of the metamorphoses of Vishnu, it partakes at the same time of the essence of all the other deities, and through it *puja* can be offered to all of them. There is nothing more efficacious for the remission of sins, no matter how grievous they may be, than to possess some water in which the *salagrama* has been washed. Forgiveness of sins may even be obtained by simply touching the water which has been thus sanctified. He who always keeps such water in his house ensures thereby perpetual wealth; and if he goes further and drinks it, he will not only obtain forgiveness of his sins, but he will also secure his happiness in this world, will always do what is right, and after death will at once enjoy the delights of *Swarga*. But before drinking this marvellous water he must not forget to address the following prayer to Vishnu:—'Narayana, you are the ruler of the world; it is your pleasure to confer blessings on all created beings. I drink this water in which your sacred feet have been washed; I drink it that I may be cleansed from my sins; vouchsafe to pardon me, who am the greatest of sinners.'

THE TULASI.

The *tulasi* (*Ocymum sanctum*) plant is to be found everywhere in sandy and uncultivated places. It is a species resembling the basil that grows in Europe. Brahmins consider it to be the wife of Vishnu, and revere it accordingly. 'Nothing on earth can equal the virtues of the *tulasi*,' say they: *Tulasi-tulana-nasty, ataéva tulasi.* *Puja* must be offered daily to it. When a Brahmin is dying one of these plants is fetched and placed on a pedestal. After *puja* has there been offered to it, a bit of its root is placed in the mouth of the dying man, and the leaves are placed on his face, eyes, ears, and chest; he is then sprinkled from head to foot with a *tulasi* twig which has been dipped in water. While this ceremony is being performed his friends cry several times aloud, *Tulasi*! *Tulasi*! *Tulasi*! The man can then die in the happy certainty that he will go straight to *Swarga*[1].

To obtain pardon of all one's sins it is sufficient to look at this sacred plant. By touching it a man is purified from all defilement, and if he perform the *namaskara* to it, any illness from which he may be suffering will be cured.

Salvation is assured to any one who waters and attends to it every day. If a branch of it is offered to Vishnu in the month of *Kartika* (November), it will be more pleasing to the god than a thousand cows. Whoever offers to Vishnu, at any time whatsoever, a spray of *tulasi* that has been dipped in saffron, is assured of becoming like Vishnu himself, and of enjoying a share in Vishnu's happiness. To give a twig of *tulasi* to any one who is in any danger, or who is suffering from anxieties and cares, is a certain means of securing for him a satisfactory ending to his difficulties.

These are only a few of the many virtues possessed by the *tulasi*.

Most Brahmins cultivate the plant in their houses, and offer it daily prayers and sacrifices. They also take care that it shall grow near the places where they perform their ablutions, and in their meeting-places, such as the *chuttrams*. The *tulasi* is usually planted on a little mound of sand, which they call *brinda-vanam*[2], or on a square pillar, three or four feet in height, hollow at the top, with its four sides facing the four points of the compass. Brahmins consider it a peculiarly meritorious act to carefully water and cultivate the plant[3].

Its leaves have a sweet aromatic scent and act as a cough elixir and cordial; indeed Hindus think that they possess many medicinal properties. Brahmins always swallow one or two after their meals, as an aid to digestion. They also eat some both before and after performing their ablutions in cold water, in order to keep up the proper temperature in the stomach and to prevent colds and chills and other maladies which might attack them without this preventative. It was

[1] This formality is observed only by the Vishnavites.—ED.

[2] This name is also given to the place inhabited by Krishna.—DUBOIS.

[3] The plant is grown in the courtyard of almost every Brahmin house, and the women offer worship to it daily.—ED.

probably in consequence of its medicinal properties that the Hindus deified the plant in the first instance.

DARBHA GRASS[1].

This plant belongs to the genus borage. It is found everywhere, especially in damp marshy ground. Brahmins always keep some in their houses, and it is used in all their ceremonies. It grows to the height of about two feet and is finely pointed at the top. It is extremely rough to the touch, and if rubbed the wrong way it cuts through the skin and draws blood.

Hindu legends differ as to the origin of this sacred grass. Some say that it was produced at the time when the gods and the giants were all busy churning, with the mountain Mandara, the sea of milk in order to extract from it *amrita* or nectar, which would render them all immortal. The story is that the mountain, while rolling about on Vishnu's back (who, under the form of a turtle, was supporting it), rubbed off a great many of the god's hairs, and that these hairs, cast ashore by the waves, took root there and became *darbha* grass. Others say that the gods, while greedily drinking the *amrita* which they had with infinite pains extracted from the sea of milk, let fall a few drops of the nectar on this grass, which thus became sacred. Then, again, others assert that it was produced at the time when Mohini—that is to say, Vishnu metamorphosed into a courtesan of that name—was distributing *amrita* to the gods. The vessel containing the nectar was supported on Mohini's hip, from which some fleshy filaments fell, and taking root in the ground, developed under the form of *darbha* grass. Be this as it may, *darbha* grass is looked upon as part of Vishnu himself. On the strength of this the Brahmins worship it and offer sacrifices to it, and, as may be remembered, make use of it in all their ceremonies, in the belief that it possesses the virtue of purifying everything. An annual feast instituted in honour of the sacred *darbha* grass is celebrated on the eighth day of the moon in the month of *Badra* (September , and is called the *Darbha-ashtami*. By offering the grass as a sacrifice on that day immortality and blessedness for ten ancestors may be secured;

[1] This sacred grass (*Poa cynosuroides*) is essential in all sacrifices.—ED.

and another result is that one's posterity increases and multiplies like the *darbha* grass itself, which is one of the most prolific members of the vegetable kingdom. I have no idea why this plant should have been selected as worthy of special honour. I have never heard of its being endowed with any peculiar properties, either medicinal, culinary, or other, which would account for its high position.

THE SACRED FIG-TREE.

There are seven different species of trees which the Brahmins consider sacred and accordingly worship; but, strange to say, they are not those which produce the best fruits. It is true, however, that their thick foliage makes a splendid shade—a priceless boon in the hot climate of India. The *aswatta*[1] comes first on the list. It is one of the most beautiful trees in the country, and grows to a huge size. It is to be found everywhere, but especially where the Brahmins perform their ablutions. Its large leaves, very soft to the touch, in colour bright green, are so light and thin that the slightest breeze sets them in motion; and as they produce an impression of most refreshing coolness, the tree is considered to possess health-giving properties. When stirred by a breeze the leaves make a pleasant rustle, which Hindu authors have sometimes likened to the melodious sounds of the *vina*. When to all these attractive natural characteristics is added the tradition that under this tree Vishnu was born, it is no wonder that the *aswatta* is regarded with great respect and veneration. No one is allowed to cut it down, lop off its branches, or even pull off its leaves unless they are to be used for acts of worship. To fell one of these trees would be an awful sacrilege, and quite unpardonable. It is consecrated to Vishnu, or rather it is Vishnu himself under the form of a tree[2]. Sometimes a solemn inaugural ceremony is

[1] It is called *arasa-maram* in Tamil; *ravi-manu* in Telugu; *aruli-mara* in Canarese. It is the pagoda fig-tree (*Ficus religiosa*), the tree of God.—DUBOIS.

[2] The *aswatta* or *pipàl*, having roots hanging from above and branches bent downwards, is allegorical. Each tree springing from an unperceived root is emblematical of the body, which really springs from and is one with the Godhead. In the *Bhagavat-gita* it is said to typify the universe. It is said to be the male of the *vata* or banian (*Ficus indica*).—ED.

gone through, called *Aswatta pratishta*, or the consecration of the *aswatta* tree. This ceremony, which is an elaborate and costly one, possesses the virtue of transforming the tree into a divinity by inducting Vishnu into it. The Brahmins assert that untold blessings will be showered upon any one who is willing to bear the expense.

I have already described, in the chapters on the *Sandhya* and on Marriage, the manner in which this tree is worshipped, and the honours that are paid to it. Sometimes it is invested, like a Brahmin, with the triple cord, the very same ceremonies being performed. And sometimes it is solemnly married. Generally a *vepu* or margosa tree[1] is selected for its spouse, and occasionally a plantain or banana tree. Almost the same formalities are observed for this curious marriage as in the case of a marriage between Brahmins. Here and there, on the high-roads and elsewhere, the *aswatta* and *vepu* trees may be seen planted side by side on little mounds. This union is not an accidental one, but the result of an actual marriage ceremony. Not thirty yards from the modest hut where I wrote these pages were two of these trees, under whose shade I have often reclined. Their trunks were so closely entwined that they had become incorporated one with another. The inhabitants of the village could remember to have seen them planted together some fifty years before, and said that they had been present at the wedding festivities, which lasted several days, and were celebrated at the expense of a wealthy person of the neighbourhood at a cost of more than 1,500 rupees.

Such, then, are the kind of good works which Hindus perform in order to obtain the pardon of their sins in this world and to ensure their happiness in the next; and such is the state of degradation to which the Brahmins, so haughty, presumptuous, and infatuated with their own ideas and opinions, have reduced a nation which is really worthy of better things[2].

[1] This is another sacred tree, which is dedicated to Siva, the *Melia Azadirachta*.—Dubois.

[2] See Racine's *La Religion*, cap. v.—Dubois.

CHAPTER VIII

The Administration of Civil and Criminal Justice.—Customs connected with Usury.—Various Kinds of Punishment.—Trial by Ordeal.—The Prevalence of Perjury.—Remarks on the European Courts of Justice.

GOVERNED from time immemorial by despotic princes, who recognized no law but their own free will and pleasure, India has been accustomed to a form of judicial administration peculiar to herself. There has been no legal code, neither has there been any record of legal usage. There are, it is true, a few works containing general legal principles, and a few wise legal maxims which have helped to guide the judges in their decisions; yet nowhere have there been properly organized courts of justice. Ordinary cases have generally been settled, without any right of appeal, by the collectors of public revenue, assisted by assessors selected from the principal inhabitants and by the military officer commanding the district.

The Hindus have neither barristers nor solicitors; neither are they compelled to submit to those long proceedings and interminable delays, the cost of which often equals the value of the matter under dispute. When it is a question of dividing property or of other business of any importance, it is generally submitted to the arbitration of relatives or of the headmen of the caste; and if the nature of the suit or the high rank of the litigants render it advisable, all the principal inhabitants of the district assemble to decide the point at issue[1].

When a case is brought before the revenue officer of the district and his assessors, no difficulty is experienced in getting them to settle the dispute if they think that they are likely to

[1] Since the Abbé's day English courts of justice have been established all over the country, and there are hosts of English barristers and attorneys and Native *vakils* practising in these courts. In the villages, however, arbitration is still resorted to in petty cases.—ED.

make any money out of it. Otherwise they will easily invent some pretext for putting off the matter till some future time when they may have more leisure to attend to it. In any important case they try their best to bring the parties to an amicable understanding; and if that is impossible, they leave the decision to a *panchayat*, or 'tribunal of five arbitrators,' which may be composed of a larger, but never of a smaller, number than five. If caste customs are the subject of dispute, the settlement devolves upon the heads of the castes.

The procedure generally followed is that dictated by common sense, by ordinary intelligence, and by such principles of equity as one always expects to find established, in theory at any rate, in all civilized countries. Besides, almost every member of a caste is well acquainted with its different customs, which are handed down by tradition from father to son, and thus are never lost. In short, the form of judicial procedure in India is less complicated than that of Europe, and would leave little to be desired if the scales of Themis were not much more easily put off their balance there than in other countries. Impartiality and disinterestedness are virtues with which Hindu judges have but a very slight acquaintance[1]. Too weak to be able to resist the bribes that are offered them, to be independent of the prejudices and predilections of their own circle, or to be above all considerations of personal interest, their judgements are rarely conspicuous for unswerving uprightness and integrity. Almost invariably it is the richer suitor who gains the day; and even the most guilty generally find some means of blunting the sword of justice.

If the parties to a suit have an equally good case or an equally bad one, the party which makes the most noise and is loudest in its abuse of its adversary usually gains the day, for eloquence at the Indian Bar consists in shouting with all the strength of one's lungs, and in pouring such a flood of invective on one's adversary that he has not an answer left.

There are two or three Hindu works which contain rules and directions concerning the administration of justice, both civil and criminal. The best known is the *Dharma-Sastras*, which contains, amongst other things, a treatise on Hindu polytheism. There are also the *Niti-Sastras*, and the *Manu-Sastras*, which

[1] Circumstances have now altered for the better in this respect.—ED.

have been partly translated into English[1]. Many legal precepts and decisions, which would be most useful helps to a judge, might be gathered from these works; but, as usual, they are immersed in a farrago of nonsense, religious and otherwise. For instance, one may find there numbers of decisions in hypothetical cases that are either perfectly ridiculous or morally impossible, and also numbers of idiotic theses propounded *ex cathedra*. Furthermore, whatever valuable information may be found here and there in these books is quite beyond the comprehension of the majority of Hindus, who do not in the least understand the learned terms in which they abound.

The Hindus, it may be remarked, recognize no prescriptive rights. A person in actual possession of any property, who happens to have no legal and authentic document stating that it belongs to him, is liable to be proceeded against judicially and evicted by the representatives of a *soi-disant* legitimate proprietor, even though the actual possessor could prove that he and his ancestors had enjoyed the property without question and in good faith for a century or more. The same principle holds in the case of debts. It is not at all an uncommon thing for creditors to sue the great-grandson of the original debtor for a debt contracted more than a hundred years before, and to force him to pay it even though he himself might be totally unaware of its existence.

Usury is a recognized institution everywhere; and there is no limit to the rate of interest. In the parts of the country where I lived the lowest rate was twelve per cent., and that they call the *dharma-vaddi* or fair interest, a rate that would not shock the most sensitive conscience[2].

Indeed to lend money at that interest is considered a meritorious action. Eighteen to twenty-five per cent. is the usual rate, and money-lenders have been known to exact the extortionate rate of fifty and even a hundred per cent. Happily the cupidity of these money-lenders often ends in their over-

[1] These and other Hindu classics have now been published in English form in *The Sacred Books of the East* series.—ED.

[2] There has been no improvement in this direction since the days of the Abbé, and various proposals have been made to legislate in the matter. —ED.

reaching themselves, for only people who are ruined and absolutely penniless will consent to pay such interest, and consequently the greedy creditor runs the risk of losing both interest and capital. Borrowers of this class do not, as a rule, offer any security which the creditor can pounce upon in case of default of payment. A Hindu's whole property generally consists of a few head of cattle; but such property is inviolable. If a creditor tried to seize a debtor's cattle, the magistrates would interfere to prevent it; not altogether in the interests of the agriculturist, but because by thus taking away the means of cultivating his fields, the creditors would, at the same time, prevent his being able to pay the taxes which belong to the State. Even the hut which the Hindu inhabits does not belong to him, but is the property of the State. When he leaves his village to settle elsewhere, he has no right to dispose of his hovel. It remains unoccupied either until some other inhabitant comes, and with the consent of the headmen of the village takes possession of it, or until it falls to pieces.

Thus it may readily be understood that usurious money-lending does not always tend to enrich the usurer. It very often happens that borrower and lender are both completely ruined together.

Nevertheless, the lenders need never relinquish all hope. The legal system of bankruptcy, which the dishonest man will so gladly avail himself of, and by which he can grow rich at the expense of his creditors, is unknown in India. If a debtor dies insolvent, his descendants to the sixth generation continue to be responsible for his debts [1].

Criminal jurisprudence in India varies greatly. In some castes, for instance, the woman who commits adultery renders herself liable to capital punishment, but neither her parents nor the headmen of her caste have to carry out or assist at her execution. Her husband alone has the right to put her to death. These severe measures, however, have never been put in practice except in countries governed by Native princes. The Mahomedans always opposed them wherever their rule extended. They thought it would be less cruel and more advantageous to the State to inflict very heavy fines for offences of this nature. Thus, a woman or girl not a prostitute by profession, who is

[1] The law on this subject is now in conformity with the English laws.—ED.

proved to have committed adultery, particularly if she afterwards became pregnant and thereby convicted herself, would be sentenced to a very heavy fine, quite beyond her power to pay; and her seducer would also be fined to the same amount. If the guilty pair were unable to find the money, the fine would fall on their nearest relatives, who would be obliged to pay it for them. The same form of punishment was meted out in any cases of a glaring nature where caste customs had been broken. These fines were collected by the revenue officer of the district in which the offences had been committed. It was further the custom for the offenders to give a feast to the headmen of their caste after their fines had been paid, in consideration of which their fault was considered to be wiped out.

There used to be, and still are in some districts, contractors who farmed the revenue derivable from such fines. These men agree to pay a fixed sum to the public treasury, and in exchange they are allowed to keep all the fines they collect for minor offences against caste customs, or other peccadilloes. One can well imagine that all their energies are directed to preventing any persons from going unpunished.

As to more serious crimes, such as theft, homicide, &c., either the ruling prince, his minister, or the governor of a province usually passed sentence on them. The governors, however, had not the right to condemn a man to capital punishment without the ruler's sanction. Thieves, as a rule, got off by giving up what they had stolen, and a good deal more besides, if they had it. The unfortunate man whose goods were stolen only received a very small portion of what he had lost, by far the larger portion remaining in the hands of the judge who had kindly consented to look into the matter. Highway robbery was punished by mutilation—the right hand, nose, and ears of the robber being cut off.

Murder itself was rarely punished by death. If the person accused was rich and knew what to give to the governor who tried the case, means could always be found to divert well-merited punishment from the culprit. If the offender was a poor man, they took away the little that he possessed and banished him and his family from the province.

Thus the most abominable outrages on society were encouraged or only lightly punished in India, whilst imaginary crimes invariably entailed punishment on any who might be accused of them. A poor Pariah was put to death in Tanjore for having hurled a stone at and killed a bull dedicated to Siva, which was devastating all the rice-fields in the neighbourhood. I knew another man of the same caste whose hand was cut off for having killed, also with a stone, a calf which was trespassing on his field. He too would have certainly lost his life had he not been able to prove that the offence was unintentional, and had not several persons of note interceded in his behalf[1].

A person condemned to capital punishment is either shot, hanged, or beheaded. There are many forms of punishment and torture prevalent in India. For instance, the offender may be banished from the country, severely flogged, or rolled naked on burning hot stones; or he may be condemned to carry a heavy weight on his head or shoulders until he faints from exhaustion; or he may be tied to a stake and exposed to the burning rays of the sun with bare head and naked body; or his hands and feet may be put into fetters tightened till they almost dislocate the joints; needles may be inserted under his nails; the pungent and acrid juice of the pepper-plant may be injected into his eyes and nostrils; or large bodkins may be plunged into the most sensitive and fleshy parts of his body, and on their withdrawal the parts be rubbed with salt and vinegar or burning acids. These are only a few of the horrors invented as punishments by the Hindus. It is not on murderers, thieves, and offenders of that class that these terrible punishments fall. They are much more likely to be inflicted on Government officials guilty of malpractices or malversation of public moneys, or on anybody who is known to be well off, but who declines to allow himself to be fleeced.

In those provinces which are still under Native government, and especially in those where the rulers are Mahomedans, no man's fortune is safe, however honestly it may have been acquired. Government agents, aided by a highly organized system of espionage, contrive to obtain most accurate information respecting the amount of every person's fortune; and whenever an unhappy individual is ascertained to have saved

[1] The Indian Penal Code effectually provides against such sentences nowadays.—ED.

enough to attract the prince's cupidity, he is denounced, arrested, and imprisoned. If these high-handed proceedings are not sufficient to induce him to transfer the contents of his strong box into the prince's treasury, harsher measures, such as torture, are resorted to.

Mahomedans treat even the Brahmins in their service with the same severity. But, it must be admitted, the latter only experience the kind of treatment that they have so often inflicted on their fellows. No one can be harder, more cruel, or more pitiless towards the poor agriculturists than a Brahmin invested with authority, when he sees a chance of wringing money from them. Nevertheless there are many Hindus, and Brahmins particularly, who endure with unshaken firmness and courage the most horrible tortures inflicted on them, even when their lives are in danger, rather than give up their treasures. I have known Brahmins who have been thus persecuted for year after year and without success. They may be seen with their bodies so covered with bruises and wounds, that they appear to be but one large festering sore, a prey to all kinds of vermin; and in this sad plight all relief is denied them, even to the extent of refusing dressing for their wounds.

If the poor prisoner survives these cruel tortures, his tormentors, astonished at his fortitude, will set him at liberty, ashamed at last of their unsuccessful efforts at coercion. This faculty of bearing the most excruciating pain with calm endurance is very common among the Hindus. There are some, however, who are not thus gifted by nature, and who, after resisting as long as possible, at length submit and come to terms with their oppressors. These weaker members receive a present, perhaps, of a new turban or a piece of new cloth. Their persecutors express much regret at having been obliged to resort to such harsh measures, remarking at the same time that their victims might have spared themselves much pain and torment by acceding to their requests in the first instance. The victims are then restored to their former honours and employments. Filled with the desire to recoup themselves for their losses, they seize every opportunity for extortion, until they become rich once more and are forced to disgorge their plunder. But whatever crimes they may commit or whatever tortures they may endure, no disgrace is attached to either. The penalty of death itself leaves no stain on the memory of the man who has undergone this supreme punishment; and, as a natural consequence, no sort of disgrace is reflected on the family of the victim. A Brahmin would be degraded and banished from his caste for having eaten food which had been prepared, or drunk water that had been drawn, by a person of lower caste; but were he convicted of stealing, of uttering vile calumnies, of attempting to take another man's life, or of betraying his prince or country, none of these offences would prevent his appearing without fear or shame in public, or would hinder his being well received everywhere.

In civil as well as in criminal cases, when the evidence does not completely establish a fact, the Hindus often have recourse to ordeals to decide the point at issue. There are four ordeals generally recognized among Hindus, namely, by the scales, by fire, by water, and by poison [1].

It is not the magistrates only who order these trials by ordeal. Any one has the right to insist on such a trial. Thus, if a theft has been committed, the head of a household compels each member to undergo an ordeal. In the same way, the head of a village may force it upon all the inhabitants on whom criminal suspicion may rest; and a jealous husband may order the same in the case of his wife whose fidelity he doubts. These ordeals sometimes produce such an effect on the real culprits that they are convinced that discovery is inevitable, and think it more prudent to confess their guilt at once than to aggravate the matter by keeping silence. On the other hand, such ordeals often occasion deplorable miscarriages of justice, and result in the conviction of innocent persons, who, strong in the knowledge of their innocence, fondly believe that the natural course of things will be reversed in their favour [2].

[1] As trial by ordeal is one of the principal features in Hindu jurisprudence, I have given a more detailed account of it in Appendix VI.—DUBOIS.

[2] This method of deciding a case, degrading example as it is of the foolish beliefs of which the human mind is capable, was common enough amongst all ancient heathen nations. Indeed it was still in existence in most Christian countries till the thirteenth century. In the belief that it was impossible, even in the most barbarous ages, for the obvious abuses of this system to have escaped the eyes of the judges who were bound to uphold it, some people have suggested that, while the long ceremonious prayers and exorcisms which

A certain young woman who lived close to my house became the victim of her husband's jealous suspicions. To prove her innocence, he forced her to plunge her arm up to the elbow into a bath of boiling oil. The unhappy woman, sure of her inviolable virtue, did not hesitate to obey, and the result was that she was most frightfully scalded. The wound became inflamed and blistered, finally mortified, and caused the unhappy woman's death.

No doubt the disregard of the sanctity of an oath prevailing among the Hindus has, to a certain extent, necessitated the adoption of this system of trial by ordeal.

Certain it is that there is no nation in the world who think so lightly of an oath or of perjury. The Hindu will fearlessly call upon all his gods—celestial, terrestrial, and infernal—to witness his good faith in the least of his undertakings; but should fresh circumstances demand it, he would not have the smallest scruple in breaking the word that he had so solemnly pledged. Woe to the imprudent person who confides to Hindus any private matter that affects his fortune, his honour, or his life! If it served their purpose, they would divulge it without any hesitation.

The unscrupulous manner in which Hindus will perjure themselves is so notorious that they are never called upon to make a statement on oath in their own courts of justice, unless they are persons who bear an exceptionally high character[1].

preceded the ordeals were going on, the judges were able to determine the guilt or innocence of the accused by their demeanour, and that in the former case they left them to the ordeal, while in the latter they found means, either by the application of medicines or drugs or by some other trickery, to ensure their passing through the ordeal safe and sound. It appears moreover that Hindu judges used to protect by other means the accused who were to undergo any dangerous ordeal. Thus, for instance, in some provinces, if a stolen object was of small value, such as a gold ornament, the judges would order a vessel full of water to be brought, and each suspected person received a smaller vessel of soft clay, which he had to place in the larger vessel. These soft earthen vessels were easily dissolved in the water, and the lost property was generally found at the bottom. Thus the culprit escaped undiscovered, and there was no need for the ordeal to take place.—DUBOIS.

The detection of crime by ordeal is not entirely dead even now. But it is not, of course, recognized in the regular courts, and in fact is illegal. —ED.

[1] In *India: What can it teach us?* Professor Max Muller defends with no little skill the general credibility of the Hindus. He quotes, *inter alios*, Sir

But the jurisprudence of the Hindus, like the rest of their political institutions, has undergone a complete change since a great European Power has dominated the country. Regular courts of justice have been established at great expense in every district to protect the rights and settle the differences of persons of all classes, irrespective of rank, position, and caste. And this is, undoubtedly, one of the greatest benefits that a just and enlightened Government can bestow on any country. However much opinions may differ as to the usages of these courts, it seems to me that no one can deny that they have already been productive of immense benefit. Nowadays every member of society can rest assured that, sooner or later, the wrongs under which he suffers, either in his person or his property, will be redressed, and he can also rely unreservedly upon the impartiality of his judges, an advantage he was far from enjoying under the iron rule of his former despotic masters. At the same time, it must be admitted that the present judicial system has by no means realized all the objects for which it was established. Indeed, how could any one reasonably expect that such a huge measure of reform would be sealed with perfection from its very commencement? Every creation of the human brain can always be improved upon when the light of experience has shown up its defects and revealed the mistakes that have been committed. For example, the fact cannot be disguised that the slow and cautious method of procedure which is customary in a European court of law is by no means adapted to the majority of Hindus, who from their straitened circumstances and the nature of their occupations cannot afford such long and expensive modes of litigation. Is it likely that they would find it convenient to wait about at the place where justice is dispensed, it may be for many days, till their turn to be heard comes, leaving, as they must, in the mean time their families without any means of subsistence? From this point of view the new system is all to the advantage of the rich and influential and to the detriment of the poor, against whom the former can bring vexatious suits

John Malcolm, who asserted: 'I have hardly ever known, where a person did understand the language, or where a calm communication was made to a native of India through a well-informed and trustworthy medium, that the result did not prove that what had at first been stated as falsehood had either proceeded from fear or from misapprehension.'—ED.

with impunity. So great is the dread amongst the poorer Hindus of these lengthy processes, and of the prolonged absences from their homes which they entail, that when they are cited to appear as witnesses before these new tribunals, they will often spend large sums in bribing the official who brings the summons, if any means whatever can be found by which they can elude the hateful business. If brawls or quarrels arise in a village, the neighbours, far from interposing and trying to restore peace, retire promptly to their own houses, terribly afraid lest they may be called as witnesses in court, and thus waste much precious time which otherwise might be profitably employed in the fields or in the house.

The conclusion to be drawn from this seems to be that under the new system of judicial administration sufficient attention has not been paid to the peculiar character, disposition, and prejudices of the people for whose benefit it was devised. It was not sufficiently borne in mind that nowhere in the whole world is there another race of men so obstinate, so deceitful, and so litigious as the Hindus, partly from faults of training and partly from their deep-seated attachment to caste customs. What we should think trifles appear to them of the utmost importance, and are often the cause of lawsuits. I defy the most active, zealous, and intelligent judge, especially in view of the enormous tract of country over which he has to administer justice —I defy him, I repeat, to hear one-fifth of the grievances, either real or imaginary, which people are ready to pour into his ears. Three-fourths at least of the legal proceedings have to do with the most petty concerns, though they are far from being regarded as such by the complainants. They are usually about small debts, quarrels, slanders, trifling assaults without bloodshed, petty larceny, &c. The settlement of these small matters might very well be removed from the jurisdiction of the higher courts and placed in the hands of village *panchayats* or petty courts of arbitration, composed of the best materials available; or they might, in part at any rate, be left to the village headmen, whose judgements in either case would be expeditious and without appeal. It could certainly not be expected that these subordinate courts would fulfil their duties with very scrupulous integrity or strict impartiality; but the parties concerned would always have as compensation for the small injustices of which they might now and then be the victims the immense advantage of not losing their time or being put to an expense which more often than not is out of all proportion to the value of the matter in dispute.

Of the penalties sanctioned by the European courts of justice, imprisonment for debt, amongst others, strikes the Hindus as a ridiculous expedient, and it is one at which they often laugh. To be deprived of liberty without any additional coercion or torture appears to them no punishment at all. Any Hindu who has sufficient private means would be quite contented never to leave his house night or day; he would be in a state of indolent repose, chewing betel, smoking his pipe, eating, drinking, and sleeping without taking the least interest in what was going on in the world outside.

There are two classes of persons who are imprisoned for debt: *firstly*, those who are fraudulent debtors, who can pay, but refuse to do so, and whom torture alone would bring to their senses; and, *secondly*, those who are absolutely insolvent. The first of these two classes will go to prison with the utmost indifference, while the second are positively delighted to be sent there, because the aggrieved party is obliged to feed them while they are in prison. And what can be more pleasing to Hindus than to be maintained in idleness? It must be borne in mind that most Hindus, when they borrow money, do so with the lurking hope that circumstances will arise, or that they will think of some expedient, by which they will be able to elude repayment. Thus strong measures have to be resorted to as the only means by which payment can be exacted from such very unscrupulous debtors. When the time for payment comes and the creditor demands his money, the debtor declares he has none and begs for further grace, swearing by all his gods that he will pay everything, capital and interest, at the time stipulated. More time is granted, once and even twice, and each time the debtor's fine promises end in smoke. At last the creditor becomes tired of these interminable delays, grows angry, and arrests the debtor in the name either of the ruler of the country or of the governor of the province[1]. The creditor

[1] This method of arrest is very common. 'I arrest you,' one Hindu will say to another, 'in the name of the King or the East India Company, or in the name of the Collector of the district,' &c. The person to whom the

forbids his debtor to eat or drink without his permission, and at the same time he himself is bound to fast. If this method does not succeed, the creditor places a huge stone on the debtor's head and a similar one on his own, and thus burdened they remain motionless opposite each other, exposed to the heat of the sun; or they walk till one of them faints from exhaustion; or they both stand on one foot like cranes; or sometimes the creditor seizes the debtor's cattle and shuts them up, forbidding any one to feed them until payment has been made in full. At last the debtor is so worried that he is unable to bear it any longer; he comes to terms, pays a large sum on account, and gives good security for the remainder. Creditor and debtor then part on the best of terms. Very often the creditor is so hard pushed himself that he is obliged to relinquish a part of what is due to him in order to get back some of his money.

Is it likely, I may ask, that men who carry obstinacy and tenacity to such lengths would be alarmed at the prospect of enjoying a few idle weeks in prison?

The only object of a prison, according to the Hindus, is to prevent the accused or the criminal running away. No disgrace is attached to imprisonment, and consequently it is no punishment at all. In fact mere imprisonment is not looked upon as a punishment even by magistrates in native provinces. Every one condemned to prison has to undergo more or less severe torture according to the gravity of his offence. If it is but a trifling misdemeanour, the delinquent is beaten and then set at liberty.

All intelligent Hindus are agreed that the penal laws introduced by Europeans into their country err considerably on the side of leniency. They consider them quite inadequate to protect society against evil-doers. To keep peace and order amongst a nation constituted like the Hindus, they say, much harsher measures must be resorted to.

Even capital punishment appears to produce no impression whatever on these apathetic people. The sight of an execution,

summons is addressed is obliged to obey it, to leave his business, and to place himself at the disposal of his adversary. If he attempted to escape, he would render himself liable to be punished for contempt of the law.—DUBOIS.

No such private arrests are now permitted by law.—ED.

far from moving the spectators to feelings of pity or compassion, is only looked upon as an amusement; and they are even much diverted by the convulsive contortions of the poor wretch who is hanging on the gallows. Perhaps the utter want of feeling shown by the crowd under these circumstances was one of the reasons why native princes so rarely resorted to capital punishment. Probably they reflected that punishments were inflicted quite as much for the sake of their deterrent effect on others as for the chastisement of the guilty. Mutilation appeared to them to be a much more efficacious way of repressing vice. Criminals deprived of nose, ears, or right hand, dragging out their miserable existence before the eyes of all men, were living and lasting witnesses of the severity of the law, and their woeful appearance served as a daily example to others. See, they seemed to say to every passer-by, what a sad fate awaits those who break the laws!

The death penalty, on the other hand, barely excites a passing terror, and I very much doubt whether the fear of it ever restrained any Hindu who was bent on committing a crime.

CHAPTER IX

The Military System of the Hindus.—Ancient and Modern Methods of Warfare.—The Material formerly composing their Armies.—The Military Game of Chess invented by the Hindus.—*Pohgars.*—Different Weapons that have been in Use at various Times in India.

HERE my self-imposed task should have been brought to a close, for it is hardly to be expected that I can treat the subject-matter of this chapter satisfactorily, seeing how foreign it is to my profession. However, as nearly all the public monuments of India, both civil and religious, commemorate some war, and as all the Hindu books are filled with descriptions of feats of arms and accounts of battles, I thought that a few details on this subject would not be entirely out of place in such a work as the present.

The Kshatriyas, or kings, and their descendants the Rajputs formerly held undisputed sway in India, and they alone had a right to follow the military profession. All this, however, has nowadays undergone a complete change, ambition having found a way through this hard and fast rule. At the present time there are very few native rulers who belong to the old warrior caste. In this case, as in many others, the strongest have seized the reins of government. Indeed, in many provinces one may find princes of very low origin, who by their courage, their talents, or their intrigues have raised themselves to their high position. In the same way the profession of arms has now been thrown open to men of all castes, from the Brahmin to the Pariah. On the one hand one may see a Brahmin who has attained the rank of commander-in-chief of an army, while on the other hand, especially in the Mahratta armies, you may see them serving as common troopers.

Though the habits of the Hindus appear more likely to impair their courage than to make them good soldiers, the art of war nevertheless seems to have been as well understood by them from very early times as any other, and those who followed the military profession have always been held in high esteem. In fact, military officers took rank in the social scale immediately after the priesthood. The Brahmins themselves, actuated by motives either of gratitude or of self-interest, allowed them to participate in some of their own high prerogatives, such as the valued privileges of being allowed to hear the Vedas read and of wearing the triple cord. But however much the Hindus may have honoured the profession of arms, and however full their national histories may be of wars, conquests, sieges, battles, victories, and defeats, it is nevertheless remarkable that no nation has shown at every epoch in its history so little skill in military science. When pitiless conquerors, at the head of savage and warlike hordes, forced their way over the northern mountains and spread themselves like a devastating torrent over the fertile provinces of India, the peaceable and docile inhabitants were unable to offer any effectual resistance. They saw their towns and villages ravaged by fire and sword, while rivers of blood, ingloriously and fruitlessly spilt, deluged their fields. The readiness with which they bent their necks beneath their oppressors' yoke, and the feebleness of the efforts which they put forth to recover their independence, proved how inferior they were in courage and discipline to the proud Tartars who invaded and conquered them.

The wars of India may be classified under three heads: those of the mythical ages, those of the ancient kings, and those of modern times. By the last I mean only the internecine wars between native princes before the time when these princes, convinced of the superiority of European military science, determined to introduce foreigners amongst their troops, and to this end enlisted in their service those European adventurers who offered to help them in their undertakings. It was an imprudent policy, and the native princes did not see until too late the danger of surrounding themselves with such intriguing and ambitious auxiliaries.

I will say nothing about the wars of the gods and the giants, which the majority of Hindu books describe with equal bombast and prolixity. Such exaggerated flights of imagination can hardly be considered worthy of a place in serious history. It is always the same story of armies of giants whose heads touched the stars, and who were mounted on elephants of proportionate size. One of these giants, for example, is depicted as upheaving the very firmament with his shoulders, giving it such a violent shock as to overthrow all the gods who dwelt therein, and thereby warning them of what they might expect from an adversary of such prowess. On the other hand, a god who is about to engage these formidable enemies takes the earth for his chariot, a rainbow for his bow, and Vishnu for an arrow. He shoots this extraordinary missile, and with one shot overthrows an immense city, in which all the villains that he is pursuing are entrenched, burying them all in the fallen ruins of the city.

Ab uno disce omnes. I do not think that the history of the wars of the ancient kings of India is one whit less absurd. It is only the poets who have undertaken the task of transmitting details to posterity, and as Hindu poets are not wont to do things by halves, they have freely availed themselves of the privilege of exaggeration and embellishment. Facts are so interwoven with foolish and senseless efforts of the imagination that it is impossible to disentangle the truth. Why should one feel astonished at Xerxes being able to gather together and maintain a million soldiers when he set forth to conquer Greece? Such an army would have formed only a small detachment of one of the armies of the kings of India. These latter never took the field at the head of less than several hundreds of millions of fighting men! If the reader will recollect what I have remarked several times, namely, that only that which is extraordinary and extravagant has the power of pleasing the Hindu, he will hardly be astonished at the strange mania which has induced Hindu authors to carry exaggeration even to puerility. In every country writers adapt their work to the taste of the public, being anxious to gain from them the greatest possible approbation. The maxim

> 'Rien n'est beau que le vrai, le vrai seul est aimable,

would be rank heresy in good Hindu literature.

The one fact that I have been able to glean for certain is that the armies of the ancient Hindu kings were divided into four arms or sections, of which the whole formed a *chatur-angam.* These four corps were the elephants, the chariots, the cavalry, and the infantry. Such, indeed, were the component parts of the army of Porus, who was vanquished and taken prisoner on the banks of the Hydaspes by Alexander.

No one at the present day denies the fact that the Hindus invented the military game of chess[1].

It is very evident that it was the composition and tactics of the ancient Hindu armies that originally suggested the game. The Hindus, in fact, called it *chatur-angam.* Though with some few small variations we have adopted their method of playing, it must be admitted that the innovations which we have introduced in the shapes and names of the pieces are certainly not happy. What can be more ridiculous than the castles which move about from place to place, the queen who rushes about fighting with the king's people, or the bishops who occupy such an exalted position?

As with us, the most important piece on the Hindu chess-

[1] The following is the story, according to Oriental writers, of how this game was invented. At the beginning of the fifth century of the Christian era a very powerful young monarch was reigning in India, who was of excellent character, but who allowed himself to be corrupted by flatterers. This prince soon forgot that the love of the people is the only sure support of a throne. The Brahmins and Rajahs uttered many remonstrances, but in vain. Intoxicated by his greatness, which he fancied was unassailable, he despised their counsels. Accordingly a Brahmin named Sissa undertook to open the young monarch's eyes by strategy. To this end he invented the game of chess, in which the king, though the most important of all the pieces, can nevertheless neither attack nor defend himself without the assistance of his subjects. This game speedily became famous, and the king expressed his anxiety to learn it. Sissa while teaching him the rules, made him realize some important truths which up to that time he had failed to grasp, and the monarch wishing to show his gratitude to the Brahmin asked him what he would like as a reward. Sissa replied that he would be satisfied with as much rice as could be placed on the sixty-four squares of the chess-board by putting one grain on the first, two on the second, four on the third, and so on, the number on each square always doubling. The king cheerfully agreed to such an apparently modest demand. But the treasurers soon convinced their master that he had pledged himself to an act of munificence which, in spite of all his treasure and vast estates, he would be quite unable to fulfil. Sissa at once seized the opportunity of pointing out to the monarch how easy it was to abuse the best intentions of a sovereign if he were not perpetually on his guard against those who surrounded him.—DUBOIS.

board is the king[1]. The second piece, which we call the queen[2], they term the *mantri*, a title which signifies a minister of state, who is also commander-in-chief of the army. Chariots[3] occupy the place of our bishops. Like us, the Hindus have knights, but instead of our battlemented castles they have elephants[4]. The pawns or foot-soldiers are, as with us, the simple rank and file of which the army is composed. The chess-board is called by the Hindus the *por-sthalam*, or field of battle.

But to return to the ancient Hindu armies. In the first line came the elephants. It is certain that these animals carried castles or howdahs on their backs, containing several men armed with javelins. But I think it would be wrong to suppose that these castles or howdahs were of any great size, as might be imagined from certain illustrations. Like those which may still be found in the present day amongst the armies of some Eastern princes, these towers or howdahs resembled large boxes without lids, as long and as broad as a large bed, placed crosswise on the back of the elephant, and capable of holding six or seven archers when sitting in Oriental fashion. Though an elephant is very strong, so as to be able to carry two small cannons and their carriages, there is nevertheless a limit to its powers; and naturally a much larger erection, with a still larger number of men in it, would be a burden under which even an elephant would succumb. And there is yet another point, namely, the difficulty of fixing a lofty structure with any degree of security on an elephant's back, a difficulty which would be rendered practically insurmountable by the brusque movements and rolling gait of the animal. Be this as it may, elephants in days gone by were formidable adversaries amongst these half-disciplined nations. They broke the ranks, frightened the horses, trampled the soldiers underfoot; and at the same time it was very difficult to wound them, on account of their hard and horny epidermis. These powerful creatures are still employed in the armies

[1] The Arab and Persian name for chess is 'the king's game.'—DUBOIS.

[2] In Low Latin this piece was called *fercia*, from the Persian *fers*, which means *minister of state, visir*.—DUBOIS.

[3] In many Eastern countries these are elephants.—DUBOIS.

[4] Amongst other Asiatic nations these are camels ridden by a man with a bow and arrow in his hand.—DUBOIS.

of native princes, but rather from ostentation than from any warlike purpose that they serve. A native general or senior officer considers an elephant to be the only mount befitting his dignity; the animal being usually covered with magnificent trappings. It is only with great difficulty that elephants can be made to stand fire, though every method is employed to familiarize them with it. Without these precautions the rattle of firearms and the squibs that are hurled at them would excite them to frenzy, and would consequently cause the death of their riders.

They were also used for battering the gates of besieged towns; and it was with a view to counteracting this that most of the gates were thickly studded on the outside with long and stout iron spikes.

In the Mogul armies, before the introduction of European tactics, an elephant always marched in the van, bearing on its head a long pole, from which floated a large flag. Sometimes this was followed by another elephant carrying a rich howdah, on which was placed a box containing a priceless relic, which usually was, if one may believe it, an actual hair from Mahomet's beard.

The chief service which these animals render nowadays is in the transport of artillery and equipage. When a swamp, a ditch, a canal, or any other obstacle arrests the progress of the bullocks that drag the cannon, one or more elephants are brought up to push the gun-carriage with their heads and trunks and thus help them over the difficulty. When rivers which are not fordable have to be crossed, elephants are often used to carry men and heavy baggage over on their backs. But the services of these animals are dearly bought, considering the vast expense which their food and keep entail. Thus they are falling more and more into disuse. Every day the camel is growing in favour as being more patient and tractable.

Chariots formed the second division of the ancient Hindu armies. If one may believe what early Hindu writers say, these chariots were used in considerable numbers and were of considerable size. That of the king was the most magnificent. The rest belonged to his subordinate chiefs. When two hostile armies met, the leaders on each side were in the habit of interchanging compliments with each other before joining battle. One, for instance, would drop an arrow just short of his adversary's chariot, and the other would return the salute. Splendid horses were harnessed to these war-chariots. One reads in the *Bhagavata* that one of the old kings of India, when setting out on a campaign, harnessed a troop of demons to his chariot, to ensure the pace being good. The chariots were usually ornamented all round with large bells, which made a great noise, and this custom is still occasionally observed at the present time in the case of private carriages. The latter, however, in no way resemble the ancient war-chariots, about which I have not been able to collect any trustworthy information.

The cavalry formed the third division. Indian generals in ancient times, however, did not rely much on this arm. The infantry played the principal part in their wars, which is contrary to the practice of more modern times, for until quite recently no use whatever was made of infantry, only a few undisciplined regiments of followers being maintained to pillage, ravage, and destroy all the villages in their way, and to devastate the enemy's country. This idea they had evidently borrowed from the Tartars, who had invaded their country, and whose superiority in arms they had been forced to acknowledge to their cost.

The Moguls and Mahrattas, the two rival powers who for a long while disputed the supremacy of India, placed on some occasions as many as 100,000 horse in the field. The Mahratta princes combined could have commanded as many as 300,000 horse. But they never knew how to utilize this unwieldy multitude to its full advantage, because they did not understand how to manœuvre it in a scientific manner. The lessons which the European invaders gave them time after time, for more than 300 years, seem hardly to have taught them to appreciate their mistakes. Even at the end of this long period, and when it was too late to mend matters, there was a vast inferiority in their tactics compared with those of their dreaded opponents. They never could be brought to understand the value of strict discipline, good tactical handling, orderly arrangements in marching and camping, and, in short, all the skilled dispositions by which it is possible to manœuvre large bodies of troops without confusion. They thought their work was done when they had collected a miscellaneous horde of men, who marched to battle in a disorderly mass and fell upon the enemy without any method or concerted plan.

Indian armies always contain a large number of chiefs who command as many troopers as they are able to raise at their own expense. Each recruit brings his own horse, which remains his private property. He receives a fixed sum for himself and for the keep of his horse. If he happens to lose his horse, he is dismissed as useless. This plan certainly puts the State to little expense, but it renders the cavalry as a body less effective, for at close quarters the rider's first care is for his horse, which belongs to himself; nay, often, when he sees that there is much danger, he will take to flight at the first order to charge. Desertion indeed is very common in the armies of Indian princes. As a rule, little trouble is taken to catch deserters; nor are they severely punished when caught. In order to ensure fidelity amongst their troops the chiefs are in the habit of keeping their pay in arrear; and this prevents a large number of mercenaries from deserting, as they fear to lose what is due to them. Nevertheless, whole armies have been known to throw down their arms in face of the enemy and refuse to take them up again until they had received their pay. It is by no means a rare occurrence for large bodies of troops to refuse to set out on a march for a similar reason. Mutinous soldiers, too, frequently put their generals under arrest, send them to prison, menace them sword in hand, or try to intimidate them by loud threats and insults. The generals, strange to say, will calmly and patiently put up with these mutinous outbursts. Usually they will pay the mutineers a part of their arrears and promise the rest in a short time. Quiet is then restored, and the men return to duty until another such occasion presents itself.

Although these undisciplined mercenaries make very inferior troops, still there are instances on record of honourable and brave conduct among their chiefs, especially among Mahomedan chiefs of high rank. The latter never cry for quarter; and, even when the day is going against them, they will not retreat a step as long as they have the support of a few of their followers. Flight or retreat under such circumstances is considered by them even more ignominious than it is by their European opponents.

The ordinary cavalry troopers, be they Mahomedan or Mahratta, are usually very badly mounted, and their equipments are still worse. Nevertheless, their weedy-looking chargers are so inured to fatigue and so accustomed to privation that they will make, with only a little coarse hay for food, a succession of forced marches which would be quite beyond the capabilities of our best European cavalry, covering as they sometimes do as much as sixty miles a day. Mounted on these wretched animals, detachments of troops are able to cover great distances, and to sweep down suddenly on districts from which they were supposed to be far away. It must not be supposed that there are not very good horses to be found, especially in the Southern provinces of India; but they are only to be bought for very high prices that are quite beyond the means of ordinary persons. Only the chiefs possess really fine horses. They take remarkably good care of them. They usually decorate them in various ways, and often paint their bodies in different colours. They train them in an extremely clever manner, and ride them most gracefully. Many indeed would be able to carry off prizes in our European riding-schools. The Mahrattas, for instance, accustom their horses to stop at a given signal. The rider dismounts and goes away, leaving his steed loose Sometimes for hours together the animal will remain as still as a milestone until his master returns. A horse-stealer who one day came across a solitary steed, which had thus been left without any one to look after it, mounted it and galloped off. The owner of the horse, seeing from a distance what had happened, thereupon gave the call by which he always stopped the animal. At the sound of its master's voice the horse perceived its mistake and stood stock still. In spite of every effort on the part of the thief it refused to budge; whereupon the latter thought it more prudent to take to flight on his own two legs.

The troopers, Mahomedan and Mahratta, are armed with lances, javelins, and *katharis,* or daggers. Some few have blunderbusses in addition, while others have indifferent sabres. A few may be seen armed with nothing but the whip or switch which they use in urging on their horses. Each man, in short, is expected to arm himself at his own expense, and consequently a remarkable variety may be noticed in the equipments of a troop of native cavalry.

They march in the most irregular fashion, and have no idea of regular military movements. Indeed, any such knowledge would be of little or no use to them, for they very rarely take part in a pitched battle. All their campaigns are reduced to mere skirmishes and constant surprises on one side or the other, in which very little blood is shed. The chief operations of native armies are confined to ravaging the country that they happen to be passing through, without distinction of friend or foe, and pillaging without mercy all the defenceless inhabitants, who are put to inconceivable tortures in the attempt to force them to disgorge imaginary treasure that they never possess.

The infantry is, if possible, in even a worse plight; or at any rate it was up to the time when native princes were induced to admit European adventurers into their service, to reorganize and drill their armies.

The ancient kings of India placed most reliance on their infantry. It formed the fourth division of their armies, and was numerically larger than the other three. It formed, in fact, the main strength of the combined forces. At the present day, too, it constitutes the principal, and indeed almost the only, force of the smaller native princes who are known by the name of *Poligars*[1]. These *Poligars* rarely have any cavalry, the smallness of their revenues and the character of the country they inhabit rendering it almost impossible to maintain them.

The *Poligars* in many respects resemble the European barons of the Middle Ages, who from their strongholds ventured boldly to defy the royal authority. They are fairly numerous in the various districts of the Peninsula, and they were much more numerous before the great European Power extended its dominion over the territories in which they were established and subdued the greater number of them. These petty despots waged almost incessant war against each other. Safely ensconced in deep jungles or on inaccessible mountain-tops, they were able to defy the princes whose territories surrounded them; and the latter, unable to suppress these turbulent vassals for fear that they would pillage and devastate their own states, tried to live amicably with them.

These *Poligars* or self-styled princes made war according to

[1] These inhabit the southern districts of the Peninsula.—ED.

methods of their own. The use of cannon was unknown to them; their only arms being arrows, pikes, and flint-locks. They never risked a pitched battle. When attacked by a superior force they took refuge in their jungles or on their mountains. Their object would be to surprise the advancing enemy in some defile. Lying in ambush behind trees or thick brushwood, they would pour well-directed volleys upon their opponents, forcing them to retire in disorder with considerable loss. It was in the midst of their jungles or on the tops of their mountains that the English, after much labour and the loss of many men, managed to lay hands upon these brigand chiefs and their lawless followers. Only by these means were the new-comers able to restore peace and tranquillity in provinces which had previously been the scene of perpetual outrages.

The art of laying out camps is as little known to Indian generals as that of marching an army. The greatest confusion always reigns both in their encampments and on the march. When an army makes a halt, the most important point, of course, is to see that there is a good supply of water close at hand. This is not always to be found where it is wanted, especially at certain times of the year, and whole armies have been reduced to the direst straits by being temporarily deprived of this indispensable element, the want of which is much more keenly felt in a tropical climate than elsewhere.

An officer usually goes on ahead, selects a suitable site for the camp, and there sets up a large flag, which is visible from a long distance. Each division then encamps in any sort of order beyond this landmark. Each chief pitches his tent in the midst of his own followers, and hoists his distinctive banner. Confusion and disorder prevail everywhere. Things are, however, a little more orderly around the commander-in-chief's tent. Fairly good discipline is also maintained in the spot set apart as a market-place. Here provisions and commodities of various kinds, pillaged from the country through which the army has passed, are exposed for sale; for the progress of an Indian army is always attended by fire, sword, and robbery. In fact, it is considered unnecessary and troublesome to establish regular depôts for provisions, or in fact to make commissariat arrangements of any kind. It was only when an army was obliged to pass through a country which had already been devastated that these precautions were considered necessary. Strings of bullocks were then employed with the army to carry its provisions. At all other times the chiefs relied for their commissariat on a crowd of purveyors attracted by the hope of gain, and especially on the *Lambadis*, or *Sukalers*, professional pillagers, whom I have already described, and who kept the camp market well supplied by their continual raids on the unfortunate inhabitants of the surrounding country.

The most abominable debauchery is openly authorized among the soldiery, especially in Mahomedan armies. A special quarter in the camp is set apart for the vile and depraved wretches who give themselves up to this hideous form of prostitution.

Charlatans of all kinds swarm in these disorderly camps. There are conjurers, soothsayers, astrologers, tight-rope dancers, acrobats, quacks, pickpockets, fakirs, religious mendicants, blind men; and furthermore, each soldier is generally followed by his whole family. Thus you may often see an army of from twenty-five to thirty thousand soldiers with three hundred thousand followers of all sorts and conditions in its train, who, profiting by the confusion which reigns in the camp, devote their whole time to robbery with impunity. The Mahratta armies are less troubled with these encumbrances, for they often make forced marches, and it would be impossible for the followers to keep up with them.

The generals' tents, especially in the case of Mahomedans, are very large and commodious. Oriental taste and luxury are conspicuous in them. They are richly adorned, and provided with every kind of comfort. They are divided into several compartments, some of which are destined for the wives or concubines of these pleasure-loving commanders, who are almost invariably accompanied by their women. Even in the midst of a tumultuous camp, Indian princes and generals never neglect anything that can pander to their sensuality.

One may well believe that it is easy to surprise a camp composed of such a rabble. There are rarely any outposts. The spies who are maintained in the hostile camp partly supply this deficiency; for, as soon as they perceive anything unusual going on, they hurry off to warn their employers, who are thus prepared to receive the enemy. The latter usually retire as soon as they perceive that their opponents are on the alert.

Moreover, surprises and night marches are not at all to the taste of Indian warriors, who do not like to be deprived of their sleep. Thus it has sometimes happened that a mere handful of Europeans has thrown into disorder and routed a whole army by unexpected attacks of this nature.

Nevertheless, however inferior the people of India may be in discipline and courage, they have one great advantage over Europeans, which, had they only known how to make use of it, would certainly have rendered the struggle between them and their formidable adversaries much less unequal. I mean their extreme temperance in eating and drinking. Give an Indian soldier three or four pounds of rice per week with a little salt, and on that, with the addition of a little water, he will keep himself in good health, be active, cheerful, and in condition to undertake forced marches for several days consecutively, without suffering any inconvenience. What a fund of latent force the Indian armies possessed in this useful faculty for the purpose of harassing and annoying an enemy whom they were afraid to meet in pitched battles, but who, infinitely less abstemious, would soon have become disheartened without a plentiful supply of substantial food!

The art of fortifying, besieging, and defending strongholds was equally neglected in India. The method generally followed was to invest a town and trust to famine to force the besieged to capitulate. To take a place by assault appeared far too dangerous a proceeding to Indian tacticians; consequently it frequently happened that a wretched little fortified town, surrounded by nothing but mud walls and defended by a few hundred peasants armed with a few worn-out matchlocks, was able to hold out for months against the attacks of a host of assailants, who, tired out at last by the perseverance of their adversaries, were obliged to ignominiously raise the siege. Even in recent times, though they might have learnt by sad experience to what horrors a town taken by assault is exposed, several Indian generals have been known to shut themselves up behind walls of mere mud or earth, and obstinately refuse to listen to any suggestion of capitulation, treating the European besiegers with insolent bravado, and fearlessly awaiting the chances of an assault.

It is true, however, that the honour of the commandant of

any fortress is at stake on such occasions. However advantageous the conditions offered to him might be, he would never willingly capitulate; for should he be weak enough to do so, he would find it difficult to escape the suspicion, on the part of his king and of the people, that he had acted with treachery or cowardice, and consequently his good name would be for ever tarnished.

Nevertheless, the art of approaching a fortified position by mines and entrenchments has long been known to Indian generals. When such works have been carried as close to the main fortress as possible, the besieged and the besiegers delight in insulting and challenging each other by word of mouth. For instance, the Hindus will say to the Mahomedans: 'If you do not now take the place, it will be as great a slur on your good name as if you had eaten pork.' And the besiegers will answer: 'If we take the place, it will be as great a disgrace to you as if you had eaten cow's flesh.' Another proof that bluster is no indication of courage.

A device upon which Indians place great reliance under such circumstances is enchantment. The magicians of either party are called upon to exercise all the resources of their black art. But unfortunately the sorcerers of the besiegers are nearly always as clever as the sorcerers of the besieged. One charm is consequently nullified by a countercharm, and it comes to the same thing in the end, namely, which side is able to display the greater amount of courage and skill. Whatever the result may be, however, the magicians always enjoy a large share of the glory of success or bear the greater part of the shame of defeat. These absurd illusions were still in vogue when I left India.

The fortifications of the most important strongholds, even up to recent times, consisted of one or two very thick walls with round or triangular towers at the angles, on which were placed a few guns very badly served. The fort was surrounded by a broad and deep moat, but as the natives of India did not understand the use of the drawbridge, the ditch was spanned by a road leading to the main entrance, which was hidden by a curtain wall to prevent its being visible from a distance.

In several places in the Peninsula strongholds may be seen which owe little of their strength to the skill of the engineer, being situated on the top of steep and almost inaccessible hills. These fortresses are called *durgams*. Alexander besieged a fortress of this kind on the banks of the Indus, and found great difficulty in capturing it[1]. But there is one great drawback to these *durgams*. The air is always cold and damp, even when extreme heat prevails in the plains below, and this renders them most unhealthy to live in, the men who garrison them being subject to long spells of fever which are difficult to cure.

The people of India have lately learnt from Europeans the warlike art of exterminating the human species in a more scientific and practical manner. They have introduced great changes in their methods of attack and defence, and, in fact, in the whole of their military system. A sad and fatal gift, which they may perhaps one day use against those who brought it to them!

Before finishing this subject I will add a few words on the different kinds of weapons that have been used in India at different times. I have already mentioned that there are thirty-two different kinds of old-fashioned weapons, each of which has a name and shape peculiar to itself. Models of these are to be found in the hands of the principal idols. Each deity is provided with the one that he most affected. As my readers would find no counterpart to them in a European armoury, it would be difficult to describe them without illustrations. All that I can say about them is that besides many instruments for cutting, there were others for hacking, stabbing, and felling.

Among Indian arms of more modern times the most important defensive ones are the helmet and the shield. The latter is made of leather, and ornamented in the centre with large bosses. Most Indian soldiers can use it very skilfully. Some wear a thick-quilted corselet as a cuirass or breast-plate, which, it is said, is impervious both to sword and arrow[2]. But as this breast-plate affords no protection against a bullet and is undeniably most uncomfortable to wear in a hot climate, its use has been almost entirely abandoned. Among the offensive weapons of India are bows and arrows. The bow measures only about two feet and a half when strung, and each arrow is nearly two

[1] See Quintus Curtius, viii. 11.—DUBOIS.

[2] The Greeks, and Romans, and many other nations of old used this sort of cuirass, but they also wore metal ones of different shapes.—DUBOIS.

feet long. These are but poor specimens of the weapons which history credits the Hindu gods with using. The bow used by Rama, for instance, was so enormous that the fifty thousand men who were employed to bring it to him succumbed beneath the burden. Vishnu's favourite weapon was the *chakram*, and many of his devotees have it branded on their shoulders with a red-hot iron. It is still used in some parts, and consists of a metal disk about nine or ten inches in diameter, with well-sharpened edges. There is a hole in the centre, and through this is passed a stick by means of which a rapid rotatory motion is given to the disk, which flies off and inflicts a severe cut on any one that it strikes.

Large grenades or squibs are also frequently used, eight or ten inches long, and armed at one end with a keen-edged crescent-shaped blade. These are fired off horizontally, and are used to produce confusion amongst bodies of cavalry. They are less effective than our hand grenades, but carry very much further. According to Hindu authors, these grenades, called *vanams*, were used in very early times. The *Ramayana* speaks of Rama's *vanam* as one of his most important weapons. It is therefore to be inferred that gunpowder was known in India in very early times. It is quite certain that the Hindus possessed the secret of compounding explosive substances long before the invasions of Tartars or Europeans. Still they can hardly have been aware of the terrible effect which these inflammable materials can produce when enclosed in a metal tube: it was reserved for those who conquered this peaceable nation to teach them the power of this agent of destruction.

The Hindus still use the pike, the dagger, and the sword. The last is at present their favourite weapon, and they have fencing-masters who can teach them to use it with great skill.

The gun is also much used by them, although in their hands it is not a very deadly weapon. Until quite recently they only used matchlocks, and their gunpowder was extremely bad, as indeed it is even at the present time. Amongst Hindu soldiers musketry practice is unknown, as their princes consider that it is a useless expense to employ powder for this purpose.

Europeans have recently introduced bronze and cast-iron cannon. In former times Indian cannon were made of iron, and were of enormous calibre. From these wretched guns they fired stone balls more than a foot in diameter. They took no trouble whatever to learn how to aim. I have read in a manuscript written nearly eighty years ago that the Rajah of Tanjore, having declared war against the Dutch, sent an army to besiege their fortress at Negapatam. When it drew near, the Dutch fired an ill-directed salvo from the top of the ramparts. The Rajah's troops, observing that the balls passed well over their heads, thought that they had nothing more to fear from the enemy's artillery, and labouring under this delusion, they boldly approached the glacis. Just at that moment the garrison fired a few well-aimed volleys of grape-shot which annihilated the rash assailants, who learnt to their cost that a cannon can be aimed both above and below its true level. The author adds that the palanquin of a Brahmin who held a high command in the Rajah's army, and who had approached a little too close to the fortress, was struck by a cannon ball and shattered to pieces. The Brahmin got off scot-free with only a fright; but his alarm was so great that he ran off as fast as he could, and, when he found himself in a place of safety, swore by his three hundred and thirty million gods that never again would he venture within ten miles of any place inhabited by those dogs of Feringhis.

APPENDIX I

The Jains.—Differences between them and the Brahmins [1].

THE word Jain, or Jaina, is a compound word denoting a person who has given up living or thinking like other men *. A true Jain should entirely renounce all thoughts of self. He should rise superior to the scorn or opposition to which he may be subjected on account

[1] Jainism is a heretical offshoot of Buddhism, and presents resemblances to both Brahminism and Buddhism, which have been summarized as follows in Elphinstone's *History of India*: 'They agree with the Buddhas in denying the existence, or at least the activity and providence, of God; in believing in the eternity of matter; in the worship of deified saints; in their scrupulous care of animal life and all the precautions which it leads to; in disclaiming the divine authority of the Vedas; and in having no sacrifices and no respect for fire. They agree with the Buddhists also in considering a state of impassive abstraction as supreme felicity, and in all the doctrines which they hold in common with the Hindus. They agree with the Hindus in other points, such as division of caste. This exists in full force in the south and west of India, and can only be said to be dormant in the north-east, for, though the Jains there do not acknowledge the four classes of the Hindus, yet a Jain converted to the Hindu religion takes his place in one of the castes from which he must all along have retained the proofs of his descent, and the Jains themselves have numerous divisions of their own, the members of which are as strict in avoiding intermarriages and other intercourse as the four classes of the Hindus. Though they reject the scriptural character of the Vedas, they allow them great authority in all matters not at variance with their religion. The principal objections to them are drawn from the bloody sacrifices which they enjoin, and the loss of animal life which burnt-offerings are liable (though undesignedly) to occasion. They admit the whole of the Hindu gods, and worship some of them, though they consider them as entirely subordinate to their own saints, who are, therefore, the proper objects of adoration.'

The following is from Mr. J. A. Baines's Census Report for 1891:—

'A second offshoot from the earlier Brahminism is found in the Jain, a

* This is not the true etymology. Jina is 'one who has overcome human infirmities and passions'; and *Jaina*, appertaining to *Jina*.—POPE.

of his religion, the principles of which he must preserve and guard unaltered even to death, being fully persuaded that it is the one and only true religion on earth, that is, the true primitive religion which was given to all mankind.

In the course of time, the Jains say, the primitive religion gradually became considerably corrupted in several essential points, and was superseded by the superstitious and detestable sophistries of Brahminism. The ancient dogmas were forgotten or put aside by the Brahmins, who invented an entirely new system of religion, in which only a shadowy resemblance can be traced to the old Hindu faith.

It is the Brahmins who invented the four Vedas and the eighteen Puranas, the *Trimurti*, and the monstrous fables connected with it, such as the *Avatars* of Vishnu, the abominable *lingam*, the worship of the cow and other animals, the sacrifice of the *yagnam*, &c., &c. The Jains not only reject all these spurious additions, but look upon them with absolute horror.

The Brahmins introduced all these sacrilegious innovations very gradually. The Jains were formerly in close communion with the

form of belief that still subsists and flourishes in India to this day. Its origin is veiled from us, but it bears a strong family likeness to the earlier form of Buddhism, and it is a question amongst scholars whether it rose about the same time or a little earlier. At all events it seems to have been unpopular with the Buddhists, and to have diverged less from Brahmanic orthodoxy. The monastic system was not countenanced, but ritual was simplified and women were allowed to share in it. As in Buddhism, however, the larger section of the Jains decline to allow that women can attain *Nirvana*. The latter, however, is with them perpetual bliss, instead of complete annihilation. Caste amongst the Jains is maintained, and though they have no special reservation of the priesthood to a class, there is a general tendency in that direction, and in some cases Brahmins even are employed. In later years the Jai s seem to have competed with the Brahmins in literature and science, so that they fell into disfavour, and would very probably have succumbed but for the advent of the Mussulman power. In the north and west of India they are still a cultivated class, most engaged in commerce, whilst in the south, where they share with the Buddhists, who preceded them, the credit of forming the Canarese and Tamil literature, they are as a rule agriculturists. Except in a few of the larger cities of the north there seems to be little sectarian hostility between them and the orthodox; and in the west, where they are still closer in customs and observances, the line of division is scarcely traceable. In parts of both tracts there is, in the present day, a tendency for Jainism to regard itself as a sect of Brahminism, in spite of the non-recognition of the divine authority of the Veda. It is probable that in compliance with this tendency many have returned their religion as Hindu of the Jain sect, so that where sect is not separately compiled, as in the imperial series of returns, the total of the Jain religion is reduced by that number. As it is, the number of Jains is given as about 1,417,000.'

Brahmins both in faith and doctrine, but they opposed these changes from the very first with all their power. Then, seeing that their remonstrances produced no effect and that these religious innovations were daily making progress among the people, they found themselves reduced at last to the sad necessity of an open rupture with the Brahmins. The immediate cause of this rupture was the introduction of the *yagnam* sacrifice, at which some living creature must be immolated[1]. This, they contend, is directly opposed to the most sacred and inviolable principles of the Hindu religion, which forbids the destruction of any living thing, for any reason or on any pretext whatever.

From that moment things came rapidly to a climax; and it was then that the defenders of the pure primitive religion took the name of Jains, and formed themselves into a distinct sect, composed of Brahmanas, Kshatriyas, Vaisyas, and Sudras. They were the descendants of the Hindus of all castes who originally banded themselves together to oppose the innovations of the Brahmins, and they alone have preserved the religion of their forefathers intact to the present day.

After the schism the Jains, or true believers, perpetually taunted the Brahmins with their debased religion, and what at first merely furnished subject-matter for scholastic disputes finally became the cause of long and bloody hostilities. For a long time success was on the side of the Jains, but in the end, the majority of the Kshatriyas and other castes having seceded and adopted the innovations of the Brahmins, the latter gained the ascendant and reduced their adversaries to the lowest depths of subjection. They overthrew all the temples of the Jains, destroyed the objects of their cult, deprived them of all freedom, both religious and civil, and banished them from public employment and all positions of trust; in fact, they persecuted them to such an extent that they succeeded in removing nearly all traces of these formidable antagonists in several provinces where formerly they had been most flourishing.

When these persecutions and wars began is a question that I am unable to answer with any degree of accuracy; but it appears that they lasted a long time and only came to an end in comparatively recent times. Not more than four or five centuries ago the Jains exercised sovereign power in several provinces of the Peninsula. Nowadays the Brahmins are the masters everywhere; the Jains, on the other hand, are absolutely powerless, and it would be impossible to find one occupying a position of any importance. They have become merged in the lower middle classes. They devote themselves to agriculture, and even more to trade, which is the special

[1] It is generally a ram.—DUBOIS.

profession of the Vaisyas, among which caste the greater number of these sectarians are now to be found. Their principal trade is in kitchen and household utensils of copper and other metals.

There are very few of the Brahmin caste who hold the opinions of the Jains. There is a village, however, called Maleyur, in South Mysore, which contains between fifty and sixty families of them. They have a famous temple there, of which the *guru* is a Brahmin Jain. In the other more important temples of the Jains, such as those at Belgola, Madighery, and others, the *gurus* or priests are recruited from the Vaisyas, or merchants. The Vaisya Jains are regarded by the Brahmins of the same sect as *patilas*, or heretics, because they have thus usurped the priestly office, and also because they have altered the religion of the true Jains by introducing some of the innovations of their Brahmin adversaries[1]. This divergence of opinion, however, has not led to any serious differences between them.

The Jains are divided into several sects or schools, which differ on the subject of perfect happiness, and on the means of attaining it. One of these sects, known by the name of *Kashtachenda Swetambara*[2], teaches that there is no other *moksha*, that is to say, no other supreme blessedness, than that which is to be obtained from sensual pleasures, particularly that which is derived from sexual intercourse with women. This sect is, it is true, not numerous.

The school of the *Jaina-bassaru* is the most numerous, and it is subdivided into several others. Its tenets differ very little from those of the *Vedanta* school of Brahminism. It recognizes the different stages of meditation as taught by the latter, and enjoins very much the same means of attaining everlasting felicity, by which they understand reunion with the Godhead.

The Religious System of the Jains.

The Jains acknowledge one Supreme Being, to whom they give the names of *Jaineswara, Paramatma, Parapara-vastu,* and several others expressing the infinity of his nature.

It is to this Supreme Being alone that all the prayers and sacrifices of the true Jains are offered; and it is to him that all the marks of respect which they pay to their holy personages, known as *Salokapurushas,* and to other sacred objects represented under a human form, are really addressed; for these, on attaining *moksha* (supreme blessedness) after death, have become united with and incorporated into the Supreme Being.

The Supreme Being is, they say, one and indivisible, a spirit

[1] *Patitas* literally means 'the fallen.' —Ed.

[2] *Swetambara* literally means 'clad in white.'—Ed.

without corporal parts or limitations. His four principal attributes are:—

1. *Ananta-gnanam*, infinite wisdom.
2. *Ananta-darsanam*, infinite intuition, omniscience, and omnipresence.
3. *Ananta-viryam*, omnipotence.
4. *Ananta-sukham*, infinite blessedness.

This noble being is entirely absorbed in the contemplation of his infinite perfections, and in the uninterrupted enjoyment of the happiness which he finds in his own essence. He has nothing in common with the things of this world, and does not interfere at all in the government of this vast universe. Virtue and vice, good and evil, are indifferent to him.

Virtue being essentially right, those who practise it in this world will find their reward in another life, either by a blessed reincarnation, or by immediate admittance to the delights of *Swarga*. Vice being essentially bad and wrong, those who give way to it will be punished in another world by an unhappy reincarnation. The worst offenders will go straight to *Naraka* after death, there to expiate their crimes. But in no case does God intervene in the distribution of punishments or rewards, or pay any attention to the good or evil done by men here below.

Matter is eternal and independent of the Godhead. That which exists now has always existed and will always exist.

And not only is matter eternal, but also the order and harmony which reign throughout the universe—the fixed and unchanging movements of the stars, the division of light from darkness, the succession and constant renewal of the seasons, the production and reproduction of animal and vegetable life, the nature and properties of the elements; in fact, all things visible are eternal, and will continue to exist just as they have existed from all time.

Metempsychosis.

The fundamental doctrine of the Jains is metempsychosis. Their belief in this differs in no way from that of the Brahmins. But they do not agree with the latter with regard to the four *lokas* or worlds. These they refuse to recognize. They also reject the three principal Abodes of Bliss—*Sattya-loka*, *Vaikuntha*, and *Kailasa*, that is to say, the paradises of Brahma, of Vishnu, and of Siva. They recognize three worlds only, which they describe by the generic name of *Jagat-triya*, and which are the *Urddhwa-loka* or superior world, the *Adha-loka* or inferior world, which they also call *Patala*, and the *Madhya-loka* or middle world, that is to say, the earth where mortals dwell.

Urddhwa-loka.

This world, which is also called *Swarga,* is the first of the *Jagat-triya,* and Devendra is lord of it. There are sixteen distinct abodes in it, in each of which a different degree of happiness is enjoyed in proportion to the merits of the righteous souls who are admitted. The first and highest of these habitations is the *Sadhu-dharma.* Only the very purest souls have access to this, and they there enjoy unbroken happiness for thirty-three thousand years. The *Achuda-karpa,* which is the last and lowest of the sixteen habitations, is destined for the souls of those who possess exactly the requisite amount of merit, neither more nor less, necessary to procure their admittance into the *Urddhwa-loka.* They there enjoy for one thousand years the amount of happiness which is their portion. In the other intermediate habitations the degree and duration of happiness are fixed in relative proportion to the merits of those who are admitted.

Women of the rarest beauty adorn these Abodes of Bliss. The blessed, however, have no intercourse with them. The sight alone of these enchanting beauties is sufficient to intoxicate their senses and plunge them into a perpetual ecstasy that is far superior to all mere earthly pleasures. In this respect the *Swarga* of the Jains differs little from that of the Brahmins.

On leaving the *Urddhwa-loka* at the expiration of the period assigned to them, the souls of the blessed are born again upon earth and recommence the process of transmigration.

The Adha-loka.

The second world of the *Jagat-triya* is the *Adha-loka,* also called *Naraka,* and sometimes *Patala.* It is the lower or inferior regions, the abode of great sinners : that is, of those whose crimes are so heinous and so manifold that they cannot be expiated by even the lowest forms of reincarnation.

The *Adha-loka* is divided into seven dwelling-places, in each of which the severity of the punishments is proportionate to the gravity of the offences. The least terrible is the *Retna-pravai,* where erring souls are tormented for a thousand consecutive years. The torture gradually increases in intensity and duration in the other abodes, until in the *Maha-damai-pravai,* the seventh, the punishments reach a point of awfulness which is beyond all description. It is there that the most villainous sinners are sent, and their horrible sufferings only terminate at the end of thirty-three thousand years. Women, who from their constitutional weakness are not able to endure such extremes of suffering, are never sent to this awful *Maha-damai pravai,* no matter how wicked they may have been.

THE MADHYA-LOKA.

The middle world, the *Madhya-loka*, is the third of the *Jagat-triya*. It is there that mortals live, and that both virtue and vice are to be found.

This world is one *reju* in extent; a *reju* being equal to the distance over which the sun travels in six months. *Jambu-Dwipa*, which is the earth on which we live, occupies only a small part of the *Madhya-loka*. It is surrounded on all sides by a vast ocean, and in the centre of it is an immense lake extending for a hundred thousand *yojanas*, or about four hundred thousand leagues. In the middle of this lake rises the famous mountain *Mahameru*. *Jambu-Dwipa* is divided into four equal parts, which are placed at the four cardinal points of *Mahameru*. India is in the part called Bharata-Kshetra.

These four divisions of *Jambu-Dwipa* are separated from each other by six lofty mountains, which are called Himavata, Maha-Himavata, Nishada, Nila, Arumani, Sikari, all running in the same direction from east to west, stretching across *Jambu-Dwipa* from one sea to the other.

These mountains are intersected by vast valleys, where the trees, shrubs, and fruits, which all grow wild, are of a beautiful pink colour. These delicious retreats are inhabited by good and virtuous people. Children of either sex living there arrive at maturity forty-eight hours after their birth. The inhabitants are not subject to pain or sickness. Always happy and contented, they live on the succulent vegetables and delicious fruits which nature produces for them without any cultivation. After death they go straight to the delights of *Swarga*.

A spring rises on the top of *Mahameru* which feeds fourteen large rivers, of which the principal are the Ganges and the Indus. All these rivers pursue a regular and even course, which never varies. Unlike the false Ganges and the false Indus of the Brahmins, the waters of which rise and fall, the Ganges and Indus of the Jains can never be forded, and their waters always maintain the same level.

The names of the fourteen rivers of the Jains are the Ganges, the Indus, the Rohita-Toya, the Rohita, the Hari-Toya, the Harikanta, the Sitta, the Sitoda, the Nari, the Narikanta, the Swarna-kula, the Rupaya-kula, the Rikta, and the Riktoda.

The sea which surrounds *Jambu-Dwipa* is two hundred thousand *yojanas*, or eight hundred thousand miles long.

Beyond this ocean there are three other continents, separated from each other by an immense sea. They closely resemble *Jambu-Dwipa*, and are also inhabited by human beings.

At the far end of the fourth continent, called *Puskara-varta-Dwipa*, is situated *Manushy-otraparvata*, a very lofty mountain which is the extreme limit of the habitable world. No living being has ever gone beyond this mountain. Its base is washed by an immense ocean, in which are to be found an infinite number of islands which are inaccessible to the human race.

THE SUCCESSION AND DIVISION OF TIME.

Time is divided into six periods, which succeed each other without interruption throughout eternity. At the termination of each period there is an entire revolution in nature, and the world is renewed. The first, called *Prathama-kala,* lasted for four *kotis* of *kotis,* or forty million millions of years; the second, *Dwitiya-kala,* thirty million millions; the third, *Tretiya-kala,* twenty million millions; the fourth, *Chaturtha-kala,* ten million millions, minus forty-two thousand years. The fifth period, called *Panchama-kala,* the period of inconstancy and change, is the age in which we are now living. It will last twenty-one thousand years. The present year (1824) of the Christian era is the year 2469 of the *Panchama-kala* of the Jains.

The comparatively recent date of the commencement of this period seems to me to be worthy of note. I am inclined to think that it is the date of the schism between the Brahmins and the Jains. Such a memorable event may well have been considered as giving birth to a new era. If this conjecture were confirmed it would be easier to fix the time when the principal myths of Hindu theology originated. There is no doubt that the new ideas introduced by the Brahmins into their religion occasioned the schism which exists to this day.

The sixth and last of these periods, the *Sashta-kala,* will also last twenty-one thousand years. The element of fire will then disappear from off the earth, and mankind will subsist entirely on reptiles, roots, and tasteless herbage, which will only grow sparsely here and there. There will then be no caste distinction or subordination, no public or private property, no form of government, no kings, no laws; men will lead the lives of perfect savages.

This period will terminate with a *jala-pralaya,* or flood, which will deluge the whole earth, except the mountain of silver, called Vidiparta. This flood will be caused by continuous rain for forty-seven days, which will result in a complete upsetting of the elements. A few people living near the silver mountain will take refuge in the caves which are hidden in its sides, and they will be saved amidst the universal destruction. After the catastrophe the elect will come forth from the mountain and will repeople the earth. Then the six periods will begin over again, and follow each other as they did before.

THE LEARNING OF THE JAINS.

The philosophy of the Jains is contained in four Vedas[1], twenty-four Puranas, and sixty-four Sastras. The Puranas take the names

[1] These are not called Vedas, but Agamas.—ED.

of the twenty-four *Tirthankaras*[1], or saints. A Purana is assigned to each of them, and contains his history.

The names of the four Vedas are *Prathamani-yoga, Charanani-yoga, Karanani-yoga*, and *Draviani-yoga.* These four books were written by Adiswara, the most ancient and most celebrated of all the holy personages recognized by the Jains. He came down from *Swarga*, took a human form, and lived on earth for a *purva-koti*, or a hundred million million years. Not only did he compose the Vedas, but it was he who divided men into castes, gave them laws and a form of government, and laid down the lines of social order. In short, Adiswara is to the Jains what Brahma is to the Brahmins; one of them having most probably been modelled from the other.

The Sixty-three Saloka-purushas.

Besides Adiswara, who is the holiest and most perfect of all beings who have appeared on the earth in human form, the Jains recognize sixty-three others, whom they describe by the generic name of *Saloka-purushas*, and whom they also worship. Their history is contained in the *Prathamani-yoga.*

These venerable personages are subdivided into five classes: twenty-four *Tirthankaras*, twelve *Chakravartis*, nine *Vasu-devatas*, nine *Bala-vasu-devatas*, and nine *Bala-ramas.*

The twenty-four *Tirthankaras* are the holiest, and to them most honour is paid. Their position is the most sublime that a mortal can aspire to. They all lived in the most perfect state of *Nirvana.* They were subject to no infirmity or sickness; they felt no want, no weakness, and were not even subject to death. After having lived for a long time on earth they voluntarily quitted their bodies and went straight to *moksha*, where they were united with, and incorporated into, the Godhead.

All the *Tirthankaras* came down from *Swarga* and took human forms among the Kshatriya caste; but they were subsequently incorporated into that of the Brahmins by the ceremony of the *diksha*[2]. During their lives they were examples of all the virtues to other men, whom they exhorted by their precepts and their actions to conform strictly to the rules of conduct laid down by Adiswara, and to give themselves up entirely to meditation and penitence.

Some of them lived for millions of years; the last of them, however, only attained the age of eighty-four.

They were in existence during the period of *Chaturtha-kala.* Some

[1] *Tirthankaras* means those who have 'passed over' the gulf which separates human beings from the Godhead.—Ed.

[2] This word literally translated means 'initiation.'—Dubois.

were married, but the greater number remained celibate, being professed *sannyasis*.

The twelve *Chakravartis*, or emperors, recognized by the Jains were contemporaries of the twenty-four *Tirthankaras*. They shared amongst them the temporal government of *Jambu-Dwipa*. They came straight from *Swarga*, and when on earth belonged to the noble caste of Kshatriyas. Some were initiated into the Brahmin caste by the ceremony of the *diksha*, completed their lives as *Sannyasi Nirvanis*, and after death obtained *moksha*, or supreme happiness. Others returned to *Swarga*. But three of them, having lived extremely wicked lives on earth, were condemned to the tortures of *Naraka*.

The twelve *Chakravartis* were often at war with one another, but they had more especially to fight against the nine *Vasu-devatas*, the nine *Bala-vasu-devatas*, and the nine *Bala-ramas*, who all governed different provinces in India[1].

The second Veda, or *Charanani-yoga*, contains the civil laws, also regulations relating to social status, caste, &c.

The third Veda, or *Karanani-yoga*, is a dissertation on the nature, order, and component parts of the *Jagat-triya*.

The fourth, or *Draviani-yoga*, contains the metaphysical theories of the Jains and several controversial subjects.

The State of Sannyasi Nirvani.

The most holy and sublime state to which man can possibly attain is that of *Sannyasi Nirvani*, which means 'naked penitent.' In embracing this state a man ceases to be a man; he begins to be a part of the Godhead. As soon as he has attained the highest degree of perfection in this state, he frees himself voluntarily, without any trouble or pain, from his own self, and obtains *moksha*, thus becoming incorporated for ever into the Divine Self. There is no real *Nirvani* existing in this *yuga*. Those who aspire to this state must pass through twelve successive degrees of meditation and corporal penance, each one more perfect than the last. These degrees are a kind of novitiate, and each of them has a special appellation. Having at last become a *Nirvani*, the penitent no longer belongs to this world. Terrestrial objects make no impres-

[1] Rama of the Brahmins is one of the nine *Bala ramas* of the Jains, and their Krishna is one of the *Vasu-devatas*. The Jains say that the Brahmins borrowed these two names to make up the *Avatars* of their god Vishnu. They assert generally that the Brahmins have stolen from them all the knowledge concerning which they so particularly pride themselves. —Dubois.

sion on his senses. He regards the good and evil, virtue and vice, to be found on this earth with equal indifference. He is freed from all passion. He scarcely feels the wants of nature. He is able to patiently endure hunger, thirst, and privations of all kinds. He can live without food of any sort for weeks and months together. When he is obliged to eat he partakes indifferently of the first animal or vegetable substance that comes to hand, however filthy or disgusting it may seem to ordinary people. He has neither fire nor sleeping place. He always lives in the open on the bare ground. Though absolutely naked from head to foot, he is insensible to cold and heat, wind and rain. Neither is he subject to sickness or any bodily infirmities. He feels the most profound contempt for all other men, no matter how exalted their rank may be, and he takes no account of their doings, good or bad. He speaks to no one, looks at no one, and is visited by no one. His feelings, his affections, and his thoughts are immutably fixed on the Godhead, of whom he considers himself as already a part. He remains absorbed in the contemplation of God's perfections, all earthly objects being to him as though they did not exist.

By a long course of penance and meditation the material part of the *Nirvani* gradually dissolves, like camphor when it is put in the fire. At last all that remains of the penitent is the semblance or shadow of a body, an immaterial phantom, so to say. Having arrived at this pitch of perfection, the *Nirvani* quits this lower world and proceeds to unite himself inseparably with the Godhead, where he enjoys eternal and ineffable happiness.

Jain Rules of Conduct.

In many respects Jain rules of conduct are similar to those followed by other Hindus, and particularly the Brahmins. The Jains recognize the same observances with regard to defilement and purity. They perform the same ablutions and recite the same prescribed *mantrams*. Most of their ceremonies relating to marriage, funerals, &c., are the same. In fact, all the rules of social etiquette and the general customs in use in ordinary life form part of their education.

The Jains differ from their compatriots in several particulars, of which the following are the most remarkable:—

Under no circumstances do they take any solid food beween sunset and sunrise. They always take their meals while the sun is above the horizon.

They have no *titis* or anniversaries in honour of the dead. As soon as one of them is dead and his funeral is over, they put him out of their memories and speak of him no more.

They never put ashes on their foreheads, as do most Hindus; they are satisfied with making with sandalwood-paste the little round mark called *bottu*, or else a horizontal line. Some devotees put these marks on their forehead, neck, stomach, and both shoulders in the form of a cross, in honour of their five principal *Tirthankaras*.

The Jains are even stricter than the Brahmins in regard to their food. Not only do they abstain from all animal food, and from vegetables the stalks or roots of which grow in a bulbous shape, such as onions, mushrooms, &c., but they also refrain from eating many of the fruits which the Brahmins allow on their tables, such as the *katri-kai*, or brinjal, called *beringela* in Portuguese, the *pudalan-kai*, &c. Their motive is the fear of taking the life of some of the insects which are generally to be found in these vegetables and fruits. The principal, and indeed almost the only, articles of food used by the Jains are rice, milk, things made with milk, and peas of various kinds. They particularly dislike assafoetida, to which Brahmins are so partial[1], and honey is absolutely forbidden.

Whilst they are eating their food some person sits beside them and rings a bell, or strikes a gong. The object of this is to prevent the possibility of their hearing the impure conversation of their neighbours, or of the passers-by in the street. Both they and their food would be defiled if any impure words reached their ears while they were eating.

Their fear of destroying life is carried to such a length that the women, before smearing the floor with cow-dung, are in the habit of sweeping it very gently first, so as to remove, without hurting them, any insects that may be there. If they neglected this precaution they would run the risk of crushing one of these little creatures whilst rubbing the floor, which would be the source of the keenest regret to them.

Another of their customs, and one which, though for a very different motive, might be advantageously introduced into Europe, is to wipe most carefully anything that is to be used for food, so as to exclude as tenderly as possible any of the tiny living creatures which might be found in or on it.

The mouth of the vessel in which water for household purposes is drawn is always covered with a piece of linen, through which the water filters. This prevents the animalculae, which float or swim on the surface of the well, from getting into the vessel and being after-

[1] This resinous gum, the smell of which appears to us so abominable that we have called it *stercus diaboli*, strikes the smell and taste of the Hindus and almost all Asiatics very differently. They consider it to be possessed of an agreeable perfume and an exquisite flavour. The ancient Greeks and Romans shared their partiality for this substance; for it seems certain that the *σίλφιον* of the former and the *laser* of the latter were nothing more or less than assafoetida.—Dubois.

wards swallowed. When a Jain traveller wishes to quench his thirst at a tank or stream, he covers his mouth with a cloth, stoops down, and thus drinks by suction. This cleanly custom is highly to be recommended everywhere, apart from the superstition which prompts the Jains to practise it.

The Jains form a perfectly distinct class. Brahmins never attend any of their religious or civil ceremonies, while they, on their part, never attend those of the Brahmins. They have their own temples, and the priestly office is filled by men professing the same tenets as themselves.

Amongst these temples there are some which are richly endowed and very famous. The Jains make pilgrimages to them, sometimes from great distances. There is a very remarkable one in Mysore, at Sravana Belgola, a village near Seringapatam. It is between three mountains, on one of which is an enormous statue, about seventy feet high, sculptured out of one solid piece of rock. It must have been a tremendous piece of work; for to execute it, it was necessary to level the ground from the top of the mountain to below the base of the statue, and there form a sort of terrace, leaving in the centre this mass of rock which was to be carved into the shape of the idol. It is a very fine piece of Hindu sculpture. Many Europeans who have seen it have greatly admired the correctness of its proportions. It represents a celebrated *Nirvani* called Gumatta, a son of Adiswara. The figure is absolutely nude, as are most of the idols to which the Jains offer adoration, and which are always likenesses of ancient penitents belonging to this sect. In those days it would have shocked them to represent these penitents as wearing garments, since they made it a point of duty to go absolutely naked. Childless women may often be seen praying to these indecent idols, in order that they may become mothers.

This temple of Belgola, being only a day's journey from Seringapatam, has been frequently visited by Europeans. It was a great source of grief to the devotees of the sect to see this *punyasthala* (holy place) defiled by a crowd of unbelieving visitors. And what was still worse, these inquisitive foreigners were often accompanied by their dogs and their Pariah servants. In one resting-place they would cook a stew, in another they would roast a piece of beef under the very nose, as it were, of the idol, whose sense of smell, the Jains thought, was infinitely disgusted by the smoke of this abominable style of cooking. At last the *guru* attached to the temple, shocked at all this desecration, fled from the unhallowed spot, and retired to some solitary place on the Malabar coast. After three years of this voluntary exile, he returned to his former abode on the assurance that Europeans had ceased to visit the place, and that the temple had been thoroughly purified. Now, I ask you whether it is not the duty of any well-conducted man, even if he does not respect them, at least not to openly outrage the prejudices, feelings, and customs of any people amongst whom he may happen to be thrown, no matter how peculiar or ridiculous they may appear to him. What pleasure could be derived, or what good could be gained, by exciting the anger and contempt of those from whom one has nothing to fear, and who cannot retaliate?

An invalid European officer, who was going to the Malabar coast for change of air, on passing near Belgola, was seized with the idea of spending a night in the temple, which he did, in spite of much opposition on the part of the inhabitants. Two days afterwards the officer died on the road, to the great delight of all the natives, who, of course, attributed his death to a miracle, and looked upon it as a direct retribution from their outraged deity. This just and condign punishment, said they, would inspire with wholesome fear others who might be tempted to try a similar experiment.

The idols of the Jains differ in many respects from those of the Brahmins. Almost all have curly hair like Negroes. They wear neither ear-rings, necklaces, bracelets, nor bangles on their ankles, whilst the Brahmins, on the other hand, overload the objects of their devotion with such ornaments.

APPENDIX II

The *Eka-dasi*, or Eleventh Day of the Moon.

THE eleventh day of the moon is religiously observed, not only by Brahmins, but by all those castes which have the right to wear the triple cord. They keep a strict fast on this day, abstain entirely from rice, do no servile work, and give themselves up wholly to devotional exercises. The following is what the *Vishnu-purana* says on the subject:—

The *Eka-dasi* is a day specially set apart for the worship of Vishnu; those who offer him *puja* on this day ensure for themselves immortality. Even before the creation of the world the 'Man of Sin' was created by Vishnu to punish mankind[1]. He is of enormous stature, with a terrific countenance and a body absolutely black; his eyes are wild and glaring with rage; he is the executioner of mankind[1]. Krishna, having seen this 'Man of Sin,' became thoughtful and

[1] See the description in the chapter on the *Sandhya*.

pensive. Touched by the woes with which mankind was overwhelmed, Krishna resolved to remedy the evil. With this end in view he mounted the bird Garuda, son of Binota, and went in search of Yama, the King of Hell. The Child of the Sun, delighted at this visit of Narayana, who was master and *guru* of the world, hastened to offer him *puja*, and placed him on a massive throne of gold. No sooner had Krishna seated himself thereon than he heard the most piteous and plaintive cries. Moved with compassion, he asked the King of *Naraka* whence these lamentations proceeded, and what caused them.

'The lamentations that you hear, O Lord of the World,' replied Yama, 'are the tears and groans of the unfortunate beings who, having spent their whole lives in sin, are now suffering the tortures of Hell, where they are treated according to their deserts.'

'Then,' said Krishna, 'let us go to this place of torment, that I may see for myself what these sinners are enduring.'

And he did see, and his heart was softened.

'What!' cried he, overcome with grief, 'is it possible that men, who are creatures and children of mine, are enduring such cruel agony! Shall I be a witness of their sufferings and do nothing to help them? Cannot I give them some means of avoiding them in the future?'

Thereupon he considered how he might bring the reign of the 'Man of Sin' to an end, he being the sole cause of all mankind's misfortune. Accordingly, to preserve henceforth the human race from the torments of *Naraka* he transformed himself into the *Eka-dasi*, or eleventh day of the moon. This is, therefore, the blessed day that Vishnu has selected in his mercy to redeem and save mankind. It is the happy day that procures the pardon of one's sins; it is the day of days, since one must look upon it as being Krishna himself.

The inhabitants of Hell, full of gratitude for the kindness that Vishnu had showed towards them, worshipped him and chanted his praises loudly. Thereupon Vishnu, being much pleased by their prayers and praises, wished to give them an immediate proof of his goodness. Turning to the 'Man of Sin,' he addressed him in the following words:—

'Begone, wretched being, begone! Thy reign is over. Till now thou hast been the tormentor of mankind; I command thee to let them live in peace for the future. They are my children, and I desire them to be happy. I wish, nevertheless, to assign to thee a place where thou mayest live, but thy place shall be unique; it shall be here. The *Eka-dasi*, or eleventh day of the moon, is myself in another form. It is the day that I have chosen, in my mercy, to save men and deliver them from their sins. Nevertheless, in order that they may be worthy of so great a favour, I expressly forbid them to eat rice on this day. I ordain that thou shalt dwell in this rice. This is the abode that I assign to thee. Whoever shall have the temerity to eat this food, thus defiled by thy presence, will incorporate thee with himself, and will forfeit all hope of pardon.'

Thus spake Vishnu; and the following is the sentence of life and death which he pronounced, and which cannot be too strongly impressed on the attention of mankind:—

'I repeat, therefore, again, because I cannot say it too often: Do not eat rice on that day; whoever you are, be your position and condition what they may, do not eat rice. Once more I say, do not eat rice.'

To fast on this holy day and to offer *puja* to Vishnu is to ensure the forgiveness of sins and the gratification of all one's wishes. Moreover these further observances must be followed. On the tenth day the *sandhya* must be performed, and only one meal must be eaten, and that without salt or any kind of peas or vegetables. It must only be seasoned with a small quantity of melted butter, and it must be eaten quickly. In the evening one must visit a temple dedicated to Vishnu, and, holding some *darbha* grass in one's hands, must meditate for some time on the greatness of the deity, addressing to him the following prayer:—

'Behold me in thy presence, great god! I prostrate myself at thy feet. Hold out a helping hand to me and remove the obstacles which I encounter at each step. My feeble will is often led astray by the passions that influence me. Thou alone canst give it strength to resist such weaknesses, and keep it straight in the path of virtue.'

This prayer being ended, some *darbha* grass must be offered to Narayana, and the worshipper must prostrate himself before him with his face to the ground.

Making a bed of this same grass at the feet of Vishnu, he must pass the night upon it. On rising in the morning he must wash his mouth out twelve times and perform the usual ablutions. During the day he must fulfil his ordinary religious duties, the chief of which is the sacrifice to Vishnu. He must fast for the whole of the day, eating and drinking nothing. The night of the eleventh day must also be spent in a temple dedicated to Vishnu. The whole family—father, mother, wife, brothers, and children—must remain together in the presence of Vishnu, and remain awake.

The wife who performs this act of devotion along with her husband will, on her reincarnation, have a husband who will make her very happy, and by whom she will have a numerous family. After her death she will be conveyed to *Vaikuntha*, and be reunited to her first husband.

Whoever during this night shall occupy himself in drawing the emblems of the *chakra* and *sankha*, which Vishnu carries in his hand, will obtain the remission of his sins committed in former generations. Whoever shall make a model of these two weapons with dough of rice flour, in several colours, shall receive a much greater reward, for his sons and his grandsons shall enjoy prosperity on earth, and occupy after their death a high place in *Vaikuntha*.

If any one places little flags of various colours in Vishnu's temple he will eventually be born again king of a fine country. And if any one allows the cloths and flags that have been offered to Vishnu to flutter freely in the wind, he will receive pardon for all his sins, however heinous they may have been. Any one who places an umbrella over Vishnu's head will be reborn rich and powerful, and will himself have the right to use one.

To employ oneself during this same night in making a little house of flowers for Vishnu is as meritorious a work as if one had sacrificed a horse a hundred times over. And if any one should make this house in cloth, he will himself have a house of bricks in *Vaikuntha*.

On the *salagrama* stone or on the image of Vishnu must then be poured some *pancha-amrita*, that is to say milk, melted butter, curds, honey, and sugar mixed together. The image must then be adorned with rich stuffs and precious jewels, and a fan must be placed before it. Having performed the *sam-kalpa*, and purified by the *santi-yoga*[1] the five elements of which man is composed, the worshippers must fix their thoughts on Vishnu, and, holding flowers in their hands, must meditate for some time on the perfections of the deity. They must picture him to themselves in their mind's eye as seated on a golden throne with his daughter by his side, casting around the effulgent light that encircles him, having sometimes two and sometimes four arms. To this Supreme Lord of the Universe must their homage be addressed.

This act of meditation ended, the worshippers must offer him *puja*, beginning with the *Swagata*; that is to say, they must ask the god whether he is in good health, and has accomplished his journey safely.

They will then present to him water to wash his feet, and to refresh him after the fatigues of his journey. They must say: 'God of Gods, receive this water to wash your feet; it is pure and sweet, and will refresh you, and it will remove the dust which has covered you on your way.'

They will then give him water for rinsing out his mouth, and more water and flowers to put on his head; some milk, honey, and sugar, mixed together, to quench his thirst; and various kinds of food to satisfy his appetite. It is thus, at intervals of three hours, that they

[1] See the description in the chapter on the *Sandhya*.

must offer *puja* to Vishnu. Everything that is offered to him must be the very best that can be procured.

I have already said that they must pass the night without closing an eye for a moment; they must spend it in dancing and singing to the sound of musical instruments. It is sufficient to repeat Vishnu's names, or even to hear them repeated, to obtain the remission of all one's sins and the accomplishment of all one's desires. It is considered a meritorious action even to go and look at persons who are spending the night in the performance of these pious exercises.

Great care must be taken on this holy day not to speak to any one who is not a true worshipper of Vishnu. To address even one word to unbelievers would cause Vishnu's worshippers to lose all the benefit of their devotion.

He who on this day hears the sound of musical instruments played in honour of Vishnu and is not enchanted, is like a dog when it hears the *vina*. The pious man should delight in listening to a symphony which is in itself capable of remitting sins, because it adds to the glory of the Lord of the World. He should join in the saintly throng of worshippers, when they with one accord hasten to show their devotion and their zeal by their dances, songs, and hymns in honour of the great deity.

He who objects to such acts of worship is the greatest of sinners. He who, while not actually disapproving, refrains from taking part in them, and occupies himself instead with other matters, will be punished for his indifference by being reborn as a cock in another life. He will be reborn dumb if he does not contribute as much as ever he can towards the pomp and ceremony of the *Eka-dasi*.

Every kind of musical instrument must be played on that night, and in fact everything that is possible must be done to contribute to Vishnu's pleasure. The worshippers must walk round the image of the god several times in procession; they must prostrate themselves before it, and from time to time they must pour milk upon its head. Each worshipper, at the conclusion of the ceremony, must give a present to the Brahmins in proportion to his means.

Ordinary food may be taken on the twelfth day in the afternoon, but not before, on pain of forfeiting for a hundred generations all the blessings which should flow from these ceremonies[1].

Those who faithfully observe the fast of the *Eka-dasi* in the manner described will make sure of salvation. If any one has killed a Brahmin or a cow, taken away the wife or property of another, committed fornication with the wife of his *guru*, drunk intoxicating liquors, caused abortion in a pregnant woman; all these and other similar

[1] This is incorrect. Those who fast on the eleventh day break their fast before sunrise on the twelfth day.—Ed.

sins, no matter how numerous or heinous they may be, will be entirely absolved by the fast of the *Eka-dasi*, and by sacrifices offered to Vishnu on that day.

. . . .

Such, in brief, is what Markandeya teaches us.

Before leaving this subject I ought to mention that the precepts contained in these instructions are not strictly kept, except by a very small number of devotees. The *Eka-dasi*, it is true, is kept as a holy day by Brahmins, and by all persons who have the right to wear the triple cord, and even by a few Sudras of good position, but they content themselves with spending the day in performing a few religious rites and in amusements. Nevertheless they all abstain from eating rice. Towards evening, however, they have a meal composed of cakes and fruit, which greatly modifies and simplifies the severity and length of the fast prescribed by the *Vishnu-purana*.

APPENDIX III

Siva-Ratri, or Siva's Night.

THE feast of *Siva-Ratri* is celebrated with great ceremony, especially by the Sivaites. This is what we read in the *Skanda-purana* on the subject:—

There is in *Jambu-Dwipa* a large town known by the name of Varanasi, where dwelt a man belonging to the *boya* or huntsman caste, who was short of stature, very dark in complexion, and of a most violent and passionate temper. One day when out hunting in the woods, as was his wont, he killed such an enormous quantity of birds of all kinds that he was hardly able to carry them, and was obliged to sit down and rest at almost every step. Dusk was coming on while he was still in the middle of a thick forest, and anxious not to lose the spoil of his day's hunting or to become a prey to the wild beasts that infested the place, he went up to a *vepu*[1] or margosa-tree, hung his game upon one of the branches, and climbed up into the tree, intending to spend the night there. Now that night happened to be the night of the new moon of the month of *Phalguna* (March), a time of year when dew falls heavily and the nights are chilly. The hunter, benumbed with cold, tormented by hunger (for he had eaten nothing during the day), and half dead with terror, passed a very miserable night. At the foot of the tree was a *lingam*, and this circumstance

[1] It should be the *bilva*, not the *vepu*.—ED.

proved to be the salvation of the hunter. The discomforts that he was enduring obliged him to change his position frequently, and the shaking of the branches of the *vepu*[1] caused some drops of dew, together with some leaves, flowers, and fruit, to fall on the *lingam*. This fortunate accident was sufficient to win Siva's favour and to obtain for the hunter absolution for all his sins. For Siva, to whose worship this night was specially consecrated, was much gratified at the offering thus made to his adored symbol; and he ordained that he who had made it, involuntary though his offering was, should be rewarded, and that his long fast and attendant anxieties should be reckoned in his favour. The hunter regained his house the following morning, and died a few days afterwards. Yama, King of Hell, on hearing of his death, immediately sent his emissaries to secure him and bring him away. But Siva, on hearing of this, also sent his own emissaries to oppose those of Yama and to claim the dead man. Yama's messengers declined to yield, and a violent quarrel ensued between them and the emissaries of Siva. From insults they quickly proceeded to violence. Siva's party, being the stronger, put the agents of *Naraka* to flight, after severely punishing them. The latter, in shame and bitterness, went and told their story to their master, and to excite his wrath showed him the wounds that they had received in the combat. Yama, beside himself with indignation, went at once to *Kailasa* to make complaint to Siva in person. At the gate of the deity's palace he found Nandi, the prime minister, to whom he explained the object of his visit, at the same time expressing his surprise that Siva should thus declare himself the protector of a common *boya*, a hardened sinner, whose trade necessitated the slaughter of many living creatures.

'King of Hell,' replied Nandi, 'it is true that this man has been a great sinner and that he has not scrupled to shed blood; but before he died he, fortunately for himself, fasted, watched, and offered a sacrifice to the *lingam* during the night consecrated to Siva. This meritorious action has obtained for him the remission of all his sins, the protection of Siva, and an honourable place in *Kailasa*.'

When Yama heard Nandi's words, he became thoughtful, and withdrew without uttering another word.

This is the origin of the feast of *Siva-Ratri*, or Night of Siva. In commemoration of the fortunate *boya* the devotees of Siva spend the night and the preceding day in fasting and without sleep, entirely absorbed in worshipping the god, in offering him sacrifices, and presenting him with the bitter leaves of the *vepu*[1] or margosa-tree as *neiveddya*, which they afterwards eat.

[1] It should be the *bilva*, not the *vepu*.—ED.

APPENDIX IV

Rules of Conduct for Women during their Periodical Uncleanness.

When a woman is in a state of periodical uncleanness, she is isolated in some place apart, and may have no communication with any one during the three days that her defilement is supposed to last. The first day she must look upon herself as a Pariah. The second day she must consider herself as unclean as if she had killed a Brahmin. The third day she is supposed to be in an intermediate state between the two preceding ones. The fourth day she purifies herself by ablutions, observing all the ceremonies required on these occasions. Until then she must neither bathe nor wash any part of her body, nor shed tears. She must be very careful not to kill any insect, or any other living creature. She must not ride on a horse, an elephant, or a bullock, nor travel in a palanquin, a dooly, or a carriage. She must not anoint her head with oil, or play at dice and other games, or use sandalwood, musk, or perfumes of any kind. She must not lie on a bed or sleep during the day. She must not brush her teeth or rinse out her mouth. The mere wish to cohabit with her husband would be a serious sin. She must not think of the gods or of the sun, or of the sacrifices and worship due to them. She is forbidden to salute persons of high rank. If several women in this unclean state should find themselves together in one place, they must not speak to or touch each other. A woman in this condition must not go near her children, touch them, or play with them. After living thus in retirement for three days, on the fourth she must take off the garments that she has been wearing, and these must be immediately given to the washerman. She must then put on a clean cloth and another over it, and go to the river to purify herself by bathing. On her way there she must walk with her head bent, and must take the greatest care to glance at nobody, for her looks would defile any person on whom they rested. When she has reached the river she must first enter the water and fill the copper vessel, or *chembu*, which she has brought with her from the house. Then, returning to the bank, she must thoroughly cleanse her teeth, rinse out her mouth twelve times, and wash her hands and feet. She must then enter the water and plunge twelve times into it, immersing the whole of her body. She must take the greatest care while doing this not to look at any living soul, and to this end each time her head rises above the water she must turn her eyes towards the sun. On coming out of the water she must take a little fresh cow-dung, some *tulasi*, and some earth. These she must mix together in a little water, until they make a thin paste, and with this she must thoroughly rub her hands and feet and then her whole body. After this she must re-enter the water, and completely immerse herself twenty-four times. When she again leaves the water she must rub herself over with saffron, and again dip three times in the water. Then mixing saffron in a little water, she must drink some and pour the rest on her head, after which she must put on a pure cloth freshly washed and the little bodice called *ravikai*. She may then paint the little round red mark on her forehead called *kunkuma* and return home. On entering the house she must take special care that her eyes do not rest on her children, for they would thereby be exposed to the greatest danger. She must immediately send for a Brahmin *purohita* so that he may complete her purification. On his arrival this venerable person first plaits together thirty-two stalks of *darbha* grass, to make the ring called *pavitram*, which he dips in consecrated water that he has brought with him. The woman then takes another bath, drinks a little of the consecrated water, places the *pavitram* on the ring finger of the right hand, and drinks some *pancha-gavia* or some cow's milk. After these ceremonies her purification is complete.

APPENDIX V

Remarks on the Origin of the Famous Temple of Jagannath.

THE Province of Orissa, in which the temple of Jagannath is situated, is called in Hindu books Utkala-desa. Indra-mena, say these books, reigned over the country. Inflamed with desire to save his soul, the prince saw with dismay that he had as yet done nothing which would ensure his happiness after death. This thought troubled him exceedingly, and he confided his anxiety to Brahma with the Four Faces, who was his favourite divinity. Brahma, being greatly touched by the sincere regrets and fervent piety of the prince, addressed him one day in the following consolatory terms:—

'Cease, great king, from troubling thyself about thy future state; I will point out to thee a way of assuring thy salvation. On the sea-coast is a country called Utkala-desa, and therein rises the mountain sometimes called Nila and sometimes Purushottama, which is a *yojana* or three leagues in length. It is called by the latter name after the god who formerly took up his abode there. This mountain is a holy place, and the sight of it has the virtue of taking away sins.

In former *yugas* there was a temple of solid gold upon it, dedicated to Vishnu. This temple is still in existence, but has been buried in the sand cast up by the sea, which renders it invisible at the present time. Restore this temple, cause its ancient glory to be revived, renew the sacrifices which were formerly offered there, and thou shalt thus ensure thyself a place of felicity after death.'

The king, Indra-mena, delighted with what he had heard, asked Brahma who was the founder of this magnificent temple, and where the exact spot was on which it had been built. Brahma responded:—

'It was thy ancestors, great king, who erected it in the preceding *yuga*, and who by this means procured for mankind the ineffable happiness of seeing the Supreme Being on this earth. Go, then, and reclaim this venerable spot from oblivion; cause the deity to descend there anew, and thou shalt procure a similar happiness for the human race.'

'But how,' again asked the prince, 'can I discover a temple which is completely buried in the sand, unless you yourself help me to find it?'

Thereupon Brahma gave him a few directions, and added that he would find, not far from the mountain of Nila, a tank wherein lived a turtle as old as the world, who would give him more definite particulars.

Indra-mena thanked Brahma and at once set forth to find the tank. Hardly had he arrived on its banks when a turtle of enormous size approached him, and asked who he was and what he wanted in that desert place.

'I am,' replied the prince, 'by birth a Kshatriya and sovereign of a great kingdom, but the enormity of my sins and the remorse that I feel oppress me and make me the most miserable of men. Brahma with the Four Faces has given me some vague information respecting a holy place near the mountain of Nila, assuring me that I shall be able to obtain from you all the necessary directions to guide me in my search.'

'I am delighted, O prince,' replied the turtle, 'to have an opportunity of contributing to your happiness. Unfortunately, however, I am unable to satisfy you upon all the points about which you seek information, for my great age has caused a partial loss of memory; yet the indications that I can give may, perhaps, be useful to you. It is quite true that in former days there existed a temple near the mountain of Nila, which was famous for its wealth. The God with Four Arms, the God of Gods, the Great Vishnu, had taken up his abode there. All the other gods resorted to it regularly to do him honour, and it was also a spot which they greatly affected for indulging in their amours. But for a long time past the sand thrown up by the sea has covered this sacred pile, and the god, finding that he no longer received the accustomed marks of respect, left it and returned to *Vaikuntha.* All that I know is that this edifice is buried a *yojana* (three leagues) deep in this sandy soil. I have lost all trace of the site that it formerly occupied. Nevertheless there is another and a certain way by which you can discover it. Go to the tank called Markandeya; on its banks you will find a crow which has been gifted with immortality, and which can recall everything that happened in the most distant times. Go and inquire of it and you will obtain all the information you want.'

The king hastened to the tank Markandeya and there found the crow, which from its extreme age had become quite white. Prostrating himself before it, he joined his hands in a supplicating manner and said:—

'O crow, who enjoyest the gift of immortality! you see before you a king who is a prey to the deepest despair; and only you can comfort him!'

'What,' said the crow, 'is the cause of your sorrow? What can I do for you?'

'I will tell you,' replied Indra-mena; 'but do not hide from me, I implore you, anything that I want to know. Tell me first of all, who was the first king who ever reigned over this country, and what he did that was remarkable?'

The crow, well versed in ancient history, had no difficulty in satisfying the monarch, and answered in the following terms:—

'The first king of this country was called Chaturanana. He had a son called Visva-Bahu, who in turn had a son called Indra-mena, a prince who, having always shown great devotion to Brahma with the Four Faces, was thought worthy after death to be admitted to the presence of the deity. The reign of Chaturanana was a period of great happiness. He dealt with his subjects as a tender father deals with his children. Amongst the many praiseworthy acts which made his reign remarkable was one by which his name will be for ever remembered. It was he who had the honour and glory of inducing the God of Gods to come down to earth from *Vaikuntha.* He built for him a dwelling-place at the foot of the mountain of Nila, a magnificent temple, the walls of which were of massive gold, while the interior was embellished with most precious stones. Time, that universal destroyer, has respected this edifice, and it is still in existence perfectly uninjured. But for a long time past it has been swallowed up by the sands of the sea. It is true that the god who inhabited the sacred spot has ceased to dwell there; nevertheless, he could not entirely forsake a mountain that had once been consecrated by his presence, and he has taken up his abode there in the shape of a *vepu* or margosa-tree. One day the famous penitent Markandeya, who for many centuries did penance on this mountain, perceiving that this tree gave no shade, was roused to indignation, and breathing upon it he partially reduced it to ashes. This tree, however, was Vishnu, the Supreme Being, and consequently immortal. The penitent could not, therefore, entirely destroy it, and the trunk still remains. The only thing that I do not know is the exact spot where this tree grew.'

Here Indra-mena interrupted the crow, and asked if it could recognize the spot where the temple stood. The crow replied in the affirmative. So they both set out together to find the site. At the place where they stopped the crow set to work to dig into the sand with his beak to the depth of a *yojana*, and at last succeeded in disclosing in its entirety the magnificent temple which had formerly been the abode of Narayana, the God of Gods. Having shown it to the king, the crow covered it up again as before.

The king, convinced of the truth of all that the crow had told him, and enraptured at having found that for which he had been seeking so earnestly, questioned his guide as to what steps he should take to restore to its former state of splendour and fame a place which had been so venerated.

'What you now ask of me,' the crow replied, 'is beyond my province. Go and find Brahma with the Four Faces, and he will tell you how to accomplish your desire.'

Indra-mena followed this advice. He again sought Brahma, and having offered him worship several times, he said:—

'I have now seen with my own eyes near the mountain Nila that superb temple which was formerly the abode of the great Vishnu, and am come to consult you, great god, on the course that I should pursue in order to rekindle in the heart of the people the holy fervour which this sacred place inspired in former times. If I build a town, what name shall I give to it? Vishnu, I know, will return and honour the place with his presence under the form of the trunk of a tree, but how will he come, and what sacrifices and offerings must be made to him? Deign to enlighten me, great god, and help me in this difficulty.'

'To accomplish the praiseworthy object that is in thy mind,' said Brahma, 'thou must erect a new temple on the very spot where the old one is now buried. Thou shalt give it the name of Sridehul. It is not necessary to make it as costly as the former one, because the present inhabitants of the country, being reduced to great poverty, would remove it piecemeal, and thy labour would be lost. It need only be built of stone. In order to provide the necessary accommodation for the crowd of devotees who will visit it, thou must build near the temple a town which will receive the name of Purushottama. The moment the work is finished the trunk of a tree, that is to say

Krishna himself, will appear on the sea-shore. This thou must remove with much pomp and ceremony into the new temple. The carpenter Visvakarma will come and work at it, and will fashion it into the face and form of the god. Thou shalt place beside this god his sister Subadra and his brother Balarama. Thou must offer sacrifices to the god day and night, but especially in the morning, at noon, and in the evening. This will be a sure and certain means of securing for thyself, and for all those who follow thy example, a place in *Vaikuntha*, the Abode of Bliss. As Vishnu will not be able to consume the enormous quantity of food that will be offered to him as *neiveddya* by the multitude of his devotees, men may therein find a means of purifying themselves and obtaining the remission of their sins by eating the remnants. Happy is he who shall secure for himself the smallest particle, for he will certainly go to *Vaikuntha* after death. To give thee some idea of the inestimable value of the remnants of Krishna's food, let me tell thee that if by accident or inadvertence some fragments should fall to the ground, the very gods themselves would strive for them, even if the dogs had already devoured a portion. In short, if a Pariah were to take some rice destined for Krishna from the mouth of a dog and put it into that of a Brahmin, this rice would be so pure, and would possess so many virtues, that it would immediately purify that Brahmin. The goddess Lakshmi cooks and prepares the food destined for Krishna, and the goddess Annapurni waits upon him. A portion of the tree *kalpa* will come down from *Swarga* and take root in the centre of thy new city. Thou knowest that this tree is immortal, and that thou hast only to ask it for what thou desirest to be sure of obtaining it. The mere sight of the temple that thou art about to erect will be sufficient to procure inestimable blessings. Even to be beaten with sticks there by the priests who serve the temple will be reckoned of peculiar merit. Indra, and the gods who follow in his train, will come and live in thy new city, and will be company for the god Krishna. The side of the city which faces the sea will be much more sacred than the other parts. Those who live on this side of it will daily increase in virtue. The sand which the sea deposits there thou shalt call *kanaka*, or gold dust. Any one who shall die on this sand will assuredly go to *Vaikuntha*. This, prince, is my answer to thy requests. Go at once and execute all my commands. In the meantime Vishnu, under the guise of the tree which is to form the trunk of which I have spoken, will grow and become fitted for the purpose for which it is destined.'

Indra-mena, having offered thanks to Brahma, set about to obey him. The temple and the new city were built with the utmost celerity. Yet when the work was completed the god did not appear. This delay began to cause the prince some uneasiness, when one day, having risen very early, he perceived on the sea-shore the trunk of the tree for which he was watching so impatiently. He prostrated himself several times before it with his face to the ground, and in the fullness of his joy cried: 'O happiest day of my life! I now have certain proofs that I was born under a lucky star, and that my sacrifices have been pleasing to the gods. Nothing can equal the happiness that I derive from this; for with my own eyes I see the Supreme Being, him whom the most favoured and the most virtuous among men are not permitted to see.'

Having thus rendered to the trunk of the tree these preliminary acts of worship, the king put himself at the head of a hundred thousand men, who marched to the new deity and placed him on their shoulders. He was thus removed to the temple with the greatest pomp.

The famous carpenter, Visvakarma, speedily arrived and undertook to carve the face and figure of the god Krishna on the tree which had just been deposited in the temple. He promised to finish the work in one night; but only on condition that no one looked on while he performed his task. A single inquisitive glance, he said, would be sufficient to make him abandon it, never to return.

This was agreed upon, and Visvakarma at once set to work. As he made no noise about it, the king, who was in a constant state of anxiety, imagined that he had run away and was not going to fulfil his promise; so to make sure, he crept softly up to the temple and peeped through the cracks in the door. To his great delight he saw the carpenter quietly at work, so he retired at once. But Visvakarma had caught sight of him; and, angered at this breach of confidence, he left the work as it was, roughly hewn out, with only an indistinct indication of a human form. And so the trunk of the tree remained much as it was in its original state, and just as it may be seen at the present day.

Indra-mena was vexed at this untoward occurrence, but in spite of it the tree-trunk became his god, and he gave it his daughter in marriage; the wedding being celebrated with the utmost magnificence.

This, then, is the history of the foundation of the city of Purushottama, now called Jagannath, and of the tree-trunk which is worshipped under the name of Jagannatha, or Lord of the Universe.

APPENDIX VI

Trial by Ordeal.—Its Different Forms.

When the evidence against a man accused of either a civil or criminal offence is not sufficiently strong to convict him, the Hindus often have recourse to trial by ordeal, this method of settling doubtful cases being a regular part of their judicial system. The principal ordeals are those by scales and weights, by fire, by water, and by poison[1]. The following are the rules to be observed. The months of *Cheitra*, *Vaisaka*, and *Margasira* (April, May, and December) are the most favourable for ordeals, though that of the scales can take place at any time when there is not too much wind. The ordeal by fire should be practised during the rainy season, that by water in the hot weather and in autumn, that by poison in winter and in foggy weather. If careful attention is not paid to these points grave errors are liable to occur. An ordeal which took place at an unfavourable moment would be of no assistance in ascertaining the truth. The accused who is to be tried by ordeal prepares himself by fasting and ablutions. He then goes to a Brahmin *purohita*, explains the circumstances of the case, and receives his advice and instruction. After this he offers a sacrifice to all the Brahmins present, asks for their *asirvadam* (blessing), and then speaks as follows:—'Say that this day shall be a fortunate one for me, a day of virtue, a day on which it will be recognized that I am innocent of the crime of which I am accused, a day on which I shall receive many blessings.'

To this the Brahmins reply three times:—

'May this day be a fortunate one for thee, a day of virtue, a day on which thy innocence will be proved, a day on which thou shalt receive many blessings.'

This preliminary ceremony, which is called the *sasti-vassa*, being ended, they offer *homam* in honour of the nine planets. The scales are then brought in. Over them is a little white flag, and a stake is driven into the ground to support them. The *purohita* presiding over the ceremony takes a vessel containing water, rice, and flowers, and turning towards the east, says:—

[1] There are ten forms of trial by ordeal:—*Tula*, 'the balance'; *Agni*, 'fire'; *Jala*, 'water'; *Visha*, 'poison'; *Kosa*, 'drinking water in which an idol has been washed'; *Tandula*, 'ejecting chewed rice grains'; *Tapta masha*, 'taking a *masha* weight of gold out of heated oil'; *Phala*, 'holding a hot ploughshare'; *Dharma dharma*, 'drawing concealed images of Virtue and Vice out of a vessel filled with earth'; *Tulasi*, 'holding the leaves of holy basil.' This holy basil is sacred to Vishnu.—Ed.

'Glory to the three worlds[1]!

'Goddess of Virtue, approach this place, come near, accompanied by the eight divine guardians of the eight corners of the world, and by the gods of wealth and of winds.'

He offers *puja* to the goddess of Virtue; then turning successively to the eight principal points of the globe, he says:—

To the east, 'Glory to Indra!' (the king of the gods).

To the south, 'Glory to Yama!' (the Hindu Pluto).

To the west, 'Glory to Varuna!' (the Hindu Neptune).

To the north, 'Glory to Kubera!' (the Hindu Plutus).

To the south-east, 'Glory to Agni!' (fire).

To the south-west, 'Glory to Nairuta!' (the Chief of the Devils).

To the north-west, 'Glory to Vayu!' (the wind).

To the north-east, 'Glory to Isana!' (the Destroyer).

He then offers *puja* to these eight deities. He also offers it to the eight gods of wealth, to the twelve suns[2], to the twelve Rudras, to the sixteen mothers, to Ganesha, and finally to the eight winds[3]. He offers to Virtue the lesser *puja*, that is to say, sandalwood, flowers, incense, a lamp, and *neiveddya*.

Then follows the *homam*. The fire having been consecrated and purified by the *purohita* according to Vedic rites, and the *gayatri mantram* having been recited, they throw into the fire a hundred and eight, or twenty-eight, or at least eight pieces of the *villi* tree, dipped in a mixture of butter and rice. At this juncture presents must be given to the Brahmins.

Then the accused, who must be fasting and be wearing very damp clothes, is placed on that side of the scale which is towards the west. They then put bricks and *darbha* grass on the other side until a perfectly just balance has been obtained. The accused then leaves his scale and is sent to perform his ablutions without taking off his garments. During this interval the *purohita* writes in two lines of equal length, and each containing an equal number of letters, the *mantram* of which the following is a translation:—

'Sun, moon, wind, fire, *Swarga*, earth, water, virtue, Yama, day, night, dusk, and dawn, you know this man's deeds, and whether the accusation is true or false.'

He then specifies below the offence which the accused is supposed to have committed. This writing must not be in black ink; ink of some different colour must be used.

[1] The three worlds, called the *tri-loka* when spoken of collectively, are *Swarga*, *Bhu-loka*, and *Patala*—heaven, earth, and hell.—Dubois.

[2] Mitra is one of the most common names for the sun. It is also the Persian name for this luminary, which peculiarity strikes me as noteworthy.—Dubois.

[3] Amongst these winds there is one called *anima*, which, I think, is also worth noticing.—Dubois.

The *purohita* places the writing on the head of the accused, and addresses the scales in these words:—'Scales, you know everything that is in the hearts of men; you know their vices and their virtues. What escapes man's perspicacity is not hidden from you. Behold a person who is accused of a crime of which he declares himself to be innocent, and who desires to prove his innocence to the public. If he is not guilty, justice demands that you should pronounce in his favour.'

The duty of watching the movements of the scales must be left neither to a religious recluse, nor yet to a person of doubtful honesty. The former would be too likely to be influenced by compassion; the latter would not scruple to trifle with his conscience. A Brahmin of tried wisdom and virtue is therefore chosen to fill the office, and he in his turn makes this speech to the scales:—

'Scales, the gods have appointed you to dispense justice to mankind and to reveal the truth. Show it, therefore, on this occasion; and if the man you are about to try is really guilty, do not allow him to preserve his equilibrium, but make the weight of his sin turn the scale against him.'

The *purohita* then puts the accused again in the scales. He chants five times a stanza suitable to the occasion. If the scale on which the accused is standing forthwith drops, he is declared guilty; if the contrary is the case, he is declared innocent. If the scales remain equal, he is considered to be partially guilty; and if the rope breaks, he is reckoned altogether guilty.

The ceremony, as usual, terminates with a distribution of presents to the assembled Brahmins.

In the ordeal by fire they first of all draw eight circles on the ground, each sixteen fingers in diameter, leaving the same amount of space between each. Fire is the presiding genius of the first circle. Varuna, the wind, Yama, Indra, Kubera, the moon, and Savitru preside over the seven others.

These eight circles are arranged in two parallel lines. A ninth, placed by itself, is dedicated to all the gods. All the circles are purified by being smeared over with cow-dung, on the top of which they scatter *darbha* grass. They then offer *puja* in turn to the deity presiding over each circle.

Meanwhile the person about to undergo the ordeal bathes without removing his clothing, and while still quite wet places himself in the first circle of the line on the west side, his face towards the east. They then dip his hands into wheat flour mixed with curdled milk, and cover them over with seven leaves of the *aswatta* tree, seven leaves of *choni*, and seven stalks of *darbha* grass.

A blacksmith then heats a small iron rod in the fire to a red heat. The rod should be about eight inches long, and the weight of fifty rupees. Then the *purohita* places some fire purified according to the rites of his Veda to the south of the ninth circle and performs the *homam*. He invokes the goddess of Virtue in the same words as those used in the ordeal by scales. He throws the red-hot iron into water; and after it has been re-heated to the same degree, he speaks as follows:—

'Fire, you are the Four Vedas, and as such I offer you *homam*. You are the countenance of all the gods, and you are also the countenance of all learned men. You take away all our sins, and that is why you are called pure and purifying. I am the greatest of sinners, but I have the happiness to see you. Purify me from all my sins, and if this man who is about to undergo this ordeal is really innocent, refrain for his sake from making use of your natural power of burning, and do him no harm.'

He finishes his discourse by doing homage to the power which this element possesses of penetrating into the inmost recesses of the human heart and discovering the truth. Then he says:—

'Glory to the three worlds!' and finally pronounces this evocation: 'O fire, come near! come near and stay here! stay here!' and he offers *puja*. The accused places himself in the first circle, and the *purohita*, taking up the bar of hot iron with some tongs, says again: 'O fire, you know the secrets of men! reveal the truth to us on this occasion!' At the same moment he puts the red-hot iron on the hands of the accused, who then, still keeping hold of the iron, runs over all the circles, in such a manner as to place his feet alternately on all. Arrived at the eighth circle he throws the iron into the ninth on to some straw, which should be set on fire by the contact.

In the case of the accused dropping the iron before he has covered the whole distance, the trial would have to begin over again. If, on an inspection of his hands, it is seen that the iron has not injured the skin, he is considered innocent. An accidental burn on any other part of his body would not count. To make quite sure that contact with the red-hot iron has produced no sensible effect on the skin, the accused is given some unhusked rice, which he has to rub vigorously between his hands to separate the grains from the husk.

The preparatory formalities for the ordeal by water are much the same as the preceding ones. For this they draw a single circle in which they place flowers and incense. A stake is also driven into a tank or a river where the current is not too strong. Near this stake the accused must place himself, the water being up to his waist. The *purohita*, with his face to the east, then speaks these words:—

'Water, you are the life of all that has life; you create and destroy at will; you purify everything, and we may always be sure to learn the truth when we take you for judge. Settle the doubtful question which now concerns us and tell us whether this man is guilty or not.'

Some one is then told to go a certain distance and to return. During the time so occupied the accused must immerse himself completely, holding on to the bottom of the stake fixed close to him. If he raises his head above the water before the person returns, he is accounted guilty; if he comes up afterwards, he is declared innocent.

If both accuser and accused are condemned to undergo the ordeal, they must both go under the water at the same time, and he who first comes to the surface to breathe is considered guilty.

The ordeal by poison is preceded by all the usual ceremonies. A little powdered arsenic is mixed in some melted butter. The *purohita* then says :—

'Poison, you are a harmful substance, created to destroy the guilty and impure. You were vomited by the great snake Vasuki to cause the death of guilty giants. Behold a person who is accused of a crime of which he declares himself to be innocent. If in reality he is not guilty, divest yourself of your injurious qualities and become to him as *amrita* (nectar).'

The accused then swallows the poison; and if, though he may feel unwell, he survives for three days, he is proclaimed innocent.

There are also several other kinds of trial by ordeal. Amongst the number is that of boiling oil, which is mixed with cow-dung, and into which the accused must plunge his arm up to the elbow; that of the snake, which consists in shutting up some very poisonous snake in a basket, in which has been placed a ring or a piece of money which the accused must find and bring out with his eyes bandaged; if, in the former case, he is not scalded, and in the latter is not bitten, his innocence is completely proved.

INDEX

THE END

OXFORD
PRINTED AT THE CLARENDON PRESS
BY HORACE HART, M.A.
PRINTER TO THE UNIVERSITY

SACRED BOOKS OF THE EAST

TRANSLATED BY

VARIOUS ORIENTAL SCHOLARS

AND EDITED BY

F. MAX MÜLLER.

⁂ *This Series is published with the sanction and co-operation of the Secretary of State for India in Council.*

REPORT presented to the ACADÉMIE DES INSCRIPTIONS, May 11, 1883, by M. ERNEST RENAN.

'M. Renan présente trois nouveaux volumes de la grande collection des "Livres sacrés de l'Orient" (Sacred Books of the East), que dirige à Oxford, avec une si vaste érudition et une critique si sûre, le savant associé de l'Académie des Inscriptions, M. Max Müller.... La première série de ce beau recueil, composée de 24 volumes, est presque achevée. M. Max Müller se propose d'en publier une seconde, dont l'intérêt historique et religieux ne sera pas moindre. M. Max Müller a su se procurer la collaboration des savans les plus éminens d'Europe et d'Asie. L'Université d'Oxford, que cette grande publication honore au plus haut degré, doit tenir à continuer dans les plus larges proportions une œuvre aussi philosophiquement conçue que savamment exécutée.'

EXTRACT from the QUARTERLY REVIEW.

'We rejoice to notice that a second series of these translations has been announced and has actually begun to appear. The stones, at least, out of which a stately edifice may hereafter arise, are here being brought together. Prof. Max Müller has deserved well of scientific history. Not a few minds owe to his enticing words their first attraction to this branch of study. But no work of his, not even the great edition of the Rig-Veda, can compare in importance or in usefulness with this English translation of the Sacred Books of the East, which has been devised by his foresight, successfully brought so far by his persuasive and organising power, and will, we trust, by the assistance of the distinguished scholars he has gathered round him, be carried in due time to a happy completion.'

Professor E. HARDY, Inaugural Lecture in the University of Freiburg, 1887.

'Die allgemeine vergleichende Religionswissenschaft datirt von jenem grossartigen, in seiner Art einzig dastehenden Unternehmen, zu welchem auf Anregung Max Müllers im Jahre 1874 auf dem internationalen Orientalistencongress in London der Grundstein gelegt worden war, die Übersetzung der heiligen Bücher des Ostens' (*the Sacred Books of the East*).

The Hon. ALBERT S. G. CANNING, 'Words on Existing Religions.'

'The recent publication of the "Sacred Books of the East" in English is surely a great event in the annals of theological literature.'

Oxford

AT THE CLARENDON PRESS

LONDON: HENRY FROWDE

OXFORD UNIVERSITY PRESS WAREHOUSE, AMEN CORNER, E.C.

FIRST SERIES.

VOL. I. The Upanishads.

Translated by F. MAX MÜLLER. Part I. The *Kh*ândogya-upanishad, The Talavakâra-upanishad, The Aitareya-âra*n*yaka, The Kaushîtaki-brâhma*n*a-upanishad, and The Vâgasaneyi-sa*m*hitâ-upanishad. 8vo, cloth, 10*s*. 6*d*.

The Upanishads contain the philosophy of the Veda. They have become the foundation of the later Vedânta doctrines, and indirectly of Buddhism. Schopenhauer, speaking of the Upanishads, says: 'In the whole world there is no study so beneficial and so elevating as that of the Upanishads. It has been the solace of my life, it will be the solace of my death.'

[See also Vol. XV.]

VOL. II. The Sacred Laws of the Âryas,

As taught in the Schools of Âpastamba, Gautama, Vâsish*th*a, and Baudhâyana. Translated by GEORG BÜHLER. Part I. Âpastamba and Gautama. *Second Edition*. 8vo, cloth, 10*s*. 6*d*.

The Sacred Laws of the Âryas contain the original treatises on which the Laws of Manu and other lawgivers were founded.

[See also Vol. XIV.]

VOL. III. The Sacred Books of China.

The Texts of Confucianism. Translated by JAMES LEGGE. Part I. The Shû King, The Religious Portions of the Shih King, and The Hsiâo King. 8vo, cloth, 12*s*. 6*d*.

Confucius was a collector of ancient traditions, not the founder of a new religion. As he lived in the sixth and fifth centuries B.C. his works are of unique interest for the study of Ethology.

[See also Vols. XVI, XXVII, XXVIII, XXXIX, and XL.]

VOL. IV. The Zend-Avesta.

Translated by JAMES DARMESTETER. Part I. The Vendîdâd. *Second Edition*. 8vo, cloth, 14*s*.

The Zend-Avesta contains the relics of what was the religion of Cyrus, Darius, and Xerxes, and, but for the battle of Marathon, might have become the religion of Europe. It forms to the present day the sacred book of the Parsis, the so-called fire-worshippers. Two more volumes will complete the translation of all that is left us of Zoroaster's religion.

[See also Vols. XXIII and XXXI.]

VOL. V. Pahlavi Texts.

Translated by E. W. WEST. Part I. The Bundahis, Bahman Yast, and Shâyast lâ-shâyast. 8vo, cloth, 12*s*. 6*d*.

The Pahlavi Texts comprise the theological literature of the revival of Zoroaster's religion, beginning with the Sassanian dynasty. They are important for a study of Gnosticism.

VOLS. VI AND IX. The Qur'ân.

Parts I and II. Translated by E. H. PALMER. 8vo, cloth, 21*s*.

This translation, carried out according to his own peculiar views of the origin of the Qur'ân, was the last great work of E. H. Palmer, before he was murdered in Egypt.

VOL. VII. The Institutes of Vishnu.

Translated by JULIUS JOLLY. 8vo, cloth, 10*s*. 6*d*.

A collection of legal aphorisms, closely connected with one of the oldest Vedic schools, the Kathas, *but considerably added to in later time. Of importance for a critical study of the Laws of Manu.*

VOL. VIII. The Bhagavadgîtâ, with The Sanatsugâtîya, and The Anugîtâ.

Translated by KÂSHINÂTH TRIMBAK TELANG. 8vo, cloth, 10*s*. 6*d*.

The earliest philosophical and religious poem of India. It has been paraphrased in Arnold's 'Song Celestial.'

VOL. X. The Dhammapada,

Translated from Pâli by F. MAX MÜLLER; and

The Sutta-Nipâta,

Translated from Pâli by V. FAUSBÖLL; being Canonical Books of the Buddhists. 8vo, cloth, 10*s*. 6*d*.

The Dhammapada contains the quintessence of Buddhist morality. The Sutta-Nipâta gives the authentic teaching of Buddha on some of the fundamental principles of religion.

VOL. XI. Buddhist Suttas.

Translated from Pâli by T. W. RHYS DAVIDS. 1. The Mahâ-parinibbâna Suttanta; 2. The Dhamma-*k*akka-ppavattana Sutta. 3. The Tevi*gg*a Suttanta; 4. The Âkaṅkheyya Sutta; 5. The *K*etokhila Sutta; 6. The Mahâ-sudassana Suttanta; 7. The Sabbâsava Sutta. 8vo, cloth, 10*s*. 6*d*.

A collection of the most important religious, moral, and philosophical discourses taken from the sacred canon of the Buddhists.

VOL. XII. The *S*atapatha-Brâhma*n*a, according to the Text of the Mâdhyandina School.

Translated by JULIUS EGGELING. Part I. Books I and II. 8vo, cloth, 12*s*. 6*d*.

A minute account of the sacrificial ceremonies of the Vedic age. It contains the earliest account of the Deluge in India.

[See also Vols. XXVI, XLI.]

VOL. XIII. Vinaya Texts.

Translated from the Pâli by T. W. RHYS DAVIDS and HERMANN OLDENBERG. Part I. The Pâtimokkha. The Mahâvagga, I–IV. 8vo, cloth, 10*s*. 6*d*.

The Vinaya Texts give for the first time a translation of the moral code of the Buddhist religion as settled in the third century B.C.

[See also Vols. XVII and XX.]

VOL. XIV. The Sacred Laws of the Âryas,

As taught in the Schools of Âpastamba, Gautama, Vâsish*th*a, and Baudhâyana. Translated by GEORG BÜHLER. Part II. Vâsish*th*a and Baudhâyana. 8vo, cloth, 10*s*. 6*d*.

VOL. XV. The Upanishads.

Translated by F. MAX MÜLLER. Part II. The Ka*th*a-upanishad, The Mu*nd*aka-upanishad, The Taittirîyaka-upanishad, The B*ri*hadâra*n*yaka-upanishad, The *S*vetâ*s*vatara-upanishad, The Pra*sñ*a-upanishad, and The Maitrâya*n*a-brâhma*n*a-upanishad. 8vo, cloth, 10*s*. 6*d*.

VOL. XVI. The Sacred Books of China.

The Texts of Confucianism. Translated by JAMES LEGGE. Part II. The Yî King. 8vo, cloth, 10*s*. 6*d*.

[See also Vols. XXVII, XXVIII.]

VOL. XVII. Vinaya Texts.

Translated from the Pâli by T. W. RHYS DAVIDS and HERMANN OLDENBERG. Part II. The Mahâvagga, V–X. The *K*ullavagga, I–III. 8vo, cloth, 10*s*. 6*d*.

VOL. XVIII. Pahlavi Texts.

Translated by E. W. WEST. Part II. The Dâ*d*istân-î Dînîk and The Epistles of Mânû*s**k*îhar. 8vo, cloth, 12*s*. 6*d*.

VOL. XIX. The Fo-sho-hing-tsan-king.

A Life of Buddha by A*s*vaghosha Bodhisattva, translated from Sanskrit into Chinese by Dharmaraksha, A.D. 420, and from Chinese into English by SAMUEL BEAL. 8vo, cloth, 10*s*. 6*d*.

This life of Buddha was translated from Sanskrit into Chinese, A.D. 420. It contains many legends, some of which show a certain similarity to the Evangelium infantiae, &c.

VOL. XX. Vinaya Texts.

Translated from the Pâli by T. W. RHYS DAVIDS and HERMANN OLDENBERG. Part III. The *K*ullavagga, IV–XII. 8vo, cloth, 10*s*. 6*d*.

VOL. XXI. The Saddharma-pu*nd*arîka; or, The Lotus of the True Law.

Translated by H. KERN. 8vo, cloth, 12*s*. 6*d*.

'The Lotus of the true Law,' a canonical book of the Northern Buddhists, translated from Sanskrit. There is a Chinese translation of this book which was finished as early as the year 286 A.D.

VOL. XXII. *G*aina-Sûtras.

Translated from Prâkrit by HERMANN JACOBI. Part I. The Â*k*ârâṅga-Sûtra and The Kalpa-Sûtra. 8vo, cloth, 10*s*. 6*d*.

The religion of the Gainas *was founded by a contemporary of Buddha. It still counts numerous adherents in India, while there are no Buddhists left in India proper.*

[See Vol. XLV.]

VOL. XXIII. The Zend-Avesta.

Translated by JAMES DARMESTETER. Part II. The Sîrôzahs, Ya*s*ts, and Nyâyi*s*. 8vo, cloth, 10*s*. 6*d*.

VOL. XXIV. Pahlavi Texts.

Translated by E. W. WEST. Part III. Dînâ-î Maînôg-Khira*d*, *S*ikand-gûmânîk Vigâr, and Sad Dar. 8vo, cloth, 10*s*. 6*d*.

SECOND SERIES.

VOL. XXV. Manu.

Translated by GEORG BÜHLER. 8vo, cloth, 21*s.*

This translation is founded on that of Sir William Jones, which has been carefully revised and corrected with the help of seven native Commentaries. An Appendix contains all the quotations from Manu which are found in the Hindu Law-books, translated for the use of the Law Courts in India. Another Appendix gives a synopsis of parallel passages from the six Dharma-sûtras, the other Smritis, the Upanishads, the Mahâbhârata, &c.

VOL. XXVI. The *S*atapatha-Brâhma*n*a.

Translated by JULIUS EGGELING. Part II. Books III and IV. 8vo, cloth, 12*s.* 6*d.*

VOLS. XXVII AND XXVIII. The Sacred Books of China.

The Texts of Confucianism. Translated by JAMES LEGGE. Parts III and IV. The Lî *K*î, or Collection of Treatises on the Rules of Propriety, or Ceremonial Usages. 8vo, cloth, 25*s.*

VOL. XXIX. The G*ri*hya-Sûtras, Rules of Vedic Domestic Ceremonies.

Part I. *S*âṅkhâyana, Â*s*valâyana, Pâraskara, Khâdira. Translated by HERMANN OLDENBERG. 8vo, cloth, 12*s.* 6*d.*

These rules of Domestic Ceremonies describe the home life of the ancient Âryas with a completeness and accuracy unmatched in any other literature. Some of these rules have been incorporated in the ancient Law-books.

VOL. XXX. The G*ri*hya-Sûtras, Rules of Vedic Domestic Ceremonies.

Part II. Gobhila, Hira*n*yake*s*in, Âpastamba. Translated by HERMANN OLDENBERG. Âpastamba, Yag*ñ*a-paribhâshâ-sûtras. Translated by F. MAX MÜLLER. 8vo, cloth, 12*s.* 6*d.*

VOL. XXXI. The Zend-Avesta.

Part III. The Yasna, Visparad, Âfrînagân, Gâhs, and Miscellaneous Fragments. Translated by L. H. MILLS. 8vo, cloth, 12*s.* 6*d.*

VOL. XXXII. Vedic Hymns.

Translated by F. MAX MÜLLER. Part I. 8vo, cloth, 18*s.* 6*d.*

VOL. XXXIII. The Minor Law-books.

Translated by JULIUS JOLLY. Part I. Nârada, B*ri*haspati. 8vo, cloth, 10*s.* 6*d.*

Vol. XXXIV. The Vedânta-Sûtras, with the Commentary by *S*ankarâ*k*ârya. Part I.
Translated by G. Thibaut. 8vo, cloth, 12*s.* 6*d.*

Vols. XXXV and XXXVI. The Questions of King Milinda.
Translated from the Pâli by T. W. Rhys Davids. Part I. 8vo, cloth, 10*s.* 6*d.* Part II. 8vo, cloth, 12*s.* 6*d.*

Vol. XXXVII. Pahlavi Texts.
Translated by E. W. West. Part IV. The Contents of the Nasks, as stated in the Eighth and Ninth Books of the Dînka*r*d. 8vo, cloth, 15*s.*

Vol. XXXVIII. The Vedânta-Sûtras. Part II. 8vo, cloth, with full Index to both Parts, 12*s.* 6*d.*

Vols. XXXIX and XL. The Sacred Books of China. The Texts of Tâoism. Translated by James Legge. 8vo, cloth, 21*s.*

Vol. XLI. The *S*atapatha-Brâhma*n*a. Part III.
Translated by Julius Eggeling. 8vo, cloth, 12*s.* 6*d.*

Vol. XLII. Hymns of the Atharva-veda.
Translated by M. Bloomfield. 8vo, cloth, 21*s.*

Vols. XLIII and XLIV. The *S*atapatha-Brâhma*n*a.
Parts IV and V. [*In the Press.*]

Vol. XLV. The *G*aina-Sûtras.
Translated from Prak*ri*t, by Hermann Jacobi. Part II. The Uttarâdhyayana Sûtra, The Sûtrak*ri*tâṅga Sûtra. 8vo, cloth, 12*s.* 6*d.*

Vol. XLVI. Vedic Hymns. Part II. 8vo, cloth, 14*s.*

Vol. XLVII. Pahlavi Texts.
Translated by E. W. West. Part V. Marvels of Zoroastrianism. 8vo, cloth, 8*s.* 6*d.*

Vol. XLVIII. Râmânu*g*a's *S*rîbhâshya.
Translated by G. Thibaut. [*In preparation.*]

Vol. XLIX. Buddhist Mahâyâna Texts. Buddha-*k*arita, translated by E. B. Cowell. Sukhâvatî-vyûha, Va*g*ra*kkh*edikâ, &c., translated by F. Max Müller. Amitâyur-Dhyâna-Sûtra, translated by J. Takakusu. 8vo, cloth, 12*s.* 6*d.*

Anecdota Oxoniensia.

ARYAN SERIES.

Buddhist Texts from Japan. I. Vagrakkhedikâ; *The Diamond-Cutter.*

Edited by F. MAX MÜLLER, M.A. Small 4to, 3s. 6d.

One of the most famous metaphysical treatises of the Mahâyâna Buddhists.

Buddhist Texts from Japan. II. Sukhâvatî-Vyûha: *Description of Sukhâvatî, the Land of Bliss.*

Edited by F. MAX MÜLLER, M.A., and BUNYIU NANJIO. With two Appendices: (1) Text and Translation of Saṅghavarman's Chinese Version of the Poetical Portions of the Sukhâvatî-Vyûha; (2) Sanskrit Text of the Smaller Sukhâvatî-Vyûha. Small 4to, 7s. 6d.

The *editio princeps* of the Sacred Book of one of the largest and most influential sects of Buddhism, numbering more than ten millions of followers in Japan alone.

Buddhist Texts from Japan. III. *The Ancient Palm-Leaves containing the* Pragñâ-Pâramitâ-Hridaya-Sûtra *and the* Ushnîsha-Vigaya-Dhâranî.

Edited by F. MAX MÜLLER, M.A., and BUNYIU NANJIO, M.A. With an Appendix by G. BÜHLER, C.I.E. With many Plates. Small 4to, 10s.

Contains facsimiles of the oldest Sanskrit MS. at present known.

Dharma-Samgraha, *an Ancient Collection of Buddhist Technical Terms.*

Prepared for publication by KENJIU KASAWARA, a Buddhist Priest from Japan, and, after his death, edited by F. MAX MÜLLER and H. WENZEL. Small 4to, 7s. 6d.

Kâtyâyana's Sarvânukramanî of the Rigveda.

With Extracts from Shadgurusishya's Commentary entitled Vedârthadîpikâ. Edited by A. A. MACDONELL, M.A., Ph.D. 16s.

The Mantrapāṭha, or the Prayer Book of the Āpastambins.

Edited, together with the Commentary of Haradatta, and translated by M. WINTERNITZ, Ph.D. *First Part.* Introduction, Sanskrit Text, Varietas Lectionis, and Appendices. Small quarto, 10s. 6d.

Oxford

AT THE CLARENDON PRESS

LONDON: HENRY FROWDE

OXFORD UNIVERSITY PRESS WAREHOUSE, AMEN CORNER, E.C.